A History of Management Thought

For the past three thousand years people have been thinking about the problems of management. This book shows how thinking about management has evolved and changed. It shows how changing social, political and technological forces have challenged people to think about management in new ways, and how management thinkers have responded. Sometimes their responses missed the mark and, occasionally, great ideas about management failed to be picked up and were lost along the way. Sometimes, truly original and creative, even world-changing ideas appeared.

Following key currents in management thought from the origins of civilization to the present day, the book begins in the ancient world, when people were wrestling with the problems of organization and leadership. It continues through the Middle Ages, East and West, as people pondered on how to manage risk and think strategically, and on the role of business in society. It shows how the Industrial Revolution led to the emergence of scientific management, and how political and social events of the twentieth century shaped management thinking right up to the present day.

From the pyramids to Facebook, from military strategy to managing for sustainability, *A History of Management Thought* tells the fascinating story of how management thinking has changed, shifted, evolved and developed down through the centuries. Students taking classes in the history of management thought will find this text to be the perfect accompaniment to their studies and will be a captivating read for anyone else.

Morgen Witzel is a Fellow of the Centre for Leadership Studies, University of Exeter, UK. A writer, lecturer and consultant on business and management, especially on the history of management, he is the author of hundreds of articles for the academic and popular press and has written eighteen books, including: *Doing Business in China*; *Management: The Basics*; and *Management History*, all available from Routledge.

A History of
Management Thought

Morgen Witzel

Routledge
Taylor & Francis Group

LONDON AND NEW YORK

First published 2012
by Routledge
2 Park Square, Milton Park, Abingdon, Oxon OX14 4RN

Simultaneously published in the USA and Canada
by Routledge
711 Third Avenue, New York, NY 10017

Routledge is an imprint of the Taylor & Francis Group, an informa business

British Library Cataloguing in Publication Data
A catalogue record for this book is available from the British Library

Library of Congress Cataloging in Publication Data
Witzel, Morgen.
A history of management thought / Morgen Witzel.
p. cm.
Includes bibliographical references and index.
1. Management—History. 2. Management science—History. I. Title.
HD30.5.W577 2011
658.009—dc23
2011025919

ISBN: 978–0–415–60057–6 (hbk)
ISBN: 978–0–415–60058–3 (pbk)
ISBN: 978–0–203–14560–9 (ebk)

Typeset in Times New Roman
by Keystroke, Station Road, Codsall, Wolverhampton

Contents

Acknowledgements

Over the course of nearly fifteen years of studying and thinking about the history of management, I have been influenced by many people and many ideas. I should like first of all to thank my professors and lecturers in history at the University of Victoria in Canada, who first made me realize that history is not just a collection of interesting stories, but a rich source of knowledge that can, should we care to do so, be applied to the problems of the present and even the future. Whether they meant to or not, they turned me into an applied historian.

My views on business and management were formed while working, first as a research officer and then on contract, at London Business School. While there, I learnt to appreciate the power of management education – and also, some of its failings. My subsequent years of lecturing on management history and other subjects at the University of Exeter Business School confirmed my belief in the utter necessity of management education, while at the same time enhancing my understanding of the weaknesses of the current system. And along the way, I became even more convinced that the application of lessons from history can solve some of those weaknesses.

I want to pay a special tribute to the University of Exeter MBA students who took my module, *From the Medici to Microsoft: The Making and Integration of Management*, from 2003–11. Their views, their ideas and their understanding helped to shape my own thinking to a great degree.

Many other people have been generous with their time and thoughts over the years, all adding in some way to my own knowledge and/or my understanding of why management history is important. They include Tim Ambler, Mie Augier, George Bickerstaffe, the late Edward Brech, Peter Case, John Child, Tim Dickson, Jonathan Gosling, Kris Inwood, Donna Ladkin, Ronnie Lessem, David Lewis, Raoul McLaughlin, Karl Moore, James Pickford, Sasaki Tsuneo, Bodo Schlegelmilch, Jonathan Schroeder, J.C. Spender, Billy So, Peter Starbuck, Malcolm Warner, Daniel Wren, Chao Xi and Milan Zeleny, and almost certainly many others whom I have overlooked.

I would like also to thank Terry Clague of Routledge, who commissioned this book, for giving me the opportunity to write it and for his support through the process.

Marilyn Livingstone has been a constant source of ideas, inspiration, critical comment and help and support when needed. To her, as ever, my eternal thanks and gratitude.

1   Introduction

A sense of the past . . . is essential to anyone who is trying to understand the here-and-now of industrial organisation. What is happening now is part of a continuing development.

(Tom Burns)

Any history of management thought needs perforce to begin by defining what is meant by 'management thought', and then explain what it is about the history of management thought that makes it important and worthy of study. There are two ways of defining 'management thought': we can take it to mean coherent theories or systems of management, or we can broaden the scope of the term and refer more generally to 'thinking about management', ideas about the meaning, purpose, function and tasks of management which are important and relevant but do not necessarily amount to a coherent overall theory.

The problem, though, is defining where the boundary lies. The year 2011 marks the 100th anniversary of the publication of arguably the most influential work of management thinking of all time, Frederick Winslow Taylor's *The Principles of Scientific Management*. Scientific management was one of the first major systems of thinking about management to be developed, though it must be pointed out that it emerged at a time which was very rich in thinking about management generally. Taylor's contemporaries included people such as Harrington Emerson, Henri Fayol, Lyndall Urwick and others who developed their own concepts of management. As we shall see later in this book, scientific management was the concept that proved to be most durable.

If we take the first definition of 'management thought' given above, then our study should commence with scientific management a century ago and move forward in time from there. But how and why did scientific management emerge? To answer that question, we need to go back to the late nineteenth century and the first calls for improvement in management methods. And what led to those calls for improvement and change? To answer *that* question, we find ourselves back in the heart of the Industrial Revolution. Should we start with Charles Babbage, who defined the need for knowledge in management and called for a more scientific and rigorous approach to management? Or do we go back further to Robert Owen, who developed ideas on how to manage people effectively and humanely? Or Adam Smith, who redefined the division of labour; or the French physiocrats who also wrote on the division of labour and developed the first ideas on entrepreneurship? Or back to ancient China, where at least one key physiocratic idea, the notion of laissez-faire, has its roots?

Before we know it, we are on a journey back in time, far earlier than the emergence of scientific management. Early twentieth-century writers on management, including some exponents of scientific management, knew this. 'The art of administration is as old as the human race' wrote Edward D. Jones in 1912.[1] Thomas North Whitehead thought that 'structure arises as soon as people begin to do something together'.[2] Harrington Emerson, Lyndall Urwick and James Mooney among others believed that the roots of management and administration could be traced back to the beginning of civilization. Likewise, modern theories and systems of management thought have their roots in much older 'thinking about management'. The two cannot be separated, not without risk of creating an artificial divide. The fact is that pretty much since the beginning of civilization, people have been writing and thinking about problems in management and how to solve them. The duties and functions of a manager, the principles of organization, markets and prices, the management of people, the importance of knowledge, strategic thinking, the management of money and finance, international trade, leadership: all of these problems and many more were pondered by people around the world and far back in time. Among them were Confucius, Plato, Ibn Khaldun, Thomas Aquinas, Machiavelli, Adam Smith, Samuel Taylor Coleridge, Florence Nightingale and Leo Tolstoy, to name but a few.

When we go back to these earlier writers and thinkers, however, we are looking at something very different from Taylor's *The Principles of Scientific Management* or the many other books on management and aspects of management that began to appear from the 1890s onward. Most earlier authors did not set out to write works on management (and we should remember that the words 'management' and 'manager' were not coined until quite late, first appearing in English in the late sixteenth century, gradually replacing older words such as 'administration' and 'stewardship').

Some people, such as the medieval scholar and lawyer Walter of Henley, did deliberately sit down to write handbooks or manuals which would help guide administrators and managers; but most offered their comments in a much broader context. Often their ideas on management have to be disembedded from a broad range of ideas on many subjects. An example is the Italian friar San Bernardino of Siena whose sermons cover subjects such as economics, theology, ethics, social mores and codes of behaviour, as well as a highly original definition of the qualities of a manager seemingly at random. The often quite profound comments by Confucius and Thomas Aquinas on the role of business in society represent tiny portions of much larger bodies of work. As Liana Farber points out in her painstaking collection and analysis of medieval European writings on trade, scholars often have to read through many lengthy discussions of almost every topic under the sun before finding a few paragraphs which offer ideas on business and management.[3] Nonetheless, those few paragraphs are often extremely significant. Through them we can trace back concepts such as the division of labour, or the metaphor of organizations as biological organisms, or theories about the relationship between price and value, or the need for reporting and control, or the role and function of the leader – to take just a few examples – for hundreds of years, sometimes thousands of years.

Why a history of management thought?

The first and most commonly used justification for the study of the history of management thought is that it provides context. We cannot fully understand the present without knowing something about the past. 'The objective is to place management thought in the context of its cultural environment and thereby to understand not only what management thought was and is, but also to explain why it developed as it did', declared the management historian Daniel Wren.[4] He refers to 'the past as prologue', the foundation on which the present is built.

The past does provide context, most certainly, and it can be used to illustrate present themes and ideas; elsewhere, I have argued that the past can be used as a mirror or a lens, to illuminate and examine the present more effectively.[5] 'A sense of the past . . . is essential to anyone who is trying to understand the here-and-now of industrial organisation', wrote Tom Burns in 1963. 'What is happening now is part of a continuing development.'[6]

But the past also provides influences. Ideas about management do not – by and large – spring fully formed from the heads of their creators, like Athena from the head of Zeus. As Daniel Wren suggests, they evolve. Each new generation of theorists applies new ideas to the existing body of theory. Very often, these new ideas are conditioned, or at least influenced, by the world in which the thinkers live and work. Much has been written about the persistence of Confucian intellectual current in East Asia, China in particular. Chinese management thought remains under the influence of the ideas of Confucius and other early philosophers, notably Laozi (Lao Tzu) and Han Fei, to this day. Japanese business leaders continued to be influenced by Sunzi, early Buddhist writers and the Japanese swordfighter Miyamoto Musashi into the twentieth century. Nor are we in the West beyond the influence of the past. The philosopher Alfred North Whitehead – whose son became a notable management thinker in his own right in the 1930s – once remarked that all of subsequent European thought 'consists of a series of footnotes to Plato', so complete is the latter's domination of our systems of thought and education.[7] Several of the people mentioned above – John of Salisbury, Aquinas, Machiavelli – were directly and heavily influenced by Plato. The Prussian strategy writer Karl von Clausewitz in turn was influenced by Machiavelli, and Clausewitz went on to influence generations of military and business strategists and managers. One of his followers, Field-Marshal Helmuth von Moltke, the victor of the Franco-Prussian War of 1871, was a strong influence on American management thinkers of the late nineteenth and early twentieth century, and Pierre du Pont's multidivisional form (M-form) organization betrays the influence of military organization. Thus there is an intellectual chain stretching between Plato and Alfred Chandler, the later twentieth-century expositor of the M-form. These chains of influence are complex and not always visible; that does not make them any less important.

The past also reminds us of the importance of continuity. Too often in the modern world, we fall victim to the belief that the past is somehow less than relevant, that the pace of technological advances, globalization and so forth mean that the world today is so different from the world of the past that we have little to learn from the latter. 'The past is a foreign country', wrote L.P. Hartley in his novel *The Go-Between*, 'they do things differently there'. That is both true and at the same time not true. Human society, culture, perceptions have all changed and evolved. The world is not the same as it was in 500 BC, or AD 1500, or even AD 1900. Many, many things have changed. Yet some things remain the same, and sometimes it can be helpful to isolate those things that have *not* changed, and try to understand why. One of the paradoxes of management is the need to focus on both continuity and change, simultaneously. To neglect change in favour of continuity risks falling under the dead hands of tradition and stagnation; but focusing only on change and dismissing continuity poses the equal risk of a continuous and ultimately destructive reinvention of the wheel.

And when we stop and consider them, the continuities almost reach out and slap us in the face. Here is how Violina Rindova and William Starbuck conclude their study of organization and control in ancient China:

> it seems that the similarities between the ancient and the contemporary are at least as great as the differences. The differences seem to fit a model that says people from different times have to restate knowledge anew, in their own language and citing current examples. The similarities suggest that modern people can understand and appreciate the

insights of their ancestors. The ancient theories are as complex as modern ones and supported by reasoning that we can appreciate even when it differs quite bit from our own.[8]

'Management thinkers are very good at reconceptualizing old ideas, giving them a new twist and packaging them for an audience that wasn't exposed to the original idea', commented Michael Mol and Julian Birkinshaw in *Giant Steps in Management*.[9] They likened this phenomenon to the propensity for Hollywood film directors to remake classic films with younger actors or contemporary settings. This would be forgivable if the intention were to improve on the original. All too often, one suspects, it is evidence of a paucity of ideas among contemporary thinkers. Understanding the continuities in management thought, the ideas that have always been and remain forceful and important, can help us to distinguish genuinely creative ideas from glossy but ultimately valueless shams.

Challenge and response

There is to my mind a further justification for a history of management thought. It can help us to understand why and how new theories and ideas about management emerge. Again the point must be made: management theories do not emerge from nowhere. New ideas about management emerge because new ideas about management are needed. Challenges in the business environment provoke a response from thinkers and practitioners. Here is how economic historian Sidney Pollard describes the managerial response to the Industrial Revolution:

> The responses to the managerial challenges . . . were immensely varied. Not all were equally successful, and some were undoubtedly responsible for the failures of that period as well as its achievements . . . The pragmatic discovery of new methods was no doubt adequate, but management appears everywhere to have adapted itself merely to the needs of technology, discipline or financial control.[10]

In other words, there was no attempt to go beyond what was needed at the moment. This is true not just of the Industrial Revolution, but of all time. In the ancient world, people evolved techniques of controlling organizations so as to carry out the tasks necessary for civilization building. In the Middle Ages business people adopted new accounting techniques to allow them better financial control in times of high risk, while the monastic orders created new forms of organization which allowed for the governance of very large and widely dispersed organizations. Scientific management emerged as a response to the need for better management of America's newly emerging large corporations. Management science in its turn emerged at least in part as a response to the intellectual and political climate of the Cold War. Post-war Japan, needing to develop world-class industries capable of competing with the West, evolved management methods that enabled it to do so, provoking a reaction from a new generation of Western management thinkers, and so on.

The entire history of management thought is thus a history of challenge and response. The challenge come nearly always from the environment: from new technologies sometimes, but more often from shifting political and social forces. Nor should this be surprising. Another thing that the history of management thought teaches us is that management is a social activity. Businesses and other organizations are not closed systems. They interact constantly and continually with the society – or societies – in which they are located. How those organizations are managed is a direct reflection of the social forces which are brought to bear on the organization. The trend in recent decades towards more participative management and democratic workplaces reflects very strongly the 'end of history' and the prevailing world-view that democracy is the best and highest form of governance. Suppose that communism had triumphed at the end of the Cold War, and capitalism had collapsed. Would management theorists still be writing about participation and democracy? From what we know of the communist governments and their own ways of managing, it seems unlikely.

Lost along the way

This brings us to a final reason why the study of management history is important, namely the light it can shed on why some ideas and concepts in management survive and are widely adopted, while others disappear. In some cases the answer is obvious. In the 1890s the Polish mining engineer Karel Adamiecki designed, entirely independently of the work of Taylor and his colleagues in America, a management system which he called the 'theory of har-monization'. His theory is startlingly similar to scientific management, even to the point of using charts called 'harmonograms' which are nearly identical to Gantt charts (a staple recording tool used by scientific managers, see Chapter 5). Harmonization was used with considerable success in a number of mines and steel mills in Tsarist Russia, where Adamiecki was employed. But after the 1917 revolution, the new leader of Russia, V.I. Lenin, preferred the American brand of scientific management. Adamiecki's ideas were consigned to the scrapheap of history. Similarly, Nazi autarky was responsible for the end of the revolutionary management systems developed at Carl Zeiss Jena in Germany and the Bat'a shoe company in Czechoslovakia. Both companies were put under state-guided, command-and-control management systems, and so thorough was the wreckage that it has taken modern historians many years to piece together the original management systems and how they worked.

In other cases, the reasons for the disappearance are harder to fathom. In the early twentieth century, three systems of management thought emerged almost simultaneously: Taylor's scientific management, Fayol's theory of general and industrial administration, and Emerson's philosophy of efficiency. The first became very popular in many countries including America, France, Russia and China, and went through a number of later iterations and evolutions. Some of its techniques such as time-and-motion study are still used by consultants today. Fayol's system was widely admired and much discussed in Europe but barely caused ripples in North America, and in the end even in his native France scientific management became the dominant philosophy. Still more surprising is the complete disappearance of Emerson's theories of efficiency, a holistic approach to management that was in many ways more sophisticated than scientific management (see Chapter 5). At one point, Emerson's methods were in use in more industrial establishments in America than were Taylor's. But 'Emersonism' never took off, and in the 1970s Claude George allocated Emerson no more than a walk-on role in his history of management thought. Today, Emerson is rarely studied or discussed even by management historians.

In the 1920s there was a flourishing school of management thought in Britain, with figures such as Seebohm Rowntree, Lyndall Urwick, John Lee and Oliver Sheldon commanding international respect and American luminaries such as Mary Parker Follett and Henry Metcalfe coming to Britain to meet and share ideas. By the 1950s, apart from the work of a few industrial sociologists such as Joan Woodward, this school had virtually died out. What happened to it? Earlier, in the late nineteenth century, George Cadbury and his son Edward had turned the chocolate maker Cadbury Bros. into the world's largest confectionery firm, using a unique system of participative labour management that brought worker commitment and innovation to new heights. 'At Cadbury, everybody thinks', said the consultant Herbert Casson. Why did not other firms step up and adopt Cadbury's methods? Why, when Robert Owen pointed out to his fellow industrialists the undeniable fact that a worker who worked ten hours a day was more productive and delivered more value to his or her employer than one who worked fourteen, did the industrialists not respond at once by cutting hours? A few did, but most waited until the Factory Acts compelled them to do so. Why, when the Lyons company introduced the first business computer, the Lyons Electronic Office (LEO) in the 1950s and showed the savings and benefits that it could generate, did not management scholars produce coherent theories of how computer technology could impact on management? Again a few did: but most kept their powder dry, and computers did not figure largely in management thinking until at least the 1980s.

Management thought evolves; and as in any other evolutionary process, there are casualties along the way. Not every new life form is able to flourish; not every new idea is recognized and taken up. There, however, the parallel with evolutionary theory must end. If we follow the Darwinian view of survival of the fittest, we would accept that the 'best' theories and ideas are the ones that survive, while those that fall behind are in some way weak or flawed. This manifestly is not so. The long path of management thought is littered with the wreckage of good ideas that failed. What happens? By what criteria do we select those ideas that we will keep, and those that we will throw away? A study of the history of management thought can not only provide some clues as to how the process works, but might even aid better decision making and selection of ideas in the future.

Structure of the book

This book starts from the premise stated above, that 'thinking about management' has been going on in some form since the beginnings of civilization itself. From there, I have attempted to show how, and why, management thought has evolved and developed. The approach is broadly chronological but with some thematic elements. The style is narrative: I have tried to follow Theodore Levitt's dictum that 'colorful and lightly documented affirmation works better than tortuously reasoned explanation'.[11]

The book begins with the idea of management as one of the elements of civilization, and shows what the early civilization builders, in the Middle East, Egypt, India, China, Greece and Rome, thought about management. We move forward to the beginnings of the age of commercial expansion, which began around the sixth to eighth centuries and is still going on today, returning again to the Middle East before turning to Western Europe. Here, ideas about business and management were often deeply embedded in broader ideas about society and how it worked; but in both the Islamic world and parts of medieval Europe, such as Italy and England, we begin to get glimpses of the study of management as management.

While the dominant administrative models in India and China evolved slowly, if at all, the Enlightenment in Europe overturned previous theories about the world and society. The spirit of inquiry which lay at the heart of the Enlightenment led to advances in science and technology which precipitated the Industrial Revolution, but also to advances in ideas about governance and management. Some thinkers and writers, and a few practising managers too, tried to apply the ideals of the Enlightenment directly to business and management. They did so with mixed success, but the spirit of inquiry persisted.

That same spirit emerged in force in the late nineteenth century when, as a result of the rapid and chaotic growth of many organizations, it became clear that a more systematic approach to management was needed. The result was an unprecedented flourishing of ideas, especially in America but also in many parts of Europe, and the spreading influences were felt in Japan, China, India and Latin America, at least. Scientific management rose to become the dominant model in America and France, but was challenged by the human relations school which felt that scientific management was too mechanistic and ignored the human element in organizations.

The tension between mechanistic and organic, human-centred models of management persisted after the Second World War with the parallel developments of management science and other approaches based on open systems and contingency theory. Meanwhile, 'management' as a discipline was beginning to fracture. Individual disciplines, notably personnel management, marketing and corporate finance, had sprung up semi-independently of general management theory and been gradually affiliated with the latter in terms of thinking and research. But as time passed more disciplines – strategy, leadership, knowledge management, to name but a few – emerged, each with its own body of theory and its own literature. There was a tension too between the academic specialists and the so-called 'gurus'. Although some of these came from specialist backgrounds, they tended to take more general approaches and they tried to speak directly to managers and offer practical management solutions rather than engage only in theory building.

And so we come to the present day, when general management thinking has declined in favour of highly specialized research, teaching and study. This is a difficult period for a general study such as this one to describe accurately, and I fear I have not tried to cover the whole picture; rather, I have stuck to my theme and focused on a few current developments in management thinking which take us back to the notion of how and why management theories are formed. My conclusion is that external, environmental forces are still dominant, and that most thinking about management emerges from the same process of challenge and response: witness the scramble to come up with coherent theories about e-commerce in the aftermath of the rise of the Internet, or the current, somewhat lumbering response by management thinkers to pressures for sustainability.

The story ends there, somewhat abruptly, for of course the story of management thinking is not finished – though as I point out at the very end, formal and systematic management thinking will face an increasing challenge to its legitimacy if it can no longer respond to the challenges faced by management in practice. In the conclusion, I try to draw out lessons from the history of management thought and discuss what light it sheds on management today or even, however dimly, on management in the future.

This is, as I have said, a general survey, not an encyclopaedia. In trying to describe trends and processes I have inevitably left out some works and thinkers whom others will consider to be of major importance. Some readers may be shocked too by the fact that little-known figures such as Karel Adamiecki or Ibn Khaldun receive as much coverage or more than well-known writers and theorists such as Herbert Simon or Peter Drucker. But in this work, the importance of figures is not directly correlated with the number of paragraphs devoted to them. In some cases the little-known figures are given greater coverage precisely because they are little known, while much more detailed coverage of the significant figures is available elsewhere. Again, the purpose here is to describe the emergence of ideas, not create a canon of management thinkers.

Although I have made reference to developments in management practice, on the whole I have tried to concentrate on developments in thinking about management. Thus I have glossed over the development of mass production, for example, which some readers might think is rather perverse of me. But mass production to me is a matter of management practice, an evolution in production methods that developed out of new technologies and the increasing scale of business enterprises. Mass production was one of the issues that management thinking had to face as it tried to cope with the new conditions. How could mass production be managed efficiently? How could its products be marketed? How should these new large enterprises be financed? In terms of challenge and response, mass production was very much part of the challenge to management thinking, not the response.

Some of the disciplines within management have received short shift too. I have said very little about developments in accounting, largely because there are already some excellent histories of accounting thought. Corporate finance has received fairly limited coverage too, especially in the later period; as the long-standing editor of a corporate finance journal, I ought to feel embarrassed by this, but I do not. I appear to have said almost nothing about the development of logistics and supply chain management, and equally have ignored modern theories on innovation and technology management. I could have included these, of course, and left out other examples; but I think that the conclusion of the book would be still be very much the same.

That is, I think, quite enough justification and rationale. It is time to begin the narrative, to tell the story of thinking about management as it has emerged over time. We shall begin at the beginning, when civilizations first began to emerge and when written historical records begin to show us the shape and pattern of these new social orders.

2   Early management thought

A city comes into being because each of us is not self-sufficient but needs many things.
(Plato)

The earliest literature of most civilizations can be divided into two categories. First, there are devotional works, such as the Indian *Rig Veda* (composed sometime before the tenth century BC), the Book of Genesis, which was probably composed over a period of time leading up to the fifth century BC, or the earliest Egyptian papyri and tomb inscriptions such as the so-called Pyramid Texts (the oldest of which date to about the twenty-fourth century BC). These works and others like them attempt to establish a relationship between the civilization and its environment. They answer questions such as, why are we here? Who made us? They provide a cosmological explanation of how the world came to be and how it is meant to work. In doing so, they give the civilization a dominant ideology, and through this ideology, a sense of purpose and identity.[1]

The second class of literature consists of what we might call 'heroic tales', myths and stories about leaders who, by force of character and personal example, rose to positions of power. Examples of this latter genre include the *Epic of Gilgamesh* from Sumeria, which in its earliest form dates back to at least 2000 BC; the *Iliad* and the *Odyssey* from Greece in the eighth century BC; the *Kojiki* (Record of Ancient Matters) from Japan around the same time, which tells of Jimmu, the legendary first emperor of Japan and his descendants; the *Mahabharata* from India, written possibly around the fifth century BC; early Chinese texts referring to Huangdi, the Yellow Emperor, the legendary first emperor of China and supposed inventor of Chinese traditional medicine; and some of the other early books of the Old Testament, particularly the Book of Exodus which tells the story of how Moses led the Israelites out of slavery in Egypt.[2]

Although these texts vary widely in terms of content and form, there are common themes that run through all of them. In each case, a strong leader – Gilgamesh, Moses, Odysseus, Arjuna, Huangdi – emerges and gives leadership to people at a time of crisis, bringing order out of apparent chaos. Some lead their people to freedom, others provide defence against foes, others lay down laws and give their societies form and structure. In many cases these written works are continuations of older oral traditions, which used example and precept to remind people of their duties and responsibilities to the society in which they lived.

Today, these works tell us what these early societies expected from their leaders. Again, there are common themes. Pretty much across the board, these ancient societies demanded that their leaders demonstrate virtues such as competence, courage, integrity, responsibility, fair and honest dealings with their own people, wisdom, justice and strength of character. Other texts made the duties and responsibilities of the leader even more clear. For example, a series of ancient Egyptian 'instructional texts' – including the *Maxims of Ptahhotep*, composed around 2400 BC, the *Instructions of Kagemni* (possibly composed as early as 2600 BC but likely of later date) and the later *Instructions of Amenemope* (probably written between 1300 and 1100 BC) – offer guidance as to how leaders should conduct themselves and maintain relationships with subordinates.[3] Scholars have noted a strong correlation between the *Instructions of Amenemope* and the Old Testament Book of Proverbs, suggesting that the influence of these instructional texts spread beyond Egypt.[4]

These Egyptian texts are the earliest works in a long tradition of instructional texts for leaders and would-be leaders that extends forward to Roman collections of homilies, medieval Islamic and Christian 'mirrors for princes', Rochefoucauld's *Maxims* and Samuel Smiles's *Self-Help*.[5] It might seem fanciful to compare these ancient texts to modern works on leadership such as Goffee and Jones's *Why Should Anyone Be Led by You?* or Lynda Gratton's *Glow*, yet there are most definitely common themes: the emphasis on personal integrity and fairness, the need to build trust between leaders and followers, the need for wisdom.[6] If we no longer imbue our leaders with divine qualities, as the Egyptians and Sumerians did, it seems that we still expect them to behave according to our expectations, and reserve the right to withdraw our loyalty from them if they do not. The implicit contract between leaders and followers was clearly understood, even at this early stage.

As civilizations grew and progressed, however, it became apparent that personal leadership was not sufficient. Leaders could not be everywhere, nor could they necessarily expect everyone to follow them through sheer force of character and personal example. Leaders appointed ministers, advisers and councillors to whom some of their duties were delegated. More, as societies became more complex, records needed to be kept, reports needed to be analysed and data needed to be collected in order to make certain that all members of society were paying their taxes, reporting for military service and so on. Societies needed order and structure if they were to last. In each society, as it progressed, a new generation of texts began to appear, each pondering how to create order and stability.

Egypt and the Near East

As Karl Moore and David Lewis have described in their book *The Origins of Globalization*, there has survived a considerable stock of records of trade in and between Sumeria, Babylon, the Phoenician cities, Egypt and their neighbours from as early as 3000 BC.[7] Thanks to these records, we know a fair amount about how business was conducted and organized in these regions. These were not mere subsistence economies: long-distance and international trade is as old as civilization itself. The Phoenicians ranged across the Mediterranean and probably as far as the British Isles; the Egyptian pharaoh Nekko sent an expedition to try to circumnavigate Africa (it failed), and trade links between the Middle East, India and China were established at a very early date, at least as early as the tenth century BC. We also see a variety of economic structures beginning to emerge. In Egypt, for example, the economy was centrally planned and controlled by the pharaoh and his officials.[8] In the Phoenician city-states, the theocratic rulers of those cities also exercised a high degree of control and were directly involved in trade and finance. Moore and Lewis make the point that in the Phoenician cities, the war leaders, heads of the civil administration, high priests of the temples and senior traders and bankers were very often the same people, fulfilling all four roles at once. In Babylon, by contrast, private merchants known as *tankārum* dominated economic activity and there was more separation of functions.[9]

Methods of economic governance varied accordingly. In Babylon, the rulers used legal codes and regulations to govern business behaviour. As Moore and Lewis comment:

> Laws sometimes multiply when people are enjoying a measure of freedom and prosperity. Legal systems, with their conservative tendencies, are much in evidence when there is something to conserve. The archaeological testimony to the longevity of the Sumerian–Assyrian–Babylonian *tankārum* could be celebrated as an expanding economy's inherent bias towards delegation, privatization and a measure of entrepreneurial capitalism.[10]

The most famous law code of this period is the Code of Hammurabi, composed around 1790 BC at the behest of Hammurabi, ruler of Babylon.[11] It consists of around 300 laws (in the most complete surviving version). The general purpose of the Code might be described as the preservation of order. There are laws prohibiting people from offering violence to each other, laws governing marriage, laws concerning the transfer of goods and chattels and many laws – at least 20 per cent of the total by my own estimate – governing the conduct of trade. The Code fixes wages to be paid to workers (perhaps it is not quite such definite evidence of entrepreneurial capitalism as Moore and Lewis suggest) and also sets out the conditions under which money can be lent and penalties for misuse of other people's money and possessions and for fraud.

The main point of the Code of Hammurabi and other similar law codes, at least so far as business is concerned, is to stabilize and rationalize relationships between business people and the rest of society. There is a clearly reflected concern that, if left unchecked, business people will sell shoddy goods or otherwise cheat their customers. One often-cited article from the Code of Hammurabi requires that if a builder builds a house which then collapses and kills the owner, the builder shall be put to death. Not all penalties are so draconian, but the principle remains: business people are an essential part of society, but they also need to be regulated, for their own good and the good of society. The enforcement of these codes of law was handled by an increasingly detailed and complex bureaucracy, as described for example in the Old Testament Book of Daniel (3:1–3).[12]

When it comes to bureaucracy, however, the Egyptians were the masters of the art. As noted, the pharaohs – who were recognized as divine beings – exercised tight central control. There were, so far as we know, no codes of laws as there were in Babylon and Assyria. 'While there were certainly legal rules (*hpw*)', writes the historian Aristide Théodoridès, 'their nature is uncertain'.[13] Théodoridès feels that it is 'inconceivable that nothing would have been legally codified in such a remarkably centralised country', and believes that there were law codes but none have survived. On the other hand, we know that the pharaohs ruled by decree, and it is possible that Egypt was governed by precedent, relying on knowledge of past decrees, rather than formal codes.

Ancient Egypt's bureaucratic system, on the other hand, was remarkably complex.[14] That bureaucracy emerged very early, and this emergence was probably driven to some extent by the need to manage very large building projects such as the pyramids and other royal monuments and tombs, and to manage complex irrigation projects along the banks of the Nile. As noted, the pharaoh issued decrees and gave orders; the function of the bureaucracy was to execute his orders and enforce those decrees. Even the highest officials had no authority to issue decrees or make laws of their own. 'The delegation of executive power was strictly authoritarian', says Eva Martin-Pardey, 'from the king to the highest officials of the state and from them to their subordinates.'[15]

We can get a glimpse into the inner workings of the Egyptian bureaucracy from a remarkable text, the *Duties of the Vizier*, composed by a senior official during the second half of the reign of the Pharaoh Ahmose (*c*.1539–1514 BC), founder of the 18th Dynasty.[16] It seems likely that the text was written on the instructions of Ahhotep, Ahmose's mother, who administered the kingdom during her son's lengthy absences from court while leading military campaigns. It can be hypothesized that, in the absence of the powerful authority of the pharaoh, Ahhotep intended to remind high officials of their duties and to make it clear that they were not excused those duties just because the pharaoh was not physically present.

Much of the *Duties of the Vizier* focuses on the official known as the *t3ty*, which we translate today as 'vizier'.[17] There is a lengthy summary of his duties and lists of the other officials over whom he has the power of appointment and who report to him. But there are also some fascinating insights into how power was exercised. While no lower official could refuse to receive a messenger from the vizier, at the same time the vizier is enjoined to be fair and equitable in his dealings with subordinates. For example, lower officials are not allowed to discipline poorly performing subordinates; they must refer their cases to the vizier, who would hear both sides and judge impartially. Full records must be kept of all transactions, and unless the pharaoh specifically dictates that the matter is to be kept secret, reports and messages must be delivered and read aloud publicly, thus ensuring transparency.

There is no direct statement of philosophy or purpose in *Duties of the Vizier*, but we can infer a few things from both the fact that the work was written at all, and by its relatively wide dissemination (several copies have survived, found in the tombs of later viziers, and we can assume that many other copies have since been lost). Ahhotep and her advisers were clearly bent on creating a stable system based on good practice that would function with minimal oversight. The vizier would run the administrative system, leaving the pharaoh to get on with making policy. That was the function of bureaucracy thirty-five hundred years ago; it continues, in theory at least, to be its function today.

Thus in these two different economic systems, we can see two different approaches to organization: one comparatively decentralized and relying on a system of regulation and enforcement, the other heavily centralized and relying on a system of direct bureaucratic control.

India

Classical Indian texts such as the *Rig Veda*, the *Mahabharata* and the *Upanishads*, a collection of theological and philosophical texts, had much influence on early Indian thinking on politics and society. Indeed, they continue to do so. Mahatma Gandhi, when charting the future of an independent India in the 1920s and 1930s, very often drew lessons and parallels with the modern day from these ancient texts.[18] Today, texts such as the *Mahabharata* and especially the *Bhagavad-Gita* remain influential.

The *Bhagavad-Gita* is part of the *Mahabharata*, though some scholars believe it is a later addition, possibly from the second or third centuries BC.[19] It takes the form of a dialogue between the god Krishna and his friend and follower the warrior Arjuna. As the text begins, Arjuna is reluctant to engage in a holy war, for it will mean fighting against his own kin and people whom he likes and admires. Krishna recalls Arjuna to his duty: he was born into the warrior caste, and therefore he must fight because that is his purpose in being. He tells Arjuna to banish all emotion and perform his duty with detachment and a calm mind. 'Be steadfast in yoga, O Arjuna. Perform your duty and abandon all attachment to success or failure. Such evenness of mind is called yoga . . . He who is without attachment, who does not rejoice when he obtains good, nor lament when he obtains evil, is firmly fixed in perfect knowledge.' Lust, greed and anger are the paths to ruin; renunciation of the senses leads to inner peace and tranquillity.[20] The message for leaders is that they must remain steadfast and do what is morally right, even if it their duty is distasteful to them personally.

There is another message in the *Bhagavad-Gita* too, one which is sometimes overlooked. All people in society have duties laid upon them by God and by their rulers. They should strive to perform those duties as well as possible, and not to seek to change the course of their life. 'It is better to engage in one's own occupation, even though one may perform it imperfectly', Krishna tells Arjuna when the latter expresses doubts about his path as a warrior, 'than to accept another's occupation and perform it perfectly . . . by following his qualities of work, every man can become perfect'.[21] This very much includes merchants. Swami Prabhupada, in his notes on his own translation of the work, comments that it is permissible for merchants to tell lies should this be necessary in order to make a profit, just as it is permissible for warriors to kill in order to be victorious. Again, merchants should simply accept that this is their lot and not express hankerings to become warriors or priests.[22] It should be noted that the *Bhagavad-Gita* is a description of how its authors feel that things should be, not how they actually were; later Indian works such as the *Kathasaritsagara* from the eleventh century AD show merchants and trade in a rather different light.[23]

The major text on administration to emerge from the classical period in India is the *Arthashastra*, composed around 300 BC. This work consists of fifteen books, further subdivided into 150 chapters of various lengths.[24] Its author, Kautilya, was a senior civil servant – according to some accounts, he held a post equivalent to that of prime minister – in the Mauryan kingdom, established in northern India by the warlord Chandragupta Maurya in the wake of Alexander the Great's invasion of India in 327–326 BC. Chandragupta had briefly been an ally of Alexander, but after the Macedonian king's abrupt withdrawal from India following a mutiny in his army, Chandragupta took advantage of the ensuing chaos to carve out a kingdom for himself. His successors went on to conquer most of the Indian subcontinent and establish a stable state that lasted for almost a hundred and fifty years.

Some sources ascribe that stability and success to the remarkably efficient bureaucracy developed by Kautilya and his officials early in Chandragupta's reign. There is no way of knowing how true this is, but we can be certain that on the whole the Mauryan kingdom *was* stable and well managed, and that the *Arthashastra* was widely read and apparently even used as an instructional text through much of that period.

The great majority of the *Arthashastra* is taken up with very detailed descriptions of the duties, roles and responsibilities of the king and his administrators. It includes instructions and procedures for collecting revenue, issuing writs and decrees, treasury management including detailed audits of receipts and expenses in order to prevent theft or fraud, the recruitment and pay of civil servants, and the composition of the royal court in minute detail, right down to the number of mistresses the king should be allowed. There are also chapters discussing the management of such economically important industries as agriculture, mining, forestry and jewellery manufacture.

But there is also a strong streak of philosophy running through the work. Kautilya is concerned not just with *how* the administration should function, but *why*. His is one of the first administrative treatises to consider not just function and procedure, but also purpose, aims and goals. It may come as a surprise to learn that Kautilya was not an absolutist. Unlike the Egyptian pharaohs, the Mauryan kings were not above the law. In Kautilya's conception, the king's purpose was to provide leadership and direction, but above all to uphold the *dharma*, an Indian term that we can define as 'righteous duty', something akin to the Western concept of natural law.[25] There is a natural order of things that is right and good: the king's duty is to make policy to achieve and maintain that natural order, and the duty of the bureaucracy is to support and implement that policy. In practical terms, this means that the king and his administrators should defend the state from attack, promote peace, order, justice and prosperity and, interestingly, 'encourage moral, religious and material progress'.[26] The purpose of this bureaucracy, then, was not just to administer things as they were ordered but to help promote change and make it happen.

Was Kautilya influenced by outside ideas? Two powerful philosophical systems had emerged not long before, that of Plato in Greece and that of Confucius in China. We know that there was substantial trade between India and China, and that philosophical and intellectual ideas were transmitted along those trade routes; it is not impossible that Kautilya was familiar, even if only at second or third hand, with some of the ideas of Confucius. As for Plato, Chandragupta's ally Alexander the Great had been tutored by Aristotle, himself a pupil of Plato. Although there is no proof, it is not impossible that some of Plato's ideas made themselves felt in the Mauryan kingdom, and there are some similarities between the ideas of the *Arthashastra* and those of the *Republic* (see below).

Certainly Kautilya himself had a lasting influence. For example, the *Yajnavalkya Smrti*, composed by the sage Yajnavalkya probably a hundred years or so after Kautilya, shows clear evidence on the influence of the *Arthashastra* in its discussions on the order and structure of society and on economics and banking.[27] The *Yajnavalkya Smrti* in turn influenced other works including the Tibetan Buddhist work the *Mulasarvastivada-vinaya*, which among other things details the ways in which monasteries are to be organized and discusses their economic organization and business activities. There are strong similarities between *Mulasarvastivada-vinaya* and the Rule of St Benedict, developed by the Christian monk St Benedict of Nursia some three centuries later (see Chapter 3).[28]

China

Ancient China produced not one but three important systems of thought, and all three offered comments on administration and management. Confucius, like Plato (and indeed, but with much greater coherence, like the writers of ancient Egypt and the Near East) sought to create an orderly social system that would endure. As well as civil administration, he commented directly, if briefly, on the role to be played by business people. Laozi (Lao-tzu) by contrast argued for a social system with minimal control where people are free to make choices, and supported the concept of natural law. The third writer, Han Fei, was a ruthless pragmatist who set out a detailed philosophy of bureaucracy.

By the time Confucius, Laozi and Han Fei appeared on the scene, Chinese civilization was well established. The Shang Dynasty ruled what is now north-eastern China in the valley of the Yellow River from about 1600 until 1046 BC, when it was overthrown by the Zhou dynasty. It was probably during the Shang period that the first texts of what later became known as the *Yijing* or *I Ching* (Book of Changes) appeared. The text was refined and developed during the Zhou dynasty and reached its final redaction during the Han dynasty in the first century AD. Essentially the *Yijing* is a divination text, which ancient kings and officials used in an attempt to understand and predict the future. However, its underlying principles including the concepts of *yin* and *yang*, the light side and the dark side, informed both Daoist and Confucian philosophies (see below), and it seems that its most important purpose was to force people to concentrate on fundamental issue of personality and interaction. The *Yijing* stresses the unity and harmony of creation; the efforts of all should be devoted to preserving harmony. There is thus a strong ethical theme to the work, and readers are constantly reminded that success depends on integrity. The work is full of often-quoted aphorisms such as 'to achieve great success by being upright and true is the way of heaven' and 'you will have good luck if you nourish what is right and true'.[29] As Mu-Lan Hsu and Kwan-Yao Chiu have shown, the *Yijing* has a long history as an aid to decision making by both administrators and business people in China.[30]

Several other works on administration emerged during this period, one of the oldest of which is the *Great Plan*, which again appeared in its final form in about 1120 BC but parts of which date back long before the Shang, perhaps as far as 2500 BC.[31] This short text is in part an exhortation to rulers to be virtuous and humble, but it also offers some thoughts on the role of administrators and officials.[32] Kao Yao, a government official active around 2200 BC, likewise urged rulers to be virtuous and lead by example.[33] More important still is *The Officials of Zhou*, composed around 1100 BC, which Violina Rindova and William Starbuck identify as the founding text of Chinese bureaucracy. In a similar fashion to the *Duties of the Vizier* but in more detail, *The Officials of Zhou* catalogues all the officials of the Kingdom of Zhou (which would shortly go on to conquer the Shang dynasty) and identifies their duties and reports and also procedures by which their work can be checked and audited. It remains one of the most sophisticated documents on organizational structure to have survived from ancient times.[34] These and other writings on administration formed the intellectual basis from which two of China's most important thinkers, Confucius and Laozi developed their ideas.

Confucius

The scholar, teacher and courtier Master Kong, better known to the world as Confucius, lived from 551–479 BC. He lived and wrote at a time when the Zhou dynasty was declining, on the eve of the era known as the 'Warring States' period when China fragmented into a number of small states, each fighting for control. It seems that Confucius was well aware of what was to come, and on one level his work can be seen as an attempt to stave off the coming chaos. His solution was to go back to the past, to try to reassert the values that – or so he believed – had given China its strength and unity. 'Confucius was an idealist trying to solve problems', write Karl Moore and David Lewis. 'Seeing warfare and quarrelsome folk all around him, he looked back to the wisdom and ritual ways of China's past.'[35]

Much of Confucius's thinking was directed to the search for a philosophy, a 'way' by which order and peace could be restored. Although he had little influence in his own lifetime, his teachings, collected by his followers under the title *Analects*, became one of the foundation texts of Chinese philosophy and education, and influenced not just China but much of the Far East. His later followers, including Mencius and Xunzi, helped transmit his ideas and added concepts of their own. His ideas on ethics, politics, society and relationships are complex and detailed.[36] Here I propose to discuss just two ideas, the notion of the family, which remains central to Chinese society and business today, and Confucius's own ideas on the role of business in society.

> Confucius begins from the insight that the life of every human being is played out within the context of their particular family, for better or for worse. For Confucius and generations of Chinese to come, it is one's family and the complex of relationships that constitute it, rather than the solitary individual, that is the basic unit of humanity.[37]

In the age-old debate as to who has priority, the individual or the group, Confucius comes down firmly on the side of the group. The concept of the 'self' is downplayed. Rather than personal *rights*, Confucius speaks of the individual's *responsibilities* to the *group*. In practical terms, this means that those at the head of any institution – the family, the state, a business enterprise, a school – have a responsibility to lead, and those who follow that lead are required to obey. Children should give unquestioning obedience to their parents; pupils should regard their teacher with reverence and never contradict him; ministers should obey the orders of the king. But this is not just a matter of blind obedience. Like the author of the *Great Plan*, Confucius also believes that parents – and teachers, and kings, and employees – have a duty to uphold the institutions they lead, and to protect and guide those who follow them. An essential quality of any leader, in Confucius's view, is wisdom. The perfect leader is the 'sage-king', who uses wisdom to guide him along the *dao*, the 'Way' of right thinking and behaviour.[38] The ultimate aim is the 'Golden Mean', a society that existed in perfect harmony, ruled by peace and wisdom. According to one of Confucius's disciples, Master Yu:

> It is honouring parents and elders that makes people human. Then they rarely turn against authority. And if people do not turn against authority, they never rise up and turn the country into chaos. The noble-minded cultivate roots. When roots are secure, the Way is born. To honour parents and elders; is that not the root of humanity?[39]

By 200 BC, if not earlier, Confucius's works were a standard part of the curriculum in Chinese schools, and have remained so until the present day.[40] For many centuries, candidates for the Imperial Chinese civil service were required to read Confucius along with other Chinese classics such as the *Daxue* (Great Learning) and *Zhongyong* (Doctrine of the Mean). They were then examined on their knowledge of these classics, and it was proficiency in such knowledge that ensured whether they passed and were accepted into the civil service. The Imperial bureaucracy – until the ending of this system after the 1911 revolution – was thus populated entirely by convinced Confucians. Nor was the influence of Confucius restricted only to the civil service. The notions of filial obedience and responsibility to the group permeated virtually every aspect of society, including business. Prior to 1949 and the establishment of the communist state, virtually all Chinese businesses were organized using the family model, and even after that date the model continued in use among the economically powerful overseas Chinese communities of South-East Asia.[41] The 'Chinese family business' remains a model which has been widely discussed and studied by academics. As Malcolm Warner has recently shown, Confucian values such as interpersonal relationships (*guanxi*), obligations to other people and reciprocity play a direct role in Chinese methods of human resource management.[42] The direct influence of Confucian thinking on modern business thought and practice in east Asia is hard to overstate.

The other aspect of Confucius which deserves mention here is his attitude to business in society. It was, and sometimes still is, assumed that Confucius was essentially 'anti-business'. This assumption is present, for example, in the work of the German sociologist Max Weber, whose *The Religion of China*, first published in 1915, portrayed Confucian thought as hidebound by tradition, more focused on the worship of ancestors than on the present day, tending to stifle creative thought and innovation.[43] This remains the standard view of Confucius today, but the view is certainly open to challenge. Important here are the views of Chen Huan-Chang, a classically trained Confucian scholar who had fled China after an abortive revolution in 1895. Arriving in America, Chen went on to complete a Ph.D. in political economy at Columbia University, where he created a new interpretation of Confucian thinking in the light of contemporary Western economics.[44] In Chen's view, Confucius was by no means antipathetic to business, though he did believe that business ought to be restricted and controlled; Chen went so far as to claim that principles of 'Confucian socialism' can be identified in the Confucian thinking.

Confucius was clearly alive to the importance of wealth generation. When asked by a follower what should be done to improve the lot of the people, Confucius replied that there were two essentials: educate the people, and make them wealthy. Education was required in order to understand how to use wealth wisely, not squander it on personal pleasures; wealth, in its turn, paid for education and made it possible. The two combined together would lead to personal enlightenment. Confucius also argued that virtue created wealth, not the other way around. He cited a passage from the Daxue in support of his views: 'The superior man must be careful about his virtue first. Having virtue, there will be the man. Having the man, there will be the land. Having the land, there will be wealth. Having the wealth, there will be its use. *Virtue is the root, and wealth is only its outcome*' [my italics].[45]

Like the lawmakers of Babylon, though, Confucius believed that economic activity could not exist unrestrained. The business people and landowners who generated the wealth were exposed to temptation and greed, and unless they were sufficiently enlightened, they could not be trusted to behave in a virtuous manner. Therefore, business people should submit themselves to the authority of the 'sage-king' who would rule over them and provide guidance just as a father would to a son. In turn, the sage-king would remain outside the economic system and would eschew personal wealth. Without wealth of their own, the sage-kings would have no personal interest in economic activity and would therefore act according to wise precepts rather than in hopes of personal gain.

Confucius believed in a regulated economy. He also eschewed competition, which like many later thinkers (including many capitalist ones) he regarded as harmful and wasteful. As part of the pursuit of the Golden Mean, he argued for a balance of supply and demand; when perfect equilibrium between the two was reached, competition would be eliminated. Unlike later Western economic thinkers, who argued for adjusting supply to match demand, Confucius called instead for the regulation of demand so that it would match supply. This meant both economic controls to restrict access to some goods, especially luxury goods, and a call to people to exercise personal restraint and be modest in their demand, and hence their spending habits. (The same call has, of course, been heard from some thinkers in the late twentieth century; reduced personal consumption has been seen as one way of tackling environmental degradation and climate change, for example.)

Two of Confucius's followers also deserve mention here. The first is Meng Ke or Mengzi, better known in the West as Mencius. He is known to have been active in the fourth century BC. A famous quote attributed to him, and quoted later by management historian Claude George, is said to anticipate one of the central ideas of scientific management:

Whoever pursues a business in this world must have a system. A business which has attained success without a system does not exist. From ministers and generals down to the hundreds of craftsmen, every one of them has a system. The craftsmen employ the ruler to make a square and the compass to make a circle. All of them, both skilled and unskilled, use this system. The skilled may at times accomplish a circle and a square by their own dexterity. But with a system, even the unskilled may achieve the same result, though dexterity they have none.[46]

The similarities with scientific management (see Chapter 5) are there, though to my mind the parallels with Harrington Emerson's efficiency movement (see Chapter 5) are even stronger. It needs to be added, though, that Chen Huan-Chang (whom George cites) paraphrased this quotation very heavily from the Mencian original,[47] and that both Taylor's *Shop Management* which first set out some of the principles of scientific management and Emerson's *Efficiency as a Basis for Operations and Wages* were in print at the time Chen was writing.[48] It is possible that Chen, knowing of scientific management, over-egged the pudding in order to make a point about how advanced Chinese thinking was.

However, Mencius did talk a great deal about the need for systems, particularly in the management of agriculture and land tenure, and he clearly believed in the use of a more systematic approach to administration rather than simply managing ad hoc. In that sense, he can be fairly seen as anticipating some of the ideas of Taylor and Emerson. Mencius also went much further than Confucius in his ideas on economic management, urging rulers to govern their economies well, to create conditions in which businesses could flourish and to keep taxes to moderate levels in order to encourage commerce and craftwork. He also paid a great deal of attention to ethical issues and argued that to behave ethically and morally was one of the first duties of a ruler.

The other writer, Xunzi, who was active during the third century BC, took a much softer line than Confucius on regulation. He believed that rules and regulations were only necessary to provide people with guidelines as to correct behaviour in uncertain times. When there was a stable political and social order, people would know naturally what was best and would behave correctly.[49] Xunzi does not discuss business directly, but there are clear implications for the conduct of business and for economic regulations. Regulations are needed when times are hard; when times are good, they can be relaxed or dispensed with.

Laozi

Details of the life of Laozi are scarce, and it is not even certain if he existed at all; if he did, then he probably lived slightly earlier than Confucius. The work attributed to him, the *Daodejing* (or *Tao Teh Ching* – literally, The Book of the Way and Virtue) was probably compiled around 300 BC, or possibly slightly earlier, probably from other texts and/or from material transmitted orally.

Daoists (or Taoists), as the followers of Laozi are known, take quite a different view of society from the Confucians. Whereas Confucians believe in the need for regulations, laws, rituals and ceremonies as guides to order and good conduct, the Daoists believe these things actually lead people astray. It was not lack of ceremony and rules that led Zhou society to break down, Laozi says, but too much of them, and not enough focus on the things that matter. The only sure guide to good conduct is to find the Way, or in practical terms, to find the right way of living and to stick to that:

> Failing the Way, man resorts to virtue.
> Failing virtue, man resorts to humanity.
> Failing humanity, man resorts to morality.
> Failing morality, man resorts to ceremony.
> Ceremony is the merest husk of faith and loyalty.
> It is the beginning of all confusion and disorder.[50]

Daoists also believed in government taking a light hand, and intervening in society and the economy as little as possible. They espoused the principle of non-action, or *wu-wei*:

The highest type of ruler is one of whose existence the people are barely aware.
Next comes one whom they love and praise.
Next comes one whom they fear.
Next comes one whom they despise and defy.
When you are lacking in faith,
Others will be unfaithful to you.
The Sage is self-effacing and scanty of words.
When his task is accomplished and things have been completed,
All the people say: 'We ourselves have achieved it!'[51]

Daoism became one of those philosophies that people loved to discuss but rarely practised. As we have seen, and shall see again in a moment, Chinese government and business alike turned their back on this model of leadership and opted for something altogether more authoritarian and structured. Daoism, with its love of paradox and its dislike of authority and control, was not well suited to the needs of ordinary Chinese, who craved authority and control as a defence against the troubled times in which they lived. Another Daoist philosopher, Zhuangzi, made a powerful argument for a connection between virtue and knowledge; only what he called an 'authentic person' could understand and interpret knowledge in such a way as to lead people effectively and in the 'right' way. (Again, there are echoes of Rob Goffee and Gareth Jones and their insistence that leaders must be 'authentic'.)[52]

However, Daoism did have one surprising and very powerful later influence. In the seventeenth century, a French Jesuit missionary in China translated the *Daodejing* as *Le livre du ciel* (The Book of Heaven). Back in France this was read by the political economist François du Quesnay, who was particularly taken with the concept of *wu-wei*, which the Jesuit translator had rendered as *laissez-faire*. In his own book, *Le despotisme de Chine*, first published in 1764, Quesnay argued that the perfect monarch 'should do nothing but let the laws rule', the laws in this case being the natural ones which, if conformed to without interference, would see society exist in perfect harmony.[53] Laissez-faire is of course one of the cornerstones of free-market capitalism as it exists today, and influenced the Scottish economist Adam Smith when he coined his own term, the 'invisible hand' (see Chapter 4).

Han Fei

The third important Chinese figure from this period is Han Fei, who died in 233 BC.[54] Unlike Confucians and Daoists, Han Fei did not believe that people could be expected to follow a system of ethics. Following the precepts of an earlier thinker, the statesman Shang Yang, Han Fei doubted the Confucian and Daoist view that human beings are essentially good. He suggested that the only way to achieve conformity to required standards and norms was through force of law – with draconian punishments for those who failed to obey the law.

Han Fei's system comprised three elements: (1) *fa*, meaning 'prescriptive standards', which includes both the legal systems and the punishments for failure to obey the law; (2) *shi*, meaning 'authority' or 'power', which was exercised to enforce the law; and (3) *shu*, a method of controlling bureaucracy by comparing 'word' with 'deed', or in other words, measuring actual performance against expectations. Needless to say, those that did not perform according to expectations were liable for punishment.

Han Fei believed explicitly in systems. Everyone should know what was expected of them, and perform their duties exactly as required. 'Things have their proper place, talents their proper use', he declared. His system had the advantage of clarity, in that no one could complain that they did not know what to expect. But Han Fei also decreed penalties for those who used their own initiative. This was expressly forbidden: acting without orders could lead to deviant behaviour and imperil the entire system, even if the action was for the best of reasons.

> Marquis Zhao of Han got drunk and fell asleep. The keeper of the royal hat, seeing that the marquis was cold, laid a robe over him. When the marquis awoke, he was pleased and asked his attendants, 'Who covered me with a robe?' 'The keeper of the hat', they replied. The marquis thereupon punished both the keeper of the royal hat and the keeper of the royal robe. He punished the keeper of the robe for failing to do his duty, and the keeper of the hat for overstepping his office. It was not that he did not dislike the cold, but he considered the trespass of one official upon the duties of another to be a greater danger than cold.[55]

Conformity was everything; failure to conform, in any way, was dangerous. Today we would call this a 'machine bureaucracy', but Han Fei suggested that his system is a natural one, based on celestial harmony. A person acting on their own was like a star losing its place in the sky; it upset the natural order of things. And Han Fei did not mince words when it came to the means to enforce conformity. It was a simple matter of carrot and stick. Succeed and you will be rewarded; fail and you will be punished.

> The enlightened ruler controls his ministers by means of two handles alone. The two handles are punishment and favour. To inflict mutilation and death on men is called punishment; to bestow honour and reward is called favour. Those who act as ministers fear the penalties and hope to profit by the rewards.[56]

Nor did Han Fei have time for such concepts as fairness, openness or transparency. It was not only acceptable for leaders to deceive their followers and play one off against the other, it was desirable and even essential. The leader should never let his followers know what he is thinking, or give them any indication of his plans. They did not need to know these things. It was enough that they should obey.

Han Fei was writing at the height of the Warring States period when central political control had failed completely in China. His book, like the much later work of Machiavelli (see Chapter 3), is in part a call for a strong leader to restore order and end the chaos. Unlike Confucius – or indeed Machiavelli – Han Fei's ideas had real impact, even if he did not live to see this happen. Near the end of his life, Han Fei became an adviser to King Zheng, leader of the kingdom of Qin, who took Han Fei's ideas to heart and built his own state bureaucracy based on Han Fei's precepts (which today form the school of philosophy known as Legalism). Ten years after Han Fei's death, Zheng forcibly unified all the warring states of ancient China and proclaimed himself emperor with the title Qin Shi Huangdi. He became one of China's most powerful emperors: his legacies include the Great Wall, the Grand Canal and the 'terracotta army' of figurines buried around his tombs. A terrifying tyrant, he also laid the foundations for the Imperial Chinese bureaucracy that survived until the revolution of 1911 (and arguably beyond; many Chinese claim that the bureaucracy of the Communist Party, especially through the Cultural Revolution, exhibited strong Legalist tendencies). Violina Rindova and William Starbuck describe Chinese bureaucracy in the centuries following Han Fei as 'a continuing contest between Legalism and Confucian values . . . neither side won this contest, and the contest continues today'.[57] And although there is no question of direct influence – Han Fei's ideas were not known or studied in the West until the late nineteenth century – there is no question too that his ideas resonate when compared with some of the bureaucratic systems developed in the West. Robespierre, the leader of the French Revolution, never heard of Han Fei, but he almost certainly would have admired him. So too would J.P. Morgan and John D. Rockefeller (see Chapter 4).

Reflections

The persistence of bureaucracy

'Using Creativity to Outsmart Bureaucracies' is the subtitle of the book *Beating the System*, published in 2005 by Russell Ackoff and Sheldon Rovin.[58] The fact that two such important scholars – Ackoff is one of the founding fathers of operations research, Rovin an expert in healthcare management – have produced this book illustrates how 'bureaucracy' has, in the modern world, become a dirty word. To describe an organization as a bureaucracy is to suggest that it is stagnant, moribund, inefficient, stifling creativity and demanding conformity, devoted to perpetuating itself rather than to achieving goals. Bureaucracy is something that has to be 'beaten', got around, outsmarted, or if this does not work, stamped flat and destroyed.

This is a very recent development. As we have seen, bureaucracy is nearly as old as civilization itself. 'Ancient organizations could be well-defined, complex, and bureaucratic', comment Rindova and Starbuck, adding that 'some managerial philosophies popular today have clear antecedents running back 4000 years.'[59] Ahhotep, Hammurabi, Kautilya and Han Fei all used bureaucracy as a means of bringing order and structure to nascent societies. Bureaucracy was a bulwark against chaos. Bureaucracy promised stable government over the long term.

In primitive tribal societies, blood kinship and strong leadership were enough to hold relatively small social units together. But as these social units began to coalesce, forming cities and states, these ties were no longer sufficient. Families were still useful social units, they could and did run businesses and till the land, but they could not manage the whole apparatus of state. Strong leaders could hold a city or a state together for while, but if they died or retired and there was no other strong leader to follow them, then the polities they led tended to collapse. Even in later years this remained true. For example, in the early fifth century the war leader Attila united the nomadic tribes of eastern Europe and modern-day Russia, and for a time his Hun kingdom posed a serious threat to the Roman Empire. But when Attila died his kingdom fragmented, each tribe going its own way once more. The Roman Empire, which still had a strong and stable administrative system survived, at least for a little longer.

Bureaucracies, as we saw in the cases of China and India, became indispensable tools in the process of nation building. The same was true in later centuries elsewhere. In the twelfth century, the English crown created a small but highly efficient bureaucracy that was the envy of Europe, and enabled the relatively small kingdom of England to often punch above its weight, both militarily and diplomatically. Powerful Italian cities such as Venice and Florence relied on bureaucracies for administration: Machiavelli, one of the leading thinkers on administration of the sixteenth century, was a bureaucrat.

Even by the early twentieth century, bureaucracy was still very much in vogue. The sociologist Max Weber in his book *Economy and Society* outlined some of the reasons why bureaucracy has persisted as an important organizational form.[60] First, as discussed, the presence of a bureaucracy allows administration to carry on uninterrupted, even if there is an interregnum or the leader goes missing. Every member of a bureaucracy has a set of clearly defined duties and responsibilities, which eliminates duplication of effort and leads to efficiency. Bureaucracies also keep records, which means greater accountability and transparency.

Half a century on, and a sea change was taking place. In his witty and acute assault on bureaucracy, *Parkinson's Law*, the historian C. Northcote Parkinson accused bureaucracy of being pretty much the opposite of what Weber had described: inefficient, inept, dedicated solely to self-perpetuation rather than to achieving goals.[61] In the 1980s and 1990s the American management guru Tom Peters declared war on the concept of bureaucracy, calling for an end to formal organizational structures and the abolition of middle management.[62] Others such as Rosabeth Moss Kanter called for businesses to adopt more fluid and flexible organizational models.[63]

So, after four thousand years of service to civilization, has bureaucracy's day come? Is it really no longer relevant to the needs of modern business or government? Many argue that the answer is yes. But it is worth taking another look at why the institution of bureaucracy was created in the first place. Bureaucracy offered a systematic and rational solution to many of the problems of administration: the need for control, for accountability, for transparency and above all for security and continuity. It may be that other organizational forms now offer those same benefits. But we should make sure of this, before we consign bureaucracy entirely to the scrapheap.

I suspect that Max Weber was right, and that bureaucracy speaks to some fundamental need for security and certainty that many of us share. Parkinson and Peters described bureaucracies that had lost their purpose, their *raison d'être*, and were simply marking time. But sometimes, as in modern China, bureaucracies also get things done; we may not like the *way* they get them done, but that is a separate argument. Hating bureaucracy is not the orthodox thinking, but how many of us stop to consider, really consider, *why* we hate bureaucracy? And we might want to consider that the problem may lie not with bureaucracy as a concept, but how we use that concept and implement it, before we dispense with this ancient organizational form altogether – and risk throwing the baby out with the bath water.

Chinese writers on strategy

No tour of ancient Chinese writings on management would be complete without mention of Sunzi (Sun Tzu). As with Laozi, there is considerable debate as to who Sunzi was or even whether he existed at all. He is sometimes identified with Sun Wen, chief minister of the kingdom of Wu in the sixth century BC, but most authorities agree that the book known as *Sunzi Bingfa* (literally The Military Methods of Master Sun, but known more commonly as The Art of War) was composed sometime in the fourth century BC, at the height of the Warring States period. If so, then either a different Master Sun was involved, or the book is a compilation of oral accounts handed down from an earlier period. In the late second century

AD the work was heavily revised by the general Cao Cao, who used it as a manual of instruction for his officers. Cao Cao's version has been handed down through the centuries, and remains widely read across the Far East. Since its first translation into English in the early twentieth century, the book has been in print almost continuously in the West as well.[64] The book has been popular with business and political leaders, as well as military officers.

Sunzi believed in a systematic approach to warfare. One of the first essentials was planning and calculation:

> Now the general who wins a battle makes many calculations in his temple ere the battle is fought. The general who loses a battle makes but few calculations beforehand. Thus do many calculations lead to victory, and few calculations to defeat: how much more no calculation at all! It is by attention to this point that I can foresee who is likely to win or lose.[65]

Another essential is good intelligence: the successful general must be fully aware of his enemy's capabilities, the capabilities of his own army and officers, the ground on which the war will be fought, and the weather and any other environmental conditions that might interfere with his plans. 'If you know the enemy and know yourself', Sunzi wrote, 'you need not fear the result of a hundred battles. If you know yourself but not the enemy, for every victory gained you will also suffer a defeat. If you know neither the enemy nor yourself, you will succumb in every battle.'[66]

Yet another of Sunzi's essentials was method and discipline. He advocated the organization of the army into divisions, with all ranks including officers knowing their tasks and roles. He also wrote on what we would now call logistics or supply chain management, maintaining that good lines of communication and supply were vital to maintaining an army in the field. Control of expenditure was important too: generals had in effect to become financial planners so as not to waste resources.

Unlike other ancient Chinese texts such as *The Thirty-Six Stratagems*, Sunzi does not offer any particular strategic precepts. There is no sense that he is trying to create strategic options which can be chosen and applied to particular situations. Instead, he argues for thorough preparation, planning and system. The general who can master these will emerge victorious, especially if his rivals cannot master these essentials. This is likely to be the secret of the book's enduring success. The principles of planning, preparation and knowledge are easily applicable in many other fields of endeavour, including business.

Most later Chinese writing on strategy and military management did not move much beyond Sunzi. Cao Cao, one of the most successful military leaders in Chinese history, sometimes known as the Napoleon of China (which is a bit unfair on Cao Cao; unlike Napoleon he emerged undefeated and his descendants became emperors of China), simply revised and adapted Sunzi for his own purposes. The only other figure of note to emerge was Zhuge Liang, one of Cao Cao's principal opponents, who became famous for his mastery of deceit and delaying tactics to counter Cao Cao's more rigorous and systematic methods of war. The story of their struggle is told in the thirteenth-century Chinese epic *The Three Kingdoms*, which is also sometimes read by students of strategy.[67]

Greece and Rome

The Greek poet Hesiod, who lived in the eighth century BC, marks that transition we saw earlier in the Near East, between the 'heroic' literature of his predecessor Homer and a new body of work preoccupied with understanding society and seeking ways of making it work better. His *Works and Days* is similar to the early Egyptian instructional literature, and it is not impossible that it was influenced by Egyptian texts. What has most excited modern attention is Hesiod's descriptions of the rural economy, and he has even been called the first economist. That is probably stretching matters, but at the heart of the work there is some very interesting material on the management of agricultural estates.[68]

The early philosophers known as the Pre-Socratics did not consider management and administration directly, but they did come up with some concepts that had influenced management thinking in later years. Particularly important from the fifth century BC are the Sicilian biologist and cosmologist Empedocles whose observations led him to conclude that the world, including all nature and people themselves, were involved in a ceaseless cycle of change and flux, and Heraclitus, a philosopher from the city of Ephesus in modern-day Turkey, who argued that the cycle of flux included two countervailing forces, one of which brought things together while the other pulled them apart. Both have had some influence on modern theories of change management, and in his book *Images of Organization* in 1986, Gareth Morgan referred specifically to Heraclitus as the inspiration for his own ideas on organizational change and flux.[69]

The two Greek writers who have most to say about administration and management, however, are Plato and Xenophon. The first speaks from a largely theoretical point of view, the latter is more practical in outlook.

Plato

Plato, who lived from 427–347 BC, wrote on many subjects and is still recognized as one of the most influential philosophers in the Western tradition. His ideas ranged across an immense range of subjects, and there is no space here to go into all of them, not even in summary form.[70] The work that considers the problems of administration in greatest detail is the *Republic*, probably written sometime between 380 and 370 BC. Here Plato and his companions, including their master and mentor Socrates, try to identify the perfect form of governance for a city.[71]

Cities, and by extension nations and any other large organization, are created when people realize that they need to work together. 'A city comes into being because each of us is not self-sufficient but needs many things', says Plato.[72] It follows as a matter of course that in a city, people will take on specialist jobs: some will be labourers, others will be shopkeepers and traders, others will be craftsmen. Markets serve as the natural medium of exchange so that each specialist can sell his own produce and buy what he needs from others.

This apparently simple concept is in fact the first known direct statement of the division of labour. The concept had of course been known before. The Egyptian tomb workers in the Valley of the Kings a thousand years before had had specialist tasks,[73] and the vivid and probably fairly historically accurate account of the building of the Temple of Solomon in the Old Testament Book of Kings also demonstrates the division of labour in action. But Plato was the first to consider this concept in philosophical terms. His conclusion, as Nickolas Pappas points out in his study of the *Republic*, is that people are naturally disposed to perform certain tasks, and not to perform others (compare this to the *Bhagavad-Gita*'s insistence that people should only perform the tasks they are born to do).[74] Far from being an artificial imposition, as we so often see it today, Plato sees the division of labour as entirely consistent with human behaviour and natural law. In other words, it is a good thing.

The city exists, therefore, to satisfy the needs of its people, needs they can meet only by coming together and sharing and exchanging goods and labour. Those who rule the city should make this satisfaction of wants their ultimate goal. A corrupt or tyrannical city is one where the wants of only a few are met, while other people go without. Justice must be at the heart of all administration. And it should come as no surprise too that Plato believed in order and hierarchy as necessary for efficient administration. Finally, Plato argued that it was the duty of administrators to educate the people, so that they could take their full part in political life.

Plato was a political and social radical, whose mentor Socrates was executed for his heterodox views. Unlike Confucius or Kautilya, he never held office, and his attempts to persuade other rulers to put his ideas into practice failed utterly. Yet his influence has been very powerful, not least on his own student, Aristotle.

Xenophon

Like Plato, Xenophon (*c.*430–354 BC) was a follower of Socrates for a time, though the two later had a falling out. Xenophon then changed career from philosopher to mercenary soldier, and was one of the commanders of a force of Greek infantry that fought during a civil war in Persia in 401 BC. When all the senior Greek officers were killed, Xenophon was elected as one of the commanders of the force and brought the remains of the army safely home. In his later years Xenophon devoted himself to writing and produced several works on Socratic philosophy. His *Oeconomicus* (Economics) contains some interesting material on household management, and was later used as a model by several Roman writers.

His most influential work was the *Anabasis*, his own account of the Persian war and the retreat of the Greek mercenaries.[75] Although the text has interesting material on the organization of the Greek army, it was particularly admired for its thoughts on leadership. Possibly because of his youth and lack of experience, Xenophon did not at first have the full confidence of his men. He won their trust over the course of the long campaign by consulting them frequently, listening to their views, and imposing his ideas through persuasion rather than merely giving orders and expecting to be obeyed. The *Anabasis* was widely read and admired by Roman military commanders, including Julius Caesar.

Another and more curious work by Xenophon, *The Education of Cyrus*, also sheds some light on contemporary thinking on leadership. *The Education of Cyrus* is a work of fiction which purports to describe the ideas and views of Cyrus the Great (*c.*600–530 BC), the founder of the Achaemenid Persian empire. According to Xenophon, Cyrus refused to rule as a tyrant. He believed that the king ought to rule like the master of a household. Social bonds, not command and control, were to be the primary mechanisms of governance. Slavery should be abolished, and all those who serve the king should do through a sense of 'willing obedience'. Here is one speech which Xenophon puts into Cyrus's mouth:

> We are different from slaves in that slaves serve their masters unwillingly, but for us, if indeed we think we are free, it is necessary to do everything willingly which we think is worthwhile to do.[76]

Given that this is a work of fiction, and his own experiences in Persia, we are entitled to believe that these sentiments are in fact Xenophon's own. But is he in fact advocating a society based on cooperation and 'willing obedience'? Lynette Mitchell, in her detailed study of this work, thinks not. She believes that Xenophon is in fact satirizing the concepts he puts into Cyrus's mouth, perhaps even satirizing the notion of democracy and arguing for a more authoritarian approach. His own heroes appear to be, not the democratic masters of Athens who arranged the judicial murder of Socrates, but the tyrant kings of Sparta.

Roman writers

The Roman Empire was one of the most economically powerful entities of the ancient world. There was a huge volume of internal trade within the empire, in bulk commodities such as Egyptian corn and Spanish olive oil but also in luxury goods. Individual mercantile concerns might have operations in two, three or more parts of the empire depending on their line of business. And as Raoul McLaughlin has shown in his fascinating study, *Rome and the Distant East*, Roman trading interests extended right across Asia to India and China.[77] Roman embassies visited China in the second century AD, and Chinese embassies also came west at least as far as Central Asia; in both cases, extending and expanding trade was one of the main motivations.

Given this vast and wealthy complex of businesses and business relationships it seems strange, even perverse, that Rome did not produce much in the way of notable work on business. Nor did it produce many works of note on political administration. There are several possible reasons for this. First, with respect to business in particular, the Claudian Law of 218 BC forbade the upper classes, the senators, to engage in commerce. Thereafter any senator wishing to become involved in commerce had to do so through an intermediary. Noblemen and women therefore had no reason to read books about commerce. Second, those few writers who did venture comment on political matters, such as Seneca the Younger (d. AD 65) often found themselves on the wrong side of the establishment; death or exile was frequently the result. Therefore there was little incentive to write on these topics. Roman writers tended to stick to safe topics such as history, law and the natural world, which were less controversial and therefore less deadly. Third, there was the influence of another powerful political figure who also came to an untimely end thanks to his opposition to Julius Caesar, Marcus Tullius Cicero (106–43 BC). His writings on law and ethics and virtue were immensely influential, especially among the upper classes whose members continued to regard him as a role model for centuries to come. For Cicero, virtue and integrity were everything; nothing else mattered. Later writers often copied his model without amendment. That most cerebral of Roman emperors, Marcus Aurelius (AD 121–80), devoted his *Meditations* not to problems of governance and power, but to matters of the spirit.

It has often been observed that the Roman Republic and Empire inherited much of their philosophy and culture from Greece. Certainly in terms of writing on administration and management, the Hellenic influence is very visible, and though many Roman writers were fine stylists, they seldom went beyond the Greeks in terms of ideas. Virgil's *Georgics*, for example, contains much material on the management of agricultural estates, but the ideas do not go much beyond Hesiod's *Works and Days*. The two most important works on agricultural management, Marcus Porcius Cato's *De Re Rustica* and Marcus Terentius Varro's *Res Rustica*, both from the second century BC, are standard instruction manuals detailing the best times of the year for sowing and harvesting, urging that roads and walls be kept in good repair and so on.[78] Varro did mention briefly that it is useful to have knowledge of local markets and prices, and that where it is necessary to hire foremen or overseers, these men should be knowledgeable and competent in their jobs. Both Varro and Cato assumed that the estates they are discussing were run using slave labour.

Biographies and histories also give a few clues as to Roman attitudes to administration. These have to be read carefully, as the authors are usually concerned with either glorifying or vilifying their subjects (depending on how the prevailing political wind was blowing at the time). But Tacitus's portrayal of his father-in-law Julius Agricola, the Roman governor of Britain, offers some insights into the Roman style of leadership which was, surprisingly in that highly bureaucratic polity, very personal and 'hands on'.[79] Arrian's *The Campaigns of Alexander*, a full-length biography of Alexander the Great, likewise concentrated heavily on Alexander's leadership style and the methods he used to persuade people to follow him.[80]

One field where Roman writers did produce several original and influential works was military strategy and organization. The two best-known works are the *Strategemata* of Sextus Julius Frontinus (AD 40–103), best known in his own day for his work as engineer in charge of the Roman aqueducts, and the *Epitoma Rei Militaris* (Epitome on the Art of War) of Vegetius, a landowner and bureaucrat active in the early fifth century AD.[81] The two take very different approaches. Although Frontinus talks briefly about the need for discipline and organization, he is mostly concerned with strategic options. He imagines a number of different situations, and then lays out what generals in the past have done when faced with that same situation. The reader can choose whichever seems most appropriate given one's time and circumstances. Vegetius, on the other hand, has more in common with Sunzi. The bulk of his book deals with preparation and planning: he covers subjects such as training, discipline, logistics, equipment and organization. The army that is well equipped, well trained and well prepared, says Vegetius, will triumph over the one that is not.

Of the two works, it is that of Vegetius that lasted longest and had most impact. For all his attempt to be practical, in fact Frontinus's book lacked practical value. Knowing what a commander had done in similar situations a hundred years ago did not always help when choosing what to do now. Vegetius, on the other hand, offered a system based on organization, planning and control. Copies of his book were still being read in Europe during the Middle Ages and through to the Renaissance.

Before leaving this discussion on Roman writings on administration, it is perhaps appropriate to discuss the most famous quote on Roman organization, attributed to the satirist Gaius Petronius Arbiter (d. AD 66) (another who was forced to end his own life after aiming jibes at the Emperor Nero in his *Satyricon*):

> We trained hard, but it seemed that every time we were beginning to form up into teams, we would be reorganised. I was to learn later in life that we tend to meet any new situation in life by reorganising; and a wonderful method it can be for creating the illusion of progress while producing confusion, inefficiency and demoralisation.

This quote appeared in books on organization and eventually in newspaper and magazine articles quite frequently in the 1970s and 1980s; I recall seeing it posted, in large print, behind one of the issue desks at the British Library in London in 1989. Doubts began to set in during the 1990s, and extensive campaign to find where this quote came from turned up no evidence that Petronius had ever written it. The earliest genuine sighting appears to come from a bulletin board in a British army barracks shortly after the Second World War, and one theory is that its author, a disgruntled soldier and student of classics, attributed the quote to Petronius in order to deflect attention from himself. Despite the false attribution, the quote remains as truthful as ever. As one anonymous observer remarked in an Internet discussion over the controversy, doubtless Petronius *would* have written these words if only he had thought of them. The past influences the present, even if only indirectly.

Conclusion

We have seen how the first tentative ideas on management, in the Near East and Egypt, stemmed from a need to create order and permanence and enable the nascent civilizations of those regions to survive and grow. Other parts of the world then followed suit. Of all the civilizations of this period, it is China that has left us with the richest legacy from this period: two distinctive models of organization, the family business and bureaucracy; two different theories of economic control, central planning and laissez-faire; and some enduring work on strategy. India too had its founding father of administrative thought, Kautilya. In classical Greece we saw the first conceptualization of the division of labour, which was seen as a natural outcome of civilization. The Greeks also commented on the role and purpose of markets, and contributed some early thoughts on leadership. These were developed a little more fully by the Romans, who although essentially imitative, did find in Vegetius an original writer and thinker on military science and organization.

We have seen the foundation stones laid for theories about organization, leadership and strategy. Why these three in particular? Because these were the fields where ideas were most needed. Leadership was needed to hold societies together and to help create the dominant ideology that would bond members to each other as well as to the leader. Strategy was needed in order to defend the nascent civilizations from threats (including, of course, threats from other civilizations). Organizations were required in order to get things done and give society stability and permanence, and creating organizations that were effective and that could last was a priority from the time of Ahhotep and Hammurabi on down. William Starbuck has commented that although people have been writing about organizations for at least three thousand years, the idea of a general theory of organizations has only developed since the 1930s: 'when the writers did make statements about organizations, they did not generalize. They wrote about specific organizations.'[82] My own view is that this may be overstating the case. Some texts, such as *Duties of the Vizier*, are indeed descriptions of particular organizations. But Plato, Confucius and Kautilya, at least, were certainly searching for general principles. Han Fei, whether we approve of him or not, absolutely did lay down some general principles of organization; he was describing royal government, but those principles translate into any organizational setting. And even if it is argued that Kautilya and the others fell short of finding those principles, they deserve credit for at least setting the lines of inquiry in motion.

One thing that has been significantly missing from most of the writings we have discussed so far is the management of commercial enterprises. Most of the writers we have discussed have been preoccupied with civil and military administration, and have treated commercial activity only in the context of the role of government. As we shall see in the next chapter, that begins to change and we see a growing awareness of commercial management as a field of inquiry it its own right; and that awareness comes first in a place that some readers may find surprising.

3 Management thought in the age of commerce

Assign every matter its proper place and do every job at the appropriate time.

('Ali ibn Abi Talib, fourth caliph of Islam)

The period from the third to the sixth centuries AD was one of geopolitical shift and transformation across much of Europe and Asia. Under pressure from Germanic and Slavic peoples migrating west, the western half of the Roman Empire gradually dissolved and became a series of independent states. The eastern half, which historians later named the Byzantine Empire, survived but was challenged for dominance in the Middle East by a new Persian dynasty, the Sassanids. In India the Mauryan Empire was followed by others such as the Kushan Empire and the Gupta Empire, but although these were politically strong and culturally brilliant, they did not succeed in unifying India to the same extent. The Han dynasty, which had succeeded the Qin in China, collapsed in AD 220, and lasting reunification of the country came only with the advent of the Tang dynasty in 618.

Industry and trade did not cease during this period, but there were significant disruptions, especially in China where the population declined by about one-half during Warring States period after the fall of the Han dynasty,[1] and in parts of Western Europe including Britain. But there were shifts in patterns as new economic centres rose and others declined. New polities also faced new challenges in terms of civil and military administration. These new polities did not forget the lessons of the past, but they reinterpreted, revised and expanded the works of previous writers and also came up with some genuinely new ideas. By the seventh and eighth centuries a new order was beginning to emerge, one that looks rather like the one we have now in Europe and Asia.

The next seven or eight centuries were a period of growth. Populations and economies expanded; even if, as in the case of China above, or the European famine and Black Death in the fourteenth century, there were also some violent contractions. Economic historians have often followed the late Angus Maddison and depicted the world economy as growing only at a snail's pace, if at all, before the advent of the Industrial Revolution.[2] In overall global terms this may be so, but this overall picture hides a great deal of rapid economic growth in many parts of the world at various times. The economy of England, for example, grew at an average rate of about 5 per cent per annum during the twelfth and thirteenth centuries.[3] And, just as today, growth brought its challenges. Government administrators and business leaders alike had to adapt to the challenges of rising populations, higher volumes of trade and increasing urbanization.

And adapt they did, inventing new forms of organization, new methods of accounting and new financial instruments, theorizing about government and the morality of business and the role of business in society, and leaving behind a significant body of records which allow us to gauge their progress. One economic historian, Roberto Lopez, coined the term 'commercial revolution' to describe the period from 950–1350, but it is hard to see why those dates have particular significance.[4] The entire period from 600–1600 is one of ongoing change and development in the commercial world, and in government and public administration too.

I have called this period rather arbitrarily as the age of commerce because of the importance of trade, especially long-distance trade, to the world's major economies.[5] But mining and manufacturing remained important – products such as silk and pottery were major exports from China, and Gene Heck argues, not uncontroversially, that the Arabian peninsula had a number of strong domestic industries at the time of the rise of Islam[6] – and agriculture was still the dominant sector almost everywhere, save in a few special cases such as the maritime city of Venice. There were advances in management in these sectors too, and we will consider these in this chapter.

I referred above to governments and business people adapting to meet new circumstances. Nowhere was this adaptation more significant or more rapid than in the Arab world following the emergence of Islam. For a time, roughly from AD 700–1100 if not longer, the Islamic states were the world's centre of economic gravity. As K.N. Chaudhuri has described, Muslim merchants dominated the maritime trade of the Indian Ocean, and acted as middlemen in the ever-growing trade in eastern spices, drugs and textiles between their producers in eastern Asia and the growing body of consumers in Europe, trading first with the Byzantine Empire and then with the Italian cities, Venice, Genoa, Pisa, Ancona and others.[7] We will come on to discuss Muslim business in a moment, but we need first to look at how theories of public administration evolved under Islam.

Islamic leadership

The expansion of Islam out of the Arabian peninsula in the seventh century and the creation of the first Islamic state have been described many times.[8] The pace and scale of that expansion posed challenges to that state's new leaders. Many of them came from mercantile backgrounds. The Prophet Muhammad's tribe, the Quraysh, contained many notable merchants and traders, including his own wife Khadija, a respected merchant in her own right. Muhammad himself had been involved in trade, and the first four caliphs who succeeded him after his death also had backgrounds in trade. But they had little experience of civil administration, especially not of a polity that by the end of the century covered most of the Middle East and North Africa.

Accordingly, although the Muslim rulers co-opted Greek and Egyptian bureaucrats into their own system, there is a strong sense that they were making it up as they went along. This is very much evident in the *Nahj al-Balagha* (Peak of Eloquence), the collected letters, sermons and other writings of 'Ali ibn Abi Talib, fourth caliph of Islam and son-in-law of the Prophet.[9] Included in this collection, compiled after his death in AD 660, are the so-called 'Document of Instruction' written to the governor of Egypt, several letters to officials including army officers and tax collectors, and a moving letter to his son al-Hasan, written while 'Ali himself was dying of wounds inflicted by an assassin.

The letter to al-Hasan consists in part of a series of maxims on how a leader should conduct himself, and is revealing on that account. 'Ali never ceases to remind his heir that, just as the people are accountable to him, so he in turn is accountable to God. The leader should be prepared at all times to render an account of himself and face God's justice. As well as a powerful statement of ethical principles, 'Ali also espouses a concept that would later become known as the 'servant-leader'. The good leader, the leader who would win merit in God's eyes, was the one who put himself at the service of the people.

Much the same tone is evident in the 'Document of Instruction'. Mercy and justice, says 'Ali, are the most important principles of governance. But there is a hint, too, of the need for a systematic approach to administration:

> Avoid haste in matters before their time, slowness at their proper time, insistence on them when the propriety of action is not known or weakens when it becomes clear. Assign every matter its proper place and do every job at the appropriate time.

Idealized portraits of later Islamic leaders often assigned the same qualities to them. A biography of Salah al-Din Yusuf (1138–93), better known in the West as Saladin, describes him as being pious, physically brave, yet gentle in manner, compassionate, generous, well spoken and a master of all forms of knowledge.[10] The same qualities are ascribed to the Abbasid Caliph Haroun al-Rashid and to many other admired leaders. It should of course be added that these accounts suggest what people wanted their leaders to be like, and were not portraits of them as they actually were. (Saladin, for example, could be very ruthless, and as well as being a pious man he could also be quite intolerant, as evidenced by his ordering the execution of the essentially harmless Sufi mystic Shams al-Din Suhrawardi on a charge of heresy.) But these idealized portraits are nonetheless important, for they tell us what society expected from its leaders.

Administration in early Islam

In the early period at least, Islamic rulers borrowed heavily from Greek ideas, and Greek philosophy became both popular and influential in the Arab world and was taught in many schools. By the time of the establishment of the Abbasid caliphate in Baghdad in 762, says C.E. Bosworth, there was 'a symbiosis in the administrative field of the non-Arabs and the Arabs'.[11] Islamic administrators, like Islamic philosophers, took Greek ideas on board and adapted them to their own needs. Al-Farabi, who died in 950, was one of the most important of these later Islamic philosophers, and his book *Al-madina al-fadila* (The Virtuous City) is one of the most important works of Islamic political philosophy.[12] Al-Farabi was clearly influenced by Plato's *Republic*, and there are similarities between the two works. Notably al-Farabi, like Plato, believes that the task of the ruler is to ensure that the inhabitants of the city have their needs met and can achieve happiness. His ideas on just and enlightened rule influenced many later Islamic writers.

The influence of Plato was not welcomed by all Islamic scholars, however. Under the influence of the scholar al-Ghazali (1058–1111), whose book *Tahafut al-falasifa* (The Incoherence of the Philosophers) claimed that philosophy was incompatible with faith, Greek philosophy began to fall out of favour. At the same time there was a rise in more mystical forms of belief such as Sufism.[13]

Another source of ideas was Persia, where the Sassanid empire had been conquered by the Muslim Arabs. Partly because they lacked administrators of their own, the latter had left most of the old Sassanid bureaucrats in place, and then began to hire them into leading positions elsewhere in the Islamic state. Persian bureaucrats were prominent at the courts of the Abbasid caliphs in Baghdad from the mid-eighth century onward, and their traditions and experience of civil administration played a major role in creating the organizational structure that sustained the Islamic state. The Barmakid family, for example, seem to have been a sort of hereditary dynasty of bureaucrats, and some of its members held high office under Haroun al-Rashid (d. 809), arguably the most powerful of the Abbasid caliphs and himself of Persian descent. Yahya ibn Khalid, a Barmakid and vizier to Haroun al-Rashid, collected Indian and Chinese texts as well as Islamic ones and led an attempt to try to synthesize learning on administration and many other subjects.

Central to Persian thinking about administration was the concept of *adab*, which the scholar G.E. von Grunebaum defines as 'the general knowledge of everything'.[14] *Adab* complemented *'ilm*, the knowledge of a particular branch of sciences. A scholar might concentrate on *'ilm*, but the *katib*, a term meaning 'secretary' but used more generally to include pretty much all middle-ranking and senior members of the administration, 'had to be erudite, and his erudition had to be exactly that mosaic of miscellaneous information kept in place by mastery of form and diplomatic grace that *adab* offered.'[15] Grunebaum goes on to note how the roles of courtier, scribe and poet often overlapped. Clearly this was a society that valued generalists, and encouraged those in places of responsibility to have general knowledge. Scholars have identified eight separate categories of knowledge covered by *adab*, a solid knowledge of political theory and the science of administration being one of them.[16]

Manuals on *adab* and its uses were widely read. Abu 'Abdallah al-Khwarazmi's *Matifah al-ulum* (Keys to the Sciences), written in the late tenth century, is one of the best surviving examples.[17] This is aimed specifically at secretaries and administrators and lays out their duties. Particular attention is paid to record-keeping, and there are chapters on how to compile registers of financial transactions and how to keep records of salaried personnel. Chapter 4 on the *kitaba*, the art of the secretary, starts with a discussion of accountancy and accounting procedures, the compilation and presentation of records and reports, as well as a description of the taxation system, and then goes on to describe accounting and reporting systems used for the postal systems, the department of lands, the army and the department of waterways. There is also a section on maintaining correspondence and keeping records, so that at all times there will be an orderly record of what has been done. This is one of the cornerstones of any administrative system, and we can be quite sure that books like the *Matifah al-ulum* were read by business people as well as civil servants.

At a higher level there are books on governance and leadership. Two of the best known are the *Siyasat Nama* (Book of Government) by the Nizam al-Mulk, written some time before 1092, and the *Qabus Nama* (Mirror for Princes) by Kai Kaus ibn Iskandar, which has been dated to 1082. Both were originally written in Persian rather than Arabic.[18]

The Nizam al-Mulk, whose real name was Abu 'Ali al-Hasan al-Tusi, was a Persian administrator who rose to be chief minister of the Seljuq Turkish state. The Seljuqs were a nomadic Turkish people from Central Asia who conquered much of modern-day Iran and Iraq and set up their own state. Like the early civilizations we saw in Chapter 2, the Seljuqs had a tradition of personal leadership and their literature fell into the 'heroic tales' mode of the early Greeks and Sumerians. An example is the so-called *Book of Dede Korkut*, a set of tales about a heroic chieftain and his companions which shows, among other things, that the early Turks had little in the way of formal organization.[19] The *Siyasat Nama* is basically a handbook on how to run a government. There are chapters on every aspect of ruling a state, including land management, law and justice, how to run an intelligence agency, the employment of messengers, how to hold audiences with subjects, even a chapter on how to arrange drinking parties. One chapter advises the ruler against giving orders while he is drunk. Others urge that decisions should be made carefully and with due consideration of all the facts, and there is much emphasis on justice and fairness in decision making. Once again, the Nizam al-Mulk is describing the Seljuq state – or the Seljuq state as it ought to be – but he is reaching back to a long tradition of Persian bureaucracy and administration stretching right back to Cyrus the Great fifteen hundred years earlier. He is trying, in other words, to lay out a set of principles that will enable the fledgling Seljuq state to settle down and become stable and permanent. It should be added that he did not succeed; he was assassinated in 1092, the Seljuq sultan was likewise assassinated a month later and the Seljuq state fragmented soon after.

Kai Kaus, who bore the title Prince of Gurgan, had seen his own state on the south shore of the Caspian Sea conquered by the Seljuqs and become a tributary state. *The Mirror for Princes* was probably written in reaction to the violent and chaotic events during and after the Seljuq conquest, again motivated in part, at least, by a search for peace and stability. His modern translator, Reuben Levy, thinks that Kai Kaus was influenced by the Greek philosophy of Plato and Aristotle as well as earlier Persian works, and there certainly seem to be strong echoes of the *Republic*, particularly in chapters on the qualities of leaders and their relationships with the community. Statements such as 'as long as a man lack accomplishments he remains without value' could have come straight from Greek philosophy.[20] At the same time, the chapter on the art of the secretary comes straight out of the tradition of *adab* (see above) and there is a section on Sufi mysticism.

Unusually for this sort of text, Kai Kaus includes a chapter entitled 'Being a Merchant'. 'Although commerce is not an occupation which can with complete accuracy be called a skilled craft', he writes, 'yet properly regarded it has its laws just as the professions have'.[21] He clearly has much respect for merchants, and cites an Arab proverb: 'were it not for venturesome men [i.e. merchants prepared to take risks], mankind would perish'.[22] He lists some of the qualities that a good merchant must have: the ability to accept risk, insight and judgement, proper knowledge of markets and prices, a desire for profit, the avoidance of extravagance and – repeated several times – honesty. 'Although the basis of trade is gain, lofty principle in the matter of gain is a guarantee of wealth and a safeguard to one's dignity', he writes, adding, 'the ultimate destiny of the man who defrauds his fellows is humiliation'.[23]

The Islamic merchant

The respect that Kai Kaus has for business people is a common theme in much literature during the classical Islamic period. Unlike China, India or most of Western Europe, where merchants were kept firmly in their place (usually) well down the social scale, Islamic society respected and esteemed merchants. Gene Heck, citing the Qur'an and a host of Islamic legal and other scholars, has demonstrated that business people were expected to play an important role in society, and that making a profit was not only allowed but was seen as something virtuous in its own right – particularly if the merchant then used that profit to support his family or gave generously to charities. He cites sayings from the *hadith*, the body of narratives concerning the life and teachings of the Prophet, such as 'to seek lawful gain is the duty of every Muslim', 'the best of works is lawful gain' and 'to seek lawful gain is *jihad*', or in another words, that to make a profit in a way that is legal and ethical is as virtuous as fighting to defend Islam against its foes.[24] 'The trustworthy merchant will sit in the shadow of Allah's throne on Judgement Day', says another *ahadith*; 'the honest and truthful merchant will stand with the martyrs on the Day of Judgement'.[25]

A body of texts make clear the role of the merchant in society, as well as society's expectations of the merchant. Examples include the *Kitab al-iktisab fi al-riza al-mustatab* (Acquisition through an Agreeable Livelihood) by the Iraq legal scholar Muhammad ibn al-Hasan al-Shaybani, sometime before 805; the *Fi madh al-tujjar wa dhamm 'aml al-sultan*

(In the Praise of Merchants and Condemnation of the Work of the Ruler) and *Al-tabassur fi al-tijjarah* (A Clear Look at Trade), both by the Basra-born scholar and polymath al-Jahiz in the middle of the tenth century; *Al-ishara ila mahasin al-tijjarah* (Reference to the Virtues of Commerce) by the Syrian jurist and proto-economist Abu al-Fadl al-Dimashqi in the eleventh century; the *Kitab al-amwal* (Book of Revenue) by the Persian physician Abu Ubayd in the eleventh century; *al-Akham al-sultaniyya* (The Laws of Islamic Governance) by the scholar and administrator Abdul Hasan al-Mawardi in the eleventh century, and many others.[26] On top of this, there is a sizeable list of works by travellers who describe trade and trading conditions across the Muslim world as well as Europe and China. For those fluent in Arabic, it is possible to know an immense amount about trade and trading conditions in the Islamic world, as Gene Heck's *Islam, Inc.* demonstrates.[27]

What can we say about management thought in Islam? In the first instance, Islamic writers were strongly in favour of free and unregulated markets. According to the *hadith*, 'the dearness and cheapness of prices are in the hands of Allah'.[28] Writers such as al-Dimashqi and al-Jahiz, as well as the famous early fourteenth-century legal scholar Ibn Taymiyyah, interpreted this to mean that prices fluctuated according to the natural scarceness or abundance of goods (and al-Dimashqi makes it clear that this is nothing new, that people in ancient times had known this as well).[29] It is clear that they understood that the value of money also fluctuates according to the same rules. For merchants and bankers, then, there is a simple rule: buy low, sell high. Rather than having states regulate markets to control them, Islamic authors urged instead that merchants study fluctuations in prices and make their profit from them.

Riba, the prohibition on usury (lending money at interest) required Islamic writers to think carefully about how capital investment could be raised. Over time, a variety of legally sanctioned instruments emerged which enabled backers to invest in a merchant venture without charging interest. Most common was some form of partnership, whereby the backer took a stake in the venture and thus received a share of the profits. These *mudarabah* (profit-sharing) schemes existed in the Arabian peninsula before the rise of Islam, as is clear from the fact that Muhammad and his wife Khadija both participated in such schemes during their mercantile careers.[30] Another scheme, which not everyone agreed was strictly legal, was for an investment to be made in cash and paid back in goods in excess of the value of the original investment, the 'interest' to be found in whatever profit the investor could make from selling the goods on.

To some later scholars, Muslim and non-Muslim, this looks like cheating. If the rule says there is to be no lending of money at interest, why should people try to get around it? But I am not convinced that al-Dimashqi and his fellows saw it that way. There seems no need to question their religious beliefs in this way. Rather, they knew what was prohibited; and in the open space of activities that were *not* prohibited, they crafted new and legal financial instruments. Al-Dimashqi is quite clear that these new systems of investment arose because there was a demand for them. After all, Muslim traders were competing with Greek and Indian and Chinese traders where there was no such prohibition, and thus no barrier to the supply of capital.[31] One of the most important lessons to come out of Muslim management thought, then, is that in order to grow a business must have access to ready supplies of capital.

Riba has been seen as a factor holding back business in the Muslim world, but there is an argument for claiming that during Islam's classical period it sometimes acted as a blessing in disguise. Islamic lawyers and business people were forced to be creative in order to comply with *riba* and still follow the Prophet's injunction to get out into the world and trade and make money. So, Muslim scholars and bankers became financial innovators. Forms of capital investment became highly sophisticated, with different types evolving to meet different investment needs, and were transmitted throughout the Muslim world, to India, South-East Asia and Indonesia. Today, some of these investment schemes are still used by Islamic banking establishments.

Different types of partnership were also developed, and the partnership became the dominant form of business organization. Some of these partnership forms were borrowed by the Chinese, and there was also an influence on trading partners in Christian Europe, particularly in the Italian city-states where partnership became a standard form of business organization by about 1200, if not earlier. (Some of these organizational forms were then re-exported to the Islamic world; according to the historian Halil Inalcik, Ottoman Turkish business ventures adopted partnership contracts from their Italian trading partners and rivals.)[32] Partnerships did not necessarily mean that all parties supplied capital; some partners might supply labour or market knowledge, for example. Most of the authors cited above discuss both the role and functions of partnerships in some detail.

Mention too should be made of advances in accounting thought and practice, with the first advances being made in civil administration but quickly spreading to the business world as well. One important advance in the eighth and ninth centuries was the adoption of what we know today as Arabic numerals, and which early Muslim writers in turn referred to as 'Hindu numerals'.[33] These allowed quicker and easier calculations, and the Muslim development of the concept of 'zero' was also a useful step. Both Arabic (or Hindu) numerals also began making their appearance in Western Europe in the twelfth century, although their diffusion was slow; as late as the fourteenth century, English bureaucrats were still keeping records using Roman numerals.[34]

Ibn Khaldun

Many of the ideas discussed above – the traits of the virtuous leader, the role of *adab* or general knowledge, the role of the merchant in society and the importance of the profit motive, the need for free markets and advances in management techniques – are summed up in the *Muqaddimah*. Its author, the historian and philosopher Ibn Khaldun (1332–1406) devotes long sections to administration and commerce – nearly four hundred pages in one modern translation[35] – and describes various crafts as well as the functions of trade and the duties of administrators. Ironically, though he agreed with al-Ghazali that philosophy and faith were incompatible, Ibn Khaldun appears to incorporate several concepts from the *Republic* concerning the need for rulers to provide safety and security for their people and to facilitate the exchange of goods and services.

'All markets cater to the needs of the people', says Ibn Khaldun.[36] He offers a theory of supply and demand, and says that when cities, and countries, are large and their populations are prosperous, demand will increase and this will force up prices for both goods and labour. Acutely too, he points out that in prosperous economies some people will accumulate wealth faster than others, and that these people will become the target of jealousy and envy by others. One of the duties of the ruler is to protect these accumulators of wealth, because through their activities they also generate wealth for others. He describes the workings of commerce, and says that merchants can obtain profit in two ways: (1) by accumulating goods and storing them until the price has risen beyond what the merchant paid in the first place; or (2) by buying goods in places where they are cheap and then transporting them to places where they can be sold for a higher price. Either way, he says, the rule is the same: 'Buy cheap and sell dear'.[37] He favours the latter method, and comments that the long-distance trade in luxury goods seems more profitable than short-haul trade in bulk goods; in other words, the former trade offers higher margins.

Ibn Khaldun also comments on the personal qualities of successful business people.[38] They must know the law, and not be afraid to enter into legal actions and to fight their case if they know they are right, for this is the only way to deter other, more unscrupulous traders. The courage to stand up and fight back against competition is another important quality. However, Ibn Khaldun cautions against too aggressive an approach. In a comment that modern-day bankers and investors might take to heart, he points out that those who are not afraid of risk will of course take more risky decisions, and are therefore more likely to suffer losses. The more cautious and risk-averse investors are less likely to suffer damage.

Later Islamic thought in the age of commerce

Ibn Khaldun represents something of a high-water mark in terms of Islamic thinking on administration and business. After a period of internal turmoil and wars with the crusaders and Mongols, the western Islamic world settled down into three distinct polities: Ottoman Turkey; the Mamluk rulers of Egypt, who came to power in the mid-thirteenth century; and the Safavid Empire in Persia. Each produced its own writings on these subjects, but most of the ideas are heavily reliant on earlier times, and there is little in the way of innovation.

Founded in the late thirteenth century, the Ottoman state had at first been a very simple one, with organization consisting of the sultan, the army and a few key administrators. The personality and leadership of the sultan had been essential in holding the state together. With expansion and conquest came the need for more permanent structures. Some attempt to found a regular civil administration had begun under Sultan Mehmet II in the fifteenth century following the establishment of the Ottoman capital at Constantinople, but the key figure is Sultan Suleiman I (1494–1566). In the West he is known as Suleiman the Magnificent and remembered for his military conquests, but in Turkish history he is known as Suleiman Kanuni, Suleiman the Lawgiver. He succeeded in establishing a professional administration and civil service, which held Turkey together for several more centuries during the rule of his – not always entirely competent – successors.[39]

Turkish administration and management unsurprisingly inherited a great deal from earlier Arab and Persian ideas and practice, but there were borrowings from Europe as well. Again, this must be largely inferred from observations of practice.[40] Turkish writers on management are surprisingly rare, but at least two Turkish writers of note set out their own commentaries on administration. Yahya Efendi Bostanzade (d. 1639), himself a Turkish administrator, wrote a book entitled *Mir'at al-ahla*, which makes explicit the duties and ethical responsibilities of administrators.[41] The government minister Mehmed Raghib Pasha (1699–1766), produced a series of letters and observations on civil administration which were influential for later ministers.[42] On the whole, though, there is little literature on this subject in Turkey, which is surprising given the richness of earlier Persian and Arabic sources. It is possible that Turkish administrators and merchants simply referred to these earlier sources. The Nizam al-Mulk's *Siyasat Nama* was certainly familiar to Ottoman rulers and higher administrators.[43] As far as trade goes, there is little firm evidence but it seems likely that the ideas of al-Dimashqi, al-Jahiz and others were still being followed. Thabit Abdallah's fascinating study of trade in eighteenth-century Basra, *Merchants, Mamluks and Murder*, suggests that very little had changed in terms of thinking about business and management.[44]

The most important writer for our purposes to come out of Mamluk Egypt is probably Ahmad al-Qalqashandi (d. 1418). His *Kitab subh al-a'sha* (Dawn for the Blind) is an encyclopedic work – fourteen volumes in the modern Arabic translation – firmly in the tradition of *adab* described earlier in this chapter. It is a compendium of knowledge meant to assist the professional administrator/secretary, and according to one scholar, 'contains practically all that it is necessary to know on the subject'.[45] One interesting addition to the corpus of general knowledge is a detailed section on cryptography, suggesting that the Mamluk administration – and possibly business people too? – used codes and ciphers when transmitting information. One of al-Qalqashandi's sons also wrote on administration and seems to have been involved in the production of handbooks for professional administrators which provided set forms for the drawing up of documents and decrees, in effect an attempt to create a standardized system of reporting and control. An analysis of Mamluk administrative documents in the archives of the monastery of St Catherine's at Mount Sinai suggests that these forms were still being followed decades or even centuries later.[46]

The Safavid Empire, founded around 1500, produced its own administrative literature too, the most prominent examples being the *Tadhkirat al-muluk* (Memorial of the Kings), written probably in 1725, and the *Dastur al-muluk* (Regulations of the Kings) by a prominent administrator in the Safavid government, Mirza Rafi'a and written sometime before 1733.[47] Again, both are compendia of useful knowledge in the *adab* tradition, and despite their great length, both are derivative of earlier sources and neither offers much that is new in terms of thinking about administration, although they do offer a detailed account of how the Safavid Empire was administered. Both are written in Persian. Curiously, both where written in the immediate aftermath of the collapse of the Safavid Empire, destroyed by an invading Afghan army in 1722. Were these works written, like those of Machiavelli (see Chapter 4) to assist princes and ministers who sought to re-establish the old order?

Medieval Europe

The period from the fourth to the sixth centuries was one of dual change in the territories of the old Roman Empire in Europe. First came the full emergence into public life of Christianity, which was officially tolerated from 313 and made the official state religion in 380. Within a very short space of time thereafter, Christian priests and bishops were also stepping into important administrative roles in the empire; and senior bureaucrats were likewise becoming priests and bishops. The faith of these men was new, but their education and training were firmly grounded in the past. St Ambrose, who became Bishop of Milan in 375, was a Roman nobleman through and through, educated in the Greek and Roman classics, and had been a senior administrator in the Roman civil service before his conversion and appointment as bishop. He was far from unique in this.

The second change was the dissolution of the empire itself and its replacement with a series of independent states. The most important of these was the Frankish kingdom of Gaul, which in turn spawned two very important later polities, the Kingdom of France and the Holy Roman Empire. These new independent states were originally pagan but quickly adopted Christianity, and played a major role in spreading Christianity into northern and eastern Europe.[48]

These changes did not happen without a certain amount of turmoil. This is the period formerly known as the 'Dark Ages', a term which thankfully is disappearing. This period of history was not noticeably darker than any other, but there was a great deal of shifting and readjustment. The new polities were founded by 'barbarian' leaders such as Clovis and Theodoric who were used to a very personal style of leadership. To govern their new kingdoms they needed professional administrators. Lacking these among their own peoples, they followed a time-honoured practice and recruited administrators from their new subjects. Just as in late Roman times, many of these were Christian clergy. Thus in terms of administrative thought in practice there was a clear continuation from Roman, and Greek, practice in antiquity into the medieval period.

The monastic rules

Monasticism, the creation of religious communities where people of faith may live apart from the world, has its origins in India, probably in Buddhism. The idea was absorbed into early Christianity through trade and other contacts between the Middle East and India. The first Christian monasteries were established in Egypt early in the fourth century, and in 356 the so-called Rule of St Basil, the first Christian monastic rule, was promulgated in Cappadocia (part of modern-day Turkey). This was not so much a rule of conduct as a set of guidelines, aids to those who wished to know what the ascetic life entailed. The rule included the taking of vows of poverty, chastity and obedience, but offered little in the way of advice on governance.

Early monasteries could be unruly places. When in the early sixth century the Roman nobleman and monk Benedict of Nursia accepted the post of abbot on one monastery in central Italy, he found the monks without discipline and ignoring both religious observance and their vows. When he tried to enforce order, the monks rebelled; according to some accounts, they attempted to poison him. Benedict withdrew and then set about creating a new monastic community at Monte Cassino south of Rome, which he hoped would serve as a model for other monasteries.

Central to the new establishment was its rule, now known as the Rule of St Benedict.[49] This simple but extremely effective document served as a combination of mission statement, organizational map and job description for all members of the community. Its seventy-three precepts begin with the mission statement, which is quite simple: the monks are to dedicate their work to the glory of God. All else follows from that. The rest of the Rule states how that mission is to be carried out. It specifies times of work, meals, prayer and rest; it lays out the duties of the abbot himself, his senior administrators such as the treasurer, and then the general body of monks, known as the chapter. One interesting feature is that Benedict insisted that leadership be consultative: the monks were to obey the orders of the abbot, but the abbot in turn had to explain his orders to the chapter, and listen to the views of the other monks if they disagreed.[50]

Did Benedict know of the *Mulasarvastivada-vinaya*, the Buddhist monastic rule discussed in Chapter 1? It is possible that he knew about it, even if only indirectly, but how strong the influence was is hard to tell. Reading the Rule today, this looks more like back-of-the-envelope stuff. Here is a man facing an administrative challenge, looking back at his own experience and at the world around him, and coming up with a simple scheme: this is our purpose, this is what each of us must do to achieve that purpose, these are the penalties for those who do not pull their weight. Modern-day writers of mission statements and strategy documents could profit by this example of brevity and clarity.

Simple, effective and powerful: the Rule of the order at Monte Cassino was widely imitated. By the time of Benedict's death in 547 more than thirty other monasteries had adopted the Rule; by the year 600 there were more than 200 monasteries and nunneries and the number eventually reached more than 1000, collectively known as the Benedictine Order.

Other religious orders followed in Europe. The variety and function of these is astounding. There were orders of canons such as the Augustinians and Praemonstratensians, and orders of friars, the most important being the Dominicans and Franciscans. There were orders dedicated to nursing the sick and caring for the poor, like the order of nursing sisters founded at Marburg in Hesse by St Elizabeth of Hungary; at the other end of the scale there were military orders such as the Knights Templar and the Knights of Calatrava whose purpose was to fight crusades against Muslims; and there were hybrid orders like the Knights of St John and the Teutonic Knights whose purpose was to do both. All of these organizations had rules, and though the rules varied from case to case depending on the purpose of the organization, the fundamental principles were those laid down in the Rule of St Benedict.

One of the most successful of these later orders was the Cistercian Order, founded at Cîteaux in France in 1098.[51] Rather than relying on lands donated to them by lay nobles, as the Benedictines and others did, the Cistercians developed a new concept. They acquired tracts of waste ground – forests, heathland, swamps – and set about converting these into productive land. They diversified from pure agriculture into fishing, iron and coal mining, vineyards and even banking. The Cistercian order ultimately grew to about 750 monasteries and nunneries, using a simple but very effective organizational form. As each monastery grew to capacity, members would go out and found what were known as 'daughter houses'. As these daughter houses grew, they would found more daughter houses and so on, creating a pyramid form of organization. Each founder house was responsible for supervising and auditing the accounts of its daughter houses, and in return reported to its own founder house, and so on up the line to the original foundation at Cîteaux.

'You will find in the woods something you will never find in books', wrote the Cistercian Order's great ideologue, St Bernard of Clairvaux. 'Stones and trees will teach you a lesson you never learned from your masters at school. Honey can be drawn from rock, and oil from the hardest stone.' Meeting the challenge of clearing and draining wastelands turned the Cistercians into the foremost technological innovators of the day. The historian of technology Jean Gimpel credits them with a leading role in the development of water power and hydraulic machinery, and water remained the standard source of power in Europe until the introduction of the steam engine.[52] Gimpel also points out that, for all their piety, the Cistercians were also a very successful commercial organization. Their estates were highly productive; the total financial turnover has never been calculated, but it must have been enormous.

Monasteries were not just places of worship and contemplation. They owned lands and resources, and lived off the revenue from these. Those lands and resources had to be managed. Consider that some monasteries owned tens of thousands of acres of land, and that estates in excess of 100,000 acres were not unknown. The numbers of monks (or canons or friars) and nuns in even the largest monasteries seldom exceeded a few hundred. The monastery of Leibus in Germany had 600,000 acres of land, and at the very height, not more than five hundred monks and lay brothers, meaning there was an average of at least 1,200 acres per member of the monastery. The working of the lands was done by a combination of tenants and hired labours, under the supervision of the members of the monastery. The monks accordingly became very skilled and efficient administrators, and developed a body of knowledge about administration that was passed down from generation to generation within each monastery. They used standard documents, known as formularies, to ensure standard forms of reporting and control across the organization. Buildings and facilities were standardized too; Cistercian monasteries were always built to the same ground plan, and it was said at the time that if you took a blindfolded Cistercian monk out of his own monastery and put him down in any other monastery in Europe, he could at once find his way around the building.

Religious orders played a prominent role in education. The children of nobility were usually educated at religious schools or by tutors who came from the religious orders. The first universities, Bologna (1080), Paris (1150), Oxford (1167), Cambridge (1208) and others were staffed almost entirely by members of religious orders. The Franciscans and Dominicans were particularly renowned for their learning and formed a high proportion of the teaching staff at Oxford. The universities drew their own model of organization from the religious orders, and even today we still use terms such as 'college', the word originally referring to religious bodies such as the College of Cardinals.

Businesses were also influenced. Medieval society was highly corporatist, and in urban settings at least, everyone belonged to something: the upper and middle classes had guilds, the lower classes had local confraternities. Merchants and craft workers were organized into guilds too. In larger centres merchants in particular sectors would join together: in the city of Florence, for example, there were guilds of physicians, of bankers, of woollen cloth manufacturers and of silk cloth manufacturers, among others. Smaller centres might have a single guild of merchants to which all business owners belonged. According to the historian S.R. Epstein, these guilds had many roles and were an important economic force.[53] They co-ordinated the activities of members, provided financial support including credit and investment in new businesses, acted as clearing houses for information, and were centres of technical and organizational innovation. They were also organized along much the same lines as religious institutions. Each guild had an article of association which stated its purpose and laid out the duties of members and the penalties for failure to abide by the guild's rules, very much in the same manner as the Rule of St Benedict. Like monasteries, these guilds were also closed to outsiders; people could only join with the consent of the guild master and senior members. It should be emphasized that these similarities to religious institution are not accidental. As the most advanced form of organization in society, religious institutions naturally served as a model for others.

Clerical administrators

It became traditional for kings and princes to employ bishops, priests and monks as administrators at every level of government; indeed, until the fourteenth century at least, it is rare to find a senior administrator who had *not* taken religious orders. (It should be added that these clerical administrators usually also drew income from church benefices, and therefore did not have to be paid a salary by the crown, which may also have helped explain their popularity as civil servants.) Administrative practices developed in the churches and monasteries soon formed the heart of royal administration in virtually every country in Christian Europe. Techniques such as standard forms of reporting and control, specialization of the civil service into different departments and regular auditing of accounts, all developed in religious institutions and became standard parts of civil service practice. Even the basic techniques of writing and record-keeping may have had their origins in these religious institutions.[54]

More importantly still for the purposes of this book, these clerical administrators began laying down their ideas for others to follow. England, which had one of the most efficient bureaucracies of medieval Europe, was particularly well served in this respect. Richard Fitz Neal (or Fitz Nigel), believed to be an illegitimate son of the Bishop of Ely, took holy orders and rose to be archdeacon of Ely himself. He also served as treasurer of England for more than forty years.[55] His *Dialogus de Scaccario* (Dialogue Concerning the Exchequer), written around 1177 and reworked again before his death in 1198, was a manual describing in detail how the exchequer worked, defining key terms, spelling out the roles of officials and describing procedures for, say, collecting on debts owing to the crown. The manual is written in simple language in a question-and-answer format, suggesting that it might have been used for educational purposes, for example for training new recruits to the clerical staff. Standardized practices and reporting methods are emphasized, as Fitz Neal makes clear in the preface to the work:

> We know, indeed, that chiefly by prudence, fortitude, temperance, and justice, and other virtues, kingdoms are ruled and laws subsist; wherefore the rulers of the world should strive after these with all their strength. But it happens at times that what is conceived with sound counsel and excellent intent is carried through by, so to say, a routine-like method.[56]

The philosophy of standardization and routine in administration was driven through other parts of the civil service by Fitz Neal's contemporary Hubert Walter, chancellor of England under Kings Richard I and John. He is another who had parallel careers, rising through the church to become Archbishop of Canterbury. Michael Clanchy in his superb study of medieval literacy, *From Memory to Written Record*, identified Walter as the moving force behind the development of much of the record-keeping apparatus of English government.[57] Fitz Neal, Walter and their colleagues were responsible for founding the English civil service, a highly efficient and effective body which, as I have said elsewhere, enabled the small country of England to punch above its weight in Europe through the Middle Ages and long beyond.[58] Reporting and accounting methods developed in the twelfth century were still in use in the nineteenth century; some are still in use today.

Right across Western Europe, the civil services and universities we have today still betray the evidence of medieval thought and practice. Should we pay more attention to this heritage? Some scholars think that we should. Katja Rost and her colleagues, writing in the *Journal of Management History* in 2010, argued that modern corporations would do well to study the effective corporate governance mechanisms of the Benedictine Abbeys, while in the same journal in 1999 Michael Kennedy argued that the influence of medieval management practices on business today is still detectable, comparing the Rule of St Benedict with the management ideas of Henri Fayol (see Chapter 6).[59]

The biological organization: John of Salisbury

A little younger than either Fitz Neal or Walter, John of Salisbury (d. 1180) was an administrator within the church hierarchy rather than the civil service, a friend of the controversial Archbishop of Canterbury Thomas Becket and later himself Bishop of Chartres. He had been educated at the famous cathedral school at Chartres, where his masters had included Peter Abelard, Thierry of Chartres and William of Conches, leaders of the revival of the ideas of Plato and the originators of a medieval brand of humanism.[60]

It was Plato's *Republic* that John had very much in mind when he wrote the *Policraticus*, his master work on political philosophy, completed in 1159.[61] The overt purpose of the book is an attack on princes and other leaders who govern according to 'worldly excess' rather than philosophy: that is, they indulge their personal whims rather than governing according to principles. That there are such principles – that is, things which are fixed, absolute and always true – is beyond doubt, says John. We need only look at the world around us. There are principles in mathematics, in astronomy, in the natural world. God made these other phenomena; and as God made us, human beings, it follows that our lives and work are governed by principles as well. The study of philosophy, particularly that of Plato and Aristotle, enables us to understand what those principles are, and in the text John lays out a number of these: truth, generosity, respect for others, living a righteous life and so on.

At first glance this looks like just another 'Mirror for Princes' in the same tradition as John's near contemporary Kai Kaus of Gurgan, or indeed the early Egyptian texts discussed in Chapter 2. But there is more to it than that. In an effort to prove his point, John revives and greatly expands an idea derived from Aristotle, namely that human organizations can be compared to biological organisms. He uses the metaphor of the human body to describe how the state functions. The prince is the head of the state; the senate or other representative body is its heart; the soldiers and agricultural workers are the equivalent of the limbs, and so on. What John creates – even if unintentionally – is a simple but coherent theory of organization. It was, moreover, one that continues to have a long life. Andrew Ure referred to this concept in the nineteenth century, as did Harrington Emerson and Charles Knoeppel in the early twentieth, and Gareth Morgan lists the biological organism as one of his eight metaphors of organization.[62]

Medieval theories about business

It was long thought that the Catholic Church, and society in general, were antipathetic to merchants and trade. True, the threefold order of society – nobles and knights, priests and monks, peasants and workers – had no place for them, and true, the other three orders did occasionally look on merchants with distrust. There is a strand in medieval literature which suggests that merchants seek only profit for themselves, and therefore are guilty of the sin of avarice. In the minds of some this made merchants legitimate prey. 'And it will be good to live [when war breaks out]', wrote the poet and knight Bertran de Born in the late twelfth century, 'for one will take the property of usurers, and there will no longer be a peaceful pack-horse on the roads; all the townsmen will tremble, and the merchant will no longer be safe on the road to France', before adding wittily, 'war without plunder is like sausages without mustard'.[63] More darkly, the Catholic Church's prohibition on usury did not extend to Jews, and though only a tiny fraction of the Jewish population of Europe worked as moneylenders, this was enough to ensure that Jews were often targets for robbery and violence.

But this was by no means the whole picture, as Liana Farber has shown in her detailed examination of medieval writers on trade.[64] There were indeed writers such as the scholastic Peter Lombard in the twelfth century who maintained that all forms of trade were sinful, but there were others such as the Catalan Dominican friar Raymond of Penyafort (or Peñafort) or the English cleric, teacher and writer Thomas of Chobham who argued the opposite. One of the early 'Church Fathers', St Augustine of Hippo (354–430), had sneered down his aristocratic nose that all traders were practitioners of deceit and fraud, but even he admitted that trade itself was essentially a sinless act; it was the unethical practices of traders themselves that led to sin.[65] This was the view taken, in more detail, by Penyafort and Chobham.

The thirteenth century saw a further shift. Reinterpretations of the works of Plato and Aristotle – aided in part by the translation of new editions of their works from Arabic into Latin, and almost certainly influenced by the commentaries of Islamic scholars; recall that Islamic thought was very much supportive of trade and commerce – focused in particular on the ideas of Aristotle's *Nicomachean Ethics*. According to this, business activity was not only a moral activity but a very necessary one. Business, as Islamic scholars had argued earlier, was essential to society. The fourteenth-century scholar Nicholas Oresme, for example, thought trade a natural human activity, and believed that trade evolved when a country had an abundance of one product and a scarcity of another.[66]

This led to the creation of value and exchange, when one party valued that which it did not have and was prepared to offer a commodity of which it has a surplus – such as money – in exchange. The thirteenth-century Dominican scholar St Thomas Aquinas famously expanded on this concept in his two major works, *Summa Theologiae* and *Summa Contra Gentiles*. Value, argued Aquinas, lay in exchange, and was determined by how much the purchasing party was prepared to offer. He rejected the notion of intrinsic value, that is, that objects have an inherent value that never changes. If that were so, said Aquinas, then a mouse would be more valuable than a pearl, for a mouse is a living thing and a pearl is not. In fact, this is ludicrous; pearls are rare and beautiful, mice are plentiful and not particularly useful, and thus much less valuable. Instead of inherent value, Aquinas came up with the idea of the 'just price'. This is the price created through the interplay of supply and demand, and it reflects natural justice for both buyer and seller. Aquinas accepted that this would not always appear to be fair; in times of scarcity, the price of wheat might rise and people be forced to pay more, but that is how the market works.

One important innovation was Aquinas's belief that sellers of goods can add value, as we would say today, by influencing the availability, nature or quality of goods, and also by assuming greater risks of times of uncertainty – for example, by importing food from other places to help feed people during a time of famine. This added value would enable the seller to charge a higher price. In his attempts to justify the purpose of trade in society, Aquinas had inadvertently stumbled across one of the core precepts of modern marketing: that customers are willing to pay more for additional value.[67]

Once Aquinas had nailed down the religious and ethical justification for trade, others such as Nicholas Oresme and especially St Bernardino of Siena began to consider the nature of trade in more detail. St Bernardino, who lived from 1380–1444, deserves special mention as one of the first to consider the role of the manager in a business context. A member of a religious order known as the Observant Friars, Bernardino spent much of his career as an itinerant public preacher in northern Italy. His collected sermons, *De Evangelio Aeterno* (Concerning the Eternal Gospel) were not written by himself but were taken down verbatim by a devoted follower who copied down faithfully every word to come from the preacher's mouth, so much so that in the middle of one sermon we hear him asking his audience to quiet a barking dog which is distracting him, while in another he scolds a group of children who are playing noisily and interrupting the sermon.[68]

One series of sermons within this larger body is a group entitled *De Contractibus et Usuris* (On Contracts and Usury). In these sermons Bernardino expands on the views of Aquinas, in particular the idea that business is a legitimate activity and benefits society as a whole. However, business only does so if it is done honestly; fraud and deceit by one business person will harm the whole community. In a passage which sounds familiar today, Bernardino urges business people to show that they are honest, keeping accounts and records so that they can prove their own integrity if required. In modern parlance, we would say that Bernardino was asking people to be more transparent.

In Sermon 33 he touches another familiar nerve, arguing that to be successful, business leaders also have to be competent, and he bemoans the fact that there are not enough competent business people to go around. What are the qualities that make for a good business leader? Bernardino lists four: (1) the leader should be efficient; (2) the leader should accept the responsibilities of his (or her) position; (3) the leader should be a hard worker; and (4) the leaders should be ready and willing to accept risk, for risk is an inevitable part of business (and as Aquinas had suggested, the assumption of risk is one way in which businesses create value for customers).[69] Other writers had set out lists of managerial duties, but in my view, Bernardino is the first to define managerial competence.

Both Aquinas and Bernardino, along with just about every other writer of the period, stresses the central importance of ethics in business. Trade was beneficial to society, but only so long as it was conducted honestly; the good merchant was *ipso facto* an honest merchant. But there were ethical dilemmas still unsolved, as Aquinas found when he came to consider the example of food prices rising in times of scarcity; rising food prices might indicate the workings of an efficient market, but this would be small comfort to the poor who could no longer afford to buy bread.

Another ethical paradox was encountered by the Englishman Thomas of Chobham (d. 1236), another of our clerical administrators who had worked for Fitz Neal at the English exchequer and was also a deacon at Salisbury cathedral. In his *Summa Confessorum*, Thomas considers a controversy that arose in Paris when a group of prostitutes offered to pay for a stained-glass window in the new cathedral of Notre Dame. The bishop of Paris had been uncertain of whether he could take the money; could wages from reprehensible trades be considered honest money?

Thomas, in an interesting reversal of the view of St Augustine – that trade itself was honest but the people engaged in it were immoral – argued that in this case the trade itself was reprehensible but the labour contributed by the worker was honest and had to be considered as such. 'Prostitutes . . . hire out their bodies and supply labour . . . Whence this principle of secular justice: she does evil in being a prostitute, but she does not do evil in receiving the price of her labour.'[70] If the prostitute admitted to enjoying her labour, or if she used measures 'to attract with false allures' such as perfumes or cosmetics – Thomas seems to consider these a form of false advertising – then indeed the money would have been earned sinfully. Otherwise, though, the prostitute was entitled to her reward: a fair day's work receives a fair day's wage.

Teetering on the brink of justifying prostitution, Thomas 'finally gets hold of himself', in the words of historian Jacques Le Goff, and remembers that there are arguments for condemning prostitution itself. Le Goff believes this is a rather extreme and absurd example, but in fact it shows real insights into medieval attitudes to trade, labour and exchange. It is also a good example of the kinds of pitfalls that lie in wait for thinkers about business ethics.[71]

Reflections

From the 'good merchant' to compassionate capitalism

The phrase 'compassionate capitalism' started to appear in writing about business in the very early years of the twenty-first century. A number of books and articles have been published on this subject since 2002, including Marc Benioff and Karen Southwick's *Compassionate Capitalism* and Daniel Goleman's *Social Intelligence*.[72] Sometimes also called 'capitalism with a human face', the term refers to the need to make the capitalist system more fair and able to provide help to those who are in need. In conventional capitalism, writes Goleman, 'empathy is sacrificed in the name of efficiency and cost-effectiveness'.[73] Proponents of compassionate capitalism believe that the market is not necessarily the fairest way of redistributing resources, and that we need to find ways of making sure that our economic institutions are connected to our social needs. That, it is said, is the key task facing capitalism in the years to come. Goleman speaks of 'ways we might reengineer social institutions for the better'.[74]

Would this same debate have happened eight hundred or nine hundred years ago? It seems very unlikely. For one thing, most thinking people took it for granted that economic institutions existed with the sole purpose of serving social needs. 'All markets cater to the needs of the people', said Ibn Khaldun, and Nicholas Oresme argued that markets had emerged in order to facilitate exchange for the good of all participants. Over and over, writers such as al-Dimashqi and Thomas Aquinas emphasized that the 'good' merchant was one who served society, not one who served only himself. The message was clear: the economy was there to serve the people, not, as some economic and political theorists today would have it, the other way around. Indeed, one of the functions of the merchant guilds was to remind members of their responsibilities to society and ensure that they played their part in meeting these (a function still filled by the livery corporations of the City of London today).

There were exceptions, of course. There were theorists such as Peter Lombard who believed that all merchants were motivated by greed. And there were greedy merchants, and corrupt merchants. There were landlords who sweated their peasants for labour. There were nobles who robbed their own people, though contrary to several generations of Robin Hood films, they were not the norm. There were oppressive employers, and there were strikes and riots by aggrieved workers. Slavery was widespread; it became less common in medieval Europe, but it did not disappear entirely. It could be argued that Ibn Khaldun and the scholastic writers were living in a fool's paradise, preaching ethical behaviour while in fact business leaders were just as avaricious and solely profit-driven as they are today.

Against that, I would advance two arguments. First, I do not believe that most business leaders today are avaricious and solely driven by profit. Second, I do not believe that most business leaders in the Middle Ages were either. It is easy to concentrate on the exceptions, and forget about men such as Francesco Datini, who gave away much of his wealth to support charitable institutions while he lived, and left more in his will. And in the Middle Ages, too, the social pressure to recognize duties to society was very severe. There was pressure from the church, from the state, from one's own peers in the guild merchant, all combining to ensure that from time to time, at least, business people had to acknowledge their social role – even if unwillingly.

There were merchants who acquired overwhelming power, such as Cosimo dei Medici in Florence and Jakob Fugger in Augsburg. But it is interesting to see how these men used their wealth. Cosimo dei Medici created much of the Florence that we see today. The palaces, the artworks, the lavish public buildings were his gift to the city. Less visible but no less important were the gifts to religious foundations, schools and hospitals. A medieval merchant who failed to support charities would have been a monster, shunned by his colleagues.

In the writings of lawyers, priests and scholars, and of business people too, we can see an implicit social contract. Businesses existed to serve the community, both directly by creating value and providing goods and services people needed – which, Aquinas reminds us, is itself a socially responsible thing to do – and indirectly through charity and good works. But somewhere along the way, that social contract was broken. What happened? Perhaps, as Max Weber seems to suggest, the new individualism that accompanied the Protestant Reformation began to privilege the individual over society rather than the other way around.[75] Certainly the concept of 'compassionate capitalism' seems to be more familiar to – and is discussed with less embarrassment by – many Asian businessmen. When Ratan Tata, the outgoing leader of the Tata group, talks of his group's commitment to the communities it serves and adds that 'profit is a by-product of what we do', he is not just stating his own beliefs, he is reaffirming his group's core values that have existed since its foundation.[76]

The study of management history suggests another possibility. The definite breakage of the social contract seems to come in the Industrial Revolution (see Chapter 4). This period saw the emergence of new industries led by a new generation of 'self-made men'. The power of the guilds had weakened and the mechanisms to apply pressure to business people to recognize their social role had weakened too, or disappeared in entirely. The new entrepreneurs regarded their businesses as their own property, to dispose of as they wished. The same applied to their profits – and, very often, to their workers. Some learned the hard way that this was not the case; Arkwright became a kinder and gentler employer after his striking workers burned his mill down. Others did not. When Robert Owen called for more humane treatment of workers, other mill owners branded him a class traitor. And when Henry Heinz supported legislation to prevent the harmful adulteration of food and drugs that was killing dozens of people in America each year, his fellow food producers likewise accused him of treason.

This state of mind, the view that the purpose of a business is to make money and return value to shareholders, and that no outsider has the right to interfere in that, will have to change before the concept of 'compassionate capitalism' has a chance of succeeding. And for that change to occur, we will need to fundamentally shift the relationship between businesses and society, including our concepts of why businesses exist and what they are for, back towards something like the views of al-Dimashqi and Thomas Aquinas. Do not mistake me. I am not advocating a return to the Middle Ages when life was poor, nasty, brutish and short, as Thomas Hobbes put it. I am saying that, if we are serious about this concept of compassionate capitalism, then we need to look back to a time when economic institutions were expected to serve social needs first and foremost and then figure out how to rewrite the social contract between business and society.

'Were it not for venturesome men, mankind would perish', wrote Kai Kaus. Society needs business people. But business people need to remember that they also need society, for without society to support them they would have no business. One thing the age of commerce teaches us, I feel, is that we need to stop studying business as an isolated phenomenon and start putting it into social context. Business studies needs to broaden its scope of inquiry.

Managing commercial enterprises

As I have described elsewhere, it is possible to know a good deal about business practice in Europe in the later Middle Ages and the Renaissance, especially in southern Europe, thanks to some remarkable document survivals such as the collected papers of the merchant Francesco Datini of Prato and the archives of some of the major trading centres, especially Venice, Florence and Genoa.[77] Here there was no question of merchants being second-class citizens. Merchants dominated the governments of the major cities, either indirectly in the case of Florence, or directly in Venice and Genoa, where the nobility and the merchant princes were usually one and the same person.[78]

'Medieval merchants were seldom concerned with abstract economic theory or ethics', wrote Roberto Lopez and Irving Raymond in their edited collection of medieval Italian business records. 'They wrote heap upon heap of bills, promissory notes, books of accounting and other business records besides a small number of manuals of business practice.'[79] The problem is compounded once again by the lack of separation of functions. Merchants, especially in the maritime centres of Venice, Genoa and Pisa, were also officials of government, war leaders, diplomats and many other things besides. The career of Benedetto Zaccaria of Genoa is a case in point. He was a successful merchant trading in alum (an important mineral used in drugs and dying cloth), commander of the Genoese navy, successful pirate, diplomat and secret agent on behalf of the Byzantine Empire – sometimes all at the same time.[80] A later historian, John Guilmartin, commenting on the difficulty of telling the difference between maritime commerce, naval warfare and piracy, suggested all three should be discussed together under the single rubric of 'armed violence at sea'.[81]

Through the vast body of records that have survived we can understand a great deal about managerial practice, and from that we can infer a good deal about thinking and principles. Management historian Claude George, for example, looked at the operations of the Arsenale, the Venetian state-owned shipyard founded in 1104. He concludes that the Venetians were well aware of issues such as cost control, inventory control, standardization and the assembly line, and had an efficient system for personnel management. His description of standardization, as evidenced in records of the fourteenth century, is particularly interesting:

> That the advantages of standardization were recognized is evident in the policy drawn up by the Arsenal's planning committee. This policy stated that (1) all bows were to be made so that arrows would fit any of them, (2) all sternposts [for ships] were to be built to the same design so that each rudder would not have to be specially fitted to its sternpost, and (3) all rigging and deck furnishings were to be uniform.[82]

One can infer a certain amount about strategic thinking and, especially, methods of managing risk by examining how companies behaved. For example, most managers in medieval Italy would have rejected the idea of core competencies set out by C.K. Prahalad and Gary Hamel.[83] Diversification was what everyone did; it was a way of laying off risk. Diversification into new business lines and new markets ensured that if something went sour in one market, profits from others would keep the business afloat. One famous metric used by Venetian merchants was to calculate profits in such a way that if five ships were sent out and four were lost in storms or taken by pirates, the profit from the cargo of the fifth would allow the business break even, is illustrative of this attitude.

Assessment of risk in turn required knowledge of market conditions, and we can see the importance of this in the letters of Francesco Datini, whose personal collection of 150,000 business letters, 500 account books, 300 deeds of partnership, 400 insurance policies and several thousand other documents is not just one of the most important business archives of the Middle Ages, but one of the most important in all of history.[84] Datini estimated that he spent half of his time on the task of collecting information to enable his business decision making. Larger businesses such as the Medici Bank had elaborate systems of couriers to enable information to be passed quickly from branch offices around Europe back to headquarters at Florence. In the sixteenth century the House of Fugger, based in Augsburg and like the Medici Bank engaged in a range of activities from mining to manufacturing and banking, also spent much time and effort on collecting information. One of the family, Philip Eduard Fugger, seems to have done this almost as a full-time job. He was responsible for the so-called Fugger Newsletters, a remarkable collection of digests of political and economic news gleaned from all around Europe and compiled in Augsburg for use by senior management.[85] There were also public sources of information such as the Italian *praticas*, which described market conditions, local products, currencies, systems of weights and measures and local regulations on trade across Europe and sometimes further afield as well. The famous *Pratica della Mercatura* by Pegolotti in the fourteenth century offers information on markets in Europe, North Africa, the Middle East and Central Asia.[86] All of this demonstrates the importance that business people of this period attached to knowledge.

The need to manage risk as well as the need to leverage capital and knowledge probably lay behind the dominant form of organization used by Italian merchants, the limited-life partnership, or *commenda*.[87] Francesco Datini tells us in great detail how he used these partnerships, and like the Muslim merchants before him, sometimes used them to bring in other capital partners to share the financial risk, or sometimes to bring in people with specific knowledge and skills deemed vital to the business. The Medici Bank, Europe's largest business enterprise with branch offices all over western Europe and agency relationships as far away as Timbuktu, Reykjavik, Tabriz and Beijing, was in fact a vast series of interlocking partnerships, dominated by the top-level partnership of the *maggiore*, the equivalent of the board of directors, who were to a greater or lesser extent partners in all the other partnerships within the enterprise. All partnerships were of limited duration, usually only three years, renewable only at the consent of all parties. Here we see evidence of the need for flexibility and response to change; prosperous parts of the business could be easily reinforced, while unprofitable ones could be dumped without harming the integrity of the business.[88]

Developments in accounting thought played a major role in the so-called commercial revolution that took place in medieval Italy and eventually spread to the rest of the continent. We saw earlier that Italian merchants adopted Arabic numerals and other accounting practices from the Islamic world.[89] A key advance was the development of double-entry bookkeeping, which was in use in the Arab world by at least the year 1000 and probably earlier. Advances in accounting also led towards developments in management education. The comparatively complex new accounting methods required training, and institutions known as *scuole d'abaco* (abacus schools) were developed in many major centres in Italy. Textbooks known as *abaci* (abacus books) were also produced; among the first of these was the *Liber abaci* by the mathematician Leonardo Fibonacci.[90] Many others followed, most importantly the *Summa de arithmetica, geometria, proportioni et proportionalita* (Summa of Arithmetic, Geometry, Proportion and Proportionality), written by the Franciscan friar and mathematician Luca Pacioli, a friend of Leonardo da Vinci, and published in 1494.[91] Pacioli's work was enormously influential, and he has been described as the 'father of modern accounting'.

I have concentrated here on Italy because that is where some of the best business records have survived, and also because it is here that some of the major advances in thinking originated. But we can be fairly sure that these developments affected the rest of Europe too, perhaps even transmitted by Italian merchants trading in the north and west. E.M. Carus-Wilson's study of merchants in Bristol shows that English traders too were aware of the importance of risk management and of knowledge,[92] and James Masschaele's study of internal trade in medieval England shows that even small traders were aware of the basic principles of competition and engaged in resource-seeking behaviour in order to gain competitive advantage.[93]

Management and agriculture

It is also possible to trace developments in management thought in the agricultural sector, especially in England. Contrary to what most of us were taught at school, agriculture in England was a progressive sector characterized, at least at the top end, by technological and managerial innovation. David Stone has shown how 'farm managers . . . managed the production of crops in a remarkably sensitive and sophisticated way'.[94] Stone demonstrated that farm managers were aware of market movements, followed prices keenly and constantly changed the quantities of particular crops sown as they tried to anticipate likely future demand. These farm managers were usually professionals and often highly trained, and had a good deal of independence. As Dorothea Oschinsky says, 'few landlords with sufficient land to employ a staff of officers . . . would themselves have the time or inclination to take an active part in the administration and farming of their manors'.[95]

By the end of the thirteenth century farm managers, stewards and bailiffs also had a body of written knowledge to sustain them. Robert Grosseteste, Bishop of Lincoln, had compiled a set of rules for the administration of his own household and estate, and around 1240–2 he produced a more detailed practical manual, known today simply as the 'Rules', for the local landlord, the Countess of Lincoln. Dorothea Oschinsky thinks it likely that a professional farm manager had a hand in the compilation of this document, which enshrines best practice rather than being innovative.[96] Another and longer document, the *Seneschaucy*, by an unknown author probably in the 1260s or early 1270s, describes how agricultural estates should be organized and administered, including lists of key officers and their duties, and a third, known as the *Husbandry*, offers advice on keeping accounts. Oschinsky has also translated more than thirty other documents on accounting for managers of landed estates from this period, including some that give formularies and advice on best practice in accounting and reporting.

The most famous book from this period is the treatise of Walter of Henley, who was probably born around 1240 and was the steward of a large estate somewhere in southern England; he may also have been a Dominican friar.[97] The treatise we have today originally took the form of a lecture, probably delivered at the University of Oxford as part of a course in estate management. Many students who read law at Oxford also trained as estate managers there, and it is not unreasonable to state that a kind of proto-business school existed at Oxford at the time, with estate managers learning law, accounting, the rudiments of agricultural science and the duties of estate management. Later copies of Walter's work divided into four sections. The first deals with general management of manors and offers guidance on surveying the estate and on choosing and hiring personnel. The second is a largely technical section on arable farming, while the third is concerned with the management of livestock. The fourth section gives information on accounting and the financial management of estates, and also describes how managers should watch markets, monitor prices and try to anticipate demand.

Oschinsky believes that Walter's treatise is at times theoretical and may not represent a true picture of agricultural management at the time. This may be so, but my reading of Walter is that he was trying to introduce theoretical concepts that would improve management practice. It seems likely that his theoretical concepts had their origins in observed best practice at professionally run estates such as that of the Bishop of Winchester. This large ecclesiastical estate was an innovator in many ways, adopting the accounting and reporting techniques pioneered in central government by Fitz Neal and Hubert Walter at the end of the twelfth century (see above). The Winchester estate is also known to have hired many Oxford graduates as administrators, and Walter of Henley's treatise might have been a way of feeding lessons from best practice back into classroom teaching. He was, in other words, trying to create a body of theory about estate management that could inform future practice. As Oschinsky says, the work 'must be taken as an indication of the intellectual level of the students of estate management for whom Walter of Henley wrote and also the high level of efficiency demanded of the profession of estate managers at that time.'[98] It is also worth noting that Walter of Henley's work was copied repeatedly in the decades to come and directly influenced writers on estate management for the next three centuries at least.

Elsewhere in the world

Given the lengthy treatment of Indian management ideas in the previous chapter, it may be thought that they have been given rather short shift in this one. Certainly there was no lack of writing on administration in India during this period. The problem, as Padma Udgaonkar points out in her study of political institutions of northern India, is that few later writers attempt to go beyond the *Arthashastra*.[99] Kautilya's masterwork remained enormously influential, and some later writers on administration did little more than copy out parts of the *Arthashastra* and put their own name on them. Examples include the *Kamandakiya Nitisara* (Elements of Polity) written around the tenth century by Kamandakya, himself probably a senior administrator;[100] the *Nitivakyamrita*, written in the tenth century by the poet Somadeva, who comments a little acidly that even an unintelligent king can succeed if he surrounds himself with wise counsellors;[101] the *Rajadhharmakanda of Krityakalpataru*, composed by Lakshmidara, foreign minister of the kingdom of Gahadvala in the twelfth century; the *Manasollasa,* attributed to King Somesvara III of Western Chalyuka in the early twelfth century, which gives some details on the qualities needed by a king along with chapters on other subjects including fishing;[102] or the *Purusarthasara*, which also lists the qualities required of a king including truthfulness, magnanimity, purity, competence, respect for the righteous, straight thinking, restraint from evil and self-control. Such lists, says historian C.V. Ramachanran Rao, 'are not free from romantic idealism'.[103] True; but as with other such texts, they tell us what traits society expected from its leaders, even if it did not always receive them.

The most sophisticated of these works is the *Sukraniti*, a work of very uncertain origin composed most likely between 800 and 1200.[104] About the author, Sukra, only the name is known. Nonetheless, Udgaonkar calls this the most comprehensive book on Indian political science after the *Arthashastra*. Though drawing heavily on the latter work, Sukra also offers his own ideas on the organization of the kingdom, the role of the king and the duties of ministers. Central to his conception is the concept of *niti*, similar to *dharma* but which Sukra believes is the source of *dharma*. He likens *niti* to a set of rules or guidelines which kings can follow in order to be sure they are behaving in a righteous manner, and cautions rulers against straying from the path of *niti*, for this is sure to lead to trouble.

Other works, including writings by travellers and epic poems, offer us fascinating insights into the rich commercial life of medieval India, and it is possible to learn a great deal about, for example, the commercial guild system, its relation to the caste system and how the guilds interacted with one another. There were big businesses in India too, such as the Chettiahs of the Coromandel and the Chands of Bengal (the latter, who bore the title Jagat Seth, or 'Bankers to the World', were estimated by a British contemporary to be more wealthy than the Bank of England), although Irfan Habib maintains that India failed to develop a capitalistic class in the same way that Europe did.[105] However, there is little to be gleaned from any of these sources on management thought, and one is left with the conclusion that Indian management thought remained stuck firmly in the age of Kautilya. It should be added, however, that Indian business historians are analysing many of these sources anew, and that it is quite possible that this conclusion will be overturned in the near future. Readers are advised to watch this space.

Buddhism arrived in China in the third century AD and managed to get itself established in Chinese thought just as the Han dynasty collapsed and the Chinese empire disintegrated. Chinese Buddhist philosophy concentrated on issues such as knowledge and enlightenment, and classics such as the *Dasheng qixunlun* (Awakening of Faith in Mahayana), composed in the sixth century, were widely read by the intellectual elite, interested in the processes by which knowledge is created an understood.[106] Buddhist intellectual thought gradually fused with Daoism, with which it had much in common, and as China reunified under the Tang and then the Song dynasties, there developed a more general search for common principles under which all of China's competing philosophies could be unified. This culminated in what modern historians of philosophy call the 'neo-Confucian synthesis', a harmonizing of Confucian, Daoist and Buddhist ideas, a project carried to completion by the writer Zhu Xi (1130–1200).[107]

There is a perception that after Confucius and Han Fei, Chinese thought became increasingly ossified, but that simply is not so. Admittedly there was a great deal of reworking of older themes and ideas, and no thinkers of similar stature appeared, but we saw in Chapter 2 how Cao Cao took Sunzi's ideas on strategy and drastically reworked them to form an essentially new work. The Emperor Taizhong of the Tang dynasty (d. 649) produced several notable works including the *Difan* (Models for the Emperor), a manual of instruction in the 'mirrors for princes' mode, and the *Zhenguan zhengyao* (Essentials of Government of the Zhengguan Period).[108] Again, this work draws heavily on earlier sources but Taizhong reinterprets and reworks them heavily for his own time. The work was read widely right to the end of the Chinese empire and was also circulated in Japan and Korea. According to Professor Billy So of Chinese University of Hong Kong, the *Zhenguan zhengyao* was also read by business people.[109] Going forward into the Song dynasty one finds more tracts on agriculture and administration.

Then came more instability, and the disaster of the Mongol invasion and ensuing famine which may once again have cost the lives of half the population of China.[110] The restoration of unity under the Ming dynasty was accompanied by no corresponding restoration of the spirit of intellectual inquiry. Under the Ming, intellectual life became increasingly mimetic. The neo-Confucian synthesis dominated, and was not to be challenged. Administrative training consisted in studying the ancient classics, with little new work being produced. There were original thinkers, such as Won Yomei (1472–1528) who wrote about self-consciousness and the unification of knowledge and action, but in a purely philosophical and theoretical way with little attempt to relate to the real world. Technological regression set in, most notably when the later Ming emperors disbanded the country's famous navy and forbade further exploration of the Indian Ocean, surrendering control to the Arabs and later the Europeans. Under the Qing dynasty, which came to power in the later sixteenth century, China again actively discouraged intellectual inquiry, especially in connection with the outside world. A popular manual for magistrates, *A Complete Book Concerning Happiness and Benevolence* published in 1699, shows us that by far the greater majority of businesses were small family affairs. Larger enterprises did exist in sectors such as pottery and textiles, but these sectors were heavily regulated and there is little evidence of advances in management thinking or methods. When the Emperor Qianlong told the British ambassador in 1798 that China had all it needed and could think of nothing that it wanted from the rest of the world, he was talking not just of goods, but of ideas.

To get an idea of intellectual life in the Qing area, one could do no better than to read Cao Xueqin's classic novel, *A Dream of Red Mansions*, written in the late eighteenth century. Whereas European literature of this period is full of restless energy, striving after new ideas and inventing new concepts, Cao Xueqin's work is almost entirely backward-looking, a beautiful, elegiac and somewhat sad book which yearns for the past. Thus China, until the European threat arrived in the nineteenth century.[111]

Japanese ideas on administration and management differ little from those of China during this period. Japanese culture was heavily influenced by Confucian and Daoist ideas imported from the mainland, and even more by Buddhism, which arrived from India by way of China. Buddhist ideas about the harmony of the universe found a natural partner in the ideas of Shinto, Japan's indigenous religion, which among other things emphasized the divine nature not only of the emperor but of the country itself. Japan, in the words of the fourteenth-century writer Kitabatake Chikafusa, was especially protected and favoured by the gods.[112] This encouraged, even more than in China, a sublimation of self to the greater good and obedience to the divine rule of the emperor. All institutions, private and public, were clearly subordinated to the emperor.

The most important document on administration from this period is the so-called Shotoku Constitution of AD 604, issued by Prince Shotoku, regent for the Empress Suiko. Its seventeen articles summarize neatly the Japanese approach to administration.[113] Like *The Duties of the Vizier* or the *Arthashastra*, it is intended as a guide for officials, not so much a procedures manual but a series of precepts that they should follow. Article 1 begins by declaring that the achievement of harmony is the primary purpose of government, and all else that follows is subordinated to this idea. Officials are told to be reverent, to conduct their business with decorum, to be neutral and impartial in making decisions, to be hard-working and punctual, and to set aside private ambitions and work solely for the good of the state. Article 11, probably influenced by Han Fei's Legalism, says that those who do their work well will be rewarded, while those who do not will be punished.

Later Japanese writings on administration add little to this. Nor did the structure of Japanese administration and society change greatly until the early fourteenth century, when a series of revolts weakened the power of the emperor and led to a general breakdown of administration. From 1467–1600 Japan was wracked by a series of civil conflicts that became known as the *Sengoku Jidai*, the Age of the Country at War. The eventual victor, Tokugawa Ieyesu, took the title of *shogun* and ruled the country in all but name, reducing the emperor to the status of puppet. The dominant social class now were the *samurai*, the warriors who had ruled the country during the *Sengoku Jidai* and still wielded much power. These produced their own literature, some of which influenced management thought and practice. In the mid-seventeenth century the master swordfighter Miyamoto Musashi wrote the *Gorin no sho* (Book of Five Rings) as a manual for swordfighters; it became much admired for its

insights into the psychology of competition and suggestions on how to anticipate an oppo-
nent's moves.[114] The book was and still is widely read by business people. Miyamoto was
perhaps the most famous of the swordfighters, but the lives and careers of many others were
studied too. For example, Sugawara Makoto's *Lives of Master Swordsmen* contains a series
of biographies of swordfighters and offers lessons from the careers and techniques of each.[115]

Later still, the *Hagakure* (In the Shadow of Leaves) of Yamamoto Tsunetomo emphasized
the need for order, structure and obedience to hierarchy. Beginning with the comment that
'The Way of the *samurai* is found in death', Yamamoto goes on: 'We all want to live. And
in large part we make our logic according to what we like. But not having attained our aim
and continuing to live is cowardice.'[116] Like Miyamoto, Yamamoto writes at length about
personal mastery, the need to understand and control oneself and one's own impulses before
one can hope to lead or influence others. His work, though castigated by some in the twentieth
century as having contributed to the militaristic culture of early Japan, does have useful
insights into leadership and organization. But like the *Gorin no sho*, it is at heart a work of
medieval Japan despite its late authorship. Not until the nineteenth century would any further
significant work on administration emerge in Japan.

It is possible to say a word about administration in the new world societies, but little more
than that. Aztec Mexico seems to have had an elaborate civil service dominated by its priestly
caste, but the conquering Spaniards destroyed virtually all evidence of this; only a handful
of documents such as the so-called Codex Mendoza remain.[117] These give us an idea of how
the country was administered, but no idea as to what the intellectual principles of administration were, or even if there were any. A similar destruction took place in Inca Peru.[118] It
may be that more information will be uncovered in the future, but it is likely to be found by
archaeologists rather than historians.

Conclusion

Through the course of this chapter we have seen ideas about business and management
advanced by lawyers, teachers, theologians, preachers, princes, civil servants, mathematicians, swordfighters, monks and even a few business people. Most continued to focus on the
three essentials of strategy, organization and leadership, but other themes began to emerge.
We have seen people beginning to wrestle with the complexities of market behaviour, and to
ponder on the roles and traits of the business manager, as opposed to the civil service
administrator.

We have seen too how heavily business thinking and practice was influenced by other
types of organization. One lesson we can draw is that much of our early understanding
of management came from the palace, the church and the military camp, rather than the
marketplace. How strongly are we still influenced by those ideas today? Marketers do not sit
down and read Thomas Aquinas, nor do management search agencies consult the principles
of San Bernardino. Yet it seems clear that these early writers did stumble across some
fundamental ideas about how organizations are managed and governed. They did so by
drawing on ideas from a wide range of sources as well as from practical experience, and came
up with some remarkable insights. Another lesson might be that we need to broaden our own
scope of inquiry today, and seek insights from comparably diverse sources.

4　Management thought in an age of enlightenment

A king is the slave of history.

(Leo Tolstoy)

Dare to know.

(Immanuel Kant)

The Enlightenment is the name given to the intellectual and cultural movement that swept across Europe during the late seventeenth and eighteenth centuries. It was a time of intellectual curiosity and scientific advancement. The term is often used carelessly, the suggestion being that before the Enlightenment came along European society was somehow 'endarkened', which it emphatically was not; the roots of Enlightenment thinking are to be found in the Middle Ages. Nor did intellectual curiosity cease during or after the French Revolution, the traditional endpoint for the Enlightenment period used by most historians; the scientific revolution of the nineteenth century was the Enlightenment's direct inheritor. The chapter title has been phrased so as to indicate that we are covering a broader period: an age characterized by critical thinking, not just the Enlightenment per se.

For one leading thinker of the time, the German philosopher Immanuel Kant (1724–1804), the spirit of the Enlightenment was summed up in a single phrase: 'dare to know'. The Enlightenment was passionate about knowledge, especially new knowledge. One of its foremost tenets was that everything was open to criticism, including the church, the crown, the administration, previously held tenets of scientific knowledge, relations within society, the lot. René Descartes (1596–1650) set things in motion with his famous statement, 'cogito ergo sum' (I think, therefore I am). The belief that the possession of a thinking, rational mind was one of the defining features of what it meant to be human was advanced by David Hume (1711–76), particularly in his *Enquiry Concerning Human Understanding*, and by Kant in his *Critique of Pure Reason*.[1] With that belief came a similar, equally powerful belief that people had a duty to use their minds, to seek truth, to learn. Not for the Enlightenment the mystical beliefs of China, India and Islamic Sufism, which held that some phenomena were mysteries that could be known but not explained. The Enlightenment hated mysteries, and even when enlightened philosophers and economists such as Quesnay and Montesquieu studied mysticism, it was with the purpose of trying to explain it.

The spirit of inquiry

Descartes is sometimes held to be the first Enlightenment philosopher, but to understand the intellectual atmosphere of the age we need to go back much further, at least to the Polish astronomer Nicolaus Copernicus (1473–1543), whose book *On the Revolutions of the Celestial Spheres* challenged established notions of cosmology. After him came Galileo, Kepler, Newton and others who between them reshaped our entire notion of the universe.

At the same time, our knowledge of the world itself was changing even more rapidly. The Portuguese prince Henry the Navigator (1394–1460) sponsored a series of expeditions to explore the Atlantic with a view to finding a way around Africa to open up a maritime trade route to India and China. Other countries, especially Spain, sent out expeditions of their own. In the space of just thirty years, from 1492–1522, the sea route around the Cape of Good Hope was opened up and maritime routes opened between Europe, southern India and South-East Asia; European navigators had made landfall in both North and South America, settlements had been established and Cortez had conquered Aztec Mexico; and Magellan's expedition had returned from its circumnavigation of the world. The world looked very different from how people had imagined it just a few decades earlier, and now people such as the Dutchman Gerardus Mercator were inventing new ways of mapping and describing that world.[2]

With old perceptions about the world and the universe changing, it was perhaps inevitable that Descartes and those who came after him would continue the process of questioning, and to search for knowledge that would help them find answers to their questions. Once Descartes had argued successfully that the mind and body were two separate things, medical scientists began to examine both, if only to try to understand how the two interacted and influenced each other. Natural scientists began to study the animal and plant worlds, making discoveries that would ultimately lead to Darwin's theory of evolution – which itself would go on to influence thinking about economics and business. Advances in physics and mathematics led to technological advances in metallurgy and engineering, which in turn led to new industries. And the spirit of the enlightenment also considered human society and looked for ways in which it could be improved, and that included discussions of politics, economics and business. Not the least of the advances of this time was the development of the science of demography by John Graunt from the 1660s onward.[3] This was the very beginning of an attempt to classify the population according to age, means and needs; a classification on which marketers, among others, continue to rely today.

A passion for classification arose more generally. The Swedish natural scientist Carl Linnaeus, in his *Systema Naturae* (Natural Systems) published in 1735, offered a method of classifying plants according to the characteristics they shared; classifications were soon introduced into every other science too, geology, zoology, medicine, meteorology, chemistry. Classification meant that a mass of knowledge could be given order and structure, making it easier to teach and understand.

A few notes of caution are in order. For all that it saw itself as a new age of light and reason quite different to the age that had gone before – Kant referred to humankind waking up from an age of ignorance and error and free at last to use its reason – there were at least as many continuities from as differences between the Enlightenment and the age just ended. In his separation of mind and body, Descartes was picking up on a theory advanced by Plato; at times, when discussing the role of critical reasoning, Hume might have been echoing the medieval philosopher Peter Abelard: 'by doubting we come to examine, and by examining so we reach the truth'. Nor were scholars of the European Enlightenment immune to influences from further afield. In France especially, translations of Turkish, Persian, Indian and Chinese literature were enormously influential, especially on the French political theorist Baron de Montesquieu (1689–1755) in his book *Lettres persanes*,[4] and we saw in Chapter 2 how the economic concept of laissez-faire was derived from Quesnay's reading of the *Daodejing*.

It should be added too that the atmosphere was not always conducive to free thinking and free speech. Sometimes – in England, quite often – it was. But elsewhere people could be and were punished for their ideas, as the persecution of Galileo by the Inquisition amply demonstrates. When Kant said, 'dare to know', he really did mean 'dare'. The passion with which many thinkers of the Enlightenment expressed their views can in part be explained by the fact that in expressing them they often laid their careers, and sometimes their lives, on the line.

Nor was this a time of enlightenment and advance and freedom for everyone. Some believed that such a time would come. William Godwin (1756–1836) and the Marquis de Condorcet (1743–94) argued that humanity was now on course to develop a truly perfect society. Science made great strides forward, and European prosperity began to rise; but the impact of colonialism and conquest meant that the prosperity of many others around the world declined correspondingly. Advances in technology enriched some but impoverished others. Not everyone believed that society was, every day and in every way, becoming better and better. In her novel *Frankenstein*, Godwin's daughter Mary Shelley offered her own dark interpretation of where the excesses of scientific knowledge and personal freedom might lead. Her work was enormously influential on later writers on dystopia including Aldous Huxley and Lewis Mumford.

How does all of this relate to management thought? It does so in two ways. First, just as in every age, the philosophical 'software of the mind', to borrow Hofstede's later phrase that is embedded in each of us through our culture and upbringing and education conditions how we think, including how we think about management.[5] A good example of this is the Lunar Society of Birmingham, the so-called 'Lunar Men' where scientists, philosophers and business leaders including Josiah Wedgwood, Matthew Boulton and James Watt gathered to exchange ideas.[6] Nor was the influence solely contemporary. In the twentieth-century writers such as the French exponent of scientific management Charles de Fréminville, for example, referred explicitly back to Descartes as a source of knowledge. Second, the spirit of inquiry that led to new technologies had a direct impact on the world of business through the Industrial Revolution of the eighteenth century, the Scientific Revolution of the nineteenth century, and the era of colony and empire that spans both.

During this era, we see management thinking begin to broaden out. Along with the old concerns of strategy, organization and leadership we now see recognition of the need to manage technology, to manage knowledge, and above all to manage people. There was also a greater complexity of both scale and scope. There had always been large businesses, often trading over large geographical areas; but there were more of them now, and in new sectors such as steel making, shipping, railways that offered their own managerial challenges.

Economists and management

In the absence of specific works on the subject, there is quite a lot to be learned about management thought at this time from the works of economists, although just as with the works of the scholastic philosophers in the Middle Ages, one often has to search diligently to find it.

Economics – political economy, as it was known until fairly recently – emerged as a discipline in its own right around this time. The first 'economists' were polymaths, men such as Sir William Petty, one of the founders of the Royal Society in England in the aftermath of the English Civil War, who wrote on subjects as diverse as taxation, music, medicine, politics and money. Not surprisingly given his interests in medicine, Petty offered a comparison between organizations and the human body, continuing in the tradition of Aristotle and John of Salisbury. He also dabbled with ideas on specialization in trade and discussed how a business that specialized in one trade could generate a surplus that could be reinvested and help to fund expansion.[7]

Petty was a member of a school of economic thinkers known as the mercantilists, who flourished especially in England, Scotland and France in the seventeenth and early eighteenth centuries. The English economy had grown in the later Middle Ages on the back of the wool trade. When this declined the economy declined too, and by the end of the sixteenth century the public and private finances of the country were in a desperate state; the civil conflicts of the seventeenth century and defeat in foreign wars by the Netherlands and France made the situation still worse. There was a crippling shortage of circulating currency, making investment and growth very difficult. Many of the mercantilists argued for the development of a banking system, finally getting their way with the establishment of the Bank of England (1694) and Bank of Scotland (1695).

The second mercantilist aim was to readjust the balance of trade so that England exported more than it imported, thus ensuring a net inflow of money. Some writers such as Josiah Child (1630–99) and Andrew Yarranton (1616–85) argued that this should be done by stimulating domestic manufacturing industries and investing in infrastructure such as roads and canals.[8] Child argued for free markets, but Yarranton wanted more regulation, including legislation to compel the poor to work for the national good. Other writers such as Charles Davenant (1656–1714) thought the answer lay in restricting imports, either through high tariffs or outright bans, while Gerard de Malynes (d. 1641) wanted restrictions on the export of currency. What all the mercantilists had in common was the need to rebuild the shattered economy, and the important role that private sector businesses must have in that process. In a later work, *The Elements of Commerce, and Theory of Taxes* from 1755, Josiah Tucker referred to the English, with obvious approval, as a 'nation of shopkeepers'.[9] Like Child and Yarranton, Tucker argued for a more rigorous approach to banking, trade and commerce. Child and Yarranton stop short of calling for a theory of business or theory of management, but they are certainly pointing in that direction. Business needs to be conducted, they and others such as William Petty argued, in a way that benefits the country; and this requires that businesses be efficient and make profits.

Tucker went rather further. Long before the scientific management movement, he argued that commerce was a science and that it was possible to discern scientific principles that governed its conduct. One of those principles he refers to as 'self-love', the motivating force that causes people to seek wealth or personal benefit through economic activity. The French economist Jean-Baptiste Say (1767–1832) renamed this term 'self-interest', and later economists have described this as the profit-seeking motive of the entrepreneur. Tucker had thus hit upon the beginnings of a theory of entrepreneurship. He also used the same concept of self-love to begin to develop a theory of labour, arguing that self-seeking behaviour was responsible for tensions between workers and employers as each tried to maximize their own self-interest at the expense of others, a concept that later influenced Karl Marx.

The term 'entrepreneur' had been introduced a few decades earlier by the French banker and economist Richard Cantillon in his *Essai sur la nature du commerce en général* (Essay on the Nature of Trade in General), first published in 1755 but written earlier.[10] Cantillon was one of a school of French economists known as the physiocrats – François de Quesnay, whom we met in Chapter 2, was another – who believed that agriculture was the only real source of wealth and all other wealth was derived from it. Like the mercantilists, they called for more rigour and the application of scientific principles to commerce and trade and, unsurprisingly, to agriculture in particular. But they were also advocates of free markets – hence Quesnay's coining of the term laissez-faire. Here we can see quite clearly the impact of Enlightenment philosophy more generally. Voltaire, Montesquieu, Rousseau and others were calling for less government, or at least, for governments to rule with a lighter hand. Likewise, the physiocrats argued that government should not interfere with the economy.

The physiocrats were an important influence on the Scottish Enlightenment philosopher and economist Adam Smith. His *Inquiry into the Nature and Causes of the Wealth of Nations*, published in 1776, remains a landmark in economic thought. His significance lies not in the fact that he himself was a highly original thinker – many of the concepts ascribed to him, such as the division of labour, free trade or the 'invisible hand' had been developed long ago by others – but rather in his ability to combine these and other elements into a coherent system.[11] With hindsight he got some things wrong – he saw no future for joint stock corporations, for example, believing that individual entrepreneurs were the way of the future – but he delivered a compelling account of an economic system with some powerful managerial ideas as well.[12]

Chief among these is his exposition and development of the ancient idea of the division of labour. Smith saw specialization not just as a necessity in order to achieve complex tasks, but as a creator of value in its own right. His famous example is that of a manufacturer of pins. To make an individual pin requires eighteen separate operations. Working on his own, a man might make only twenty pins in a day, surely not enough to support him and his family. But if workers combine and each takes on one of the eighteen operations – one draws the wire, one cuts it, one straightens it, and so on – they can speed up productivity. Smith calculated that a series of workers operating in this way could make 4,800 pins in a day, far more than the same group could make if each worked individually. Of course, what Smith is describing is not just the *division* of labour but also the *concentration* of labour, the factory system which even then was being born in northern England and his own native Scotland.[13]

Smith influenced an entire generation of economists across Europe including David Ricardo, Jeremy Bentham, James Mill and the latter's son, John Stuart Mill. Another follower was Thomas Robert Malthus, most famous for his theories on population but also noted for *The Principles of Political Economy*, published in 1820. Malthus is one of the first writers to introduce motivation as a factor in theories of exchange. Rejecting Jean-Baptiste Say's view that supply creates its own demand, Malthus argued that exchange is not created just by the presence of supply and demand, but by the will, intent and ability of both parties to make the exchange. He describes demand as 'the will combined with the power to purchase', while supply is 'the production of commodities combined with the intent to sell them'.[14] In other words, people make markets. Their ability to participate in those markets depends on their relative power, affluence and – especially – their desire to make an exchange. This very human-centred view of markets is found also in early twentieth-century marketing theory, and continues to resonate today.

Malthus has a further claim to fame as a founding member of staff of the first business school in the modern sense, the East India Company staff college at Hayleybury in Hertfordshire. The company had earlier tried to found a training college in India, but this had failed. However, the directors agreed that there was merit in the idea of giving some training to newly recruited managers and agents rather than simply sending them out to India and hoping they would learn on the job, and Hayleybury was founded with this purpose. Trainee administrators undertook a two-year programme during which they were taught law, history, political economy, mathematics and accounting, natural sciences, literature and Oriental culture and languages. Malthus taught political economy there until his death in 1834; the college itself lasted until the demise of the East India Company in 1858.

Unsurprisingly given this association, Malthus was a believer in education and knowledge and thought that these had economic value. So did his younger contemporaries, notably Nassau Senior (1790–1864), who believed that knowledge was essential in order to co-ordinate and control the work of others: in other words, in order to manage people one must have knowledge. Later still, Karl Marx pointed out that there was no distinction between 'mental work' and physical labour: both created value.[15] One might expect the beginnings of a theory of knowledge management to emerge at this point, but curiously the subject was not picked up by management until much later.

A curious amalgam of the influence of Adam Smith and the mercantilists also deserves a mention. The Italian writer Melchiorre Gioia (1767–1829) had been a civil servant in the Cisalpine Republic, a puppet state of Napoleon's First Empire. Unsurprisingly, he was a proponent of state control and state intervention. But he also wrote in detail on the division of labour, and followed Smith in most matters apart from free trade. He picked up on the logical consequence of Smith's concentration of labour and insisted that large, highly centralized enterprises were the most efficient and most productive form of business. The debate as to whether this was actually true would heat up later in the century, especially in America (see below).[16]

Managing labour

By the mid-nineteenth century at least, economists were beginning to look at issues surrounding the management of labour. The relationship between labour and value creation had been understood for some time but, with a few rare exceptions such as Josiah Tucker, it was more or less taken for granted that workers would work: that was their role in life. There had been little progression beyond the 'three orders' system of the Middle Ages. The freedom preached in the brave new world of the Enlightenment did not extend to the working classes, save in the works of radicals such as Thomas Paine, Rousseau and the ideologues of the French Revolution or the early English socialists.

In 1848 the English economist John Stuart Mill foresaw the day when workers, rather than being content to work for the owners of capital, would pool their own capital and start their own firms, and he approved of ideas such as the cooperative movement.[17] It apparently did not occur to him that a rethinking of the relationship between employers and workers might be an option. Nor did it to Karl Marx, who seems to have regarded relationships between capitalists and workers as being too far gone to be worth salvaging. Marx, taking his cue in part from Josiah Tucker and in part from the French Revolution, argued that the self-interest of the capitalist and working classes meant that they would always be at each other's throats. Famously, he believed that in the end the working classes would seize control of the means of production from the capitalists and become themselves the owners of capital.

From the perspective of managerial thought, however, Marx's real innovation is to introduce the worker as a self-motivated actor in the workplace. Workers are no longer pawns to be used or machines to be driven. They have their own motives, their own purposes for working, their own roles to play in the workplace, which are often directly opposed to those of the employer. Marx believed this problem had only one solution: revolution. Others thought differently; and indeed, it was precisely this problem that scientific management first set out to solve (see Chapter 5).

Mention should be made of another biting attack on the contemporary system of labour by the American economist Henry Carey, one of the first economists of distinction to emerge in America. By the time of his book *The Slave Trade* in 1853, slavery had been outlawed in the

British empire but still existed elsewhere, notably in the southern United States. Carey's attack is both moral and pragmatic. He is perfectly happy to accept what he calls the 'local division of labour', the concentration of workers in factories, but attacks the 'territorial division of labour', or the migration (usually forced) of people to other parts of the world to work in industries where their labour is needed; incidentally thus crippling the countries they have left and where their labour is also needed. But Carey also makes the point that workers need to be treated well if they are to work effectively. He argues that there is little moral or practical distinction between the slave plantations of southern America and the sweatshops of the north. Also, neither sweated labour nor slavery makes economic sense. Carey calculates that one free worker, well fed and well paid, will do the work of four underpaid workers or unpaid slaves, at less cost to the employer. Why do employers then continue to sweat workers or employ slaves? Carey thinks that it is because short-term cost pressures force employers to behave in ways that can only harm their own interests in the long term. 'Cheap food and slavery go together', he says, 'and if we desire to free ourselves from the last, we must commence by ridding ourselves of the first'.[18]

The scaling up of enterprises

Other issues caught the attention of American economists as time went forward. One of these was the increasing scale of enterprises. This issue roused less interest in Europe, but there had long been an uneasy tension in America between business – especially big business – and the rest of society. For example, America had been slow to develop a banking system thanks to the opposition of people such as Thomas Jefferson, third president of the United States, who vigorously opposed the use of paper money and credit and was antagonistic to large businesses. He preferred the idea of small cottage industries or even self-sufficient households. As he wrote in 1812:

> We have reduced the large and expensive machinery for most things to the compass of a private family. Every family of any size is now getting machines on a small scale for their household purposes . . . my household manufactures are just getting into operation on the scale of a carding machine costing $60 only, which may be worked by a girl of twelve years old, a spinning machine . . . to be worked by a girl also . . . We consider a sheep to every person as fully sufficient for their woollen clothing.[19]

The 'girl' of course was not a member of Jefferson's family, but one bought in the market-place.

A later president, Andrew Jackson, blocked an attempt to establish a central bank in America on the grounds that such a powerful institution would be a threat to American liberty.[20] As historian Robert Wright describes in his study of the financial community in Philadelphia, nascent financial centres did emerge, but they often did so in spite of rather than because of governmental and public support.[21] John Jacob Astor, founder of one of the first large diversified business empires in America, retired to Europe after he sold his business, preferring the more business-friendly atmosphere there.

Several things then happened. The American Civil War forced a scaling up on the part of businesses, especially manufacturing firms, in the northern states in order to feed and clothe the Union army. Second, the tide of immigration into America began to rise steadily not long after the war, and the population grew at an unprecedented rate. Another scaling up was required to feed the population of America's rapidly growing cities. The third was the introduction of new European ideas, most notably from the German Historical School, which influenced the post-Civil War generation of economists and which were much more friendly to the concepts of big business and industrial concentration. Francis Amasa Walker, founding president of the American Economic Association in 1885, was deeply influenced by the German economists.[22]

Whether America wanted big businesses or not, it now had them. Asked to give his verdict on these large entities – many of which were monopolies or near-monopolies – were good or bad for the country, Walker responded by trying to evade the issue. 'Political economy has to do with no other subject, whatever, than wealth', he wrote. 'Especially should the student of economics take care not to allow any purely political, ethical or social considerations to influence him in his investigations.' We have come a long way from al-Dimashqi, Ibn Khaldun and Aquinas, who insisted that ethical and social considerations lay at the heart of business and economics! Indeed, it seemed that Walker had gone too far; he was widely castigated for his view that business was somehow ethically neutral (though they would later be revived in various forms, notably by Milton Friedman). Other economists such as Jeremiah Jenks and William Graham Sumner were caught in a dilemma.[23] Both espoused free trade and believed like Adam Smith that the government should not intervene in the economy. And yet, unregulated capitalism seemed to lead to concentration, monopoly and the stifling of the very principle of competition that was so dear to them. How should they respond? Both Sumner and Jenks responded, after some hesitation, by calling for government intervention to prevent monopolies.

The economic debate about the impact of large businesses and monopolies exposed a deeper issue pertaining more directly to management. What are the responsibilities of businesses and managers to society? In the past, most societies had regulations and systems to inform managers of those responsibilities and how to discharge them. Post-Civil War America seemed to lack these. The kind of capitalism described by William Fowler in *Twenty Years of Inside Life in Wall Street* in 1880 was certainly not ethically neutral, and the men who dominated the market – Cornelius Vanderbilt, Jay Gould, Daniel Drew – seemed subject to no law but that of the jungle. Fowler makes an explicit reference to the Darwinian concept of 'survival of the fittest', and suggests that this is about the only law that operated on Wall Street.[24]

In this context, it is useful to refer to the writings of the lawyer and economic historian, John Davis. He too was influenced by the German Historical School, and his early history of the Union Pacific Railway is an interesting attempt to use historical principles to explain organizational evolution.[25] The Historical School tended to concentrate on economies and systems, but Davis showed that its methods could be used to show how organizations change and grow. His later book *Corporations*, published posthumously in 1905, was written in light of the increasingly fierce debate about the role of large business entities in society.

Davis argued that all corporations are social forms. There are several consequences of this. First corporations evolve and adapt over time: 'Like all other social forms, corporations are subject to modification: (1) internally, by the influence of their content, the social activity exercised by them, and (2) externally, by the influence of other social forms and social activity.'[26] Social forms have a close relationship with their environment and, like species in the biological world, can undergo changes through contact with other forms. Second, there is a direct link between form and function:

> Social forms and social functions are intimately interdependent. Lack of adaptation of either to the other must result in modifications in one or the other or both . . . If the form,

whether originally or as the result of a subsequent more or less arbitrary modification, is unsuitable for a particular function, it must be altered to conform to the character of the function, or perish – unless it be adapted or adaptable to some other social function to which it may be readily transferred.[27]

(1905: 11)

This adaptation, Davis says, is a historical process: 'Corporate forms and functions and the environment by which they are influenced are all products of time. They are all meaningless except as they register past experience or predict future social growth, stagnation or decay. They must therefore be subjected to historical treatment.'[28] Each historical era develops the corporations which suit its particular needs for social forms. But – and this is the critical point – each era also discards those corporations it no longer needs, or which are not seen as contributing to society in some way. Davis's description of the dismantling of the European monasteries can be taken as a coded warning to big businesses: if you persist in putting your own self-interest ahead of the interests of society, society will turn against you. And, indeed, in some cases society did just that; in some countries such as Russia and China, the entire free market system was swept away by revolution.

I have treated Davis at some length, in part because his books are little read today, and in part because I feel he makes some profound points about the location of businesses within evolving social systems. For those interested in corporations as social systems, his work continues to have much value.

Andrew Ure and Charles Babbage

The same is true of our two final writers in this section, Andrew Ure and Charles Babbage. Ure was an internationally reputed chemist, whose work as a consultant to manufacturing businesses led him to an interest in the problems of industry. He wrote several books on the subject, the most important of which is *The Philosophy of Manufactures*, published in 1835.[29] Noting that the government of France was taking steps to encourage the dissemination of scientific knowledge in the business community, he warned that this would give French industry an advantage. (As Daniel Wren points out, Ure was probably thinking in particular of his friend Charles Dupin and his colleagues at the Conservatory of Arts and Professions, a kind of rudimentary business school in Paris.)[30] His purpose in writing was to encourage similar dissemination in Britain. Interestingly, Ure tells us that he spent more than a year doing field work, visiting dozens of factories and deducing general principles from his observations.

Ure's philosophy is divided into three sections, or 'principles of action': the scientific, the moral and the commercial. His commercial philosophy is largely a rehash of earlier writings on political economy, and his moral philosophy seems to be largely derived from the work of Robert Owen (see below). It is the first section, which Ure calls the 'scientific economy of manufactures' that is most interesting. Here he shows how principles of chemistry and mechanics can be used to make manufacturing more efficient. He also introduces concepts from biology, and yet again we see the biological metaphor of organizations raising its head. According to Ure his three principles of action, the scientific, moral and commercial

may not unaptly be compared to the muscular, the nervous, and the sanguiferous system of an animal. They also have three interests to subserve, that of the operative, the master, and the state, and must seek their perfection in the due development and administration of each. The mechanical being should always be subordinated to the moral constitution, and both should co-operate to the commercial efficiency. Three distinct powers concur to their vitality – labour, science, capital; the first destined to move, the second to direct, and the third to sustain. When the whole are in harmony, they form a body qualified to discharge its manifold functions by an intrinsic self-governing agency, like those of organic life.[31]

This holistic view of organization was a major influence on the later thinking of Harrington Emerson (see Chapter 5).

Charles Babbage was one of the foremost mathematicians of his day, Lucasian Professor of Mathematics at Cambridge and a founder of both the Astronomical Society and the Royal Statistical Society. He is best known for his interest in computers and designed two seminal machines, the difference engine, a highly advanced form of calculating machine, in 1822 and the analytical engine, the first programmable computer, in the 1830s.[32] Like Ure, Babbage was concerned that Britain was losing its competitive edge to countries such as France and Germany which were investing more heavily in technology and education and where businesses often had close ties to universities and other centres of knowledge. He believed that more needed to be done in order to disseminate scientific and technical knowledge as widely as possible. He sets out his views in two works in particular, *The Economy of Machinery and Manufactures* and *The Exposition of 1851*.[33]

In *The Economy of Machinery and Manufactures*, Babbage makes it clear that business should be conducted according to rational and scientific principles. 'Science' in this context means not just technology but the application of scientific methods to the study of business and markets. Babbage never directly sets out the scientific principles that he believes should govern management, but they can be picked out of the text. One of the most important is the need to make effective use of technology. Babbage argues – accurately as it turns out – that machines such as his analytical engine would be very valuable for both generating and disseminating knowledge. Analytical engines would enable managers to have more knowledge, and this would enable better decision making. Technology could also be used to improve the lot of the workers by reducing the amount of manual labour required and making work less strenuous. This was not just wishful thinking. Babbage was well aware of the work of the automated weaving looms developed in France by Joseph Jacquard in 1801, controlled by series of punch cards (the same punch cards that Babbage used to control the analytical engine and continued to be used with computers up to the 1980s). Jacquard looms required less labour, increased productivity and improved quality. Babbage felt that this kind of technology should be adopted more widely in Britain.

In terms of labour, Babbage believes in profit sharing. He argues that a rational society was also a fair one, and that people had the right to profit from their own work:

It would be of great importance if, in every large establishment the mode of payment could be so arranged, that every person employed should derive advantage from the success of the whole; and that the profits of each individual, as the factory itself produced profit, without the necessity of making any change in wages.[34]

Babbage also offers some original ideas on marketing and customer value. In two chapters in *The Economy of Machinery and Manufactures*, 'On the Influence of Verification on Price' and 'On the Influence of Durability on Price', he argues that quality affects the price that goods can command in the market. He makes clear that it is not just the actual quality of the product, but how quality is perceived by customers that really matters. The key concept here is verification: do customers have the ability to make an accurate assessment of quality before making a purchase? If they do not, then there will be higher levels of uncertainty for the customer and, he says, the price the customer is willing to pay will be lower. On the other hand, if customers can make an accurate assessment of quality, then they may be willing to pay more for the reassurance this brings. Babbage argues that sellers need to send signals of quality to customers, using methods such as trademarks which reassure customers as to the provenance of the goods and make a promise on quality. Babbage is the first writer on management to make an explicit connection between product quality, price and profit, and in doing so he begins to explore issues such as branding and customer loyalty.

Babbage was a supporter of the Great Exhibition of 1851, which was intended to showcase the best of British workmanship but actually reinforced the point that Britain was losing the technological and productivity race to its main continental competitors, France and Germany. His book *The Exhibition of 1851* repeats many of his earlier points about technology, knowledge and value, and again stresses the role of education in disseminating new scientific knowledge – including knowledge about business – as widely as possible. He offers some further thoughts on marketing, including on pricing strategy, pointing out that the notion that businesses should sell their products for the highest possible price was wrong, as this would not result in market growth: 'a high price limits the extent of the sale. Their [the sellers] object is that the profit on each article, multiplied by the number sold, shall be the greatest possible.'[35]

He also describes a version of the product life cycle, noting that new industries begin with high-priced goods; then the price falls in order to attract more customers, more competitors then enter the market and the price falls still further. In order to stay ahead of the competition, says Babbage, companies that enter the market first should reinvest part of their capital in 'a succession of moderate improvements, which exciting no immediate inquiry or rivalry, shall increase the per centage of his products, thus constantly keeping his manufactory one, or at the utmost, only two steps in advance of his customers'.[36] In other words, he is arguing for continuous, incremental innovation; exactly the strategy that modern companies such as Procter & Gamble and Apple have used with great success.[37]

In his writings on markets and branding, on technology and knowledge and on the need for scientific principles in management, Babbage was ahead of his time by several decades at least. Lyndall Urwick and Edward Brech later identified Babbage as one of the precursors of scientific management.[38] He is also one of the first really systematic thinkers about business management. Babbage's legacy to management encompasses much more than just the computer.

Thinkers on strategy and leadership

While the economists were introducing new notions about knowledge, technology, markets and labour into management thought, the discipline of strategy was also evolving. In Chapter 2 we saw examples of strategic thinkers in the ancient world, particularly Sunzi and Vegetius, who continued to be read through the medieval period into the modern world. Other ancient writers were widely read too. The library of Matthias Corvinus, King of Hungary from 1458–90, included Vegetius's *Epitoma Rei Militaris*, Frontinus's *Strategemata*, Arrian's *The Campaigns of Alexander* and Xenophon's *The Education of Cyrus*.[39] In Western Europe, however, one later writer on strategy would have a profound and lasting effect. That man was Niccolò Machiavelli.

To say that Machiavelli lived in turbulent times is an understatement. During much of his lifetime (1469–1527) the city-states of Italy were almost continually at war with the French, the Spanish, the papacy and each other. This was an era when a pope thought nothing of donning armour and aiming his own artillery during a battle.[40] Machiavelli himself rose through the ranks of the Florentine civil service to become a member of the high council known as the Ten of War, and served on several diplomatic missions. His career survived two revolutions in Florence but not a third; in 1512 he was arrested, stripped of his offices and titles, tortured and sent into exile. He spent the rest of his life living quietly in a rural villa, but he never stopped hoping for a return to high office. Meanwhile he devoted himself to writing, producing three notable books: *The Art of War*, *Discourses on the First Ten Books of Livy* and, famously, *The Prince*. Only the first of these was published in his own lifetime.[41]

The Art of War is actually the least interesting of the three for our purposes, being mostly a discussion of the arming and preparing of troops and the relative merits of citizen armies and mercenaries. His key ideas on strategy and leadership are contained in *The Prince* and *The Discourses*. It is *The Prince* that has attracted the most attention, largely because of Machiavelli's assertion that 'the end justifies the means'. He is willing to accept the use of deceit, subterfuge, lies and even torture, if this is what is required to ensure the safety of the state. It is granted that these things are wrong. But suppose their use is the only way that the prince can ensure the survival of the state? If he does not sanction the use of lies and torture, the state might fall to its enemies, in which case many and far greater wrongs might ensue.

The ethical implications of this are profound, and it is easy to see why Machiavelli's contemporaries criticized him harshly and banned his books. But, as James Burnham and others have argued, when Machiavelli says that the end justifies the means, he is expressing an inconvenient truth.[42] The first duty of a ruler is to ensure that his or her state survives. A failed state, no matter how high the ethical and moral standards of its ruler, is still a failed state. The same is true in business. As a Danish journalist colleague once commented, a business may have a high and noble purpose, but it will never achieve it if the business itself is also a basket case. But does this mean that we simply accept Machiavelli's arguments without question? The same argument has been used very recently by political leaders to justify the waterboarding of terrorist suspects. More pertinently for our purposes, it is also used by those who defend the act of taking or paying bribes in order to secure business; paying bribes is wrong, but we must do it in order to get contracts and secure jobs for our people. Five centuries on, Machiavelli still leaves us feeling uneasy about the nature of right and wrong.

Machiavelli's thinking about strategy continues to resonate. Success in any enterprise, he says, is down to a combination of two factors. The first is *fortuna*, literally 'luck' but in fact a combination of circumstances and environmental factors that affect our thinking and actions. The second is *virtù*, by which means not just integrity but also intellect, strength and mental resilience. It is *virtù* that enables leaders to see threats and opportunities posed by *fortuna* and then gather the resources required to meet them. The successful leader, then, is one who is always on the lookout for strategic opportunities and can move swiftly to take advantage of them. Machiavelli actively eschews planning: 'he errs least and will be most favoured by fortune who suits his proceedings to the times'.[43]

There is a direct line between this approach to strategy and the late twentieth-century concept of emergent strategy espoused by Henry Mintzberg and others.[44] There is also to my mind a strong link with the concepts of strategic thinking discussed by Kenichi Ohmae in *The Mind of the Strategist*. 'Success must be summoned: it will not come unbidden or unplanned', writes Ohmae. 'To become an effective strategist requires constant practice in strategic thinking. It is a daily discipline, not a resource that can be left dormant in normal times and then tapped at will in an emergency.'[45] This could be a partial definition of Machiavelli's concept of *virtù*.

Though his works were officially on the Catholic Church's list of prohibited books, Machiavelli's ideas were still well known to statesmen and military commanders. They influenced the *Memorie della guerra* of the Italian general Raimondo Montecuccoli (1609–80), which was translated into several languages in the eighteenth century and became a popular manual of organization and strategy. But by the eighteenth century too we can see a trend for thinking about strategy, and warfare more generally, to become more analytical and scientific. In part this is because of the changing nature of war itself. Improvements in gun-founding, artillery and fortifications meant that a range of sciences from chemistry and metallurgy to engineering were becoming more important; the Dutch stadtholder Maurice of Nassau went so far as to establish training courses in siege warfare at the University of Leuven. Machiavelli's 'emergent' strategy was set aside in favour of a search for a set of scientifically based principles on which all strategy rested. This was the preoccupation of Antoine-Henri Jomini (1779–1869) who served on the staff of the French commander Marshal Ney in the Napoleonic Wars, and also of the Prussian officer Heinrich von Bülow who compared warfare to commerce. The military force of a nation is its capital, he said; just like capital, military force needs to be concentrated at the right time and place in order to yield a return on investment.'[46]

The dominant writer on strategy in the nineteenth century was the Prussian staff officer Karl von Clausewitz, whose book *Vom Kriege* (On War) remains a classic of strategic thinking.[47] Clausewitz too was in search of universal principles. The two most important principles he identifies are: (1) that strategy is subordinate to purpose; and (2) that the achievement of any given strategic goal is never certain. Clausewitz is adamant that war is not an independent phenomenon; it is waged for a purpose, one that is determined by the will of the commander and ultimately by the political leaders of the state. There is a difference between the purpose of war and war itself; the latter is simply 'an act of violence meant to force the enemy to do our will'.[48] The sense that strategy is not an end in itself but is always subordinate to purpose and mission remains fundamental to strategic thinking today.

Clausewitz is also doubtful about the value of planning. The problem is that all plans, however well researched and well formulated, begin to unravel as they are put into execution; as Clausewitz's later disciple the Prussian field-marshal Helmuth von Moltke commented, 'no plan survives contact with the enemy'. Probably drawing on Machiavelli's concept of *fortuna*, Clausewitz identified the concept of friction, which he defines as 'countless minor incidents – the kind you can never really foresee – combine to lower the general level of performance, so that one always falls far short of the intended goal'.[49] Friction, he says, is what distinguishes real war from war on paper. As friction builds up, success will depend not on previously laid plans but on factors such as courage and spirit of the leader and the skill and spirit of the troops. This concept too became influential in later writing, and Igor Ansoff's concept of 'turbulence' owes much to Clausewitz's 'friction'.[50]

'Everything in strategy is very simple', says Clausewitz, 'but that does not mean that everything in strategy is very easy'.[51] He places much emphasis on the ability of the leader to understand what is going on in the field and take steps to counter threats and take advantage of opportunities; in other words, he is returning to the ideas of Machiavelli.

Another writer doubted whether even this was possible, and questioned whether leaders themselves were free agents. Count Leo Tolstoy had served as an officer in the Russian army during the Crimean War of 1854–5, which may have coloured his later views. In the novel

War and Peace – which as well as being a work of fiction is also a platform for much of Tolstoy's own philosophical thought[52] – he describes two contrasting leaders, Napoleon and the Russian field commander, Marshal Kutuzov.[53] Napoleon, says Tolstoy, believed himself to be always in control, and that his military victories and conquests were due to his own genius. In 1812 Napoleon claimed to have won the Battle of Borodino but in reality, says Tolstoy, Napoleon was far from the front lines, his view of the battle was entirely obscured by smoke, and he did not give a single order that materially affected the outcome of the battle. Kutuzov, on the other hand, recognized that his powers were limited. Tolstoy depicts him as waiting until the Russian army itself was clear as to its own purpose and what it wanted to do, and then giving only a single order, to advance. With its unity of purpose established, the Russian army defeated the French at Malo-Yaroslavets and precipitated the disastrous French retreat during the winter of 1812.

Even the war itself, said Tolstoy, had not begun spontaneously, nor were the two rival sovereigns, Napoleon and Tsar Alexander I, in control of events:

> The deeds of Napoleon and Alexander, on whose fiat the whole question of war or no war apparently depended, were as little spontaneous and free as the actions of every common soldier drawn into the campaign by lot or by conscription. This could not be otherwise, for in order that the will of Napoleon and Alexander . . . should be effected a combination of innumerable circumstances was essential, without any one of which the event could not have taken place . . . The more we strive to account for such events in history rationally, the more irrational and incomprehensible do they become to us.[54]

Tolstoy argued for the existence of a kind of path dependency, where decisions taken at one point in time have unintended consequences far in the future, and the combination of such consequences forces leaders down a predetermined route or chain of decisions, often without their being aware of it. Far from being a powerful free agent, he declared, 'a king is the slave of history'.[55]

Textbooks and handbooks on management

We saw in Chapter 3 the emergence of the first practical books for managers, the *praticas* or handbooks for merchants first published in Italy, and the handbooks for agricultural estate managers such as the *Seneschaucy* and the work of Walter of Henley. The tradition of handbooks and dictionaries for merchants continued, with one notable example being *Le parfait négociant* (The Perfect Merchant) by Jacques Savary, published in Paris in 1675.[56] Savary, a successful businessman himself, served for several years on a commission advising the French government on revising the laws governing trade and commerce, and wrote a number of papers on various aspects of trade for the benefit of his fellow members. *Le parfait négociant* is in part a collection of those papers, which include some works on the best and most efficient methods of managing businesses. The book remained popular in France through the eighteenth century.

A number of English-language dictionaries from the eighteenth century still exist, the best of which is Malachy Postlethwayt's *The Universal Dictionary of Trade and Commerce* from 1751 with chapters on a variety of economic and commercial subjects. This book filled much the same role in Britain as *Le parfait négociant* did in France, going through numerous editions. There is nothing systematic about either work, but it is possible in both to gain a good idea of the prevailing levels of knowledge about management.[57] The same is true of

Postlethwayt's *The Merchant's Public Counting House, or New Mercantile Institution*.[58] Thomas Mortimer's *A General Dictionary of Commerce, Trade and Manufactures* adds little that cannot be found in Postlethwayt, but his earlier work *The Elements of Commerce, Politics and Finances* is interesting as it is clearly intended for educational purposes, though at what sort of institution we do not know. Another of his works, *Every Man His Own Broker* is likewise an attempt to educate investors about securities markets so that they will not be taken advantage of and lose their money (as happened once to Mortimer himself).[59] This book ran to thirteen editions in the forty years after it was published. The most scholarly of the later English works is John Ramsay McCulloch's *A Dictionary of Commerce*. Published in 1871, it had wide circulation on both sides of the Atlantic, and was a direct influence on later works such as John Lee's *Dictionary of Business Administration*, and possibly too on W.D.P. Bliss's *New Encyclopedia of Social Reform*.[60]

The steady flow of textbooks on estate management continued. In the early twentieth century a survey by Donald McDonald counted over a hundred such texts in England alone between 1600 and 1900.[61] Most are simply technical works about farming, and many are largely copies of earlier works. Others expanded on particular themes. Samuel Hartlib (1600–62) and Gervase Markham (d. 1637) both made the point that farmers require knowledge in order to farm efficiently and that many of the inefficiencies found in farming are due to ignorance of best practice. Jethro Tull (1674–1740) is credited with introducing the experimental method into agriculture, searching for more efficient ways of tilling and sowing, for example, and then communicating what he found. Arthur Young (1741–1820), who became Secretary of the Board of Agriculture, followed this example and urged farmers to conduct their own experiments and exchange information.[62]

Other works were devoted more specifically to land management. For example, Edward Lawrence's *The Duty and Office of a Land-Steward*, published in the early eighteenth century describes not only the day-to-day duties of a land steward but also the purpose of his job.[63] He argues that the land steward must have a complete range of general agricultural knowledge and knowledge about his particular estate: 'no one should undertake the business of a steward till he is fully acquainted with country-affairs, so as to be able upon all occasions, to direct and advise such tenants as do not understand the best and latest improvements in husbandry'.[64] He stresses the need for continuous improvement; there is always room for innovations which will make the estate more productive and more profitable, and the steward should be constantly looking for opportunities. At the same time, he must have a care for the tenants and ensure their safety, health and well-being, making sure that the children are educated and the elderly cared for. This is enlightened self-interest; if farmers have fewer things to worry about, then they will concentrate on farming and do a better job of it.

There were also handbooks on the management of forestry, mines, shipyards, hospitals, schools and charitable institutions, the home and even the nursery. Hundreds of these handbooks were published in Britain between 1600 and 1900, and many more in Europe and, after about 1750, in America. There were also numerous textbooks on accounting, starting with Hugh Oldcastle's *A Profitable Treatyce* in 1543, Richard Dafforne's *Merchants Mirror* of 1636 and John Collins's *An Introduction to Merchants Accounts* from 1653, all of which owe something to Pacioli's earlier Italian work.[65] By the nineteenth century there were scores of these works, some meant for use as textbooks in the bookkeeping schools which had begun to spring up in Europe and America by about 1850.

Mention should be made too of books of advice to ambitious people who wished to get ahead and to know the principles of governance and leadership. The ancient and medieval 'mirrors for princes' had filled this role, and the tradition continued with books such as *The*

Book of the Courtier by Baldesar Castiglione (1478–1529).[66] He advises that to get ahead in life, one should be well educated, presentable, have good manners and behave as a gentleman. A rather different picture is painted by Eustache de Refuge (d. 1617), whose *Treatise on the Court* is a kind of survival guide to life at court and gives advice on subjects such as how to avoid getting attached to the wrong party in a dispute, how to come out on the winning side in a conflict, how to curry favour with the monarch and, importantly, how to recognize that one's career has peaked and to make a graceful exit.[67] *Treatise on the Court* is a bleak look at a court ruled by self-interest – and almost certainly more realistic than the flowery *Book of the Courtier*.

These early works were aimed at courtiers and nobles, but as time passed self-improvement books for the middle classes began to appear too. The most important of these for our purposes was *Self-Help* by Samuel Smiles, first published in 1859.[68] Smiles argues that 'the spirit of self-help is the root of all genuine growth in the individual; and, exhibited in the lives of the many, it constitutes the true source of national vigour and strength. Help from without is often enfeebling in its effects, but help from within invariably invigorates.'[69]

Smiles encourages his readers to learn from examples of the past: 'Biographies of great, but especially good men are nevertheless most instructive and useful, as helps, guides and incentives to others. Some of the best are almost equivalent to gospels – teaching high living, high thinking and energetic action for their own and the world's good.'[70] In a chapter on 'leaders of industry', he urges would-be business leaders to learn from experience rather than precept: 'a steady application to work is the healthiest training for any individual'.[71] The book is full of case studies of people who made good by following these precepts, and Smiles urges his audience to follow their example.

The book has both its good and bad points. On the one hand it encourages people, especially young people, to see the world as a place of limitless possibilities. Neither poverty nor class need prove an impediment: work hard enough and you will succeed. That optimistic spirit was clearly a source of inspiration to many tens of thousands of young people who set forth in life with a copy of *Self-Help* in their pocket. One of these was William Pirrie, who was given a copy by his mother on the day he joined the shipyard Harland &Wolff as a gentleman apprentice; he rose to become chairman of the firm. On the other hand, Smiles's relentless insistence on innate qualities and his belief that hard work rather than training was the key to making a successful manager undoubtedly helped to reinforce the barriers to professional management training in Britain for decades to come, and his belief that leadership consists in following the examples of 'great men' is now widely discredited.[72]

Nonetheless the book was hugely popular: it sold 20,000 copies in its first year alone and went through numerous editions and translations. In 1870 the work was translated into Japanese. It had an immediate resonance in Japan where, after the Meiji Restoration of 1868, the country was now racing to modernize and catch up with the West. Business people had been considered as third-class citizens in Japan after the sixteenth century, when the Tokugawa shoguns took power, although the position had improved somewhat thanks to the ideas of Ishida Baigan (1685–1744), who clarified the social role of the merchant while at the same time reminding merchants of their duties and urging them to be honest and frugal.[73] (Ishida had also advanced a doctrine of personal self-reliance, which may also have helped to create a reception for the ideas of Samuel Smiles.) Now there was a passion for all forms of Western knowledge, especially knowledge about business.

At the centre of this new movement was Fukuzawa Yuichi, writer, translator and educationalist who did more than other single individual to bring Western knowledge about management to Japan in the nineteenth century. Born in 1835, he had his first contact with the outside world in Nagasaki, the only port in Japan then open – on a very limited basis – to foreign traders. He had visited America and Europe even before the Meiji Restoration, and naturally found himself at the centre of the reform movement. He translated books on political economy and bookkeeping, taught at Keio University and helped establish a publishing company to disseminate translations of Western works; it was this company that published the translation of *Self-Help*. Fukuzawa and his colleagues were grabbing, seemingly almost at random, books of knowledge useful to business people, translating them and pushing them out onto the market. He also wrote a number of books and essays of his own. He argued in favour of free trade and urged business people to take the lead in the great project of transformation, but, perhaps following Ishida again, he also urged them to be virtuous and have integrity. Over and over again he urged the power of education, which could transform people and, through them, the nation. Shunsaku Nishikawa believes that this amounts to an agenda for building a stock of human capital.[74]

A similar though much smaller-scale project of modernization was embarked upon in the Ottoman Empire in the second quarter of the nineteenth century. The Egyptian scholar Rifa'a al-Tahtawi (1801–73), a leading figure in the *Nadha* (Islamic Renaissance) movement, spent several years studying in France and, upon his return, began teaching Western ideas and also began a programme of translation of Western books, including books on administration. Like Fukuzawa, he believed in the power of education to bring about social and political change. He had the support of the Ottoman governor of Egypt, Muhammad 'Ali, but after the latter's death his successors were more lukewarm. However, the *Nadha* movement continued and a later generation of Egyptian scholars, notably Muhammad 'Abduh (see Chapter 7), grew out of this milieu.[75]

There was a similar transmission of ideas in India, mostly through the medium of British-established schools where administration and bookkeeping were often taught. Some Indians also travelled to Britain to study. The Hindu religious movement known as *Brahmo Samaj* became a centre for social reformers, and probably influenced later thinkers such as Swami Vivekananda (1863–1902). The latter visited the USA and Japan and met the Indian industrialist Jamsetji N. Tata (see below), who may well have had an influence on him; he was also impressed by what he saw at the Chicago World's Fair in 1893. Vivekananda's views are an interesting mix of mercantilism and free trade. He believed that the best way for India to gain wealth was to become a manufacturing centre and to export to the rest of the world; the wealth earned from exports could eradicate poverty. But this could only happen if Indians had access to the highest-quality technical and scientific knowledge, which would enable them to compete with the rest of the world. There are similarities here with the work of Charles Babbage, though it is not at all certain that Swami Vivekananda was familiar with his work. But at the same time he looked back to the Vedas and other ancient Indian texts, which he saw as embodying the spirit of India which would need to be awakened. Although much of his writing deals with Indian society as a whole, it is clear that his ideas could also be applied to individual businesses and to people as individuals. Today, there is a new interest in his ideas among business people in particular.[76]

Returning to Britain, there is one last text which does not really fit into any category at this stage, but deserves a mention. Henry Sampson's *A History of Advertising from the Earliest Times*, published in 1874, is as far as I know the first attempt at general business history (apart from the history of business institutions). Arguing that 'advertisements give a real insight into the life of the people' – a position later echoed by Marshall McLuhan – Sampson sets out to describe the evolution of advertising from ancient times, including changes in technology and venue and changes in subject matter.[77] The work is, as he says, full of insights and it is possible to see how businesses communicated with their customers and appealed to them. The work remains very much worth reading today.

Management in the Industrial Revolution

The spirit of inquiry in its various forms, philosophical, scientific and commercial, converged in organizations like the Lunar Society of Birmingham, founded in 1765. Its members were young, often in their thirties or early forties, intelligent and ambitious, and they were interested in everything from free will and the nature of society to physics and the mechanics of the universe. Jenny Uglow, in her study *The Lunar Men*, describes how one member, Matthew Boulton, wrote essays or even just jotted down ideas on scraps of paper concerning, literally, everything under the sun: precipitation, the freezing and boiling points of various liquids including mercury, the nature of sunbeams, how to make phosphorus, the difference in human pulse rates. He tested different types of scales, and built his own thermometers.[78]

Boulton, already a prosperous hardware manufacturer, used his scientific knowledge to build an improved version of Thomas Newcomen's steam engine. He then joined forces with fellow Lunar Society member James Watt, who had also come up with his own improved steam engine, and the two men began manufacturing steam engines. By the end of the century they had sold several hundred engines to factory owners and laid the ground for a trans-formation of industry as the primary power source changed from waterpower to steam. But it is not so much for what they did, as how they did it, that Boulton and Watt are interesting. They brought the same scientific approach and spirit of inquiry to the design of their factory, the Soho Engineering Foundry. Their sons, Matthew Robinson Boulton and James Watt the younger, who took over the factory around 1795, turned it into a model of industrial organization. 'They brought to the task of organisation an entirely new outlook', says Erich Roll, an outlook based on scientific analysis of the workplace and the tasks required.[79] Lyndall Urwick credits them with understanding of a lengthy list of management concepts including market research, site location, production planning, standardization of product components, training for workers, work study and payment by results.[80]

Another of the Lunar Men, the potter Josiah Wedgwood, moved his growing business to a greenfield site near Stoke-on-Trent. As well as a new factory, Wedgwood also built housing for his workers and provided them with meals and decent wages. His village of Etruria was one of the first 'model villages' for workers. Again, this was enlightened self-interest very much as Edward Lawrence described it above. Clean, safe, healthy, well-fed workers were more productive than half-starved ones. They were more innovative too, and Wedgwood relied on continuous innovation, both in new designs and new ceramics materials to produce lighter, harder and more durable dishes. Today Wedgwood is best known for his ground-breaking neoclassical designs that made his work internationally famous and brought him a series of 'reference clients' including Tsarina Catherine the Great of Russia who bought a 952-piece dinner service for more than £2,000. But Wedgwood was well aware that reputa-tion and brand had to be backed up with product quality.[81]

We infer the kind of management thinking used by men such as Boulton, Watt and Wedgwood from occasional letters and documents and from their actions. On the whole, like the Italian merchants of the Middle Ages, they were too busy writing about other things to write much about their businesses. Richard Arkwright, one of the central figures in the early Industrial Revolution, left behind only some correspondence. Occasionally someone did set down his thoughts on paper: Robert Owen left an autobiographical account and some essays, and the Dundee flax-spinner William Brown wrote papers on the organization of a factory and duties of under-managers.[82] But these are rare.

Nevertheless, the economic historian Sidney Pollard and the consultants-turned-business historians Lyndall Urwick and Edward Brech agree that there was some highly sophisticated management thinking going on right from the beginning of the Industrial Revolution. Pollard points out that managers in the Industrial Revolution faced three challenges. The first of these was the mastery of the use of advanced forms of new technology. Following on from this, the second challenge was size. Businesses had to scale up in order to take advantage of the new technology and make it economical to use, but size brought its own complications in terms of organization and managing people. Third, these large organizations extended well beyond the owner's span of control, and required a class of professional managers to oversee them. Arkwright, for example, was at one time or another a partner in more than a dozen ventures; it is doubtful if he visited some of them more than once.[83] Robert Owen recalled that when he managed Drinkwater's mill in Manchester the owner appeared at the plant just three times in four years.[84]

To overcome the second problem in particular, it seems that the early factories were carefully designed and planned. Arkwright's genius was not so much for technological innovation – some of his technology was 'borrowed' from the designs of others – but for combining technologies into a single efficient system. His factories were considered marvels of efficiency and order. Arkwright, like Boulton, was another man fascinated by science, very much in keeping with the spirit of inquiry of the times. What both worked out how to do was to combine technologies in ways that were economically efficient, or as we might say today, they were able to commercialize their innovations.

Designing and using technology and managing large concerns required training. There were rare individuals such as Robert Owen who were self-taught, but as Sidney Pollard points out, in the eighteenth century Britain had a widespread and varied system of technical and scientific education encompassing grammar schools, academies and universities.[85] Most factories also operated schemes for management apprentices, sometimes also known as 'gentleman apprentices'. This carried on into the nineteenth and early twentieth centuries, and some firms, such as Charles Parsons, the turbine maker, ran large-scale apprenticeship schemes for potential managers.

'British society at the time of the Industrial Revolution was vigorous, mobile and inventive', says Sidney Pollard. 'The responses to the managerial challenges were immensely varied. Not all were equally successful, and some were undoubtedly responsible for the failures of that period as well as its achievements.'[86] In other words, managers in the Industrial Revolution did what managers have always done before and since; they experimented. Sometimes they got it wrong, sometimes they came up with ideas of lasting significance.

One area where experimentation was surely needed lay in the managing of people. This was one area where the managers of the Industrial Revolution had little to guide them. Large-scale concentrated organizations were not new in human history – we can think of the thousands of workers employed to build the Egyptian pyramids, or the large cloth-making ventures in medieval Flanders and Italy – but there were few of them in Britain at the time. Entrepreneurs and managers with experience of managing a few dozen people at most now had to manage several hundreds on a single site, in operations that ran twenty-four hours a day. There were no systems and no body of experience for them to draw on. As discussed in Chapter 2, the tendency on the part of these entrepreneurs was to treat the factory or mill, and the workers, as their own property to dispose of as they wished. The duty of the workers was to work, and do what they were told. Much has been written on the quality of life for workers in the early textile mills and factories, and there is no need to go into it in detail here.[87] But in terms of management thought, there were two consequences.

The first is that some experimenters, including Josiah Wedgwood and especially Robert Owen, hit upon methods that worked. Famously, Owen cut working hours at his New Lanark mill and found that productivity went up; when he cut hours further, productivity went up again. He also banned child labour in his mill, and like Wedgwood insisted that his workers were clean, healthy and well nourished. Owen concluded that investment in labour was just as important as investment in technology, and claimed that he was getting returns of up to 50 per cent on capital invested, far higher than the 20 per cent or so that was the average at the time.[88] New Lanark was admired by philosophers, social reformers and politicians, but not by most mill owners. When Owen published his views on management he was met with derision and abuse.[89] He was eventually ejected from his own business at New Lanark by his partners, one of the reasons being that they objected to his spending money from the business to educate the children of mill workers; that money, they felt, belonged rightfully in their own pockets.[90]

Owen's ideas at New Lanark were not without influence. He became something of a role model for later enlightened capitalists, including George Cadbury, Titus Salt and William Lever, to name just a few. Model villages of the Etruria/New Lanark type sprang up around the country as business owners realized that catering for the needs of their employees could lead to better workplace relations. Owen's influence also spread to the continent. Alfred Krupp, head of the steel-making firm Krupp of Essen was an autocratic business owner who laid down strict rules for his employees but also paid them well and provided them with housing and amenities. Krupp also tried to instil a sense of elitism among his employees and make them proud of the firm for which they worked.

Krupp set down his own theories in a work usually known as the *General Regulations*, an attempt to create an all-embracing system of management: 'no case should occur for many years, for a century, which has not been foreseen in this compilation. No post should exist, from that of general manager to workman, as to the duties of which this collection of rules does not give precise information.'[91] The result of this ambition was a rigid and inflexible doctrine of business management that Krupp's own successors eventually abandoned, but there are some surprises. Krupp too believed that a business could be compared to a living organism, even to a human being:

> The spirit which inspires all, from the top to the very bottom, must be permeated throughout, in particular, by respect for morality and the law. A sound ethical outlook, closely allied to discipline and loyalty, makes for prosperity and contentment. Without it, frustration, disorder, vice, perfidy and corruption ensue.[92]

At the other end of the scale from Krupp in terms of political beliefs and personal philosophy, the Indian businessman Jamsetji Nusserwanji Tata also derived some of his ideas indirectly from Robert Owen.[93] As a young man Tata spent three years in Britain, from 1865–8. He steeped himself in liberal philosophy and also visited many of the mills of northern England. One particular influence was Thomas Carlyle, who in his novel *Sartor Resartus* had expressed the idea that 'the nation that gains control of iron soon acquires the control of gold.' In other words, iron and steel, being vital industries, are important sources of wealth. This idea too gained wide currency and was adopted by a number of writers around the world, as diverse as Aikawa Yoshisuke the Japanese industrialist and the Zionist ideologue Vladimir Jabotinsky.[94]

Returning to India, Tata set up a series of business ventures that today form the core of the Tata group. His own philosophy is expressed in his letters and occasional speeches, perhaps most clearly in a speech of 1895 when he stated:

> We do not claim to be more unselfish, more ungenerous or more philanthropic than other people. But, we think, we started on sound and straightforward business principles, considering the interests of our shareholders our own, and the health and welfare of our employees the sure foundation of our prosperity.[95]

His companies were the first in India, and among the first in the world, to introduce concepts such as company pensions, sick pay, paid annual holidays and other benefits. When Tata Iron & Steel Company was founded, Tata also built a model town to house his workers and insisted that there be a full range of benefits, including places for exercise and places of worship. He was particularly adamant that there be plenty of trees and green space. His beliefs may have been influenced to some extend by the 'garden city' concept developed by Ebenezer Howard at the end of the nineteenth century.[96] The town, Jamshedpur, went on to become a template for other 'model towns' in India. Like so many others, Tata never wrote down his principles of management, but it is clear that he understood that sound employee relations were essential to good management of the overall business.

The second of the two consequences referred to above was that workers did not take their treatment lying down. When their treatment reached extremes, they could and did turn on their employers. One of Arkwright's first mills was burned to the ground during a strike. When government sided with business owners, sometimes using military force against strikers as during the Luddite attacks in 1811–12 or at Peterloo in 1819, workers began to organize. Robert Owen, giving up on his attempt to persuade his fellow industrialists to see reason, went over to the side of the workers and helped to organize trade unions. Other radical politicians joined in. European workers began to unionize as well, and socialist and communist ideas began to circulate ever more widely, given a considerable boost during and after the revolutions of 1848 by works such as Marx and Engels's *The Communist Manifesto*.[97] By the third quarter of the century it looked increasingly as if organized labour and capital were on a collision course. A managerial response to the problem was called for, as we shall see in Chapter 5.

Reflections

Foxes and hedgehogs

In his 2010 book *Obliquity*, the economist and – I hope he will not mind being called this – philosopher John Kay writes despairingly of architects and town planners that their work is based on 'crass simplification and the reiteration of familiar themes'. He goes on:

> The same combination of simplification and reiteration is found in the thinking of gurus who believe that they can re-engineer large corporations, ideologues who see all political events through the same lens and visionaries who project some current technological or geopolitical trend with exaggerated pace to exaggerated

extent. All lack the real imagination to understand the complexity of their environment.[98]

Kay is dismissive of big ideas. He cites with approval Isaiah Berlin's essay on Tolstoy, expounding on the latter's contrast between the fox and the hedgehog.[99] The hedgehog, says Berlin, views the world through a single lens, shaped by a single idea or ideology. The fox has many ideas and draws on many sources of learning, and so is wedded to no one defining ideology. Kay believes this makes hedgehogs more inflexible and more prone to keep doing what has always been done, while foxes are more reactive and flexible and more capable of change.

Businesses, and business thinkers, can be categorized in the same way, of course. Some businesses are inflexible and can only think of doing things one way. Others react, adapt, engage in continuous innovation. We see this around us in the world today, but we can see it very plainly in the Industrial Revolution too. The difference between people such as Joseph Jacquard, Robert Owen, Josiah Wedgwood, Jamsetji Tata or even Alfred Krupp, on the one hand and the mass of rigidly inflexible manufacturers and industrialists on the other, the mill owners who sweated their workers, the monopolists who refused to see that their system was not working, is like the difference between night and day.

What separates the two? One theory is that difference lies in attitudes to the uses of knowledge. A century and a half after economists had begun writing about it, the management world finally woke up to the importance of knowledge in the 1980s. Arie de Geus, writing in *Harvard Business Review* in 1988, stated that in the future the most important source of competitive advantage would be a company's ability to learn, and in 1990 Peter Senge called for the creation of 'learning organizations'.[100]

De Geus's concept makes sense, and I have often referred to it when teaching MBA students. But . . . why only in the future? Knowledge has *always* been a source of competitive advantage. The best firms, the best organizations, are built on embedded knowledge that is constantly renewed and refreshed. Take for example the optical equipment maker Carl Zeiss Jena, founded in 1846. The success of this firm was based on its relationship with the University of Jena, which ensured a flow of high-level technical knowledge into the firm. Innovation at Carl Zeiss Jena was something done by everyone, all the time. It was as commonplace as breathing. And Zeiss and Ernst Abbé, the directors, made sure they created an atmosphere where people felt free and were encouraged to innovate. George and Edward Cadbury did the same at their chocolate-making works in Britain, as did the chain maker Hans Renold. All these companies thrived on knowledge.

The question is, what knowledge made them successful? The problem facing the learning organization is: what knowledge do you learn? What do you need to know? For the Lunar Men and others in the age of enlightenment the answer was: everything. No fact was too small, no concept too abstruse as to escape their attention. Go back still further to Copernicus, astronomer, mathematician, philosopher of science, administrator and on one occasion, military commander. Think of the vast range of interests of Leonardo, or the Arabic writers stressing the importance of *adab*, general knowledge about everything.

The Industrial Revolution was born out of the spirit of inquiry that shaped the Enlightenment. It is almost inconceivable that the Industrial Revolution would have happened without it, or at least that it would have taken the form that it did. There were plenty of hedgehogs in the Industrial Revolution, stubborn men who kept on trying to manage new enterprises in old ways, men such as Samuel Oldknow; and very often they went broke. The foxes, the ones who capitalized on widespread experience and new learning in every form, such as Ernst Abbé or Henry Heinz or Matthew Boulton, built businesses that in some cases continued to flourish long after they themselves had turned to dust. They were full of the spirit of inquiry, and they were interested in everything under the sun.

What is the lesson for the internet age? To me, it is this. Somehow, despite the almost overwhelming tide of information that laps around us each day, we must find ways of continuing to learn from as many sources as possible. No one theory about management, no one school of thought, no one idea is sufficient. As Gareth Morgan pointed out, we need many theories, many lenses through which to view the world.[101] We need to remember the example of the Lunar Men. We need to be more like foxes.

Advances in marketing

Another group of business leaders deserves mention as well for their contributions to management thought. Rising populations and an increasingly affluent middle class saw new business forms emerging in both retailing and wholesaling and advances in branding and marketing. In the late nineteenth century Andrew Pears and William Lever both showed that they understood the value of branding and mass advertising as soap made the transition from high-priced luxury good to mass-market consumer good. Around the same time Henry J. Heinz introduced the principles of branding into food production, creating one of the world's most enduring portfolio brands, H.J. Heinz. New product and service categories emerged and showed themselves to be equally amenable to branding, as Thomas Cook demonstrated in the newly created industry, package tourism, and Julius Reuter showed when creating the first global news agency.

Advances in transportation opened up new channels. Montgomery Ward and then Sears developed catalogue retailing or mail-order retailing, also in the late nineteenth century. One of the most innovative new retail forms was the department store. Arguably the world's first department store was Echigo-ya in Tokyo, established in the seventeenth century, and some large retailers offering multiple product categories had appeared in America in the 1830s and 1840s. Credit for introducing the first department store in the modern sense must go to Aristide and Marguerite Boucicaut with the founding of Au Grand Marché in 1852. The Boucicauts evolved their model over time, creating an institution that combined visual appeal, high standards of service and luxury goods at affordable prices; 'the democratisation of luxury', as one observer called it.[102] Their concept soon spread to Britain, Germany, America, Japan and Hong Kong, all of which had department stores by 1900. One particular aspect of marketing that the Boucicauts understood well was the building of customer relationships in order to generate repeat business.

Business and society

Jamsetji Tata, discussed above, was both an enlightened employer and a patriot. His chief goal was to see a strong and independent India, and the purpose for which he created his businesses was, as his biographer says, the creation of wealth, not for himself but for the people of India.[103] He was an early supporter of the Congress party, and his son Sir Dorajbi Tata helped to fund some of Gandhi's early work in South Africa. Moving around the world, we can see the same in other rapidly modernizing and advancing economies, such as Japan where the banker and industrialist Shibusawa Eiichi threw himself into the project of strengthening Japanese industry so as to strengthen the nation.[104] There were many others like him; modernization was a project that seemed to unite the Japanese people very strongly.[105]

The Chinese minister Li Hongzhang attempted similar projects in China. Li was a proponent of the economic philosophy of *guandu shangban*, or 'government supervision and merchant operation'; that is, the government would set the agenda and define the economic goals, and the merchants would work at government direction to achieve those goals. It was once thought that the Chinese economy in the later Qing period was largely moribund, but revisionists such as Thomas Rawski have argued that there was in fact considerable economic growth in the second half of the nineteenth century.[106] The chief barriers to further growth were lack of capital and lack of institutional structures to support business. Nearly all Chinese businesses, including banks, were small family firms. Li's most famous venture was the China Merchants' Steam Navigation Company, a shipping firm founded in 1872. Li introduced the Western model of the joint-stock corporation while sticking firmly to the principle of *guandu shangban*, with the purpose of competing with Western shipping firms but also, it seems, with the idea that this might serve as a model for other enterprises that could aid China's modernization and development.

Li was thwarted in the end by his own bureaucracy. When the company began to make a profit it was suggested that the government, which had backed the company with loans, should convert those loans to stockholding and in effect take over the company. The private sector partners then began to withdraw their own capital, and the company declined and eventually disappeared around 1902.[107]

Li was not alone in his efforts. A number of traders and merchants wrote on the need for change and reform of the business system if China was to compete with the Western and Japanese firms now trading on its soil. *Fuguo Ce*, Wang Fengzao's translation of Henry Fawcett's *Manual of Political Economy* published in 1880, urged institutional reform to allow the establishment of large businesses. In another work of 1894, *Shengshi Weiyan* (Warnings to a Prosperous Age), the merchant Zheng Guanying called for the introduction of joint-stock companies on a much wider basis. He believed these to be the key to Western, especially British, business success. Zheng was fluent in English, and appears to have derived at least some of his ideas from Western business thought. His ideas seem to have had some effect, and joint-stock companies were formally recognized by Chinese law in 1902. In 1897 the diplomat Song Yuren argued for the foundation of chartered companies such as the now-defunct East India Company to take advantage of trading opportunities overseas. Another writer, Chin Chi, urged the establishment of a banking system along Western lines to provide capital, and his efforts too bore fruit with the establishment of the Commercial Bank of China in 1897.[108]

Despite these efforts, a combination of shortage of capital, bureaucratic inertia and outright opposition from the regent, the Empress Cixi, led to little change in the business environment in China until the revolution of 1911, which swept away the Qing dynasty.[109] As we shall see in the next chapter, despite political turmoil the environment was now much more business-friendly and China began rapidly to adopt elements of Western management thinking. Even then, however, Chinese businesses and the state were closely linked and shared common goals with nation-building high among them.

The situation in America is often portrayed as being quite different. Government control over business activity was much more limited than in Europe, Japan or China. The post-Civil War period, especially from 1800 onwards, is often portrayed as the era of the 'robber barons', railway owners such as Cornelius Vanderbilt and Daniel Drew and industrialists such as John D. Rockefeller, Andrew Carnegie and Daniel Guggenheim. They were described at the time by opponents such as the socialist journalist Henry Demarest Lloyd as greedy capitalists whose sole intention was the amassment of personal wealth.[110] That point of view is still largely followed today. The most recent biographer of the financier J.P. Morgan, Jean Strouse, admitted that when she set out to research her subject she started from a position of considerable antipathy.[111]

It must be recognized, however, that there was a strong strain of business and economic thought which supported their activities. The period 1880–1903 saw increasing levels of concentration in many sectors of the American economy, leading to monopolies or near-monopolies in many including some of those most vital to the economy: oil, steel, food production.[112] In the process were created some very large businesses, the largest the world had yet seen in terms of capital, production capacity and numbers of employees. The creation of these dominating business entities was supported by Francis Amasa Walker and some (though not all) other leading economists on the grounds of national interest. It was widely believed that unrestricted markets were wasteful, creating product shortages and driving prices up. America, growing as rapidly as it was, could not afford shortages of vital commodities such as food. The result could be social unrest and starvation. Unspoken but implicitly recognized by Walker and others too was that America still had no centralized institutions to exercise economic governance. That role had to be filled by the private sector companies acting in concert. In 1894, for example, J.P. Morgan personally rescued the American government from bankruptcy. And finally, there was the hope that powerful large businesses could check the rising power of organized labour and the spectre of socialism that lay behind it.

All of these ideas were mooted by business leaders as well. J.P. Morgan was among the foremost to push the case for less competition and more concentration. It is difficult to know his views exactly, as he destroyed his personal papers before his death, but enough can be reconstructed to know that he was a strong supporter of monopoly. So was Charles Flint, founder of the company that later became IBM, who unlike Morgan was only too eager to go on record to push the case for monopoly.[113] The monopolists had allies in the press as well, such as Ivy Lee, who helped Rockefeller manage his public image in the aftermath of the attacks of the Muck-Rakers and Herbert Casson, whose portrayal of the steel industry *The Romance of Steel* included a vigorous defence of concentration.[114]

Two points need to be made. First, it is open to discussion whether the monopolists truly believed what they said or were simply searching for an ideological justification for lining their own pockets. Fowler's description of the 'law of the jungle' on Wall Street tends to reinforce the latter position, as do incidents such as the sale of Carnegie's company to United States Steel where J.P. Morgan is alleged to have earned a profit of $25 million for acting as broker. Second, there is the undeniable fact that most of the big monopolies were financially unsound and, far from creating economic efficiencies, were very inefficient. Before IBM Flint had founded two large combinations, both of which failed. By some estimates, more than half of these large combinations were technically insolvent by 1900. Their catastrophic financial management led to a scrambled search for solutions and a number of textbooks on financial management appeared over the next decade, notably Edward Meade's *Corporation Finance* and William Lough's *Corporation Finance*.[115] These and other texts, as well as the establishment of specialist institutions for the study of finance such as the Wharton School at the University of Pennsylvania, paved the way for further thinking about corporate finance.

Yet the notion of the efficiency of concentration did not entirely reach a dead end in management thinking. The virtues of scale efficiency are now well known, and the value of strategic alliances and collaboration is widely discussed, particular in fields such as supply chain management and R&D and even marketing.[116] At least in part, the failure of those first generations of big business must be traced to problems of competence. The arrogance of those who led these giant business combinations was not always matched by their skill. American industry had a severe shortage of capable managers, and few facilities for training them. That challenge too was recognized, and would be rectified (see Chapter 5).

This seems a good place to describe another American philosophy of management, one which until fairly recently was largely overlooked. Native American culture, though vastly simpler than the culture that replaced it, had its own concepts of organization and leadership. In the past twenty years, works by Russell Edmonds, Michael Bryant and Tracy Becker have led to a re-evaluation, especially of Native American views of leadership and decision making.[117] Stephen Ambrose's study in contrasts of General George Custer and the Lakota war leader Crazy Horse also has much to offer.[118]

From these works we can see that the idea of the 'servant leader' was very much alive and well, and that across most cultures leaders were expected to lay problems before their fellows so that decisions could be reached by consensus. This in turn ensured 'buy-in'; all who participated in the decision were expected to abide by it, and decisions once reached had a spiritual, even sacred force. Spiritual qualities were highly valued, and leaders were expected to be deeply spiritual people, as the Lakota leader Black Elk recounted in his own memoirs.[119] Finally, we note that Native American society was highly egalitarian. It is interesting to see that some scholars are now working to apply lessons from American Indian society to their own organizations; for example, Darrell Steele has demonstrated that there is a fit between the organizational principles of Native American society and his own organization, the US Air Force.[120]

The critics

As noted earlier, the advances of the Enlightenment did not spread their benefits evenly. Workers reacted, sometimes violently to attempts by employers to enforce excessive control. The Luddite movement of 1811–12 saw widespread damage to mills and factories, with some burned to the ground. Although the general view is that the Luddites were reacting against the introduction of new technologies which they felt would threaten their own livelihoods by forcing them to accept lower wages, the historian E.P. Thompson has argued that the Luddites were in fact targeting particular employers who were notable for treating their workers badly.[121]

In France the introduction of the Jacquard power loom met with similar resistance from workers who thought the new looms would put them out of work. Some threw their wooden shoes or *sabots* into the looms to break them; from whence comes our word 'sabotage'. Resistance to Jacquard looms died away once it became apparent that, in Paul Mason's words, 'Jacquard's invention had automated not the physical labour of weaving but the process of implementing a design. Far from deskilling weavers, Jacquard had preserved the skill of their hands.'[122] Mason credits Jacquard with preserving an industry, and jobs, that would otherwise have disappeared.

Intellectuals wondered whether the rise of factories and big businesses was entirely in keeping with the Enlightenment vision. Mention has already been made of the dystopian vision of Mary Shelley's *Frankenstein*. William Blake's poem *Jerusalem*, published in 1804, also rejected the industrial age, and called for change; Blake knew about working conditions in factories, and there can be no doubt about the meaning of the phrase 'dark satanic mills'.[123] In his *A Lay Sermon*, Samuel Taylor Coleridge referred to 'an over-balance of the commercial spirit' and felt that society was becoming too dominated by commercial values.[124] His brother-in-law the poet Robert Southey argued that although the factory system had undeniably added to the wealth of the country, 'in a far greater degree [it] has diminished its happiness and lessened its security. Adam Smith's book is the code, or confession of faith, of this system; a tedious and hard-hearted book, greatly over-valued even on the score of its ability, for fifty pages would have comprised its sum and substance.'[125] Southey also felt that the factory system was concentrating power in the hands of a few owners of capital and discouraging the spirit of entrepreneurship; in other words, people who went to work in factories were unlikely to start businesses of their own, especially not if the system trapped them in a cycle of poverty and dependence.

Southey's views have much in common with the later views of Robert Owen, and we have already discussed Karl Marx's view that there was no hope of reconciling the capitalist and working classes. But how much was this an economic problem, and how much a problem of management? Was the factory system itself at fault, or was it being badly run? Marx believed that the factory system was a deliberate attempt by the capitalists to exercise greater control over labour, and this certainly happened, but there are grounds for believing that this was an outcome of the factory system, not a cause. Richard N. Langlois believes that the factory system arose as an economic and managerial response to the problem of rising demand, coupled with the need to control quality.[126] And as the disparate examples of Robert Owen and Joseph Jacquard show, the capitalists could provide decent employment and working conditions and save jobs which might otherwise have been lost.

What the Luddites, Owen, Coleridge, Southey and Marx were all, from various points of view, objecting to was the breaking of that implicit social contract that had existed in earlier ages. The capitalist who obeyed no law but his own became a standard hate figure in late nineteenth and early twentieth-century literature, for example in works such as Émile Zola's *Germinal* (1885) and Upton Sinclair's *The Jungle*.[127] Nor was the problem confined to factories and mines; Zola's *Au bonheur des dames* paints an equally unpleasant picture of working conditions in a Paris department store.[128]

One critic maintained that the problem lay less in the form that business organizations took, but in *how* companies were managed, and even more importantly, *why* they existed. The American liberal journalist Ida Tarbell published a detailed critique of Standard Oil, one of the largest American corporations, in the pages of *McClure's* magazine in 1903.[129] Standard Oil was an exception to the general rule of monopolies in that it was extremely well run and efficient. Acknowledging this, Tarbell declared that this was precisely why it was so dangerous. The other trusts and conglomerates were so ramshackle that they would fall apart of their own accord, but Standard Oil was not. She felt that the concentration of power in the hands of a few was a threat to democracy. In one important passage, she hits on what may be the heart of the problem: a lack of moral compass on the part of managers.

> There is something alarming to those who believe that commerce should be a peaceful pursuit, and who believe that the moral law holds good throughout the entire range of human relations, in knowing that so large a body of young men in this country are

consciously or unconsciously growing up with the idea that business is war and morals have nothing to do with its practice.[130]

Despite what some of her critics have said, Tarbell was not anti-business. She wrote often on business matters, including a book on business ethics and a series of articles on the role of women in business for the magazine *Industrial Management*.[131] What angered her was the lack of morality and the 'law of the jungle' mentality – the overbalance of the commercial spirit that Coleridge had referred to – which she felt was making society worse rather than better. Her later article 'Commercial Machiavellianism' is in part an attempt to remind business people of the duties they owe to society.[132] She also wrote an approving biography of Owen Young, chairman of GE and founder of RCA; she admired Young, she wrote, because he took his duties to society seriously and was not out to simply make money for himself. As a result, he and his businesses were forces for good in American society.[133]

All of these issues – the threat to traditional ways caused by technology, the economic dominance of large businesses, poor working conditions and poverty, and the lack of moral compass – came together in the ideology of William Morris (1834–97). Morris was, if such a thing is possible, a practical utopian; that is, he did more than dream of a perfect society, he took concrete steps to try to make it happen. A talented writer, poet, painter and architect, Morris made his name in the decorative arts and set up a highly profitable business making a range of home furnishings including fabrics, furniture, wallpaper and stained glass. He established a very strong brand and a highly profitable business. He believed in quality and his products offered value for money. His name became one of the most popular and widely known brands in Victorian London. It was not uncommon for people to furnish entire houses from top to bottom solely in William Morris designs.

But he also believed that business had a purpose, and that the mere making of money was almost an incidental outcome. Morris once stated that it was his goal that all of his workers should be able to take pleasure in their work, and that as their employer his own task was to find ways for them to be creative and use their own talents to the fullest. Again, there is an element of self-interest here: Morris's brand was based on design and product quality, and he knew that workers who were stimulated to use their creative talents to the fullest would give it to him. He also paid high wages, introduced profit-sharing for managers and full-time workers, and urged the piece-workers involved in craft production to work at their own speed and take time off when it suited them. His encouragement of people to take ownership of their own work was one of the inspirations for the Arts and Crafts movement which spread from Britain to Europe and America.[134]

Conclusion

A curious combination of romantic dreamer and acute businessman, Morris believed that craft working was a viable alternative to the factory system and could ultimately replace it. For a number of reasons, this never happened. He made a profit, certainly, but few industrialist were tempted to follow his lead. Yet it is worth remembering the alternative system that Morris created, for in the spirit of inquiry we do need to recall from time to time that the economic and managerial systems we have today did not come about because they are perfect. They evolved from a combination of economic, political and social pressures and, quite often as in the case of Morris, personal beliefs and worldviews. Challenges emerged and solutions were found. As Sidney Pollard says, sometimes those solutions worked and sometimes they did not. We shall see this same pattern of challenge and response when we come to discuss scientific management in the next chapter.

5   Scientific management

Scientific management rests on the fundamental economic principle that harmony of interests exists between employers and workers.

(Robert Hoxie)

Efficiency, like hygiene, is a state, an ideal, not a method.

(Harrington Emerson)

In 1886, Henry Robinson Towne, co-owner of the lock-makers Yale & Towne, stood before his colleagues of the American Society of Mechanical Engineers and delivered a paper entitled 'The Engineer as an Economist'. He stated his position bluntly. American industry was in a mess. There was no professional management, poor organization and control, a great deal of waste and often incendiary labour relations. 'The management of works', he said, 'is almost unorganized, is almost without literature, has no organ or medium for the interchange of experience, and is without association or organization of any kind'.[1]

Something had to be done to improve the quality of American management. As no one else was prepared to rise to the challenge, Towne believed that he and his fellow engineers would have to do it themselves. Indeed, he said, because engineers understood both the technical and non-technical aspects of management, they were uniquely qualified to do so.

Towne had laid down the challenge: to fix the broken management system in American industry. Before we proceed to discuss how that challenge was answered, though, we need to stop to consider why it had come about and why engineers in particular were being tasked with coming up with a solution.

Scientific management was defined by an outside observer, the economist Robert Hoxie, in 1915 as 'a system devised by industrial engineers for the purpose of subserving the common interests of employers, workmen and society at large, through the elimination of avoidable wastes, the general improvement of the processes and methods of production, and the just and scientific distribution of the product'.[2] As this definition hints, the concept of scientific management did not originate in a vacuum.[3] It evolved as a specific response to problems facing industry, American industry in particular: the need for efficiency, and the need to find a solution to what many referred to as the 'problem of labour' but which, as Bernadette Longo points out, could equally be called the 'problem of capital'.[4] As to the importance of the former point, there is no lack of testimony. Frederick Winslow Taylor, on taking up his first post as an engineer, noted that every worker seemed to be content to work at their own speed, meaning that it took a long time for even simple processes to be completed.[5] There was a lack of reporting and control procedures, a lack of accountability and a great deal of waste. Herbert Casson later recounted what he first found when visiting industrial plants:

Managers had never studied management. Employers had never studied employership. Sales managers had never studied the art of influencing public opinion. There were even financiers who had never studied finance. On all hands I found guess-work and muddling . . . A mass of incorrect operations was standardized into a routine. Stokers did not know how to stoke. Factory workers did not know how to operate their machines. Foremen did not know how to handle their men. Managing directors did not know . . . the principles of organization. Very few had learned how to do what they were doing.[6]

Frederick Taylor put it slightly more artfully but with equal force:

Probably a majority of the attempts that are made to radically change the organization of manufacturing companies result in a loss of money to the company, failure to bring about the change sought for, and a return to practically the original organization. The reason for this being that there are but few employers who look upon management as an art, and that they go at a difficult task without either having understood or appreciated the time required for organization or its cost, the troubles to be met with, or the obstacles to be overcome, and without having studied the means to be employed in doing so.[7]

We saw the rising self-awareness and power of labour in the previous chapter. Strikes happened everywhere, but those in America increased in frequency and violence. The Homestead Strike of 1892 saw workers and the company using rifles and heavy weapons against each other; the Pullman Strike of 1894 saw 250,000 workers on strike across the country, and military intervention led to thirteen deaths.[8] Such strikes were costly in monetary as well as human terms. The assassination of pro-business President William McKinley by an anarchist and a number of assassination attempts on prominent business leaders including Henry Frick and Jack Morgan, son of the banker J.P. Morgan, can only have heightened tensions. Some in America began to fear the prospect of outright revolution.[9]

The task, then, was to make management more efficient and to restore harmony with workers. Why did engineers decide they were the ones to solve it? In part this has to do with the prevailing climate of the times. The rapid advances of science in the nineteenth century had produced a heady sense that science could do anything. Electricity, railways, the telephone, the telegraph, advances in medicine had all changed people's lives; the aeroplane and the motor car were both in prototype stages. Jules Verne was awakening people to the prospect of opening up new worlds through undersea exploration and space flight. The watchword of the day was expressed by Lord Kelvin: 'science begins with measurement'. If one could measure a problem, then one could design its solution. And who, with their training and technology such as slide rules and stopwatches, was better at measuring and designing things than engineers?

That in essence was the logic that drove Towne and his fellow engineers. Towne made a first attempt, developing a concept that he called 'gainsharing' similar to the profit-sharing schemes coming into fashion in Europe (indeed, he may have had the inspiration for the idea during a visit to the Paris Exhibition in 1889).[10] Horace Drury, the early chronicler of scientific management, describes gainsharing as follows: 'His plan was to isolate in the bookkeeping those components of cost which the laborer has it in his power to influence, and base the division of profits upon the amount in reduction of these costs.'[11] It seems clear that this was intended to be a short-term or temporary expedient to reward workers for efficiency gains; Towne believed that there were limits to the efficiency gains that could be realized, and once those were reached there would be no point in trying to continue the system. Drury comments that the plan probably left too much power in the hands of the employer, who determined the levels of efficiency to be achieved and the level of the bonus in a somewhat arbitrary fashion.

Another engineer, Frederick Halsey, believed that the best way to achieve efficiency was to provide financial rewards for increased output. This would achieve a double goal, as increased productivity for the company would also result in better pay for workers, which should help to reduce tensions in the workplace. In a paper first presented to the American Society of Mechanical Engineers in 1891, Halsey set out what he called the 'premium plan'.[12] The standard method of payment by performance at the time was the piece-rate system, in which workers were paid by result. If an employer wished to sweat more labour out of workers, he or she could simply cut the piece rate, forcing workers to do more for the same amount of money. Halsey tried to create a fairer system based on a combination of standard daily wage plus piecework bonuses if tasks were completed more quickly. One significant development was the setting of a standard benchmark in terms of the time each task should take to complete.

The premium plan seemed to work, and factories that adopted it reported efficiency gains. Companies in Germany and Britain as well as America began to adopt it. But effective though it was, the premium plan was still only a tool. Towne had called for a complete rethink of the nature and role of management. As Bernadette Longo says, 'The idea of the engineer as economist placed the engineer/manager between labor and capital when dealing with the "labor problem" . . . engineers needed to design an organization in which capital controlled how work was done on the shop floors. This meant that engineers had to design a new relationship between capital and labour.'[13] But there was even more to it than this. Management also had to examine itself, its own role and function, and try to come up with a set of guiding principles. That is the task which was attempted by Frederick Winslow Taylor.

Taylor and his ideas

Taylor is one of the most widely discussed, and probably one of the most widely vilified, figures in the history of management thought. His critics are legion, and though some such as biographer Robert Kanigel are harsh but fair, others have had a tendency to criticize what they thought Taylor said, rather than what he actually said.[14] I do not intend to go into Taylor's ideas in detail here, but I hope that by referring back to Taylor himself rather than to his numerous critics, we can make his position and ideas clear.

Born in 1856 into a Quaker family, Taylor had a good education which included several years spent in Europe. He had intended to go to Harvard University, but then for reasons that are not entirely clear he chose to apprentice as a machinist instead (conventional wisdom has it that he suffered bouts of ill health including headaches which prevented him studying, but the work of a machinist hardly seems suitable for someone in that condition). After his apprenticeship Taylor took a job at the Midvale Steel Works in Philadelphia.[15] He was promoted to foreman and then to chief engineer, and also took a degree in mechanical engineering from the Stevens Institute of Technology. He thus acquired a high degree of technical knowledge, both theoretical and practical. During his time at Midvale too, as he tells us in his later writings, he began to consider the problem described by Towne in his paper in 1886. Taylor left Midvale and had several other jobs before setting up his own engineering consultancy, and it was not until 1895 that he had leisure to organize his thoughts and present his own paper, 'A Piece-Rate System', to the American Society of Mechanical Engineers.[16]

Taylor, like Halsey and Towne, was searching for a system that would enable workers to be rewarded fairly for their work. The principle of fairness runs right through 'A Piece-Rate System', and indeed, through much of Taylor's later writing as well. A workplace in which people are managed fairly and receive what is due to them is a workplace that should be both efficient and free from strife. It is worth dwelling, though, on what Taylor means by 'fairness'. In both 'A Piece-Rate System' and his subsequent book *Shop Management,* he is clear that the concept is very much an individual one. Taylor rejected European-style profit-sharing plans, in which a percentage of profits is put into a pot and then shared out equally among all employees, as fundamentally unfair. In any workplace – and it is clear that Taylor is speaking from his personal experience at Midvale – there will always be some who work hard and conscientiously and some who drag their feet and do not contribute their fair share of labour. An equal share of profit for all meant that the hard workers would not get as much money as they deserved, while the slackers would be rewarded for doing less; and this last in particular was repugnant to Taylor's Puritan soul.

Like Halsey, Taylor was well aware of the tendency of unscrupulous employers to cut piece rates in order to force employees to work harder, and workers had to be protected from this. Taylor's solution was the differential rate system, which he explains as follows:

> The differential rate system of piece-work consists briefly in offering two different rates for the same job: a high price per piece, in case the work is finished in the shortest time possible and in perfect condition, and a low price, if it takes a longer time to do the job, or if there are any imperfections in the work. (The high rate should be such that the workman can earn more per day than is usually paid in similar establishments.) This is directly the opposite of the ordinary plan of piece-work, in which the wages of the workmen are reduced when they increase their productivity.[17]

Just as with Halsey's system, Taylor found he needed benchmarks. He began time trials with a stopwatch, measuring how long it took workers to perform tasks, and set up a small department to record and analyse the results. By creating a run of data through these time studies, Taylor was able to arrive at optimum times for each task.

Not long after the publication of 'A Piece-Rate System' Taylor was contracted to improve the efficiency of operations at Bethlehem Steel, a much larger operation than Midvale. Here he was able to further develop his system. As he tells us in *Shop Management,* the idea for a simple system of rewarding employees now developed into a fully fledged theory of organization. Taylor's approach was atomistic. One started with the smallest possible units: one man, one task, and one analysed that task and determined how quickly in optimal conditions the man could perform it. He gives several examples both here and later in *The Principles of Scientific Management.* The most famous case, which both supporters and critics of Taylor tend to cite, is that of a steelworker whom he calls 'Schmidt'. This man carried an average of 12.5 tons of pig iron to the smelters each day. Once Taylor's team had re-engineered his task, he was able to carry 47 tons a day. This meant that Schmidt was now considerably better paid. On the other hand, one is entitled to wonder what physical effect this additional labour had on Schmidt; Taylor himself does not tell us.

If there were barriers preventing people from working at optimal speed, then these had to be removed. So Taylor began redesigning plants and developing new processes that would speed work. This in turn necessitated a redesign of the overall organization so that all the redesigned processes would work together in harmony. This last point is important. Taylor's approach to organization, as he tells us in his final book *The Principles of Scientific Management*, is very much to build from the ground up:

> Perhaps the most prominent single element in modern scientific management is the task idea . . . These tasks are carefully planned, so that both good and careful work are called for in their performance, but it is distinctly to be understood that no workman is to be called upon to work at a pace which would be injurious to his health. The task is always so regulated that the man who is well suited to his job will thrive while working at this rate during a long term of years and will grow happier and more prosperous, instead of being overworked. Scientific management consists very largely in preparing for and carrying out these tasks.[18]

It follows that everything else in the business is there to support the proper carrying out of tasks. This is clear too from Taylor's description of the duties of managers:

> *First.* They develop a science for each element of a man's work, which replaces the old rule-of-thumb method.
>
> *Second.* They scientifically select and then train, teach, and develop the workman, whereas in the past he chose his own work and then trained himself as best he could.
>
> *Third.* They heartily cooperate with the men so as to insure all of the work is done in accordance with the principle of the science which has been developed.
>
> *Fourth.* There is an almost equal division of the work and the responsibility between the management and the workmen. The management take over all work for which they are better fitted than the workmen, while in the past almost all of the work and the greater part of the responsibility were thrown upon the men.[19]

Doing these things is not quick or easy. In *Shop Management*, Taylor observes that 'it is not at all generally realized that . . . the building up of an efficient organization is necessarily slow and sometimes very expensive.' But this is an investment, he feels, that will pay dividends, and he criticizes business owners who will invest in machinery but not in organization. They can see and feel and touch machinery and so know where their money has gone, but 'putting money into anything so invisible, intangible . . . as an organization seems almost like throwing it away. There is no question that when the work to be done is at all complicated, a good organization with a poor plant will give better results than the best plant with a poor organization.'[20]

   To sum up, the four principles on which scientific management rests are: (1) the scientific design of tasks; (2) the scientific selection of workers; (3) training workers in a scientific manner; and (4) willing cooperation between workers and management.[21] This last point is stressed over and over in Taylor's writings. Without the cooperation of workers, Taylor says, it is quite simply impossible to manage scientifically. This last point is often overlooked by critics, who concentrate on the abuses to which scientific management was later put. It is possible to criticize scientific management as a theory on a number of levels, but when doing so we should be careful to acknowledge Taylor's original intent. Robert Hoxie, who had studied under Thorstein Veblen and was sympathetic to the cause of labour, acknowledged this when he wrote: 'Scientific management rests on the fundamental economic principle that harmony of interests exists between employers and workers . . . it substitutes exact knowledge for guesswork and seeks to establish a code of natural laws equally binding upon employers and workmen.'

A number of Taylor's letters and speeches survive today, but the three critical works that established his reputation and ensured the dissemination of scientific management are the three discussed above: 'A Piece-Rate System', *Shop Management* and *The Principles of Scientific Management*, the latter published in 1911 a few years before Taylor's death. The first set out the foundation of his ideas; the second was widely read at the time and was very influential on engineers and business leaders alike. It is the third book which has proved most enduring. *The Principles of Scientific Management* was reprinted dozens of times through the course of the twentieth century, and remains one of the most influential books on management ever written.

The Taylor circle

Scientific management was not solely the creation of Taylor, even if it is sometimes referred to as Taylorism. He himself acknowledged the influence of a number of people, including Halsey, Towne and also the army officer Henry Metcalfe, whose book on workshop management he admired.[22] Taylor also cites Field-Marshal Helmuth von Moltke, the victorious commander in the Franco-Prussian War of 1870–1, who all of the founders of scientific management regarded as practically one of their own thanks to his rigorous and methodical approach to war. The most important influences, believed by many to be on a par with Taylor himself in terms of their influence on the development of scientific management, were Frank and Lillian Gilbreth. They too took a task-based approach to analysis, but whereas Taylor had initially concentrated on the time it took to carry out a task, the Gilbreths concentrated on the movements of workers while performing the task.

Frank Gilbreth had become interested in this subject while working for a firm of builders, watching the movements of bricklayers transferring bricks from a pallet to the wall they were building. He worked out a way of reducing the number of movements, which both speeded up the task and reduced levels of fatigue for the bricklayers, and in doing so realized that there were some fundamental principles involving space and motion that could be applied to all work. He and his wife Lillian began to analyse these, and came up with a set of generic classifications of movement – turn, lift, load and so on – which they named 'therbligs' (an anagram of 'Gilbreths'). By breaking each task down into its component parts, the Gilbreths were able to re-engineer the task so as to make it more efficient and reduce fatigue.[23] The combination of Taylor's time study and the Gilbreths' motion study became time-and-motion study, a tool still widely used by consultants today.

The Gilbreths went on to do much important work on industrial efficiency and became particularly interested in the problem of fatigue and how to reduce it.[24] From simple motion study they proceeded to study the design of working spaces and how these could be reconfigured to reduce the physical impacts of work on employees. They are widely credited with pioneering the concept of ergonomics. Lillian Gilbreth wrote a highly original work on the psychology of management (see below), and was also a pioneer in the field of home economics. Frank Gilbreth also wrote one of the more popular textbooks on scientific management, *Primer of Scientific Management*, which sums up the main principles in a more practical way than Taylor.[25]

Another key figure in the circle around Taylor was Henry Gantt, who had worked with Taylor at Midvale and succeeded him there as chief engineer; he later worked closely with Taylor at Bethlehem Steel.[26] Gantt made two significant improvements to Taylor's system. One was the Gantt chart, a simple device for showing the progress of work, which Lyndall Urwick described as 'simple but revolutionary'.[27] The other was a simplification of Taylor's differential rate system, which Gantt felt was too complex. In his description of the work at Bethlehem, he described exactly the problem that Taylor had anticipated: because the workers did not understand what Taylor and his engineers were doing, they were unco-operative and therefore there was little chance of achieving anything meaningful. Gantt developed the 'task and bonus' system, which promised a specific reward for work conducted within a set standard time, and a further bonus if the work was performed more quickly. This system proved more popular than the differential rate system, and was in widespread use by 1915.[28]

Gantt's major work, *Work, Wages and Profits*, is a detailed description of these and other ideas, and shows Gantt to be particularly preoccupied with the problem of labour. He understood the mentality of workers better than Taylor, and was more sympathetic to their needs. His own four principles of scientific management show his thinking:

> First – complete and exact knowledge of the best way of doing the work, proper appli-ances and materials. This is obtainable only as a result of a complete scientific investi-gation of the problem.

> Second – an instructor competent and willing to teach the workman how to make use of this information.

> Third – wages for efficient work high enough to make a competent man feel they are worth striving for.

> Fourth – no increase of wages over day rate unless a certain degree of efficiency is maintained.[29]

Gantt also stressed that managers need to understand not just the system of scientific management but the principles that underlie it:

> The man who undertakes to introduce scientific management and pins his faith to rules, and the use of forms and blanks, without thoroughly comprehending the principles upon which it is based, will fail. Forms and blanks are simply the means to an end. If the end is not kept clearly in mind, the use of these forms and blanks is apt to be detrimental rather than beneficial.[30]

(1910: 8)

In his final years Gantt's interests broadened. He became interested in mysticism and dabbled in politics. His final book, *Organizing for Work*, published just before his death in 1919, includes a plea for businesses to be more responsible: 'the business system must accept its social responsibility and devote itself primarily to service, or the community will ultimately make the attempt to take it over in order to operate it in its own interests'.[31] As Daniel Wren points out, as he wrote these words Gantt was watching the capitalist system under assault, in Russia, Germany and even in America. The answer, he believed, was for business to devote itself to the needs of society, rather than trying to set itself apart from society.

A few others of the circle around Taylor also deserve mention. The mathematician Carl Barth worked with Taylor and Gantt at Bethlehem Steel and went on to become an independent consultant, where he developed his own wage system, the Barth standard wage scale.[32] He also made some practical and technical improvements to the scientific man-agement system. Morris Cooke showed that Taylor's principles could be applied in public administration, and with direct support from Taylor undertook a major programme of scientific management-based reforms in Philadelphia from 1911 onward; these are described in part in Cooke's book *Our Cities Awake*.[33] Cooke went on to hold senior posts in the administration of US President Franklin D. Roosevelt. Horace Hathaway, who worked with Taylor for a number of years, wrote an article on the need for planning and preparation when introducing scientific management to an organization as well as a number of specialist articles.[34] Sanford Thompson introduced Taylor's principles into the construction industry, and is also credited by Taylor with influencing his own work.

Broadening the scope of scientific management

The ideas of scientific management soon spread far beyond Taylor and his circle. This was intended; Taylor, the Gilbreths and Gantt were quite clear that they were on a mission to improve all of business, not just the ones they could reach, and their writings were widely disseminated. Others took up the same themes, and in the two decades after the publication of *Shop Management* in 1903 there was an explosion of books and articles on the subject. Magazines such as *System*, *Industrial Management*, *American Machinist* and *Engineering Magazine* ran hundreds of articles by writers great and small. Many of these books and articles were on highly technical aspects of scientific management, or else on its implementation in a particular industry; some are entirely derivative and little more than restatements of the principles of Taylor and his circle.

A few stand out, and C. Bertrand Thompson's collection of articles published under the title *Scientific Management* in 1914 contains a selection of some of the best and most original. Hugo Diemer's *Factory Organization and Administration* draws directly on Taylor and attempts to expand and further develop the principles of scientific management.[35] Alexander Church's *The Science and Practice of Management* is an attempt to marry the principles of scientific management to some of the more holistic management thinking coming out of Europe (see Chapter 6), and also to introduce principles of cost accounting into the system; despite some interesting ideas, the book was not a success.[36]

A significant influence on the spread of scientific management was the lawyer Louis Brandeis, who in 1911 represented a group of businessmen before the Interstate Commerce Commission in Washington to argue against a proposed increase in shipping rates by several eastern railways. Brandeis argued that the increase was not justified, and that if the railways were to adopt the methods of scientific management they would become more efficient and save more money than they would gain from a rate increase. Before making his case, Brandeis contacted Henry Gantt and arranged a meeting with Gantt and others of the Taylor circle in order to be briefed on what their theories entailed. It was at his instigation that the group agreed to adopt the term 'scientific management' as an umbrella term to cover all their activities, which went on to feature in the title of Taylor's famous book later that year.

As David Savino has pointed out, Brandeis's interest in scientific management did not end there. A progressive lawyer who later became a Supreme Court judge, Brandeis was interested in anything that promised to bring reform and enlightenment, and it is clear from his own writings that he saw scientific management as having the potential to do just that. Perhaps paradoxically, Brandeis was no friend to big business; he fought against monopolies, attacked mass consumerism (and by extension mass production), and like Ida Tarbell believed that big businesses where a threat to society. *Other People's Money* is a savage attack on large banks and bankers, especially J.P. Morgan. What appealed to Brandeis about scientific management, perhaps, is that it could be used by small and medium-sized businesses; and might give them an efficiency edge in competition with large firms.[37]

The influence of scientific management is strongly visible too in *Budgetary Control* by James O. McKinsey, lecturer in accounting and later founder of the consultancy firm McKinsey & Company.[38] *Budgetary Control* sets out generic principles for budgeting and then integrates these into a broader theory of organization that owes much to Taylor. There are echoes too of the earlier work of British accountant Lawrence Dicksee (see Chapter 6), though it is not at all certain that McKinsey was familiar with Dicksee's work. McKinsey went beyond Taylor, however, in showing how all the parts of a business organization are interconnected and how problems in one part of the business can have knock-on consequences elsewhere. McKinsey's contribution to the development of general management thought has perhaps not been fully appreciated.

One significant development was the introduction of psychology to scientific management. Two nearly contemporary books, Hugo Münsterberg's *Psychology and Industrial Efficiency* and Lillian Gilbreth's *The Psychology of Management*, show two different aspects of the relationship between psychology and management.[39] Münsterberg, a German experimental psychologist who taught at Harvard for a number of years, was interested in how psychology could be used to influence workers and their attitudes to work, and also its potential uses in vocational training. Some of his ideas clearly anticipate the later work at Harvard by Roethlisberger and Mayo (see Chapter 7).

Lillian Gilbreth took a somewhat different approach. In the course of completing a Ph.D. in psychology, she came to the conclusion that psychology had a central role to play in management. She stated her reasons as follows:

> It has been demonstrated that the emphasis in successful management lies on the *man*, not on the *work*; that efficiency is best secured by placing the emphasis on the man, and modifying the equipment, materials and methods to make the most of the man. It has, further, been recognized that the man's mind is a controlling factor in his efficiency, and has, by teaching, enabled the man to make the most of his powers.[40]

It follows therefore that 'management is a life study of every man who works with other men. He must either manage, or be managed, or both; in any case, he can never work to best advantage until he understands both the psychological and managerial laws by which he governs or is governed.'[41]

In *The Psychology of Management*, Gilbreth gives a detailed exposition of the principles of scientific management, much more detailed than Taylor himself ever did. She includes chapters on motivation and on the welfare of workers – the latter clearly a subject about which she feels very strongly. She expands Taylor's original four principles out to nine: individuality, functionalization, measurement, analysis and synthesis, standardization, records and programmes, teaching, incentives and welfare.

One of the more curious chapters is that on individuality, where she discusses motivation. She takes it as axiomatic that all human beings are individuals, and argues that individuality is a fundamental principle of scientific management. Under 'traditional' management, she says, all workers are paid the same and treated the same. Under scientific management, each is rewarded for individual performance, thus ensuring a truly fair and free system. There are 'at least 50 or 60 variables' in human nature and conduct, and she says the onus is on supervisors to carefully select men who have the right traits to perform specialized work. She accepts, if somewhat obliquely, that there is a contradiction between the individual nature of people and the kind of standardized work that scientific management designs into the workplace; she is not entirely comfortable with this paradox and never really resolves it, except to call for more psychological and physiological studies to investigate the impact of stand-ardized work on the mind and body.[42] But she reiterates strongly her view that scientific management is more tolerant of individuality and idiosyncrasy than 'traditional' management.

Gilbreth goes so far as to call scientific management the 'ultimate' form of management. She and her husband also coined the term 'one best way' to describe scientific management.[43] Her own philosophy, and that of her colleagues, is grounded squarely in the thinking of the Enlightenment and the scientific revolution of the nineteenth century: it is possible, by studying a problem using scientific methods, to come to a solution; and if the methods used have been truly scientific, then the solution will be the best possible one. That belief lay at the heart of scientific management.

The Psychology of Management is an extraordinary book in many ways, one of the most profound to come out of the early period of scientific management. It nearly did not see the light of day. At least one publisher turned it down on the grounds that no woman could write a credible book on engineering and management, and when the book finally was accepted both the American and British publishers, Sturgis & Walton and Pitman, gave her name on the cover as 'L.B. Gilbreth' with, as Simone Phipps says, no indication that the author was a woman.[44]

The spread of scientific management

Managers and engineers outside of the US were quick to pick up on the ideas of scientific management. *The Principles of Scientific Management* in particular was translated into many languages. Two of the most prominent magazines supporting the scientific management movement, *System* and *Engineering Magazine*, both published British editions. Taylor and Frank Gilbreth visited Britain in 1910 to give lectures.

Despite their efforts, scientific management received a mixed reception in Britain. The general view today, that there was widespread resistance to scientific management, is prob-ably overstating the case, as we shall see in Chapter 6. However, there was no widespread take-up of the whole system and its ideology. A variety of reasons have been advanced, including cultural ones. Margaret and Alan McKillop – another husband-and-wife team of consultants, this time British – suggest in their own contemporary book on scientific management that British employers and workers alike may have been more comfortable with pooled profit-sharing than the individual reward systems proposed by Taylor and Gantt.[45] British managers and management thinkers were certainly aware of scientific management (see Chapter 6) and were happy to borrow some of its ideas, but they were not interested in adopting the system wholesale.

In France, by contrast, scientific management quickly found passionate adherents. The most important of these was the metallurgist Henri Le Châtelier, a professor at the École des Mines. Under the influence of *Shop Management*, and possibly some of Taylor's earlier work too, he became an ardent supporter of scientific management. He used the journal he had founded and edited, *Revue de métallurgie*, as a vehicle for broadcasting Taylor's ideas (his own ideas are summarized in his later book, *Le taylorisme*).[46] Later he had *The Principles of Scientific Management* translated into French, and founded the Conférence de l'Organisation Française to help promote scientific management, and especially technical training and education.[47]

Those influenced by Le Châtelier included Charles de la Poix de Fréminville, who wrote a number of articles in his own right and also an important book, *Quelques aperçus sur le système Taylor* (Fundamental Principles of the Taylor Method).[48] Against those who attacked scientific management as an American import and defended the home-grown management system of Henri Fayol (see Chapter 6), Fréminville asserted that Taylor's principles were universal. There was nothing uniquely American about them. Indeed, Fréminville argued, the roots of scientific management went right back to the Enlightenment and to the concepts of knowledge expounded by René Descartes. There seems little doubt that this convinced at least some of his readers that they could adopt scientific management with a clear conscience. French firms such as Michelin and Renault certainly did so, though with mixed results in the case of the latter. Scientific management also had support at first from figures in government, notably from Albert Thomas who served as minister of munitions during the First World War.[49]

French engineers were prominent at the first International Management Congress at Prague in 1924, which led to the foundation of the Comité International de l'Organisation Scientifique (CIOS), an international body dedicated to the promulgation of scientific management worldwide; Fréminville later served as the president of CIOS. This organization sponsored conferences on scientific management and encouraged the formation of national organizations like those already existing in France.

During the 1930s, however, interest in scientific management declined. Despite Fréminville's best efforts, scientific management continued to be regarded as an American import in many circles. The rising tide of anti-American sentiment in France, typified by books such as *Scènes de la vie future* and *Les Etats-Unis d'aujourd'hui* – both strongly critical of the American economy and society[50] – meant that American methods for everything were going out of fashion. Not until after the Second World War did intellectual interest in scientific management revive, this time under the direct stimulus of American efficiency experts brought in under the Marshall Plan.

German engineers were interested in scientific management from an early stage, and were almost certainly applying it in some plants before the First World War. A German translation of *Shop Management* appeared as early as 1904.[51] Interest resumed after the war, and several engineers wrote widely on the subject. Among them were Carl Köttgen, an engineer with Siemens who became interested in scientific management during a visit to America after the First World War and helped to found the *Reichskuratorium für Wirtschaftlichkeit*, or German Institute of Management, and Kurt Hegner and Waldemar Hellmich who established the REFA, or German Institute of Work and Time Study. Friedrich-Ludwig Meyenberg, who had taught engineering at Göttingen before going into industry, was also a moving force behind the latter organization, and perhaps the most prolific of the German writers on scientific management, producing five books and more than a score of articles. Some of his work is in English, as he spent the Second World War as a refugee in Britain. His most complete work is *Industrial Administration and Management*, published shortly after his death.[52] Although it describes scientific management in detail, the book is notable for its insistence on what the author calls 'the human factor' in business. There are influences of Lillian Gilbreth, Emerson and the human relations school (see Chapter 7) as well as Taylor.

Some German firms such as Siemens did adopt scientific management, but hyperinflation followed by economic depression and increasing political turmoil in Germany meant the movement made little headway. Adolf Hitler was opposed to the idea of scientific management, as indeed he was to most non-German ideas; though as Robert Conti says in his study of Taylor, it seems clear that some of the methods of scientific management were used by Nazi economic planners.[53] Foreign consultants were banned from working in Germany apart from the firm of Charles Bedaux, which used an advanced form of scientific management. A much warmer reception was found in Russia, where Lenin was a strong admirer of Taylor and ordered *The Principles of Scientific Management* to be serialized in *Pravda* in Russian translation. Stalin was also an admirer, and the management methods described by Taylor and Gantt were widely used in Soviet industry. Walter Polakov, an engineer who had trained with Henry Gantt, was instrumental in developing methods of reporting and control in Soviet factories. The widespread adoption of scientific management in the Soviet Union led to some considerable horrors, but it may also have played a role in Soviet industry's effective response to the German invasion in 1941.[54] Before leaving Europe, mention should be made of Francesco Mauro, who founded ENIOS, the Italian Institute for Scientific Management in 1923 and wrote widely on the subject. Included in his more than twenty books are translations of all of Taylor's major works, a biography of Taylor and also an intriguing book on the state of development of Japanese industry and management.[55]

It was perhaps inevitable that Japan, still in the throes of rapid industrialization and suffering a scarcity of raw resources, should become interested in industrial efficiency. The extent of the influence of scientific management on Japanese management thinking in the first three decades of the twentieth century is hard to measure, but certainly seems to have been extensive. Contrary to received wisdom, says William Tsutsui, Japanese management before and after the First World War was very much alive to outside influences and absorbed them eagerly.[56] This was entirely in keeping with the philosophy of Fukuzawa in the previous century, who had borrowed wholesale from Western economic thought. Now Japanese scholars and consultants did the same with management thinking.

The Principles of Scientific Management was translated into Japanese by Hoshino Yukinori within a year of its first publication, and many other Japanese books and articles followed. Several research institutes were set up to study scientific management, which was also taught at training colleges and universities. A key figure in these developments was the pioneering Japanese industrial psychologist Ueno Yoichi, who corresponded with Lillian Gilbreth and was much influenced by her; he also translated works by Frank Gilbreth, Taylor and Münsterberg. He was founding president of the Industrial Efficiency Research Institute in 1922, later taking over ownership of the Institute when it ran into financial problems. This institute trained hundreds of Japanese engineers in the methods of scientific management. During the 1920s Ueno travelled widely in America and Europe to learn about scientific management, and also encouraged many American industrial engineers and efficiency experts to come to Japan, and it is clear that there was a considerable transfer of knowledge and ideas. Regrettably, none of Ueno's extensive writings on Taylor and scientific management have been translated into English.[57]

Another important figure was Araki Toichiro. Trained as a chemist in Japan, he came to America to do graduate studies at the University of Ohio, but on learning about scientific management changed his specialism to industrial engineering. He studied with Lillian Gilbreth, who by this time had become involved in teaching as well as writing and consulting, and continued to correspond with her after his return to Japan. Here he set up a consulting firm modelled on Taylor's, and also wrote extensively on scientific management.[58] He was a founding member of the Industrial Efficiency Research Institute and worked closely with Ueno. Influenced by the Gilbreths and Harrington Emerson – of whom more anon – as well as Taylor, Araki seems to have adapted what he learned quite freely. He too found Taylor's differential rate method too clumsy, preferring a version of the premium plan. He introduced scientific management methods into scores of firms large and small across Japan. The list of Japanese firms that adopted scientific management is extensive, and the influence was long-lasting.[59] Robert Conti believes there is a direct link from scientific management, Japanese style, to the production methods pioneered at Toyota in the 1930s,[60] and the enthusiasm with which Japanese business took to statistical control and other similar ideas after the Second World War is likely to have been in part due to preconditioning by scientific management.

In the aftermath of the 1911 revolution and the opening up of China, Chinese engineers and managers also took an interest in scientific management. The engineer Yang Xingfo, while studying at Cornell University, took Dexter Kimball's course on works administration and went on to take an MBA from Harvard Business School. His article on 'personnel efficiency' for the Chinese journal *Kexue* (Science) in 1915 is believed to be the first publication on scientific management in Chinese.[61] The businessman Mu Xiangyu, who had read *The Principles of Scientific Management* while studying in America in 1914, was already at work on his translation of that work, which was published in 1916. Mu also set up several businesses in Shanghai where he introduced scientific management. Among other things he required his managers to undertake technical training and ensured better working conditions and treatment for his workers, and generally tried to bring about a more professional approach to management. He was involved with several industry bodies in an attempt to disseminate the ideas of scientific management still further, and Stephen Morgan in his study of scientific management in China lists a number of enterprises that adopted scientific management, sometimes with considerable success. There was also a steady flow of articles on this subject in the Chinese press. By the mid-1920s there were a dozen Chinese journals and newspapers devoted to business and management issues in Shanghai alone, with scientific management being a major topic of discussion.[62]

Mu was also a founder of the China Industry and Commerce Management Association (CICMA) in 1930, which had the backing of the Ministry of Industry and Commerce, and both Mu and Yang Xingfo served as board members. CICMA encouraged companies to adopt scientific management, published its own journal and sponsored a number of publications including a three-volume *Anthology of Chinese Business Management*. The period 1930–7 saw a steady flow of ideas and discussions about scientific management, although as Stephen Morgan says, 'ideas may have been more talked about than practiced'.[63] The outbreak of war with Japan brought these initiatives to an end, but it is interesting to note that in the wake of economic reform, interest in scientific management in China has revived strongly. As Morgan points out, scholars and managers alike may find that they have a rich tradition of scientific management in their own country that can be revived.

Scientific management also found favour in Brazil, thanks to the patronage of Armando Salles de Oliveira, an engineer turned politician. In the aftermath of the revolution of 1930 that brought the progressive Getulio Vargas to power, Oliveira founded IDORT, the Brazilian institute for the study of scientific management, in 1931. Others prominent in the founding of IDORT included the businessman and economist Roberto Simonsen and the lawyer Clovis Ribeiro. IDORT had good relations with other management institutes in Europe, but its publications on management were relatively few. It seems likely, however, that IDORT played an important role in the industrialization of Brazil that took place under the Vargas regime.[64]

As Judith Merkle has described, scientific management became more than just a set of theories about management.[65] It became an ideology, one that eventually circled the globe. Its influence was not universal, and there are some surprising gaps in that influence. One might have expected the modernizing government of Kemal Ataturk in Turkey, which took power in 1923, to have expressed an interest especially given the industrialization and economic reforms which his government introduced. But this was not the case; more than thirty years elapsed before a translation of Taylor into Turkish was published. Nor was there much interest in India, although some Indian businesses did import American engineers who had been trained in scientific management methods.

The influence of the scientific management movement was profound, and stretched far beyond management itself. In 1934 the sociologist Lewis Mumford dreamed of a day when science, including scientific management, would lead to the triumph of democracy and freedom around the world.[66] There is a strong argument for suggesting that scientific management had an impact on the entire modernist movement, as Mauro Guillén points out in his study of Taylorism and modern architecture.[67] Images reflecting the impact of scientific management abound in art, music and cinema, including Maurice Ravel's *Bolero* with its rhythms suggestive of factory machinery, and the Charlie Chaplin film *Modern Times*. But, just as with the Industrial Revolution, not all of those impacts were positive and not everyone liked scientific management or its effects.

Analysis of scientific management

Scientific management probably would not have developed – and certainly would not have developed the way it did – had the Industrial Revolution never happened. Scientific management was a direct response to the crises in plant efficiency and labour management that the Industrial Revolution had created. The question is: did scientific management solve those crises, or did it exacerbate them? The debate continues today, and it is probably safe to say that the balance of opinion favours the latter view.

That may be an overly harsh judgement, but there were flaws in scientific management right from the start. Scientific management reflects very strongly the characteristics of those who founded it. They were tough-minded rational pragmatists, yet there were also idealists whose belief in the perfection of science flows from every page of their books. They truly believed that they had found the ultimate form of management, the one best way. And that itself was dangerous, because when things went wrong in practice, the response of the scientific management community could be summed up as: don't blame the theory. If something has gone wrong, then it must be because people don't understand the theory or are implementing it in the wrong way. Hence another constant strain in the writings of Taylor and his circle: the system will only work if everyone is truly committed to it and fully understands it.

That is the first flaw. As Sigmund Wagner-Tsukamoto suggests, one of the first mistakes that Taylor and the others made was to overestimate managers.[68] Taylor thought that all managers were rational beings who would act in the best interests of both the organization and its employees and recognize that there were bonds of mutual self-interest between them. In this, he was quite wrong. Many managers, as Robert Hoxie found in his survey, did not recognize these bonds. In part we have to consider the times, and the often violent antipathy between managers and workers that had been building up for several decades. It was hard for each side to trust the other, and yet Taylor had said that trust and understanding were absolute prerequisites for success.

Because the workers did not trust management's motives in introducing scientific methods, they resisted. Sometimes they went on strike, as at Watertown Arsenal in 1911 or Renault in 1913. Sometimes they sabotaged the work of the time-and-motion study experts: there are numerous tales of workers moving more slowly while being studied, stealing timesheets and stopwatches, or even threatening the engineers with violence.[69] And sometimes unscrupulous managers really did try to subvert the principles of scientific management and use it as a way of sweating more labour out of workers. The most extreme example is the Stakhanovtsy system developed in the Soviet Union, which had its origins in scientific management but which set near-impossible production targets for workers, with the threat of deportation to labour camps for them and their families if they failed to meet those targets.[70]

The career of Henry Ford shows how after a good beginning, the ideals of scientific management could become subverted. The supreme egoist, Ford rarely gave credit to anyone else and insisted that most ideas were his own. But there is no doubt that Ford's Highland Park plant, built for the production of the Model T, was designed using the principles of scientific management. Ford's achievement was to bring together scientific management and the techniques of mass production which had been developed – or more correctly, further developed – by earlier entrepreneurs such as Colt and McCormick and fashion these into a coherent system; he was, in effect, the Richard Arkwright of his time.[71] Ford did not pay piece-rates or production bonuses, insisting on a standard but very high daily wage, but in most other ways he conformed to the principles of scientific management. The company even had a sociology department devoted to studying the workplace and improving operations.[72]

In the early years Ford was a model employer in many ways, and his workers liked and trusted him. But as time passed, megalomania and – very probably – mental illness began to take their toll and Ford's character began to change. Wages were progressively reduced in terms of real earning power. Relations between Ford and his workers broke down. The sociology department changed from being an institution devoted to workplace betterment to one whose purpose was repressive control – all still within the framework of scientific management.

'In defence of Taylor, these are consequences he neither intended nor could have predicted', argue Michael Mol and Julian Birkinshaw.[73] Lyndall Urwick and Edward Brech put it even more strongly: 'The methods of scientific management can of course be abused. They can be applied ruthlessly and for purposes of exploitation, but to describe such abuse as scientific management is no more accurate than to describe the use of poison gas in warfare as chemistry.'[74] This is of course an ethical problem which scientists face all the time. If the scientist creates an invention with the intent to do good, and others take that invention and use it to do harm, is the scientist responsible for the damage done? In this particular case, I do not believe it is at all fair to hold Taylor responsible for Stakhanovtsy, or even for Ford. But at the same time, it was obvious to many – not least to many workers – that the system inevitably *would* be abused. Taylor and his colleagues knew this; so much is obvious from the writings of Taylor, Gantt and Lillian Gilbreth. Yet they thought the perfectness of their system would rise above the imperfections of people. As Wagner-Tsukamoto says, they failed to account for the fact that not all human beings were as high-minded and principled as themselves.

Robert Hoxie, who surveyed thirty-five American factories where scientific management had been introduced, stated bluntly that Taylor's ideas on workplace harmony were 'a Utopian dream'.

> In their attitude towards industrial democracy as a practical matter, scientific managers are divided; a very few are truly democratic in spirit and purpose; some think themselves democratic, but analysis of their ideas and attitude shows them to be in reality adherents of a benevolent despotism; more are definitely committed to the autocratic attitude of employers generally.[75]

In other words nothing had changed, save that task analysis had given employers greater control and weakened the position of the worker. Modern critics sometimes argue that this was the goal all along. Hoxie does not accept this; he is quite ready to accept that the intentions of Taylor and his circle were good. But he accuses them of a narrow world-view, rooted too deeply in engineering and mechanical sciences and displaying a 'naive ignorance of social science and the social effects of scientific management', along with an arrogant refusal to accept that their system had flaws.[76]

Here is the heart of Hoxie's criticism.

> We speak of modern industry as though it were all of one piece. But in fact, there is no single necessary or logical line of industrial development; no perfectly uniform set of conditions and problems in different industries or even in different shops with the same general productive output. There can, then, be no single system of organization of methods equally applicable to all industries and to all shop conditions. Adequate management as applied to any shop is not a ready-made garment to which it can be made easily to conform, but must be worked out by the slow and painful process of cut and try. It is not a surprising thing, then, to find that the most fundamental methods of scientific management as at present practiced, especially those which bear most directly on labour and labour conditions, have a limited sphere of applicability.[77]

The search for the one best way, then, is the quest for a phantom. No single management theory can be applied in every circumstance. Yet this did not prevent the scientific management community from trying, coming up with ever more elaborate modifications to the core principles as they tried to realize their dream of creating an all-embracing managerial theory for everything. For example, one criticism of the original Taylor method was that performance of tasks would vary over time, particularly during the course of a shift as workers grew more fatigued. Workers could of course take rest breaks, but this muddied the waters still further as no one was quite certain how much rest was needed to ensure optimal performance. Charles Bedaux, working as a manager at a furniture factory in Michigan, worked out a way of factoring rest time into task time, using what he called a 'relaxation curve'. Once this had been done, said Bedaux, tasks could be broken down into universal units called 'work units' or 'B units'. Bonuses were paid if workers could exceed the established optimal speed for each B unit.[78]

Bedaux set up his own consultancy unit in 1918, and enjoyed great success. More than a thousand firms around the world adopted his methods; the Bedaux system was popular with employers in Germany and, paradoxically, in Britain even though Taylorism had earlier been rejected. But the system was even more complex to administer than the original Taylor system; workers understood it less and trusted it less; and strikes and industrial disputes were more frequent and more bitter.[79] This did not stop employers from trying to bring in the system, as the hope of productivity gains overcame their fear of industrial unrest. It is debatable, however, as to how many companies that employed the Bedaux system actually saw the gains they hoped for.

There are two reasons why it is important to consider the flaws in scientific management as a theory, as well as the mistakes made in implementation. The first is that scientific management remains very much alive and well, in different forms, all around the world. The second is that the same flaws in reasoning that characterized scientific management may lie dormant in other, later theories. My own view is that a full-scale critical re-evaluation of scientific management is necessary, if for no other reason than to force us to analyse how management theories are made, what forces lead to their creation and evolution, and whether there are any similar systemic mistakes in how we evaluate and disseminate them.

Again, the foregoing may seem overly harsh. Taylor and his circle deserve credit for a great deal, not least for forcing managers to become more systemic and more rigorous in their thinking. There is no doubt that scientific management helped to expose and, at least in some cases, eliminate a great deal of sloppy practice. The ideal of fairness and collaboration between managers and workers was taken up by other schools of thought, notably the human relations school (see Chapter 7). And there was also a strong link between scientific management and the founding of professional management training and education, which we will come on to in Chapter 8. But the time has now come to leave scientific management, as practised and preached by Taylor and his circle and their followers, and move to the other big management theory of the day, the efficiency theory of Harrington Emerson.

The gospel of efficiency

Emerson is often portrayed as one of the scientific management circle, and is sometimes described as a follower or disciple of Taylor. That he emphatically was not. The two men detested each other personally, and Emerson's writings are full of veiled – and sometimes open – rejections of the atomistic approach followed by scientific management. Emerson had his own ideas, his own consultancy company and his own followers, and he went very much his own way. When Robert Hoxie approached Taylor, Gantt and Emerson and asked each to state the advantages of his system of management, he received a vigorous response from Emerson:

> Mr. Emerson does not subscribe to any definite and detailed system, but asserts that he is engaged merely in the application of fundamental principles to the industrial process. On his own testimony, he has not worked out a complete set of invariable methods and devices to which he is wedded and which he is bound to defend. 'We have no system', he states. 'What we attempt to do is to apply certain principles. We are willing to adopt any methods, any device, if it is advantageous . . .' He takes it for granted that the ideal is never attained. In fact he deprecates the idea that 'shops can be found which will exactly represent the different systems' . . . in his belief there is not more than one existing plant 'which [exactly] represents the ideas of any scientific manager.'[80]

Emerson himself attacked Taylor's vision of scientific management in *The Twelve Principles of Efficiency*:

> Efficiency, like hygiene, is a state, an ideal, not a method; but in America we have sought our salvation in methods. American industrial organization, even when it has good methods, cannot use them, because the organization . . . is so defective in theory as to make the application of the principles as well as of good methods impossible.[81]

Emerson was born in 1853, the son of the political economist Edwin Emerson. His father had a lengthy career as a lecturer in Europe, and Emerson was at various times educated in Paris, Siena and Athens before taking a degree in engineering from the Royal Polytechnic in Munich. The formative influence of his early years, as he tells us, was witnessing the Franco-Prussian War at first-hand.

> It is not the pomp and glory of that campaign that appealed to me as I intimately and personally, both in Germany and in France, watched it from start to finish, for there was little of either; but the calm, merciless skill of the play showed me what principles could

do when carried into effect by a suitable and competent organization. It was not the German soldiers who won the war; von Moltke would have won equally well had he applied his principles to Italian, Austrian, French, Russian, Japanese or Americans. It was not the German drill or tactics that won the war – mere methods, both long ago superseded. It was not the German equipment – mere devices – that won the war . . . It was not German money that won the war, for France was at once richer and had far better credit. It was von Moltke's principles and organization that won.[82]

Emerson concluded that Moltke had succeeded because he had four things:

1   A definite plan or ideal, or standard.
2   An organization or a form capable of attaining and maintaining the ideals through the application of principles.
3   Equipment of men, money, materials, machines, and methods to enable the organization, through the application of principles, to attain and maintain the ideals.
4   Leaders, competent and forceful, making the organization and equipment attain and maintain ideals.[83]

From this springs Emerson's own philosophy of management. The first step is to set a goal; the second, to develop an organization capable of meeting those goals; the third, to give it the tools it needs; and the fourth, to give it leaders to steer it on its path. All these activities are guided by twelve fundamental principles which, if put into practice, will lead to efficiency:

1   *Clearly defined ideals.* The organization must know what its goals are, what it stands for, and its relationship with society.
2   *Common sense.* The organization must be practical in its methods and outlook.
3   *Competent counsel.* The organization should seek wise advice, turning to external experts if it lacks the necessary staff expertise.
4   *Discipline.* This refers not so much to top-down discipline as to internal discipline and self-discipline, with workers conforming willingly and readily to the systems in place.
5   *The fair deal.* Workers should be treated fairly at all times, to encourage their participation in the efficiency movement.
6   *Reliable, immediate and adequate records.* Measurement over time is important in determining if efficiency has been achieved.
7   *Dispatching.* Workflow must be scheduled in such a way that processes move smoothly.
8   *Standards and schedules.* The establishment of these is fundamental to the measurement of progress towards efficiency.
9   *Standardized conditions.* Workplace conditions should be standardized according to natural scientific precepts, and should evolve as new knowledge becomes available.
10   *Standardized operations.* Likewise, operations should follow scientific principles, particularly in terms of planning and work methods.
11   *Written instructions.* All standards should be recorded in the form of written instructions to workers and foremen, which detail not only the standards themselves but the methods of compliance.
12   *Efficiency reward.* If workers make progress towards efficiency, then they should be duly rewarded.

On the surface there seems to be much in common with scientific management, and so the confusion between it and Emerson's efficiency theory becomes understandable. But there are several key differences. First, despite his training as an engineer, the 'science' that Emerson favours is biology. Darwin, not Kelvin, is his household god. Over and over again he draws parallels between how biological organisms evolve and interact, and how the parts of organizations do likewise. He eschews the crude 'survival of the fittest' model and instead talks about Darwinian concepts such as cooperation and sympathy. He revives the centuries-old biological metaphor for organizations and speaks of organizations having circulatory and nervous systems: even, at one point, as having a soul.

The principles of efficiency, Emerson believes, were found everywhere in nature, in art, in music, in military science. Because of this, he urges managers to look outside their own milieu in order to learn. He himself borrows eclectically from these disciplines and more. Sometimes his eclecticism leads him into difficult terrain; he is also under the influence of Galton, and his musings on eugenics sometimes have an unpleasant tone to them. But sometimes his borrowings are significant. One concept from military science is an idea he credits specifically to Moltke, the concept of the 'line and staff' organization. The line is the part of the organization that executes tasks, does the actual work; the hands and feet, in Emerson's terms. The staff is the thinking brain that plans work, reacts to changing circumstances and gives the organization direction. His model looks very similar to that being developed by Du Pont and his colleagues, first in embryonic form at E.I. du Pont de Nemours and then later at General Motors. There are strong similarities between the line-and-staff model and the multidivision or M-form organization, and later organizational models that distinguish between core and field or periphery operations. His comments on overall organization design seem to foreshadow the much later concept of 'organizational fitness for purpose' described by Miles and Snow.[84]

The biggest difference of all, however, lies in the fundamental approach. Taylor starts with the task. He atomizes the organization and then builds it up slowly from constituent parts. Emerson starts with the goal. The first of his twelve principles is 'clearly defined ideals', and in his view, nothing else can be done until this step has been completed. Then one designs an organization which is fit for purpose. And only when this has been done does one approach the subject of tasks and standards. He also believes that standards should never be cast in stone: they should alter as circumstances dictate, as new technology becomes available or as workplace conditions change. At the same time, standards should not be used as a bar on a high jump, constantly raised as workers attain the desired level. Standards are there for guidance, not as challenges or methods of compulsion.

Emerson did not regard management as the application of high science, but rather of common sense and universal principles. Efficiency, he believed, was the natural order of affairs, in both the human and the natural world. Inefficiency was first and foremost a human creation, caused by ignorance, lack of ability, unwillingness to learn, greed and short-sightedness. To get to a state of efficiency was almost like going back to a state of nature: rather than building up artificial systems to achieve efficiency, as Taylor did, Emerson thought efficiency could be achieved through a clean, orderly simplicity allied to vision and clear principles. Ultimately, as we saw above, Emerson believed that efficiency was an ideal to be striven for, a journey rather than a destination.

Emerson's theories were picked up by others, the most important of which were two members of his own consulting practice, Herbert Casson and Charles Knoeppel. Casson tried to persuade Emerson that the principles of efficiency could be applied to marketing and advertising; when Emerson expressed doubts, Casson developed his own theories all the same and then left to set up the advertising agency Casson & McCann (later McCann–Erickson). He later moved to Britain where he did the bulk of his writing, and we will encounter him again in Chapter 6 (and in Chapter 8 when we return to the origins of marketing).

Charles Knoeppel, a draughtsman who rose to become a manager at the Parkhurst Boiler Works in Oswego, New York, was initially a keen supporter of Taylor. After using Taylor's system to improve productivity in his own firm, he set up a consultancy firm of his own to help other companies do the same. In 1909 he became a convert to Emerson's efficiency theory and spent two years working for Emerson before setting up on his own once more. His subsequent writings betray the emphasis of Emerson very strongly. His book *Organization and Administration* is one of the first to focus on the principles of organization. Rather than focusing on control, he broadens the scope of inquiry and attempts to understand the human element in organization using concepts from psychology and sociology. Anticipating Mary Parker Follett (see Chapter 7) by several years, Knoeppel emphasizes coordination rather than control. Coordination and control are, he says, mutually interdependent and neither can exist without the other; but he gives primacy to coordination as it is only through the latter that the efforts of the organization can be harnessed to achieve its product.

Knoeppel also develops on the biological metaphor of organizations. The three key elements of the human body to him are as follows: the brain, which functions as guide and controller; the senses, which process information and are the means by which we gain knowledge; and the organs and limbs, which perform the functional tasks. When the three work together, the entire body is thus harnessed to the process of achieving a single goal. Based on this biological metaphor, Knoeppel sets out his six principles of organization:

First: INVESTIGATION: Finding out what to do.

Second: ORGANIZATION: Building the machine that will properly carry out what should be done.

Third: RECORDS: Gathering facts and statistics to be used by this organization in arriving at the right kind of conclusions in carrying out what should be done.

Fourth: PLANNING: Logically arranging and co-ordinating all details so that the various steps can be rapidly and efficiently carried out.

Fifth: STANDARDIZATION: Carrying out the steps determined or actually doing the work in a proper manner.

Sixth: INCENTIVES: The results of the successful application of the other five.[85]

Knoeppel stands halfway between scientific management and the human relations school, and there is evidence of a strong if indirect influence on thinkers like such as Follett. In this way, elements of efficiency theory survived. They survived too in other forms; Lyndall Urwick and the economist Philip Sargant Florence were both impressed by Emerson's line-and-staff model and urged its adoption. But even these ideas have not proved durable.

Emerson was writing and thinking at almost exactly the same time as Taylor. His *Efficiency as a Basis for Operations and Wages* was published in 1909, and *The Twelve Principles of Efficiency* came out in 1913, two years after *The Principles of Scientific Management*. Both books were very popular, and for a time Emerson's consultancy company had more clients than did Taylor's. Yet by the time Emerson retired from active life in the early 1920s, his ideas were fading from view. Very few succeeding management theorists make reference to them, and today his works are read only by historians of management.

Paradoxically, it was scientific management that evolved and adapted to suit the changing environment, and efficiency theory which became extinct.

Conclusion

The period between 1890 and 1920 was one of immense intellectual ferment where management is concerned. It is probably safe to say, indeed, that this was the most intense period in the entire history of management thought. Huge conceptual advances were made, and entirely new ways of thinking about management were advanced. Management itself was now seen as an object of systematic scientific inquiry. Earlier writers on management had come up with some profound and lasting ideas, but with a few exceptions they did so in isolation. Now, schools of thinking about management were emerging, aided in part by the permanent establishment of management thought as an academic discipline. We will return to this period again over the next three chapters of this book, as we consider the emergence of still other schools of thinking and of new disciplines within management. In the next chapter, we shall look at alternatives to scientific management that emerged in Europe, and consider their fate.

Reflection

Survival of the fittest

We are all familiar with fads in management, ideas that pop up, are discussed and adopted and then fade away as the next fashion comes along. Adrian Furnham, in his book *Management and Myths*, does a masterly job of analysing fads and how and why they emerge.[86] But what about the opposite side of the coin? What about the genuinely good and respected ideas in management that fail to make any impact and then fade from view and are forgotten?

One of the most admired management books of the 1990s was Ikujiro Nonaka and Hirotaka Takeuchi's *The Knowledge-Creating Company*.[87] It showed how Japanese companies organize for innovation, and linked this to their commercial success over the previous twenty years. The book was widely discussed and its implications for Western companies were analysed. Then . . . nothing. The book is still read and frequently cited – though less often of late – in scholarly books and articles. But where is the impact? Where are the knowledge-creating companies that this book should have created? Why did this much admired idea simply fade from view?

At least Nonaka and Takeuchi are still read. Arie de Geus's *The Living Company*, which advances on his earlier concept of the 'learning organization' and shows how companies can create a 'harmony of values' with their stakeholders that can be an additional and very powerful source of learning, was well reviewed and equally admired.[88] Today it is rarely cited, even by scholars with similar interests, and very few in professional management have ever heard of it.

Henry J. Spooner's *Wealth from Waste*, published in 1918, is a book with a theme that is immediately familiar today.[89] Spooner recognized that industrial waste was a worldwide problem, and he urged businesses to re-examine their waste products. Some of the things they were throwing away were actually valuable and could be sources of further income. The book caused a bit of a stir at the time; Lord Leverhulme, one of Britain's senior business leaders, wrote the introduction, and a few other publications followed. Then interest died out. Today this is a critical issue to which many businesses are turning their attention, but why did the idea languish for so long?

Which brings me to Emerson and efficiency theory. I am not saying that Emerson is right and Taylor wrong, or that either theory should have replaced the other. My question is, why did Emerson's ideas disappear off our intellectual radar screens, so completely that today he is barely even discussed?

In order to work this out, let us look at the key differences again. Taylor's theory is atomistic; it starts at the smallest possible level, the worker and the task, and then builds up. Understanding the process requires fairly simple linear thinking; there is nothing terribly complex about scientific management in its most basic form, and we can go through the theory in an orderly fashion. Emerson, on the other hand, requires us to start with ideals and goals, considering the purpose of the business and refashioning the whole organization. Comprehending his theory requires holistic thinking. Taylor tells us to look at the ground beneath our feet. Emerson urges us to stare towards the far horizon.

Emerson's theory is therefore full of risk. He makes no bones about this; as he told Robert Hoxie, there are no certainties. Taylor promises certainty; in fact, he tells us that if we follow his methods we will assuredly find it. Emerson's theory is complex; just as de Geus and Nonaka's theories are complex. Taylor's system appears to be simple, just as its intellectual successors the Bedaux system and business process re-engineering appear to be simple. (Never mind the fact that they are not simple or risk-free at all; it is the promise theories hold out that determines their survival.)

We might conclude from this that managers like systems that are simple and eschew those that are complex. But do we not *need* complexity? Think back to the previous chapter, to Isaiah Berlin and his fox and hedgehog. Taylor, with his one big idea, his one best way, is certainly the hedgehog; Emerson, with his eclectic drawings on many sources, is the fox. Only in this case, it is the hedgehog who has survived and the fox has become extinct.

And that has been management thinking's loss, for despite all scientific management's excellent qualities and the advances in thinking that it represents, the promise of certainty that it offers is, as Robert Hoxie said in 1915, a vain one. No one theory can encompass every possibility. In his book *World Out of Balance* the chairman of A.T. Kearney, Paul Laudicina, talked about 'wild cards', events that can disrupt any system or any plan.[90] To rely on one system or idea only is to court disaster. Fox-like adaptability and flexibility is critical to survival.

And that, again, means that we need not one theory of management but many. Privileging one theory about management and forgetting or letting go of others risks reducing the scope and thence the flexibility of our thinking about and understanding of management problems. We need more managerial biodiversity, the circulation of as many management models and paradigms as possible. Quite possibly some of them will turn out to be fads. But the good ones have something to offer, and those need to be kept alive, nurtured, discussed and circulated.

6 European management thought

> The advance of science and the cult of efficiency have tended to obscure the fundamental humanity of industry. We have paid in largely to our account of applied industrial science, but we are bankrupt of human understanding.
>
> (Oliver Sheldon)

The same challenges that beset American industry in the late nineteenth century – the need for greater efficiency and the need for workplace harmony – were present in Europe also, in equal measure. The impacts were slightly different. In America, weak central government, lack of effective regulation in many cases, and institutional voids in some areas such as central banking meant that businesses had more power but were also more exposed to risk. In most European states, especially Britain, France and Germany, strong central governments and regulatory frameworks meant that government could exercise more control over the 'problem of labour'.

This did not mean that there was more labour peace – there were many bitter and brutal strikes and other disputes – or that workers in Europe were better off than in America. But the dynamic of the confrontation between business and labour was different. Organized labour had more political representation and a louder voice in both the French Third Republic and in Britain, where groups such as the Fabian socialists espoused its cause, and this may have functioned to some extent as a safety valve for bleeding off tensions. In Germany, Chancellor von Bismarck and his successors kept the labour movement firmly repressed, but Bismarck was also wise enough to make concessions, such as his programme of state pensions and other reforms, at least some of which were derived from the policies of the company Carl Zeiss Jena.[1]

The need for labour peace and greater efficiency remained largely unmet, but by the end of the century both issues were being widely discussed; and more, it was generally assumed that the labour peace and efficiency went hand in hand and that the same solutions could be used to solve both problems. But rather than a single group such as engineers taking the lead, the need for efficiency became a more general concern. Capitalists and socialists, labour leaders and business leaders, economists and clergymen and politicians all had views on the subject, and sometimes those views were very rich and diverse.

One theme which runs strongly through European management thought from this period is the need to focus on the human element. Whether management is considered an art or a science – and there was some debate on this point – the role of human beings as principal actors in organizations is always under the microscope. There is a strong historical element too, with many writers harking back to older philosophies and views of society (though some, like Walther Rathenau, thought that this was the wrong approach).

Yet for all its richness and humanity, this early twentieth-century flowering of European management thought did not last. Management thinkers continued to emerge in Europe right through the century, but after 1939 there were no more big ideas, no more major schools of thought – possibly excepting the industrial sociologists who followed Tom Burns and Joan Woodward (see Chapter 9) for several decades after the Second World War. We will come back to the reasons for this decline at the end of this chapter, but first let us consider the European responses to the managerial challenges thrown up by the Industrial Revolution. Rather than re-engineering the workplace, like Taylor, European management thinkers on the whole focused on the human element: the person took primacy over the task. And they strove too, especially in Britain, to rebuild the implicit social contract that had fallen by the wayside early in the Industrial Revolution. There was a direct attempt to reconnect business with society. That too failed, but along the way many interesting ideas and concepts were generated.

There was an intellectual movement which urged employers to take more responsibility for their workers, and some did. Some of their efforts were undoubtedly paternalistic, and some worker welfare programmes disguised quite ruthless attempts to gain still more control over employees. But some business leaders such as Titus Salt, George Cadbury, William Lever, Alfred Krupp or the Italian textile magnate Cristoforo Crespi at Crespi d'Adda in Lombardy were, by delivering things their employees needed, able to reap genuine rewards in terms of efficiency, innovation and profitability. Profit-sharing was widely discussed and often practised, and by the 1880s if not earlier people were beginning to discuss the merits of co-partnership, where workers would have a greater say in the running of the businesses for which they worked. This was widely advocated by left-wing intellectuals, and also by some surprising figures within industry such as the shipbuilder and shipowner Christopher Furness and the department store owner John Spedan Lewis. Co-partnership was a difficult thing to do well; Lewis developed the idea successfully, but Furness abandoned the idea after less than a year. We will come on to their ideas in more detail below.

Meanwhile by 1890 a few people around Europe – again mostly engineers – were working on the problem of efficiency. One of the most interesting of these is the engineer Karel Adamiecki who, at almost exactly the same time as Taylor and in many of the same ways, came up with his own version of scientific management.

Harmony of spirit

Adamiecki was born in 1866 in Dabrowa Gornicza, one of the cluster of mining and smelting towns around the great Polish industrial city of Katowice.[2] He studied engineering in St Petersburg, taking a degree from the university there and returning to Dabrowa Gornicza in 1891, where he became engineer in charge of the rolling mill at the Bank Smelting Works and was set the task of increasing productivity. Rather like Taylor at Midvale, he evolved his own ideas through observation and a certain amount of trial and error. As I have pointed out elsewhere, thanks to the late arrival of the Industrial Revolution in Russia, Adamiecki had very little in the way of previous experience and ideas to go on. Further, as a Pole in the Russian Empire Adamiecki was very much a second-class citizen and had no opportunity to travel abroad and learn from developments in other countries. Any influences that did trickle through to occupied Poland would have been very faint. In the 1890s, Adamiecki addressed a problem and developed a solution based on his own observations and skill.

He seems to have been successful; he moved on to a senior position at a much larger mill in Lugansk in 1899, and then in 1903 was appointed technical director for all the rolling mills in the Russian city of Ekaterinoslav, which was then emerging as a major industrial centre.

Again like Taylor, this time at Bethlehem, Adamiecki was able to hone his ideas and develop them into a coherent system.

Adamiecki called his system 'the theory of harmonization'. The aim, he said, was to ensure that all employees throughout the company were working efficiently towards the same goal. Adamiecki argued that 'harmony' had to exist across three dimensions. First there was 'harmony of choice', a slightly strange phrase which actually means 'standardization'. Rather than everyone choosing their own tools, methods, ways of reporting and so on, all work processes should be standardized or 'harmonized'. The second dimension was 'harmony of doing'. This essentially meant coordination of work across all departments – essential in a complex operation like a rolling mill, where delays in one area had knock-on effects for others – with coordination being handled by a central 'staff' within the business. Adamiecki developed a graphic representation, the harmonogram, which could be regularly updated so as to show workflow and progress at a glance. There are strong similarities between the harmonogram and the Gantt chart, which is not surprising given that both were designed for pretty much the same purpose.

Thus far the similarities between harmonization and scientific management are striking. Where Adamiecki goes just a little further than Taylor is in the third dimension, 'harmony of spirit'. Taylor argued that management and the workers needed to recognize that they were bound by common economic interests, but Adamiecki elevates this to a slightly higher plane, believing that workers and managers must share the same values if they are to succeed. It seems clear that he is talking about social as well as economic values. He emphasizes that organizations are composed of human beings, and are thus ultimately social constructs. Bringing people who share the same values together to work in teams is central to the theory of harmonization.

Adamiecki's ideas were published and widely discussed in Russia, and it seems that his system did have some dissemination elsewhere in Russian industry. Then came the First World War and the Russian Revolution, and all his work in Russia was swept away; the incoming Bolshevik regime under Lenin replaced it with Taylor's scientific management. Quite why Lenin should have decided to replace a home-grown system of scientific management with a foreign import is not at all clear. Adamiecki himself continued to have influence in his native country, to which he returned in 1919 after Poland became independent. In 1922 the Warsaw Polytechnic created a chair in industrial administration and management – itself a fairly radical development in European terms – and Adamiecki held this chair until his death in 1933, writing and publishing on his theory of harmonization. Then came the Second World War followed by more than four decades of communist government, and Adamiecki's achievements in Poland were swept away too. He is still remembered there, but it is doubtful if his theory is even discussed save by a few historians. Another strong and coherent management idea was lost, this time buried by the forces of history itself.

Looking around Europe as the nineteenth century turned into the twentieth, we see others working in the same direction, trying to achieve efficiency but tempering their efforts with humanity and a clear sense of social responsibility. Among this group were men such as the Belgian engineer Ernest Solvay, who insisted that technical systems alone were not the solution to the problem of efficiency; there had to be greater attention to the human factor. Solvay also advocated closer ties between government and industry in order to foster a stronger sense of social responsibility.[3] Lyndall Urwick, who may have known Solvay towards the end of the latter's life – he died in 1922 – described him as 'an idealist for whom money-making was incidental to the search for near-perfection in every activity, whether it was the processing of the materials of industry or the solution of the problems of society'.[4]

Another example from slightly later is Tomás Bat'a, who combined influences from Taylor and Ford with his own natural humanism to create a spectacularly successful business system based on advanced technology, organizational efficiency and employee commitment. Innovations included an internal market, with each shop and department an independent accounting unit and all linked to each other by contracts; a system of instant communication using pagers and telephones which meant that people could talk to each other right across the business; and direct contact between top management and the workers. Famously, Bat'a had his office at the company's main plant at Zlín in Czechoslovakia installed in a lift; when workers wanted to talk to the boss they did not come to him, he went up and down between floors to see them. In 1924 when introducing the company's first profit-sharing scheme he told his employees:

> We are granting you a share of the profits not because we feel the need to give money to people out of the goodness of our hearts. No, in taking this step we have other goals. By doing this, we want to achieve a further decrease of production costs. We want to reach the situation in which shoes are cheaper and workers earn even more. We think that our products are still expensive and workers' salaries too low.[5]

Bat'a was another idealist, dedicated not so much to profit but to wealth generation and building a future for the new nation of Czechoslovakia. His system too lasted until 1939, when it was dismantled first by the Nazis and then the post-war communist government.

Rather than go on citing individual examples from around Europe, however, I would like to take a different approach. The three countries where thinking about management was most widespread, and where it probably reached the highest stages of development – excepting the individual effort of Adamiecki – were Britain, France and Germany. We saw in Chapter 5 the varying receptions accorded to scientific management. In this chapter we shall look at the progress of 'home-grown' management thought in each of the three, starting with Britain.

The evolution of British management thought

The origins and growth of British management thought have been studied in detail in recent years, first in Edward Brech's monumental five-volume *The Evolution of Modern Management* and then by John Wilson and Andrew Thomson in *The Making of Modern Management*.[6] Both of these works take a fairly pessimistic view of their subject. Among the faults they find are the lack of a coherent system of thought, lack of a knowledge base, lack of training in management per se, and a lack of institutions to support the dissemination of knowledge and encourage the growth of professionalism. Wilson and Thomson believe that British management took a largely defensive stance, concerned mostly with justifying itself and demonstrating its own legitimacy to society at a time when socialist thought and influence was on the rise.

I take a somewhat different view. First, I find little that is defensive about British management thought at this time. The level of engagement between left-wing thinkers and economists such as Graham Wallas and Sidney Webb on the one hand and thinkers about business on the other hand – at venues such as the Rowntree conferences, for example – was high, probably as high as anywhere in the world. My interpretation is that people from both sides of the political spectrum were thinking about the problems of management and trying, often quite collaboratively, to come up with solutions. And to rehearse the point again, one thing they were trying to do was rebuild the social contract between business and society. Far from being a purely defensive move, I see this as a positive step.

British management thought produced no detailed thought system of the likes of scientific management. But, was that the aim? I argue that, apart from the fairly small group who believed entirely in scientific management and wanted to adopt the model wholesale, British management thinkers were trying to find a broader and more eclectic model which took account of variations in institutions and people, rather as Emerson had tried to do. Writers such as Oliver Sheldon and Lyndall Urwick looked to many different sources for inspiration (in this respect again resembling Emerson much more than Taylor).

As for a coherent knowledge base, I would argue that one was beginning to emerge, but that it had several formidable obstacles to overcome. One of these was the lack of an institutional framework and training programmes, and here I concur very definitely with Brech, Thomson and Wilson. The British management community's pig-headed insistence that managers are born and not made, the refusal to countenance anything other than technical training and the absence of journals and other vehicles for dissemination meant that, even if a strong knowledge base had been created, there were few ways in which that knowledge could be shared. Heroic efforts were made by the likes of John Lee, Lyndall Urwick and Benjamin Seebohm Rowntree. All too often, though, British management thought was in the position of a tree falling in the forest, but with no one within earshot to hear it fall.

It will be recalled from Chapter 4 that in the 1830s both Andrew Ure and Charles Babbage had issued clarion calls to British business to improve both technical knowledge and managerial knowledge. For a time around the Exhibition of 1851, momentum appeared to be building. The late Edward Brech believed that much of the responsibility for this rested with Prince Albert, the consort of Queen Victoria and a highly progressive thinker in his own right.[7] Albert was an important supporter of the Exhibition, which he hoped would wake British industry up to the need for improvements, including improvements in the way that businesses were run. But this momentum slowed after Albert's death in 1861. Brech notes that from 1874 there was a steady trickle of calls for the provision of more administrative skills to engineers and others in charge of works, but little was done to meet this increasingly apparent need.[8]

There were exceptions. For example, there had been significant advances in accounting. William Deloitte, in his work with Great Western Railway in the 1840s and 1850s developed the concept of externally audited company accounts, so successfully that this became enshrined in law. Edwin Waterhouse, senior partner of the London firm Price, Waterhouse & Co., made further refinements to the audit process and also played a key role in the development of the concept of the limited liability company. Waterhouse also provided research on companies that were targets for takeovers, and helped change the role of accountants from mere monitors and recorders to providers of managerial knowledge. Both Deloitte and Waterhouse had expanded their practices to America by the end of the nineteenth century. Some sectors were more advanced than others. Shipbuilding, an industry in which Britain led the world, was singled out by Sidney Pollard and Paul Robertson as being an example of a well-managed and efficient sector.[9]

Then in the 1890s come the stirrings of a more general change. Why then? External political events are likely to have been a factor. In that decade, Britain began to realize that its political and economic power were both under threat. France and its ally Russia were still political foes, Russia because of the threat it theoretically posed to British India, France out of the habit of centuries. In 1898 France and Britain came to the brink of war over the Fashoda Incident, involving colonial claims along the upper reaches of the Nile.[10] Both

France and Russia were industrializing at a rapid rate. Much more significant was the rise in industrial power and, simultaneously, the rise in bellicosity of Germany.[11] The novel *The Riddle of the Sands*, published in 1903 and warning of the prospect of a German invasion of Britain, shows how tense the situation had become – and the novel itself did nothing to quell those tensions.[12] Nor was America a certain friend; the American government was believed to still harbour designs on Canada, and the rapid growth of American industry was perceived by some to be a threat as well. Another novel, *The Naval Engineer and Command of the Sea* from 1896 described the hypothetical case of the Royal Navy fighting a war on two fronts against France and America.[13]

The author of this last work, Francis Burton, was a naval engineer and also one of those who was calling for more efficient administration and more training. If it came to war with Germany or France, or even America, could British industry cope with the demands that would be made on it? Burton believed that British industry needed to become more efficient if Britain were to compete in a time of war. Like many others, he believed that Britain's commercial, economic and political interests were all intertwined. He himself wrote a number of books and articles on management, and was particularly keen to introduce new concepts from cost accounting into more general management use. His most important work, *The Commercial Management of Engineering Works*, begins by offering one of the first attempts to define general management. It is worth quoting at length here:

> The term 'Commercial Management' is a very comprehensive one, and includes a great deal more than making office arrangements, compiling catalogues, purchasing stores and selling products . . . It has its *content* in a profitable workshop, and therefore includes everything which affects the profit and loss account, whether it be initially of a technical or commercial character. It is supreme over technic, in so far as the employment thereof is concerned; it is subordinate to technic, because no commercial management can in these days be successful which is purely empiric in character and neglectful of scientific deduction and knowledge. The problem presented is a very wide one, and requires in its solver broad and extensive observation of men as well as books, as well as *the possession of personal qualifications which may be indicated but which cannot be imparted.*[14]

In other words, 'management' covers everything that affects the firm: technical systems, commercial operations, finance, people. But note the final passage, which I have put into italics. The manager needs to study and needs experience, but there is still an 'it' factor, a personal quality that every manager has. Good managers are born with this; unsuccessful ones are not.

Burton follows these themes through much of the book. He emphasizes the need for generalists as well as specialists, and says that business enterprises need both for success. He makes an explicit link between staff morale and productivity, and argues for the importance of justice; workers must feel they are being treated fairly and honourably, or else no system of discipline can be expected to work smoothly. In their study of early British management literature, Lyndall Urwick and Edward Brech were dismissive of Burton's book, but some of his ideas on general management are quite novel.[15] Burton also tries to take a holistic approach to the management of firms, something which would characterize other British management thinkers as time passed.

In this particular respect Burton was undoubtedly building on an earlier work, *The Commercial Organization of Factories* by another engineer, Joseph Slater Lewis.[16] Lewis argued that the general manager of a factory needed to be a good administrator, and that administrative skills were more important than technical ones, though these were by no means unnecessary. The general manager needed to know what was going on in the factory at all times. The most important factor of all, though, is that the general manager needed to be a strong disciplinarian. He should be fair but firm, and should not hold back from handing out punishments when they were due. This makes the general manager sound rather like a Victorian paterfamilias, which is presumably what Lewis intended, but it is hardly progressive in terms of management thinking.

Lewis also argued in favour of more business education, particularly in an article in *Engineering Magazine* in 1900, where he argued that it was not enough to know how to make a product well; one also had to know how to sell it: 'Commercial traffic takes the line of least resistance, and neither technical education, specialized machinery, nor anything else will enable a man in India to make money by manufacturing snow-balls for Icelanders.'[17] Urwick and Brech report that Lewis's work was popular in America; his books were reprinted there and he wrote a number of articles for American engineering journals. He was almost certainly read by Taylor, though the latter does not mention him.

Handbooks, textbooks and articles began to appear, at first sporadically but then in increasing numbers. There were even series of books such as the Harmsworth Business Library, launched in 1911 with the publication of J.W. Stannard's *Factory Organisation and Management*, a standard primer on organization and production management.[18] Burton produced a second edition of *The Commercial Management of Engineering Works* in 1905, including a chapter on Taylor and a summary of his ideas from *Shop Management*, and also a chapter on German manufacturing companies, contrasting their efficient management with the state of British firms.

Another engineer, Alfred Liversedge, wrote a series of articles on management for the magazine *Mechanical Engineer* which were published under the title *Commercial Engineering*. Much of this work is a discussion of factors of production, particularly labour and capital and how they function, along with information about the business environment. In the opening chapter Liversedge emphasizes the importance of knowledge: 'other things being equal, the success of a business will be proportionate generally to the extent and accuracy of the knowledge by which it is directed'.[19] Liversedge divides business knowledge into two parts, technical knowledge and commercial knowledge, or the knowledge of how to run a business, and in this latter category he includes everything from financial management to sales and marketing (this is one of the first British handbooks to mention the latter). While the system of education for technical knowledge in Britain is generally good, he says, the system for providing commercial knowledge is non-existent, and he compares Britain unfavourably to Germany in this respect.

Lawrence Dicksee, who taught accounting at both the London School of Economics and the University of Birmingham, produced a number of textbooks on accounting and also a more general work, *Business Organization*. This work may have been influenced by continental, especially German, attempts to site business management within the broader discipline of economics. Dicksee takes an economics perspective on subjects such as accountancy and organization, and attempts to show students how an organization should be structured and managed. There are elements of scientific management present in his thinking, but once again this book is human-centred rather than task-centred. Dicksee urges business owners to invest in training and skills provision, and in providing good pay and benefits as well as clean and safe working conditions. They are quite prepared to invest money in buying and maintaining machinery, he says; they should be prepared to spend equal if not greater amounts on the people who operate those machines.[20] A similar point was made in the following year by Emerson in America.[21]

Partners in enterprise

A few years earlier the shipbuilder and shipowner Christopher Furness published his first book, *The American Invasion*, which in places strongly prefigures Servan-Schreiber's *Le défi américain*.[22] Still smarting from a recent fight with J.P. Morgan, who had attempted to force Furness to join his proposed monopoly of Atlantic shipping, International Mercantile Marine, Furness warned of the rising competitive challenge coming from America. To meet that challenge would require British companies to be more flexible and more entrepreneurial, and Furness also echoed a point made by Slater Lewis; the country needed more and better training for managers.

Furness also argued for a less adversarial approach to management-labour relations, citing again the need for management and labour to stand together against a common foe. This theme is taken up in more detail in his second book, *Industrial Peace and Industrial Efficiency*. Here he argued that capital and labour both share the same goals, stating a little vaguely that both 'came together at the summons of enterprise'.[23] Those goals are best achieved if both work in partnership. He tried to start a co-partnership scheme at his own business, but was unable to overcome the scepticism of either workers or managers and the scheme was abandoned after less than a year.

Co-partnerships were a hot topic in Britain in the decades before the First World War, and were linked to the wider cooperative movement, which traced its intellectual roots back to Robert Owen. Many firms experimented with them, and even some sceptics came around to the idea. William Lever at Lever Brothers, by then the world's largest manufacturer of soap with operations in America, Africa and the South Pacific, was against profit-sharing as he felt it was too complicated in a firm of that size. But in 1909 he was persuaded to introduce a limited form of co-partnership whereby each employ received shares but Lever was left with a controlling interest. To his surprise, he found that productivity and employee relations both improved.[24]

There were alternatives to employee ownership, demonstrated most dramatically at the chocolate maker Cadbury. The Cadbury firm has often been studied in terms of its commitment to social responsibility and social welfare. It is regarded as a 'good' firm, and along with other Quaker-owned chocolate firms such as Fry and Rowntree is regarded as the embodiment of so-called 'Quaker capitalism'.[25] But as Edward Cadbury makes clear in his book *Experiments in Industrial Organization*, there was far more to Cadbury than social welfare.[26] Providing housing and benefits for workers was just one pillar of an elaborate organizational edifice.

The other pillars were a reward system that included a good basic rate of pay plus performance-related bonuses and then a third, much more unusual feature: merit pay based on quality of work done, not quantity. The third pillar was a system of employee involvement and industrial democracy that itself had several mechanisms including a highly transparent employee suggestion scheme which allowed employees themselves a say in which suggestions were acted upon, and works committees that included some members elected from the shop floor and which were required to approve all major decisions. Edward Cadbury, a passionate believer in women's rights, made certain that the women workers' committee had equal status and equal voice to that of the men; indeed, the purpose of setting up a separate committee for women was to ensure that their voice was heard and they were not shouted down by their male colleagues.[27] The fourth was a highly effective and well-organized back office and marketing function. Together, these turned Cadbury from a small regional firm into the world's leading confectionery maker, a position it held for several decades. Lyndall

Urwick and Edward Brech praised Cadbury Brothers for its innovations in personnel management in 1947, but a contemporary, Herbert Casson, got to the heart of the matter when he pointed out that the Cadbury personnel system was what made Cadbury Brothers one of the most innovative companies in the world.[28]

Cadbury had an ambivalent view towards scientific management. In his book *Sweating*, he warned obliquely of the dangers that scientific management could lead to, and a later paper, 'Some Principles of Organisation' in 1914, made it clear that he thought that scientific management was too focused on processes and tasks and not enough on people.[29] This view was a common one; the previous year the economist J.A. Hobson had expressed similar sentiments in an article for the *Sociological Review*.[30] Yet Cadbury also found things to admire about scientific management, and as Michael Rowlinson says, he adopted elements of scientific management into his own system at Cadbury.[31] And why not? Cadbury was a progressive and ambitious employer who was clearly willing to be pragmatic and adopt elements of any system that he thought would be beneficial to his firm. What he was not prepared to do was swallow scientific management whole. He already had a functioning business system which (a) worked and (b) was suited to his own ideology. For him to have scrapped this system and brought in scientific management in its entirety would have been perverse.

Much the same can be said of Hans Renold, whose company was one of the world's largest makers of drive chains for bicycles, automobiles and, later, tanks. Renold went further than Cadbury in endorsing scientific management, and introduced a number of reporting and statistical control techniques into his factories. But his system too was very much human centred. Rather than spending vast amounts of time on task analysis, Renold concentrated on training and growing talent in his workforce and then letting them get on with it. He once commented that 'it is not our job to make chains, it is to make men and women – they will make the chains for us'.[32] Lyndall Urwick, who had a great admiration for Renold, regards him as a kind of fusion between scientific management and the European humanistic approach to management, but with the latter clearly dominant. Once again, there was no reason for Renold to make wholesale changes to a management system that was clearly working well for him.

And here, in pre-war Britain, is the crux of the problem for those who believed in scientific management. The concept had its appeal, and as Kevin Whitson has pointed out, there were a number of articles in British journals around the time of the publication of *The Principles of Scientific Management* indicating that scientific management was widely discussed, largely in positive terms, among engineers.[33] But unlike in America, engineers were not the only force driving the debate. Economists, labour leaders and their allies, and industrialists such as Cadbury, Renold and Furness were also involved and had powerful voices. These other groups were prepared to admit merit to elements of scientific management, but they were not prepared to adopt it as a doctrine.

Acceptance of this came in 1914 with the publication of the engineer Edward Elbourne's *Factory Administration and Accounts*. This work became a surprise bestseller when it was spotted by a senior civil servant at the Ministry of Munitions just after the outbreak of the First World War, and strongly recommended it to those running factories on government contracts. It became in effect a handbook for managers, especially those involved in the armaments industry, and 10,000 copies were sold between 1914–18. Although most of the book is devoted to accounting and control procedures, there is little evidence of direct influence by Taylor; this despite the fact that Elbourne had visited America before the war to observe factory management.[34] Had Elbourne decided that his book would be more acceptable if he adopted a broader approach to management? That certainly is what he did, offering a threefold conception of managerial tasks: works administration, sales administration and financial administration. He also made a plea for more and better education and training in all three fields, a theme that would occupy much of his later writings and work. *Factory Administration and Accounts* is an entirely pragmatic work, offering ideas on how to manage well rather than urging the merits of a particular theory or school of thought.

Oddly, one of the strongest cases for scientific management from this period comes from the Fabian socialist Sidney Webb, who along with his wife Beatrice was one of the founders of the London School of Economics. In 1898 the Webbs had published a book entitled *Problems of Modern Industry* which had highlighted issues such as low pay, sweated labour and the inferior position of women in the workplace.[35] Sidney Webb, himself the son of an accountant, seems to have become convinced that the solution to the abuses he had seen was to change the way that businesses were run. In his later book *The Works Manager To-Day*, based on a series of lectures given to managers during the First World War, Webb began by offering his own definition of management:

> Arranging and directing the activities of a band of producers, including both brain-workers and manual workers, so as to create among them the most effective cooperation of their energies in achieving the common purpose.[36]

This is an interesting anticipation of later definitions of management such as that of Lawrence Appley, 'getting things done through other people'.[37] It also highlights the role of cooperation and coordination rather than control; compare with the work of Charles Knoeppel in America at about the same time (see Chapter 5). That is a theme which runs through the rest of the book. When it comes to scientific management, Webb probably summed up the view of many, capitalists and socialists alike:

> the matter is well worth study by every British professional manager – he cannot fail to pick up hints that will be useful to him. But I am afraid that a lot of rubbish has been talked about under cover of the phrase 'scientific management'. I am told by those who have visited a great many American works in different industries that some of those that profess the most, in the way of 'scientific management', have really achieved nothing at all superior to what we have done quietly in our own way over here.[38]

This may be bombast, although Daniel Nelson cites the American engineer Dwight Farnham, writing in 1921, who believed that British industry was on a par with American industry in terms of its adoption of scientific management.[39] Webb argued that scientific management has much to teach in terms of 'its insistence on the perfect organization of the factory, use of the best machinery, consideration of the conditions of greatest efficiency for each worker, prevention of any loss of time, and prompt application of labour-saving appliances'.[40] He was also in favour of work-study so long as it had the genuine goal of discovering how waste can be prevented or time saved, but cautioned against any attempt to use work study to lower rates or sweat more labour: 'Remember always that your workmen are not horses. If once they believe you are playing tricks with them, you are – from the standpoint of maximising production efficiency – undone.'[41]

Here, however, Webb departed from the standard doctrine of scientific management to urge a fusion of its methods with a human-centred philosophy of management. Critical to success, he said:

is to take care that every operative is in a position to render, consciously, his or her services in the most efficient manner. To this involves perfect physical health, an untroubled mind, and a cheerful disposition. The wise works manager, in the United States even earlier and more extensively than in the United Kingdom, has necessarily realized that the establishment was as much interested in the health and well-being of its operatives as they were themselves . . . This is partly philanthropy, or rather common humanity; and partly – we had better be candid about it – a way of increasing industrial efficiency. Those benevolent and far-sighted firms [such as Cadbury, Rowntree and Lever] have found their expenditure well repaid . . . in the increased productiveness of their establishments.[42]

Post-war British management thought

Following the First World War there was a surge in interest in management thought in Britain, in part because of the experience of the Ministry of Munitions. Here, a combination of scientific management-based production techniques, the accounting and control techniques advocated by Elbourne and the emphasis on the human element had – not without problems along the way, such as the unrest in the Clydeside factories in 1916 – worked efficiently. There was much discussion, in particular of the Ministry's industrial welfare department headed by Benjamin Seebohm Rowntree. One of his first actions had been to cut the excessive hours worked by munitions workers, with the result that productivity had increased; Urwick and Brech comment a little acidly that munitions factory managers seemed to have forgotten the lesson learned by Robert Owen.[43]

Many of the pre-war writers returned to publication, their ideas expanded in part by the experience of war. Lawrence Dicksee's *The True Basis for Efficiency* argues that the key elements for business success are training, equipment, leadership and morale, and of these leadership is most definitely *primus inter pares*.[44] He calls on managers and leaders to win the trust of their staff and build personal relationships with them, just as army officers do with their men in wartime. He also argues that there is a spiritual dimension to management, a theme that is returned to in the work of other later British writers. Edward Elbourne, now a tireless promoter of the cause of management education in Britain, published two more notable books including the first major British book on marketing, *The Marketing Problem* (which includes among other things a twenty-five page bibliography of works on marketing, mostly American in origin) and his final book, *The Fundamentals of Industrial Administration*.[45] In this last book Elbourne attempts to establish a link between the principles of management and economics, perhaps owing a debt here to the industrial economist Philip Sargant Florence. He lists the principles of management as investigation, goal-setting or 'objective', organization, direction, experiment and control. 'Experiment' refers to what we would now call continuous improvement: 'If the principles of continuity and mobility are to be observed it is necessary to make arrangement for constant experiment with a view to improving features of the organization or system.'[46]

Philip Sargant Florence also had considerable influence in the pre-war period, starting with his early works on industrial fatigue and unrest. His *The Logic of Industrial Organization* betrays some influence of the German Historical School (see below), which is unsurprising given that he was largely educated in America, where adherents of that school were prominent in the field of economics.[47] One of the most interesting passages in his work is a discussion of efficiency where – once again – we read that true efficiency is not just a matter of technical systems but also of human systems; the most efficient factory is not necessarily the one with the best cost ratios. He also reminds readers that people are often illogical in their behaviour, a factor which affects not only supply and demand but operations as well. This comes through most strongly in his discussion of organizations as political systems, in which political factions form and vie for dominance. His ideas here may owe a debt to Mary Parker Follett, and are part of a longer chain of thinking that stretches back to Machiavelli, at least, and forward through Tom Burns, Gareth Morgan and many others to the present day.

The eminent economist Alfred Marshall also included a chapter on organization in his book *Industry and Trade*, in which he is particularly critical of mass production and repetitive work, claiming that it dulled the mind and made workers less efficient. He praised the craft-working model employed at Carl Zeiss Jena and held it up as an alternative. He also listed the qualities that senior managers should have, including judgement and prudence, technical knowledge, an ability to organize, 'in which system plays a great part, but "always as a servant, never as a master"', the ability to manage people including qualities of trust, tact and sympathy and finally diligence and attention to detail.[48] Marshall, like Elbourne, pleaded the case for business education: 'The creation of vast businesses involves great risks unless there is good reason to expect that men competent to manage them, will be forthcoming. It is often assumed that they are sure to be forthcoming, but history gives little support to this belief.'[49]

Management philosopher: Oliver Sheldon

Elbourne also acknowledged the influence of another British writer, Oliver Sheldon, and quoted him at length. Elbourne, like Sheldon, reckoned that scientific management was an important tool, but no more. The key to management lay in the management of people; all else followed from that.

Sheldon himself was one of the most thoughtful writers on management of his generation. After serving in the British army during the war, he joined Rowntree and held a senior post there, absorbing many influences and almost certainly influencing in turn. His book *The Philosophy of Management* was widely admired and quoted in Britain, though it seems to have made little impact elsewhere. This is a pity, because Sheldon was anticipating a great deal of later thinking about management, from Mary Parker Follett to Peter Drucker. He starts by restating, rather elegantly, a by now common theme in British management thought, that human systems must always take primacy over technical systems:

> Industry is not a machine; it is a complex form of human association. The true reading of its past and present is in terms of human beings – their thoughts, aims and ideals – not in terms of systems or of machinery. The true understanding of industry is to understand the thoughts of those engaged in it. The advance of science and the cult of efficiency have tended to obscure the fundamental humanity of industry. We have paid in largely to our account of applied industrial science, but we are bankrupt of human understanding.[50]

This does not mean that he was opposed to scientific management, or to technology. Businesses use machines; indeed, he says, organizations themselves can be likened to a kind of tool or machine. Scientific management itself is likewise a tool: 'Undoubtedly there is a science of management, but it is to be sharply distinguished from the art which employs that science. A profound knowledge of the ascertained and codified facts of management does not necessarily entail a capacity for management.'[51]

He states explicitly that management is an art, not a science, but he then goes further still. Management is something that is intrinsically linked with organizations. One thing that all people have in common is the tendency to organize. It follows, says Sheldon, that 'management is the natural outcome of our association'.[52] One could go so far as to say that the art of management is part of our humanity. Sheldon does not say so explicitly, but he does argue that management is a continuous theme in human society that can be traced right back through time. For this reason he urged managers to study history:

> Industrial history . . . is necessary to place the present in the right focus . . . history gives the necessary background and places events in their true perspective. It gives proportion and a sense of relative values. It shows the forces which have fostered the growth of what to-day are problems . . . Management, without a broad knowledge of industrial history, is apt to be impressed only with the vivid colours of the present.[53]

Economics, business ethics, the science of management and industrial history, he says, are the four subjects that every manager should study. Like Elbourne, he is passionate about the need for training. Training leads to the stimulation of thinking and ideas, and shows managers how to use concepts and principles to guide their actions. This deep and creative thinker about management was influential on a number of others, including Elbourne, John Lee and Lyndall Urwick.

John Lee took some of Sheldon's ideas still further. He is best known for editing the two-volume *Dictionary of Industrial Administration*, an attempt to go beyond purely business encyclopedias such as *Harmsworth's Business Encyclopedia*.[54] The latter, in five densely packed volumes, had almost nothing to say about management and administration. Lee's aim was to create a knowledge base for managers by summarizing as much as possible of what was known of the art and science of management under one cover. Today the book remains a splendid snapshot of the state of the art of management knowledge in Britain and suggests, to me at least, that British management thinking was not only alive and well but eclectic and sophisticated. In 1969 John Child maintained that up to that time, 'there is nothing else to compare with this work in the history of British management thought'.[55] I agree, but I think one could with justification remove the word 'British' and the statement would still be true. This is a remarkable book on anyone's terms.

Lee was also one of the first British management thinkers since Slater Lewis to make an impact in America. Two of his earlier works, *Management* and *Industrial Organisation*, had sold well there, and Lee became known as a contributor to periodicals; he was on his way to a speaking tour in America when he died of a heart attack in 1928.[56]

It is worth mentioning also Lee's best-known work today, the essay 'The Pros and Cons of Functionalization', which was published after his death. Here Lee muses on the fit between his own Christian values and management thought. Although he understands the need for functionalization and specialization, he questions the psychological and moral impact that these have on people, urging managers always to remember 'the sacredness of man'.[57]

Around the same time that Lee was writing these words, John Spedan Lewis was embarking on the most daring experiment in co-partnership so far, devolving ownership of his entire department store business to his employees. His starting point was his personal belief that a business 'is a living thing with rights of its own'.[58] Far from owning the firm, Lewis believed he was merely its custodian; the real owners were the people whose labour was responsible for creating its profits. Over the course of 1928–9 he established the John Lewis Partnership, which gave equal shares in the business to every employee, including himself. This was partly an ethical view and partly a practical one: Lewis believed that this move would lead to greater involvement and commitment by employees, who would reap the direct reward of their efforts. He also believed that this system encouraged the generation and circulation of managerial knowledge.[59] Writing much later, he felt that his views had been justified: during the Great Depression, the John Lewis business remained highly profitable and expanded rapidly across the UK. It is worth noting that the John Lewis Partnership remains in existence and that, during the economic downturn of 2008–9, the John Lewis Group grew faster than any other retail chain in Britain.

The American entrepreneur Gordon Selfridge, founder of the eponymous London department store, did not go so far as Lewis, but he offered his employees good wages and a variety of other benefits. He also believed in leading by example, and demonstrated his own commitment and enthusiasm not just for his own company but for business in general. He set out his own philosophy in his book *The Romance of Commerce*, published just at the end of the First World War. Selfridge believed that the war signalled a turning point; the old order was ending and a new era beginning. Leadership in that new era, he believed, would come not from the aristocracy or politicians but from leaders of commerce. Most of the book is devoted to a very detailed history of business and commerce which Selfridge hoped would inspire young men and women to take up business as a career. The book is very detailed, and Selfridge went to the extent of having the Fugger newsletters (see Chapter 3) translated into English to aid his research. Interesting from our perspective is the final chapter in which he describes the organization of a department store – presumably his own – in great detail. We can see a separation between line and staff functions, and Selfridge also has a great deal to say about the importance and roles of both the sales manager and personnel manager. The detailed organization chart makes it clear that Selfridge was also using a kind of multidepartmental structure with each function having its own separate department.[60]

One more post-war writer deserves a brief mention, even if only for his prolificity. Herbert Casson, Methodist minister turned socialist writer and agitator turned management consultant, had sold his interest in Casson & McCann (see Chapter 5) and emigrated to Britain in 1914. Intending to retire, he instead got caught up in war work and became a consultant to British manufacturers, urging them to adopt scientific methods including Emerson's philosophy of efficiency. He continued in like vein after the war, founding and editing *Efficiency* magazine. He wrote more than seventy books and hundreds of articles and papers before his death in 1951; if British management lacked a knowledge base, it seemed, Casson was trying to remedy this all on his own. Many of Casson's works are repetitive or derivative, but the best of them show a highly creative mind in action.

In *How to Get Things Done*, for example, Casson proposes a much more dynamic idea of management than we have seen yet; only Sidney Webb, from the opposite side of the political fence, runs him close. Management, says Casson, is purposive action; it is about getting things done. He defines action as 'the creation of causes that are likely to produce a certain desired effect'.[61] The task of the manager is to first define the desired effect – the goal – and then create the causes that will bring about that effect. Those causes require action, and he defines two types of action: *routine* action, or that which has been done before, and *creative* action, or doing something new. Ideally a mixture of both is required, routine action to keep things running smoothly, creative action to help take the enterprise forward. Creativity and innovation are themes that come up repeatedly in Casson's writing, and in his usual direct style he emphasizes the need for continuous learning:

> If a man says: 'I know all about my own business' he is ready to die; he is finished; he cannot go on amongst ordinary men any more; he knows too much. The only finished man is a dead man.[62]

Sharing knowledge: Benjamin Seebohm Rowntree

Many of the themes we have seen above – the debate about scientific management, the need for more efficient accounting and costing, the human factor, the need for leadership, creativity and innovation, the spiritual dimension to management – were summed up in a single remarkable institution, the Oxford management conferences sponsored and organized by Benjamin Seebohm Rowntree. As noted, Rowntree had headed the industrial welfare department at the Ministry of Munitions during the war; the Reverend Robert Hyde, founder of what later became the Industrial Welfare Society, was one of his assistants. Rowntree himself was very much cast from the same mould as his bitter commercial rival Edward Cadbury, a Quaker businessman with a strong social conscience and desire to serve society, and, at the same time, a hard-headed man of commerce. Both these sets of values are reflected in his own major work, *The Human Factor in Business*. The key themes of this work – the need for production efficiency, the need for industrial democracy and so on – have been described so often above that it would be wearisome to summarize them again here. Rowntree's account of his attempts to introduce industrial democracy at his company are interesting, but one thing that stands out clearly is his statement of the purposes of business and management:

1   Industry should create goods or provide services of such kinds, and in such measure, as may be beneficial to the community.
2   In the process of wealth production, industry should pay the greatest possible regard to the general welfare of the community, and should pursue no policy detrimental to it.
3   Industry should distribute the wealth produced in such a manner as will best serve the highest ends of the community.[63]

After the war Rowntree began to organize conferences for managers, most likely for those from his own firm at first, bringing in experts in various fields to give lectures and impart knowledge. These became more popular, and the conferences moved to a larger venue at Balliol College Oxford and became open to all. The conferences were biannual, each usually featuring from eight to ten speakers with discussions following each paper, and they were very well attended with many of the leading names in British industry appearing in the lists of attendees. The speakers were eclectic in the extreme, and showed the range of Rowntree's own interests. Elbourne, Oliver Sheldon, John Lee, Lyndall Urwick and Herbert Casson were among them, and intense commercial rivalry did not prevent Edward Cadbury or his father George from giving lectures on several occasions. The left-wing labour economist Graham Wallas shared a platform on one occasion with the now very right-wing Herbert Casson. Sir William Beveridge, architect of many later social reforms in Britain, Hans Renold's son and successor Charles Renold, the economists J.A. Hobson and G.D.H. Cole and a range of engineers and technical specialists all gave papers. The list of papers at one conference in 1924 is illustrative:

1   The economic consequences of modern political thought
2   Scientific salesmanship as a factor in regularizing the demand for goods
3   Industrial peace
4   Need movement study dehumanize industry?
5   Can the severity of cyclical waves of trade depressions be lessened?

6   Industry as a service
7   Controlling production within the factory
8   The mental process of responsible decision making[64]

European and American thinkers on management also appeared on the platform. The two most notable Americans were Henry Dennison and Mary Parker Follett, both of whom we shall encounter again in Chapter 7. Follett in particular was received enthusiastically, so much so that she was encouraged to move to Britain, spending the years 1928–33 teaching at the new department of business administration at the London School of Economics. The first series of conferences, which ran from 1919–32, saw more than three hundred papers presented. For reasons unknown, there was then a brief hiatus. A second conference series ran until the outbreak of war in 1939, but the quality of speakers and the number of papers was greatly reduced. The early period, however, marks a period in British management thought when the quality and quantity of thinking was clearly very high.

A life devoted to management: Lyndall Urwick

From this milieu came the man who can with some justification be regarded as Britain's most impressive management thinker, Lyndall Fownes Urwick. His work and ideas have been neglected in the past, but fortunately a definitive biography has now been published.[65] Its authors tell us how Urwick came to be interested in the problems of management. After attending the University of Oxford he joined the British army upon the outbreak of the First World War, and saw frequent service on the Western Front. In April 1915 he came across a copy of Taylor's *Shop Management*, which he read by candlelight while his platoon took shelter in a ruined stable. As he recalled later, 'That was it! It answered the problem which had worried me at Oxford, how to reconcile a business career with being useful to society. It made management "an intelligent occupation". I determined then and there that if I survived, I would devote my life to management.'[66]

Following the war, Urwick continued to read and develop his own ideas. In April 1921 he gave a paper entitled 'Management as a Science' at an Oxford management conference. Although he never lost his admiration and respect for Taylor, it is already possible to see other influences coming through along with Urwick's own original thought. The paper was well received and resulted in a job offer at Rowntree, where he was able to rub shoulders and exchange ideas with the likes of Benjamin Seebohm Rowntree and Oliver Sheldon. Thereafter Urwick found himself at the heart of not just the British but the European management movement. He helped to establish the Management Research Groups in Britain and was for more than five years director of the International Management Institute in Geneva. In 1934 he established his own management consultancy, Urwick Orr, which became one of Britain's largest consulting firms and by the 1950s was operating inter-nationally. He continued to be in demand as a speaker and lecturer, including in America where he remained popular into the 1950s.

Urwick is sometimes portrayed as merely a British apostle of scientific management, but that is not strictly speaking true. As noted, he admired Taylor and was heavily influenced by him, and he called repeatedly for a more scientific and rigorous approach to management; as his biographers note, he brought a similarly rigorous tone to his own consulting work. But his article entitled 'Principles of Direction and Control' for John Lee's *Dictionary of Industrial Administration*, shows strong evidence of Emerson and the French management thinker Henri Fayol as well as Taylor.[67] Other influences included Gantt, the Gilbreths, Mary

Parker Follett, Henry Dennison, Edward Filene and many others, as well as British contemporaries like Rowntree, Sheldon and Lee. He was, in short, an eclectic thinker.

Urwick wrote twelve books and a wide range of articles and papers on subjects ranging from marketing to office administration and production as well as general management and the history of management. Perhaps his most important book was *Management of Tomorrow*, 'Urwick's first and only full presentation of a personal philosophy of management', written while Urwick was director of the International Management Institute and, incidentally, struggling to keep that institution afloat in the face of political dissension and the Great Depression.[68]

Here he offers his own definition of scientific management: 'the substitution, as far and to the full extreme which our knowledge allows, of analysis and a basis of fact for opinion'.[69] This, it is clear, is a highly personal statement: this is what scientific management means to *him*. Note the implication that the quest for knowledge is essential; without it, nothing can happen. Elsewhere he enlarges on this view: 'Knowledge of the facts is insufficient. Thought and experiment are alike hampered by outworn conventions and traditional practices.'[70] Empiricism on its own is not enough, theory and concepts are needed too, and this is one of the reasons why Urwick, like Elbourne, believes that management courses at university level are essential.

Urwick also tries to define the key tasks facing managers. He devotes an entire chapter to research, and two more to the principles of organization, expounding on Emerson's principle of the line-and-staff organization. To Taylor's insistence on scientifically based method and Emerson's views on flexible organization, he adds Fayol's emphasis on the role played by leadership and top management. There is a chapter on marketing in which he urges readers to adopt a 'marketing point of view'.[71] Here we might see the emphasis of his old mentor Rowntree, who had been instrumental in adapting American marketing methods in order to fight off his rival Cadbury.[72] Interestingly, though, Urwick also thinks that adopting a marketing point of view is a matter of recovering some of Britain's own management heritage. He sees little in current marketing thought that was not already present in marketing practices in the past, going right back to the eighteenth century. What we have now, he thinks, is more scientific knowledge of that practice, and more ability to apply that knowledge.

In terms of organizations, Urwick is rather more radical. He believes that existing forms of organization are outmoded, and must change in order to accommodate new social and political realities. At times he almost forecasts the era of globalization, talking of how improvements in education and communication mean that people are more knowledgeable and have a greater sense of expectation and entitlement. 'Men and women have changed', he says. 'There are greater general knowledge and wider expectations of life which cynicism may easily ferment into despair and disorder. Broadly speaking, large populations have become at the same time and for the first time intercommunicating and economically conscious.'[73] The historian in Urwick knows that predicting the future is impossible. Rather than trying to anticipate the future, we should concentrate on getting our methods right and making sure we have the education and knowledge to anticipate change. The new organizations of the future, he says, will only function effectively if they are 'mixed in the crucible of fact and cast in the mould of effective action'.[74]

Urwick's dream of creating an eclectic theory of management which brings together the strands of Taylorism, Fayolism, Emerson's efficiency theory, the human relations school and much more comes closest to fruition with *Papers on the Science of Administration*, which he edited along with the doyen of American public sector management theorists, Luther Gulick.[75] This collection of essays by such luminaries as Fayol, Dennison, John Lee, Elton

Mayo, Thomas North Whitehead and James Mooney, sometimes described as the *éminence grise* of General Motors, along with a virtually unknown Lithuanian engineer named A.V. Graicunas, who wrote on the subject of the managerial span of control. Between them the papers cover both technical and social systems more comprehensively than any book yet published up to that time, in either Europe or America.

And, finally, Urwick needs to be credited as the first true historian of business. His work with Edward Brech, *The Making of Scientific Management*, offers both an interesting critique of American scientific management from a non-American viewpoint, and a clear – if at times biased – view of the development of scientific management in Britain. His subsequent work, *The Golden Book of Management*, rescued from obscurity a number of figures and ideas who might otherwise have been lost to view altogether, including Karel Adamiecki, with whom this chapter began. If for no other reason, for reminding us of the diversity of management thinking in the past, Lyndall Urwick deserves recognition.

French positivism: Henri Fayol

Urwick was also responsible for the first translation into English of the foremost work of French management thought in the early twentieth century, Henri Fayol's *Administration industrielle et générale* (General and Industrial Administration), first published in its entirety in 1916.[76] Urwick was the first to introduce Fayol's thought to the English-speaking world, and, as noted, respected Fayol equally alongside Taylor as a management thinker. He felt that their work was 'complementary, in that while Taylor looked mainly at production processes, Fayol looked at the organisation as a whole'.[77]

Born in 1841, Fayol trained as an engineer at the École Nationale des Mines and in 1860 joined the large French mining firm of Commentry-Fourchambault. He rose through the ranks to become managing director, and was still associated with the firm at the time of his death in 1925. As managing director he rescued the firm from near-bankruptcy, guided it through the takeover of another firm and oversaw its steady growth up to the end of the First World War.

Fayol's own management experience was thus very different from that of either Taylor or Emerson – or Urwick. Of the four, Fayol was the only one who had top-level management experience and had actually run a very large business. Taylor's focus was the shop, the production facility; Fayol's focus was the whole firm, and in each case that focus is directly reflected in the management theories they developed. Taylor searched for a theory of how to make businesses efficient at the lowest level, believing as an act of faith that the sum total of each individual efficiency would lead to overall efficiency. Fayol was at the other end of the looking glass; his search was for an overarching set of principles that would lead to efficient management of the whole firm, with efficiency cascading down through the organization as a result.

Fayol himself credited his business success to his understanding of general management and administration, not technical knowledge.[78] In fact he was a notable scientist in his own right, who made new discoveries in geology and pioneered new techniques for fighting fires in coal mines. Jean-Louis Peaucelle and Cameron Guthrie are right to call attention to the fact that Fayol 'had the spirit of an experimental scientist'.[79] His theories are not 'folklore' as some later critics, notably Henry Mintzberg, would have it.[80] Rather, they are the result of decades of experience, analysed and carefully shaped into theory.

Nor was Fayol creating a theory out of nothing. His ideas are firmly grounded in the philosophy of the Enlightenment, and are permeated by the spirit of inquiry. Like many

French engineers of his day, Fayol was influenced by the French utopian socialist Henri de Saint-Simon, who had argued that the highest form of thinking was that based upon scientific research, and had called upon industry to lead the way in creating a better world. Saint-Simon believed that a new 'industrial class' was emerging, composed of both owners and workers who shared a common interest in business success.[81] Another influence was Saint-Simon's follower the positivist Auguste Comte (1798–1857) who believed that humankind was entering the third stage of its development, the positive stage, in which science and rationalism would rule.[82] A third important influence was Fayol's near-contemporary the sociologist Émile Durkheim, who used positivism to explain social organizations. Durkheim criticized the social effects of the division of labour and argued for greater unity in society.[83] These were no mere passing influences. Positivism – briefly, a philosophy which suggests that the only true knowledge is that which can be verified scientifically – had a profound effect on artists, musicians and writers (including Karl Marx) and on scientists and engineers. Followers of Saint-Simon and Comte were prominent among lecturers in French engineering schools throughout the nineteenth century and their influence shaped French business and management thinking.

In *Administration industrielle et générale*, Fayol takes a process-based view of management; that is, he sets out to analyse what it is that managers do. He classifies management into five types of activity. The first of these is *prévoyance*, which earlier translations render as 'planning' but which in fact means looking forward or anticipating what is to come. The second, on which Fayol spends a great deal of time, is organization. The third is coordination, making sure that all parts of the organization are working in harmony with each other and also, Fayol says, with the business environment around them; coordination means not just internal coordination but keeping pace with external events and forces. The fourth is generally translated as command, although *commander* can also imply the giving of instructions or the general causing of things to be done; in other words, leadership. Interestingly, in light of later debates over the differences between leadership and management, Fayol seems to be insisting the leadership is one of the tasks of the manager. The fifth type is *contrôler*, which Peaucelle and Guthrie translate as 'verification', checking that tasks have been completed rather than 'controlling' in the English literal sense; 'to see that everything occurs in conformity with the defined plans, the established rules and the given orders, and the accepted principles'.[84]

Much as with Taylor, there are at least two different ways of interpreting this fivefold scheme. Some have seen this as confining and constricting version of management which emphasizes top-down control. Others, including Urwick, have argued that this was not Fayol's intention at all and that his system emphasizes coordination and harmonious interaction rather than direction, following the notions of a unified society as described by Durkheim. As noted above, how Fayol has been translated has affected how people have viewed his ideas. The earliest translations, sponsored by Urwick, tended to use words like 'planning' and 'control', possibly because the English-language management vocabulary of the time offered no alternate choices.

Fayol also described the qualities that make a good manager, including good health, intellectual ability, perseverance and strength of will, management ability, general knowledge and functional knowledge. He was opposed to too much specialist management, and in fairness to his critics he did believe in unity of command and argued that an organization must have one point of central control, the general manager. He was emphatic on the need for management training, and wrote in detail on this in *Administration industrielle et générale* and elsewhere.

The culmination of *Administration industrielle et générale* is the famous Fourteen Points, which Fayol believed to be general principles of management applicable across all organizations in all sectors. Summarized very briefly, these are as follows:

1   Division of labour, but within limits. He accepted the need for the division of labour; specialization led to efficiency, but overspecialization led to problems of coordination and control that actually reduced efficiency.
2   Authority and responsibility. Fayol emphasized the need for personal authority, not just official authority.
3   Discipline, ensuring that rules are followed and agreements honoured.
4   Unity of command. Each worker should have only one supervisor, so that there is clarity in the hierarchy.
5   Unity of direction. One person only is responsible for ensuring that strategic goals are met. This and the previous point show the influence of Durkheim.
6   Subordination of individual interests to the interests of the group.
7   Fair remuneration for work.
8   Centralization, but again with limits. Top managers make the big decisions, but other decisions should be devolved to local managers.
9   Scalar hierarchy, with everyone aware of their position in the organization.
10   Order and orderliness, with the right people in the right places at the right time.
11   Equity; all employees are to be treated fairly and with justice.
12   Stability of employment and low staff and management turnover. This reduces development costs and captures knowledge.
13   Initiative. Staff and managers are to be encouraged to think for themselves and take appropriate action in the best interests of the firm.
14   Morale and esprit de corps. Everyone should be engaged with the firm and share its interests. This is an early description of what we would now call corporate culture, but is also very much in the spirit of Saint-Simon and his industrial class.

Both directly and indirectly, Fayol's ideas have been very influential. Michael Kennedy suggests that Fayol had hit upon certain principles of organization which can be identified in the work of many thinkers and practitioners going back as far as St Benedict in the sixth century.[85] Mildred Pryor and Sonia Taneja identify influences of Fayol in the works of Mary Parker Follett and, much later, Michael Porter; and we have already referred to Henry Mintzberg's negative response.[86] There is a clear link too with a later set of Fourteen Points, those of W. Edwards Deming (see Chapter 10) and there is no doubt of the influence of Fayol on one of the leading figures in thinking on public administration, Luther Gulick (see Chapter 8). Fayol too was interested in public administration and tried to apply his principles to the public sector. At the First International Congress of Administrative Science in Brussels in 1910, he had argued – following Durkheim's view that the principles of positivism were applicable to all the sciences, physical and social – that the principles of business management and government administration were the same. Gulick took the same view, adapting and expanding on Fayol's ideas notably in his own contribution to *Papers on the Science of Administration* (from which we may reasonably conclude that it was Urwick who introduced Fayol's ideas to Gulick).

The slow decline of management thought in France

As we saw in the previous chapter, scientific management was introduced into France principally through the work of Henri Le Châtelier, who began publishing articles on the subject in the *Revue de métallurgie* as early as 1909. He and Charles de Fréminville were vocal advocates of scientific management at a time when Fayol was committing his own ideas to writing in a series of journal articles. Unlike in Britain, where many writers sought to pick out the useful parts of scientific management and blend them with home-grown ideas about how to manage, in France there soon developed a split into two rival camps, those dogmatically for scientific management and those equally solidly set against it. Le Châtelier's Conférence de l'Organisation Française, founded in 1920, represented the interests of scientific management, while Fayol's Centre d'Études Administratives, founded in the same year, represented his ideas and those of his supporters. Fayol's supporters included many of the older generation of French positivists who felt that Taylor's theory focused too much on the division of labour; their opponents were often younger engineers who pointed to the scientific and technical feats achieved by French industry during the First World War by the use of Taylor's methods.

Much has been made of this split, which seems to have happened against the wishes of either Fayol or Le Châtelier, and indeed it did not last long. At the Second International Conference of Administrative Science in Brussels in 1925, Fayol stated publicly that there was no fundamental disagreement between his theory and that of Taylor, and the two rival organizations were then merged. Fayol's death later that year, and Le Châtelier's a few years later, ended the discussion.

Thereafter, intellectual interest in management in France went into a decline. This should not be taken to mean that management itself declined in France; in fact, French industry as a whole in the 1930s was probably more technically and educationally advanced than its British counterpart. Scientific management, often with Fayolist overtones, continued to be practised in France at firms such as Michelin and by the railway engineer Raoul Dautry. The American consulting engineer Wallace Clark, who had trained with Henry Gantt, set up an office in Paris which functioned right through to the outbreak of the Second World War.[87] Both he and French consulting engineers such as Fréminville built successful practices.

As far as business education goes, France was again in the forefront. As Sasaki Tsuneo comments, 'France is an advanced nation in both the study of business administration and in management education. Regrettably, however, this fact is not well known, and many people are unaware of it.'[88] The École Supérieure de Commerce, founded in 1819, and the Hautes Études Commerciales, founded in 1881, are among the world's oldest business schools. Following Fayol's calls, the technical and engineering schools began to teach management in the 1930s, and a series of management research institutes was established in the 1950s, again following in part the initiative begun by Fayol.

But the intellectual conversation and debate about management thinking in France ground to a halt. Partly, as we saw in Chapter 5, this was a matter of fashion: rising anti-Americanism in France in the late 1920s and early 1930s disinclined people to debate the merits of scientific management publicly. The gloom of the Great Depression cast doubt on whether the better society advocated by the positivists could ever come to pass.

Scientific and technical perspectives on management thinking faded away. A new model did emerge after the Second World War, this time grounded in economic theory. One of the foremost thinkers of this new generation was Gabriel Campion. Born in 1896, he studied law and economics and then went on to a long career with the French Ministry of Finance as a specialist in banking and auditing. Like Fayol he reached back into the nineteenth century, but his source of inspiration was the economist Léon Walras and his general equilibrium theory. His book *Economie privée*, first published in 1943, is an attempt to harmonize general equilibrium theory with Fayol's theory of administration, making links between how firms are managed and how they perform.[89] He follows Fayol in dividing firms into two distinctive aspects, the technical and the commercial, and believes that the combination of the two should result in a whole greater than the sum of its parts. Ensuring that this combination is effective is one of the tasks of the manager. The other is to ensure that the firm responds effectively to challenges from the environment. Here the key determining factors are the degree of autonomy the firm enjoys and the appetite for risk displayed by its managers. Campion portrays the firm as seeking two states of equilibrium; internal harmony between all of the factors of production, and external harmony with the environment.

Thus with Campion we see the focus in French management thought shift away from the technical aspects of management towards theories of the firm. French writers in the 1950s and 1960s continued to discuss management, but with nothing like the vigour or originality of Fayol and his colleagues.

German management thought

Economics too played a leading role in German management thought, which had also begun to develop in the decade before the First World War. The dominant school of economic thinking was the German Historical School, founded by Wilhelm Roscher (1817–94) and his followers.[90] The Historical School rejected the classical economics of Adam Smith and his followers, opposing in particular the view that the principle of self-interest would lead markets to become self-regulating. History, it was suggested, proved otherwise. Roscher, one of the founders of the theory of economic cycles, and his colleagues advanced a much more pessimistic view, namely that markets guided by self-interest tended to the work to the advantage of a few, and against the interests of the many. Not surprisingly, many of them were of strongly socialist leanings, and they were also violently opposed to the Austrian School, the followers of Carl Menger (1840–1921) who followed on from the classical school and favoured free markets.

Followers of the Historical School were prominent among the founders of Germany's first business school, Leipzig Commercial College, in 1898. Similar establishments in Hamburg and Berlin soon followed. The College produced several notable German management thinkers including Heinrich Nicklisch and Eugen Schmalenbach, both of whom were members of the class that joined in 1898.

This development came at a time when German industry was growing and expanding rapidly, and was attracting attention from outside the country. In the second edition of his *The Commercial Management of Engineering Works* the British engineer Francis Burton included a chapter on German industry and noted the close ties between business and state. In particular, business seemed to have borrowed some of the efficiency methods of the German army, and he commented on the quasi-military nature of some German plants.[91] This could have been propaganda, intended to alert British business to the threat Burton believed it faced, and it should be noted that there were other German businesses such as Carl Zeiss Jena which were run on very democratic and meritocratic principles with only loose direction from the top.

The corporatist nature of the German economy may have been a reflection of the influence of the Historical School, which held that business management was an economic discipline and that there was no difference between public and private sector management; the economic principles of political economy that governed each were entirely the same. The arrival of scientific management in Germany after 1904 (see Chapter 5) posed a direct challenge to this way of thinking. The first economists to break ranks and challenge the Historical School were two professors at the University of Freiburg, Moritz Weyermann and Hans Schönitz in 1912, who argued that there was such a thing as 'private economics' that was distinct and separate from political economy.[92] Weyermann and Schönitz called for research into the technical aspects of how businesses functioned, in much the same manner that scientific management advocated.

Their work was roundly castigated by other members of the Historical School, but Weyermann and Schönitz had set a train of ideas in motion. In the 1920s Heinrich Nicklisch insisted that public administration and business enterprise were two separate things, and gave priority to the latter as the prime generator of national wealth. Rather like the positivists, Nicklisch saw businesses as communities, combinations of capital and labour to achieve a stated goal. He discussed the factors of production that lead to profit, which must be the end goal of all enterprises. But profit is not the only goal. Nicklisch also believed that businesses exist in order to serve the people who work for them, and should of necessity seek to improve the lives and living standards of workers.[93] Fritz Schonpflug, who graduated from Berlin Economic University after the First World War, accepted what was in effect the scientific management position, that there was a normative science of business administration.[94] Rather than try develop principles of business administration, however, Schonpflug went on to develop a research agenda and suggest how academics could contribute to the development of such a science.

We must be careful not to go too far here. For all of their acceptance of a separate, normative management science, Nicklisch and Schonpflug were still arguing that businesses were ultimately social organizations comprising human beings or, as Bøje Larsen says, they were part of an organic rather than a mechanistic paradigm.[95] The same was true of Eugen Schmalenbach, an alumnus of Leipzig Commercial College and well known for his writings in the post-First World War period on accounting. His development of the dynamic balance sheet was a major step forward, and he also made important contributions to the theories of costs and prices. In his final book, *Über die Dienstellengliederung in Grossbetrieb* (On the Division of Departments in Big Business), Schmalenbach set out his own view that the purpose of business is to satisfy the needs of the community. To the end he also argued against bureaucracy and for the decentralization of large organizations, as he felt that bureaucracies restricted freedom and were not progressive or supportive of the Enlightenment ideals that he himself held. Both Schmalenbach and Nicklisch referred back specifically to Immanuel Kant and his ideas on personal freedom and the power of knowledge.[96]

Another who considered the problems of freedom and bureaucracy was Max Weber, who studied problems of sociology and economy using the methods of the Historical School but often arriving at rather different conclusions. In his most famous work, *The Protestant Ethic and the Spirit of Capitalism*, influenced in part by a visit to America in 1904, Weber asks why the European and American economies have come to dominate the world.[97] The answer, he believes, lies in the development in the West of rationalism and rational systems. He links these in turn to the rise of Protestantism, but it seems clear that the kind of rationalism he describes owes much to the Enlightenment, which was not a uniquely Protestant phenomenon. Rational systems, first and foremost bureaucracy, are the instruments of social control which have enabled to the West to harness its latent economic power. He contrasts the use of rational and legal authority in the West with the more traditional charismatic and personal types of authority which are found in other cultures, and indeed were found in the West before modern times.

There is much that is contradictory about Weber. He criticizes Chinese and Indian societies for failing to keep up with the West, and believes that Confucianism has smothered enterprise and initiative in China.[98] Yet he is clearly unhappy about the spread of bureaucracy in the West and its tendency to trap people in an 'iron cage' of rules and regulations; like Schmalenbach, he deplores the loss of freedom that this entails. The dehumanizing and restrictive qualities of bureaucracy and large organizations are one of the features of Weber's thought that are most commented on today, and many observers believe that they are still very much present in the modern world.[99] Michel Foucault in particular expanded on Weber's concept of rationalism to create a picture of how organizations exert control and enforce conformity; George Orwell did the same in *Nineteen Eighty-Four*.[100] Yet it is not quite clear what Weber himself wanted to see happen. Was he advocating a return to more personal forms of authority as in the past? Or was he advocating the end of capitalism and a form of benevolent state bureaucracy as envisioned by colleagues such as Werner Sombart? No, these did not seem to find favour with him either. He seems to have agreed with the view of his colleague Robert Michels, who posited the 'iron law of oligarchy': according to Michels, the control of information and authority vested in leaders, coupled with the deference shown them by followers means that over time all organizations, including political parties and trades unions, will turn themselves into oligarchies.[101] Weber was describing the world as it is, but it is clear that he did not like it very much and would have preferred to find another, more human-centred paradigm.

A more humanistic approach can be found in the work of Joseph Schumpeter. He was one of the second generation of Austrian School economists, along with people such as the ultra-free marketeer Ludwig von Mises and the more liberal Adolph Drucker. Although from the opposite side of the methodological fence, he and Weber shared some views and worked together on at least one occasion. Like Weber, he too was influenced by what he found in America, where he emigrated in 1932, but whereas Weber was appalled at the dominance and power of big corporations, Schumpeter was fascinated by American entrepreneurs. In his writing he expressed scepticism about the economic contribution of the big bureaucracies, and placed more emphasis on the role of the entrepreneur. Although he did not invent the term 'entrepreneur' itself, Schumpeter came up with a highly developed theory of entre-preneurship which includes an analysis of the relationship between entrepreneurs, capital and innovation, and of how entrepreneurs create economic value.[102]

Rathenau and rationalism

While this ferment of activity was going on, scientific management was gaining favour among engineers and industrialists. Guido Buenstorf and Johann Peter Murmann argue that Ernst Abbé had introduced a form of scientific management at Carl Zeiss Jena; the argument is an interesting one, but Abbé – like Adamiecki – developed his theories independently without direct reference to Taylor.[103] Other large firms such as Siemens and AEG did employ industrial engineers to bring in the techniques of scientific management before the First World War. Frank Gilbreth is believed to have spent part of 1913 and 1914 working in Germany with a subsidiary of AEG.[104] Following the war, as noted in Chapter 5, a number of German engineers picked up on the ideas of scientific management again and began to develop them. The economic theories of the Historical School and its followers were useful in explaining how firms functioned, but they could not explain how to run a machine shop;

and that kind of detailed, low-level managerial knowledge is always where scientific management has had the most to offer.

An attempt to fuse the two systems together was made by Walther Rathenau. As chairman of the supervisory board of AEG, he almost certainly had contact with Frank Gilbreth during the latter's work with the company; he may even have been responsible for hiring Gilbreth in the first place. During the war, like Benjamin Rowntree in Britain and Albert Thomas in France, he worked for the government, helping to organize the flow of raw materials to munitions factories. His books *Von Kommenden Dingen* (In Days to Come), *Die Neue Wirtschaft* (The New Economy) and *Der Neue Staat* (The New Economy), written shortly before the end of the war and the collapse of the German Empire, were widely read.[105] After the war he was one of the leading figures in the reconstruction of the German economy, going on to serve as Minister for Reconstruction and then Foreign Minister, taking up the latter post not long before his assassination by the Nazis in 1922.

Rathenau explicitly rejected the Historical School. 'The historical outlook has served our thought for a century', he wrote. 'It is now degenerating, and is becoming harmful, especially when applied to institutions.'[106] In the wreckage of the old European order at the end of the war it was clear that a new way forward was needed. Like Saint-Simon and Fayol, and Nicklisch, he believed that industry should now take over from the aristocracy as the leading class in society. Like Weber, he thought that the new industrial age was dehumanizing and was enclosing workers in a cage of formal rational rules. Although in favour of many aspects of scientific management, he rejected Taylor's time–study methods as these meant that workers were being valued for nothing but their labour. A truly fair system would only result when workers could take pride in their work and feel part of a genuine partnership between capital and labour.

A progressive employer himself, Rathenau admired people such as Robert Bosch and, earlier, Alfred Krupp who took care of their employees and provided benefits beyond just pay.[107] But he also argued that in a new society, workers needed things to give more meaning and purpose to their lives. One radical idea was that workers should spend part of their time doing manual labour and the other part doing 'intelligence work' which would allow them to learn and acquire new skills. This would be particularly important for those who came from humble backgrounds and had not been able to avail themselves of higher education.

Rathenau argued that a new kind of rationalism was needed, one based on symbiotic, voluntary relations between people. Instead of capital and labour, there would simply be society, unified and whole. Business organizations should function in much the same way, without internal class divisions. Business organizations are human organizations, said Rathenau, and what we all have in common is our humanity.

Rathenau also advocated more use of professional managers, and argued that these tend to make rational decisions which are good for the whole organization, whereas owner-managers are more likely to take decisions based on self-interest. It was he who coined the term 'separation of ownership and control', which went on to become part of orthodox thinking in Western management circles (though not without opposition, as we shall see in Chapter 8).

Rathenau's murder robbed Germany of a talented business and political leader, and also once again choked off a new and potentially promising line of thinking. Thereafter, hyperinflation and growing political instability both worked against the development of new ideas, and after 1933 the Nazis stifled any ideas which did not fit with their own narrow ideology, including Rathenau's liberalism and scientific management. As noted, all foreign consultants were expelled from Germany save the Bedaux company, which survived only because Charles Bedaux had friends in high places in Germany; but even the Bedaux consultants were strictly supervised and controlled. Adolph Drucker's son Peter, then a journalist in Germany, watched all this with dismay. After publishing a stinging attack on Hitler, he quickly departed for Britain and ultimately America; others followed. For those who remained, there was often little time to write or reflect. Shortly after the publication of *Über die Dienstellengliederung in Grossbetrieb*, Schmalenbach and his wife were forced to go into hiding from the Gestapo.

Post-mortem

In Britain, France and Germany, the first three decades of the twentieth century saw a lively interest in management thinking, with home-grown ideas about management both competing and fusing with scientific management and other American ideas. In all three countries there was a lively discussion as to the best ways to manage and the purpose and ends of management itself. From the mid-1930s onwards, however, these movements began to decline.

Again, we must be careful not to overstate the case. The aftermath of the Second World War was far from the barren period that is sometimes portrayed. There were many talented people in Europe doing work on various aspects of management. In Germany, Edmund Heinen and Erich Gutenberg continued the development of business economics and analysis of management as an economic, value-creating activity, while Erich Kosiol refined Schmalenbach's ideas on accounting and developed a theory of organization based on the idea of networks of relationships.[108] In France, Campion continued to work on management as an economic activity and Michel Crozier and Michel Foucault advanced our knowledge of the sociology and psychology of organizations.[109] Labour and human problems of industry in Britain were studied by Hugh Clegg and Allan Flanders; Joan Woodward helped lay the groundwork for contingency theory, Patrick Blackett advanced the science of operations research, Peter Checkland and Geoffrey Vickers developed ideas on systems thinking, and Ronald Coase developed his idea of the firm as a nexus of contracts.[110]

There were people in Europe thinking about management, quite deeply and profoundly. But they were often working in near isolation, or in little clusters. European management theory had lost whatever cohesion it had developed in the early part of the century. There were no more big theories, no more big schools of influence. The human relations school, the development of management science, advances in marketing, corporate finance, strategy and leadership would have their centres of gravity in North America. European scholars would participate in these movements, but as junior partners.

Why, after a promising beginning, did European management thought decline? A number of reasons have been given over the past sixty years by scholars on both sides of the Atlantic. The reasons offered include: dominance by American ideas such as scientific management which effectively pushed the home-grown theories of management to one side; lack of relevance of the theories themselves; resistance by business and other elites who refused to acknowledge the value of the new theories; the low social status of business people in Europe; resistance by organized labour, which foiled attempts at reform of the business system; political turmoils; the impact of economic downturns, especially the Great Depression; and lack of institutional support, including from educational institutions, to enable dissemination of new ideas.

Some of these factors have been exaggerated, or were not relevant at all. The class system has been blamed for most things, but it was not a factor here. Aristocrats have always sneered at new money; witness the low status of merchants in ancient India and China, or how the Daughters of the Revolution looked down their noses at the arriviste business barons of the

Gilded Age; or the famous remark by a British politician of Deputy Prime Minister Michael Heseltine that 'the trouble with Michael is that he had to buy his own furniture'. If this were a factor, there would have been no advances in management thinking ever. Furthermore, by the 1890s, as Gordon Selfridge and Walther Rathenau saw, the business elites were increasingly taking over leadership of society. The businessman W.H. Smith rose to high political office in Britain, while others like Pirrie, Furness, Northcliffe and Lever were ennobled.

There was resistance by conservatives in government, business and labour circles alike, as there always is to any new idea, but I feel the extent of this has been overplayed. Urwick and Brech, and others since, have been highly critical of business leaders in Britain for failing to show more interest in scientific management. But this does not equate to a lack of interest in management thinking generally. The volume of the Harmsworth Business Library containing Stannard's *Factory Organisation and Management* also contains a series of essays from luminaries of British business including Lord Northcliffe, Lord Furness, Sir Hiram Maxim, Sir Joseph Lyons, Sir Thomas Dewar and Sir Thomas Lipton, all of them household names. The list of attendees at Rowntree's conferences in Oxford shows similar interest. Resistance by organized labour was certainly encountered, particularly by engineers trying to bring in the Taylor and Bedaux systems, but more typical was the attitude of Sidney Webb; the new management methods were more professional, and on the whole were in the best interests of workers. A full study of European labour's attitude to new management methods, not just scientific management, remains to be done but one suspects the results would be interesting and counter-intuitive.

Of course, there is an open question as to whether this interest led to any real and positive action, and it is quite likely that there was a gap between the two. But this same charge can be levelled at almost every theory of management, including scientific management. The number of firms that were 'Taylorized' between 1905 and 1925 looks impressive; until one compares it to the total population of firms. One of the inescapable facts about management theories is that, throughout history, people have been more ready to talk about them than to put them into practice. Even Rowntree, earnestly advocating co-partnership, admitted that he had not yet got around to doing anything about it at his own company.

The decline in management thinking that occurred in Britain, Germany and France took different forms, and I do not think it is possible to assign a single cause that covers all three countries. In Germany, the decline is almost certainly down to environmental factors, the political and economic turmoil of the 1920s and the assumption of power by the Nazis in the 1930s. On one level it is possible to draw a contrast between Germany in the 1920s and America in the 1880s. In the latter case a body of people, the engineers, had stood up and taken on the role of leadership for change, evolved the theories and then driven them forward and popularized them through their own institutions and their own journals and magazines. Germany had economic, engineering and educational institutions that could have taken this lead, but they did not. Did Rathenau's murder make people cautious about calling for change? Certainly after his death, no one else of similar stature came forward to take the lead.

France also lost its most effective thought leaders, Fayol and Le Châtelier, in the 1920s, and once again no one came forward to pick up the reins. The economic gloom of the Depression, rising anti-American sentiment and a general and growing sense of pessimism among French elites probably contributed to this. As we saw, French consultants got on with things and were making a fair job of modernizing French industry before the war came, but no more thought leaders emerged.

Britain, by contrast, had plenty of thought leaders. What it lacked was an institutional and educational structure to disseminate ideas. In *The Evolution of Modern Management*, Edward

Brech documents repeated attempts to set up institutions that would play the same role that the American Society of Management Engineers or the French and German institutes had played. Despite interest in new methods of management, nothing happened. The most effective institution in Britain was almost certainly the Oxford management conferences, set up by Rowntree and run out of his own office.

And while America, Britain and France had all developed networks of business schools before the First World War, not until the very end of the 1920s did the first business courses become established at British polytechnics, followed by the London School of Economics. And even when initiatives did get off the ground, they often failed; Brech documents the unseemly haste with which many training programmes and courses were shut down in 1939 following the outbreak of war (just when management training was probably needed most). The reason for this is simple: even progressive thinkers such as Burton and Liversedge insisted that management could not be taught. Either one had a natural facility, a gift for management, or one did not. The role of education was to provide technical and commercial skills such as accountancy and sales; it was not to teach people how to manage other people. When, years later, the Federation of British Industry passed a resolution at one of its conferences advocating support for more business training its director, Charles Renold, resigned in protest.

Britain had gifted thought leaders but was plagued by institutional voids; France and Germany had strong institutions but, for different reasons, a second generation of thought leaders failed to emerge. It is worth remembering not only that there was a rich diversity of management thought in early twentieth-century Europe, but also why that diversity declined and why Europe surrendered thought leadership to America.

Reflection

The light that failed

It started, as these things so often do, with a cup of coffee. A colleague and myself had been reviewing the last 50 years of the literature on leadership, and it had struck both of us that there was comparatively little research on European leadership, at least compared with the oceans of material from the USA. It was also clear that American examples were far better known than those from Europe, and were more widely quoted and used.

As a result, there has been a tendency to think of leadership in 'universal' terms, based on a largely American model. But almost any serious piece of leadership research published in the last 20 years – whether American or European – has said that leadership is contextual . . . And if it is true that situation and context have a major effect on leadership, why are we Europeans using material and ideas on leadership that are based largely on research done on Americans, by Americans, in America?[111]

Phil Hodgson's article from a few years ago on the quest for a European model of leadership has stuck in my mind from the moment I first read it. We know that context is important; thanks to the work of Geert Hofstede and many others who have come after him, we know that national and local cultures have an impact on how we manage. Yet in leadership studies and in many other fields too – marketing, finance and supply chain management are three that come at once to mind – there is a tendency still to look for one universal model, one best way. And very often, that way comes from America.

This is not a criticism of America. I have the highest admiration for (most of) American business scholarship over the past century. The groves of American business academe have been graced with a seemingly endless number of makers of wisdom. But unless we subscribe fully to the one-best-way model – the hedgehog rather than the fox – we must recognize the need for a plurality of theories and ideas to help us manage in different circumstances. And as Hodgson says, too often we find there is a void, and we have to fall back on the only ideas out there – the American ones – and try to adapt them to our own circumstances.

During the twenty-first century this will undoubtedly change. In 2011 there are stirrings in India, a gradual building up of ideas that might in time lead to a distinctly Indian theory of management. Some have detected a similar movement in China.[112] But the theory makers and thought leaders in these countries need to be aware of what happened in Europe in the early twentieth century, and note just how easy it is for such schools of thought to lose momentum and vanish. Or look too at Japan, and how quickly the innovative Japanese school of management thinking lost momentum once Japan's economy began to struggle. There are many fine Japanese business scholars, but even they would have to admit that they no longer dazzle the world as they once did.

For a school of management thought to really take hold, it would seem that three things are needed. One is a continuing succession of thought leaders, people who will reshape old theories and come up with new ones and then take lead responsibility for promulgating and disseminating them, including working on a hands-on basis with practitioners. The second is an effective set of institutions and media for dissemination of ideas, primarily educational institutions and a captive press that is read by a wide audience. The third element is the ability to evolve and move on, to contextualize old idea and turn them into new ones to meet changing times (and not just pour old wine into new bottles).

On the whole, for the past century America has been very good at both of these things. The Europeans have failed over the long run. And unless Europe can relearn how to do these things, the idea of turning Europe into a cockpit for innovation and making it competitive with America, India and China in the coming century is likely to fail also. Phil Hodgson quotes Jeremy Rifkin's book *The European Dream*:

> My personal belief is that Europe is best positioned between the extreme individuation of America and the extreme collectivism of Asia to lead the way into the new age. European sensibility makes room for both the individual spirit and collective responsibility . . . its dream will become an ideal for both West and East to aspire to.

But that will not happen of its own accord. It will not happen at all, unless European thought leaders and institutions conspire to create and disseminate a set of valid ideas that are, as Lyndall Urwick said, 'mixed in the crucible of fact and cast in the mould of effective action'.

7 Management thought and human relations

The ramifications of modern industry are too widespread, its organization too complex, its problems too intricate for it to be possible for industry to be managed by commands from the top alone.

(Mary Parker Follett)

One of the themes running through almost all of European management thought, as we saw in Chapter 6, was the recognition of the human element in management and organizations. The notion that business organizations have a responsibility to ensure the physical, mental and spiritual well-being of their employees was commented on repeatedly. But there was also a strong awareness that organizations themselves are composed of human beings, that they are social and political systems as well as technical systems, and that people are the most important part of any organization. 'It is not our job to make chains, it is to make men and women – they will make the chains for us', Hans Renold had said, and a few years later Thomas Watson of IBM echoed him: 'it is human ability above all else that will make this company succeed'.[1]

This human-centred view of society was very much in accord with the ideals of the Enlightenment. It was of course not unique to the Enlightenment; one can find similar expressions in other cultures too. Jamsetji Tata had put the interests of his employees at the heart of his growing business empire, partly for idealistic reasons and partly in the knowledge that the health and welfare of his workers was 'the sure foundation of our prosperity'.[2] 'Shame on you for trying to make human beings work by wage incentives', the superintendent of one Japanese plant told the industrial engineer Araki Toichiro when he learned of plans the engineer had to introduce a bonus scheme for workers. 'You should have them work by means of spiritual guidance, not treat them as mere material resources.'[3]

The superintendent's comment was not untypical of reactions to scientific management around the world. Sidney Webb felt that for all its technical brilliance, scientific management had overlooked the human element; André Siegfried argued that scientific management and mass production had given America in particular vast material wealth, but at a human cost.[4] The same feeling was also spreading in America itself. The businessman James Clark exploded with rage after seeing a works superintendent bullying young female employees: 'You are deliberately hammering flat the very spirit which set your forefathers in revolt and led to the founding of this republic . . . One rejoices to see the spark of liberty burning so brightly in the countenances of even the humblest of these young citizens; and at the same time one stands aghast at the immeasurable folly that would actually extinguish so vital a flame.'[5]

Among observers and thinkers about management in America, unease was beginning to grow. There was a feeling that perhaps management had taken a wrong turning, or rather, had started from the wrong place. Organizations were human institutions and needed to be studied as such; or as the theologian Pierre Charron had said as far back as 1601, 'the true science and study of man is man'. The study of tasks had taken management forward, but only so far. It was time to see what the study of people might do.

Managing people

By 1916 a steady stream of articles was appearing in American periodicals calling for a different approach to managing people. Such calls were not entirely new. It was understood well before that time that there were benefits to building relationships with employees and treating them well. John Patterson of National Cash Register, writing in *Engineering Magazine* in 1902, commented that 'the problems of today in factory management are not so much problems of machinery as of men: not so much of organization as of personal relations'.[6] Patterson, a hard-nosed competitor, was also a model employer, and he urged the use of employee consultation and suggestion schemes, including the famous one at Eastman Kodak (he appeared not to know of the one at Cadbury Brothers).

As with the Webbs in Britain, there was also interest among those involved in industrial welfare, and many early labour managers and personnel managers had backgrounds in public or industrial welfare. Daniel Wren has pointed out the important contribution of the social welfare movement to ideas about personnel management in America.[7] We should particularly remember the pioneering – and too often overlooked – contribution made by women in this field. Many, perhaps even a majority of early personnel managers were women, and they made notable contributions to research as well. One group of researchers was affiliated with Hull House in Chicago and included Sophonisba Preston Breckinridge, who studied the economic consequences of deprivation, and her colleague Edith Abbott, whose *Women in Industry* argued that there was a growing class consciousness among women workers which would ultimately lead to their standing up and demanding their rights – for example, equal pay for equal work.[8] A century on, it would seem that Abbott's prediction has still not fully come true.

But by 1916 this issue was starting to preoccupy managers and management thinkers much more widely. Claude George is almost certainly right in suggesting that increased production during wartime was putting labour management systems under increasing strain. Once again, a challenge had arisen, and management had to come up with a response.[9] One duly came. Most of the May issue of the *Annals of the American Academy of Political and Social Science* in 1916 was devoted to articles discussing the management of people. In one article Ernest Nicholls, president of Dartmouth College, pointed out that poor methods of managing people were leading to inefficiencies as great as those found in poorly designed factories. Staff turnover alone was a major cost to industry, a cost which could be avoided by managing people more effectively.[10] In another article William Redfield, Secretary of Commerce in the Wilson administration at the time he was writing, commented on the care and attention to detail paid by owners when buying a new machine, and added:

> How many of us apply the same kind of thinking to the man or the woman we take into our shops, so infinitely more complex a machine than the loom or the shaper or the planer or the paper machine, an infinitely more complex thing with all sorts of qualities to which most of us pay no attention? In fact, there is a word we use in that connection which by its very use shows the limitation of our thought. We say we employ so many 'hands'. The very use of the word shows that we do not appreciate the situation. We are not

employing 'hands'; we are employing brains and hearts and dispositions, and all sorts of elements that make for personality – we are employing them all.[11]

Meyer Bloomfield, a lawyer and writer who was already beginning to make a name for himself, argued in that same journal that labour management, or personnel management as it was beginning to be called, needed to become more professional and management as a whole needed to take this specialism more seriously. 'Employing people and understanding them have not been generally regarded as more than an incident in management', he wrote. 'Duties of this nature have been looked upon as unproductive, if not as a necessary evil. In consequence, the men placed in charge of this work were not always the best type procurable nor of the education the work calls for.'[12]

After the First World War, Bloomfield went on to become a leading figure in the development of better education for personnel managers, and helped it to become recognized as a discipline in its own right. His book *Men and Management* became a widely read textbook.[13] Another writer and educator beginning to make his mark around this time was Ordway Tead. Still only in his late twenties, he had worked for the Bureau of Industrial Research during the First World War, and had already produced one well-regarded book, *Instincts in Industry*, an attempt to apply the principles of psychology to the world of work.[14] Reading this book, one is reminded that psychology too was a young discipline still finding its feet. The major works of the functionalist school, James Sully's *Outlines of Psychology* and William James's *The Principles of Psychology*, were only a few decades old.[15] The work of Freud was known but not widely understood, and it was to the functionalists that people such as Tead and Lillian Gilbreth turned in their attempts to understand the personal dynamics of organizations. Among the subjects discussed by the functionalists were things such as consciousness, how thought changes and evolves, and self-awareness. William James described the relationship between the material self and the social self, and argued that the mind does not merely 'know' things, it acquires knowledge in order to take action.[16] All of this was directly relevant to those trying to understand the psychology of the workplace.

In 1920 Tead took up a post as lecturer on industrial administration at Columbia University, where he continued to teach for more than thirty years. His book *Personnel Administration* was published that year. Like Bloomfield's work, it was intended as a teaching textbook but it also sums up the state of art and practice at the time. Tead and his co-author Henry Metcalf define 'personnel administration' as 'the direction and coordination of the human relations of any organization with a view to getting the maximum necessary production with a minimum of effort and friction, and with proper regard for the genuine well-being of the workers'.[17]

The authors are in no doubt that there is a need for this new form of management, and implicitly accuse the scientific management school of overlooking the human factor:

> The logical necessity of centering attention in industry upon the effectiveness with which human labor is applied, has been the basic cause of a shift of managerial emphasis which has really only begun. Industrial management is thus far little beyond the threshold of a new method and a new evaluation of administrative ability. The new focus in administration is to be the human element. The new center of attention and solicitude is the individual person, the worker. And this change comes about fundamentally for no sentimental reasons, but because the enlistment of human cooperation, of the interest and goodwill of the workers, has become the crux of the production problem.

Clearly, therefore, it is not a more penetrating conception of management which has to be justified or to prove its case; it is rather managers themselves who are today realizing how large a share they must shoulder for the responsibility which is upon us all for the confusion and conflict into which industry has fallen . . . the conspicuous part which wise administration must play – especially the administration of those affairs directly touching workers – in the upbuilding of a more stable and equitable industrial order, has been long enough ignored. It is distinctly the task of those charged with the function of management to possess themselves of a point of view and methods which give promise of better results.[18]

Chapter 2 discusses the application of psychology to management, especially to the management of people, and Tead and Metcalf argue that the study of management leads to the inescapable conclusion that work plays a central role in our development as people. Managers must understand this responsibility and accept it:

Reinstatement of the human personality as the central value in life has a significance for industry which it is impossible to ignore. it implies that as a condition for the development of the individual, there must exist a reasonable freedom for choice of work, for leisure, for growth, for free association, for exercise of the whole gamut of human faculties. Industrial practices are, in other words, to be judged in terms of their effect on human beings.[19]

Tead continued to develop these themes in his later books and articles. In *The Art of Leadership*, for example, he stresses the collaborative nature of leadership and the responsibilities that leaders have to their followers.[20] Metcalf, in his capacity as director of the Bureau of Personnel Administration in New York, also went on to play a leading role in the drive for more professionalism in personnel management.

The use of psychology could be a two-edged sword, however. Some psychologists were experimenting with techniques of controlling people. Some at least agreed with Charles A. Elwood, who wrote in *Psychological Bulletin* in 1919 that the human character – as distinct from human nature – is not a natural part of us but is actually constructed and shaped by the forces of the society in which we lived; it follows that our human character can and should be modified by forces of social control.[21] 'The conscious and intelligent manipulation of the organized habits and opinions of the masses is an important element in democratic society', wrote Freud's nephew Edward Bernays in his book *Propaganda*. 'We are governed, our minds are molded, our tastes formed, our ideas suggested, largely by men we have never heard of. This is a logical result of the way in which our democratic society is organized.'[22] There was a danger that the discipline of personnel administration, if dominated by this kind of psychology, could turn into an instrument of repressive control. But this approach to management was vigorously and decisively rejected by one of the more remarkable figures in the history of management thought: Mary Parker Follett.

Human relations: Mary Parker Follett

Follett did not come from a business background, and she never worked in industry. Born in 1868 into an old Bostonian family, she studied economics, government and law at Radcliffe College, and spent much of her career engaged in social and community work in the Boston area, as well as writing and lecturing on society, politics and government. That she made so powerful an impact on the world of management thought is down mostly to her own penetrating intellect and the persuasive force of her ideas. Her friend and admirer Lyndall Urwick called her a 'political and social philosopher of the first rank', and recent studies including those of Pauline Graham, Joan Tonn and John Child insist that her ideas are as valid today as they were when written.[23]

In formulating those ideas, Follett turned for inspiration to a variety of sources, including the philosophy of Johann Fichte and Henri Bergson and the psychology of William James and the Gestalt school. Her second book, the one that brought her to widespread public attention, was *The New State*, which called for a breaking down of bureaucracy and a decentralization of government to put more power into the hands of the people.[24] She argued that communities – that is, people bound together by invisible networks of common interest – were the most important social unit. Her most important philosophical work is *Creative Experience*, published in 1924. This book was widely read by business leaders and management theorists alike, and Follett became a popular speaker at conferences in both America and Britain, receiving a particularly warm reception in the latter country. She wrote many papers on aspects of management, a number of which were published in collections after her death.[25]

At the heart of *Creative Experience* is the idea of integration, the bringing together of social groups which are falsely opposed to each other and creating mechanisms whereby they can work harmoniously. 'Labor and capital can never be reconciled as long as labor persists in thinking that there is a capitalist point of view and capitalists that there is a labor point of view. There is not.'[26] Unfortunately, she feels, the recent trend in society is for more and more specialization, which tends to emphasize differences and leads to conflict.

Follett criticizes scientists and other experts – and by implication, followers of scientific management – who argue that the only route to truth lies in gathering and analysing facts, and she objects too to the principle of one truth, or one best way. 'The greatest flaw . . . is the assumption that the automatic result of scientific investigation is the overcoming of difference. This view both fails to see the importance of diversity, and also ignores the fact that the accumulation of information does not overcome diversity.'[27] But the 'beneficent despot', the expert, ignores this, and so we are proceeding towards a society where 'the people, it is assumed, will gladly agree to become automata when we can show them things – nice, solid, objective *things* – they can have by abandoning their own experience in favour of a superior race of men called experts.'[28]

Experience, says Follett, is a powerful source of learning, especially when it is 'integrated'. That means integrating one's own personal knowledge as well as sharing and integrating knowledge within groups; people need to be able to 'integrate their experience' and learn from it, rather than making potentially dangerous judgements about what is relevant and what is not. In others words, she is calling for an eclectic approach to knowledge. She believes human beings are naturally inclined to live and work in groups and to share experience. She offers three concepts from psychology to support this: the notion of *circular response*, which explains how people share information and create what we would in modern parlance call 'feedback loops' of action and response; *integrative behaviour*, meaning that groups that share a common goal tend to adjust their behaviour naturally to conform to the group so that the goal can be met more easily; and the Gestalt concept of wholeness, which she believes can be applied to the collective mind of the group as well as the individual mind.

Understanding group dynamics, then, means understanding the people who make up the group. 'The behavioristic question, "What is the individual really doing?" I have changed to, What does the individual really want? – the same question in another form.'[29] Understanding what people want is not always easy, because very often they themselves do not know what they want. Here is where the group comes in; consultation with others helps people to determine their own needs. Follett resolutely opposes the idea that being part of a group involves surrendering power to that group. On the contrary, she says, being part of a group makes people more powerful as individuals.

Follett also points out that the things that people want will vary over time, particularly according to their own behaviour. To the question, 'what things do workers respond to?', she lists four factors: (1) the employer, including wages and working conditions; (2) general conditions such as cost of living; (3) his own desires and aspirations; and (4) 'the relation between his responding and the above'.[30] In other words, a person's own thought and actions help to determine their subsequent thought and actions.

Follett reiterates her belief that small groups linked by relationships are both the natural order of society and the most effective form of organization. She is often regarded as the founder of the 'human relations' school of thinking about management. One of her many later essays, 'The Process of Control', shows the direction her thinking had taken. Here she makes the argument – running somewhat against Fayol and his doctrine of unity of authority – that it is not possible for anyone to control a large organization:

> The ramifications of modern industry are too wide-spread, its organization too complex, its problems too intricate for it to be possible for industry to be managed by commands from the top alone. This being so, we find that when central control is spoken of, that does not mean a point of radiation, but the gathering of many controls existing through-out the enterprise.[31]

'Control', then, really means 'coordination'. What leaders do is to coordinate the activities of other, lower-level leaders cascading down through the organization. There are, she says, four different types of coordination:

1   coordination as the reciprocal relating of all the factors in a situation
2   coordination by direct contact of the responsible people concerned
3   coordination in the early stages
4   coordination as a continuing process[32]

The first of these is the most complex, and relates to the ideas first expounded in *Creative Experience*. When people work together they combine their thinking through a process of adjustment. In a game of doubles tennis, for example, each player has to adjust their thinking to take account of the movements and actions of their partner. In a large business orga-nization, the heads of each department constantly 'adjust' their thinking to reflect the actions and activities of their colleagues and their departments. All these different sets of adjustment, going on simultaneously, interpenetrate each other rather like circles on a Venn diagram. No department exists in isolation, nor is the organization just a set of departments; all the departments are bound together by this constantly changing cycle of action and adjustment. This in turn affects everything that the organization and its members do.

> If you accept my definition of control as a self-generating process, as the interweaving experience of all those who are performing a functional part of the activity under consideration, does not that constitute an imperative? Are we not every one of us bound to take some part consciously in this process? Today we are slaves to the chaos in which we are living. To get our affairs in hand, to feel a grip on them, to become free, we must learn, and practice, I am sure, the methods of collective control. To this task we can all devote ourselves. At the same time that we are selling goods or making goods, or

whatever we are doing, we can be working in harmony with this fundamental law of life. We can be assured that by this method, control is in our power.[33]

The Hawthorne experiments

Integration is a theme that appears in the work of the Australian psychologist Elton Mayo, who joined the faculty at Harvard Business School in 1926. He had already made a name for himself researching the causes of industrial fatigue and identifying measures that could be taken to reduce fatigue and increase productivity. His first major work, *Democracy and Freedom*, published while he was still working in Australia, touched on many of the same themes as Follett.[34] Mayo was not happy with the idea of separate technical and social systems in the workplace, and sought to find ways of bringing them together into a unified whole, which he felt reflected more accurately the reality of how people worked: the technical and the social constantly affected and influenced each other.

His chance to demonstrate this came in 1927 when he was approached by the management of Western Electric, a subsidiary of AT&T engaged in making telephone equipment including receivers and switches. Influenced by some of the new writings on psychology, Western Electric's management had begun conducting their own experiments in an effort to learn whether changing workplace conditions or layout would lead to higher productivity. The results were baffling. For example, the company experimented with changing the lighting in one workshop, expecting to find that increased levels of lighting would result in higher productivity. In fact the results appeared to show the opposite: reducing lighting levels increased productivity. Yet when interviewed, workers said that they like the brighter light and found it more stimulating. Several other experiments yielded similarly inconclusive results.[35]

Western Electric turned to Mayo for help. He and a team of Harvard academics including Fritz Roethlisberger and Thomas North Whitehead conducted a series of experiments over the course of several years. In an early article, Mayo describes one experiment wherein a researcher monitored the activity of a team of six young women assembling telephone relays. The researcher noted that the productivity of one woman fell dramatically during a two-week period when she was suffering problems at home, but rose to former levels once the problems were resolved. He also noted a steady rise in productivity coupled with a change in the attitude of the young women:

> The girls soon came to feel that the observer was there as a sympathetic listener and not as a gang-boss with fixed ideas about production. They talked freely every day, they lost their original shyness, and they confided to him most enlightening stories of the effect on them and others of 'holly-ragging' methods of supervision. That their liking for their work increased is shown not merely by these confidences but also by their record of absences which is only a fraction of the department average or of their own former habit.[36]

'So', said Mayo, 'the provision of an impartial person to observe change became itself the greatest change'. Accordingly the investigation changed its focus. As Roethlisberger and Dickson put it in the final report on the experiments:

> No longer were the investigators interested in testing for the effects of single variables. In the place of a controlled experiment, they substituted the notion of a social situation which needed to be described and understood as a system of interdependent elements. This situation included not only the external events but the meanings which individuals assigned to them: their attitudes toward them and their preoccupations about them.

Rather than trying to keep these 'psychological' factors constant, the investigators had to regard them as important variables in the situation.[37]

The findings were conclusive: social and psychological factors had a very powerful impact on production.[38] Mayo recounts another case of a young woman whose output had been falling, and which suddenly shot up to far higher than average. It was later found that she was living unhappily at home, and had then decided to share an apartment with some friends. Her personal happiness was reflected in her work. Mayo also makes the point she took the decision to change her life on her own, without any intervention from her employers.

As a result of the findings, Western Electric introduced a radical programme to interview each of its 40,000 employees. Mayo's team trained the interviewers for this task. There was no set programme, no questionnaire; employees were allowed to talk about whatever they wished. The result was a massive boost in productivity.

In subsequent work, Mayo emphasized the role of the supervisor: 'The method of the supervisor is the single most important "outside" influence. Home conditions may affect the worker and his work; a supervisor who can "listen" and not "talk" can in many instances almost completely compensate such depressing influences.'[39] Roethlisberger and Dickson went on to describe in more detail the social system at Hawthorne. They accepted the separation of technical and social systems, but argued that the latter was much more important. Among other things, relationships between employees, quite independent of any relationship with the supervisor, were also observed to have a strong effect.

Thomas Whitehead, son of the philosopher and mathematician Alfred North Whitehead, developed on all these ideas still further in his book *Leadership in a Free Society*, where he searched for general conclusions that could be drawn from the Hawthorne experience. He concluded that organization is one of the features of human civilization: 'structure arises as soon as people begin to do something together'.[40] Whereas the early psychologists, including Mayo in his earlier days, had focused on the individual, Whitehead followed Follett and shifted the focus to the group. He concluded that there were two kinds of groups: primary groups whose members were all in close proximity and knew each other, and secondary groups, whose members were dispersed inside larger organizations such as large companies, and did not know each other but nonetheless shared a common identity. It is these groups and the relations between them which are at the heart of the social dynamic in organizations. Whitehead believed that all organizations are composed of social relationships and social action; even a simple matter like exchanging tools in the workplace is a social act. 'It is the economic motive *within a social setting* that is of importance to human beings'[41] he wrote (1936: 21). He goes on to state that:

> *Business is the universal pattern of stable social organization everywhere and always.* Men seek the society of their fellow creatures, but they need something more than mere physical propinquity. To be satisfying, social contacts must provide for activities performed in common which lead to an immediate pleasure in the exercise of social skills and sentiments, and which are also logically ordered in terms of an ulterior purpose; by these means, stable relationships between persons become established. The ulterior purpose is to contribute to the future social situation.[42]
>
> (Ibid.)

One of the of the human relations school has been this notion that job satisfaction, and not mere wages, is an important motivator for workers.

Reflection

The limits of theory

How much impact did all of these good ideas and good intentions really have? It is easy to be cynical about the human relations school; as historians of labour tell us, conflicts between capital and labour continued, and in Britain in particular they increased in number after the Second World War. There are plenty of examples of firms that adopted enlightened employment policies; there are even more examples of those that did not. As pointed out earlier in this book, the same is true of scientific management; only a few hundred companies, certainly no more than a thousand, directly absorbed and applied the principles advocated by Taylor and his school.

So does this mean that management theories are just so much talking? Are they truly more discussed than acted upon? That danger of course exists, but it might be that management theories are important not for their direct impact on companies, but on the intellectual atmosphere within which those companies operate. They do not change management, except in a few cases. But what they do, if they survive and are disseminated, is change *thinking* about management.

In a thoughtful article in 2003, Paul Adler identified what he called Kondratian cycles in attitudes to human resource management and organization in the twentieth century.[43] First there was the industrial welfare movement which emphasized the role of the workers. Then came scientific management, which put the emphasis on technical systems. Human relations then drew the emphasis back to social systems, only to be succeeded by the systems rationalization movement in the 1950s and 1960s. In the 1970s and 1980s the emphasis switched back to people with a new interest in employee involvement, only for business process re-engineering (BPR) in the 1990s to turn the focus back to technical systems.

Adler is describing differences in emphasis, of course, not total revolutions. As we shall see, the human relations movement did not advocate the full uprooting of scientific management so much as modifying it to make it more human centred. But the picture described by Adler raises two interesting issues. First, as he says, it is possible to link each of these changes in direction with broader economic and social forces. Scientific management was a response to the needs for efficiency and labour peace and offered a rational solution. The human relations school emerged, even if only subconsciously, as a response to the threats of tyranny and the need for freedom and democracy. The systems rationalization school emerged from the Second World War and in response to the Cold War; the revival in interest in employee involvement came about as a result of worsening industrial relations in the 1970s, and BPR was at least in part a response to the challenge being posed by Japanese management; having tried and largely failed to absorb Japanese methods, Western management had to find its own solution.

That brings us to the second point. In each case, management thinkers were still chasing the phantom of a perfect solution. Companies must be technically efficient, comes the cry, or else they cannot compete and will fail. No, comes the answer, true efficiency comes from people; look after people and nurture them and they will grow your business for you. If the past hundred years have taught us anything, surely it is that both statements are true simultaneously. Organizations need both technical solutions and social solutions, and cannot do without both.

Elton Mayo and Mary Parker Follett disliked the polarization of social and technical solutions and sought ways of fusing them. Neither succeeded, in part because they made it clear that they privileged social systems heavily over technical solutions. The search for the right balance goes on, for example in the work of the Tavistock Institute (see Chapter 10); and of course, theorists are shooting at a moving target because as Chester Barnard reminds us (see below), the point of balance is always changing.

But, to come back to the original point: the legacy of the human relations school is still present in the debate. When, today, managers and educators and policy makers speak about empowerment and participation and the rights of the employee, they are – whether they know it or not – using the concepts and sometimes the exact words of the human relations school; just as when they talk about efficiency and training and the need for accurate data and information, they are harking back to scientific management. The truth is that most managers are using human relations concepts in their own vocabulary, every day.

Insights from practitioners

The works of the earlier industrial psychologists, Follett and the Hawthorne team were all widely read and discussed. Roethlisberger and Dickson's final report on Hawthorne, *Management and the Worker*, was a bestseller and was reprinted several times. In some ways, though, the Hawthorne team were merely codifying and reinforcing conclusions that others had come to earlier. This is not meant in any way to play down the achievements of Mayo and his colleagues; rather, the presence of so much evidence from so many other sources tends to confirm and reinforce their findings.

To their credit, some members of the scientific management school quickly picked up on these new concepts and incorporated them into their own thinking. Frank and Lillian Gilbreth, in a contribution to the May 1916 issue of the *Annals of the American Academy of Political and Social Science*, advanced an idea for worker selection and promotion based on psychological insights.[44] Dexter Kimball's popular textbook *Principles of Industrial Organization*, based on the course he taught at Cornell University, made the point that 'while no doubt some form of organization must always be employed, especially for the rank and file of the workers, care should be exercised that the administrative methods do not throttle the initiative and enthusiasm of even the lowest subordinate. Genius does not work well in harness, and men are always more important than machines or methods.'[45] It may have been Kimball who first coined the term 'human relations' to describe the new way of thinking.

That scientific management and the human relations approach could coexist in the same workplace was shown at Joseph & Feiss, a garment manufacturer in Cleveland. Richard Feiss, vice-president of the company, was an enthusiastic proponent of scientific management, introducing task analysis and a differential rate system. When workers struck against the introduction of the new system, Feiss realized that he needed to get their support. He created an employment and service department and in 1913, on the advice of Meyer Bloomfield, hired Mary Barnett Gilson to run it.[46]

Feiss and Gilson based their philosophy on the concept of 'personal relationships' between managers and employees. There were several elements to this. One of the key concepts was organization fitness, which Gilson divided into two types: fitness for one's position – i.e. how well one could do a particular job – and fitness for the organization, or in other words 'fitting' with the organization's culture and values. Gilson created a detailed framework for assessing fitness and managing people more generally, including physical and mental fitness tests for new recruits, interviews, orientation and training programmes, home visits by welfare workers, employee counselling for those who needed it, and employee participation in decision making. She stressed that this last had to be done in the genuine spirit of collaboration; there must be no sense that employers were condescending to their workers when asking for their views. As Simone Phipps says, 'she understood the spiritual value of democracy' in much the same way that Follett did.[47]

Gilson was also very much aware that what happened in the workers' homes affected their work. Hence she tried to keep in touch with what was happening in their daily lives through conversations and home visits. Given that she had begun developing this system in 1913, it is hardly surprising that in 1940 she criticized Roethlisberger and Dickson's *Management and the Worker* for 'discovering the obvious' and remarked that the researchers seemed to lack experience in industrial practice.[48]

Gilson was also aware of her own responsibility; by becoming involved with her employees on such a personal level, she was in effect acquiring power over them, and that power needed to be used wisely. A popular textbook, Henry Dutton's *Principles of Organization*, also warned students of the human consequences of their actions as managers:

> Dealing thus with people, having the power to move them to action which may be beneficial or harmful to them, the organizer or executive assumes a responsibility which is not light. Organization is a technique, a tool, which may be used for evil as well as good.[49]

One of the leading lights in the business world to contribute to the human relations movement was Henry Dennison, described by John Kenneth Galbraith as 'arguably the most interesting businessman in the United States at the time'.[50] Dennison broke ranks with the prevailing movement of the time which favoured individual reward systems such as the premium plan and the differential rate system, and brought in a pooled profit-sharing system for employees in 1911; around 1924, he introduced a complex employee shareholding system which allowed employees to own part of the company but had safeguards to prevent a hostile takeover. Dennison's writings on employee ownership and co-partnership betray a high level of understanding of psychological and organizational concepts. He recognized the need for job satisfaction, and reached independently the same conclusion as the Hawthorne researchers, namely that relationships between workers and supervisors and between workers themselves were an important factor in productivity. Kyle Bruce argues that Dennison should be recognized as an important contributor to the human relations school.[51]

Much the same can be said of Edward Filene, the Boston department store owner whose book *Successful Living in this Machine Age* set out his own personal philosophy. Filene admired Taylor and scientific management, and succeeded in applying some of the techniques of scientific management to sales and marketing.[52] Filene believed that mass production would ultimately have a liberating effect, creating wealth and eradicating poverty, and that freedom would follow on from the higher standards of living thus achieved. But, this goal would only be achieved if businesses recognized their own responsibility, paid good wages and helped their employees to improve their lives. He too recognized that employees longed to find value and meaning in their work, and were motivated by more than just wages: 'we are all employers or workers or consumers, to be sure, but most of us are something vastly more. Most of us are human beings, and because we are human beings, we long to rise above the mere job of staying alive.'[53]

Two executives with the Metropolitan Life Insurance Company, Lee Frankel and Alexander Fleischer, were also emphatic about the need to consider motivational factors in their book *The Human Factor in Industry*. By finding ways of increasing production, they write, scientific management had solved one problem and created another. Workers did not work to increase production, they worked for reward which would allow them to enjoy their leisure time. Any move to increase production that does not also increase employee happiness is doomed to failure:

> The individual employé cannot abstract himself from his labor power, he cannot look at it as a commodity, and when an employment manager or a scientific manager assumes the authority of an expert in devising means by which the employé may double or quadruple his labor power, the latter naturally looks for the personal benefit to be derived therefrom.[54]

In advance of her time too was Cornelia Stratton Parker, widow of the economist Carleton Parker, who entirely on her own initiative decided to conduct studies into the motivations of workers, especially women workers. The results were published as *Working with the Working Woman* in 1922. This remarkable book, now seldom read, is in its way as revealing as the accounts of the Hawthorne experiments. Parker's single-handed study was much smaller than the latter, but reached many of the same conclusions.

Parker had become disenchanted with the literature on work, believing that much of it was too theoretical and had little grounding in practice. 'Suppose that for the moment your main intellectual interest was to ascertain what the average worker . . . thought about his jobs and things in general. To what books could you turn? Indeed I have come to feel that in the pages of O. Henry there is more to be gleaned on the psychology of the working class than books to be found on economics shelves.'[55]

Her solution was to spend time with women in the workplace, talking to them and also observing what they did and how they did it. The result is a series of chapters which portray working women, partly in their own words, and reveal a great deal about their own attitudes and thoughts. Parker argued that this methodology ought to be used more widely; because labour is a dynamic process, very much linked to human nature, its study should be dynamic too. She called for more understanding and cooperation between workers and employers, and like nearly every writer of her time, believed that such cooperation would result in more energetic and committed workers and, hence, higher productivity.

Even some of the most conservative employers began to recognize the need for change. Daniel Guggenheim, chairman of the mining corporation ASARCO, had long advocated using force to break strikes, but the wave of violent strikes which swept through his industry in 1911–13 which resulted in the deaths of a number of workers and company security guards seems to have brought about a change of heart. In 1914 Guggenheim and John D. Rockefeller, Jr of Standard Oil met with Samuel Gompers of the American Federation of Labour to discuss a plan for general industrial peace.

This was the start of a Damascene conversion for Guggenheim, who startled the Commission on Industrial Relations in 1915 by stating in evidence that workers were justified in organizing into unions when they were treated badly by employers. 'The men want more comforts', he said, 'more of the luxuries of life. They are entitled to them. I say this because humanity owes it to them.'[56] That same year, 1915, he wrote in an article, 'I think the difference between the rich man and the poor man is very much too great, and it is only by taking steps to bridge the gulf between them that we shall be able to get away from the unrest now prevailing among the working classes.'[57] By this point Guggenheim was thinking about more than just ending labour unrest. In his view, bringing capital and labour together to work for a common interest required an understanding of worker motivation, and a recognition that workers had rights equal to those of capitalists. Guggenheim also believed that the problem was too big for industry to fix on its own, and he called on government, workers and capitalists to work jointly for a solution.

The younger John D. Rockefeller was another who recognized that change was needed. In 1914 he called in the noted labour lawyer and future prime minister of Canada, William Lyon Mackenzie King, to work out a peace plan between employers and workers at one of his companies, Colorado Fuel & Iron. Mackenzie King's proposals required Rockefeller and his directors to recognize the legitimacy of worker interests and, more, to begin to treat workers as partners in enterprise. As Daphne Taras says, 'enlightenment had to occur at the top'.[58] Mackenzie King's idea was to set up a series of councils with equal representation by managers and workers, which would help to ensure cooperation. But Mackenzie King was adamant that such a plan would only work if both sides were willing to make it work (and indeed, as Taras says, the plan was only a partial success for that reason). In his later book *Industry and Humanity*, Mackenzie King argued that the current relationship between capital and labour is based on fear, and called for a new relationship based on faith and trust.[59]

Exhortations to both sides to remember their essential humanity make Mackenzie King's book worth reading today. Worth reading too is Esther Lowenthal's article on the employment policies at the Oneida silver works in New York.[60] The business had been founded by the utopian socialist Oneida commune, and continued as a joint-stock company after the commune broke up. Lowenthal describes how some of the ethos of the commune continued to permeate management thinking, particularly about labour relations. Oneida workers were paid good wages plus a share of the profits and had the opportunity to buy shares in the company, but they were also treated almost as family by managing director Pierrepont Noyes and his senior staff. The atmosphere was inclusive rather than paternalistic; Noyes put key decisions to his workers, asked for their opinions and listened to their voices. As a result, staff turnover was almost non-existent and worker grievances were rare; one union organizer, after visiting the company and talking to its workers, reported back to his headquarters that there no point in even trying to form a union at Oneida. The company was also highly profitable.

The human relations movement in the wider world

The human relations school drew some of its inspiration from the Enlightenment and European philosophy, but it was also a very strongly American school in terms of both context and ideals. It is probably no coincidence that it emerged in its fullest form in the aftermath of the First World War, when ideals such as peace and harmony and collaboration were very much in the public consciousness in America. There is a natural fit between the ideals of the human relations movement and those of, say, the League of Nations. As totalitarian governments began to strengthen their grip in Russia, Germany, Italy and Japan, America's view of itself as the beacon of democracy grew stronger, and this too provided the human relations school – itself based on the ideals of democracy and freedom – with a further push.

That the human relations school did not catch on widely elsewhere in the world – save for Britain, which we shall come onto in a moment – is thus unsurprising. The notion that workers should have a voice and participate in decision making was hardly going to find favour in the repressive regimes then emerging. Indeed, as we saw in Chapter 6, humanistic management and industrial democracy were one of the casualties of totalitarianism in Europe. There were exceptions; for example, managers in Finland were aware of the human relations school from the early 1930s onward, and its ideas were discussed and written about there.[61]

Yet we should not be too pessimistic. There were management thinkers elsewhere in the world who did come up with ideas that bear striking similarities to the human relations school. In Japan, the textile mill owner Ohara Magosaburo evolved by about 1919 a concept he called *rodo riso shugi*, or 'labour idealism'. Harmony between capital and labour was one of the key platforms of labour idealism. Ohara introduced an extensive employee welfare scheme, and also provided education for his employees and their children. He was associated with the Ohara Institute for Social Research and the Kurashiki Institute for the Science of Labour, the latter founded in 1921. Ohara was a committed Christian and personal belief played a large role in his ideas, but both institutes also used techniques from psychology to study the workplace and interpersonal relations. It seems likely that there was at least some influence from America during the 1920s, but in the 1930s as Japan became increasingly militaristic this research was halted.[62]

An interesting precursor to Follett and some of the other writers of the human relations school comes from the Middle East before the First World War. Here the Nahda (Awakening) movement was attempting to both modernize Islam and revive national pride among the Arabic and Persian peoples with a view to recovering their lost independence. The three key figures in this movement were the Egyptian scholar Muhammad 'Abduh, the Lebanese writer and journalist Muhammad Rashid Rida and the Persian scholar and politician Jamaluddin al-Afghani. Rida wrote several books including an important book on women's rights, and al-Afghani was known as a political and legal modernist, but for our purposes it is 'Abduh who is most interesting. His book *Risalat al-Tawhid* (Theology of Unity), published in 1897, advocates a kind of integration in society that would have appealed to Mary Parker Follett. He also believes that community is the natural form of organization for human beings, and that belonging to a community makes us stronger, not weaker. 'Man has a natural propensity for community', says 'Abduh. 'But unlike bees and ants, for example, he has not been granted the instinctive facility for what community requires.'[63] Successful organizations require leaders, and 'Abduh talks at length of the qualities required in a leader, reviving the old Islamic notion of the servant-leader (see Chapter 3).

'Abduh's ideal organizations and communities are held together not by self-interest or gain, but by love. He describes love as a kind of strong force that draws people together and makes them desire to associate with each other; and it is also the basis of the bond between leaders and followers. Developing genuine bonds of love within an organization is, for 'Abduh, one of the highest goals of leadership.

Around the same time as 'Abduh was writing, Mohandas Karamchand (Mahatma) Gandhi arrived in South Africa to begin practising as a lawyer. Gandhi was a specialist in labour law, and between 1893 and 1915 he worked with labour movements as well as opposition political groups. Returning to India, he worked with a number of labour unions, most famously the textile workers union at Ahmadabad, and served as a conciliator helping to resolve labour disputes. One of the core elements of Gandhi's personal philosophy was the need for peaceful coexistence and mutual cooperation between all groups in society, and he used this philosophy to good effect as a conciliator.

Like many in the human relations school, Gandhi believed that capital and labour shared common interests and a common goal, the creation of prosperity. For either to achieve prosperity at the expense of the other would be a violation of the principle of *satyagraha*, or 'holding fast to truth'; in other words, we might say that it would be a violation of natural law. His usual method of resolving a dispute was to identify the common interests and common ground between the parties, and then persuade them to recognize these common interests too; from there, a solution to the dispute could be worked out. To employers, he argued the need for profit-sharing and facilities such as education that would help employees to enrich their lives; to workers, he stressed the need for discipline and harmony. He was a particular advocate of *sanyyam* or self-discipline, 'blossoming where there is an inner harmony as a result of inner strength'.[64]

Rather than emphasizing self-interest, then, Gandhi took a position that both parties were equal, and that the only fair result was one that rewarded both equally. He took a similar view of leadership, a subject on which he wrote frequently. His writings on leadership show an eclectic range of influences from classical Hindu and Jain philosophy and modern European figures such as John Ruskin and Leo Tolstoy; he is quite at home quoting Euclid and the *Bhagavad-Gita* in the same article. Rather like 'Abduh, Gandhi extols the virtues of the servant-leader, and argues too that the process of becoming a leader is never complete:

> The goal ever recedes from us. The greater the progress, the greater the recognition of our unworthiness. Satisfaction lies in the efforts not in the attainment. Full effort is full victory.[65]

Leadership, like life, is a journey rather than a destination, a journey spent in the constant pursuit of wisdom. Gandhi's ideas continue to exert much influence in India, and many Indian business people look to him as role model, even though his own socialist economic views are somewhat at odds with Indian capitalism as practised today.

There is less evidence of progressive thinking in China where many industries, especially in mining and manufacturing, used a form of contract labour where the business owner bought in labour from a third-party contractor. This contractor continued to be responsible for the pay, feeding and discipline of the workers, and in some cases for providing the tools with which they worked. In this way, writes Tim Wright, the managers were able to avoid responsibility for their workers entirely.[66] This system was widely abused. Some of the workers received no pay at all, and barely enough food to keep them alive; conditions in many workplaces amounted to little more than slavery, while the contractors enriched themselves by pocketing the money intended to pay wages and buy food and tools. Small firms used an apprenticeship system, and the lot of the apprentices was often equally grim; apprenticeship contracts were known as *maishenqi*, or 'body-selling' contracts.[67]

However, as Min-Ch'ien Tyau reported in his book *China Awakened*, published in 1922, there were signs that China was beginning to absorb lessons from the West. An organization called 'The Union for the Improvement of Chinese Labour' in Shanghai had been founded for the purpose of lobbying for better working conditions for all workers. Enlightened employers such as Sincere, the Hong-Kong based department store that also had a branch in Shanghai, and the Commercial Press were following the example of American and British firms. The Commercial Press, indeed, allowed women workers who became pregnant to take two months' maternity leave and gave them a small amount of maternity pay; both these practices were far from standard even in the West. Tyau notes too that the Commercial Press had loyal employees and was paying an increasingly large dividend to its shareholders as a result of high productivity. Tyau also quotes H.Y. Moh, the 'Cotton King of China', as saying:

> The modern capitalist values highly the energy of his employees because it is the unseen capital of industry. The employees must be trained to exert their energy scientifically or economically. It should not be wasted. The employer should always be on the alert as to the increase of his employees' energy through proper boarding, sanitation, peace of mind and timely rest. Human efficiency can be increased through education. It is the duty of the employer to educate the laborers. The more he tries to do so, the more efficient they will become.[68]

Speaking at the opening of a new cotton mill, Moh stated:

> This mill is not only owned by the shareholders, but by the employees; not only jointly owned by the shareholders and employees but by the people of this city. So this mill should be considered public property, from which people can get money for their labour.[69]

Tyau was painting a deliberately rosy picture, trying to improve his country's image in the West while simultaneously trying to persuade his own people to undertake further social and political reforms. Nevertheless, there is at least some evidence that elements of human relations thinking had reached China, though the onset of war with Japan and the military occupation of much of the country would soon snuff out this small beginning.

Attempts at fusion

Of all the countries outside America, however, it is probably Britain where the movement had the most impact. As we saw in Chapter 6, Mary Parker Follett and Henry Dennison both lectured in Britain and were warmly received; Follett spent several years at the London School of Economics before her death. And as we saw in Chapter 6 too, the humanistic element was already pretty well engrained in homegrown British management thinking, so there was a natural fit with human relations thinking. John Lee and Lyndall Urwick in particular were well received in America.

An ambitious attempt to pull together British and American human relations thinking and combine them with scientific management, Fayol's theory of general management, Emerson's efficiency theory and older concepts of the firm is James Mooney and Alan Reiley's *Onward Industry!* first published in 1931. Mooney was president of General Motors's overseas division, supervising operations in more than a hundred companies, and one of the senior team around Alfred Sloan at GM. It is believed that most of the ideas in *Onward Industry!* are his.

Opinion is divided as to the significance of this work. Some believe it to be a throwback to Taylorism, and management historian Daniel Wren maintains that the book 'became a building block for a formalistic view of organizations'.[70] It is true that Mooney and Reiley do take a more formal and bureaucratic view than, say, Mary Parker Follett, but there is plenty of evidence of other ideas too. One important influence is John Davis, the American lawyer and historian whose book *Corporations* clearly helped to shape their thinking about the role and purpose of organizations. Like him, Mooney and Reiley see organization as a natural part of civilization, the 'form of every human association for the attainment of a common purpose'.[71]

Mooney and Reiley trace the origins of the modern business organization, which they see as being a direct descendant – in terms of organizational form – of the medieval monastic orders such as the Benedictines, and the professional military organizations of the nineteenth century, such as the Prussian army of Clausewitz and Moltke. They adopt the line-and-staff model from Emerson, but with some strong modifications; the role of the staff is not that of director or general, but rather it serves to coordinate and to transmit information: 'The line and staff . . . must not be thought of as segregated functions. The idea of a staff that simply recommends, or of a line that simply does what the staff recommends, would be an absurdity in organization.'[72]

Despite the bureaucratic form that modern organizations appear to take, Mooney and Reiley are advocates of decentralization and delegated authority in terms similar to those used by Follett. They also use the biological metaphor of organization, again adapting from Emerson. In their conception, management is the 'vital spark' that animates and moves an organization; elsewhere they refer to management as a 'psychic force'.

> The technique of management, in its human relationships, can be best described as the technique of handling or managing people, which should be based on a deep and enlightened human understanding. The technique of organization may be described as that of relating specific duties or functions in a completely coordinated scheme. This statement of the difference between managing and organizing clearly shows their intimate relationship. It also shows, which is our present purpose, that the technique of organizing is inferior, in logical order, to that of management. . . . The prime necessity in all organization is harmonious relationships based on integrated interests, and, to this end, the first essential is an integrated and harmonious relationship in the duties, considered in themselves.[73]

This is pure human relations school thinking (note again that this work appeared prior to the first studies of the Hawthorne project). Mooney and Reiley go on to discuss the human factor in the workplace, and conclude that the three principles of personnel management must be 'universal adequacy of compensations, the adjustment of each compensation to the merit of the service, and the recognition of the right of every man to grow'.[74] The second principle could have come straight from Frederick Taylor; the third sounds more like Jean-Jacques Rousseau, or even Kautilya and his concept of the king as keeper of the *dharma*. Mooney and Reiley argue that businesses have a duty not just to help the mental and spiritual development of their employees; they also have a duty to stimulate the desire to grow, to encourage people to do more than just exist and make a living. The church, they say, has as part of its mission the stimulation of spiritual growth among the people. Industry should take on some of that same role.

In a later paper, Mooney expands on this view: 'Worthiness in the industrial sphere can have reference to one thing only, namely the contribution of industry to the sum total of human welfare. On this basis only must industry and all its works finally be judged.'[75] Here again he is following John Davis, and beyond him a tradition of thinking going back at least to the Middle Ages concerning the relationship between business and society. Mooney himself seems to have understood and taken that relationship and responsibility seriously. Upon the outbreak of the Second World War he used his personal connections to secure interviews with both Hitler and Mussolini in a vain attempt to persuade them to halt military action. These attempts were complete failures, as Mooney must have known they would be. What is interesting is his view that given his unique position and contacts, it would be morally wrong for him not to at least try to avert war.[76]

If Mooney was looking back to older views on the relationship between business and society, Luther Gulick was looking forward to the development of a new discipline, public administration, whose sole purpose was to serve society. Prior to Gulick's day, there had not been many significant advances in thinking about 'public sector management' since the days of Fitz Neal and Hubert Walter. A few individuals do stand out. Following the Crimean War of 1854–5 Florence Nightingale, learning the lessons from her own (not always successful) interventions in the conflict, helped to lay the ground for more professional management in health care, and more advances were made by doctors in Europe and America as the century wore on. Also in Britain, Octavia Hill and Ebenezer Howard had begun to develop theories about housing and public services.[77]

In America, the rapid growth of cities put pressure on the authorities to come up with more systematic approaches to public administration. In New York, the Bureau of Municipal Research was founded as a private organization in 1906, with the remit of coming up with more rigorous and systematic methods of managing public expenditure and delivering public services. To what extent the Bureau was directly influenced by scientific management is not clear, but George Hopkins's description of the Bureau in 1912 shows that they definitely shared common principles.[78] By 1911 the Bureau had established a training centre for public employees. Gulick took charge of this training centre upon his return from military service in 1919, and became director of the Bureau itself in 1921. In 1924 the Bureau became the National Institute for Public Administration, and Gulick soon became known as one of the leading international figures in this field.

In earlier times, business leaders had borrowed ideas about management from the public sector. By the 1920s the shoe was on the other foot; management thinking in the business world had advanced far beyond that of the public sector. Gulick borrowed theory and ideas from many different sources, including Urwick, Fayol, Mooney, Follett and scientific management. He himself did not do a great deal of theorizing; in a professional career spanning more than seventy years he produced a great many articles and reports, but most are technical works on specific subjects. In his collaboration with Urwick, however, Gulick also produced some notable ideas on public organization. He was responsible for elaborating on Fayol's original five categories of managerial responsibility, expanding this to seven using the acronym POSDCORB: planning, organizing, staffing, directing, coordinating, reporting and budgeting.[79]

Gulick argues that there was no essential difference between public organizations and businesses; both sought to reach their goals as efficiently as possible. Organizations to Gulick are tools, means to achieving an end. He is of the view that one determines the end result desired and then builds an organization capable of meeting, clearly prefiguring the 'structure follows strategy' approach of Alfred Chandler.[80]

Gulick inclines towards a holistic view of organization. He borrows some ideas from scientific management, and accepts that the division of labour is necessary in order to achieve efficiency, but argues against the more atomistic approach of Taylor. Sometimes, he says, division of labour simply makes no sense. For example, it might be technically more efficient to have the front half of the cow out in the pasture grazing at the same time as the rear half is in the garden being milked, but in reality any attempt to divide a cow in this fashion was clearly doomed to failure.

All the efforts of labour, divided or no, must be harmonized towards the organization's goals. Gulick is clearly influenced by Follett's ideas on coordination, and himself comes up with a fourfold classification of coordination: coordination by purpose (that is, by the aims of the unit); coordination by process (what the unit actually does, such as engineering or accounting); coordination by persons or things (customers served, products made and the like); and coordination by geographical place or location. However, he says, it is not quite that simple. At any given time, two, three or all four of these methods of coordination may be necessary at once.

This of course greatly complicates the task of the manager, but fortunately there is a fifth means of coordination which can itself help to unify the other four: coordination through ideas.

> Any large and complicated enterprise would be incapable of effective organization if reliance for co-ordination were placed in organization alone. Organization is necessary; in a large enterprise it is essential, but it does not take the place of a dominant central idea as the foundation of action and self-co-ordination in the daily operation of all parts of the enterprise. Accordingly, the most difficult task of the chief executive is not command, it is leadership, that is, the development of the desire and will to work together for a purpose in the minds of those who are associated in any activity.[81]

Ideally, says Gulick, each organization should have a single guiding idea which is universally understood by all its members. In a later work, *Administrative Reflections from World War II*, Gulick attributes the Allied victory to the fact that the Allied armies were united by a single strong idea.[82] Finally, Gulick lists the factors which hinder or prevent coordination from being carried out. There are five of these: uncertainty about the future, lack of knowledge on the part of the leaders of the organization, lack of management skills on the part of the leaders, lack of management skills elsewhere in the organization, and finally 'the vast number of variables involved and the incompleteness of human knowledge, particularly with regard to man and life', Clausewitz's friction in another form.[83]

A year after Gulick and Urwick published *Papers on the Science of Administration* the most ambitious attempt yet at synthesizing management theory was published. Chester Barnard's *The Functions of the Executive* is generally agreed to be one of the most profound books on management ever written – as well as one of the most difficult to read. This dense, multilayered work is capable of a number of interpretations, and thanks to Barnard's inclusive approach to his subject, modern writers in subjects as diverse as organization theory, strategy, leadership, ethics and marketing have claimed him as a tutelary deity. He himself acknowledged a vast number of intellectual influences, including earlier writers on scientific management and human relations, psychologists, writers on law and politics and philosophers stretching back to Plato and Aristotle.[84]

Barnard spent much of his career as a senior executive at New Jersey Bell Telephone, becoming its president in 1927. In the course of his wide reading, he became concerned that much of current theory on organization was too theoretical and not realistic. There was too much emphasis on rational behaviour. Scientific management in particular seemed to rest on the view that people would always act in their own self-interest. This did not accord with his own view, and in the 1930s he began developing his ideas, first as lectures and then as his major work, *The Functions of the Executive*.

Barnett, like Follett and Fayol, believed that cooperation and coordination were the main tasks of management. He cautioned that successful coordination, while very easy to talk about and describe, is very hard to achieve – and in fact, most organizations never achieve it. 'Successful cooperation in or by formal organizations is the abnormal, not the normal condition', he says. 'What are observed from day to day are the successful survivors among innumerable failure.'[85]

All organizations seek to achieve a dual equilibrium. Like Fayol, Barnard maintains that organizations require external equilibrium – that is, to be in harmony with their external environment, markets, social pressures and so on – and internal equilibrium, meaning that the parts of the organization have to work together in harmony. Yet this is not easy, for pressure of events means that the situation is always dynamic. Coordination plays a vital role in making certain that equilibrium is maintained; one is reminded of Follett and her doubles tennis players constantly reacting to each others' movements. Barnard calls this the theory of 'dynamic equilibrium', and the concept remains present in much thinking about organization today.

Barnard also draws a distinction – perhaps for the first time – between *effectiveness* and *efficiency*. Effectiveness refers simply to the organization's ability to carry out its purpose and meet its goals. His views on efficiency are interesting, and rather ahead of their time. True efficiency, Barnard suggests, stems not from technical systems but from the willingness of people to contribute to the organization in terms of time, labour and skills.

That willingness in turn depends on what people themselves receive from the organization. That means money, but also more than money; satisfaction and other motivating factors are present too. As Andrea Gabor and Joseph Mahoney point out, Barnard anticipates the theories of Maslow and Herzberg, both of whom posited complex series of motivational factors;[86] and, as we have seen, other business leaders including Henry Dennison and Edward Filene had earlier reached much the same conclusion.

The role of the leader, the executive, is to manage this process of dynamic equilibrium so as to ensure efficiency and effectiveness both are maintained. Barnard's views of how leaders actually work are interesting, and in some ways anticipate those of Bennis and Mintzberg (although Mintzberg was critical of Barnard).[87] He stresses the need for trust and empathy, and acknowledges that some decisions are intuitive rather than rational; he sees no harm in this. He also writes of the importance of faith, not necessarily religious faith, but faith in the organization and its purpose; one of the tasks of the leader is to create that faith (recall Muhammad 'Abduh and the need to create love). His worldview, showing now the influence of Plato, is grounded in conceptions of morality. 'Organizations endure, however, in proportion to the breadth of morality by which they are governed', he says in one famous passage. 'This is only to say that foresight, long purposes, high ideals are the basis for the persistence of cooperation.'[88]

Conclusion

The human relations school and scientific management are sometimes seen as competing or opposing paradigms. That is too simplistic. Many members of the human relations school were directly or indirectly critical of scientific management as a body of thought for lacking awareness of the human factor, or even lacking in humanity. The purpose of human relations theory was to fill that gap and to 'humanize' management thinking. It did so quite successfully, as we have seen; even some of the scientific management school shifted position to accommodate these new ideas.

The human relations school did not supplant scientific management. Nor did it continue to exist as a coherent school of thought for much longer; Barnard's work was in effect its completion. The post-Second World War period saw attention turned in different directions. As we shall see in the next chapter a process of 'divisonalization' was taking place in management thought, with thinkers concentrating on particular aspects of management rather than management in the round.

8　The growth of management disciplines

Practiced experience, as well as the best economic theory, lays emphasis upon the importance of an able manager.

(Thomas L. Greene)

Thus far, we have discussed ideas about management as simply 'management', with only occasional allusions to accounting, marketing and so on. We have looked at theories which discuss how firms should be run, to what purpose or end, and by whom. But this is not the full picture. From the beginning of the twentieth century, other thinkers were beginning to consider aspects of business, marketing and corporate finance in particular, but also other subjects such as corporate governance, business economics and theories of the firm, international business, business education and, eventually and rather belatedly, business strategy. All of these grew into managerial disciplines in their own right, with their own bodies of theory and their own practitioners, consultants, educators and students.

In this chapter, we shall look at a few of these disciplines and how they grew, up until roughly the early 1960s. It is not my intention to give a comprehensive history of each and every discipline associated with management: that is a task for an encyclopedia of the history of management, not a general survey such as this book. The purpose of this chapter is to describe a further stage in the overall evolution of management thought, the process of divisionalization into separate disciplines and to consider how – and more importantly why – this evolution happened.

Theories about people

The Hawthorne experiments had awakened the interest of many psychologists in the problems of human relations in the workplace, and following the Second World War this became an important field of research. Whereas before the war there had been inputs from economics, from broader management theory and from direct managerial experience, like that of Fayol, Mooney and Barnard, in the 1940s and 1950s this field became heavily scientized, largely the province of psychologists and sociologists. This is very likely the effect of the Hawthorne studies themselves, or rather of the publications that came out of those studies, which were very widely read. Many succeeding studies used the Hawthorne methodology, or variants on it.

Studies in the 1940s and 1950s generally fell into one of two types. First, there were studies which focused on groups and group dynamics. These studies were especially influenced by the German-born psychologist Kurt Lewin, who taught at Massachusetts Institute of Technology until his death in 1947. Lewin came from the same Gestalt tradition that had influenced Mary Parker Follett, and he took a holistic view of groups and organizations. He sought to bring together techniques from psychology and sociology, showing how individual motivation was affected by external factors, including the actions and views of others in one's social network. Lewin influenced other groups, most notably the Tavistock Institute of Human Relations, founded in Britain in 1946. The Tavistock Institute devoted much of its time to field work, studying group dynamics and the processes of cultural formation and cultural change. One early work, *The Changing Culture of a Factory* by Elliott Jaques, discussed how one business managed an effective process of cultural change to achieve both better human relations and greater business efficiency.[1]

We will come back to the Tavistock Institute later in this book, as the most important works of its members were not published until the later 1960s and 1970s. The group context continued to be important for some American thinkers too, notably Keith Davis whose *Human Relations in Business* focused on groups rather than just on individuals.[2] During the 1950s, as a result of field work in both France and America, Michel Crozier developed his theory of 'systems of actions' which describes how the collective behaviour of groups responds to various stimuli, including changes in relative power within organizations.[3]

The second group of studies focused first of all on the motivation of individuals, and considered groups largely in terms of how their behaviour might affect individuals. The key question most researchers in this group were asking was: what motivates people to work – and in particular to work effectively? This was the question the Hawthorne researchers had stumbled across, and now psychologists attempted to answer it more fully. An important influence here was the behavioural psychologist Abraham Maslow. Rejecting the Freudian view that most human behaviour was driven by physical needs such as hunger or sex, Maslow constructed his famous 'hierarchy of needs', a fivefold ascending classification beginning with basic physical needs, followed by the need for safety, the need for society and companionship or love, the need for self-esteem and finally the need for self-actualization. As each lower-level need is satisfied, people turn to the fulfilment of the next need in the hierarchy: for example, if we have enough to eat and a roof over our heads, our next need will be for the company of others, and so on.[4]

Maslow's theory reinforced earlier ideas that people go to work for reasons other than money; they work because they seek the society of others, because their work makes them feel good about themselves and they find it personally fulfilling. His work was advanced and developed by Frederick Herzberg, who posited two types of motivational factors at work, actualization factors and environmental or 'hygiene' factors. The first group concerns things that people desire, such as achievement and recognition for achievement, responsibility and the possibility of personal growth. Environmental factors are things external to the person but which affect motivation, such as the quality of management in a firm, pay, working conditions, job security and factors in one's personal life.[5]

The third pre-eminent figure from this period is Douglas McGregor. He argued that there are two competing theories of how to manage people, Theory X and Theory Y. Theory X assumes that most people are lazy and work-shy and also lack ambition; they will only work productively if they are coerced into doing so. Theory Y assumes that work is a natural human function, that most people will work effectively if motivated to do so and, what is more, most will naturally seek responsibility and try to rise to positions where they can exercise their own creativity and find more personal freedom. Theory X assumes people are motivated only by low-level physiological needs; Theory Y assumes that they are seeking self-esteem and self-actualization. Fairly obviously, McGregor thinks Theory Y is the way forward. Under Theory Y, organizations in effect become living systems, self-regulating and self-organizations, whereas Theory X organizations are mere machines.[6]

As well as Maslow, McGregor was also drawing on Chris Argyris, who had earlier argued that people whose motivations are on the upper end of the hierarchy of needs will not fit well into mechanistic organizations.[7] McGregor himself influenced Rensis Likert, who expanded on Theory X and Theory Y to create a fourfold classification of management systems: exploitative systems, benevolent systems, consultative systems and participative systems. Again, there is little doubt as to which Likert thinks is best.[8]

Maslow, Herzberg and McGregor were, and are, powerful influences on thinking about human behaviour in the workplace and the management of people. All three give us a highly optimistic picture. All people, or nearly all people, aspire to higher things. They cherish freedom and responsibility and they desire to be creative. The task of the manager is to motivate and inspire, and to give people the freedom to grow and develop. These views become more interesting when we look at the times and their own backgrounds. All three did most of their research and idea formation in the late 1940s and 1950s; McGregor's *The Human Side of Enterprise* was published the year John F. Kennedy was elected, 1960. They were writing at a time when America once again seemed to be the bastion of freedom and democracy, locked in struggle with repressive regimes in the Soviet Union and China. Maslow was the son of Jewish immigrants who had fled the pogroms in Russia; Herzberg, also the child of immigrants, had witnessed the horrors of Nazi death camps at the end of the Second World War. McGregor had been a professor at Antioch College, a very liberal institution which valued freedom, equality and self-expression.

All three were thus preconditioned towards a belief that freedom is a natural state and that all human beings, if given freedom, will aspire to higher things. Did this background affect their theories? It would be surprising if it did not. It is interesting to see how, with the passage of time, the beginnings of the Vietnam War, the protest movements of the later 1960s and Watergate, the picture becomes a little less rosy. The later work of David McClelland, for example, focus on motivational factors such as the need for achievement and the need for power, while Amitai Etzioni explored motivations for dissent and the impact of protest movements.[9] Both McClelland and Etzioni argued too that one could not understand organizations by looking at individual motivation alone. Eventually, the study of individual motivation and of group dynamics would join forces.

Marketing

Marketing's emergence as a discipline was almost exactly contemporaneous with that of scientific management. For most of two decades the two evolved pretty much independently, and only gradually did marketing become subsumed into the more general discipline of management.

Leading marketing theorists have advanced the view that marketing emerged when it did because the technological advances of the Industrial Revolution had led to first, an excess supply of goods over demand, meaning businesses had to resort to marketing techniques in order to create new demand and shift stock, and second, adequate transportation links so that goods could be shipped and sold over long distances.[10] There is some truth to the latter point, very little to the first. This is an example of what David van Fleet refers to as the problem of management scholars writing about history when they do not know enough history.[11] I have pointed out the fallacy of this view elsewhere, and will not belabour the point again; suffice it to say that in Chapters 2–4 of this book we saw plenty evidence of awareness by business leaders and thinkers about the behaviour of markets, price sensitivity, fluctuations of supply and demand and the like.[12] Lyndall Urwick believed that there was evidence of marketing being practiced at least back to the eighteenth century, and more recently Hamilton and Lai have described sophisticated marketing practices in China going back to the tenth century.[13] The owners of the Tongrentang pharmacy, founded in the seventeenth century, were certainly aware of most of the principles of marketing.[14]

Paul Cherington, appointed first professor of marketing at Harvard Business School in 1918, agreed that the work of he and his fellow marketing scholars was to understand and codify best practice, not invent a new field. He believed that the greater concentrations of capital and labour brought about by modern corporations meant that overproduction was now more likely than before, but accepted that this was not a new phenomenon. To Cherington, the decisive change in recent years was the breaking of the personal linkage between producers and consumers. Up to the middle of the nineteenth century, most businesses in America were small affairs selling primarily into local markets. These producers knew their customers and could anticipate demand with a fair degree of accuracy and manage their own production accordingly. Big manufacturers, however, produced goods for consumption not immediately but at some indefinite point in the future. They faced the task of trying to ensure their goods were sold at a price which recouped the costs of production, transport, distribution and storage.[15]

This probably holds true for America, which had a different development trajectory from Europe or Asia. As far back as antiquity, we have seen goods traded over long distances within and between Europe, the Middle East, India and China. By the eighteenth century the list of such goods being traded in bulk included corn, textiles, ceramics, glass, timber, salt, steel, leather, wine and spirits, sugar, spices, pharmaceuticals and tea among others. And yet, neither Europe nor China nor India developed a theory of marketing. Why then did one emerge in America, and why in the early twentieth century?

Cherington's separation between buyer and seller is part of the answer, but we must look at the demand side as well as the supply side. In the fifty years from the end of the Civil War, America's population more than doubled, from 39 million to 92 million.[16] Much of that population was concentrated in urban centres, and needed a steady supply of food and other commodities. Moreover, many of the millions of new arrivals in the country had come from small and impoverished communities in Eastern and Central Europe where they were used to buying goods from local producers or peddlers. Arriving in America and speaking little English, they found distribution and retail systems that were quite foreign to them. The challenge to business, then, was a social as well as an economic one. Businesses had to find a way not only to meet demand, but to make people aware of where and how they could purchase the goods they needed.

This is evident in Paul Cherington's description of marketing. The purpose of marketing, he says, is 'to effect a transfer of ownership of goods in exchange for what is considered to be an equivalent'.[17] The aim of the marketer is 'to bring a buyer and a seller together in a trading mood'; that is, to locate people who want to make a purchase and show them where and how they can buy.[18]

Bearing these principles in mind, Cherington goes on to describe the functions of marketing, which he classifies into three groups: merchandise functions, auxiliary functions and sales functions. Merchandise functions include delivery, or 'assembling', quality control, or 'grading and classing', storage and transportation. Auxiliary functions include financing and the assumption of risk. Cherington and many of his contemporaries considered both of these to be of great importance. Firms at the time tended to think of distribution as a cost-free activity, an activity which Cherington strongly corrects; large-scale distribution is very costly and requires capital, from either inside or outside the producing firm. The assumption of risk includes insurance to protect the actual goods from damage during distribution and hedging activities in case market forecasts turn out to be wrong and goods remain unsold. Finally, sales functions include selling, branding and advertising, the latter of which is essential in order to communicate with the consumer; for large producers, it replaces the face-to-face contact enjoyed by small local firms.

This is a very simple summary of this complex thinker's views, and does not really do him justice. A few other points need to be mentioned. Cherington thought it was important for consumers to educate themselves and get to know the market, and that educated consumers would in time force inefficient producers or those who produced low-quality goods out of the market. In later works he argued for the dynamic nature of demand, and also argued that free markets which do not regulate either demand or supply are most efficient, both in economic terms and in the creation of human happiness, as people are able to buy whatever they need.[19] As a side note, Cherington himself was never terribly happy with the term 'marketing' and preferred 'merchandising'; by about 1930, however, 'marketing' had finally become the accepted term.

It is also interesting that although Cherington had been researching and teaching on marketing-related subjects since the founding of Harvard Business School in 1908, it was another six years before the first specialist course on marketing was offered, and another four before Cherington was appointed professor of marketing. Even among its exponents, there was clearly some confusion as to how this new discipline fitted in with the rest of management.

Cherington and his colleagues at Harvard including Melvin Copeland took a view of marketing based on economics.[20] Another perspective came from Northwestern University where Walter Dill Scott was using psychology to investigate the mechanisms by which advertising worked. Advertising too had been around for centuries, as Henry Sampson had described earlier, but Scott was the first to try to analyse the workings of advertising in a scientific way. He argued that 'advertising is a case of mind meeting mind', and that a successful advertiser needed to understand the mind of the consumer.[21]

Scott developed a model of effect which he called 'attention-comprehension-understanding'. The message must first get the customer's *attention*, and it must do so by appealing to his or her perceptive senses. He described attention as the 'gateway' to the customer's mind, and spent some time describing how the senses work in physical terms and how they engage with the brain. Once the message is through the gateway, however, it must still be *comprehended*; that is, the customer must know what the message is about and what product it refers to. Provided the customer attends to and comprehends the message, however, there is a final hurdle to be got over; the customer must *understand* what relevance the message has to himself or herself; that is, will the product being advertised satisfy some personal need or desire? Scott seemed to take it for granted that, understanding having been achieved, action will follow. This was clearly a flaw, and a curious one. Scott was surely aware of the AIDA (awareness-interest-desire-action) model developed by Elias St Elmo Lewis a few years earlier, which made it clear that the consumer's understanding of the benefit to themselves, and taking action to make a purchase, were two different things.[22] In the end it was the AIDA model that went on to become more widely used, and is still used in advertising today. Scott and other writers based at Northwestern, most notably Fred Clark, went on to develop a school of thinking about advertising strongly grounded in psychology, just as thinkers at Harvard continued to follow Cherington's economics approach.[23]

Scientific management and marketing

Following the publication of *The Principles of Scientific Management* there were a number of attempts to apply Taylor's principles to marketing. One of the first writers to do so was the prolific Herbert Casson, who drew on Taylor as well as Emerson's efficiency theory in his book *Advertisements and Sales*. Casson took the view that the principles of scientific analysis of markets were already known to businesses: railways and steamship companies predicted the number of passengers they would carry, magazines and newspapers analysed their circulation figures and so on. Now companies had to become more systematic and efficient in their approach if they were to deal with rising competition; as he puts it, 'find better ways of doing the same old things'.[24] It is worth reiterating this point: rising competition, not rising production, is the factor forcing companies to think more rigorously about sales and marketing.

Casson's analysis is simplistic, and is more concerned with proving that it is possible to manage marketing and advertising in a scientific way than with laying down principles (although it should be added that he practised what he preached and went on to found a very successful advertising agency). A more sophisticated picture emerged in an article on retailing by C. Bertrand Thompson in *System* magazine, in which he began by broadening the concept of scientific management:

> The fundamental principles of scientific management as practised in industrial establishments are: first, the organization of the present scattered knowledge in regard to the business into a coherent science; and, second, the organization of the human and material factors involved to secure the most efficient application of the science.[25]

Exactly the same principles can be applied to retailing, said Thompson, and he went on to demonstrate this by developing a classification system for retail costs. He argued for more attention to be paid to the task element in retailing: for example, sales people should be given clearly defined tasks and set targets.

Advertising executive Charles Hoyt made many of the same points in his *Scientific Sales Management Today*, first published in 1913.[26] Hoyt suggested that sales management needs to be guided by the following four 'scientific' principles: (1) planning sales activity based on recognized and verified facts; (2) recruiting salesmen according to predetermined principles, so as to be sure to get the highest possible quality; (3) educating and training a sales force so that its members' skills are of the highest possible level; and (4) ensuring cooperation between all members of the sales force and between front-line staff and head office. Hoyt concentrated particularly on training, believing that only properly skilled staff can achieve success. To say that the methods Hoyt suggests are 'scientific' may be stretching a point, although if we accept Thompson's view that scientific management is essentially management based on the assembly and consideration of all available knowledge, then Hoyt qualifies. Certainly his emphasis on meticulousness and precision fits in with the scientific management ethos.

It should be noted that not everyone accepted that it was possible to manage sales and marketing in a scientific way. Selden Martin, a colleague of Cherington at Harvard Business School, was one of those who queried the applicability of scientific principles given that 'marketing abounds in the human equation'. Is it possible to find scientific principles, asked Martin, or do not the dynamics of human relationships between sales staff and customers mean that every case is different? What Martin seems to be pointing to is a principle that later became axiomatic in services marketing, namely that the customer is also part of the marketing process and has a direct impact on the process and outcome.[27]

The first steps towards a theory of relationship marketing had already been taken. The British businessman Arnold Brown, writing in the *Harmsworth Business Library* in 1911, described the importance of branding and reputation and suggested that manufacturers should develop close relationships with retailers, but also use advertising to develop relationships with customers.[28] Writing on the development of mail-order retailing in the same source, George Orange and J. McBain argued that mass communication does not mean customers can be treated as a single mass. They developed at length on the need for and techniques of personalizing mail-order advertisements, or 'shots'. They also pointed out that mail-order customers, if treated well and if a relationship can be developed, tend to become repeat customers:

> Usually it is possible to sell goods to people who are already customers at one-half to one-third the cost of effecting the sale in the case of a first transaction . . . It is obvious, therefore, that a mail-order advertiser of this type makes his profit out of a particular customer, not on the first sale but on the sum total of the transactions that he has with that customer.[29]

The problem of distribution

The elements of product, place, price and promotion were all well known to writers on marketing at least as early as 1920, if not further. Of the four, promotion probably received the most attention as there was a burgeoning literature on advertising, branding and public relations. Much of this followed the lead set by Walter Scott and drew on concepts from psychology. Although it was accepted that psychology could tell advertisers how the human mind worked, it was not at all clear that advertising itself could be managed scientifically. One textbook, Harry Tipper's *Advertising: Its Principles and Practice*, made the point that it was impossible to gauge the effectiveness of advertising, nor did advertising appear to be very efficient – but nonetheless, it was essential.[30] Product theory was probably least advanced. At Harvard, Melvin Copeland began experimenting with methods of segmentation – the term was in widespread use by the mid-1920s – in an attempt to define what products appealed to which consumers, but generally there was not a great deal of innovative work on this subject.

Discussions of price and distribution became bound up with each other for a time. The economist Wesley Clair Mitchell had in 1913 offered a theory of how prices are formed, discussing factors such as convenience, access, scarcity and quality.[31] But the first three of this, at least, were contingent on the effectiveness or otherwise of distribution systems, and these were still extremely crude by modern standards. The railway network represented an immense advance over previous systems, but it was not all-embracing, and delays and accidents were very common. The road network especially in America was still quite poor in many parts of the country, and the car itself was still a fairly primitive device. It was not always easy to bring buyer and seller together, as Cherington had advocated.

Controlling and managing distribution systems was a major headache for marketers, as publisher Arch Shaw observed in his book on the subject in 1912.[32] A more detailed look at distribution was advanced by the economist L.D.H. Weld in 1917.[33] Previous work on distribution had focused on the role of the various players in the distribution stream: the manufacturer, the wholesaler, the jobber, the transporter and the retailer, and had attempted to assign specific roles to each. Weld argued that distributive functions could be carried out by anyone. Manufacturers could be wholesalers, and even jobbers, if they chose; in other words, Weld was arguing that manufacturers should take greater control over the downstream parts of the value chain. Consumers also had a role to play in the distribution system and took on some distributive functions when, for example, they purchased goods in a store and then carried them home or elsewhere for ultimate use or consumption. Weld urged distributors to think about new ways of involving the consumer and, in effect, transferring some of the expense of distribution onto the consumer during the process.

To some extent Weld was describing a process that was already happening. The meat-packing trade, dominated by big firms such as Swift and Armour, urgently needed to get control of its value chain so as to reduce inefficiencies and risk spoilage of its perishable products – and, incidentally, mass starvation if meat could not be shipped quickly and cheaply from the Chicago slaughterhouses to the big cities of the east coast of America. They were already practising vertical integration, and this had begun to attract attention. Charges were levelled that the meat-packers' control over the value chain gave them too much advantage (it should be noted that Weld and his colleagues did not use the actual term 'value chain', which was introduced much later by Michael Porter; but they were describing the value chain concept nonetheless).

A sharp debate between Weld and another economist, Lewis Haney, in *American Economic Review* in 1920–1 shows the fault lines. Haney argued that vertical integration – or 'integrated marketing' as it was then known – was wasteful, did not save companies money and resulted in higher prices for the consumer. If other companies controlled parts of the value chain, this would result in competition which would drive down prices. Responding, Weld argued that controlling the value chain was a matter of reputation, not just price. The meat-packing companies had to get their highly perishable product to the market when it was still in a condition to be sold. Only by controlling the distribution process themselves could the packers ensure that their products reached the consumer in time. It was the duty of the producer to deliver not only the best price to the consumer, but also the best service. Following Mitchell – and, although he may not have been aware of it, Charles Babbage – Weld argued that customers would be willing to pay more if it meant a guarantee of a good-quality, fresh product.

Marketing and management

Just as scientific management had evolved to solve one set of problems, marketing had evolved to solve another: how to reconnect consumer and producer in an age of mass production and mass consumption, and how to secure efficient distribution to ensure that people's needs were met, bringing buyer and seller together. There had been an attempt to link marketing with scientific management, but beyond showing marketers that they needed to be rigorous and analytical – which the best of them already knew – this had not been very successful. Marketing had grown up on its own, trying to work out its own function and its own identity.

Everyone recognized that marketing was a management issue, but where did fit into the larger picture? Marketing did not feature in Fayol's fourteen points or Emerson's twelve principles of efficiency, and the human relations school had paid it no heed. How could the connection be made?

The first detailed attempt at linking marketing to management is probably W.D. Moriarty's *The Economics of Marketing and Advertising*, which takes its inspiration from the classical economics of Adam Smith, David Ricardo and Nassau Senior. According to Moriarty, professor of business administration at the University of Washington, economic theory says that utility and scarcity are the key sources of value. Marketing is directly linked to both. As to the first, 'marketing is always performing this function [utility], discovering new uses for raw materials and new uses for finished goods, as well as new places where both can be used.'[34] In other words, marketing does not just meet consumer demand, it tries to anticipate it. As for scarcity, marketing seeks to make goods more freely available (Moriarty acknowledges the existence of an 'illegitimate' form of marketing which creates artificial scarcities so as to drive up prices).

There we have it: the purpose of marketing is to create value. In terms of the functions of the business, why it exists, the purposes for which Ibn Khaldun and Thomas Aquinas and John Davis all agree that businesses were created, marketing is at the sharp end. It is the tool that businesses use to satisfy society's needs, earn profits for themselves, and legitimize their existence.

There is more to Moriarty's book than this. It is in many ways a very modern book, and some of its ideas sound very fresh. He is probably the first writer to refer to internal marketing, when he suggests that advertising can be used within the firm to increase efficiency as well as externally to increase sales. He offers a detailed analysis of price elasticity and its causes. Most important of all, however, Moriarty suggests that marketers will not be able to compete solely on price, and sustainable competition requires them to 'raise the plane' of competition and compete on issues such as quality and consumer service. He succeeds in linking all the elements of marketing together to make it a coherent discipline, and also provides the theoretical link to integrate marketing into management more broadly. His views were widely diffused and was followed by writers on marketing through the 1930s and into the 1950s.[35]

Earlier, writers such as Homer Vanderblue of Northwestern University had warned that the studies of sales, distribution, pricing and so on were in danger of going their separate ways, and argued for an integrated study of marketing which showed how all the separate elements of marketing were interwoven.[36] Moriarty showed how all the elements of marketing worked together to create value for the consumer. Later writers would simplify and reduce the concepts he set out, leading ultimately to Neil Borden's identification of the 4 Ps of product, price, place and promotion in a speech to the American Marketing Association in 1953; the 4 Ps were then enshrined by Jerome McCarthy in his 1960 textbook *Basic Marketing*. Other models have since succeeded the 4 Ps, but the premise that marketing consists of a number of different strands of thought and practice woven together remains valid today.

Yet, the unease that Lewis Haney had felt about marketing persisted for a long time, long after management thinking and marketing had begun to draw closer to each other. The suspicion that spending money on marketing and advertising was wasteful, as articulated by Haney, remained widespread. Joseph Rowntree, founder of the eponymous English chocolate company, believed that marketing put undue and unfair influence on customers; good products, he said, will sell themselves, they do not need to be promoted. Other business leaders agreed, despite the obvious examples of companies such as Pears, Lever Brothers, Singer and Heinz which had used marketing with spectacular success. This unease seeped into the general culture as well, in part thanks to the publication of Edwin Bernays's *Propaganda* which caused a public sensation when its author claimed that controlling the public mind through the media was in the best interests of society.[37] In the 1930s Aldous Huxley's satire *Brave New World* compared market segmentation to social stratification and the caste system – his system of social classification from Alpha Major at the top to Epsilon Minor at the bottom is based directly on demographic segmentation as used by marketers – and in the 1950s Pohl and

Kornbluth's novel *The Space Merchants* raised the spectre of mass mind control through subliminal advertising.[38] The same fear that marketers are trying to control us for their own nefarious reasons can be found in more modern works such as Naomi Klein's *No Logo*.[39] Others have deplored the cultural impacts of marketing and advertising in the creation of mass consumerism and the psychological impact on people more generally. A typical example is the Canadian sociologist Marshall McLuhan's book *The Mechanical Bride*:

> Ours is the first age in which many thousands of the best-trained individual minds have made it a full-time business to get inside the collective public mind. To get inside in order to manipulate, exploit, control is the object now. And to generate heat, not light is the intention. To keep everybody in the helpless mental state engendered by prolonged mental rutting is the effect of many ads and much entertainment alike.[40]

In later works such as *Understanding Media* and *Culture is Our Business*, McLuhan took a much more balanced view of marketing and advertising, but he still warned of the dangerous purposes to which they could be put.[41] Just as the human relations school had learned that influencing the minds of workers could be a two-edged sword (see Chapter 7), so marketers realized that trying to influence the minds of customers could be equally dangerous.

Marketing theory did not emerge as a subset of management theory. It emerged in its own right, in response to a different – if related – set of problems to those that Taylor, Emerson, Fayol, Follett and Mayo were trying to solve. It took some time before the relationship between marketing and the rest of management became clear, and even then there was a process of slow evolution rather than a eureka moment. And indeed, some separation does still exist. For example, in 2000 Tim Ambler believed that many companies are still focused on bottom line growth and pay too little attention to where that growth actually comes from – which is, as Moriarty pointed out long before, the market. 'Accountants seem to imagine that a pile of money will grow if only you count it often enough', was Ambler's rather acid comment.[42]

The emergence of business strategy

There is a connection between the development of marketing and the emergence of business strategy. It may seem somewhat surprising that we have had writers on military strategy giving us their theories and ideas since the time of Sunzi well over two thousand years ago, and that by 1900 military strategy was a highly developed field of study, and yet no corresponding field of business strategy emerged until the 1960s.

That does not mean that business leaders had no concept of strategy, or that they did not think strategically. There was certainly awareness of what we would now call 'business policy', the overall setting of goals and determining the purpose of the business, and this permeated non-commercial organizations too as we saw with the Benedictine and Cistercian monastic orders (see Chapter 3). But there is clear evidence that business leaders before modern times were doing more than that. They were thinking strategically: they knew how to analyse risks and offset them, they knew how to plan and execute, they knew how to make choices between strategic options.[43]

The writers we have discussed in this chapter and the previous two understood the need for strategy too. The concept of strategic thinking is clearly evident in Fayol's concept of *prévoyance*, for example, and the need to look forward is evident in Emerson's works. Chester Barnard's ideas on decision making all show clear evidence of awareness of the need to think strategically. The early marketers too, in their work on anticipating demand, clearly forecast the need to think in strategic ways. So why did not theories specifically about business strategy emerge alongside the new theories on operations, managing people, marketing and finance?

The answer, most probably, is that there was no need for them. James Brian Quinn is likely correct when he suggests that prior to the 1960s business people borrowed strategic concepts such as concentration of force and economy of force directly from military science.[44] It seems fairly clear that at least some business leaders followed Clausewitz – again, even if indirectly – and tried to first establish their business purpose and goals and then find a form of organization that was suitable for meeting that purpose and those goals. The multidivisional form, or M-form, of organization developed by Pierre du Pont at E.I. Dupont de Nemours and then from General Motors looks very similar to the divisional form already in use in modern armies. These divided troops into units by capability, function and purpose: there were separate units of infantry, light infantry, cavalry, artillery and later signals, logistics, medical staff and so on. Du Pont also used the line and staff model of organization advocated by Emerson and again drawn from Moltke and Clausewitz. We must never underestimate the influence Moltke had on early twentieth-century management thought, and we must remember too that many of the leaders of large organizations had themselves seen military service in the First World War.

More saw service during the Second World War too, and yet in the 1950s realization began to seep in that business needed its own model of strategic thinking. Daniel Wren believes the trigger point may have been a new translation of Fayol's *General and Industrial Management* which appeared in 1949 and enjoyed wider circulation than the previous effort in 1930. He traces a further influence to Peter Drucker, who in *The Practice of Management* in 1954 argued that 'the important decisions, the decisions that really matter, are strategic . . . Anyone who is a manager has to make such strategic decisions, and the higher his level in the management hierarchy, the more of them he must make.'[45]

This was no more than a passing thought by Drucker, who at this stage in his career was still working out his own much more general theory and philosophy of management. The next important step was the publication of Theodore Levitt's famous article, 'Marketing Myopia', in *Harvard Business Review* in 1960. Levitt argues here that products are important only in that they help meet customer demand. Where companies go wrong is in defining themselves by their industry or product category, rather than the benefit that they provide. Thus the railway companies defined themselves as being in the railway business when in fact they were in the transportation business, Hollywood defined itself as being in the film business when in fact it was in the entertainment business, and so on.

Levitt is not saying anything radical about marketing; these are points that had all been made before. What he *is* saying is that the top executives need to lose their 'myopia' about markets and adopt a marketing viewpoint. This in turn necessitates them rethinking their own strategic vision. Too many companies, says Levitt, regard themselves invulnerable, secure in the fact that they are in a growth industry. 'There is no such thing as a growth industry', he says bluntly, showing how changes in customer demand can cause an apparently secure industry to sag and decline.[46] No company should ever think its position is secure. Yet many think that their own technical skills and efficiency are all that is needed to ensure continued profit and growth.

> Another big danger to a firm's continued growth arises when top management is wholly transfixed by the profit possibilities of technical research and development . . . What gets

short-changed are the realities of the *market*. Consumers are unpredictable, varied, fickle, stupid, short-sighted, stubborn and generally bothersome. This is not what the engineer-managers say, but deep down in their consciousness, it is what they believe. And this accounts for their concentrating on what they know and what they can control, namely product research, engineering and production. The emphasis on production becomes particularly attractive when the product can be made at declining unit costs. There is no more inviting way of making money than by running the plant full blast.[47]

Here we see clearly the need for a new concept of strategy. In any competitive environment the winner, says Levitt, will be the one who can respond to market needs, rather than the one who can build the perfect system. He is aware of the need for control, and he criticizes companies that expand rapidly without putting in place proper control systems; but to me it seems clear that he is reacting also to the growing scientization of management, the fascination with systems thinking and operations research that was coming to dominate the world of organizational thinking in the 1950s (see Chapter 9).

In trying to build and design the perfect operating system, managers – and management thinking – were falling into the same trap that had awaited scientific management. Once again the human element was being ignored: not employees, this time, but customers. One thinker who seized eagerly on this idea was Peter Drucker, who in his next major book, *Managing for Results*, expanded greatly on Levitt and developed a concept of strategic market analysis. Indeed, says Peter Starbuck, he wanted to call the book *Strategy for Results*, but was deterred by his publishers who felt that no one would understand what the title meant.[48]

It was in this atmosphere that the business historian Alfred D. Chandler published his book *Strategy and Structure* in 1962. Chandler studied a number of large firms in early twentieth-century America, including Du Pont and General Motors, and concluded that a major factor enabling their growth was the adoption of the multidivisional form. This form of organization had enabled the perfect blend of coordination and control, which enabled these companies to move forward rapidly and become dominant in their respective industries. Chandler observed that almost every major American corporation up to 1960 had at some stage adopted the M-form, again because it was the best organizational form to support their growth strategies. His famous conclusion was that 'unless structure follows strategy, inefficiency results'.[49]

No other book of business history has had the same impact as *Strategy and Structure*, and probably no other will. Not only did it set in motion an entire generation of research into the relationship between strategy and structure, but it also had direct impact on the world of business. In particular the book was taken up by consultants at McKinsey & Company, who used it as a tool to help introduce the M-form structure at scores of companies in America and in Europe.[50] Even more, Chandler had helped to make business strategy popular. By turning it into a subject that was now popular with executives he had to some extent done what Levitt had hoped for: he had refocused business thinking away from operations and structures towards goals, businesses and markets. Nothing in *Strategy and Structure* is new or radical; Chandler was merely reporting what he saw. But the way he presented that material helped to produce a shift in business thinking.

Of course, that shift brought its own problems. Although Chandler had stressed the importance of strategy, he had not been precise as to what strategy actually was. How did a company go about developing a strategy, for example? During the late 1950s the Lockheed Aircraft Corporation had been working on a policy of diversification and two of its staff, the economist George Steiner and the engineer Igor Ansoff, who had previously worked at the RAND Corporation, came up with model of strategic planning.[51] This model had its origins in the kind of futurology-based forecasting work for which RAND was famous,[52] and Ansoff believed the same techniques could be applied to business strategy. This was the beginning of strategic planning in theory and practice, an event with somewhat mixed consequences. Strategic planning would later be savaged by Henry Mintzberg, Ansoff later repudiated it and turned to a contingency theory of strategy, and RAND itself abandoned futurology in favour of a more open approach; but strategic planning remains alive to this day.

Corporate finance

The discipline of corporate finance, or corporation finance as it was originally known, emerged from the same process of challenge and response. People had of course been writing and thinking about financial management for centuries, as Jonathan Baskin and Paul Miranti have shown in their excellent history of the subject.[53] Gabriel Hawawini and Ashok Vora have shown that mathematicians and economists were working on ways of calculating the yield from annuities and bonds as early as 1556, and probably far earlier than that.[54] Robert Wright has also demonstrated some of the richness of earlier writing on the subject.[55] There are indeed many works from this early period that describe financial instruments and financial markets, from the medieval *praticas* to Savary's *Le parfait négociant* or Thomas Mortimer's *Every Man His Own Broker*, that tried to impart lessons about financial management and financial markets (see Chapter 4).

However, much as we have seen with management theory more generally, thinking about finance in America in particular began to evolve in different directions in the late nineteenth century. As Richard Norgaard says, '1860 through 1949 was the period in which finance and finance textbooks were organized into the pattern we now observe'.[56]

We touched on the reasons why in Chapters 4 and 5. The period after the American Civil War saw very rapid growth, including the emergence of large, ramshackle monopolies or near-monopolies. Many of these were highly secretive. In *Wealth Against Commonwealth*, the journalist Henry Lloyd reproduced transcripts of evidence given by Standard Oil executives to various government commissions in the 1890s, in which they refused to divulge any financial or operational details, going so far as to pretend ignorance of where the company's headquarters was located.[57] Many of the large corporations were also very badly managed in financial terms. United States Steel, formed in 1901 through the merger of the Carnegie company with several other small steel producers, embarked on an ambitious programme of acquisition and expansion that seemed to be driven solely by, to paraphrase Theodore Levitt, the belief that money could be made by running the plants at full blast. A shareholder revolt broke out in 1910 when it emerged that the finances of the company were in chaos and no one could even agree as to what the company's value was.

Although there were a number of bookkeeping schools in America, there was no programme for training people in the complexities of financial management in large organizations until the Wharton School of Finance and Economy opened its doors at the University of Pennsylvania in 1881. Even this was not enough to meet the growing need for professional financial management. Thomas Greene, author of one of the first textbooks on corporate finance, stressed the importance of capable management:

> Practiced experience, as well as the best economic theory, lays emphasis upon the importance of an able manager. Nothing can take his place; and his rewards in the shape of salary or returns upon his shares, must be commensurate with his importance. In

building up a business the personal element is a great factor . . . When our important corporations have passed their experimental stage, proper management will be largely a question of proper payment.[58]

The comment that corporations are passing through an 'experimental phase' is an interesting one, as it shows that at least some observers were aware that American business and management were very much feeling their way, from a world of small businesses and domestic competition to one of large businesses and international markets. European business and management had taken several centuries to evolve through this process, and a body of practical, diffused knowledge had been built up. American businesses and managers were compressing the same process into about forty years. Greene's *Corporation Finance* is accordingly a textbook of the most basic sort, explaining the basic purposes and tasks of a financial manager in simple terms.

More sophisticated works were not long in coming. William Lough's *Corporation Finance* in 1909 describes a variety of debt and equity instruments and the markets for each, the processes of consolidating and merging companies, the various functions of corporate treasury. Three entire chapters are devoted to the subject of 'manipulation', discussing how executives, directors and stockholders may try to control the corporation for their own ends and there are constant warnings about the dangers of fraud. Edward Meade, who taught at both Wharton and Harvard Business School, covered many of the same points in his own book the following year. He too discussed the relationship between executives, directors and stockholders, in realistic and at times cynical terms; he commented once that 'stockholders act naturally like a flock of sheep', following the leads set by directors so long as they can see financial advantage to themselves.[59]

From then on there is a steady flow of works. In 1921 Edmund Lincoln provided a list of nearly 200 books and journals available to students of financial management. A few of these are worth mentioning in passing.[60] W. J. Jackman's *Corporations: Organizing, Finance and Management* is an early attempt to integrate financial management into organizing and managing more generally; though it has little new to say about finance specifically, it deserves attention as an attempt at integrating management disciplines. Lincoln's textbook *Problems in Business Finance* is another such attempt. Thomas Conway's *Investment and Speculation* offers a distinction between investments made with the aim of increasing share value and those made with a view to earning dividend income; it is clear that he disapproves of the latter. William H. Walker's *Corporation Finance* begins to discuss the separation of ownership and control, though he does not use that term; he describes the limits and responsibilities of both directors and shareholders, and describes the relationship between them. Two of the most widely read textbooks of the 1920s, Charles Gerstenberg's *Financial Organization and the Management of Business* and Arthur S. Dewing's *Corporation Finance* are similar in structure to Lough and Meade, but show how thinking about corporation finance was evolving as the publicly owned corporation became the dominant business model in America, at least for large businesses. Discussions of control and relationships between the owners and controllers of capital are important themes in both books.[61]

From these books and others, we can see that by the 1920s four key themes in the study of corporate finance have emerged: (1) the need for capital resources to fund expansion and growth – and in some cases, survival; (2) the need for professional financial management; (3) the need for a balance between technical and financial management; and (4) the need for accountability and openness. It is worth dwelling on this last point, for it was a major preoccupation with writers on corporate finance right up to the Second World War. Many of the leading academic figures in the field, including Meade, Lincoln, Lough, Jackman, Gerstenberg and especially the vigorous and dogmatic William Zebina Ripley from Harvard had been strongly critical of the tight and un-transparent control exercised over American business by a handful of oligarchs during the era of the trusts. They argued persistently for the introduction of publicly owned joint-stock corporations which would dilute control and also allow the daily business of business to be conducted by professional managers, especially professional financial managers. This would ensure greater financial stability for large corporations and hence greater stability for the economy generally.

This last point may well have been the reason why America adopted the public corporation model much earlier and much more widely than any other country. As Brian Cheffins has pointed out, Britain did not begin a large-scale move to the public limited company model until the 1960s and 1970s, and many countries still have not taken up this model except in a very limited way.[62] Mark Roe believes that public corporations were created as a result of political pressure: 'American politics deliberately fragmented financial institutions so that few institutions could focus their investments into inside blocks of stock. Different ways to develop corporate institutions are imaginable, but American politics cut their development paths off.'[63]

Roe's thesis, which seems to me entirely plausible, is that progressive American administrations, especially those of Franklin D. Roosevelt, remembered the overweening dominance of the robber barons and were determined not to return to that era. Weakening ownership by diffusing it across a broad and fragmented group of investors seemed to achieve that goal. There was another form of ideology too, derived in part from scientific management. The idea of the 'professional manager', disinterested and impartial with no personal stake in the business, had been developed in both America and Europe. In Chapter 6 we saw that Walther Rathenau had coined the term 'separation of ownership and control' and argued that professional managers would always act in the best interests of the business whereas owners would always be self-interested.

The term 'separation of ownership and control' was first used in America by William Ripley in his book *From Main Street to Wall Street*. Unlike Rathenau – whose work he seems to have been aware of – he was strongly against the idea. He argued that the separation of ownership and control handed power to the senior executives of the firm, particularly the financial managers. These now had the ability to dominate and impose their will on shareholders. What is more, the financial managers would always draw their salaries no matter how well or badly the company was doing, so had no reason to act in the best interests of the company, or indeed anyone but themselves. He was equally critical of shareholders for not doing more to assert their own position, accusing them of 'selling their birthrights for a mess of pottage':

> What an amazing tangle this all makes of the theory that ownership of property and responsibility for its efficiency, farsighted and public-spirited management shall be linked the one with the other. Even the whole theory of business profits, so painstakingly evolved through years of academic ratiocination, goes by the board . . . Veritably the institution of private property, underlying our whole civilization, is threatened at the root unless we take heed.[64]

Ripley's influence was acknowledged by his student Adolph Berle in the preface to the influential book *The Modern Corporation and Private Property*, written by Berle and the economist Gardiner Means a few years later. Berle and Means were also unhappy about the separation of ownership and control, which they argued tipped the balance of power too far away from owners and gave a small group of professional managers power over much of the nation's wealth. They argued that 'neither the claims of ownership or those of control can stand against the paramount interests of the community', and offered a number of measures for the protection of shareholders in order to re-establish a balance of power.[65]

An even more vigorous denunciation was launched a decade later by James Burnham, the Trotskyite-turned-libertarian ideologue whose book *The Managerial Revolution* described the emergence of a new 'middle class', 'the salaried executives and engineers and managers and accountants and bureaucrats and the rest, who do not fit without distortion into either the "capitalist" or "worker" category'.[66] He equated the new class of business executives in the West with the bureaucrats of the Nazi and Soviet systems, arguing that both had the same goal: maximizing their own power at the expense of both capital and labour. He scoffed at the idea of a viable separation of ownership and control:

> Ownership *means* control; if there is no control, then there is no ownership . . . If ownership and control are in reality separated, then ownership has changed hands, to the 'control', and the separated ownership is a meaningless fiction . . . Control over access is decisive and . . . will carry control over preferential treatment in distribution with it: that is, will shift ownership unambiguously to the new controlling, a new dominant, class. Here we see, from a new viewpoint, the mechanism of the managerial revolution.[67]

Yet despite these objections, the separation of ownership and control became the new orthodoxy, very possibly for the political reasons that Roe mentions. The debate died out after the Second World War as Richard Norgaard's 'organizational phase' of corporate finance came to an end. New thinking in the 1950s and 1960s and beyond was more heavily dominated by economics and econometrics, as we shall see in Chapter 9.

Corporate finance was slower to emerge as a discipline in Europe, probably because there was less perceived need for it (this did not mean that the actual need did not exist, however). Ownership in both countries remained concentrated and financial markets were already mature; attention focused on the internal workings of firms, especially on corporate treasury. In France and especially Britain there was a steady stream of works on accounting, many of which were textbooks on financial management by another name; there is evidence of at least some borrowing from the likes of Meade and Lough in America. German textbooks often combine an accounting approach with ideas from economics (see Chapter 6), and despite the idea having originated there, there was little separation between ownership and control.[68]

The same is true of Japan, although there was some fairly extensive borrowing from American corporate finance theory and practice. Yumiko Morii points out that there were important differences in their respective financial systems: Japanese firms were much more dependent on debt than equity, and the issue of the separation of ownership and control did not arise, for cultural as well as political reasons.[69] Accordingly, most Japanese texts from this period concentrate on issues such as banking, debt markets and corporate structure. Almost none of this literature has been translated into English.

There was also a growing interest in corporate finance in China as a result of the opening up of the country and increased exposure to foreign competition. China's banking system, which had not changed substantially for centuries, had to modernize quickly. Yu Yajing, one of the leaders of the Ningbo guild of bankers, helped to found the Shanghai Stock Exchange in 1921.[70] Other businesses had to modernize too. As Wen-hsin Yeh says:

The internationalization of the maritime trade made it necessary . . . that the Chinese state look beyond its own system and answer to other states in its dealings with its own merchants. Chinese merchants learned, for their part, to conceive of the reach of commercial activities in international terms and to consider the pragmatic benefits as well as compelling necessities to position themselves strategically (or opportunistically) among the contending states.[71]

Yeh describes the emergence of *shangxue*, or commercial knowledge, as a branch of learning in its own right: 'it no longer seemed unthinkable that superior knowledge, as opposed to greed or dishonesty, should be the primary factor of a merchant's wealth and success'.[72] Accounting and finance were a major component of *shangxue*. A leading figure in the dissemination of American ideas was Pan Xulun, who had studied accountancy and economics at Harvard and Columbia University before going on to teach at Shanghai Commercial College and Jinan University as well as running his own accounting firm. He wrote prolifically on accounting and finance, and also established his own Lixin Accounting School (now the Shanghai Lixin University of Commerce). According to Yeh, the school graduated 80,000 students in its first ten years of operation.[73] All of this activity continued right up until the Japanese conquest of Shanghai in 1937.

What is interesting about *shangxue* is that it appears to be an attempt to define management as a single subject of study, albeit one dominated finance and accounting. Elsewhere in the world, especially in America and to a lesser extent in Britain, finance and accounting were created very much as separate disciplines. As we have seen, they evolved separately from scientific management and marketing, and though they followed similar trajectories and quickly found their places in business schools, they were – and continue to be – regarded as quite separate branches of management thought and practice.

This also seems the appropriate place to describe briefly another non-American school of financial thought which emerged in the 1940s in India. Islamic finance, as this school is generally known, was an offshoot of the Nahda (Renaissance) movement for Islamic political and cultural revival that began in the late nineteenth century, led by people such as Muhammad Rashid Rida and Muhammad 'Abduh. One of those influenced by Rida was the Egyptian Hasan al-Banna', who went on to found the League of Muslim Brothers (more usually known as the Muslim Brotherhood) and wrote of the need to refound an Islamic state.[74] His message was that the recovery of Islam could only come about through political action. He in turn influenced the Indian scholar Sayyid Abul A'la al-Mawdudi, who founded the Jamaat-e-Islami political party in 1941 to campaign for independence from Britain and the establishment of an Islamic state. As al-Mawdudi himself said:

> The plan of action I had in mind was that I should first break the hold which Western culture and ideas had come to acquire over the Muslim intelligentsia, and try to instil in them the fact that Islam has a code of life of its own, its own political and economic systems and a philosophy and an educational system which are all superior to anything that Western civilization could offer.[75]

As part of his political programme, al-Mawdudi called for a system of banking and finance that was compliant with *sharia*, Islamic law. In particular, such a system would forbid the lending of money at interest. As we saw in Chapter 3, early Islamic merchants, scholars and lawyers had evolved a number of methods of financing business that were *sharia*-compliant, and in essence al-Mawdudi was calling for a return to this system.

Al-Mawdudi's concept of Islamic banking was part of a far wider programme of reform and renewal. The idea was taken up by others, notably the nationalist leader Sayyid Qutb in Egypt, various figures in Malaya (now Malaysia) and perhaps most importantly Anwar Iqbal Qureshi who went on to become economic adviser to the government of Pakistan after independence in 1948.[76] Qureshi tried to persuade the government to adapt Islamic finance as the economic model for the entire state, but without success. However, many private Islamic banking institutions have appeared, and, a variety of new instruments including *sukuk* (*sharia*-compliant bonds) have evolved over the years. Islamic finance has experienced rapid growth since the 1990s. As Hans Visser describes in his excellent introduction to the topic, opinion about Islamic finance was and is divided in the Islamic world. Some have argued that Islamic finance is an attempt to get around or evade the obligations of *sharia*; others, including many Muslims, have seen Islamic finance as a reactionary force, one which extends the power of the Muslim clergy over secular life. At least one outspoken Muslim critic of Islamic finance has been assassinated by extremists.[77]

International business

International trade and commerce had been growing steadily for centuries, and literature providing detailed knowledge about trading conditions in other parts of the world had grown along with it, from the medieval *praticas* to nineteenth-century reports on trading conditions and prices and, of course, the first international network to supply economic, financial and trade information developed by Reuters from the 1860s onward. International trade took many diverse forms. Mark Casson and Howard Cox have described the importance of networks in international trade, and Geoffrey Jones and Tarun Khanna have shown how the big European and Japanese trading companies played a key role in the advancement of world trade.[78]

As international trade began to grow more complex, more detailed books on the subject began to appear. One of the most sophisticated, British economist Barnard Ellinger's *Credit and International Trade*, describes how the slow but steady international integration of banking and financial institutions during the interwar year was leading to more connectivity between economies and markets. Ellinger anticipates globalization theory; he also anticipates Porter's value chain, showing how the transformation from raw materials to finished goods happens across and between markets.[79] Lewis and Schlotterbeck's *America's Stake in International Investments* fulfils a similar function from an American point of view.[80]

The rising industrial power of Japan and the opening up of China presented both challenges and opportunities for Western businesses, and scholars in both East and West worked to provide knowledge. To take just China as an example, a series of books beginning with H.B. Morse's *The Guilds of China* provided detailed information about the business environment there.[81] Following the 1911 revolution more books followed including many by Chinese scholars, economists and political leaders including Chong-Su See's *The Foreign Trade of China*, En-Sai Tai's *Central and Local Finance in China*, Chin Chu's *The Tariff Problem in China*, Min-Ch'ien Tyau's *China Awakened* and Sun Yat-Sen's *The International Development in China*.[82]

Not all of the impact of international trade was positive. There were those in Chinese business who resented foreign competition and wanted to re-establish the dominance of Chinese firms. Some of these drew inspiration from the *Thick Black Theory* of Li Zongwu, published first in 1911. Li advocated two traits in the successful leader: a 'thick face', which can mean both shamelessness and a willingness to do anything to achieve a goal, or strong defences that will repel attackers, and a 'black heart', or ruthlessness. Although Li was writing about politics, the book was also popular with business leaders and went through several editions before being banned by the Chinese government. Mao Zedong is believed to have studied it, and in the 1990s a highly edited interpretation appeared in English, the author maintaining that the book is still widely read in China.[83] Li has been compared to Machiavelli, and both Chinese and Western commentators have called him immoral. But *Thick Black Theory* can also be read, like Machiavelli, as a description of how the world of early twentieth-century China really worked. It is a useful antidote to the optimism of books such as *China Awakened*.

Courses on international business began to develop at business schools and colleges too, and were among the first to be offered at Harvard Business School after 1908. The main task that faced academics for a long time was the simple collection of information and case materials. When Paul Cherington and Selden Martin offered a course at Harvard Business School on business in Central and South America, they realized that there were no teaching materials. Martin's subsequent researches to collect case materials entailed a journey of 26,000 miles, including crossing the Andes six times. Gradually a body of material built up and writers such as Ellinger and Lewis were able to begin to develop a few theoretical insights. This work was then comprehensively interrupted by the Second World War.

Revival in interest in international trade came in the 1950s, firstly through increased American business contacts with Europe and Japan in the course of post-war reconstruction work, and secondly after the formation of the European Coal and Steel Community in 1952 followed by the European Economic Community in 1957. The lowering of trade barriers in Europe sparked a sudden and intense interest in international trade. John Dunning's first study of foreign direct investment, *American Investment in British Manufacturing Industry*, offered concrete evidence of the economic benefits of FDI, and this was closely followed by John Fayerweather's *Management of International Operations*, one of the first works to set out the principles of managing across borders. Richard Robinson's *International Business Policy*, reporting on a study undertaken for the US Department of Commerce, began to outline key themes in international strategy.[84] All of this work paved the way for a surge in interest in the field in the 1970s and onward by people such as Peter Buckley, Mark Casson, Geoffrey Jones and further important work by Dunning on FDI and multinational companies.[85]

Management consultancy

One consequence of the growth of scientific management and other specialisms was a rapid growth in the management consultancy industry. Management consultants were not new. Accountants such as William Deloitte and Edwin Waterhouse (see Chapter 6) had been providing consulting services on financial matters since then mid-nineteenth century, and there were also 'company doctors' such as Arthur Chamberlain who specialized in turning around failing companies. Consulting engineers had also been practising since the middle of the nineteenth century.

Scientific management led to many more consulting firms springing up. Taylor and the Gilbreths had their own firms, as did Emerson and so did many of their associates. Charles Bedaux established the first truly multinational consulting firm in the 1920s. Mention has already been made too of James O. McKinsey's establishment of his consulting organization around the same time. Several other now-famous names were already practising. The chemist Arthur D. Little established a consulting firm near Boston in 1905; his chemists made headlines in 1921 when they actually made a silk purse from a sow's ear, boiling the ears to make glue, then treating the glue with chemicals to make fibres which were woven and sewn together to make the purse.[86] Arthur Andersen established his eponymous firm in 1913, and Edwin Booz set up his company, which later became Booz Allen, in 1914. Booz originally was an engineering consultant, but soon began broadening to cover more general management issues. In 1940, Joel Dean's survey of management consulting in America found a thriving and rapidly growing profession providing a variety of services. The overwhelming majority of the consulting firms Dean surveyed were purveyors of specialist expertise in a single discipline of management.[87]

The importance of the consultancy profession lay in its dissemination of management ideas rather than its creation of them. Taylor, the Gilbreths, Emerson and McKinsey – and in Britain, Lyndall Urwick – all generated important ideas, but they did so for the most part before becoming consultants. The vast majority of consultants said little if anything that was original, but they did act as channels to spread new ideas about management and help put them into practice. This can be seen most visibly and most powerfully in McKinsey & Company's use of Chandler's ideas on strategy and organization in the 1960s. Many had close ties with leading universities and business schools: Booz was linked to the University of Chicago and Northwestern University, Arthur D. Little had a strong link with the Massachusetts Institute of Technology, and McKinsey developed an enduring relationship with Harvard Business School from the 1950s onward.[88] In general, the role of management consulting firms in spreading new ideas about management during this period should not be overlooked.

The growth of business education

At the other end of the intellectual value chain, business schools and other educational institutions also began take on a new importance. They quickly supplanted the independent thinkers such as Taylor and Urwick and became the new centres of thinking and idea formation.

Again, business schools as a concept were not new. The East India Company's training college at Hayleybury was established in 1805, and the École Supérieure de Commerce had been founded in Paris in 1819. In both Europe and America in the second half of the century there was a sudden upsurge in growth of commercial colleges; in America the number rose from 26 in 1870 to more than 400 by 1900. According to one source, in 1900 the colleges enrolled 110,000 students of whom 65,000 were men and 45,000 women. This last figure is worth noting. As Michael Sedlak and Harold Williamson point out, 'the contribution by the commercial colleges to a kind of emancipation of women during this period is noteworthy'.[89] Training enabled thousands of women to find work as clerks, bookkeepers and secretaries, and with employment came a degree of economic and personal freedom.

These schools trained accountants and bookkeepers – Frederick Taylor and Henry Heinz were among earlier graduates – but they could not supply the higher level skills that were increasingly being sought. The growing demand for specialist knowledge led to the foundation of the Wharton School in Philadelphia and the Hautes Études Commerciales in Paris, both in 1881. More foundations followed rapidly. The first business school in Germany, Leipzig Commercial College, was founded in 1898, the same year that undergraduate schools of commerce were established at the University of Chicago and the University of California. At least two more business schools were established in Germany before 1914. There were numerous schools teaching bookkeeping and accounting in Britain before the First World War, and institutions such as the London School of Economics also offered courses, though as we saw in Chapter 6 there was resistance to higher-level management education in Britain. In America schools of commerce or other programmes on management were swiftly established at University of Wisconsin, University of Vermont, New York University, University of Illinois, Cornell University, and especially Dartmouth College where the Tuck School of Business, founded in 1902, developed specialist expertise in personnel management. The Kellogg School was founded at Northwestern University in 1908, the same year that the Harvard Graduate School of Business Administration was founded.[90] In Japan Keio University, founded by Fukuzawa in 1858, offered courses in accounting and bookkeeping from an early date. Fukuzawa was also involved in the founding of Tokyo Commercial College in 1878; this was transformed into Tokyo Commercial University in 1920, ancestor of the modern Hitotsubashi University. Other commercial colleges soon followed. Nanyang College in Shanghai began offering a programme of study in 'technical management' from 1904 onward, and after the revolution of 1911 business schools and colleges proliferated rapidly. As Wen-hsin Yeh says, most of these were of a 'fly by night' nature and quickly disappeared, but by 1930 there were six departments of business studies attached to universities in Shanghai, plus two private institutions. One of these, the Shanghai College of Commerce, trained several prominent business figures in the late 1920s and 1930s.[91]

The establishment of business colleges and schools sometimes faced opposition, and not just in Britain. Faculty at the University of Pennsylvania were hostile to the establishment of the Wharton School, and opposed later plans to expand its curriculum. An attempt to establish a department of business studies at Columbia University collapsed in the face of faculty opposition. There was widespread opposition at Harvard to the foundation of a business school too and the university's president, Charles Eliot, had to do some tricky negotiating to overcome this. He struggled even to find a dean for the new school; his first choice, the Canadian labour lawyer William Lyon Mackenzie King, turned down the post and the eventual choice, economic historian Edwin Gay, accepted only reluctantly. Prejudice against the new school continued for many years. When future McKinsey managing director Marvin Bower told the dean of Harvard Law School that he planned to go to Harvard Business School after finishing his law degree, the dean responded, 'You are about to graduate from the greatest educational institution in the world, and now you're going to *that* place?'[92]

Harvard Business School nonetheless became the model for business schools around the world for much of the twentieth century. Its teaching methods, notably the case study, were widely imitated and are still in use today. It is interesting to observe how quickly Harvard and other business schools 'divisionalized', not just offering courses but setting up departments and research programmes based on individual functions of management. By about 1920 there were departments of marketing, operations, international business, corporate finance and so on, reflecting the broader divisions in management thought itself.

The early business schools were trying to reflect the world around them. As Paul Cherington said, their task was to search out best practice and try to codify it and pass it on to others. To this end, the early business schools eagerly sought out professionals in industry and invited them to come and lecture. Carl Barth, a Taylor associate, was an early lecturer at Harvard Business School and he persuaded Taylor, who was initially sceptical about the value of management education, to lecture there too. The publisher Arch Shaw, the brains behind the successful branding of Kellogg's Corn Flakes a few years earlier, was involved in the development of the case study method, and developed the 'live case study' where executives would come into the school and describe real-life problems to students.[93] Shaw's company also published *Harvard Business Review*, which likewise served as a model for other business school journals. *Harvard Business Review* was popular with managers, and academics at

Harvard and other business schools were also frequent contributors to journals such as *System* and *Engineering Magazine*.

The business schools are important for our purpose because they were disseminators of management thought, both through the classroom and through publication in the popular press. They also represent part of the pattern of challenge and response. The late nineteenth-century crisis of management, the lack of management skills and knowledge and the impact this had on business, was most acute in America. The need for business education was so overwhelming that opposition to it in most cases was stifled. On a much smaller scale we saw the same thing happening in early twentieth-century Shanghai, where the need to compete with the West was a powerful driver for education. In Europe, especially Britain, where the crisis of management was less severe, the need was felt to be less also. But this in turn represented a missed opportunity. The failure to establish a management education system meant that the quality of British management, especially middle management, began to lag.

Conclusion

We tend to think of disciplines such as marketing and corporate finance, in particular, as subsets of management. That is what they have evolved into, but it is not how they began. Marketing and corporate finance – as intellectual disciplines – evolved separately to scientific management, albeit with some connections and along parallel paths.

This might at first seem surprising. What we know about previous management practice suggests that marketing and finance – and indeed strategy – were top management functions. The leader and his or her closest associates at the top of the business took personal responsibility for these. An exemplar of this is Henry Heinz, who took lead responsibility for marketing and for the direction of the firm and also monitored its finances very closely. William Lever was another such. Henry Ford delegated responsibility for marketing and finance to James Couzens, but he and Couzens worked closely together. There was little or no separation of functions.

So, the separation into disciplines looks artificial, and to an extent it is. But the three disciplines evolved in response to separate, if related, challenges. Scientific management had little to say about marketing and finance, nor did the human relations school give them much thought beyond making the point that organizations need to be governed in a unitary manner. Yet the problems of financing and marketing were there and pressing. As a result, separate schools of thought emerged, and only gradually did their paths converge. It could be argued that this convergence is not yet complete, even today.

Reflection

The silo effect

We are all familiar with it. Vertical walls are erected inside organizations between divisions or departments, walls that block communication and leave those inside feeling out of touch and unconnected to the rest of the organization. Jeremy Holt in his study of senior finance professionals found that even at the top level many finance executives feel isolated and left out.[94] Studies of marketing professionals have reported similar findings.

Business schools suffer from the same problem. Jerry Wind, professor of marketing at the Wharton School puts it plainly:

> Typical MBA programs are still dominated by functional/disciplinary perspectives, and the schools offering them are still organized by disciplinary departments. Faculty typically publish in their disciplines, and with a few exceptions . . . most of the respected academic publications are disciplinary focused. Most core and elective MBA classes are offered by the various disciplines, and with the notable exception of a few capstone courses and projects, not much room is left for integrative thinking opportunities.[95]

Wind believes that integrative thinking is essential because that is how the world works. There is plenty of other evidence from theory and practice to back him up. Right from the beginning, thinkers about management have realized that organizations achieve strength by being more than the sum of their parts. There is no such thing as a 'finance problem' or a 'marketing problem' or a 'strategy problem'. Solving business problems requires inputs from all of these disciplines and more. Strategy, organization, employees, customers, finance, innovation, culture: all of these things are intricately interrelated and interconnected.

The evolution of these as different disciplines happened, as we have seen in this chapter, for complex reasons relating back to the cycle of challenge and response. Business schools brought these disciplines together under one roof, which was a positive step. But when it comes to integrating – or re-integrating – these disciplines into a single study of management, they have stumbled. They have so far failed to meet the challenge of developing an integrative study of management. A number of business schools have tried, and are trying. But progress has been painfully slow.

Business schools have taken plenty of criticism in recent years, and it has been argued that they should accept a share of the blame for the economic turmoil that began in 2008, for failing to turn out graduates equipped to meet the challenges of managing in the modern world. Whether a more integrative approach to management education would have improved the situation is open to discussion, but I am among those who believe that such an approach must be tried. I taught an integrative management module at the University of Exeter Business School for eight years, and I found the response from students was overwhelming; this module, they said, was exactly what they needed to help them pull together all the separate and discrete ideas they had learned in other modules. This is not to pat myself on the back, but rather to confirm the view taken by Professor Wind and others that integrative teaching is possible, and should be tried more widely.

Can business schools adapt? It is again, I believe, a matter of challenge and response. Business schools were created to solve the pressing need for a particular kind of management education and to help disseminate new ideas and best practice throughout the management community. They met that need very well. Today, they are definitely falling behind when it comes to dissemination through publication; fewer and fewer academics are willing or able to publish in anything other than 'peer-reviewed journals which only three people ever read', as one colleague puts it. If it turns out that the management education we are providing is no longer what is needed either, then business schools could face a challenge to their legitimacy, even their existence.

Breaking down the silos and introducing more integrative ways of thinking and managing is the big challenge that faces business schools right now. It will be interesting to see how they respond to that challenge over the coming years.

9　From scientific management to management science

We cannot put into words what it is that we are taking into account in doing what we are doing, and in that sense we do not know that what we are doing will get us where we want to go, will achieve the result we want to achieve. We judge that it will, we think it will, but we are not sure and *only time will tell*.

(Elliott Jaques)

The Second World War had a profound impact on management thinking. In America and Britain, the huge challenge of planning and allocating resources for the war effort tested previous assumptions about organization, systems and efficiency. The techniques of operations research, pioneered in Britain and much expanded and developed in America, were transferred wholesale from the realm of military planning and analysis to the business world after the war.

It was widely accepted that one of the factors behind the Allied victory was the industrial power which the Allies were able to harness to the war effort. Science had played an important role in the victory. Science had helped to plan and organize production and develop new tactics and new weapons systems. It had helped to break enemy codes: Babbage's dream of a programmable computer had finally been realized at Bletchley Park. And science had given the Allies the most fearsome weapon of all, the atomic bomb, the use of which had finally broken Japanese resistance and brought the war to an end.

Yet there was no respite, for almost at once a new challenge arose in the form of the Soviet Union and China. Capitalism and communism stood opposed to each other. The feeling that America was the bulwark of the free world became stronger still, especially in America itself. The free market ideology of Ludwig von Mises was very popular in America. In his book *Human Action*, published just as the Cold War was beginning, Mises argued passionately for free and unregulated markets and an end to government regulation.[1] Laissez-faire, he said, was the only economic system that could guarantee freedom. This in turn implied that businesses, especially big businesses, were themselves in some ways defenders of freedom, an idea taken up by one of Mises's most ardent followers, Ayn Rand. In her novel *Atlas Shrugged*, Rand portrays a society falling into decay as governments tax capitalists into extinction in order to prop up welfare systems. They are resisted by heroic figures such as the capitalist John Galt, who goes on to create a new and entirely free economic and social system.[2] The message is clear: capitalists are the defenders of freedom. Others agreed with this position. Ralph C. Davis, professor at Ohio State University, began his article 'The Philosophy of Management' by stating that management is a concept grounded in the free market and is irrevocably opposed to socialism.[3]

Yet there was another theme running through Ayn Rand's work too. Freedom could be preserved only at a cost. Sacrifices were required. The experience of the war tended to confirm this. The war had been won not by individual soldiers, sailors and airmen but by divisions, armies and fleets. The sacrifice of individuals was accepted and expected so long as the greater organization fulfilled its purpose. The influential writer on public administration Luther Gulick referred directly to the experience of the war when he wrote in 1948 that individual members of organizations must be prepared to sacrifice themselves for the common good, even if necessary serving as scapegoats to protect others above them:

> The prestige of top management must be maintained even though this involves a certain shifting of responsibility for individual failures and successes to subordinate organizations and men. This is cruel to those organizations and men, but it preserves the integrity of total management in a world of trial and error. In administration, as in baseball, it is the batting average that counts, not the occasional strikeout. Top management must be held accountable for the total record, not each segment.[4]

New techniques for scientifically managing production such as methods–time measurement (MTM) emerged from the wartime experience. MTM, basically an advanced form of time and motion study, had been developed at Westinghouse in an effort to speed up wartime production. After the war its inventors published a successful book. The preface of this book is worth quoting at length, for it symbolizes the new approach:

> For many years management has felt the need for a procedure for establishing production standards that would eliminate the element of judgment on the part of the production engineer. When a time-study is made under conventional procedure, it is necessary for the observer to form a judgment of how the performance of the operator compares with the average or normal performance level. Regardless of the fact that such judgments can be made quite accurately by the experienced observer, because the intangible element of judgment is involved, it is difficult to prove that a correct determination has been made. There is often a tendency on the part of the worker to question the accuracy of standards determined in this manner, particularly if industrial relations are strained, and management has no way of proving the rightness of its production requirements except by studying and restudying the job until an overwhelming mass of evidence has been gathered.
>
> This is costly and time consuming. Therefore, a procedure that eliminates the element of judgment will not only be more acceptable to labor, but it will be more economical to apply.
>
> The methods–time measurement procedure eliminates the necessity for judging the performance level at which an operator works while being observed. The procedure is simply one of determining the motions required to perform the operation and then of assigning pre-determined time standards to each limiting motion.[5]

Note that the need to 'eliminate the element of judgment' is referred to three times in this passage. Not only is the worker denied a voice in the process, but so too is the junior manager tasked with implementing this pre-set system. This, in McGregor's terms, is Theory X management. MTM was hugely popular; hundreds of American businesses adopted it, and it was one of the business methods exported to Europe by American industrial engineers and consultants during the rebuilding of the European economy under the auspices of the Marshall Plan in the late 1940s and early 1950s.[6]

Where there is judgement there is doubt, and one of the purposes of the new scientific approach to management that emerged after the Second World War was the elimination of doubt. Rational choice theory became a powerful influence on public policy, education and not least on management thought.[7] The prevailing world-view, especially in America, was in the words of Mie Augier and James March, 'the idea that society and democracy could be strengthened through the intelligent application of rational analysis to social problems. Those worldviews were reflected in words and phrases such as *interdisciplinary, behavioral and social science, problem-focused, mathematical/analytical/scientific,* and *policy science.*'[8]

Augier and March describe the enormous influence of the RAND Corporation, the private-sector research body that helped to bring scientific research methods to bear on a variety of problems in government and business, and the Ford Foundation, whose influential report of 1959 helped to change the nature and role of business schools.[9] The Ford Foundation report urged the necessity for more rigorous fundamental research, and for more interdisciplinary research. In practice as well as in theory, there were limits to interdisciplinarity. Even at landmark institutions such as the Graduate School of Industrial Administration at the Carnegie Institute of Technology, founded in 1949 and described by Augier and March as 'a "poster child" for the Ford Foundation's efforts and more broadly for the reform of business schools'.[10] Interdisciplinarity in practice meant mathematics, computer science, physics, psychology and sociology, with an occasional dash of political science. The influence of economics remained only in financial management (which we shall come onto in a moment). The organic sciences sat in the second-class seats; the liberal arts were frozen out entirely.

Nor was the move towards greater interdisciplinarity particularly successful. 'The post-war business school reformers had endorsed the twin virtues of fundamental research and interdisciplinarity', write Augier and March. 'In practice, the two proved to be largely incompatible.'[11] The need for fundamental research meant that the emphasis shifted towards specialist functional training for academics and thus further reinforced the silo effect in business schools – and, ultimately, in businesses themselves.

In terms of Paul Adler's cycles of thinking about people and organizations, then, the focus in the post-Second World War period swung strongly back towards organizational control and away from human relations.[12] This might seem odd, given the almost anarchistic form of libertarianism espoused by Ayn Rand; but in *Atlas Shrugged* she was not arguing for unlimited personal freedom, merely for freedom from state control. Market efficiency was to be the new guardian of freedom and at the same time, the mechanism through which freedom was maintained. Nor should we think that business thinking turned its back on the human element. As we saw in the previous chapter, the influence of the human relations school ran on through the work of people such as Maslow, Herzberg, McGregor and McClelland. In a recent article in the *Journal of Management History*, Patricia McLaren and Albert Mills make the point that the 'ideal manager' of the Cold War period was an educated, rational man (and it nearly always was a man) who nonetheless understood that he had a responsibility to his workers and that human relations were important to efficiency. They add, however, that 'the early years of the Cold War returned some of the absolute authority to managers that they had lost in the 1930s and 1940s. The Cold War was a battle between capitalism and communism, and the strongest proof of capitalist superiority was prosperity and consumption . . . Authority, leadership and strength were stressed as the first line of defense.'[13] We can see this clearly in works such as Gulick's *Administrative Reflections from World War II*, George Trundle's *Managerial Control of Business* and Marshall Dimock's *The Executive in Action*, all written around the end of the Second World War.[14]

But the concepts of organization that emerged in the aftermath of the war are not just scientific management 2.0. Scientific management was about exploring new *methods*; management science was and still is engaged in the quest for *systems*. The early pioneers of operations research, which at some indeterminate point evolved into management science, were indeed concerned with technical efficiency. But their primary purpose was to build efficient systems, not engineer efficient tasks. And further, the need to include social systems was understood from the beginning – indeed, hence the call for interdisciplinarity. The quest for a single way of understanding how technical and social systems combine and interact had begun, and indeed is still going on today.

Operations research

The Operational Research Society's definition of 'operational research' in 1962 defined not just that subject but an entire general approach to management thinking:

> OR [operational research] is the attack of modern science on complex problems arising in the direction and management of large systems of men, machines, materials, and money in industry, business, government, and defence. The distinctive approach is to develop a scientific model of a system, incorporating measurements of factors such as chance and risk, with which to predict and compare the outcome of alternative decisions, strategies or control. The purpose is to help management determine its policy and actions scientifically.[15]

The foundation of operations research – or operational research; both terms are used fairly widely – is usually traced to the founding of the Aeronautical Research Committee under the auspices of the British Air Ministry in 1935. The committee's purpose was to decide how to organize the air defences of Britain given limited resources and the very likely prospect of a war with Germany. One of the most prominent members of the committee was Patrick Blackett, who went on to serve in a variety of capacities during the war, advising the government on the siting of anti-aircraft guns, the development of new bombsights and tactics that convoys could use to evade U-boats, and also on whether Britain should develop its own atomic bomb. Arguing that strategic decisions should be based on facts and not emotions, he developed the techniques of data collection and analysis that became known as operations research.[16]

Operations research grew rapidly in America after that country's entry into the war in 1941. One of the key figures here was Norbert Wiener, professor of mathematics at Massachusetts Institute of Technology. A child prodigy, Wiener had written his first paper entitled 'The Theory of Ignorance' when he was 10 years old. Wiener worked on anti-aircraft defence systems for ships, developing a fire control system based on a constant series of feedback loops between radar screens and gun positions. Following the war Wiener set down the theory behind his work, coining the term 'cybernetics', meaning mathematical systems that use feedback loops to mimic biological systems.[17] This was one of the most important scientific breakthroughs of the twentieth century, and cybernetics has had many uses ranging from communications networks to medicine.

One of the first textbooks on operations research from America is *Methods of Operations Research* by Philip Morse and George Kimball, who had headed the US Navy's Operations Research Group during the war. Their book was widely used as an introduction to the subject. Another important figure was Claude Shannon, another mathematician at MIT who also worked on fire control systems and spent time working with Alan Turing on cryptanalysis;

he went on to develop a mathematical theory of communication that complemented some of Wiener's work.[18] Mention should be made too of the statisticians Walter Shewhart and W. Edwards Deming who worked together for much of the war. Shewhart was already known for his work on the use of statistical methods to control product quality, and had written several influential books and papers on the subject.[19] Deming would go on to use Shewhart's methods to great effect after the war (see Chapter 10).

Wiener's work on cybernetics and Shannon's information theory were picked up in the 1950s by Stafford Beer, who set up an operations research unit at the British firm United Steel in 1956. His first work, *Cybernetics and Management*, was a comparatively simple statement of how cybernetics can be applied to any organization, including businesses. He later developed the viable system model, which offered an understanding of how organizations adapt and evolve using feedback and control loops to process information. Management in a viable system model has five principal functions: operations, coordination, control, 'intelligence' or the gathering and processing of knowledge, and policy, or in other words setting strategy and goals. Beer believed that organizational systems contain smaller systems and subsystems, and that by and large these systems should function autonomously but still within the overall control of the main systems; an analogy might be different programmes running simultaneously on the same computer. A cybernetic system, said Beer, creates its own logic. These systems and subsystems define themselves through function, rather than being artificially established as part of an organization chart. However, in later works he made the point that cybernetic systems do not run themselves. The third of his managerial processes, control, is vitally important to steer the system towards its defined goal.[20]

Two of the most widely read authors on operations research, C. West Churchman and Russell Ackoff, expanded the concept in different directions. They founded the Operations Research Group at the Case Institute of Technology in America and produced one of the most widely read textbooks on operations research, *Introduction to Operations Research*.[21] However, both became quickly aware that operations research focusing on the internal workings of organizations could never provide the whole answer to most questions. Churchman began applying the principles of operations research to systems thinking, and his *The Design of Inquiring Systems* is an ambitious attempt to rationalize the processes whereby systems absorb information and disseminate it in order to achieve their purpose.[22] Ackoff for his part came to feel that operations research was good at solving operational and tactical problems but not strategic ones, and turned his attention to strategic thinking. Using some of the techniques of operations research, Ackoff divided strategic planning into three sections: ends planning or goal setting; means planning, or how the goal will be achieved; and resources planning, or what resources will be required to achieve the goal. Ackoff also became interested in social systems thinking, and his earlier book with psychologist Fred Emery argued that all human-designed systems are 'purposeful systems', that is, they are designed with a specific purpose and goal in mind.[23]

Another attempt to link technical and social systems was made by Jay Wright Forrester at the Massachusetts Institute of Technology. His book *Industrial Dynamics* begins with the concept of feedback loops and shows how computer modelling can explain how the nature of feedback loops changes over time as they interact with each other. But Forrester also made it clear that mental models, the assumptions people make about 'what causes what', are an important part of the system. These assumptions form the bases from which people make decisions. Forrester believed that these mental models could also be modelled by computers, which would allow managers to assess their own mental models and, if necessary, change them.[24]

The dynamic approach developed by Forrester eventually fed into the concept of business process modelling which began to emerge in the 1990s and led to a new way of thinking about organizing: organizing by process, rather than organizing by function. The concept of business processes had been understood for a long time; the Gantt chart (see Chapter 5) and Adamiecki's harmonogram (see Chapter 6) were attempts to define and monitor business processes. Software-enabled dynamic modelling helped researchers to define business processes and identify their various stages more easily. This in turn led to business process re-engineering, an attempt to reorganize businesses on functional lines. The BPR movement harked back quite deliberately to scientific management; its proponents referred back to Taylor and the industrial engineers, and regarded themselves to some extent as inheritors of Taylor.[25]

Management science, as the discipline is now generally called, is often portrayed as an entirely formal–rational system of thinking about management and problem solving. Its proponents emphatically reject this. 'In practice, formal techniques play a very small part in MS [management science] investigations', says Samuel Eilon, one of the later leading thinkers in the field.[26] Eilon also notes that there is a gap between management science *theory*, which is heavily dominated by issues such as linear programming and mathematical modelling, and *practice*, where more attention is played to social systems. He credits Herbert Simon (see below), for introducing an element of realism into the discipline. Investigations in management science tend to fall into two categories, optimizing and 'satisficing'. Optimizing investigations seek the best possible solution; 'satisficing' solutions seek the best realistic position given time and resources.

Nor should it be thought that operations researchers and management scientists were not aware of the human element. Many had high personal ideals and high ethical standards, and they valued humanity immensely. Despite winning a Nobel Prize for his work, Patrick Blackett was ostracized by the British establishment after the war for his opposition to the area bombing of Germany and the use of the atomic bomb. Churchman's work was pervaded a by a deep sense of humanity, and he believed that systems thinking was in fact ethical thinking. Thanks in large part to the work of the behavioural psychologists, the human element was still very much part of this new discipline. It is not that the early operations researchers and management scientists ignored human behaviour; rather, they believed that it could be explained and even predicted using technology and modelling.

But, rather as with scientific management, the ideas generated by management science have been used for purposes other than which the researchers intended. 'BPR became a synonym for downsizing', say Michael Mol and Julian Birkinshaw. 'Many companies in need of an excuse to cut jobs announced they would engage in re-engineering.'[27] They note how BPR became something of a fad, leading to a backlash as people turned against it. Even some of BPR's leading exponents later dissociated themselves from the concept. Similarly, mathematical modelling, a technique pioneered by management science and now very widely used in the private and public sectors alike, has been heavily criticized in the aftermath of the 2008 economic downturn as it was felt that businesses in particular had become too reliant on it. For all its attempts to recognize and deal with the human factor in business, management science ultimately failed to achieve this goal, just as scientific management did.

Financial economics

Economics also became much more scientized in the 1950s, with a much greater emphasis on mathematics, statistics and modelling. This trend had been building up for some time, at least since the days of Alfred Marshall in the late nineteenth and early twentieth centuries.

Marshall, a Cambridge-trained mathematician, applied mathematics to economic problems in a systematic way, and many others copied him.[28] The American economist Irving Fisher used mathematics to try to model stock market movements, though his predictions in the later 1920s, on the eve of the Wall Street Crash of 1929, did not prove especially accurate.[29]

Following the Second World War, and very much in the same tradition of using science to solve problems that we saw above – and for very much the same reasons, connected with freedom and democracy and demonstrating the superiority of the capitalist system – the new discipline of financial economics began to emerge. Harry Markowitz's work on portfolio selection in the 1950s is usually pointed to as the starting point for this trend.[30] Markowitz's portfolio optimization model offered a model which allowed investors to choose their portfolios depending on their own appetite for risk. Importantly, the model did not just measure the characteristics of individual investments, but also the effect that the movement of other investments in the same market might have. This in theory meant that more accurate assumptions could be made about future movements and prices. This was closely followed by the efficient markets hypothesis, developed by Paul Samuelson and others in the 1960s, which harked back to the 'random walk' model originally proposed in the 1860s and asserted that markets were efficient processors of information and that all available information was reflected in market movements; therefore, over time it was impossible to 'beat the market' and realize above-average returns.[31] A third key idea was the capital asset pricing model, developed around the same time. These three concepts together go to make up modern portfolio theory, the bedrock of modern financial economics. The option pricing theories developed by Fisher Black, Myron Scholes and Robert Merton in the 1960s were another important set of ideas to emerge from financial economics.[32]

As Geoffrey Poitras has described, the emergence of financial economics or 'new economics' was strongly challenged by proponents of more traditional economics and the earlier 'organizational' school of corporate finance. The arguments between the two schools during the 1950s were often personal and bitter. Ultimately, as Poitras says, 'teachings of the old finance school were either ignored or absorbed by the emerging scientific movement of modern financial economics.'[33]

And yet, what did this victory achieve? Financial economics is now studied and taught at most of the world's business schools. Yet after more than fifty years, says Poitras:

> use of the techniques of MPT [modern portfolio theory] in the securities markets is miniscule. Security market professionals, particularly in the equity markets, appear to adhere to techniques that were the bread-and-butter of the old finance school. Leading investment professionals, such as Warren Buffett, criticize key elements of modern financial economics such as 'beta' with dictums such as: 'it is better to be approximately right than precisely wrong.'[34]

Option pricing models such as the Black–Scholes–Merton (BSM) model were more widely adopted by the financial community, at least for a time. But as Pablo Triana describes, doubts about BSM and its effectiveness and accuracy have now emerged and, very much as above, traders are drifting back to older rule-of-thumb methods.[35] Financial economics, like management science, failed to fully account for the human and irrational elements. As a result, the discipline is facing an increasing challenge to its relevance.

Reflection

An unhealthy yearning for precision

'Most of us hate uncertainty', wrote the former derivatives trader Pablo Triana in 2009. 'The unknown, the dubious, the inscrutable. Most of us despise the immeasurable. We dislike living in a world where unquantifiable vagueness can roam freely . . . We can't accept that wild randomness and utter chaos may be all there is to it. We seek the comfort of order, and con ourselves into believing that someone, somewhere must have the answers, down to the third decimal.'[36]

Triana was writing in the aftermath of the financial crisis of 2008, and he directed his anger at the financial industry and, especially, at financial economics and its theorists who, he believes, were partly responsible for the crisis. But his comments reveal a deeper problem, one that probably bears lead responsibility for the crisis: a problem of human nature. As Triana says, as a species we hate uncertainty, and we are willing to accept anything that comes along that promises certainty – or at least, less uncertainty.

Scientific thinking was first applied to management by Taylor and his colleagues in an effort to reduce uncertainty. In the 1950s, the renewed emphasis on scientific thinking and scientific rigour, driven in part by the need to strengthen the capitalist economy and society in the face of the perceived threat from communism, sought once again to reduce uncertainty. As a consequence, people began applying scientific thinking, and especially mathematical calculation, to anything and everything. Here is management historian Claude George, writing in 1972 when management science was beginning to take firm hold:

> If we agree that managing consists of physical and conceptual acts which effect or yield physical and conceptual environments . . . then, we can express managing as
>
> $$Mg = [(Ac + Ap) \rightarrow (Ec + EP)]f(Oi, Og)$$
>
> where
>
> Ac = conceptual acts, Ap = physical acts, Ec = conceptual environment, Ep = physical environment, Oi = individual objectives, Og = group (corporate objectives), W = a weight (proportion) of P (planning), O (organizing), D (directing), and C (controlling).[37]

And that is only the beginning; there is another page and a half of equations and explanation. George's view seems to be that knowledge can only be considered to be 'proper' knowledge if can be scientifically proven and expressed in mathematical form.

Reading this conclusion to George's survey of management history, I was reminded of Isaac Asimov's invention of 'psychohistory'. In his novel *Foundation*, Asimov describes a society where psychohistory has been used to predict the future in amazing detail, so that policy makers and leaders know in advance exactly what decisions to make and when (was he thinking of the Ford Foundation when he chose the title?). Society proceeds with amazing order, until one day a rogue element that had not been predicted enters the system and turns the future upside down.[38]

Psychohistory is Asimov's satirical take on what Triana later called the 'unhealthy yearning for precision' – unhealthy because, in the view of both authors, the more we strive to eliminate chaos, the more we actually increase the chances of its happening. That is not to say that we should turn the other way and deliberately seek to create chaos. I once mortally offended a group of management consultants by suggesting that Tom Peter's *Thriving on Chaos* was a dangerous book.[39] My point was that encouraging managers to create chaos was irresponsible because very few people are capable of living comfortably with chaos, still less of managing it. Because most people are frightened of chaos, they become disturbed and unhappy when force to live with it. For both humane and practical reasons, deliberately advocating chaos as Peters did – or as Chairman Mao did during the Cultural Revolution – is in my view wrong.

We do need a degree of certainty and order and structure in our lives, and in our organizations. But the more I look at management science, financial economics and the like, the more I am reminded of the Irish story about a driver stopping a pedestrian and asking the way to Dublin and being told, 'You can't get there from here.' I think we may be starting from the wrong place. This is not to denigrate management science or financial economics, both of which have given us much valuable and useful knowledge, but we are starting from the wrong premise. We, by which I mean the community of people who think about management, have started by thinking, *how* do we do management? We should have begun by thinking, *why* do we do management? Then, once that question had been satisfactorily answered, we should have proceeded to search for the best means of fulfilling the purpose of management. In that quest, science and mathematics would necessarily have played a major part. But the depressing thought that occurs is that it may be too late to make a fresh start.

In their book *Einstein's Space and Van Gogh's Sky*, the psychologist Lawrence LeShan and the physicist Henry Margenau maintain that the problem is not all psychological: some of it is philosophical. In the West, they say, we are very good at explaining the world around us; we are very poor at explaining ourselves. 'We inevitably arrive at a situation in which we increase our understanding of matter and energy but do not increase our understanding of the minds that direct the use of matter and energy. To give one obvious example, we have greatly increased our ability to wage war since Hellenistic times, but we have not increased our understanding of the causes of war.'[40] Since the age of the ancient civilizations, we have greatly increased our capacity to manage. But how far have we advanced our understanding of what management is?

Human-centred organizations

We saw above how management science – and its cousin-german, financial economics – explored and developed systems that were grounded in mathematics and the physical sciences, and then attempted to adapt these to take the human factor into account; not always successfully. Another group of thinkers – those grounded in fields such as conventional or 'old' economics, sociology and psychology – approached the problem from another direction. They focused on the human element of organizations, but sometimes borrowed heavily from the techniques and sometimes the language of science, especially the social sciences, in order to formulate theories and test conclusions.

Economists of the traditional type, having been elbowed out by their more mathematically inclined colleagues, nevertheless made a number of useful contributions. In Britain, Philip Sargant Florence blended psychology, political science and economics in attempt to come up with new insights into human motivation and performance. He focused very much on the level of the individual. In one of his most important post-war works, *Labour*, he took a process view of labour and the human factor. He defined the 'human factor' as the combination of the worker's *capacity* to work (how much he or she *can* do) and the worker's *willingness* to work (how much he or she *will* do). Inefficiencies in labour, he says, nearly always stem from a deficiency in one or the other aspects of the human factor. These inefficiencies can be measured though the quantity and quality of output, and also through records of accidents, absenteeism, strikes and industrial disputes, and labour turnover.[41]

The influence of Schumpeter's theory of entrepreneurship remained very strong (see Chapter 6). The British economist Ronald Coase, in a 1937 paper entitled 'The Nature of the Firm', thought that business organizations consisted of a series of contracts between the entrepreneur and other members of the firm.[42] These contracts are often implicit, and quite different from formal contracts of employment; they do not always spell out in detail what is required of each party. Coase also developed his famous theory of transaction costs, which helps to explain why some firms grow in size and others stay small. There is a trade-off, said Coase, between transaction costs – the costs of buying or selling in the marketplace – and organizational costs – the costs involved in running an organization. If the former are higher than the latter, the firm might choose to expand upstream or downstream. To give an example, William Lever expanded to set up his own palm oil production facilities to supply his soap works, finding it cheaper and less risky to do so than to buy on the open market. If organizational costs are higher than transactions costs, however, then the firm is internally inefficient and it will be cheaper to buy in services or supplies on the open market than to produce them internally. This concept has had a durable effect on thinking about organizations and strategy, and among others has influenced Hamel and Prahalad's ideas on core competency (see Chapter 10). There are some similarities between Coase's work and that of Erich Kosiol in Germany, who in 1962 suggested that the human relationships, or 'nexus of contracts' in Coase's terms, within firms should be considered as dynamic and that changes within relationships over time will affect the performance of the firm.[43]

Philip Sargant Florence had been sceptical about the idea of optimality in business, and argued that decisions such as capital investment or plant location should be made on the basis of specific conditions and factors at the time and place the investment is made.[44] There are echoes of this in the general impossibility theorem developed by Kenneth Arrow, economist at Stanford University and long-time consultant to the RAND Corporation.[45] Arrow argued that it is not possible for group decisions to proceed rationally from individual preferences because, in effect, it is not possible that the decisions made by a group will match with all the preferences of all members. All organizations, he said, exist in a state of equilibrium, a tension between the needs of the group and the needs of individuals. This means that there is always an element of uncertainty and risk in any organizational situation. This idea was later expanded by the German economist Erich Gutenberg who argued that as well as an internal state of equilibrium, businesses also existed in a state of equilibrium with their environment, constantly balancing competing pressures.

Mention should be made too of Kenneth Boulding, economist at the University of Michigan who by the early 1950s was developing his ideas on economics as a set of social exchanges that would later lead him towards the idea of environmental economics (see Chapter 11). From our perspective, Boulding's most interesting work is probably *The Image*, in which he discusses how multiple perspectives on the same object can yield more know-ledge than a single perspective. He takes organizations as an example, and says that they can be perceived on seven different levels:

1 The static level; snapshot of the organisation as it is at a given moment, frozen in time.
2 The clockwork dynamic level; the organisation as a machine with moving parts all working together, but still in a fairly mindless fashion.
3 The level of 'homeostatic control'; the organisation has communications systems and feedback devices which enable it to be controlled and kept in working equilibrium.
4 The biological level; the organisation is cellular and self-maintaining, and its cells are also capable of reproduction, which enables the organization to grow.
5 The botanical level; the same, only with some cells taking different forms from others according to the functions they serve, their combined functions all supporting life and growth.
6 The animal level; a living organism that is also capable of movement, awareness and reaction.
7 The human level; as above, but also endowed with the power of conscious thought, self-consciousness and self-awareness, and the ability to create vision and set goals.[46]

There are clear parallels forward in time with the ideas of Gareth Morgan (see Chapter 10), and also backwards to the centuries-old biological metaphor of organization. Boulding's con-ception of the organization as a self-regulating, adapting entity has on one level parallels with cybernetics theory. Where it differs sharply is by introducing concepts such as evolutionary and organic growth and, above all, consciousness.

Bounded rationality: Herbert Simon

One of the most important post-Second World War thinkers on organization was the American polymath Herbert Simon. After taking a Ph.D. in political science, Simon joined the faculty of the Graduate School of Industrial Administration at Carnegie Institute of Technology (later Carnegie Mellon University) where his research interests spanned everything from conflict and decision making to computers and artificial intelligence. He is sometimes described as a positivist, and the fact that he was simultaneously a professor of psychology and computer science and that he worked on artificial intelligence means that some have claimed him as an apostle of management science. But as Hunter Crowther-Heyck and J.C. Spender have shown more recently, that is much too narrow a view of Simon.[47] He understood – even seems to have enjoyed – the fact that all human systems were prone to uncertainty and that there were always going to be grey areas. These merely represented another challenge. As Crowther-Heyck says, 'Simon was comfortable with chaos because he was always sure that an order lurked within.'[48]

Simon became interested in the problems of organization while working on his Ph.D. in political science in the 1940s, publishing his ideas in his most famous work, *Administrative Behavior*, in 1947.[49] Simon acknowledged the influence of Chester Barnard (see Chapter 7) who had argued that rational economic theory did not really explain how, or why, orga-nizations functioned. Simon took the same view. He argued that decision making is not simply a matter of choosing one option from a menu. Often it will be necessary to choose several options and pursue them simultaneously. Nor is decision making simply a matter of gathering all the information required, weighing the evidence and then making an informed choice. Simon believed that this is impossible. No single human being can possibly process all the information needed to make a rational choice about anything. We are always acting on the basis of imperfect information. Simon coined the term 'bounded rationality' to indicate that there are limits to rationality in decision making, limits which are usually the product of our inability to gather and understand all the available data.

How do we deal with bounded rationality? According to Simon, this is one of the main reasons why we form organizations. Being a member of an organization restricts our choices, and also allows us to draw on information possessed by others, not just our own. Organizations, in Simon's view, are not just tools that society uses to get things done. They are also essential mechanisms for information processing and decision making, or as J.C. Spender says, they are invented artefacts that help us cope with our own limitations.[50]

Thus organizations serve at one and the same time as enablers and limiters. Bounded rationality applies to organizations too, because even with the 'boost' that they give to information processing and decision making, it is still not possible to know everything. So we make the best decisions that we can with the information available. Simon terms this 'satisficing', a neologism combining 'satisfy' and 'suffice', meaning that we make decisions which are adequate for the time and place rather than aiming for the ideal decision. The same is true of outcomes; we accept what is 'good enough' rather than waiting for perfection.

In a later work, *Organizations*, Simon and his co-author James March explored the concept of bounded rationality still further when questioning why people choose to submit to the authority of organizations. In effect, joining an organization becomes a kind of trade-off; we accept the limitations the organization imposes on us for the security and enabling powers it gives us. But this does not mean that all is calm and peaceful within organizations. March and Simon describe organizations as resembling political coalitions. People come together for a common end, but they also jockey for position along the way. This means that organization's goals themselves are constantly shifting: 'Since the existence of unresolved conflict is a conspicuous feature of organizations, it is exceedingly difficult to construct a useful positive theory of organizational decision making if we insist on internal goal consistency. As a result, recent theories of organizational objectives describe goals as the result of a continuous bargaining-learning process.'[51]

Some of these ideas are not new. Plato and Muhammad 'Abduh, among others, had described the trade-offs between individual freedom and membership of a society or organization, and the concept of organizations as political coalitions has a long pedigree too. But Simon and March link many important concepts together, bounded rationality and satisficing, decision making, choice, authority and conflict, and present us with a concept of organization that is quite a distance from the cybernetic system described by Beer or the rational organization envisioned by the financial economists. Neither a machine nor a biological organism, the organization conceived by Simon and March is an uncertain, hesitating thing that gropes forward trying to peer through the mists that surround it while at the same time trying to resolve its own internal contradictions, and never really succeeding at either task.

Some of these themes were picked up by March and Richard Cyert in their book *A Behavioral Theory of the Firm*. Against the rational view of decision making posited by economic theory, which suggested that firms will always act in their own best interest, i.e. to maximize profits, Cyert and March argued that a range of irrational factors influences decision making. What, for example, do people do when they are required to reach several goals at once, especially if those goals might conflict with each other? How do they react when those goals are ambiguous, or subject to change, or both? The answer is that they make decisions that are not always rational, but which sometimes turn out to be right anyway. In one later article, 'The Technology of Foolishness', March wrote about the need to come to terms with and understand behaviour which violates rational expectations but is nonetheless omnipresent. Even the most formal bureaucracy, it seems, also has its irrational elements.[52]

Open systems

At around the same time as Simon was laying out the case for bounded rationality, the biologist Ludwig von Bertalanffy was developing the concept of open systems. Von Bertalanffy was reacting to a scientific world-view based on Newtonian mechanics, which perceived all systems as *closed systems*; in other words, all systems – including organizations – behaved in a manner consistent with the laws of physics, and behaved according to mechanical principles. Scientific management is an example of a fairly pure closed system. The primacy of closed systems had been challenged by natural scientists following Darwin, and in part accounts for the upsurge in interest in the biological metaphor which we saw earlier in the work of Emerson and Knoeppel and more recently, above, in the work of Kenneth Boulding.

Starting in Vienna in the 1930s and then in California in the 1950s, von Bertalanffy developed the concept of open systems. Rather than breaking the subject of study into its component parts and analysing these in detail, after the fashion of scientific management, open systems theory observes the interactions of the parts within the whole, but regards the whole entity or organization as the primary unit of study. It focuses too on the interaction of the entity with its environment. Another feature of open systems theory is its view of organizations is dynamic rather than static; organizations are constantly changing both internally and externally in response to new stimuli, whereas closed systems theory persisted in studying them as if they were frozen in time.[53] The ramifications of this are considerable. To take just a couple of points, open systems theory not only admits but expects that organizations are in a constant state of evolution and change; therefore, an assumption about an organization that is good at one moment in time may not be valid the next. Second, open systems theory imposes severe limits on predictability. As Lawrence LeShan and Henry Margenau point out, it is possible to accurately model a closed system and predict its future. But one cannot do so with an open system, because one cannot predict what elements might enter the system in the future and so change its nature and direction.[54]

The idea of open systems was quickly taken up by some writers on organization. There are important echoes of this in the work of Cyert and March, above, but von Bertalanffy was particularly influential on some industrial sociologists, who saw the value of open systems theory in explaining what they themselves were observing in organizations in both private and public sector. For example, in *Towards a Sociology of Management*, Geoffrey Vickers more or less rejected the importance of individualism as posited by the thinkers of the Enlightenment. Instead, he stressed interrelationships between people as the key factor to be studied in organizations, and described humankind as a social animal in much the same way that 'Abduh had done. He noted that over the course of time human systems – which are always open systems – develop their own unique worldviews and ways of thinking and making decisions, ways which are not easily replicated by other systems. In essence, he was describing how organizational cultures evolve.[55] Following on from Vickers, Peter Checkland developed what he called 'soft systems methodology' which explored how people identify and solve problems in climates of uncertainty; for example, where there is disagreement about the nature of the problem the organization faces, and whether there is any real need for change. Checkland also saw problem solving as an iterative process. Every solution, he warned, generates its own problems which likewise need solving, thus creating a cycle of action and reaction in which continuous thinking and learning play a key role.[56]

Open systems concepts also played a role in the thinking of Chris Argyris, whom we encountered in the previous chapter as a critic of bureaucracy. Argyris and Donald Schön were responsible for the development of concepts such as 'action research', whereby managers and workers conduct their own research into business problems and apply their own solutions rather than relying on academic experts (one feels that Mary Parker Follett would have approved). Another concept was 'double loop learning'. Single loop learning is a simple process whereby feedback from previous actions is used to alter future actions. Double loop learning uses feedback from past actions to question not only the nature of future action, but all the underlying assumptions on which future decisions are to be made. When considering feedback, researchers and managers ask not only 'what should we do?', but also 'why are we doing it?', and even more importantly, 'what else ought we to be doing?'. Only by asking these questions, said Argyris and Schön, can learning truly effective and rooted in the organization's culture.[57]

Argyris also picked up on the point made by March and Simon, that organizations limit the actions of their members and that the unresolved conflicts between members can lead to resistance by one faction to another. This can lead to conflict and obstruction, the deliberate slowing up of work, industrial action or even criminal behaviour. Many employees will perceive any change in the organization as a threat. In response, they adopt what Argyris describes as 'defensive routines', actions which can inhibit change or even prevent it entirely. Some employees will employ defensive routines for negative reasons, purely because they do not wish to upset the status quo. More dangerous, says Argyris, are those who seek to block change for what they feel are positive reasons: they may be seeking to protect colleagues who are threatened by change, or they may genuinely believe that the proposed changes are harmful and will damage the organization. Many of these defensive routines become deeply embedded in the organization's culture, so that even new employees brought in to promote change become 'infected' and thus part of the problem.[58]

Contingency theory

Bounded rationality and open systems theory formed two legs of the new human-centred theories of organization. The first rejected the idea that organizations behave rationally, the second pointed out that behaviour, whether rational or no, changes over time. The third leg, contingency theory, argued that organizations evolve and change in quite different ways, and must be managed in quite different ways, depending on a host of factors both internal and external. Contingency theory was a slap in the face to the notion of the 'one best way'. There is no 'one best way' of organizing and managing, says contingency theory, only the way that is right for the place, time and people involved.

One of the first to study the notion of contingency theory was the British industrial sociologist Joan Woodward. Her early work sought to understand the reasons why organizations chose different kinds of structure. Her findings related structure to the complexity of technology and production processes. Larger, more complex organizations using large amounts of technology – especially those engaged in mass production – tended to have strong hierarchies and large amounts of top-down control. Smaller organizations engaged in craft production, especially using simple technology, had less hierarchy and looser control. In McGregor's terms, the former were managed according to Theory X, the latter according to Theory Y.[59]

Woodward's later research on control systems followed the same theme. Large and complex organizations tend to adopt formal administrative systems of control, while smaller and less complex ones will rely on personal relationships to achieve control. On one level, this seems to affirm the validity of scientific management and other more formal forms of control. Woodward does not deny that for some organizations, formal control seems to work. But she reminds us that not every business is a large, technically complex business, and that there is no one-size-fits-all solution. Organizations seek the structure and control systems that best suit them, often in an adaptive and evolutionary way rather than implementing new structures and systems wholesale.[60]

Whereas Woodward believed there was a broad spectrum of organizational structures that could evolve, Tom Burns and George Stalker, also working in Britain around the same time as Woodward, came up with a rather more black-and-white distinction between mechanistic and 'organismic' organizations.[61] Mechanistic organizations are formal, rational and highly structured, with an emphasis on divisionalization and division of labour. They are the descendants of Weber's bureaucracies, organized along the lines suggested by scientific management. Organismic organizations, on the other hand, are less rigidly structured, and there is more integration between parts of the organization, which resemble cells rather than mechanical parts – again, we see the idea that biology offers us an alternative way of understanding how organizations work. Among other things, said Burns and Stalker, mechanistic organizations are very poor at exploiting innovation. They create R&D departments that came up with good ideas, but R&D department are always quite separate from the rest of the business and are often regarded with suspicion by line managers and workers. Mechanistic organizations are in general very bad at learning and adapting new knowledge.

Organismic systems, said Burns, 'are adapted to unstable conditions, when new and unfamiliar problems and requirements continually arise which cannot be broken down amongst specialist roles within a hierarchy.'[62] Burns believed these organizations are better suited to survival in times of uncertainty and change – which, practically speaking, means most times. There is a clear foreshadowing of later work by Tom Peters and Rosabeth Moss Kanter, in particular.[63] Burns and Stalker argued that mechanistic organizations are often unable to change; in some cases, the attempt to change only makes the organization more complex and more difficult to manage without achieving real change.

In America, Paul Lawrence and Jay Lorsch were also developing ideas on contingency theory. Organizations, they said, are characterized by 'a complex set of interrelationships among internal organizational states and processes and external environmental demands.'[64] Their study of high-performing firms across different sectors found marked differences in structure. The key determining factor seemed to be the level of uncertainty and risk found in each sector. In sectors where uncertainty was fairly low and perceived risk was low also, more formal and hierarchical structures predominated, while in high-uncertainty and high-risk environments, more open and flexible systems were common.

The work of Lawrence and Lorsch suggests, even more clearly than that of Woodward, that organizations are themselves engaged in a continuous cycle of challenge and response. Organizations adapt and evolve in Darwinian fashion to the conditions of their environments. This is a conclusion that raises almost as many questions as it answers. For example, what happens when organizations expand out of their own sector, into other sectors or into foreign markets where the environment is different? How do they then adapt, or can they adapt at all? This version of contingency theory went on to influence some later thinking about international business.

The influence of contingency theory is visible too in the work of the Tavistock Institute in Britain where a group of – mostly – psychologists, influenced by the earlier work of Kurt Lewin, began to develop a 'sociotechnical approach' to studying organizations. Like the work of McGregor and Herzberg, the sociotechnical approach focused strongly on the group, the organization, and less on the individual. Among the leading thinkers associated with the Tavistock Institute were the Australian Frederick Emery, the Canadian Elliott Jaques and the Briton Eric Trist. Emery was influenced by biology and also by Gestalt, the psychological theory of 'wholeness'. His concern was that formal and rational organizations had an 'alienating' effect on the people who worked for them, treating them like cogs in a machine, and wondered whether this was in the best interests of the organizations themselves. Following on from McGregor, he called for more openness and more democracy in organizations as a way of encouraging better relations in the workplace and hence more worker commitment.

Emery and Trist reiterated the point that technically complex bureaucracies have trouble functioning in conditions of uncertainty. They are bad at learning and innovation, and tend to alienate employees rather than encouraging them to work for the good of the organization. The sociotechnical approach argued for a more fluid kind of organization based on self-regulation rather than top down control, de-emphasizing the division of labour and encouraging people to perform more than one task, and using flexible rather than standardized methods of operation. All of this would help organizations be more responsive to change.[65]

The distinction drawn by Elliott Jaques was between 'requisite' and 'anti-requisite' organizations. The former encourage people to work together by creating an atmosphere in which trust and equity are important, the latter force people to work together by using coercion and control.[66] Even more than Trist and Emery, Jaques was concerned with the impact of work on people. In *The Form of Time* he argued that modern society placed too much emphasis on the rational and the conscious, and ignored the subconscious and reflective, 'the deeper sense of simply understanding what is right and wrong or fair or just, the sense of the reasonable, the ability to sit back and reflect and remember and to feel a part of one's past and present, and to identify with other human beings, to feel empathy and sensitivity.'[67] Jaques believed that all organizational life was characterized by uncertainty, and was especially dismissive of 'one best way' theories, or any theory which promised a definite outcome to a course of action: 'We cannot put into words what it is that we are taking into account in doing what we are doing, and in that sense we do not know that what we are doing will get us where we want to go, will achieve the result we want to achieve. We judge that it will, we think it will, but we are not sure *and only time will tell*.'[68]

Jaques' theories are complex and it is difficult to summarize them quickly, but one thing which underlines nearly all of his ideas on management is the view that most business organizations simply do not reflect how the human mind operates. The mind makes connections and draws parallels in many different ways; organizations, on the other hand, tend to be linear and highly structured and force thinking into narrow channels.

Another British initiative, the Aston Group led by Derek Pugh and David Hickson, applied elements of contingency theory to the study of organizational structure. In an article in 1973, Pugh concluded that 'context is a determining factor – perhaps overall the determining factor – which designs, shapes and modifies the structure of any organization.'[69] From the group's research, Pugh also noted that about 50 per cent of the variability of organizations is down to contextual influences, leaving top management the ability to influence the rest; a statement that recalls Machiavelli's belief that *fortuna* governs half the affairs of men, leaving them responsible for the other half (see Chapter 4).

The same view of environmental forces as a determining factor can be found in Edgar Schein's work on organizational culture.[70] Schein argued that there is a cyclical connection between people and culture. 'Individuals create organisations that develop cultures', he wrote:

> and organisations acculturate individuals. The balance between individual and organisational autonomy is a perpetual struggle forever modulated by dynamic 'psychological contracts' between employer and employed. Leadership in starting an organisation is a completely different process from leadership in a mature organisation that is trying to change some elements of its culture. Leaders create cultures through imposing their personal values and assumptions on their colleagues and employees, but as the organisation develops a shared view, i.e. 'culture', it imprints itself on its members who may then create yet other organisations on this same model.[71]

A similar theme can be found in James David Thompson's work on the interdependence between the parts of an organization. All organizations must cope with uncertainty, said Thompson, and finding ways to cope successfully was 'the essence of the administrative process.'[72] In their work on organizational ecologies, Michael Hannan and John Freeman pointed to similar linkages and interdependencies with the external environment.[73]

Contingency theory also began creeping into writing on strategy, modulating the influence of the Chandlerian dictum of 'structure follows strategy'. Examples include Jay Galbraith and Daniel Nathanson in their *Strategy Implementation* and especially Raymond Miles and Charles Snow in the *Organizational Strategy, Structure and Process*.[74] Referring to organizational variables, Miles and Snow first asked how and why these variables come to exist. They concluded that the variables are generated within organizations as part of an 'adaptive process' as each organization struggles to come to terms with its environment in a unique way. The reason such responses differ between organizations is in turn due to the complexities of the environment, which they described as:

> not a homogeneous entity but rather . . . a complex combination of factors such as product and market conditions, industry conditions and practices, governmental regulations, and relations with financial and raw material suppliers. Each of these factors tends to influence the organization in its own unique way.[75]

Organizations respond to these pressures by attempting to ensure that their own organization (structure) and technology (process) are closely aligned with the strategy they must pursue in order to respond effectively with their environment. Miles and Snow referred to this concept as 'organizational fitness for purpose'.

Reactions

Just as the human relations school had reacted to scientific management, perceiving the latter to be overly mechanistic and not enough in tune with the realities of human nature and behaviour, so the new generation of organization theorists beginning with Herbert Simon had reacted to just the same traits in the more formal theories of management derived from economics and management science. Bounded rationality, open systems and contingency theory were attempts to create a more humanistic concept of organization, one which took into account the vagaries of human nature.

Yet even these theories were, and are, too rational for some. Harold Koontz, one of the more popular American writers on management in the 1950s and 1960s, rejected the purely scientific approach; management, he said, was an art as well as a science and needed to partake of the essence of both. Following the influence of Lyndall Urwick, he called for more study of the historical evolution of management methods and the conditions under which they emerged, rather than trying to generate theories from scratch.[76] As we saw in the previous chapter, Theodore Levitt deplored the lack of realism in nearly all theories of organization, pointing out that they missed the most important element in any business: its customers. He was not the only one to feel that such organizational navel-gazing was not only wrong and dangerous; Peter Drucker urged managers to think less about organizational structure and more about purpose and objectives (see below).

A second line of criticism, articulated especially by postmodern thinkers on management, doubted the validity of the entire project of creating theories of organization. In 1985 Graham Astley doubted whether it is possible to ever reach objective truth, which is what students of management were striving for. 'The body of knowledge constituting administrative science is not an objective representation of administrative practice', he wrote. 'It does not, through literal correspondence, simply reflect events and activities in the managerial world. Instead of discovering enduring facts of organizational life and reporting them through neutral description, we actively create truth by assigning meaning to the phenomena we observe and experience . . . our *knowledge* of objective reality is subjectively constructed.'[77] In a mischievous and highly entertaining article, 'Voicing Seduction to Challenge Leadership', Marta Calás and Linda Smircich challenge the idea of a definitive organization theory. The ground is constantly shifting and changing, organizations are shifting and changing all the time too, and any theory of organization is likely to be obsolete even before it is formulated. Is there then any point to the exercise?[78]

A third criticism came from those who doubted whether either set of theories accurately reflected how organizations worked or what managers did. In *The Science of Muddling Through*, Charles Lindblom gave quite a different picture of how managers make decisions, usually concentrating on small evolutionary steps and avoiding if possible thinking or doing anything about the larger issues; a practice which Lindblom argued could be quite beneficial.[79] More than a decade after Lindblom, Henry Mintzberg referred to much of existing management theory as 'folklore', unreflective of real life. Far from being reflective practitioners, most managers are ad hoc respondents to unforeseen and emerging situations. They make decisions quickly, often on the move, usually on the basis of intuition rather than any analysis of the possible consequences. They are usually too busy fire-fighting, solving one crisis after another, to stop and think about interrelationships and interdependencies. Even satisficing is far too formal a term to describe what they do.[80]

Certainly the writings of contemporary business leaders show at best little engagement with any of the theories and ideas discussed above, and at worst outright hostility to them. Harold Geneen, the hard-boiled president of ITT, dismissed most management theories as 'baloney' and insisted that 'the old-fashioned virtues of hard work, honesty and risk-taking' were all that managers required.[81] His own management style was based on close monitoring and coordination of the different parts of his business. Andrew Grove of Intel in his first book, *High Output Management*, told his managers that knowledge of Maslow's hierarchy of needs was sufficient to help them understand how to motivate workers. The manager's job, he said, is not to generate ideas or theories, but output: all else was subordinate to that. Grove compared the task of the manager to that of a waiter serving breakfast. Both have the same basic tasks of production: 'to build and deliver products in response to the demands of the customer at a *scheduled* delivery time, at an *acceptable* quality level, and at the *lowest* possible cost.'[82] The Japanese industrialist Matsushita Konosuke kept his finger on the pulse of new developments and was an earlier adopter of elements of the Toyota system (see Chapter 10), but in his own writings he rarely mentions systems or theories. His philosophy of business is grounded in older concepts, such as the need for close relationships between employers and workers, and the social goal of business to create peace and prosperity.[83]

Matsushita would probably have agreed with the authors of an article entitled 'Our Concepts of Controlling Need Re-thinking' in 1958 who argued that human values 'serve as the master control of all organizational activity. These values as perceived by individual managers are the conscious and unconscious criteria for establishing all business objectives and policies. They are the criteria for establishing business criteria.'[84]

The purpose of management: Peter Drucker

The work of Peter Drucker stands out in stark contrast to much of the theorizing that was going on in the 1950s and 1960s. This is not to say that Drucker did not theorise: he did so profusely, but in quite different ways to the management thinkers described above. Drucker has famously described management as the last of the liberal arts, and although he had a lively interest in economics and organization theory, he also had a lively interest in everything from political science to Japanese art, all of which informed his work.[85] An eclectic thinker, he more nearly resembles Harrington Emerson or Lyndall Urwick than many of his own generation.

Drucker had an early interest in economic and organizational theories, but by the 1950s he had turned his attention to the role of the manager, not the organization. As Peter Starbuck points out, Drucker was influenced by Schumpeter's conception of the entrepreneur as a societal force and, further back, Walther Rathenau's belief that business leaders were becoming the new standard-bearers of social progress.[86]

Drucker's mature management thought is captured in three key works: *The Practice of Management, The Effective Executive* and *Management: Tasks, Responsibilities, Practices*.[87] In these three books, he quite deliberately switches the focus away from organizations and systems to tasks and, especially, purpose. Indeed, he warns managers not to become overly preoccupied with organization structure. The most important questions for him are (1) what kind of business are we? and (2) what kind of business should we be?

Drucker attempts to define what it is that managers do, or in modern terms, what value they add. His list of basic tasks of the manager is reminiscent of Fayol and Gulick: managers are responsible for setting objectives, organizing, motivating, measuring and communicating. The leaders of the organization are also responsible for setting policies (i.e. strategy), measuring performance and evaluating results. This looks at first like an old-fashioned functional approach to management, but for Drucker this is merely a necessary laying out of the managerial job description: these are the things that managers must be able to do.

Drucker believes that managers must be proactive. Again showing the influence of Schumpeter, he argues that it is up to managers to shape the organization and its environment. 'Economic forces set limits to what a manager can do', he says. 'They create opportunities for management's action. But they do not by themselves dictate what a business is or what it does.'[88] What the business does is harness resources, create production and satisfy needs. The importance of marketing lies at the heart of much of Drucker's mature work:

There is only one valid definition of business purpose: *to create a customer*. Markets are not created by God, nature or economic forces, but by the people who manage a business. The want a business satisfies may have been felt by customers . . . but it remained a potential want until business people converted it into effective action. Only then are there customers and a market.[89]

While systems thinkers tried to define the relationship between the business and its environment, Drucker simply took that relationship as read. Businesses, in his conception, are part of society; they exist to serve social needs, to contribute to progress and the advancement of civilization. The idea that business is a moral force for good runs through much of his later work, such as *The New Realities*.

In *The Practice of Management*, Drucker introduced a term which would later be controversial, 'management by objectives'. The idea of management by objectives – the setting of targets and then working towards them – was heavily criticized by later writers such as W. Edwards Deming who felt that this would lead to pressure to hit targets by whatever means necessary, which would compromise quality. Others felt that this was a return to old-fashioned top-down control, in which management gave orders and expected the workers to perform. In fairness, Drucker insisted that objectives should be discussed and agreed between management and the workers. His intention was to turn managerial focus away from rigid adherence to tasks and routines and encourage managers to think more creatively about how they reached their goals. It is easy to see how this would annoy Deming, who for all his own emphasis on creativity still believed in the importance of method (see Chapter 10).

Drucker's works were and remain highly popular; he may be the most widely read management thinker of all time, and unlike many of his contemporaries he was widely read by practising managers. One South Korean businessman was so impressed that he changed his own name to Peter Drucker; surely a unique accolade in this field. What made Drucker so popular? A clear and accessible writing style helped, but his focus on the manager as individual, quite at odds with much of the management thinking of the time, must have been refreshing to those who were tired of being described as merely part of a system. He emphasized personal responsibility and purposive action, and tried to persuade managers that their own efforts could have real impact. His methods are those of the philosopher, not the scientist, and in an era dominated by scientistic thinking he showed that philosophy still has a place in management thinking, even if only to stir and motivate managers.

Conclusion

From the 1950s onward, attempts to apply scientific research and concepts to management and organization increased in number and sophistication. As we have seen, one school of thought took principles from the physical sciences, while another drew most of its inspiration from the social sciences; a few, such as Herbert Simon, attempted to cross over and do both.

The results were mixed. At least some of those involved in operations research and management science harked back, directly or indirectly, to scientific management and the spirit of the one best way. The reaction of the other camp in some ways resembles that of the human relations school to scientific management in the 1920s and 1930s. The social scientists insisted that there was no one best way to be found, and that a plurality of structures and systems was both necessary and good. But in making that statement and gathering a mass of evidence from field studies to back it up, what did the social scientists prove? That the world was imperfect, the environment was messy and the task of the manager was uncertain. And most managers already knew this.

This period saw huge advances in our theoretical understanding of management and organizations, with breakthroughs made by both physical and social scientists. But with a few exceptions, it saw very little in the way of practical tools and applications which could be put into managers' hands – at least, as Geoffrey Poitras noted when talking of modern portfolio theory, applications that managers would accept and use. The popularity of Peter Drucker, who tried to do just that, is probably a further reflection of this increasing trend towards theory rather than practice.

Another consequence of the scientization of management was to transfer responsibility for thinking and development firmly within the bounds of academia. Even up to the 1930s, American journals and periodicals on management regularly featured articles by business leaders such as Henry Ford, John North Willys, John Patterson, Thomas Watson and other lesser names, who shared their experiences and insights. But the time was fast approaching when their work would actually be barred from academic journals because it was not considered rigorous or relevant to the task of theory building. As a result, business leaders like Geneen and Matsushita and Grove wrote their own books to share their experiences directly with their peers (or worse, did not write at all). The interaction between practitioners and theorists that had characterized the early journals was breaking down, and would soon be gone.

10   The age of the management gurus

Man's beginnings were described in the Bible in terms of conscious planning and grand
strategy. The opposing theory developed by Darwin suggested that no such grand design
existed but that environmental forces gradually shaped man's evolution.

(Henry Mintzberg)

The fault line that was opening up between theory and practice did not go unnoticed. From
the late 1970s another group of management thinkers and writers began trying to reconnect
with the business world. In doing so, sometimes quite overtly, they were following the path
already laid by Peter Drucker. The phenomenal success of his books from the 1960s onward
showed that there was an appetite for theory and ideas among practising managers, if those
theories and ideas were relevant and were presented in an appealing way. In response, from
the 1970s through to the end of the 1990s there emerged a group of thinkers who became
known – not always flatteringly – as the 'gurus'.

There is no uniform definition of what a 'management guru' is. Some canonical lists of
management gurus now include older figures such as Taylor and Urwick. For the purposes
of this discussion, I mean those influential and popular writers who emerged after Peter
Drucker's rise to prominence, who disseminated management ideas widely and became, at
least for a time, household words in management circles. Some of the gurus were academics;
others were consultants or practising managers. The majority were American, with some
Japanese and a very few British and others. There were sometimes tensions between the gurus
and the academic core of management scientists and social systems thinkers: some of these
tensions were doubtless the result of jealousy, but there was a feeling too that what many of
the gurus were doing was not empirical and not rigorous, and therefore flawed. When it later
emerged that some of the 'excellent' companies held up as exemplars by Tom Peters and
Robert Waterman in their book *In Search of Excellence* had later run into problems, the
academic community enthusiastically tore their work to shreds. Against this, the gurus could
argue that they were disseminating ideas about management in a way that many of their
colleagues were not.

In this chapter, I do not intend to give exhaustive coverage of the views of the gurus, or
even to represent them all. All were, and some still are, widely read and their ideas will be
known to many. Some who were later classified as gurus such as Edgar Schein, James March
and, of course, Peter Drucker have already been covered in the previous chapter, and some
will wait their turn until the next. The aim here is to give some idea of how and why the
gurus became popular, and an overview of some of the contributions they made to management thought in particular areas, including strategy, marketing, quality, organization
and leadership.

The challenge from Germany and Japan

There was another reason for the emergence of the gurus, especially in America. After two decades of growth, the world economy faltered in the 1970s. By the time growth resumed in the 1980s, American companies discovered that they had formidable challengers emerging in Germany and, especially, Japan. As Robert Locke has described, the myth of American managerial superiority was shattered.[1] American managers could no longer assume that their ways of doing business were better than those found elsewhere in the world.

The economy of the Federal Republic of Germany (West Germany) had been rebuilt after the Second World War with, at first, strong American assistance through the Marshall Plan. This initiative was part of the opening moves of the Cold War and was designed to strengthen the economy of Germany and turn the country into a bulwark against communism in Europe. France and Italy received similar assistance, which included the provision of American engineers and consultants and the transfer of American management methods.[2] Although much attention has been paid to this transfer and the consequent 'Americanization' of German business, less attention has been given to the revival of Germany's own management culture and the continuity of ideas from the pre-Nazi period. By the end of the 1950s Germany had developed a management culture whose key features were a strong focus on technical knowledge – most senior managers had Ph.D.s, very often in the physical sciences – a long-term approach to planning with planning horizons typically much longer than in America, an emphasis on quality and service, strong collaboration with government and a strongly consensual approach to managing people. Many companies developed sophisticated programmes of employee involvement, so much so that Alfred Chandler referred to German managerial culture – somewhat disparagingly – as 'cooperative managerial capitalism'.[3]

Earlier, in *The Visible Hand*, Chandler had described his own version of the 'managerial revolution' in America. He argued that the emergence of professional managers in the 1920s and 1930s and especially after the Second World War had been a key factor in America's industrial dominance. But Chandler misunderstood the strength of German management culture and its values. High levels of technical knowledge and a strong emphasis on technical quality gave German industry a formidable competitive advantage in areas such as automotives, electronics and especially machine tools, where it dominated the world market for decades.

German management thought harked back to Schmalenbach and Nicklisch (see Chapter 6), and even to some extent to Rathenau. Whereas American economic theory largely rejected economics, German thinkers continued to embrace economic thinking. Among the earliest post-war economic writers on management were Wilhelm Rieger and Erich Gutenberg. Rieger, like Schmalenbach, started with an interest in accounting before moving on to discuss theories of entrepreneurship. Rieger's view was that profit was the primary motive of the entrepreneur, and he concentrated on issues of technical efficiency.[4] Gutenberg developed a version of equilibrium theory, arguing that businesses constantly balanced off competing pressures from their markets and the environment more generally, and sought maximal efficiency in order to make that balance work.[5]

These highly technical conceptions of business were moderated by the work of Edmund Heinen, who added a behavioural perspective to the Gutenberg's equilibrium theory and the older ideas of Nicklisch on the social role of business. Rainer Marr has compared his approach to that of March and Simon (see Chapter 9).[6] Heinen introduced concepts such as irrational behaviour, ambiguity and decision making on the basis of limited information, thereby 'humanizing' the formal–rational ideas of Gutenberg.[7] His work also emphasized the connection with community and the need for consensus between government, industry and workers. As Marr says, Heinen's theories formed the basis of the dominant model of management thinking in Germany for several decades, and played a role in the country's industrial success up to 1991.

If the German challenge was serious, the Japanese challenge quickly assumed critical proportions, especially in sectors such as automobiles and consumer electronics where American companies watched their market share erode as low-cost, high-quality Japanese imports moved in. Fear of the Japanese threat took on extreme forms, as for example in the novel *Rising Sun* which suggested that Japan might be seeking economic domination of America.[8] The screening of a television documentary, *If Japan, Why Can't We?* in 1980 caused shock in corporate America when it revealed that Japanese industry owed much of its success to its adoption of methods advocated by two American consultants, W. Edwards Deming and Joseph Juran. This was, and is, an oversimplification. As Naoto Sasaki describes in his book *Management and Industrial Structure in Japan*, Japanese business culture has a number of strengths including the *nemawashi* system which disseminates knowledge and secures consensus and employee buy-in to key decisions, and a strong sense of organizational culture.[9] Companies such as Toyota had already been working on their own management systems before the Second World War. Now they borrowed the quality control methods of Deming and Juran – and, as is sometimes overlooked, management by objectives and other ideas from Drucker – and grafted them onto indigenous management methods to create a system which, for a time, amazed the world with its efficiency and effectiveness.

Although American aid and American technicians played a large part in rebuilding the Japanese economy, and had an impact on Japanese management thinking, the core of Japanese management thinking remained rooted in Japanese culture. Key influences were the pragmatic strategic thinking of Sunzi (see Chapter 2) which urged preparation and knowledge of oneself and of the opposition rather than formal planning, and the works of Miyamoto Musashi and other swordfighters with their emphasis on personal mastery and mental preparation, along with ideas drawn from Japan's Buddhist and Shinto heritage. Toyoda Sakichi, founder of the Toyota Spinning and Weaving Company in 1918, acknowledged two important influences, Buddhist philosophy and Samuel Smiles's *Self-Help*. Both, he said, taught him that while perfection would always remain out of reach, striving for it would nevertheless result in much good.[10]

The Toyota system

Toyoda Sakichi and his son Toyoda Kiichiro founded the Toyota Motor Company in 1937, and it was here that the first elements of what later became known as the Toyota system were developed.[11] At Toyota, necessity was the mother of invention. The Toyodas could not afford to establish a large plant – the first car production line was set up using space borrowed from the textile works – and there was no money to acquire and hold large stocks of components in the way that other mass producers did. Workers making components worked alongside the assembly line, and were told to on no account make components until they were called for. A card system, known as *kanban*, was introduced to signal when components were required. The component makers then had to work very quickly and accurately so as not to cause delays on the production line. The Toyodas also emphasized precision work and the avoidance of waste, all in the name of eliminating unnecessary costs. Toyoda Kiichiro hung a large banner with the inscription 'just in time' over the assembly line to remind everyone of the guiding principle. This system, with refinements over the next several decades, became known as just-in-time or 'lean production'.

Just-in-time was only half of the Toyota philosophy. The other half was *kaizen*, usually translated as 'continuous improvement'. Buddhist philosophy provided the inspiration for this idea; Buddhism seeks spiritual perfection, but it is not hard to transfer that same quality to the process of making things. Quality, in the Toyota vision, was a journey and not a destination; no matter how good things are, they can always be made better. There was a pragmatic reason for this idea too. *Kaizen* emerged as an important force after the Second World War, when Toyoda Kiichiro coined the slogan 'Catch Up With America'. Japan needed to export in order to prosper, and in order to gain access to the lucrative European and American markets, Japanese businesses had to meet and beat Western quality standards.

Toyota's chief engineer Ohno Taiichi played a leading role in the development of this system. Ohno coined terms such as 'zero defects' and 'wasteless manufacturing' which went on to become part of the management lexicon, and not just in Japan. He also stressed the importance of finding the fundamental sources of production problems, not just applying patches to solve the immediate problem. 'Underneath the "cause" of a problem, the *real cause* is hidden', he wrote. 'In every case, we must dig up the real cause by asking *why, why, why, why, why?*'[12] The system of inquiry that he called the 'five whys' was aimed at finding those hidden problems that were the real source of inefficiency.

There was much that was mechanistic about the Toyota system. For example, the system of *poka-yoke* or 'foolproof' assembly was designed to eliminate defects by standardizing processes of assembly so that work could only be done one way: the correct way. The emphasis on speed and absolute precision could be considered to have a dehumanizing effect on workers in the same way that scientific management had done. And Toyota had its labour problems; Toyoda Kiichiro was forced to resign as head of the company in 1950 after a series of damaging labour disputes, and his cousin and successor Toyoda Eiji had to make a number of concessions to workers in order to restore harmony.

The quality movement

Charles Darwin is responsible at least in part for total quality management. His theories of evolution led many people such as Francis Galton and, for a time, John Maynard Keynes to consider the possibilities of managing the evolutionary process in plants and animals, which they called 'eugenics'. One of Keynes's contemporaries at the University of Cambridge, the statistician Ronald Fisher, conducted a series of studies on agricultural crops and developed what he called the 'analysis of variance', by which patterns of deviance from the norm can be detected and analysed. Fisher went on to develop applications for his theories in many branches of science, and is generally known as the father of modern statistical methods; his *Statistical Methods for Research Workers* became a standard text in both Europe and America between the wars.[13]

Fisher had been publishing his work in journals since the early 1920s, and his articles came to the attention of Walter Shewhart, head of the inspection department at Western Electric's telephone components plant at Hawthorne, Illinois, more famous for the experiments on industrial efficiency which were just beginning there (see Chapter 7). Like most companies, Western Electric conducted inspections of finished products at the end of the manufacturing cycle with a view to weeding out defects. In 1924 Shewhart and his department developed a method of using variation analysis to measure defects during the production process. This in turn allowed adjustments to be made to the production process which would reduce the number of defects and improve efficiency. This process became known as statistical quality control.

The consequences of this were far-ranging. Joseph Juran was one of Shewhart's assistants and the student W. Edwards Deming, who worked at the plant during the summer, got to know Shewhart and went on to work with him in the 1930s. The influence of the inspection department at Western Electric on subsequent management thought has probably been greater even than that of the Hawthorne experiments. Juran's pamphlet 'Statistical Methods Applied to Manufacturing Problems' was written in 1928, followed by Shewhart's *Economic Control of Quality of Manufactured Product* in 1931. Interest in quality control issues began to grow in some sectors, especially in electrical engineering and also at General Motors. Deming, having worked with both Shewhart and Ronald Fisher, became a successful consultant, and Juran advanced to senior positions in Western Electric. During the Second World War statistical quality control became part of the broader programme of operations research (see Chapter 9), and led to the foundation of the American Society for Quality in 1946.

Then, at the end of the Second World War, interest seems to have died out. Armand Feigenbaum, who coined the term 'total quality control' in the 1950s and served as president of the American Society for Quality, wrote two important books on the topic that were widely disregarded by American industrialists.[14] A successful businessman himself, Feigenbaum found himself in a position resembling that of Robert Owen nearly a century and a half before: he had found ways of improving quality and efficiency, but no one wanted to hear them. This seems surprising, given the focus on operations research and technical efficiency we saw in Chapter 9; but that focus was aimed at *systems* and not at products. With the economies of Japan and Europe devastated by war, American industry had little competition. It was possible to make money, as Theodore Levitt said at the time, by keeping the plants going at full blast.[15]

Instead, interest in statistical quality control developed in two other parts of the world. One was India, where the Indian Statistical Institute, founded almost single-handedly by the mathematician P.C. Malahanobis in 1931, attracted a number of scholars after the Second World War. One of these was the eminent statistician C.V. Rao, who later went on to Britain to study with Fisher. Walter Shewhart, finding himself to some extent a prophet without honour in America, first visited the Institute in 1947–8, where he gave a number of lectures and was warmly received.[16] Ronald Fisher and the mathematician J.B.S. Haldane also served as visiting professors. Malahanobis and the Institute engaged with the Indian government and made a number of contributions to administrative practices and government planning. There was little contact with Indian industry, however.[17]

The other place where statistical quality control saw a surge in interest was Japan. Among the leading figures were Ishikawa Kaoru, who joined Tokyo University in 1947 and established the Quality Control Research Group under the auspices of the Japan Union of Scientists and Engineers in 1949, and Masuyama Motosaburo, who worked with the University of Tokyo School of Medicine. Masuyama was heavily influenced by Fisher, whom he met while he too was a visiting professor at the Indian Statistical Institute. Among Masuyama's students was Taguchi Genichi, who likewise studied with Shewhart and Fisher at the ISI and went on to develop statistical control methods for measuring manufacturing quality.

Ishikawa was also aware of the work of Shewhart and Fisher, and began giving his own lectures on quality control soon after the war. In 1947 he met Deming on the latter's first visit to Japan, and asked the latter to lecture as well. This was the beginning of a long relationship between Deming and Japan, and the latter was a frequent visitor to the country through the two decades that followed, in wide demand as a lecturer and consultant. In 1951 Juran's *Quality Control Handbook* was also picked up by Ishikawa and his colleagues and he was invited to lecture in Japan; from 1954 onward he too was a popular consultant in Japan and his books sold well there.[18]

The combination of lean production and *kaizen* with statistical quality control was a powerful one. The exact extent of the influence of Deming and Juran has been debated. Deming and Juran were both publicly praised and honoured by the Japanese government, but in a later reflection Deming believed that the Japanese scientists and managers deserved most of the credit; he and Juran had merely played supporting roles.[19] Certainly much credit must be given to Ishikawa, who played a major role in defining the concept of total quality control and the development of quality circles. One of the keys to achieving quality, he believed, was getting employees to 'buy in' and contribute ideas that would help improve quality – rather as Edward Cadbury had done so effectively in Britain before the First World War. Although Ishikawa took ideas from the Toyota system, he thought it relied too much on top-down control; employees were expected to achieve quality targets set for them, rather than having a say in the process.[20]

In the 1980s there was worldwide awareness of an interest in the Japanese 'economic miracle', and total quality control, now known as total quality management (TQM), was much discussed and talked about.[21] Attempts to implement it in the West met with mixed results. The failure of some TQM initiatives led some critics to dismiss it as a fad. TQM was also seen as a return to old-fashioned command and control management. All of this led to belated interest in the ideas of Deming and Juran, and both enjoyed second careers as gurus in North America and, to a lesser extent, Europe.

What is interesting about Deming and Juran is that by the 1980s their own thinking had moved far beyond statistical quality control. If they had an influence in Japan, then Japan had clearly also had an influence on them. In his later writing, Joseph Juran stressed the need for a company-wide approach to quality control.[22] Unlike Ishikawa but very much in keeping with the Toyota ethos, he stressed the need for top management to take the lead. Quality control initiatives would only work if the company's leadership was fully engaged in quality initiatives and helped to drive them through. Otherwise, individual departments and teams will pursue their own initiatives in an unstructured way. Juran was in favour of quality councils, groups which would help coordinate quality initiatives across the company, but was insistent that the CEO had to be closely involved.

In terms of quality itself, Juran argued that 'quality' should be defined as 'fitness for use'.[23] No matter how well-designed and highly engineered the product, if the customer does not received what he or she expect, then the product is not a quality one. This does not necessarily mean luxury, it merely means that the product meets customer needs. Showing the influence of *kaizen*, Juran also insisted that there were no absolute standards for quality, and that managers would have to improve continuously in order to keep meeting customer expectations.

For Deming, too, quality was more than just a set of techniques for quality control and standardization. Quality had to become a mindset, embraced by the entire company.[24] He also emphasized the importance of the role of the manager, and stressed his opposition to the culture of 'blame the workers' whenever things went wrong. It was management's responsibility to develop a quality system that could work, and then ensure that all staff were committed to making it work. His ultimate philosophy of quality was more of a philosophy of general management. He summed up his views in his famous Fourteen Points:

1   create constancy of purpose.
2   adopt a new philosophy for leadership and purpose.
3   cease dependence on inspection to achieve quality; build quality into the product in the first place.
4   end the practice of awarding business on the basis of price; consider the total cost of good and bad quality.
5   undertake continuous improvement of both production and service.
6   institute training on the job.
7   institute leadership.
8   drive out fear, enabling everyone to work effectively for the company.
9   break down barriers between departments.
10   eliminate slogans, exhortations and targets.
11   eliminate work standards, quotas, management by objectives and management by numbers; replace these with leadership.
12   remove the barriers that rob workers of the right to workmanship, both on the shop floor and in management.
13   institute a rigorous programme of education and self-improvement.
14   put everyone in the company to work to accomplish the transformation.[25]

Here too, in the emphasis on factors such as continuous improvement, building in quality at the beginning of the process, total company transformation and constancy of purpose, we can see the influence of Japanese total quality management thinking. Points 8–12 are particularly interesting. Deming, whom many people associate with statistical control, is arguing here for an end to statistical targets, an end to exhortations to higher productivity, and an end to barriers between workers and management. Instead he argues that managers should give workers pride in their work and managers pride in their companies. Rejecting targets and goals, and management by objectives in particular, he calls instead for an open-ended system which challenges everyone to excel, not to achieve a particular task but for the sake of doing the job well. There are strange echoes of the craftworking ideology of William Morris that does not always sit comfortably with mass production systems, and some thought Deming had gone too far. Juran, for example, thought that within limits fear could play a useful role. Fear of failure could lead people to work harder to succeed. But this is slightly to miss the point. Deming is calling here for a renewal of purpose; for managers and workers alike to remember what business is for. His last book, published in the year of his death, argued that the quality movement could act as a basis for national economic and social renewal.[26]

The importance of culture

While Ishikawa, Deming, Juran and others were developing the basis for modern theories of quality management, another guru was beginning to emerge in Europe. The Dutch engineer and sociologist Geert Hofstede joined IBM's executive development department in 1965, going on to become manager of personnel research a few years later. Hofstede was interested in the idea of culture. That organizations had their own cultures, beliefs and ways of doing things was well known, but conventional wisdom had it that national culture had only a weak effect on employee behaviour; organizational culture was a much stronger determinant. Hofstede, working with one of the world's most monolithic companies, which prided itself on its uniformity, wondered if this was true.

Hofstede undertook two surveys of IBM employees, one in 1968 and another in 1972. In all, 116,000 people were surveyed across forty different IBM companies; the people themselves came from sixty different nationalities. His conclusion was that national culture makes a powerful difference and affects how people behave and think even within the same organization. Hofstede then tried to break down the responses and develop classifications for behaviour. He concluded that cultural variations can be measured along four key dimensions:

1   Power distance, the degree to which power within a society is distributed equally or unequally, and the extent to which that society accept this distribution. High power distance societies tend towards strong hierarchies and strongly defined roles; low power distance societies have weak hierarchies and put more emphasis on individual respon-sibility.
2   Uncertainty avoidance, the degree to which members of the society require structure and boundaries in the work place. High uncertainty avoidance societies are those which are intolerant of risk, and also of ideas which may challenge accepted norms and standard ways of doing things. Low uncertainty avoidance societies, on the other hand, are more accepting and tolerant of risk.
3   Individualism/collectivism, the degree to which people act according to self-interest or the interests of the group.
4   Masculinity/femininity. Societies where earnings, promotion and status are seen as the most important work goals are classified as 'masculine', while those where quality of life and human relationships are prioritized are classified as 'feminine'.[27]

Two implications of this survey and findings stand out. The first is that, far from being dominant, organizational culture in fact has a fairly weak influence on workplace values and behaviour, at least compared to national culture. The second is that national cultures themselves cannot be defined in black-and-white terms. Cultures that score high in some dimensions score low in others. National culture is a much more complex phenomenon than anyone had previously believed.

Revision and criticism of the Hofstede model began almost at once. It was pointed out that the data he had collected in Asia was fairly weak and did not necessarily reflect Asian workplace values. Hofstede accepted this, and in subsequent works added a fifth dimension, time orientation.[28] Others added further dimensions of their own, until twelve or even sixteen dimensions were not uncommon. There have been a number of complaints about his findings, and other surveys using the same methodology have shown conflicting results. But this in a way also validates Hofstede's view that culture is very complex and has many different influences on the workplace. Hofstede's work asked more questions than it answered, and subsequent studies such as the GLOBE Project in the 1990s in part merely confirmed how complex and little understood cultural influences on management can be.[29]

One consequence of Hofstede's work was an acceptance of the fact that multinational corporations cannot be monoliths. Internal and external diversity are factors that will not go away. Nancy Adler's work on international strategy and human resource management makes this point particularly strongly. Culture affects strategic networks, partnerships, the man-agement of people; indeed, it affects companies on almost every level. Adler urged that managers come to terms with this and show more willingness and interest in working with people from other cultures.[30] From the 1990s onward there has been an increasing prolifera-tion of works urging that diversity is a positive thing and can be a source of organizational strength and competitive advantage.[31]

Reflection

Software of the mind

One of the best places to understand cultural differences and how they work is the European Leadership Conference, held each year at the IEDC business school at Bled in Slovenia. In June 2011 the special theme of the conference was relationships between the EU and Russia. Many of the speakers, both Russian and Western, described at some length the role played by cultural differences and misunderstandings as a barrier to businesses. It was clear to them that Russian and Western European culture, despite many similarities, were distinctly different.

To my mind, the most interesting thing about this was that speakers were giving the idea so much prominence. Cultural differences are an equally powerful barrier between the West and India, or the West and China. And they always have been. We have different norms, different values, different ideas of right and wrong. When the Chinese diplomat Zhang Deyi first visited London in 1868, he was perplexed by much of what he saw and heard. For example, he was horrified to find that the English used news-papers and writing paper as toilet paper. To Zhang, this showed a terrible disrespect to the persons whose views were recorded on the paper. Such a thing would never happen in China.[32]

But at Bled in 2011, the idea that cultural differences are nothing new, nor are they unique to Russia and Western Europe, was cold consolation. What mattered to the speakers and the delegates was that the barriers existed; nor did they look likely to end. They were an obstacle that had to be overcome. Yet if Hofstede is right, this barrier never will be overcome. It will never go away. Listening to the discussion, my thought was: rather than wishing culture would go away, should we not accept it, and as Nancy Adler said, try to find positives in diversity?

Proponents of globalization argue that there is a process of convergence happening around the world, and that in time cultural differences will break down. This has happened to a degree, but it is now recognized that there are limits to convergence. Indeed, in *The Next Global Stage*, Kenichi Ohmae warned that national culture is making a comeback; and not only that but within countries regional culture is on the rise too.[33] One needs only to think of the rise of Welsh and Scottish nationalism in Britain or Catalan nationalism in Spain, the paralysing strife between Flemings and Walloons in Belgium, the increased recognition of ethnic and cultural groups inside China, to be aware of this. We have become a little more like each other, in that we dress alike and drink the same fizzy soft drinks and listen to the same pop music. But we still *think* differently, just as differently as in Zhang Deyi's day.

To my mind, Hofstede's work is valuable for two reasons. Set aside his scales, his research methods and their validity; it does not matter if they are right or wrong. What matters is that Hofstede reminds us of something we should already know, which the delegates speaking at the conference in Bled certainly knew: culture matters. As Hofstede said, it is the software of the mind. It conditions how we think, how we perceive, how we act in relation to others, how we make decisions. No understanding of international business can possibly be complete without an understanding of the role of culture. Pretending that we can go abroad and do things just as we did them at home simply won't do. And yet, companies fall into this trap all the time, in Russia, China, India, Japan and many other places.

The second point is even more important. Understanding the impact of culture reminds us too that most things that happen in business do so for reasons that have nothing to do with business. Political events and social changes can exercise a powerful impact on business. But even at the micro level, businesses are affected by things that happen in their environment. Employees bring their problems at home into the workplace, and this creates disruption. Public transport strikes or epidemic illnesses can suddenly create problems that prevent them getting to work at all. Customers may suddenly and – apparently – inexplicably change their minds about what they want. Many, many other external factors can intervene, all of which make a mockery of the idea of businesses as formal rational systems. For cultural reasons alone, the idea of businesses as closed systems will never be realized.

Broadening the concept of marketing

Marketing had originally been defined by writers such as Paul Cherington and Melvin Copeland in a fairly functional way. Apart from the psychological studies of motivation and consumer decision-making from Northwestern University, studies of marketing and texts on marketing had concentrated largely on what marketers do. For example, one of the most popular textbooks, Jerome McCarthy's *Basic Marketing* in 1960, focused on the 4Ps and the tasks of the marketing manager. As Philip Kotler and Sidney Levy pointed out a few years later, 'The term "marketing" connotes to most people a function peculiar to business firms. Marketing is seen as the task of finding and stimulating buyers for the firm's output.'[34]

Kotler and Levy's article 'Broadening the Concept of Marketing', which appeared in 1969, is one of the most significant writings on marketing ever published, one which changed the perception of what marketing is.

> It is the authors' contention that marketing is a pervasive social activity that goes considerably beyond the selling of toothpaste, soap and steel. Political contests remind us that candidates are marketed as well as soap; student recruitment by colleges reminds us that higher education is marketed; and fund raising reminds us that 'causes' are marketed. Yet these areas of marketing are typically ignored by the student of marketing.[35]

'Every organization performs marketing-like activities whether or not they are recognized as such', Kotler and Levy continued.[36] They argued that marketing is not just about securing commercial transactions. Even when dealing with commercial goods and services, marketing is also a matter of transmitting and communicating social values. Every product that is made and sold performs some sort of social function; every transaction has some social aspect, and therefore social values are part of all exchanges. Marketing is a social function. Ultimately, marketing is about communication. What is being sold matters much less than to whom, and why.

Kotler and Levy's work caused a furore within marketing academia. David J. Luck rebutted the idea of broadening the concept of marketing, claiming that the broad approach meant that the concept of marketing had now become meaningless: 'If a task is performed, anywhere by anybody, [resembles] a task that is performed in marketing, that would *be* marketing ... The clergyman who had been pondering his church's programs and had considered himself to be a theologian and spiritual leader turns out to be a marketer.'[37] To refer to non-commercial activities as marketing, says Luck, is pointless. Politicians have been making decisions about communications channels and messages for thousands of years, marketing had only been around for a few decades. What right had marketing to claim these other activities as its own?

But Luck and other critics missed the point of what Kotler and Levy were trying to say. First, Kotler and Levy pointed out that the tools and techniques of marketing can be adapted to other purposes in order to make other, non-commercial organizations more effective. Kotler went on to reinforce this point in later works, and charities in particular have now become much more sophisticated in their approach to fundraising and pleading their own causes as a result. Kotler coined the term 'social marketing' to reflect this use of marketing techniques for non-commercial purposes.[38] He later redefined this as 'societal marketing' which 'holds that the organization's task is to determine the needs, wants, and interests of target markets and to deliver the desired satisfactions more effectively and efficiently than competitors in a way that preserves or enhances the consumer's or society's well-being.'[39]

Second, Kotler and his various co-writers started a redefinition of the concept of marketing itself. Instead of the old functional model, Kotler's new model of marketing was founded on a few simple common elements, regardless of what is being marketed and to whom. Those elements begin with analysis of the needs, wants and demands of the customer. *Needs*, he says, are the realization of the lack of some basic requirement; *wants* are specific requests for products or services to fill needs; *demands* are wants backed up by the desire and ability to pay or otherwise make exchange.

Next in importance come the concepts of *value* and *satisfaction*. Customers, as Juran had suggested, make their choice based on perceived value to themselves, not to the marketing company. Value thus depends on how well the product will satisfy a need, want or demand. *Satisfaction* is the extent to which actual value realized by the purchase or acquisition of the product matches the pre-purchase assessment of value. If actual value is equal to or greater than perceived value, satisfaction will result, if not, then dissatisfaction will result. Thus Kotler defines marketing as 'a social process by which individuals and groups obtain what they need and want through creating and exchanging products and value with others'.[40]

In offering this definition, Kotler was also taking an important step in reconnecting the theory of marketing with customers and ultimately with society. Marketing was no longer something that was done *to* people in order to maximize income and profit for the firm. Ten years earlier, Theodore Levitt had called for firms to pay more attention to the true source of their wealth, their customers.[41] Kotler's contribution was to establish the connection with customers more strongly, but also to remind marketers that theirs was ultimately a social function. His concepts of value and satisfaction resemble not so much marketing writers like Cherington or McCarthy, as older philosophical thinkers about the nature and purpose of business such as al-Dimashqi and Thomas Aquinas.

Refocusing marketing on the customer had several consequences. One was to highlight the importance of service. For most of the twentieth century the focus of marketing in America had been on physical products: some had even argued that services, because they were intangible, could not be marketed. Services marketing and the quality movement came together in the work of Parasuraman, Zeithaml and Berry in the 1980s who attempted to develop a scale for measuring service quality.[42] Their system has been criticized, but it did lead to further research on customer-led measures of service quality, and hence of quality more generally. Today, the notion that quality is determined by the customer is generally accepted.

A similar philosophy has pervaded much of the recent work on brands. Typical is the work of David Aaker, whose work on brand equity in the 1990s made it clear that the value of a brand rests on customers' perceptions of it.[43] Patrick Barwise reminded the marketing community that the value of a brand is directly linked to the value of a product and the rest of the firm, and more recently Mary Jo Hatch and Majken Schultz, among others, have enlarged on the concept of the corporate brand, the vehicle through which the firm engages with all of its stakeholders, including society at large.[44] Other writers have commented on the process of 'co-creation', whereby brand value is created through interactions between the firm and its customers, or even in interactions between customers quite independently of the firm itself (for example, the comments posted and read by hotel customers on TripAdvisor help to create – or destroy – hotel brand value).[45]

Kotler himself was not a typical guru. A career-long academic, he wrote mostly academic articles and textbooks. But his ideas have been read by hundreds of thousands of students around the world, who have taken his ideas and applied them directly in their own organizations. His lasting achievement has been to turn marketing from a functional to a human-centred discipline.

Emerging views on strategy

In Chapter 8 we saw how the discipline of business strategy emerged, rather late, out of more general considerations of organization. The highly formalistic school of strategic thinking now known as the 'planning school' dominated strategic theorizing for nearly two decades. In the words of Peter McKiernan:

> The planning school preached that strategy could be formulated in a deliberate manner, with implementation following in a controlled sequence. Objectives were thereby achieved and the strategy realized. There was always a danger that this could become the unchallenged entrenched view, which it did. Ironically, it is still the preferred pedagogical layout for the major teaching texts.[46]

Typical of the planning school was the Harvard Business School professor Kenneth Andrews, whose *The Concept of Corporate Strategy* became a standard textbook. Andrews described corporate strategy as 'the pattern of decisions in a company that determines and reveals its objectives, purposes, or goals'.[47] Andrews drew a distinction between corporate strategy, which affects the whole enterprise, and business strategy, which concentrates on particular markets or businesses within the larger firm. A succession of individual business strategies thus nests within a single overarching corporate strategy. Andrews's view of strategy, like that of Chandler and Ansoff before, was highly deliberate: companies scan the environment, analyse the options, take rational decisions and make formal plans which are then implemented in a linear fashion.

This view of strategy was challenged repeatedly as time went on. One early critic, Aaron Wildavsky, argued that the experience of planning suggested that the process of planning was itself flawed. In an article entitled 'If Planning is Everything, Maybe It's Nothing', Wildavsky argued that 'the planner has become the victim of planning; his own creation has overwhelmed him. Planning has become so large that the planner cannot encompass its dimensions. Planning has become so complex planners cannot keep up with it.'[48] Planners believe that planning introduces rationality to thinking about the future and enables them to control the future, yet paradoxically, they have no proof of this; their belief, therefore, is an act of pure faith in the efficacy of planning, unsupported by evidence. Commenting on public sector planning, Wildavsky observes that 'if governments perseverate in their national planning, it must be because their will to believe triumphs over their experience'.[49]

Among the most prominent and vocal critics of the planning school was the heterodox Canadian academic and writer Henry Mintzberg. In *The Nature of Managerial Work* Mintzberg challenged the received academic wisdom, not just about strategy but about organizations, decision making and management in general, claiming that what managers actually *do* bears very little relation to what academics *assume* they do. His critique of the planning school focused on the latter's assumption that top managers are capable of a kind of Olympian detachment and are able to plan strategy in a detached and emotionless way. That, says Mintzberg, simply does not happen. He compares the planning school to the creation of the world as described in the book of Genesis:

> Man's beginnings were described in the Bible in terms of conscious planning and grand strategy. The opposing theory developed by Darwin suggested that no such grand design existed but that environmental forces gradually shaped man's evolution.[50]

His own view of strategy, generally known as 'emergent strategy', saw strategy making and strategy implementation as a process of constant evolution very much in the Darwinian mode of thinking. Strategy makers respond to environmental pressures and change and adapt their strategy as they go along. Rather than formal planning, Mintzberg speaks of 'crafting' strategy, and uses the metaphor of a potter at the wheel, letting the clay take shape under his or her hands. This too is an old metaphor for creation, used among others by Omar Khayyam in the *Rubaiyat*.[51] Even more interesting, however, is the parallel which can be drawn between Mintzberg's views of strategy and those of Machiavelli nearly five hundred years earlier. The latter had also argued that the ability of leaders to make decisions and act upon them is limited and that environmental forces, or *fortuna*, shaped strategic thinking to a large extent.

Viewed in one light, then, Mintzberg can be seen as reminding managers of a long-recognized truth, that managers and leaders are at least in part prisoners of the circumstances in which they find themselves. Kotler had tried to reconnect marketing theory with the real world of customers and markets; Mintzberg was trying to do much the same thing with strategy.

Another attempt came from Kenichi Ohmae, whose book *The Mind of the Strategist* became a bestseller first in Japan and then worldwide. Ohmae, who worked with McKinsey & Company in Japan for a number of years, professed himself to be baffled by the formal, planned approach to strategy that he saw in American companies in particular. Like Mintzberg, he believed strategy to be an art, not a science, 'a thought process which is basically creative and intuitive rather than rational. Strategists do not reject analysis. Indeed they can hardly do without it. But they use it only to stimulate the creative process, to test the ideas that emerge, to work out their strategic implications . . . Great strategies, like great works of art or great scientific discoveries, call for technical mastery in the working out but originate in insights that are beyond the reach of conscious analysis.'[52]

Ohmae pointed out that Japanese companies did not have strategy departments and seldom engaged in formal planning. Instead, people in Japanese companies were trained to think about strategy on a continuous and ongoing basis. This point was particularly important. Thinking about strategy is a kind of intellectual exercise, said Ohmae, and people need to train their mental habits in order to become at once more analytical and more reflective. The most important virtues of the strategist, said Ohmae, were vision and courage. Again, there are echoes of the past here: Buddhist thinking and the works of Miyamoto the swordfighter both influence Ohmae's thinking, even if indirectly. A famous passage from *The Mind of the Strategist* shows those influences clearly and sums up Ohmae's approach to strategy:

> Strategic thinking in business must break out of the limited scope of vision that entraps deer on the highway. It must be backed by the daily use of imagination and by constant training in logical thought processes. Success must be summoned: it will not come unbidden or unplanned . . . To become an effective strategist requires constant practice in strategic thinking. It is a daily discipline, not a resource that can be left dormant in normal times and then tapped at will in an emergency.[53]

The result of these attacks was to splinter the discipline of strategy into different schools of thought. The planning school continued to have its strong adherents, but the 'emergent' concept championed by Mintzberg grew in strength. Igor Ansoff, one of the founders of the planning school, retracted many of his original ideas in a later work, *The New Corporate Strategy*, where he cast doubt on the efficacy of formal planning and argued that managers had to play more attention to 'turbulence', unforeseen events that could disrupt and delay plans (turbulence, of course, is Clausewitz's 'friction' by another name).[54]

Emergent strategy eventually became subsumed into another school known more generally as the 'learning school', which held that strategy happens as a response to social, political and other environmental forces. The idea that strategy emerges as a response to what organizations learn about the world around them was encapsulated by Arie de Geus in his article 'Planning as Learning' in *Harvard Business Review* in 1988.[55] De Geus argued that the ability to learn is a powerful source of competitive advantage – indeed, perhaps the only sustainable source of competitive advantage – as it enables organizations to look ahead and try to anticipate future changes and thus respond to them. De Geus's colleague at Royal Dutch/Shell, the economist Pierre Wack, had earlier described how scenarios can be used to model possible future events. The purpose of such modelling, said Wack, was not to predict the future – that was impossible – but rather to accustom managers to the habit of thinking about the future, much in the manner described by Kenichi Ohmae.[56]

Another sub-school within the learning school was incrementalism, which grew out of the ideas of Charles Lindblom. In his article 'The Science of Muddling Through', Lindblom had argued that no strategist can ever fully comprehend the complexities of the world in which he or she exists. Further, most strategists recognize this fact. In order to reduce risk, they will seek strategic options where they have at least some control over the variables. In practice this means a series of small, cautious, incremental decisions rather than big bold steps. Lindblom later identified a number of different forms of incrementalism, and also developed the notion of what he called 'partisan mutual adjustment', the process of negotiation and bargaining whereby organizations manage strategic change. Rather than top managers deciding on change and then giving orders to make it happen, they must persuade the rest of the organization that change is beneficial and help other members understand how their own roles will change.[57] Lindblom's approach was criticized for lacking in direction and being likely to lead to strategic 'drift', but this criticism was rebutted by James Brian Quinn, who argued that incrementalism was a logical response to uncertainty and were not incompatible with long-term thinking about the future.[58]

A third-school, the resource-based view of strategy, began to emerge in the 1980s and became popular in the 1990s. The *Strategic Management Journal* in particular published a number of articles on the subject.[59] Drawing upon earlier economic theories of the firm such as those of Philip Sargant Florence and Edith Penrose, the resource-based view argued that companies are constrained in their strategic choices by the resources – capital, human, technological and so on – that they have at their disposal. Conversely, how well they use the resources they *do* have can determine how well they can execute their strategies. This in turn led to the development of the notion of 'core competencies' by two of the most popular gurus of the 1990s, C.K. Prahalad and Gary Hamel. Rather than try to do everything, argued Hamel and Prahalad, companies should seek to find out the things they are best at doing, the things that give them a unique source of competitive advantage, and then concentrate on doing those things.[60] From this in turn came the practice of outsourcing, whereby companies contracted out ancillary and back-office functions as far as possible, enabling them to devote all their resources to their core competencies and to developing lasting competitive advantage.

A fourth school, the positioning school, went some way back towards the planning school. Although not in favour of formal planning as such, the positioning school believes that there are generic strategic options from which companies can choose, depending on where they wish to position themselves in the market. It will be recalled that Frontinus had advanced a similar proposition with relation to military strategy (see Chapter 2). Igor Ansoff had outlined some generic strategic options in the early 1960s, as had the economist Joe Bain in his book *Industrial Organization*.[61] The growth–share matrix developed by Bruce Henderson, founder of the Boston Consulting Group, in 1968, is another example which uses a simple grid to plot the strategic position of companies and business units.[62]

The best-known guru from the positioning school is undoubtedly Michael Porter. His book *Competitive Strategy* offered a few simple tools which were intended to enable companies to analyse their competitive position.[63] The 'five forces' model set out the forces that shape competition within a given industry of market: the risk of new entry by other competitors, the degree of competition between established competitors, the bargaining power of buyers, the bargaining power of suppliers and the threat of substitute products which might render one's own products obsolete. Porter went on to offer generic strategic options, depending on whether the company wished to focus on particular products and find niche markets or to appeal to mass markets.

Porter's generic strategies have proven very popular with businesses, despite widespread scepticism about them in the academic world. There Porter's ideas are seen as being overly simplistic and, rather like the planning school, too formal and not representative of how companies really think about and do strategy. However, Porter did make another important contribution with his concept of the value chain. This idea had been explored in outline by earlier writers, but Porter went into it in some detail, explaining how each stage of the production process from supplier to distributor adds value in some way – or should – for the end user. How companies position themselves within and control the value chain is a key determinant of strategic success.

The foregoing is only a brief summary of the courses taken by strategic thinkers. The gurus tried to drag strategy back to a position closer to real managerial experience, but it is not clear that they succeeded. Many more strategic schools have emerged, and are emerging.[64] On one level this might be taken as evidence of healthy debate and discussion within the discipline. On the other hand, it might be argued that business strategy is now so splintered and fractured that there is now little consensus on any issue – indeed, there is little agreement as to the definition of 'strategy' itself.

Rethinking organization

As we have seen, debates about strategy and debates about organization have tended to overlap. It was through considering the development of the multidivisional form of organization that Alfred Chandler developed his first ideas on business strategy. Chandler, it will be remembered, regarded the M-form as being the essential structure which supported the rapid growth and internationalization of (primarily) American businesses from the 1920s to the 1960s.

The M-form enabled businesses to grow. But how well would it support them in times when survival, not growth, was the main concern? In the 1970s, the twin challenges of economic recession and the threat from Japan put American businesses under severe pressure to change not only their approach to strategy but also their approach to organization. This point was made forcefully by the McKinsey consultants Tom Peters and Robert Waterman in their bestselling book *In Search of Excellence*. Rather than referring to previous academic research, Peters and Waterman delved into their own experience as consultants. They developed the 7S framework of organizational variables – structure, strategy, systems, skills, staff, style and shared values – and went on to urge a programme of radical transformation in all seven levels, but especially on the level of organization.

Like many before them, notably the writers of the human relations school (see Chapter 7), Peters and Waterman called for a loosening of formal controls. Companies should be decentralized and there should be much more emphasis on coordination rather than control. Leaders needed to learn, or relearn, to lead people by motivating them rather than disciplining them. Chandler had believed that size was important because of the economies of scale it created, but Peters and Waterman believed size could be a barrier. They described with obvious approval the German *Mittelstand* companies, the small and medium-sized companies of which Chandler had disapproved but which Peters and Waterman argued – with some justification – were the real engine of German economic growth. They also favoured the much more flexible approach to organization and leadership used by Japanese companies, although they advocated 'delayering' and stripping out tiers of middle management in order to achieve flatter hierarchies, which was quite contrary to Japanese practice.[65]

Peters went on to become one of the most popular management gurus of the 1980s and 1990s, at least in America (his work had a cooler reception in Europe, possibly in part because of the author's highly personal and very American style). His later books, especially *Thriving on Chaos* and *Liberation Management*, expanded on the themes of *In Search of Excellence*.[66] Peters attacked bureaucracy in all its forms, arguing for extreme decentralization and an emphasis on personal responsibility and independence which at times stopped just short of anarchy. He called for companies and organizations to put themselves into a perpetual state of change and revolution, and revolted against anything that smacked of tradition. Only through constant churn and transformation, he argued, could businesses get ahead and stay ahead of their competitors.

The work of Rosabeth Moss Kanter follows some of the same themes, albeit with much more restraint. Kanter had studied sociology before moving into business studies (she was also editor of *Harvard Business Review* for several years). She produced two highly popular books, *The Change Masters* and *When Giants Learn to Dance*. In the former, she argued that in order to maintain their competitive edge businesses – American businesses in particular – needed to become more innovative. The problem, she said, was that American businesses were quite bad at managing innovation, which was traditionally seen as the province of the 'lone wolf' entrepreneur. Companies needed to create an internal atmosphere where entrepreneurship and innovation were not only possible but welcomed.[67]

In *When Giants Learn to Dance*, Kanter warned organizations that they faced a new paradox: the need to do more, with less. 'This constitutes the great corporate balancing act. Cut back and grow. Trim down and build. Accomplish more, and do it in new areas, with fewer resources.'[68] She accepted the prevailing view that corporations needed to become 'leaner and fitter', but she argued strongly against what she saw as the thoughtless slashing of costs and structures without regard for the consequence; there was a difference between trimming away fat, and cutting into the bone. Downsizing and delayering were in many cases necessary, but could not be conducted randomly; instead, they needed to be conducted according to what she called 'the post-entrepreneurial principles of management'. These principles were three in number: (1) minimize objectives and maximize options so as to ensure more flexibility; (2) use coordination and influence rather than control to achieve leverage; and (3) encourage 'churn' and the continuous regrouping of people and functions and products in search of new and unexpected combinations.[69] She called for more alliances and more and better collaboration within and between companies and, like Peters, she argued for an end to bureaucracy.

Remembering the quote attributed to Petronius (see Chapter 2), we can perhaps be sceptical about the efficacy of the methods Kanter proposed, especially with regard to 'churn'. But there is no doubt that her work was widely read, even if there is little evidence that it was widely acted upon. The same is true of the Anglo-Irish guru Charles Handy, whose books became very popular in the 1980s and 1990s. His first major work, *Understanding Organizations*, was a development of the earlier work of the British industrial sociologists and the Aston Group.[70] Handy discussed organizations in terms of their cultural types, dividing them into four categories: power cultures, where most power is concentrated in the hands of one dominant individual; role cultures, which tend to be specialized and divided up along functional lines; task cultures, where the focus is on the task in hand and the organization is often split into task-focused teams and groups, and person cultures, where there is no defined leader and the organization functions largely through the personal ties between members (Handy lists barristers' chambers and hippie communes as two prime exemplars).

Unlike many earlier writers, Handy did not assert the primacy of any one of these cultures over the others. His ideal organization would have room for all four somewhere within it, reflecting the diverse nature of the groups and individuals involved. Handy did not believe that organizations are, or should be, homogeneous. That theme was brought out more strongly in a later book, *The Age of Unreason*, where he introduced the notion of the 'shamrock organization'.[71] In the future, Handy argued, organizations will consist of three types of people. The first type are 'core workers' whose skills and experience are essential to the company and are employed on a long-term basis. The second type are workers doing important work but in functions which can be contracted out or outsourced in some way; they work with the company but are not technically part of it. The third type are workers doing non-essential functions, employed directly by the company but often on a temporary or short-term contractual basis so that they can be let go quickly when their work is no longer needed. This fragmentation of the workforce poses obvious problems, and Handy argued that one of the major challenges of management in the future will be learning how to manage these different groups in a way that is fair and equitable, especially to the third group.

In his next major work, *The Empty Raincoat*, Handy focused on the management of paradox.[72] Paradox is here to stay, he argued; it cannot be avoided. He lists nine different paradoxes which challenge managers:

1   The paradox of intelligence: intelligence is the greatest single source of wealth but it is also the most difficult to own and control.

2　The paradox of work: as our society becomes more efficient, there is less work to do and consequently more 'enforced idleness'.

3　The paradox of productivity: greater productivity has been achieved by fewer people working longer hours, with a consequent increase in unemployment and underemployment.

4　The paradox of time: greater efficiency has in theory led to more leisure time, yet the pressures on our time are greater than ever.

5　The paradox of riches: the increasing concentration of wealth in the hands of fewer people is actually leading to a slackening of demand.

6　The paradox of organizations: new business organizations have to be structured yet flexible, global yet local.

7　The paradox of age: every generation believes itself to be different from its predecessor, but assumes the next generation will be the same as itself.

8　The paradox of the individual: we seek to be individuals, yet we identify with the groups and organizations to which we belong.

9　The paradox of fairness: justice demands that all should be treated equally, yet our system of distribution makes it inevitable that some will achieve and earn more than others.

Although *The Empty Raincoat* was described by reviewers as a statement of the problems of management in an age of change and flux, Handy himself made it clear that paradox is not new; indeed, paradoxes are inherent in human society. A similar view was taken by another guru, less popular than the likes of Kanter, Peters or Handy but with a strong following at the time, Gareth Morgan.[73] An academic rather than a consultant, Morgan argued that it is not possible to understand organizations simply by thinking of them as machines, or biological organisms. No single metaphor offers a complete explanation. Rather than searching for a 'one best way' of understanding organizations, Morgan argued that we need multiple metaphors and multiple viewpoints. These help us to study organizations from many different angles and so achieve a more complete understanding. As well as machines and biological organisms, Morgan offered six other metaphors of organization: organizations as brains, organizations as cultures, organizations as political systems, organizations as psychic prisons, organizations as flux and transformation, and organizations as instruments of domination. Like Handy, Morgan was not afraid to step beyond the boundaries of management theory for his ideas: the concept of the organization as a psychic prison is drawn directly from Plato, while the idea of flux and transformation was inspired by the pre-Socratic philosopher Heraclitus.

Towards a theory (or theories) of leadership

People have been writing and thinking about leadership for as long as they have been writing and thinking about management. As we saw in Chapter 2, leadership was a subject of great interest in the ancient world, and the duties and responsibilities of the leader were often commented upon. In the twentieth century many writers on management including Fayol, Emerson, Urwick and Follett also stressed the need for leadership. In the 1960s the psychologist Fred Fiedler applied contingency theory to leadership.[74] His research found that, as Tolstoy and Machiavelli had earlier indicated, leaders do not always have the ability to act freely and are often constrained by the situation in which they find themselves. His suggestion was that in these situations, instead of changing the leader, organizations should consider changing the situation so as to remove the constraints. Fiedler's work was considered controversial, and has been heavily criticized, but the concept of situational leadership continues to be discussed.[75] Other important writers of the period include James MacGregor Burns, who argued that successful leaders are those who understand their followers' needs and act accordingly, and Robert Greenleaf, whose concept of the 'servant-leader' harks back to earlier Christian, Islamic and Indian views on leadership.[76] Greenleaf believed that leaders have a duty to the organizations they lead, and are responsible to and for the members of those organizations. He also stressed the need for leaders to have a strong sense of ethics and personal values.

Several of the gurus cited above, especially Peter Drucker and Tom Peters, made the point that without leadership, organizations have little hope of achieving their primary purpose. Like Emerson and Urwick and other early writers, they talked about leadership within the larger context of management. In the 1980s, however, another group of popular writers questioned whether leadership and management were the same thing. One of the first to do so was the academic Warren Bennis, who spent much of his career working on group dynamics and organizational development and then brought that perspective to bear on leadership.[77] Bennis's view of leadership focuses on the interaction between leaders and others in the group and like Mary Parker Follett, whose influence he acknowledges, he sees the task of the leader as one of coordination rather than control. His early work focused on the role of trust between leaders and followers, but he later turned to issues such as power and reciprocity. Bennis believed that a successful leader must possess three traits: ambition, competence and integrity. Successful leaders are able to develop a vision and persuade others to share it. Most important, they have high degrees of self-knowledge; they know how to leverage their own strengths and manage their own weaknesses. Although Bennis saw leadership as being to some extent an inherent quality, he believed there were ways of developing and bringing out that quality in order to make leaders more effective.

As noted above, Bennis also drew a distinction between the role of the manager and the role of the leader. He described managers almost as functionaries; their job is to get things done, to administer and control. They have a short-term perspective and tend to focus on the bottom line. Leaders, on the other hand, are there to have vision and to look out towards the horizon. The famous comment that 'the manager does things right; the leader does the right thing' sums up his point of view.[78] This does not mean that Bennis was deliberately denigrating the role of the manager; it is clear that organizations need both managers *and* leaders. However, he argued strongly that businesses in particular need more leaders and fewer managers, more vision and less bureaucracy.

Much the same views were held by Bennis's near contemporary, John Kotter. Also an academic, Kotter formed his views on leadership after first spending some years studying the role and functions of the general manager. He too concluded that management and leadership are two different things. The role of the leader is to create change, to motivate and inspire people, to establish the direction that the organization should go and then to make sure its members are ready to make the journey. Managers, on the other hand, are there to plan, direct and control.[79]

This view has now become widely accepted; indeed it is probably true to say that this is the orthodox view of leadership and management. For example, in *The Seven Habits of Highly Effective People*, Stephen Covey says that it is the job of a manager to make sure that a ladder is erected correctly and efficiently, while it is the job of the leader to determine that it is erected against the right wall.[80] Joseph Rost rejected any linkage between management and leadership, arguing that leaders get things done by influencing people while managers get things done by exercising authority over people, while Max DePree argued that leadership consists in ensuring that things get done without necessarily managing the actual process by which they are done.[81]

Consciously or not, Bennis and Kotter were picking up on a theme which had been discussed briefly, and often inconclusively, by earlier writers. In *The Philosophy of Management*, Oliver Sheldon had suggested that there were two functions: administration, which consisted of the technical day-to-day running of organizations, and management, which was concerned with long-term vision and purpose. Emerson's line-and-staff model had also made a distinction between functional management and general management, and regarded leadership as part of task of the 'staff'. In the 1980s, this model received a twist: now it is the managers who are the hands and feet of the organization, are responsible for getting jobs done, while the leaders are the hearts and brains, the custodians of the vision and spirit of the organization.

The idea of a separation between leadership and management has had its strongest impact in America. In *The Knowledge-Creating Company*, Nonaka and Takeuchi showed that quite a different attitude to management exists in Japanese companies. In particular, managers and leaders share a common goal and vision. And while it may be the job of leadership at the boardroom level to define that vision and set it out, more junior managers exercise leadership in other ways. For example, the young middle managers whom Nonaka and Takeuchi refer to as *samurai* take the lead on innovation and knowledge-gathering projects, and effectively drive those projects within the context of the wider vision.

British attitudes show some differences too. John Adair, the doyen of British leadership theorists, developed the concept of 'action-centred leadership' in which leadership is exercised through a combination of the leader and the team: both are essential, and both play an equal role. Adair was adamant that leadership can come from anywhere in the organization; it is not the prerogative of the boardroom.[82] Like Greenleaf, he was intrigued by the concept of the 'servant-leader' and often wrote about this. Adair also used examples of past leaders, stretching back to Xenophon in the ancient world, in order to make points about leadership today. He also sought to broaden the study of leadership, arguing that leadership in business, the armed forces, government or the church is fundamentally the same; it is only the context that is different.

The separation of leadership and management is not without its consequences. In *The Change Masters*, Rosabeth Moss Kanter commented that when people are put into positions where they have little or no power, they tend to do one of two things: subside into apathy, or work out how to get promoted so that they can have access to power. This is not always the best way of ensuring good leadership. The Canadian psychologist Lawrence Peter became briefly famous in the 1970s for the Peter Principle, which states that 'in a hierarchy, every employee tends to rise to the level of his own incompetence'.[83] According to Peter, most people are promoted on the basis of their past performance; promotion is a reward for good work done and targets achieved. This ignores the fact that the person may have been very well suited for their previous job, but lacks the talent, temperament or skills to perform in the job to which they have been promoted. This usually only becomes apparent once the promotion happens. At this point, the 'level of incompetence' is discovered and the person will progress no further up the career ladder, thus (a) making them unhappy and (b) damaging the organization through incompetent management. Much the same point was made by Norman Dixon in *On the Psychology of Military Incompetence*, a bestseller which was widely read by business people as well as military officers.[84]

Conclusion

The gurus responded to the crisis of the 1970s by trying to reconnect with the world of business and develop tools and concepts which could be applied directly by managers (and leaders). How successful they were is a matter of some doubt. Certainly they sold a great many books, and their ideas were widely discussed. How far their ideas were implemented is another matter. The quality movement did have an impact, and although some sceptics dismissed total quality management as just another fad, there seems little doubt that managers in North America in particular take quality much more seriously than did their counterparts forty years ago and realize it can be a source of competitive advantage. Marketing too has felt the impact of Kotler and his successors. Although his ideas are hotly debated and heavily criticized, Hofstede did succeed in putting national culture onto the map of management thinking.

On the other hand, we have seen now the discipline of strategy has fragmented and become an arena for territorial and ideological disputes. The division between leadership and management is perhaps useful in terms of demarcating fields for academic study, but does little to help managers and leaders puzzling over how to find the right combination of the two in their own organizations.

The age of the gurus came to an end around the time of the dotcom bubble and economic downturn in 2001. This is not because the gurus had run out of ideas; far from it. Instead, managers stopped buying guru books, at least in such large numbers. In a new age of cynicism and uncertainty, it seemed that managers were no longer prepared to swallow whole the ideas of the gurus. Partly too this was a matter of oversupply. Bookshelves had become crowded with books on the Next Big Idea in business, written by consultants and academics who dreamed of becoming the next Peter Drucker, or publicizing their own consulting ventures, or both. There were too many voices speaking too many messages, and it became increasingly difficult to tell those with genuinely good ideas apart from the charlatans.

There are still plenty of popular writers on management, some based in academia, some in consulting firms or their own businesses. Some of them produce very thoughtful work. But it is almost impossible to tell whether this work has any real impact. There is simply too much out there. Most management books, whatever their quality, struggle to achieve recognition among the greater mass. To take leadership alone, Keith Grint estimated in 2006 that there were already 20,000 books on leadership in print.[85] That number will only have increased. The number of books on management more generally is probably beyond calculation. Faced with such a daunting choice of things to read, managers tend to either read what everyone else is reading – or not read at all.

11 Management thought in the internet age

Change is inevitable. In a progressive country, change is constant.

(Benjamin Disraeli)

We are now drawing very near to the present day. One of the questions that presents itself to any historian working on the very recent past is where to draw a line and bring the narrative to a close. When does the past turn into the present? At what point does history become merely slightly stale current affairs?

There is no one best answer to this question, and most historical narratives find their own convenient point at which to end depending on the subject they are describing. In this case, there are good reasons for trying to bring at least some of the narrative up as close to the present as possible, in order to illustrate both change and continuity in management thinking and also to examine some of the problems and challenges that management thinking faces.

I do not intend in this chapter to undertake a comprehensive survey of the current state of play in management thinking. Instead, I would like to pick out a few themes – only a few – and explore how they have developed, where they currently stand and where they might go. Mindful of Keith Grint and his discovery of 20,000 books on leadership alone, I will not go into much detail on individual figures and their writings, and will illustrate the main themes with reference to such works as I am acquainted with. My views on each subject should not be taken as authoritative. The purpose, once again, is to come to a better understanding of management thinking in general terms rather than to explore each and every individual strand.

The permanence of change

One of the recurring themes in management thought over the past thirty years, and especially over the past ten, is change. There is nothing particularly new about change. In ancient Greece, Heraclitus and Empedocles both stressed that the cosmos was undergoing a continuous process of change, and in 1867 the future British prime minister Benjamin Disraeli made his famous comment: 'Change is inevitable. In a progressive country, change is constant.' The early twentieth-century writers on management were well aware of the power of change; indeed, it was change in the economic and social environment that drove them to come up with new ideas about management in the first place.

The management scientists and open systems theorists of the 1950s through to the 1970s accepted the idea of change and argued that both organizations themselves and their environment were dynamic and constantly shifting. But from the mid-1980s, change became a topic of greater urgency in management thinking. Radical change was happening almost simultaneously on at least three different dimensions. First, advances in technology, especially information and communications technology, were threatening economic and social changes at least as profound as those created by the Industrial Revolution in the eighteenth century. Second, the growing integration of the world economy, accelerated in the early 1990s by the collapse of the Soviet Union and the opening up of China and India, was challenging old ways of perceiving the world. Third, the increasing strain being placed on the resources of the planet by continuous demographic and economic growth had begun to arouse fears that current levels of growth were unsustainable.

The work of the gurus of change, such as Alvin Toffler and John Naisbitt, were widely read. Naisbitt's *Megatrends* sold more than 8 million copies.[1] Among the important trends he identified were globalization, technological change, a change in emphasis from 'blue-collar' industrial work to 'white-collar' knowledge-based work, decentralization of authority, broader participation in decision making and a shift from hierarchies to networks as the dominant form of organization. In *The Third Wave*, Alvin Toffler argued that human civilization was undergoing a paradigm shift, moving from the industrial age to the information age. Knowledge and ideas, he believed, would replace land and physical labour as the new creators of value.[2]

The same themes were picked up by writers on management. As we saw in Chapter 10, Rosabeth Moss Kanter warned that companies would have to become more agile and flexible in order to adapt to their new environment.[3] Warren Bennis and Burt Nanus, surveying the changing face of leadership, made many of the same points.[4] The changing world required leaders to become more visionary, to anticipate the future rather than just reacting to events, to become better at sharing information and empowering and motivating other people. The authoritarian leaders of the past needed to be replaced by team-builders and team players. For Bennis and Nanus, the biggest threat of all was technological change. At one point they refer to a 'tsunami' of new technologies; elsewhere they describe technology as a kind of seismic activity, bubbling up in unexpected places and taking unexpected forms.

Linking the world: the technological challenge

The most important technological advances, and those which appeared to threaten existing management models most directly, were in the field of communications. Previously, the big disruptive technologies had come in the form of power generation – water power in the Middle Ages, steam at the end of the eighteenth century – or production technology such as the Arkwright factory system or the Jacquard power loom. Now, as Alvin Toffler and others suggested, the power of information and knowledge was threatening to reshape the world.

This particular trend had been in the making for a long time. In the 1830s and 1840s, Charles Babbage had argued that knowledge was a source of economic power – competitive advantage, we would call it today – and his work on computers was intended to help society harness the power of knowledge. At almost the same time as Babbage was writing, the first prototype telegraph systems were being developed by Carl Gauss in Germany, David Alter in America and William Fothergill Cooke and Charles Wheatstone in Britain.[5] The artist Samuel Morse began trials of his own system in the early 1840s, and this quickly became the international standard. Prior to the telegraph, messages could take days or weeks to reach their destination; now the same messages could be transmitted in minutes. In London, the journalist Julius Reuter founded the first international news agency in the 1850s, using the telegraph to transmit financial data and news in something close to real time.[6] Further inventions including the railway, the telephone, radio and then television helped to collapse time and space still further. In the 1960s Marshall McLuhan coined the term 'global village' to describe the process by which communications media were bringing people all around the world closer to each other and encouraging them to share the same values (with negative as well as positive consequences).[7]

The idea of networking computers goes back to the early 1960s at least, and the first computer networks were in use by the military and in academic communities by the 1970s. The Minitel system developed by France Telecom in 1982 was the first public access network, connecting about a quarter of all French households by 1990, and was imitated in other countries. The most important breakthrough came with the development of a single standard network system that could be used around the world. In the late 1980s, while working at the CERN particle physics laboratory in Geneva, Tim Berners-Lee brought the work of Babbage and Morse together through his research on hypertext.[8] The World Wide Web, created during the period 1990–3, was the outcome of this work.

Berners-Lee, like Babbage, believed that the World Wide Web would be a pool of knowledge that people could use to assist them in their work and daily lives. But during the 1990s, although much was written about the Web and the internet and the possibilities of their use by managers, there was no clear consensus as to what those possibilities were.[9] Opinions varied widely. Some writers warned of the dangers of the internet and the risks to business and commercial security in a system that was open and easy to access; Berners-Lee himself had warned of these risks. Others went the other way and envisioned a bold new world of 'e-commerce' that would render old-fashioned shops obsolete; in the future, people would buy everything from groceries to clothing to books and music over the internet. 'Clicks, not bricks', became a common watchword among writers and commentators on e-commerce.[10]

At least some of those ideas perished during the so-called 'dotcom bubble' of 2000–2001, when the share price of many new technology companies collapsed, leading in turn to the demise of many of the companies themselves. In the aftermath, it became clear that the internet was a social phenomenon which people used in different ways.[11] One of the key features of the internet was that people could configure it to suit themselves. For example, the slow growth of Amazon has shown that people have become more willing to buy books online. On the other hand, despite the development of internet shopping facilities by most chains of supermarkets, it seems clear that the great majority of people still prefer to buy their food in person. As Charles Babbage pointed out long ago, people feel the need to verify the quality of the food they are buying, and can best do so if they inspect it personally. Books, on the other hand, tend to be of uniform physical quality and therefore can be purchased without inspection.

Broadband internet and mobile telephony – and the convergence between the two – represent a further advance in technology with yet more profound social implications. At the time of writing, no one knows quite where these will lead us, or what the managerial implications will be. On the positive side, these technologies enable companies to build relationships with customers, suppliers and other stakeholders and to communicate directly with them and hear their views. On the potentially negative side, it has increased the ability of stakeholders to communicate with each other. Earlier I mentioned how the 'co-creation' of brands now takes place increasingly through the interaction of customers with each other, independent of the brand owner's influence. Other groups use modern communications too. In 1994 the Zapatista Army of National Liberation used mobile phones to coordinate activities over a wide area of southern Mexico; more recently, protest movements in Iran and the 'Arab spring' movement in Tunisia and Egypt have used sites such as Facebook and

Twitter for similar purposes.[12] Thinking back to the work of Chris Argyris and others on defensive routines and resistance to change, it is not hard to see how groups of managers and employees might use similar technologies to disrupt or even demolish change programmes. Management thought has yet to get to grips with this problem in any systematic way. The challenge is there: we are still waiting for the response.

Relationships and networks

Warren Bennis and Burt Nanus argued that new technologies would force leaders to put more emphasis on relationships. Others argued that networks both within and without the organization would take on increasing importance, and that networks would enable greater participation and involvement in decision making and determining the direction the organization should take. Such views would have gladdened the heart of Mary Parker Follett, who argued for a similar broadening of participation in decision making in the 1920s.[13] At present, much attention is focusing on the potential of social networking sites such as Facebook and LinkedIn. One view has it that these sites are used by managers in order to seek out other people who have skills or knowledge that they need in order to do their own jobs.[14]

At present, however, most of the thinking on this field is theoretical and speculative, and there is little grounding in any kind of research. As with the writers on motivation in the 1950s (see Chapter 7), whose ideas were shaped by their own context and the prevailing belief in democracy and freedom, the suspicion must be that at least some of the present theorizing on the importance of social networking rests on faith rather than evidence. Because we believe that participation and sharing of ideas are a good thing, we think that social networking, which is supposed to encourage such participation and sharing, is a good thing too. Recent media reports of information theft and bullying on social networking websites will hopefully encourage a more nuanced view in time.

It has also been argued that new technology will create new forms of organization based on networks rather than bureaucracy, and here more progress has been made. Two forms of organization, the matrix organization and the virtual organization, have been studied in some detail. Matrix organizations retain the traditional functional structure with marketing, production and so on organized in discrete departments, but they also have a multifunctional project or product structure superimposed on this. Thus an individual worker or manager in the marketing department would report to the heads of his or her department, but also to the head of his or her project team.

Matrix organizations go back at least to the nineteenth century, and probably have their origins in the military, where the increasing sophistication of weapons systems meant that specialists had to be distributed amongst fighting units. In the Royal Navy, for example, each ship had a chief engineer and a chief gunnery officer who reported to both the captain of the ship – responsible for its overall fighting efficiency – and to a squadron engineer or gunnery commander – responsible for the technical efficiency of his branch of the service across all ships in the squadron.[15] Businesses began experimenting with matrixes in the mid-twentieth century. Among the first to do so was Polaroid, which used a matrix organization to govern teams working on development projects; the example was later copied by Ken Olsen at Digital Equipment Corporation.[16] Neither of these attempts was entirely successful, but more companies and organizations began adopting versions of the matrix organization and more knowledge of the subject has gradually accrued.[17]

Virtual organizations, that is, organizations that are widely dispersed and use communications media to coordinate the activities of the various parts, have also been around for some time. In a separate work, Malcolm Warner and I argued that Reuter's news agency, founded in the 1850s, was a form of virtual organization, and Royal Air Force Fighter Command during the Battle of Britain in 1940, which used radar and radio to coordinate the movements of squadrons of aircraft from various dispersed bases, was indistinguishable from the modern virtual organization.[18] In 1994 Samuel Bleeker maintained that virtual organizations offered companies the chance to become more flexible and adapt more quickly to new technologies and meeting customer needs.[19] More recent work on virtual organization has centred on the creation of virtual teams, project groups made up of members working from various locations around the world and linked electronically, and on virtual collaboration between organizations, usually for research purposes such as the Bluetooth project.

Innovation and knowledge

The writers on change in the 1980s also stressed the importance of innovation as a source of competitive advantage in a time of rapid change. Again, it might be argued that there is nothing new here. Innovation had been equally important to success in the Industrial Revolution, and the need to keep innovating had been recognized by the likes of Richard Arkwright, James Watt and Josiah Wedgwood (see Chapter 4). However, one of the perceived strengths of Japanese and German business in the 1960s and 1970s had been in their ability to innovate, and a common theme in much of the work of the gurus was the need for Western businesses, especially American businesses, to regain the lead in innovation.

The literature on innovation since that time has been vast, and I will dip into it only briefly. One recurring theme in much of the literature has been the classification of innovations into two kinds: 'incremental' innovation which seeks to make a steady series of small improvements to existing products, and 'radical' or 'breakthrough' innovation, which seeks to develop new technologies or business processes that will transform a sector or market. The possession and exploitation of a breakthrough innovation is seen as an important source of competitive advantage, and many writers such as W. Chan Kim and Renée Mauborgne have urged companies to pursue innovations that will put distance between themselves and their competitors.[20] In contrast, Patrick Barwise and Seán Meehan suggest that most companies that enjoy long-term success do so off the back of continuous incremental innovation. Earlier, in the *Innovator's Dilemma*, Clayton Christensen had warned of a trap waiting for innovative companies; often they invest so much time and energy, and emotion, in creating an innovation that they remain wedded to it and fail to recognize when competitors are creating breakthrough innovations of their own.[21]

Another consequence of the emphasis on innovation was a re-examination of the nature of knowledge and its links with management and innovation. It will be recalled that the importance of knowledge was recognized by the economists of the nineteenth century, especially Karl Marx, but few did more than speculate briefly on how knowledge is used to create value. The exception to the rule is Charles Babbage, who made an explicit connection between knowledge and quality. The most important influence in the twentieth century was probably the philosopher Michel Polanyi who started from a conception of knowledge as being what is possible to express in words. He quickly realized that this was not the whole of the story. For example, we may recognize a person because we know their face; but if asked to explain how we relate that face to that person, we will struggle to articulate what we know. In other words, said Polanyi, 'we can know more than we can tell'.[22]

Polanyi thus classified knowledge into two types: explicit knowledge, which can be easily put into words and transmitted to others, and tacit knowledge, which is very much inherent in persons and much harder to transmit or disseminate. Later writers on management, notably Max Boisot and Ikujiro Nonaka, recognized that tacit knowledge is most important in terms of innovation, as tacit knowledge is also very hard to replicate. Boisot linked the exploitation of tacit knowledge to business culture in an attempt to explain why some businesses are good at using tacit knowledge and others are not. Nonaka and Takeuchi explored the ways in which Japanese companies unlock tacit knowledge through organizational models which encourage the spread of ideas and information.[23]

A dynamic model of how organizations acquire and use knowledge, based in part on the work of de Geus and Wack at Royal Dutch/Shell (see Chapter 10) was developed by Peter Senge at the Massachusetts Institute of Technology. Senge believes that there is an organizational learning cycle. Organizations begin by learning new skills and capabilities. As they do so, their awareness changes and they begin to view the world in new ways. This new awareness and knowledge leads to deeper changes in attitudes and beliefs, and this in turn necessitates the need to learn new skills so as to explore those new beliefs more fully. He defines learning organizations as 'organizations where people continually expand their capacity to create the results they truly desire, where new and expansive patterns of thinking are nurtured, where collective aspiration is set free, and where people are continually learning how to learn together'.[24]

In order to become true learning organizations, says Senge, organizations and their members need to master five key disciplines. The first is 'personal mastery', which includes personal knowledge and skills but also confidence and judgement; here again, one is reminded of Miyamoto and the Japanese swordfighters, who emphasized many of the same things. The second is mental models, the set of fundamental assumptions that people make about their environment, their work and so on. Following on from this, building shared vision means the creation of a single overarching mental model in which all can share. Team learning means the ability to learn together rather than as individuals; Senge cites as an example how sports teams learn to work together, thus creating a whole that is more effective than the sum of its parts. The final discipline is 'systems thinking', a concept Senge adapted from the system dynamics approach of Jay Wright Forrester, which encourages people to think in holistic terms and evaluate the impact of actions and decisions on the whole organization, not just their own part of it.

Senge's work was widely read and he became one of the most popular gurus of the 1990s. As with some of the other gurus, however, it seems that his ideas have been admired more than practised. Have he, and some of the other writers on knowledge and organizations too, set the bar too high? Is the learning organization an ideal to which companies can aspire but rarely reach? The last thirty years have seen some remarkable breakthroughs in understanding how knowledge works in businesses but – and supporters of Peter Senge would undoubtedly argue this point – we seem to still be some distance from a general set of tools that will enable companies to manage knowledge more effectively. Once again the challenge is there: we await the response.

Internationalization and globalization

Again, as we have seen earlier in this book, there is nothing particularly new about international business. The late nineteenth and early twentieth century saw many businesses expand internationally, but in the 1930s economic depression, protectionism and the threat of conflict forced a retrenchment. The establishment of the Common Market in Europe saw renewed growth at least between Western Europe and North America, and Japan also became more important as a trading partner, but barriers to trade existed across much of the world until the end of the 1980s.

Foreseeing future changes, however, some management thinkers began to develop new theories about international trade. A seminal work was Peter Buckley and Mark Casson's *The Future of the Multinational Enterprise*, first published in 1976. As Buckley and Casson themselves later commented, they were writing at a time when discussions about international business were generating a great deal of heat but very little light.[25] They cited particularly the immensely popular *Le défi américain* (The American Challenge) by Jean-Jacques Servan-Schreiber, which warned that Europe – and France in particular – was in danger of being overwhelmed by the economic power of big American businesses. It was around this time too that the American economist Immanuel Wallerstein coined the term 'globalization' to describe the spread of American economic hegemony; the economic equivalent of McLuhan's cultural 'global village'.[26] Buckley and Casson sought to inject a note of realism into the discussion. They measured foreign direct investment flows, analysed the behaviour of multinational businesses and tried to understand what determined investment decisions. A further contribution was made by John Dunning, whose eclectic paradigm sought to explain how and why firms entered international markets. Dunning argued that the choice of mode of entry – through licensing, export or foreign direct investment (FDI) – depended on the benefits that would accrue to the firm through that choice. For example, if there were advantages to setting up a plant or operation in another country in terms of cheap access to scarce resources, the firm would probably choose the FDI route, but if no such advantages existed then it would make more sense to adopt a licensing or export strategy.[27]

Theorizing about international trade and FDI was given a major boost by the Uruguay Round of the General Agreement on Tariffs and Trade (GATT) which lasted from 1986 to 1994 and led to the establishment of the World Trade Organization.[28] This in turn had been made possible by a series of remarkable political events: first, the progressive opening up of the Chinese economy, starting in 1979 and gathering in pace in the late 1980s despite the events in Tiananmen Square in 1989; second, the rapprochement between Russia and the West that began in 1985, leading to the fall of the Berlin Wall and the collapse of the Soviet Union a few years later; and third, the liberalization of the Indian economy that began, again slowly, in 1991. This series of events forced a rethink of the future of the global economy. In 1985 the Japanese consultant Kenichi Ohmae maintained that global competition would be dominated by three powers, Western Europe, North America and Japan. By 1990 he had changed his mind, and argued that a 'borderless world' was developing which would encourage competition from many places in the world as both companies and governments sought to leverage their own competitive advantages in terms of labour costs, regulator barriers, knowledge and skills, ability to innovate and so on.[29]

There was no consensus as to what these events might mean. Theorists such as Buckley, Casson, Dunning and many others made the argument that free trade would provide a spur to economic growth and advantages for companies, but there was widespread fear of the consequences of free trade. Francis Fukuyama's *The End of History and the Last Man* took a Hegelian view and argued that Western liberal democracy might well represent the final and most complete form of government which would soon spread across the world, but the economist Samuel P. Huntington took a darker view; his *The Clash of Civilizations* warned that there were plenty of societies in the world who feared and rejected Western liberal ideals and Western domination, and that there would be resistance and conflict if the West tried to proselytize or force its ideals on those societies.[30] The West had triumphed, said Huntington, not because its own values were superior but 'by its superiority in applying organized violence'.[31] The Gulf War of 1991 thus became a symbolic event, a battleground between the West and Islam; subsequent events in Iraq, Afghanistan and, quite possibly, Libya have intensified that sense of conflict.

As Paul Laudicina suggests in *World Out of Balance*, we have exchanged one set of risks for another. There now appear to be clear limits to Ohmae's concept of the borderless world, and since 2001 at least, scholarship has turned away from the idea of a single harmonious world and back towards the issue of national, cultural and other barriers. The collaborative work of Sumantra Ghoshal and Christopher Bartlett is an example of the kinds of themes that are being pursued. In *Managing Across Borders*, for example, they argue that multinational or global businesses must be endlessly adaptive, changing their methods of operation according to the requirements of each market they enter and accommodating the needs of stakeholders everywhere. Businesses, in Bartlett and Ghoshal's conception, are not bigger than society; they are part of society and must behave as responsible citizens if they are to succeed.[32]

Increasingly, the idea of global convergence of markets and cultures as envisioned by Wallerstein and McLuhan is falling out of fashion. The concept of 'thinking globally and acting locally' has been traced back to the British urban planner Patrick Geddes, who argued in 1915 that local culture is a powerful force and that any outside agency needs to assimilate that culture to a degree if it is to have a hope of establishing itself.[33] Today, once-monolithic Western companies are learning to tailor their products, their advertising or both to local market requirements; a policy of 'think global, act local' is given credit for the recent revival of the international fortunes of McDonald's, for example.[34] Managing the global–local paradox is an area where we should expect to see much more, and better, research and theorizing in the years to come.

Reflection

Black swans

Why, with all of the analytical tools we have at our disposal and with all the knowledge we have amassed, are we so bad at preparing for the future? The financial crash of 2008 has certainly wounded – perhaps fatally – our faith in models and instruments for predicting the future. Yet the models themselves are not solely at fault. With hindsight the signs of the crash were there, had been there for at least two years. But most of us chose to ignore them, and the crash duly came. At time of writing we are still living with the consequences.

That is not the only example. The terrorist attacks of 9/11 in 2001 are widely held up as an example of an unpredictable event. But is that really true? Al-Qaida had attacked the World Trade Center before. It had developed plots to hijack planes and fly them into buildings before. And as for timing, surely the assassination of the Afghan commander Ahmed Shah Massoud – who had fought first the Russians and then the Taliban for decades and was a key ally of the West – a week before the attacks should have set alarm bells ringing at intelligence agencies around the world. But there is no sign that it did. The collapse of the Berlin Wall was another seismic world event that seemed to take everyone by surprise, even though the signs of weakness in the Soviet bloc had been there for several years. Or to come back nearer the present, the explosion and fire and subsequent oil spill from the Deepwater Horizon oil rig in the Gulf of Mexico seemed to catch not only BP but the American authorities by surprise; even though similar smaller incidents had happened before.

In 2007, Nassim Nicholas Taleb wrote about the 'black swan' phenomenon.[35] Prior to the first European explorations of Australia, natural scientists had assumed that all swans were white. They had simply never imagined the possibility of black swans, which were native only to Australia. According to Taleb, this happens all the time. We cannot conceive of things that lie outside our own experience; we cannot imagine what we cannot imagine. As a result, we fall victim to what Taleb referred to as 'black swan events', unpredictable things which happen very seldom but at the same time have extreme impact. With hindsight, says Taleb, black swan events appear to be pre-dictable, but not beforehand. For example, if the 9/11 attacks had been predictable, the American government would have taken precautions to prevent the hijacking of the planes or destroy them before they reached their target.

But there is a flaw in Taleb's logic here. The failure to take action to prevent an event from happening does not mean that the event was unpredictable. History is full of examples that prove the opposite. During the Second World War, the Japanese navy planned an attack on the island of Midway in an effort to lure the American navy into battle. During a simulation of the attack, two American aircraft carriers appeared by surprise in an unexpected place and launched a surprise attack that sank two Japanese carriers. Furious, the Japanese commanders ordered the simulation to be run again, this time instructing the officers in charge of it when and where the American carriers should appear. All went well, and the Japanese navy won a victory. But in the real battle a few months later, not two but three American aircraft carriers appeared just where the original simulation had said they would, and the Japanese navy was dealt a blow from which it never recovered.[36] We are very willing to close our eyes to unpleasant portents. That is a habit of which we need to free ourselves.

We have two choices. We can sit back, rely on our systems knowing they are fallible, and resign ourselves to being prey for the occasional black swan, or we can do something about trying to predict the unpredictable – and then making sure we act on what we learn. Paul Laudicina refers to black swan events too, calling them 'wild cards', trends and events we cannot control but which affect us all the same.[37] Laudicina is in favour of scenarios, the concept first pioneered by Wack and de Geus at Shell in the 1970s. Scenarios don't tell us what *will* happen, but they help us to prepare for what *might* happen. We cannot prevent black swans or wild cards, but we *can* become better and faster at reacting to them so as to minimize the harm they cause. The kind of strategic thinking urged by Kenichi Ohmae, and practised by Andrew Grove when he was chief executive of Intel, can keep organizations agile and ready to react to trouble.[38] Indeed, as Grove says, if organizations can react quickly and well, they can not only fight off challenges but emerge stronger at the end of the process.

And one of the lessons that the history of management teaches us is that the challenges never end. Indeed, it could be argued that businesses face fewer risks today than they did seven hundred years ago, when war, famine and plague were rather more omnipresent than now and when merchants expected that if they sent out five ships, four might not return home. How did people cope with risk? What mental models did they use? How did they assess risk, and how did they lay off risk? Rather than trying to simulate the future, perhaps we need to go back to the good old days of simply thinking about the future, as often as possible, thinking the unthinkable and imagining the unimaginable. If we believe that anything can happen, and if we get better at interpreting the signs of what may happen, then when something *does* happen we should be better prepared, rather than standing in Ohmae's famous metaphor like deer caught in the headlights.

Rather than attempting to develop overall theories of global–local management, however, most writers and researchers have chosen to concentrate on the complexities of individual regions and cultures. East Asia, especially China, has received the most attention, and there is a wealth of literature on business culture, markets, economics, regulation, financial markets and structures, human resource management and many other subjects. These works fall into several chronological categories. There are first of all the 'exploration' books that began to appear soon after the opening up of China, general works whose purpose was to help Western academics and business people alike understand the complexities of this new market. Examples include John Child's *Management in China in the Age of Reform* and Gordon Redding's *The Spirit of Chinese Capitalism*.[39] Following the Asian financial crisis of 1998, a second wave of books and articles explored the roots of the crisis and tried to understand its implications. This was a matter of shutting the stable door after the horse had bolted, but some interesting lessons about financial markets in particular were learned nonetheless. In the past six or seven years a third wave of works has appeared which attempt to explore aspects of Chinese and other East Asian economies and business. Some, like Elizabeth Croll's *China's New Consumers*, offer very considerable insights into their subject.[40] Others attempt to apply Western theoretical concepts and frameworks to East Asian business in an inappropriate manner, and suffer as a result. Unfortunately, this includes some work by Chinese scholars as well.

As noted earlier in this book, Chinese business scholars have been slow to come up with their own theories and models of business, seeming for the most part content to adapt foreign ideas to their own needs. We must assume that this will change, probably in the very near future. The impact of original thinking about business from China, when it does start to emerge, will be very interesting to observe.

A different situation obtains in South Asia, where Indian academics and consultants have for some time been aware of the inadequacies of Western ideas to explain their own situation and experience. Though they remain influenced by Western ideas, they are not afraid to reshape these or even to come up with entirely new theories on a quite pragmatic basis. The consultant Rama Bijapurkar, for example, has developed her own version of Maslow's hierarchy of needs to develop a unique psychographic model of segmentation for Indian consumers. She offers five classes of customer: the 'resigned', the very poorest people on the edge of subsistence, whose only ambition is to survive; the 'strivers', those who were born into poverty but are working hard to escape its clutches; the 'mainstreamers', who earn enough money to satisfy their basic needs of food, shelter and safety and are now looking to consolidate their position and look after their families; the 'aspirers' or 'wannabes' who are upwardly mobile and trying to meet their self-esteem needs; and finally the 'successful' who have made it to the top and seek recognition for their achievement and power as well as, in some cases at least, a degree of self-actualization. This group typically use their wealth to give back to society and try to help the very poorest in some way.[41] (There is a nice circularity here, given that Maslow's knowledge of Indian philosophy played an important role in his development of the hierarchy of needs.)

One of the most original theories to come out of India is the 'bottom of the pyramid' concept developed by C.K. Prahalad. He argued that the world's poor, the 2.5 billion people who live below the poverty line, exist in poverty in part because large businesses overlook them. They are not reached by existing distribution chains, and have no access to the goods and services that might lift them out of poverty. Though their disposable incomes are small, they do nonetheless exist. Prahalad argued that companies needed to connect to these markets for two reasons: first, they could play a role in alleviating poverty, and second, they could build relationships with a new generation of customers. Today's poor, said Prahalad, are tomorrow's middle classes.[42]

The bottom of the pyramid concept has its critics, but it seems to be gathering more support. Some companies are adapting their marketing strategies; for example, Tata Beverages in India now sells single teabags to customers who cannot afford to buy an entire box. This allows those customers to participate, even if briefly, in the same lifestyle as their more affluent compatriots.[43] The bottom of the pyramid concept was also behind the development of microcredit schemes, the most famous of which is the Grameen Bank established by Muhammad Younis in Bangladesh; these schemes can now be found in many developing countries in Asia, Africa and Latin America. Microcredit schemes have had mixed fortunes, but the best of them have gone some way towards alleviating poverty.[44] Prahalad's ideas were picked up by other theorists too. In *Capitalism at the Crossroads*, Stewart Hart suggested that companies that focused on the bottom of the pyramid would also be making a contribution towards sustainable development, while in an earlier article Hart and Ted London argued that engagement with bottom of the pyramid markets would help to create social embeddedness for companies and would also constitute a valuable source of learning on how to go beyond Western business models and engage with customers in new and creative ways.[45] This too is an idea which we are likely to see more of as time goes by.

The 1980s also saw the beginning of interest in developing countries by both Western writers and writers from developing regions, the latter often based at Western universities. Most of these works were of the 'exploration' type. James Austin, Moses Kiggundu and Monir Tayeb contributed important general works on management in developing countries, focusing on issues such as regulation and the role of government and local business cultures.[46] Peter Blunt, Merrick Jones and Tayo Fashoyin wrote important works on management in Africa.[47] As with China, much of the work on Africa in the 1980s and 1990s applied Western management theory to Africa, but there is an interesting strand of work by scholars such as P.K. Odubogun and Mamadou Dia which points out that cultural and institutional differences meant that not all Western management concepts were relevant in the African context.[48] There have been some interesting case studies of individual countries too, including Piet Human and Frank Horwitz's description of South African companies in the early 1990s as the apartheid system was coming to an end, and Iyabo Oladje's account of women managers in Nigeria.[49] Many others have followed on from this, exploring management in both the private and public sectors – and reiterating the point that there is often a close relationship between the two – and more recently Vijay Mahajan's *Africa Rising* is an excellent example of the 'exploration' genre.[50] But there is a sense that studies of African business are still very much in that exploration phase, and we are still waiting for coherent theories or schools of thought to emerge from the study of African management.

The same is true of management in the Arab world, which received scant attention for many years despite Farid Muna's path-breaking *The Arab Executive* more than thirty years ago.[51] By 1990 Arab scholars were producing some very useful exploration texts which helped scholars and managers elsewhere to better understand management in the Arab world. Important early works include Abbas 'Ali's studies of decision making and managerial behaviour, Monir Tayeb's work on human resource management, M.A. al-Tawail's detailed study of public administration in Saudi Arabia and Kassem and Habib's *Strategic Management of Services in the Arab Gulf States*, which is a good introduction to Arab business culture.[52]

The picture in Latin America is slightly different. A long tradition of higher education in which economics featured strongly led to a number of economics-based studies of trade and industry generally, while American trade links with a number of Latin American countries meant that there was interest from outside the region in how management was done there. Studies of aspects of management both the region in general and individual countries began to emerge in the 1960s, early examples being Thomas Cochran and Reuben Reina's study of Argentine business culture, and Robert Shafer's work on Mexican business organizations.[53] Later significant works include the *Reference Manual on Doing Business in Latin America*, which included important articles on management and culture; Bartell and Payne's collection of chapters, *Business and Democracy in Latin America*, which explored the relationship between the state and the private sector; and Eva Kras's comparative study of American and Mexican managers.[54]

The theme of relationships between government and business has been explored many times in works in English, Spanish and Portuguese. Many of these focus on economic policy, but some do look at the role of the manager as well. Many were also written against a background of radical political change as many Latin American regimes made the transition from military dictatorship to elected democratic governments. The book *Development, Technology and Flexibility: Brazil Faces the Industrial Divide*, published in 1992, emphasized the need for better methods of organization and more skills and knowledge formation.[55] The most important and original work of this type is Rodolfo Terragno's *The Challenge of Real Development in Argentina in the Twenty-First Century*. Terragno, who served as minister in the government of President Raúl Alfonsín, the first democratic government of Argentina in the modern era, argued that the two most important requirements for any developing country were capital and knowledge. Innovation, he believed, was a pathway to national development.

Terragno believed that advances in technology were changing the nature of management. 'The postindustrial economy will not depend on the size, the vertical organization and the discipline of the companies', he wrote. 'It will demand, instead, that imagination, knowledge, and responsibilities be widespread in all productive organizations . . . Administration will become more complex, and its interdependence with science and technology will be reinforced.'[56] He foresaw an increasing interdependence between management and technology: 'The development of cybernetics and management was complementary: management created the main market for computers and, in turn, became dependent on them.'[57] He believed that managers should cooperate with scientists and become better informed about scientific developments.

Although in general he was in favour of free markets, Terragno doubted whether entrepreneurs could absorb all the new skills and knowledge they needed without outside aid. He therefore argued for public sector–private sector partnerships in the field of knowledge generation, education and innovation. His philosophy, which became known as *terragnismo*, was highly popular for a time in Argentina and his book sold more than 80,000 copies. However, probably for political reasons, succeeding governments of Argentina did not look on his ideas with favour, and the *terragnismo* project was not taken up.

Management for sustainability

Economic and managerial thinking about sustainability also has a long if somewhat patchy history. One of the first to raise this issue was the economist Thomas Robert Malthus, who, in *An Essay on the Principles of Population* in 1798, warned that based on current trends, the population of British and other European societies would grow beyond the ability of those societies to feed themselves.[58] Agricultural production was increasing arithmetically, said Malthus, while population was multiplying itself; in other words, during the time that agriculture moved from a value of 3 to 4, population increased from a value of 3 to 9. Eventually, demand would outstrip supply, leading to scarcity and higher prices and, ultimately, mass starvation. Malthus also argued that the increasing gap between the richest and the poorest in society would hasten this trend.

Malthus's book caused a furore when published and he was attacked by, among others, the perfectibilist William Godwin who believed that society was on a steady path towards improvement and freedom, and the poet Robert Southey who accused Malthus of not caring about the fate of the poor. Malthus defended himself in subsequent editions of his work, pointing that far from being uncaring he was trying to warn people of the dangers that lay ahead. To this extent he was successful. A combination of improvements in agricultural management and agricultural science and the lifting of regulations inhibiting growth in the agricultural sector resulted in rising food production, which was able to keep pace with the rapid population growth of the nineteenth century. Later in the century Europe was able to drain off some of its surplus population to the New World, and further improvements in technology meant it was now possible to import food from places such as Argentina and New Zealand; but India and China, which also experienced population growth, were repeatedly stricken by famine.

Malthus's ideas came back into focus in the 1960s and 1970s as rising world populations began once more to put strain on food production capacity. The book *The Limits to Growth* in 1972 used the Jay Wright Forrester's principles of system dynamics to analyse global population and economic systems and concluded that a new Malthusian crisis was not only possible but likely.[59] This time, however, the focus was not solely on food. Concerns that the planet's ecological systems were being damaged by human activity were voiced by activists such as Rachel Carson, whose bestselling book *Silent Spring* led to some of the first environmental protection laws.[60] There were also fears that supplies of oil, by now the main source of energy on which Western industry depended, might be beginning to run out.[61] The work of James Lovelock, Sherwood Rowland and Mario Molina on detecting the damage done by chloro-fluorocarbons to the atmosphere was the first step towards a more general awareness of the dangers of climate change. Lovelock went on to develop his famous 'Gaia theory' which saw the Earth as a single complex interacting eco-system, where damage done to one part of the system can have momentous consequences for other parts.[62] Kenneth and Elise Boulding's *The Social System of the Planet Earth* offered a similar 'one planet' approach to human society.[63]

The UN World Commission on Environment and Development, chaired by Norwegian prime minister Gro Harlem Brundtland between 1983 and 1987 urged a greater focus on 'sustainability', which it defined as 'development that meets the needs of the present without compromising the ability of future generations to meet their own needs'.[64] In the following decade the consultant John Elkington coined the term 'triple bottom line'.[65] Elkington believed that sustainability had three dimensions, economic, social and environmental, sometimes expressed as 'people, planet, profit'. Elkington acknowledged the influence of the urban planner Patrick Geddes, who had similarly argued that people's happiness depends in part on their environment; Geddes in turn was drawing on still earlier concepts such as the 'garden city' of the late nineteenth century. More recently, concern for the environment has to some extent come to dominate the other elements of the triple bottom line, especially since the publication of the Stern Report in 2007.[66]

There has been, sporadically, some highly creative thinking about sustainability and management. Among the earliest works was Herman Daly and John Cobb's *For the Common Good*, which urged managers and business to think in collective terms and focus on co-operation rather than competition.[67] That same theme was followed by two major works in the last decade, Stuart Hart's *Capitalism at the Crossroads* and Peter Senge's *The Necessary Revolution*.[68] In the 1990s Paul Hawken revived the biological metaphor of organization and economy and began working on economic systems that mimicked those found in the natural world and were thus inherently self-sustaining; his work and others led ultimately to the development of terms such as 'biomimicry' and 'natural design'.[69] Other writers, perhaps following Saudi oil minister Sheikh Yamani's comment that 'The Stone Age did not come to an end because we had a lack of stones, and the oil age will not come to an end because we have a lack of oil', have begun looking beyond the end of the age of oil and trying to find economically viable new sources of energy.[70] Recently too there has been a more general trend away from 'eco-efficiency', the mere reducing of impact on the environment, towards 'eco-effectiveness', the development of business strategies which will have a positive impact on all three elements of the triple bottom line.[71] In this respect, thinking on sustainability sometimes crosses over with thinking about the bottom of the pyramid (see above).

I say that this work is sporadic because although there are a great many people – far more than I have mentioned here – coming up with some very interesting ideas, there is often little connection between them. A look at current literature and thinking on the internet shows that there are literally hundreds of initiatives, often little more than one-woman or one-man bands trying to make their voices heard among the general noise. Some of their ideas are in conflict with each other, and there is little sense of people working together, if one may use the phrase, in a sustainable way. Thinking about management and sustainability is generating many individually good ideas, but there is no sign yet of a conceptual framework that will pull them altogether. Given the growing demand and need for sustainability, this is surely the biggest challenge to management thinking over the coming decade. Once again, it will be interesting to see how management thinkers respond – or, indeed, whether they are now capable of responding in a coordinated and practical way.

12 Conclusion

> Education is not only inevitably conditioned by time and place but should be consciously related to the needs of the particular society of which it is a function . . . the educational system itself must be fully unified and deliberately integrated as closely as possible with the life of society.
>
> (Julian Huxley)

It has been a long journey from the Bronze Age to the internet age, and I shall make my conclusion brief. We began with the civilization builders of Egypt, Mesopotamia, China, India, Greece and Rome, and we saw how they used organization as a tool for the creation of stable societies. Many of the earliest writings we have on management are in effect searches for principles of organization – or for principles of leadership and sometimes also of strategy, for leadership and organization seemed to go hand in hand, each necessary to the other, and strategy was very much something that leaders did. The challenge of creating a stable society led to the search for these principles and their recording in various forms.

The seismic political shifts of the fifth to seventh centuries led to the emergence of a new world order, one where long-distance trade was once again a key feature. The prevailing mood in one polity, the Islamic empire, saw trade and traders as being a force for good, and we see here the beginnings of a body of thought on the relationship between business and society, as well as the principles of administration and management and even some considerations on the nature of managerial knowledge. Some of these ideas spread to medieval Europe, where new power-generating technologies and new forms of organization were emerging, and where there was something of an early industrial revolution in the twelfth and thirteenth centuries. We saw how managers responded to challenge and risk, and how management thinking responded too, creating for example new forms of accounting and new financial instruments to enable trade to expand and to help business people mitigate risk.

The European Enlightenment and the spirit of inquiry that it engendered led to rapid advances in science and technology, which in turn led to the Industrial Revolution. Another transformation of thinking was required, and now as businesses grew larger and more complex, management thinking had to become more complex too. The foundations for coherent systems of management thought were laid early in the nineteenth century, if not before; by the end of the century building work had begun, and the first two decades of the twentieth century saw an explosion of ideas as people searched for ways of harnessing the power of these new industrial engines more effectively and making them more efficient – not just to generate profits for their owners, but to serve society. There was a missionary quality about many of the early twentieth-century management thinkers: they were not just generating ideas for their own sake, they genuine believed that they were helping to create a better world.

Scientific management presented a system designed to control organizations and make them less wasteful and, as is often forgotten, more equitable in terms of work and reward. Scientific management appeared to offer a simple system of control, a one best way of managing, which is probably why so many managers adopted it gratefully. The simplicity, directness and practicality of the theory are also probably the reason why scientific management spread and endured while other theories of management such as those of Emerson and Fayol fell by the wayside. But one of the criticisms made of scientific management, then as now, was that it did not take account of human nature and human frailty. The human relations school proposed a more human-centred notion of management, but one which substituted the subtleties of coordination for the presumed certainties of control. As we saw, for much of the twentieth century there was a continuing tension between management systems such as MTM and BPR which focused on process, and the work of theorists such as Herzberg and McGregor who insisted the emphasis should be on people.

In the aftermath of the Second World War as the West, and especially America, stood face to face with the Soviet bloc, the first reaction of American management thinkers was to opt for a positivist and formalistic approach to management. Rigorous research, rigorous teaching, rigorous management methods were urged by bodies such as the RAND Corporation and the Ford Foundation, and these took root in business schools and had some impact on managerial practice too. During the 1950s and 1960s, to paraphrase Theodore Levitt one last time, managers made money by running their plants full blast. Economic conditions were such that they could get away with it, for a time. But new competitive challenges emerged, in Germany and Japan, and the positivist and formal approach to management thinking had no answer. Neither really did the open systems thinkers and industrial sociologists who were trying to create a new, equally rigorous approach to management but based on social science thinking rather than the principles of physical science.

Instead there was a kind of revolt against conventional management thinking, with gurus such as Tom Peters, Rosabeth Moss Kanter, Henry Mintzberg, Kenichi Ohmae and Philip Kotler overturning previously held beliefs and arguing for more flexible and more human-centred approaches to management. Less management and more leadership; less bureaucracy and more flexibility; less mechanistic thinking and more innovation; these were the *cris de cœur* of the 1980s and 1990s. By then, too, it was clear that seismic shifts in the global order were stirring below ground. A combination of new technologies – especially but not limited to the Internet – a new political order and rising concern as to whether the planet itself could continue to support our growing economies and population led to a reappraisal of management methods and calls for radical change. At time of writing, those calls are still going on. The first footsteps have been taken towards change, no more.

We live, as the Chinese proverb has it, in interesting times. A great challenge faces the management thinkers of today, as great as the challenges of the late nineteenth century. It is no exaggeration to say that we need to undertake a root and branch re-examination of what management is, what its purpose is, what the role of management thinkers is, and how we as management thinkers can contribute to meeting that challenge. If we fail it, then not only are our businesses, perhaps society itself, put at risk, but we will have failed the test of proving our own relevance. As I mentioned earlier in the book, the financial crisis of 2008 has tested popular faith in financial economics and financial management, possibly to destruction. That same test faces all management thinkers now. We may well find that in the very near future we face a choice: be relevant, or be redundant.

Throughout the course of this book, I have generally portrayed management thinking in a positive light. That is because I believe that *on the whole* management thinking has had a positive impact on society. That does not mean that I am a perfectibilist. I do not necessarily believe that each new 'advance' in management thinking represents forward progress, nor do I necessarily believe that the way we manage now is the best possible way of managing, even given the knowledge we already have. As I said at the start of this book, one thing that the history of management teaches us is that many good ideas about management get lost along the way: forgotten, passed over, buried in the avalanche of historical events like those of Adamiecki or Bat'a or Rodolfo Terragno. Others simply fail to receive support. (This, of course, is true of all intellectual endeavour, there is nothing special about management thinking in this respect.)

But not everyone believes that management is a force for good. Running in parallel with management thinking, there is a history of dystopian ideas which draw at least some of their inspiration from contemporary thinking about management. William Blake's *Jerusalem* and Mary Shelley's *Frankenstein* were both in part reactions against the social change being wrought by the Industrial Revolution. Aldous Huxley's *Brave New World* is in part a satire on the new world of business and management. There is nothing satirical about James Burnham's *The Managerial Revolution*, just biting condemnation. In the 1930s Lewis Mumford was optimistic about the future; by the 1960s he had changed his mind and foresaw a vision of a 'megatechnic wasteland' in which people surrendered control of their lives to faceless technocrats backed up by machines.[1] Popular culture had already picked up on this theme with George Orwell's *Nineteen Eighty-Four*, it would do so many times again in works such as Kurt Vonnegut's *Player Piano*. In *Future Shock*, Alvin Toffler foresaw a society so complex and intricate that stress and disorientation would effectively cancel out the gains made by technology.[2]

Popular commentators today such as George Monbiot and Naomi Klein remain suspicious of management – and they have wide followings and reach broader audiences than most management writers do. The financial crisis of 2008 did more than create doubt about financial economics. As in the aftermath of the bursting of the dotcom bubble of 2001, there has been a popular backlash against business schools, management education and, by implication, management academia. We are seen as being partly responsible for the crisis, and for the financial and human cost of cleaning it up. It seems to me that we cannot stand aloof from that criticism or that debate. As our colleagues who study brand management know, it is important to tell your own story. I think it is time we did a little brand management of management education and management thinking. Are we a force for good, as I have said I believe we are? Then if so, we need to start telling that story.

What is management thinking for?

In *The Tacit Dimension*, Michael Polanyi recalled a conversation with the Soviet ideologue Nikolai Bukharin in 1935:

> When I asked him about the pursuit of pure science in Soviet Russia, he said that pure science was a morbid symptom of class society; under socialism, the conception of science pursued for its own sake would disappear, for the interests of scientists would turn spontaneously to the problems of the current Five-Year Plan. I was struck by the fact that this very denial of the existence of independent scientific thought came from a socialist theory which derived its tremendous persuasive power from its claim to scientific certainty. The scientific outlook appeared to have produced a mechanical conception of man and history in which there was no place for science itself. This conception

denied altogether any intrinsic power to thought and thus denied also any grounds for claiming freedom of thought. I saw also that this self-immolation of the mind was actuated by powerful moral motives. The mechanical course of history was to bring universal justice. Scientific skepticism would trust only material necessity for achieving universal brotherhood. Skepticism and utopianism had thus fused into new skeptical fanaticism.[3]

This anecdote intrigues because – as usual with Polanyi – there are multiple layers to it. There is first of all Bukharin's denial of pure science and insistence that the only valid form of science is applied science (and we can take this statement to imply that Bukharin intended the same fate for all branches of knowledge, not just science; everything was to be harnessed to the service of the state). Polanyi rejected this, and so I think would most people. Indeed, management academics and business schools have fought a long-running battle to maintain freedom of thought and avoid the domination and direction of either the state or the corporate world. Should we surrender to the demand that all our work should be applied thinking, we would become no more than corporate brain-slaves. Freedom, as we have seen over and over again in this book, is essential to creativity. It is for this reason that few if any really powerful ideas about management were generated in either the Soviet Union or Maoist China.

But what do we do with that freedom? I come back to the third paragraph of Polanyi's anecdote: 'The mechanical course of history was to bring universal justice.' Contrast this with the words of Frederick Winslow Taylor in *The Principles of Scientific Management*: 'In the past man has been first; in the future the system must be first.'[4] Both Bukharin (as Polanyi saw it) and Taylor imply that justice can only be achieved when people sublimate themselves to the mechanical system. It will be recalled that Luther Gulick made much the same argument in the aftermath of the Second World War (and that George Orwell heard that argument and rejected it violently). The management scientists of the 1950s, Taylor's intellectual heirs, were closer in mindset to their Soviet foes than they might have liked to think.

If we as management thinkers use our freedom of thought to develop constraining systems which rob human beings of the ability to be creative, to use their intuition, to be wrong, to make mistakes and learn from them; to create iron cages of bureaucracy, to contribute to the making of a megatechnic wasteland, then I would argue that we have abused that freedom. Chains are still chains, even if we put them on voluntarily. Any consideration of management needs to start with the human element. Here I worry about some of those who are doing research on management for sustainability, who in the equation 'planet, people, profit' rank them in that order. Stretch this concept to its absurd extreme and you come to the idea that people should be prepared to sacrifice themselves to save the planet. *This will not work.* We must begin at the beginning. Management thinking developed in the first instance out of the need to build civilizations. It exists, has always existed, at the service of civilization. Pure thought and applied thought both are necessary, but we must keep the end goal in mind.

There has, as we have noted, been a ding-dong battle over the years between those who regard management as a science and those who regard it as an art. I propose a third option. We need to regard management as a philosophy, as way of 'thinking about doing things'. We need a set of ideas, including moral ideas as well as scientific ideas, to show us how best to use that precious freedom of thought for the good of businesses, economies – and for the good of humanity? Why not?

In 2009 I interviewed R.K. Krishna Kumar, one of the 'grand old men' of the Tata group in India. I asked him a typical management thinker's question: what did he perceive to be the strengths of the Tata brand? 'What you must realize is that this is not a brand story', he replied. 'This is a story about good and evil.' My first reaction was an inward cringe. Good and evil? In a discussion about brands? Surely we should be talking about features such as value, integrity, trust . . . Except that, are those not features of goodness? And is not their absence what most belief systems would describe as evil? The problem was not with Krishna Kumar; it was with me. For Krishna Kumar, the Tata group existed to combat corruption, to help alleviate poverty, to generate social development and help the less advantaged communities of India catch up with their more fortunate compatriots, to help India take its rightful place in the family of developed nations. To him, at least, what he does as a manager and business leader is righteous.

And where people like Krishna Kumar lead, I believe the rest of us can follow. To repeat, management was born out of the need to build civilization, and management has existed at the service of civilization ever since. Each time our civilization has evolved and grown, it has placed new demands on managers and asked questions of management thinkers. Each time – so far – management thinkers have responded, often powerfully. Can we continue to do so? I believe that we can, but only if we find our way back to, in Oliver Sheldon's phrase, a philosophy of management. The future will call for both management as art and management as science, both guided in their purpose by management as philosophy.

And yet, I think that management thinking is going in the wrong direction.

The iron age of management thought

In his *Metamorphoses*, the poet Ovid described the progress of human civilization passing through four ages.[5] First there was the Golden Age, which 'spontaneously nurtured the good and the true' and in which people lived in complete freedom. Second came the Silver Age when the first civilizations were built and order and structure appeared. Next was the Bronze Age, which saw technological advances but also saw fragmentation, division and conflict. Finally came the present day, the Iron Age, characterized by discord, conflict and splintering of society with every person out for their own interests.

Management thinking has passed through four similar stages. First was the Golden Age, which we saw in Chapters 2 and 3 and which lasted until about 1900. Absolutely anyone who wanted to express ideas about management could do so freely and in any forum, be it works of philosophy, poetry or even as in the case of San Bernardino, in public sermons. There was a glorious confusion of ideas, though a few common themes shine through, such as the linkage of organization and civilization, and the subordination of the interests of business to society.

Then came the Silver Age, the age of scientific management and its contemporaries. Now ideas were codified into systems of thought; now there were theories, structures, models. Scientific management, efficiency theory, administration theory, the human relations school, personnel management, marketing, corporation finance: these were the creations of the Silver Age.

The Bronze Age corresponds to the period beginning in the 1930s and especially after the Second World War. Immense advances in theoretical understanding were accompanied by a fragmentation of management thinking into increasingly numerous disciplines and schools of thought. The unity of thinking about management as an art that had once existed now began to erode. By our own time, it has vanished entirely.

We now live in the Iron Age. I do not mean that we should take this literally; it is not the case that friend is not safe with friend, or brother with brother, nor do academics mix aconite to poison each other; or if they do, only metaphorically. But management thinking is increasingly becoming a closed world, and I do not think it is too strong to say that it exists for selfish ends. I have already remarked that it is rare for non-academics to be invited to write for management publications save for a few exceptions such as *Harvard Business Review*. Unless non-academics choose to write their own books – and can find a publisher – management thinking is now the province of academe.

And to what end? I have served as a commissioning editor for various management publications for more than ten years, and I have watched the slow but steady disengagement of academia from 'real-world' publishing. I have listened to academics flatly refuse to publish their ideas in any popular journal for fear of the damage it might do to their reputation. I have heard how universities discourage their younger academics in particular from writing books, or even chapters in books, or anything at all save for articles in peer-reviewed academic journals which, as one colleague remarks, are only read by three people. No matter; publication in such journals ticks boxes. It proves that the researcher has been doing research, it establishes reputation and it helps the employing university or business school bump up its own reputation and earn more money from the government or other funding bodies.

I have no objection to any of this; we all have reputations, we all have to make a living. But to *deliberately* refuse to also publish one's ideas in journals where practising managers might read one's ideas, and to prevent others from doing so – in other words, to deliberately withhold new research from the public gaze – is I fear nothing more than intellectual onanism. And it is precisely this model of research and publication that threatens the future of management thinking. I do not mean that we must all rush out and devote ourselves to the service of the Five-Year Plan; I hope I have made that clear by now. But we must remember our purpose, our philosophy. Our task as management thinkers, here and now, is to work out what management is for and what its principles are, and then to teach these to a new generation of managers and leaders so that they tackle the problems of the present and future with confidence and skill. That is our role in the battle between good and evil. Have we the moral strength to step up and play that role? As Elliott Jaques, said, only time will tell.

Notes

1 Introduction

1 Edward D. Jones, 'Military History and the Science of Business Administration', *Engineering Magazine*, 1912, p. 1.
2 Thomas North Whitehead, *Leadership in a Free Society*, 1936, p. 3.
3 Liana Farber, *An Anatomy of Trade in Medieval Writing: Value, Consent and Community*, 2006.
4 Daniel Wren, *The Evolution of Management Thought*, 1994, p. 3.
5 Morgen Witzel, *Management History: Text and Cases*, 2009.
6 Tom Burns, 'Industry in a New Age', *New Society*, 1963; repr. in Derek S. Pugh (ed.), *Organization Theory: Selected Readings*, 1997, p. 99.
7 Alfred North Whitehead, *Process and Reality*, 1929, p. 39.
8 Violina Rindova and William Starbuck, 'Ancient Chinese Theories of Control', *Journal of Management Inquiry*, 1997, p. 157.
9 Michael Mol and Julian Birkinshaw, *Giant Steps in Management: Creating Innovations that Change the Way We Work*, 2008, p. 2.
10 Sidney Pollard, *The Genesis of Modern Management*, 1965, p. 314.
11 Theodore Levitt, 'Marketing Myopia', *Harvard Business Review*, 1960 (repr. 1975), p. 14.

2 Early management thought

1 See *From the Rig Veda; From the Atharva Veda*, trans. R.C. Zaehner, 1966; Miriam Lichtheim, *Ancient Egyptian Literature: The Old and Middle Kingdoms*, vol. 1, *A Book of Readings*, 1975.
2 The dating of many ancient texts is controversial, and there are many alternative theories. See *Epic of Gilgamesh*, trans. N.K. Sandars, 1960; *The Iliad*, trans. Herbert Jordan, 2008; *The Odyssey*, trans. Robert Fitzgerald, 1998; *Kojiki*, trans. Basil H. Chamberlain, 1932; R.V. Vaidya, *A Study of the Mahabharat*, 1967; *The Yellow Emperor's Classic of Internal Medicine*, trans. Ilza Veith, 1972.
3 Parkinson, R.B., *Poetry and Culture in Middle Kingdom Egypt: A Dark Side to Perfection*, 2002; Thompson, Stephen E., 'Textual Sources, Old Kingdom', in Kathryn A. Bard (ed.), *Encyclopedia of the Archaeology of Ancient Egypt*, 1999, 801–2.
4 And, of course, biblical texts such as Proverbs influenced later thinking in Jewish and Christian circles.
5 François de la Rochefoucauld, *Maxims*, trans. Louis Kronenberger, 1959; Samuel Smiles, *Self-Help: With Illustrations of Character and Conduct*, 1889 (1859).
6 Rob Goffee and Gareth Jones, *Why Should Anyone Be Led by You?* 2006; Lynda Gratton, *Glow: How You Can Radiate Energy, Innovation and Success*, 2009.
7 Karl Moore and David Lewis, *The Origins of Globalization*, 2009; see also Moore and Lewis, *Foundations of Corporate Empire: Is History Repeating Itself?*, 2000; Morris Silver, *Economic Structures of Antiquity*, 1995; Maria Eugenia Aubet, *The Phoenicians and the West: Politics, Colonies and Trade*, 2001; Neville Morley, *Trade in Classical Antiquity*, 2007.
8 Barry J. Kemp, *Ancient Egypt: Anatomy of a Civilization*, 1992.
9 Moore and Lewis, *The Origins of Globalization*.
10 Moore and Lewis, *The Origins of Globalization*, p. 75.

11 Daniel D. Luckenbill (trans.), *The Code of Hammurabi*, 1931.

12 My thanks to Richard Taylor for drawing my attention to this passage.

13 Aristide Théodoridès, 'Law', in Kathryn A. Bard (ed.), *Encyclopedia of the Archaeology of Ancient Egypt*, 1999, p. 439.

14 Stephen Quirke, *The Administration of Egypt in the Late Middle Kingdom*, 1990; Nigel Strudwick, *The Administration of Egypt in the Old Kingdom*, 1985; Eva Martin-Pardey, 'Administrative Bureaucracy', in Kathryn A. Bard (ed.), *Encyclopedia of the Archaeology of Ancient Egypt*, 1999.

15 Martin-Pardey, 'Administrative Bureaucracy', p. 116.

16 See G.P.F. van den Boorn, *The Duties of the Vizier*, 1988. This is the date given by van den Boorn, but this has been challenged by other writers.

17 The English word 'vizier' derives from the Arabic *wazir* (minister or adviser), and only came into common English usage within the last few hundred years.

18 Raghavan N. Iyer, *The Political and Moral Thought of Mahatma Gandhi*, 1973.

19 For example, S. Radhakrishnan, *The Bhagavadgita*, 1993. Other good translations include that of R.C. Zaehner in *Hindu Scriptures*, 1966, which also includes the text of a number of the Upanishads, and A.C. Bhaktivedante Swami Prabhupada, *The Bhagavad-Gita as It Is*, 1972. See also Charles Chow Hoi Hee and Bruce Gurd, 'Leadership Essentials from Sun Zi's Art of War and the Bhagavad Gita', *Journal of Management History*, 2010.

20 Prabhupada, *The Bhagavad-Gita as It Is*, pp. 133, 143.

21 Prabhupada, *The Bhagavad-Gita as It Is*, pp. 815–16, 814.

22 Prabhupada, *The Bhagavad-Gita as It Is*, p, 816.

23 Somadeva, *The Katha Sarit Sagara*, trans. C.H. Tawney, 1924.

24 M.V.K. Rao, *Studies in Kautilya*, 1979; Umesh Kumar, *Kautilya's Thought on Public Administration*, 1990.

25 I have of course oversimplified this concept drastically; see John Taber, 'Duty and Virtue, Indian Conceptions of', in Edward Craig (ed.), *Routledge Encyclopedia of Philosophy*, 1998, vol. 3, pp. 183–7 for a more detailed discussion.

26 Kumar, *Kautilya's Thought on Public Administration*, p. 3.

27 For a translation, see Manmatha Nath Dutt, *Yajnavalkyasmrti: Sanskrit Text, English Translation*, 2005.

28 For much more detail on the business organisation of Buddhist monasteries in this period, see Gregory Schopen, *Buddhist Monks and Business Matters*, 2004. The Mulasarvastivada school was one of many early schools of Buddhism; it later declined and today has only a few adherents.

29 Thomas Cleary (trans.) *I Ching: The Book of Change*, 1992.

30 Mu-Lan Hsu and Kwan-Yao Chiu, 'A Comparison between I-Ching's Early Management Decision Making Model and Western Management Decision Making Models', *Chinese Management Studies*, 2008.

31 See Violina P. Rindova and William H. Starbuck, 'Ancient Chinese Theories of Control', *Journal of Management Inquiry*, 1997.

32 *Great Plan*, Chinese text and English translation, http://ctext.org/shang-shu/great-plan.

33 See James Legge, *The Chinese Classics*, 2001. The point about leading by example is particularly stressed by Rindova and Starbuck, 'Ancient Chinese Theories of Control'.

34 Legge, *The Chinese Classics*, 2001.

35 Moore and Lewis, *The Origins of Globalization*, p. 198.

36 D.C. Lau, *Confucius: The Analects*, 1979; David L. Hall and Roger T. Ames, *Thinking Through Confucius*, 1987; Wing-tsit Chan, *A Source Book in Chinese Philosophy*, 1963; Chen Huan-Chang, *The Economic Principles of Confucius and His School*, 1911.

37 D.C. Lau and Roger T. Ames, 'Confucius', in Edward Craig (ed.), *Routledge Encyclopedia of Philosophy*, 1998.

38 This again is a huge oversimplification. For those wanting more detail, Lau and Ames, 'Confucius', provide a good introduction, and David L. Hall and Roger T. Ames, *Thinking Through Confucius*, 1987, is recommended as an in-depth treatment.

39 Quoted in Chen, *The Economic Principles of Confucius and His School*.

40 Apart from a period during the Cultural Revolution when there was a campaign against Confucian ideas led by Mao Zedong's wife Jiang Qing, Confucius and his ideas continued to be taught even after the establishment of the People's Republic of China.

41 Richard Hughes, *Foreign Devil*, 1972; Wong Siu-lun, 'The Chinese Family Firm: A Model', *British Journal of Sociology*, 1985; Min Chen, *Asian Management Systems*, 1995; Ian Rae and

Morgen Witzel, *The Overseas Chinese of Southeast Asia*, 2008; Tim Ambler, Morgen Witzel and Chao Xi, *Doing Business in China*, 2009.

42 Malcolm Warner, 'In Search of Confucian HRM: Theory and Practice in Greater China and Beyond', 2010.

43 Max Weber, *The Religion of China*, 1964.

44 Chen Huan-Chang, *The Economic Principles of Confucius and His School*, 1911.

45 Quoted in Chen, *The Economic Principles of Confucius and His School*.

46 Quoted in Chen, *The Economic Principles of Confucius and His School*, p. 408; Claude S. George, *The History of Management Thought*, 1972, p. 13.

47 D.C. Lau, *Mencius*, 1970. I have checked several translations of Mencius and not been able to find this passage. On the other hand, I was working from translations and Chen worked from the original, so it is possible that my interpretation here is wrong.

48 Frederick Winslow Taylor, *Shop Management*, 1903; Harrington Emerson, *Efficiency as a Basis for Operations and Wages*, 1909.

49 Homer H. Dubs, *Hsüntze: The Moulder of Ancient Confucianism*, 1927.

50 Quoted in John C.H. Wu (trans.) *Tao Teh Ching (Daodejing)*, 1990.

51 Quoted in Wu (trans.) *Tao Teh Ching (Daodejing)*.

52 Goffee and Jones, *Why Should Anyone Be Led by You?*

53 G.F. Hudson, *Europe and China*, 1931.

54 For a good introduction and authoritative translation, see Burton Watson, *Han Fei Tzu: Basic Writings*, 2003.

55 Quoted in Watson, *Han Fei Tzu*.

56 Quoted in Watson, *Han Fei Tzu*.

57 Rindova and Starbuck, 'Ancient Chinese Theories of Control', p. 156.

58 Russell Ackoff and Sheldon Rovin, *Beating the System: Using Creativity to Outsmart Bureaucracies*, 2005.

59 Rindova and Starbuck, 'Ancient Chinese Theories of Control', p. 148.

60 Max Weber, *Economy and Society*, trans. Keith Tribe, 2008.

61 C. Northcote Parkinson, *Parkinson's Law*, 1958.

62 See in particular Thomas J. Peters, *Thriving on Chaos: Handbook for a Management Revolution*, 1987.

63 Rosabeth Moss Kanter, *When Giants Learn to Dance*, 1989.

64 The version I have used here was translated in 1910 and edited carefully by the American general and military historian Samuel B. Griffiths in 1963 (listed in the bibliography as Sunzi 1963), but there are many other translations and editions. See also Chow Hu Wee, Kai Sheang Lee and Bambang Walujo Hidajat, *Sun Tzu: War and Management*, 1991.

65 *The Art of War*, ch. 1, §26,

66 *The Art of War*, ch. 3, §17.

67 Luo Guanzhong, *The Three Kingdoms*, trans. Moss Roberts, 1991.

68 Martin L. West (ed. and trans.), *Hesiod: Works and Days*, 1978.

69 Gareth Morgan, *Images of Organization*, 1986. See the relevant sections in W.K.C. Guthrie, *A History of Greek Philosophy*, 1962–78; M.R. Wright, *Empedocles: The Extant Fragments*, 1981; Charles H. Kahn, *The Art and Thought of Heraclitus*, 1979.

70 For more on Plato, good starting points are W.H.D. Rouse (trans.) *Great Dialogues of Plato*, 1956; G.M.A. Grube, *Plato's Thought*, 1980; Richard Kraut, *Cambridge Companion to Plato*, 1992; Nickolas Pappas, *Plato and the Republic*, 1995.

71 Again, for the purposes of the present project, I am oversimplifying greatly; those interested in the ideas of the *Republic* should read the work itself and also Pappas, *Plato and the Republic*.

72 *Republic* 369b; Rouse, *Great Dialogues of Plato*, p. 165.

73 Morgen Witzel, *Management History: Text and Cases*, 2009, pp. 34–8.

74 Pappas, *Plato and the Republic*, p. 65.

75 Xenophon, *The Persian Expedition*, trans. Rex Warner, 2004.

76 *The Education of Cyrus*, quoted in Lynette Mitchell, 'The Education of Cyrus and the Obedience of the Willing', 2008, p. 15.

77 Raoul McLaughlin, *Rome and the Distant East*, 2009.

78 For translations of both works, see T.E. Page, *Cato and Varro De Re Rustica 'On Agriculture'*, 1967.

79 Tacitus, *The Agricola and the Germania*, trans. H. Mattingly, 1948.

80 Arrian, *The Campaigns of Alexander*, trans. Aubrey de Sélincourt, 1948.
81 Sextus Julius Frontinus, *Stratagemata*, trans. Charles E. Bennett, 1925; Vegetius, *Epitome Rei Militaris*, ed. and trans. N.P. Milner, 1993.
82 William H. Starbuck, 'The Origins of Organization Theory', in Haridimos Tsoukas and Christian Knudsen (eds), *The Oxford Handbook of Organization Theory*, 2005, p. 143.

3 Management thought in the age of commerce

1 Charles O. Hucker, *China to 1850*, 1978, p. 91.
2 Angus Maddison, *The World Economy*, 2006. In fairness, my reading of Maddison is that he believes there was economic growth in Europe after AD 1000, but this has often been overlooked by those who focus on the more 'sensational' news that China was then the world's largest economy.
3 Bruce M.S. Campbell, *English Seigniorial Agriculture 1250–1400*, 2000, who provides figures from several sets of analysis of the English economy over this period.
4 Roberto S. Lopez, *The Commercial Revolution of the Middle Ages, 950–1350*, 1971.
5 The term is not my own: 'the age of commerce' is a catch-all title which historians have used to describe particular eras when countries or regions were engaged in high-volume trade that enriched their economies. The age of commerce in Western Europe, depending on which country we are talking about, can be anywhere in the period from 1100 to 1900. Historians have identified at least two 'ages of commerce' in South-East Asia, from 900–1300 and from 1450–1680: Anthony Reid, *South-East Asia in the Age of Commerce, 1450–1680*, 1988–95; Geoff Wade, 'An Early Age of Commerce in Southeast Asia, 900–1300 CE', *Journal of Southeast Asian Studies*, 2009.
6 Gene W. Heck, *Islam, Inc.*, 2004.
7 K.N. Chaudhuri, *Trade and Civilisation in the Indian Ocean: An Economic History from the Rise of Islam to 1750*, 1985. See also Aziz S. Atiya, *Crusade, Commerce and Culture*, 1962; Hugh Kennedy, *The Great Arab Conquest: How the Spread of Islam Changed the World We Live in*, 2007; Heck, *Islam, Inc.*
8 A short and highly accessible introduction of the emergence of Islam can be found in Albert Hourani, *A History of the Arab Peoples*, 1991; a longer and more detailed treatment is Marshall G.S. Hodgson, *The Venture of Islam*, 1977.
9 'Ali ibn Abi Talib, *Nahjul Balagha* (Peak of Eloquence), trans. S.A. Reza, 1978.
10 Beha ed-Din, *What Befell Sultan Yusuf*, 1978.
11 C.E. Bosworth, *Medieval Arabic Culture and Administration*, 1982, p. i.
12 For a translation, see Richard Walzer, *Al-Farabi on the Perfect State*, 1985; see also Michael Galston, *Politics and Excellence: The Political Philosophy of Alfarabi*, 1990.
13 Michael E. Marmura, *The Incoherence of the Philosophers: Tahafut al-Falasifah*, 1997.
14 Gustave E. von Grunebaum, *Medieval Islam: A Study in Cultural Orientation*, 1953, p. 251.
15 Grunebaum, *Medieval Islam*, p. 253.
16 Grunebaum, *Medieval Islam*, p. 253.
17 C.E. Bosworth, 'A Pioneer Arabic Encyclopedia of the Sciences: al Khwarazmi's "Keys of the Sciences"', 1963; Bosworth, 'Abu 'Abdallah al-Khwarazmi on the Technical Terms of the Secretary's Art', 1969.
18 Nizam al-Mulk, *Siyasat Nama*, trans. Hubert Darke, *The Book of Government or Rules for Kings*, 1960; Kai Kaus, *Qabus Nama*, trans. Reuben Levy, *A Mirror for Princes*, 1951.
19 *Book of Dede Korkut*, trans. Geoffrey Lewis, 1964.
20 *Qabus Nama*, p. 21.
21 *Qabus Nama*, p. 156.
22 *Qabus Nama*, p. 156.
23 *Qabus Nama*, pp. 158, 163.
24 Heck, *Islam, Inc.*, p. 187.
25 Heck, *Islam, Inc.*, p. 188.
26 Not all of these works are available in translation, and I have therefore had to take on trust their importance. Al-Dimashqi's *Al-ishara ila mahasin al-tijjarah* is available in French under the title *Eloge du Commerce*, trans. Youssef Seddik, 1995. Abu Ubayd's *Kitab al-amwal* and al-Mawardi's *Al-akham al-sultaniyya* are both available in English translations from 2005. Scholarly interest has tended to focus on works on civil administration rather than on those on commerce.
27 Heck, *Islam, Inc.* This is the most complete work of its kind that I have encountered, but it is not without problems, chief among these being the author's insistence that the European commercial

growth that began in the eleventh century could not have happened without Islam. The influence of Islamic business practices is undoubted, but the author heavily overstates his case.

28 Heck, *Islam, Inc.*, p. 190.
29 Al-Dimashqi in *Eloge du Commerce*; Heck, *Islam, Inc.* p. 190.
30 Heck, *Islam, Inc.*, p. 210.
31 The Catholic Church officially prohibited usury, but there was no such prohibition in the Byzantine Empire, which though Christian was governed by civil rather than religious law. See Gerald A.J. Hodgett, *A Social and Economic History of Medieval Europe*, 1972, p. 65.
32 Halil Inalcik, *An Economic and Social History of the Ottoman Empire*, vol. 1, *1300–1600*, 1994.
33 The system of numbering we use today in the West was certainly of Indian origin, probably invented by Buddhist scholars rather than Hindu ones.
34 Documents reproduced in M.T. Clanchy, *From Memory to Written Record*, 1993, clearly show roman numerals still in use at the end of the thirteenth century. Marilyn Livingstone, who has worked extensively with English medieval records in the mid-fourteenth century, confirms that Roman numerals were used in all but a few instances in the documents she has seen.
35 Ibn Khaldun, *The Muqaddimah*, trans. Franz Rosenthal, 1986; see also Yusuf M. Sidani, 'Ibn Khaldun of North Africa: An AD 1377 Theory of Leadership', *Journal of Management History*, 2008.
36 Ibn Khaldun, *The Muqaddimah*, vol. 2, p. 276.
37 Ibn Khaldun, *The Muqaddimah*, vol. 2, p. 337.
38 Ibn Khaldun, *The Muqaddimah*, vol. 2, pp. 342–3.
39 A good account is Colin Imber, *The Ottoman Empire 1300–1650*, 2002.
40 See for example Murat Çizakça, *A Comparative Evolution of Business Partnerships: The Islamic World and Europe, with Specific Reference to the Ottoman Archives*, 1996.
41 Leyla Gurkan, 'Bostanzade, Yahya Efendi', in Oliver Leaman (ed.), *Biographical Dictionary of Islamic Philosophers*, 2007.
42 Bilal Kuşpinar, 'Raghib Pasha, Mehmed', in Oliver Leaman (ed.), *Biographical Dictionary of Islamic Philosophers*, 2007.
43 Halil Inalcik, *An Economic and Social History of the Ottoman Empire*, 1994.
44 Thabit A.J. Abdullah, *Merchants, Mamluks and Murder: The Political Economy of Trade in Eighteenth-Century Basra*, 2000.
45 M.T. Houtsma *et al.* (eds), *Encyclopedia of Islam*, 1913, p. 819. Unsurprisingly given its size, the encyclopedia has not yet been translated from Arabic.
46 D.S. Richards, *Mamluk Administrative Documents from St Catherine's Monastery*, 2011.
47 *Tadhkirat al-muluk*, trans. Vladimir Minorsky, 1980; Muhammad Ismail Marcinkowski, *Mirza Rafi'a's Dastur al-Muluk: A Manual of Later Safavid Administration*, 2002.
48 J.M. Wallace-Hadrill, *The Barbarian West*, 1952, remains an excellent account of this period; see Richard Fletcher, *The Conversion of Europe*, 1997, on the transformation and spread of Christianity.
49 See J. McCann, *Saint Benedict*, 1937; Charles Cary-Elwes, *St Benedict and His Rule*, 1988.
50 A full text of the rule can be found in Cary-Elwes, *St Benedict and His Rule*, or online at www.ccel.org/ccel/benedict/rule2/files/rule2.html, although this version has been edited and modernized to a degree.
51 See G.R. Evans, *Bernard of Clairvaux*, 2000, and Morgen Witzel, 'The Cistercian Order', in *Management History: Text and Cases*, 2009, pp. 84–9.
52 Jean Gimpel, *The Medieval Machine*, 1976.
53 S.R. Epstein, 'Craft Guilds in the Pre-Modern Economy', *Economic History Review*, 2008; see also S.R. Epstein and Maarten Prak (eds), *Guilds, Innovation and the European Economy, 1400–1800*, 2008.
54 For more on the development of record-keeping, see Michael Clanchy, *From Memory to Written Record*, 1993.
55 Marilyn Livingstone, 'Fitz Neal, Richard', in Morgen Witzel (ed.), *Biographical Dictionary of Management*, 2001.
56 From the translation by Ernest Henderson, 1896. See also Charles Johnson (ed. and trans.), *Dialogus de Scaccario*, 1950.
57 Clanchy, *From Memory to Written Record*, p. 92; see also C.R. Cheney, *Hubert Walter*, 1967; Marilyn Livingstone, 'Walter, Hubert', in Morgen Witzel (ed.) *Biographical Dictionary of Management*, 2001.

58 Morgen Witzel, *Management History: Text and Cases*, 2009.

59 Katja Rost *et al.*, 'The Corporate Governance of Benedictine Abbeys', *Journal of Management History*, 2010; Michael H. Kennedy, 'Fayol's Principle and the Rule of St Benedict', *Journal of Management History*, 1999.

60 Charles Homer Haskins, *The Renaissance of the Twelfth Century*, 1927.

61 John of Salisbury, *Policraticus*, trans. J. Dickinson, 1927.

62 Andrew Ure, *Philosophy of Manufactures*, 1835; Harrington Emerson, *The Twelve Principles of Efficiency*, 1913; Charles E. Knoeppel, *Organization and Administration*, 1918; Gareth Morgan, *Images of Organization*, 1986.

63 The latter statement became something of a catchphrase in the later Middle Ages, sometimes rendered as 'war without fire is like sausages without mustard'.

64 Liana Farber, *An Anatomy of Trade in Medieval Writing*, 2006.

65 For the full debate, see Farber, *An Anatomy of Trade in Medieval Writing*, ch. 1.

66 Farber, *An Anatomy of Trade in Medieval Writing*, p. 12.

67 A point made by even the earliest scholars on marketing; see for example W.D. Moriarty, *The Economics of Marketing and Advertising*, 1923. For more on Aquinas's economic thought, see Farber, *An Anatomy of Trade in Medieval Writing*; B.W. Dempsey, 'Just Price in a Functional Economy', *American Economic Review*, 1935; Raymond de Roover, 'Scholastic Economics: Survival and Lasting Influence from the Sixteenth Century to Adam Smith', *Quarterly Journal of Economics*, 1955; de Roover, 'The Concept of Just Price Theory and Economic Policy', *Journal of Economic History*, 1958.

68 Iris Origo, *The World of San Bernardino*, 1962.

69 Raymond de Roover, *San Bernardino of Siena and Sant'Antonio of Florence: The Two Great Economic Thinkers of the Middle Ages*, 1967, p. 13.

70 Quoted in Jacques Le Goff, *Time, Work and Culture in the Middle Ages*, 1980, p. 66.

71 Le Goff, *Time, Work and Culture in the Middle Ages*, 1980, p. 67.

72 Marc Benioff and Karen Southwick, *Compassionate Capitalism: How Corporations Can Make Doing Good an Integral Part of Doing Well*, 2004; Daniel Goleman, *Social Intelligence*, 2006.

73 Goleman, *Social Intelligence*, p. 252.

74 Goleman, *Social Intelligence*, p. 314.

75 Max Weber, *The Protestant Ethic and the Spirit of Capitalism*, 2002.

76 Morgen Witzel, *Tata: The Evolution of a Corporate Brand*, 2010.

77 Witzel, *Builders and Dreamers*, 2002; *Management History*, 2009.

78 Roberto S. Lopez, *The Commercial Revolution of the Middle Ages*, 1971, is considered the classic account of this period; see also Lopez and Raymond (eds), *Medieval Trade in the Mediterranean World*, 1955.

79 Lopez and Raymond, *Medieval Trade in the Mediterranean World*, p. 408.

80 Roberto S. Lopez, *Benedetto Zaccaria*, 1933.

81 John L. Guilmartin, *Gunpowder and Galleys*, 1976.

82 Claude S. George, *The History of Management Thought*, 1972, p. 39. For more detail on the Arsenale, one of the more fascinating organizations of the Middle Ages, see Frederic C. Lane, *Venetian Ships and Shipbuilders of the Renaissance*, 1934; Guilmartin, *Gunpowder and Galleys*.

83 C.K. Prahalad and Gary Hamel, 'The Core Competence of the Corporation', *Harvard Business Review*, 1990.

84 Iris Origo, *The Merchant of Prato*, 1957.

85 The collection of Fugger newsletters amounts to about 35,000 pages. Selections have been published, for example *The Fugger News-Letters*, 1924.

86 Francesco di Balducci Pegolotti, *La pratica della mercatura*, ed. A. Evans, 1936.

87 Lopez, *The Commercial Revolution of the Middle Ages*. For the use of these limited-life partnerships by the Datini and Medici firms, see Origo, *The Merchant of Prato*; Raymond de Roover, *The Rise and Decline of the Medici Bank*, 1962.

88 De Roover, *The Rise and Decline of the Medici Bank*, and Origo, *The Merchant of Prato*, both give good accessible summaries of the partnership system; see also Lopez, *The Commercial Revolution of the Middle Ages*. An interesting earlier view is Max Weber, *The History of Commercial Partnerships in the Middle Ages*, trans. Lutz Kaelber, 2003. My thanks to J.C. Spender for drawing this work to my attention.

89 Credit for doing so is often given to Leonardo Fibonacci at the end of the twelfth century, but Arabic numerals were almost certainly in use in Europe much earlier than this.

90 Laurence E. Sigler, *Fibonacci's Liber Abaci*, 2002.

91 A full translation can be found in Basil S. Yamey (ed.), *Luca Pacioli: Exposition of Double Entry Bookkeeping Venice 1494*, 1994; see also Yamey, *Essays on the History of Accounting*, 1978; Michael Chatfield, *A History of Accounting Thought*, 1977; F.J. Swetz, *Capitalism and Arithmetic*, 1987.

92 E.M. Carus-Wilson, *Medieval Merchant Venturers*, 1967.

93 James Masschaele, *Peasants, Merchants and Markets*, 1997.

94 David Stone, 'Medieval Farm Management and Technological Mentalities', *Economic History Review*, 2001, p. 619.

95 Dorothea Oschinsky, *Walter of Henley*, 1971, p. 9.

96 A full translation of the Rules, the Seneschaucy and the Husbandry can be found in Oschinsky, *Walter of Henley*.

97 Marilyn Livingstone, 'Walter of Henley', in Morgen Witzel (ed.), *Biographical Dictionary of Management*, 2001.

98 Oschinsky, *Walter of Henley*, p. 190.

99 Padma B. Udgaonkar, *The Political Institutions and Administration of Northern India During Medieval Times*, 1969. See also C.V. Ramachandra Rao, *Administration and Society in Medieval Andhra (AD 1038–1538)*, 1976; D.C. Sircar, *Studies in the Society and Administration of Ancient and Medieval India*, 1967; B.R. Verma and S.R. Bakshi (eds), *Administration and Society in Medieval India*, 2005.

100 *Kamandakiya Nitisara; or, The Elements of Polity, in English*, 1896.

101 See Udgaonkar, *The Political Institutions and Administration of Northern India*, p. 79. I have not been able to find an English translation of this work.

102 P. Arundhati, *Royal Life in Manasollasa*, 1994.

103 Rao, *Administration and Society in Medieval Andhra*, p. 103.

104 Krishna Lal (ed.), *The Sukraniti*, 2005.

105 See Witzel, *Management History*; Irfan Habib, 'Potentialities of Capitalistic Development in the Economy of Mughal India', *Journal of Economic History*, 1969. My thanks to J.C. Spender for drawing my attention to this article.

106 Hakeda Yoshito, *The Awakening of Faith*, 1967.

107 Wing-tsit Chan, *Chu Hsi: Life and Thought*, 1989.

108 A good summary of this work is to be found in Lily Hwa, 'State Building in the Government of Tang Taizhong', *Forum on Public Policy*, 2008.

109 Pers. comm. My thanks to Professor So for drawing this work to my attention.

110 Charles O. Hucker, *China to 1850*, 1978.

111 Cao Xueqin, *A Dream of Red Mansions*, translation n.d. The book is also sometimes known as *Dream of the Red Chamber*.

112 Paul H. Varley (trans.) *A Chronicle of Gods and Sovereigns: The Jinno Shotoki of Kitabatake Chikafusa*, 1980.

113 For an English text, see William Theodore de Bary, Donald Keene and Tsunoda Ryusaku, *Sources of Japanese Tradition*, 1958, pp. 49–53.

114 Miyamoto, Musashi, *The Book of Five Rings*, trans. Thomas Cleary, 2005.

115 Sugawara Makoto, *Lives of Master Swordsmen*, 1985.

116 Yamamoto Tsunetomo, *Hagakure*, trans. William Scott Wilson, 1979, p. 17.

117 W.H. Prescott, *The Conquest of Mexico*, 1909, describes much of what is known about Aztec administration; he draws on earlier Spanish sources such as the work of Bernardino de Sahagun. See also Frances F. Berdan and Patricia R. Anwalt, *The Essential Codex Mendoza*, 1997.

118 John Hemmings, *The Conquest of the Incas*, 1983, summarizes what little is known about Inca government and society.

4 Management thought in an age of enlightenment

1 John Cottingham, *Descartes*, 1986; David Hume, *Enquiry Concerning Human Understanding*, 1978; Immanuel Kant, *Critique of Pure Reason*, 1933. For general introductions to the period, see Norman Hampson, *Enlightenment*, 1968; Roy Porter, *Enlightenment*, 2001.

2 For a good introduction to this period, see J.H. Parry, *The Age of Reconnaissance: Discovery, Exploration and Settlement*, 1964.

3 John Graunt, *Natural and Political Observations made upon the Bills of Mortality*, 1939.

4   Montesquieu, *The Persian Letters*, 1973.

5   Geert Hofstede, *Cultures and Organizations*, 1991.

6   Jenny Uglow, *The Lunar Men*, 2002.

7   William Petty, *The Economic Writings of Sir William Petty*, 1890; Alessandro Roncaglia, *Petty: Origins of Political Economy*, 1985.

8   Josiah Child, *A Discourse of the Nature, Use and Advantages of Trade*, 1694; Andrew Yarranton, *England's Improvement by Sea and Land*, 1678. For more on mercantilism generally, see E.A.J. Johnson, *Predecessors of Adam Smith*, 1939; Lars Magnusson, *Mercantilism: The Shaping of Economic Language*, 1994.

9   Josiah Tucker, *The Elements of Commerce, and Theory of Taxes*, 1755.

10 See Anthony Brewer, *Richard Cantillon*, 1992.

11 Smith probably did coin the English phase 'invisible hand', and George R. Crowley and Russell S. Sobel, 'Adam Smith: Managerial Insights from the Father of Economics', *Journal of Management History*, 2010, credit him with so doing. But I have always been convinced that the phrase, which appears in others of Smith's books, notably *The Theory of Moral Sentiments*, has its origins in physiocratic thought, notably that of Cantillon and Quesnay. I realize that this view is not universally held.

12 Adam Smith, *Inquiry into the Nature and Causes of the Wealth of Nations*, 1776; see also R.H. Campbell and Andrew S. Skinner, *Adam Smith*, 1986.

13 Smith was professor of moral philosophy at the University of Glasgow, near one of the early centres of the Industrial Revolution.

14 Thomas Robert Malthus, *Principles of Political Economy*, 1820, vol. 1, p. 120.

15 Nassau Senior, *An Outline of the Science of Political Economy*, 1830; Karl Marx, *Das Kapital*, 1933.

16 Melchiorre Gioia, *Nuovo Prospetto delle scienze economiche*, 2010.

17 John Stuart Mill, *Principles of Political Economy*, 2008.

18 Henry C. Carey, *The Slave Trade*, 1853, p. 393.

19 Thomas Jefferson, *Writings*, ed. M.D. Peterson, 1984, pp. 1265–6.

20 Bray Hammond, *Banks and Politics in America from the Revolution to the Civil War*, 1957; Robert E. Wright and David J. Cowen, *Financial Founding Fathers: The Men Who Made America Rich*, 2006.

21 Robert E. Wright, *The First Wall Street*, 2005.

22 Francis Amasa Walker, *Political Economy*, 1887.

23 William Graham Sumner, *Collected Essays in Political and Social Science*, 1885; Jeremiah W. Jenks, *The Trust Problem*, 1900.

24 W.W. Fowler, *Twenty Years of Inside Life in Wall Street*, 1880, pp. 35–6. This may be one of the first references to 'survival of the fittest' in a business context. Of course, as Geoffrey Hodgson and Thorbjørn Knudsen point out, there is much more to Darwinism than survival of the fittest – concepts such as sympathy and cooperation play a role too; see their *Darwin's Conjecture*, 2010.

25 John P. Davis, *The Union Pacific Railway*, 1894.

26 John P. Davis, *Corporations*, 1905, vol. 1, pp. 10–11.

27 Davis, *Corporations*, 1905, vol. 1, p. 11.

28 Davis, *Corporations*, 1905, vol. 1, p. 11.

29 Andrew Ure, *The Philosophy of Manufactures*, 1835; see also his *The Cotton Manufactures of Great Britain*, 1836, and *Dictionary of Arts, Manufactures and Mines*, 1839.

30 Daniel A. Wren, *The Evolution of Management Thought*, 1994, p. 65.

31 Ure, *The Philosophy of Manufactures*, 1835, p. 55.

32 The analytical engine was never completed owing to lack of money. See Anthony Hyman, *Charles Babbage: Pioneer of the Computer*, 1985.

33 Charles Babbage, *The Economy of Machinery and Manufactures*, 1835; *The Exposition of 1851*, 1851.

34 Babbage, *The Economy of Machinery and Manufactures*, 1835, p. 251.

35 Babbage, *The Exposition of 1851*, p. 47.

36 Babbage, *The Exposition of 1851*, p. 43.

37 Patrick Barwise and Seán Meehan, *Beyond the Familiar*, 2011.

38 Lyndall Urwick and E.F.L. Brech, *The Making of Scientific Management*, vol. 1, *Thirteen Pioneers*, 1947.

39 Marcus Tanner, *The Raven King: Matthias Corvinus and the Fate of His Lost Library*, 2008.

40 As, most famously, did Pope Julius II. A good contemporary account of the era in which Machiavelli lived is Francesco Guicciardini, *The History of Italy*, trans. Sidney Alexander, 1969.

41 *The Art of War*, trans. Ellis Farneworth, 2001; *The Discourses*, trans. L.J. Walker, 1970; *The Prince*, trans. G. Bull, 1961.

42 James Burnham, *The Machiavellians*, 1943; Anthony Jay, *Management and Machiavelli*, 1967.

43 Machiavelli, *Discourses*, Book 3, Chapter 9.

44 See for example Henry Mintzberg, *The Rise and Fall of Strategic Planning*, 1994.

45 Kenichi Ohmae, *The Mind of the Strategist*, 1982, p. 78.

46 Antoine-Henri Jomini, *Traité des grandes opérations militaires*, 1805, see also Michael Handel, *Masters of War*, 2000; R.R. Palmer, 'Frederick the Great, Guibert, Bülow: From Dynastic to National War', in Peter Paret (ed.), *Makers of Modern Strategy*, 1986.

47 Karl von Clausewitz, *Vom Kriege*, 1819, ed. trans. M. Howard and P. Paret, *On War*, 1984.

48 Clausewitz, *Vom Kriege*, p. 90.

49 Clausewitz, *Vom Kriege*, p. 119.

50 H. Igor Ansoff, *The New Corporate Strategy*, 1988.

51 Clausewitz, *Vom Kriege*, p. 178.

52 Gary Saul Morson, 'Tolstoi, Count Lev Nikolevich', in Edward Craig (ed.) *Routledge Encyclopedia of Philosophy*, 1998.

53 Leo Tolstoy, *War and Peace*, trans. Rosemary Edmonds, 1957.

54 Tolstoy, *War and Peace*, p. 717.

55 Tolstoy, *War and Peace*, p. 718.

56 Jacques Savary, *Le parfait négociant, ou instruction générale pour ce qui regarde le commerce de toute sorte de marchandises de France et des pays étrangers* (The Perfect Merchant, or General Instruction regarding the Mercantile Trade of France and Foreign Countries), 1675.

57 Malachy Postlethwayt, *The Universal Dictionary of Trade and Commerce*, 1751.

58 Postlethwayt, *The Merchant's Public Counting House, or New Mercantile Institution*, 1750.

59 Thomas Mortimer, *A General Dictionary of Commerce, Trade and Manufactures*, 1810; *The Elements of Commerce, Politics and Finances*, 1772; *Every Man His Own Broker*, 1761.

60 John Lee (ed.) *Pitman's Dictionary of Industrial Administration*, 1928; William D.P. Bliss (ed.), *The New Encyclopedia of Social Reform*, 1908.

61 Donald McDonald, *Agricultural Writers from Sir Walter of Henley to Arthur Young, 1200–1800*, 1908.

62 McDonald gives more details on these and many other writers, along with lists of their works.

63 Edward Lawrence, *The Duty and Office of a Land-Steward*, 3rd edn, 1731.

64 Lawrence, *The Duty and Office of a Land-Steward*, p. 16.

65 Richard Dafforne, *The Merchants Mirror, or Directions for the Perfect Ordering and Keeping of His Accounts*, 1636; John Collins, *An Introduction of Merchants Accounts, Containing Five Distinct Questions of Accounts*, 1653. See also A.C. Littleton, *Accounting Evolution to 1900*, 1981; Morgen Witzel, 'Collins, John', in Donald Rutherford (ed.), *Biographical Dictionary of British Economists*, 2004.

66 Baldesar Castiglione, *The Book of the Courtier*, trans. Charles S. Singleton, 1959.

67 Eustache de Refuge, *Treatise on the Court*, trans. J. Chris Cooper, 2008.

68 Samuel Smiles, *Self-Help: With Illustrations of Character and Conduct*, 1889.

69 Smiles, *Self-Help*, p. 1.

70 Smiles, *Self-Help*, p. 8.

71 Smiles, *Self-Help*, p. 23.

72 Smiles did not invent the Great Man theory of leadership, but he certainly did much to reinforce it.

73 Takemura Eiji, *The Perception of Work in Tokugawa Japan*, 1997.

74 Shunsaku Nishikawa, 'Fukuzawa, Yukichi', in Malcolm Warner (ed.), *The IEBM Handbook of Management Thinking*, 1998; Yukichi Fukuzawa, *An Encouragement of Learning*, 1876.

75 Albert Hourani, *Arabic Thought in the Liberal Age*, 1970.

76 Sri Nabaniharan Mukhopadhyay, 'Swami Vivekananda's Thoughts on Industrialization', *Vivek-Javan*, 2008.

77 Henry Sampson, *A History of Advertising from the Earliest Times*, 1874, p. 2; Marshall McLuhan, *Culture Is Our Business*, 1970.

78 Uglow, *The Lunar Men*, pp. 57–8.

79 Erich Roll, *An Early Experiment in Industrial Organization*, 1930.

80 Lyndall Urwick, *The Golden Book of Management*, 1956, p. 2.

81 Uglow, *The Lunar Men*; Morgen Witzel, 'Wedgwood, Josiah', in Witzel (ed.) *Biographical Dictionary of Management*, 2001.
82 Sidney Pollard, *The Genesis of Modern Management*, 1965, pp. 293–4.
83 Richard S. Fitton, *The Arkwrights: Spinners of Fortune*, 1989.
84 Ian Donnachie, *Robert Owen*, 2000.
85 Urwick and Brech, *The Making of Scientific Management*, vol. 2, describe the extent of technical training in the nineteenth century, making again the point that by mid-century other countries were starting to provide more and better training for their managers and engineers; pp. 113–14.
86 Pollard, *The Genesis of Modern Management*, pp. 313–14.
87 An extensive range of sources can be found in Pollard, *The Genesis of Modern Management*, for example.
88 Frank Podmore, *Robert Owen*, 1924. Podmore debunks Owen's claim that his methods of people management were responsible for his success, claiming that growth in the cotton industry was so high that anyone could make money using any system. Not so; Samuel Oldknow was only one of many mill owners who saw their ventures fail during this period.
89 Robert Owen, *A Statement Regarding the New Lanark Establishment*, 1812; *Observations on the Effect of the Manufacturing System*, 1815.
90 Donnachie, *Robert Owen*.
91 Quoted in Gert von Klass, *Krupps: The Story of an Industrial Empire*, 1954, p. 91.
92 Klass, *Krupps*, p. 91.
93 See R.M. Lala, *For the Love of India*, 2004; Frank R. Harris, *J.N. Tata: A Chronicle of His Life*, 1925; see also Witzel, *Tata: The Evolution of a Corporate Brand*, ch. 2.
94 Thomas Carlyle, *Sartor Resartus*, 1838; Vladimir Jabotinsky, *Prelude to Delilah*, 1945.
95 Quoted in Lala, *For the Love of India*, p. 37.
96 Sir Ebenezer Howard, *Garden Cities of To-morrow*, 1902
97 Karl Marx and Friedrich Engels, *The Communist Manifesto*, 1998.
98 John Kay, *Obliquity: Why Our Goals Are Best Achieved Indirectly*, 2010, pp. 134–5.
99 Isaiah Berlin, *The Fox and the Hedgehog: An Essay on Tolstoy's View of History*, 1953.
100 Arie de Geus, 'Planning as Learning', *Harvard Business Review*, 1988; Peter M. Senge, *The Fifth Discipline: The Art and Practice of the Learning Organization*, 1990.
101 Morgan, *Images of Organization*, 1986.
102 Witzel, *Management History*, pp. 215–20.
103 Lala, *For the Love of India*.
104 For an account of his remarkable life and career, see Shibusawa Eiichi, *The Autobiography of Shibusawa Eiichi: From Peasant to Entrepreneur*, trans. Teruko Craig, 1994.
105 W.G. Beasley, *The Meiji Restoration*, 1972; Beasley, *The Rise of Modern Japan*, 1995.
106 Thomas G. Rawski, *Economic Growth in Prewar China*, 1989.
107 Chi-kong Lai, 'The Qing State and Merchant Enterprise', in Jane Kate Leonard and John R. Watt (eds), *To Achieve Security and Wealth: The Qing Imperial State and the Economy 1644–911*, 1992.
108 A good source for these and other writings is Pui Tak Lee, 'Understanding and Practice of "New Business" in Nineteenth-Century China', in R. Ampalavanar Brown (ed.), *Chinese Business Enterprise: Critical Perspectives on Business and Management*, 1996.
109 Witzel, *Management History*, pp. 400–3.
110 Henry Demarest Lloyd, *Wealth Against Commonwealth*, 1894.
111 Jean Strouse, *Morgan: American Financier*, 1999.
112 Richard T. Ely, *Monopolies and Trusts*, 1900, Jeremiah Jenks, *The Trust Problem*, 1900, and William Z. Ripley (ed.) *Trusts, Pools and Corporations*, 1905, is a good survey, though from a hostile point of view.
113 Charles R. Flint *et al.*, *The Trust: Its Book*, 1902.
114 Herbert N. Casson, *The Romance of Steel: The Story of a Thousand Millionaires*, 1907.
115 Edward Meade, *Corporation Finance*, 1910; William Lough, *Corporation Finance*, 1909; see also Morgen Witzel, 'Early Contributors to Financial Management: Jeremiah Jenks, Edward Meade and William Ripley', in Geoffrey Poitras (ed.) *Pioneers of Financial Economics*, vol. 2, 2007.
116 See for example *Harvard Business Review on Strategic Alliances*, 2003; Richard Gibbs and Andrew Humphries, *Strategic Alliances and Marketing Partnerships*, 2009; Yves L. Doz and Gary Hamel, *Alliance Advantage: The Art of Creating Value Through Partnering*, 1998; John Child, *Cooperative Strategy: Managing Alliances, Networks and Joint Ventures*, 2005.

117 Russell D. Edmunds, *Tecumseh and the Quest for Indian Leadership*, 1984; Miles T. Bryant, 'Contrasting American and Native American View of Leadership', 1996; Tracy Becker, *Traditional American Indian Leadership: A Comparison with US Governance*, 1997.

118 Stephen A. Ambrose, *Crazy Horse and Custer: The Parallel Lives of Two American Warriors*, 1975. For broad background, Dee Brown's *Bury My Heart at Wounded Knee*, 1970, is an excellent introduction.

119 Black Elk and John G. Neihardt, *Black Elk Speaks*, 1979.

120 Darrell C. Steele, 'Leadership Lessons of Great American Indians: An Untapped Legacy for Today's Airmen', 2006.

121 E.P. Thompson, *The Making of the English Working Class*, 1963. Useful for our context is Kevin Binfield, *Writings of the Luddites*, 2004, which summarizes what is known about Luddite thinking, particularly with reference to employer–worker relations.

122 Paul Mason, *Live Working or Die Fighting*, 2008.

123 David V. Erdman, *Blake, Prophet Against Empire*, 1991, offers a broad interpretation and suggests Blake was rebelling against the British political and imperial system more generally.

124 Samuel Taylor Coleridge, *A Lay Sermon*, 1817, in John Morrow (ed.), *Coleridge's Writings*, p. 117.

125 Robert Southey, *On the State of the Poor*, 1812, p. 111; see also his *On the Economical Reformers*, 1811.

126 Richard N. Langlois, 'The Coevolution of Technology and Organisation in the Transition to the Factory System', in P.L. Robertson (ed.), *Authority and Control in Modern Industry*, 1999.

127 Émile Zola, *Germinal*, 1885, trans. Peter Collier, 2008; Upton Sinclair, *The Jungle*, 1906.

128 Zola, *Au bonheur des dames*, 1883, trans. Brian Nelson, 1995.

129 The collected articles were published as *The History of the Standard Oil Company*, 1904.

130 Tarbell, *The History of the Standard Oil Company*, vol. 2, p. 291.

131 Tarbell, *New Ideals in Business: An Account of Their Practice and Their Effect on Men and Profits*, 1916; Tarbell, 'The New Place of Women in Industry', *Industrial Management*, 1921.

132 Tarbell, 'Commercial Machiavellianism', 1906.

133 Tarbell, *Owen D. Young: A New Type of Industrial Leader*, 1932.

134 See Charles Harvey and Jon Press, *William Morris*, 1991; Paul Thompson, *The Work of William Morris*, 1967; Eileen Boris, *Art and Labor*, 1986.

5 Scientific management

1 Henri Robinson Towne, 'The Engineer as an Economist', *Transactions of the American Society of Mechanical Engineers*, 1886, p. 428; quoted also in Urwick, *The Golden Book of Management*, 1956, p. 26.

2 Robert F. Hoxie, *Scientific Management and Labor*, 1915.

3 There is a considerable literature on the scientific management movement, beginning with contemporary works such as C. Bertrand Thompson, *Scientific Management*, 1914, Horace B. Drury, *Scientific Management: A History and Criticism*, 1915, and Hoxie, *Scientific Management and Labor*, 1915. H.G.T. Cannons, *Bibliography of Industrial Efficiency and Factory Management*, 1920, lists a large number of related publications. Among later works, Urwick and Brech's three-volume work *The Making of Scientific Management*, 1947, is a detailed account of the multinational development of scientific management. See also works on specific figures in the movement, below.

4 Bernadette Longo, *Spurious Coin: A History of Science, Management and Technical Writing*, 2000, p. 99.

5 Frederick Winslow Taylor, *Shop Management*, 1903.

6 Hebert N. Casson, *The Story of My Life*, 1931, pp. 222–3.

7 Taylor, *Shop Management*, pp. 17–18.

8 Richard Schneirov *et al.* (eds), *The Pullman Strike and the Crisis of the 1890s: Essays on Labour and Politics*, 1999.

9 Barbara W. Tuchman, *The Proud Tower: A Portrait of the World Before the Great War 1880–1914*, 1980. For a more general perspective on this period, see Charles W. Calhoun (ed.), *The Gilded Age: Perspectives on the Origins of Modern America*, 2006; Alan Trachtenberg, *The Incorporation of America: Culture and Society in the Gilded Age*, 2007.

10 Urwick, *The Golden Book of Management*, pp. 27–8.

11 Drury, *Scientific Management*, p. 39.
12 Frederick A. Halsey, 'The Premium Plan of Paying for Labour', in John R. Commons (ed.), *Trade Unionism and Labour Problems*, 1905; see also Halsey, *Methods of Machine Shop Work*, 1914.
13 Longo, *Spurious Coin*, pp. 98–9.
14 A study by Aditya Simha and David J. Lemak, 'The Value of Original Source Readings in Management Education: the Case of Frederick Winslow Taylor', *Journal of Management History*, 2010, found that most business school students study Taylor only through modern paraphrases, and rarely read his original writings. Stephanie C. Payne and her colleagues, on the other hand, felt that most textbooks were accurate but also urged more attention to Taylor's original writings rather than to modern interpretations; 'Portrayals of F.W. Taylor across Textbooks', *Journal of Management History*, 2006.
15 Robert Kanigel, *The One Best Way: Frederick Taylor and the Enigma of Efficiency*, 1997, is a good if critical biography. See also Charles D. Wrege and Ronald G. Greenwood, *Frederick W. Taylor, The Father of Scientific Management: Myth and Reality*, 1991.
16 Frederick W. Taylor, *A Piece-Rate System*, 1895.
17 Taylor, *A Piece-Rate System*, p. 35.
18 Taylor, *The Principles of Scientific Management*, 1911, pp. 21–2.
19 Taylor, *The Principles of Scientific Management*, p. 20.
20 Taylor, *Shop Management*, p. 18.
21 Taylor, *The Principles of Scientific Management*, p. 72.
22 Henry Metcalfe, *The Cost of Manufactures and the Administration of Workshops*, 1885.
23 Frank B. Gilbreth, *Motion Study: A Method for Increasing the Efficiency of the Workman*, 1911.
24 See for example Frank B. Gilbreth and Lillian E. Gilbreth, *Fatigue Study*, 1916.
25 Frank B. Gilbreth, *Primer of Scientific Management*, 1912.
26 As well as Gantt's own works, a good detailed treatment of Gantt's ideas can be found in Alex W. Rathe, *Gantt on Management*, 1961.
27 Urwick, *The Golden Book of Management*, p. 90.
28 Hoxie, *Scientific Management and Labour*; Drury, *Scientific Management*.
29 Henry L. Gantt, *Work, Wages and Profits*, 1913, p. 40.
30 Gantt, *Work Wages and Profits*, p. 8.
31 Gantt, *Organizing for Work*, 1919, p. 15.
32 Carl Barth, 'The Barth Standard Wage Scale', *Manufacturing Industries*, 1926. See also Urwick, *The Golden Book of Management*, pp. 80–5; Florence M. Manning, 'Carl G. Barth, 1860–1939: A Sketch', *Norwegian–American Studies*, 1989.
33 Morris L. Cooke, *Our Cities Awake: Notes on Municipal Activities and Administration*, 1918.
34 Horace K. Hathaway, 'Prerequisites for the Introduction of Scientific Management', 1911.
35 Hugo Diemer, *Factory Organization and Administration*, 1914.
36 Alexander Hamilton Church, *The Science and Practice of Management*, 1914.
37 David Savino, 'Louis D. Brandeis and His Role Promoting Scientific Management as a Progressive Movement', *Journal of Management History*, 2009. On Brandeis, see Thomas McCraw, *Prophets of Regulation: Charles Francis Adams, Louis D. Brandeis, James M. Landis, Alfred E. Kahn*, 1984. On his opposition to banks and big business, see Louis D. Brandeis, *Other People's Money and How the Bankers Use It*, 1914; Brandeis, *The Curse of Bigness*, 1934.
38 James O. McKinsey, *Budgetary Control*, 1922.
39 Hugo Münsterberg, *Psychology and Industrial Efficiency*, 1913; Lillian Gilbreth, *The Psychology of Management*, 1914. See also Thomas J. Van De Water, 'Psychology's Entrepreneurs and the Marketing of Industrial Psychology', *Journal of Applied Psychology*, 1987.
40 Gilbreth, *The Psychology of Management*, p. 3.
41 Gilbreth, *The Psychology of Management*, p. 4.
42 Gilbreth, *The Psychology of Management*, pp. 28–9.
43 See for example Lillian Gilbreth, *The Quest of the One Best Way: A Sketch of the Life of Frank Bunker Gilbreth*, 1924.
44 Simone T.A. Phipps, 'Mary, Mary, Quite Contrary', *Journal of Management History*, 2011.
45 Margaret McKillop and Alan D. McKillop, *Efficiency Methods: An Introduction to Scientific Management*, 1920.
46 Henri Le Châtelier, *Le Taylorisme*, 1928.

47 For more on Taylorism in France generally, see George G. Humphreys, *Taylorism in France 1904–1920: The Impact of Scientific Management on Factory Relations and Society*, 1986.

48 Charles de la Poix de Fréminville, *Quelques aperçus sur le système Taylor*, 1918; see also André Danzin, *Charles de Fréminville 1856–1936: pionnier de l'organisation scientifique du travail*, 2002.

49 Emil Walter-Busch, 'Albert Thomas and Scientific Management in War and Peace, 1914–32', *Journal of Management History*, 2006. See also Paul Devinat, *Scientific Management in Europe*, 1927.

50 Georges Duhamel, *Scènes de la vie future*, 1930; André Siegfried, *Les Etats-Unis d'aujourd'hui*, 1927. Siegfried in particular believed that America's economic progress was being accompanied by a parallel decline in its civilization, and that a large part of the cause for this lay in the repetitive working methods of scientific management.

51 Daniel Nelson, 'Scientific Management in Retrospect', in Daniel Nelson (ed.), *A Mental Revolution: Scientific Management Since Labour*, 1995.

52 Friedrich-Ludwig Meyenberg, *Industrial Administration and Management*, 1951. Biographical sketches of all four can be found in Urwick, *The Golden Book of Management*.

53 Robert Conti, 'Frederick Winslow Taylor', in Morgen Witzel and Malcolm Warner (eds), *Oxford Handbook of Management Thinkers*, forthcoming.

54 Daniel Wren, 'Scientific Management in the USSR, with Particular Reference to the Contributions of Walter N. Polakov', 1980. My thanks to Robert Conti for drawing my attention to this article. On the Stakhanovtsy system, see Arthur G. Bedeian and Carl R. Philips, 'Scientific Management and Stakhanovism in the Soviet Union: A Historical Perspective', *International Journal of Social Economics*, 1990; Morgen Witzel, 'Where Scientific Management Went Awry', 2005.

55 Francesco Mauro, *Esperienze di Organizzazione Giapponese* (The Experience of Japanese Management), 1930; see also biographical note in Urwick, *The Golden Book of Management*, pp. 248–51.

56 William M. Tsutsui, 'The Way of Efficiency: Ueno Yoichi and Scientific Management in Twentieth-Century Japan', *Modern Asian Studies*, 2001.

57 Ronald G. Greenwood and Robert H. Ross, 'Early American Influence on Japanese Management Philosophy: The Scientific Management Movement in Japan', in Sang M. Lee and Gary Schwendiman, *Management by Japanese Systems*, 1982; Malcolm Warner, 'Japanese Culture, Western Management: Taylorism and Human Resources in Japan', *Organization Studies*, 1994; Tsutsui, 'The Way of Efficiency'.

58 Andrew Gordon, 'Araki Toichiro and the Shaping of Labour Management', in Tsunehiko Yui and Keiichiro Nakagawa, *Japanese Management in Historical Perspective*, 1989; Sawai Minoru, 'Araki Toichiro', in Morgen Witzel (ed.) *Biographical Dictionary of Management*, 2001.

59 William M. Tsutsui, *Manufacturing Ideology: Scientific Management in Twentieth-Century Japan*, 1998.

60 Conti, 'Frederick Winslow Taylor'.

61 Stephen L. Morgan, 'Transfer of Taylorist Ideas to China, 1910–30', *Journal of Management History*, 2006. The following material on scientific management in China is drawn largely from this article.

62 Wen-hsin Yeh, *Shanghai Splendor: Economic Sentiments and the Making of Modern China 1843–1949*, 2008, p. 32.

63 Morgan, 'Transfer of Taylorist Ideas to China', p. 419.

64 Biographical sketches of all three, and lists of their writings, can be found in Urwick, *The Golden Book of Management*.

65 Judith Merkle, *Management and Ideology: The Legacy of the International Scientific Management Movement*, 1980.

66 Lewis Mumford, *Technics and Civilization*, 1934.

67 Mauro Guillén, *The Taylorized Beauty of the Mechanical: Scientific Management and the Rise of Modern Architecture*, 2006.

68 Sigmund Wagner-Tsukamoto, 'Scientific Management Revisited: Did Taylorism Fail Because of a Too Positive Image of Human Nature?', *Journal of Management History*, 2008.

69 See for example T. J. Watson, 'Scientific Management and Industrial Psychology', *English Review*, 1931.

70 Witzel, 'Where Scientific Management Went Awry'.

71 The debate as to when mass production first developed is a source of continuing discussion among management historians. As we saw earlier, the Arsenale in Venice was using some of its techniques including standardized components as early as the Middle Ages. Most makers of army muskets and rifles were using standardized components by the eighteenth century, and it is possible that techniques used at the Springfield Arsenal in America informed the development of mass production by private weapons makers such as Colt. In other words, mass production should be seen as the result of an evolution, not a revolution.

72 Stephen Meyer, *The Five-Dollar Day: Labor Management and Social Control in the Ford Motor Company 1908–1921*, 1981; Steven Watts, *The People's Tycoon: Henry Ford and the American Century*, 2005; Allan N. Nevins and Frank E. Hill, *Ford: the Times, the Man, the Company*, 1954; Nevins and Hill, *Ford: Expansion and Challenge, 1915–1933*, 1957.

73 Michael J. Mol and Julian Birkinshaw, *Giant Steps in Management: Creating Innovations That Change the Way We Work*, 2008, p. 16.

74 Urwick and Brech, *The Making of Scientific Management*, vol. 2, p. 104.

75 Hoxie, *Scientific Management and Labor*, p. 112.

76 Hoxie, *Scientific Management and Labor*, p. 120.

77 Hoxie, *Scientific Management and Labor*, pp. 113–14.

78 Charles Bedaux, *The Bedaux Efficiency Course for Industrial Application*, 1918; see also Ian Kessler, 'Bedaux, Charles', in Malcolm Warner, *Handbook of Management Thinking*, 1998.

79 Steven Kreis, 'The Diffusion of Scientific Management: The Bedaux Company in America and Britain', in Daniel Nelson (ed.) *A Mental Revolution: Scientific Management since Taylor*, 1995.

80 Hoxie, *Scientific Management and Labor*, pp. 12–13.

81 Emerson, *The Twelve Principles of Efficiency*, p. 23.

82 Emerson, *The Twelve Principles of Efficiency*, pp. 18–19.

83 Emerson, *The Twelve Principles of Efficiency*, p. 11.

84 Raymond E. Miles and Charles C. Snow, *Organizational Strategy, Structure and Process*, 1978.

85 Charles E. Knoeppel, *Organization and Administration*, 1918.

86 Adrian Furnham, *Management and Myths: Challenging Business Fads, Fallacies and Fashions*, 2004.

87 Ikujiro Nonaka and Hirotaka Takeuchi, *The Knowledge-Creating Company: How Japanese Companies Create the Dynamics of Innovation*, 1995.

88 Arie de Geus, *The Living Company: Habits for Survival in a Turbulent Environment*, 1997.

89 Henry J. Spooner, *Wealth from Waste: Elimination of Waste, A World Problem*, 1918.

90 Paul A. Laudicina, *World Out of Balance: Navigating Global Risks to Seize Competitive Advantage*, 2005.

6 European management thought

1 Witzel, *Management History*.

2 Morgen Witzel, 'The Unsung Master of Management', *European Business Forum*, 2006; Urwick, *The Golden Book of Management*, pp. 107–10.

3 Ernest Solvay, *Etudes sociales: notes sur le productivisme et le compatibilisme*, 1900.

4 Urwick, *The Golden Book of Management*, pp. 16–17.

5 Tomás Bat'a, *Knowledge in Action: The Bata System of Management*, 1992, p. 181.

6 E.F.L. Brech, *The Evolution of Modern Management*, 2002; John F. Wilson and Andrew Thomson, *The Making of Modern Management: British Management in a Historical Perspective*, 2006. See also Wilson, *British Business History 1720–1994*, 1995. John Child's *British Management Thought*, 1969, is also very valuable.

7 Brech, *The Evolution of Modern Management*; E.F.L. Brech, pers. comm.

8 Brech, *The Evolution of Modern Management*, vol. 1, p. 4.

9 Sidney Pollard and Paul Robertson, *The British Shipbuilding Industry 1870–1914*, 1979.

10 Patricia Wright, *Conflict on the Nile: The Fashoda Incident of 1898*, 1972, also describes the more general tensions between Britain and France. The *entente cordiale* of 1904 reduced tensions with France, but if anything increased them with Germany.

11 Paul Kennedy, *The Rise of Anglo-German Antagonism 1860–1914*, 1980; David Stevenson, *The First World War and International Politics*, 2005; Tuchman, *The Proud Tower*.

12 Erskine Childers, *The Riddle of the Sands*, 1903. As a result of the publication of this book, the British government began to prepare seriously for war with Germany.

13 F.G. Burton, *The Naval Engineer and Command of the Sea: A Story of Naval Administration*, 1896.

14 F.G. Burton, *The Commercial Management of Engineering Works*, 1899, pp. 1–2.

15 Urwick and Brech, *The Making of Scientific Management*, vol. 2, pp. 148ff.

16 Joseph Slater Lewis, *The Commercial Organization of Factories*, 1896.

17 Lewis, 'Works Management for Maximum Production', *Engineering Magazine*, 1900, p. 212.

18 J.W. Stannard, *Factory Organisation and Management*, 1911.

19 Alfred J. Liversedge, *Commercial Engineering*, 1912, p. 4.

20 Lawrence R. Dicksee, *Business Organization*, 1910.

21 Emerson, *Efficiency as a Basis for Operations and Wages*, 1909. It is not clear in which direction the influence ran, or indeed this might well have been two people reaching a similar common-sense conclusion at about the same time but independently of each other.

22 Christopher Furness, *The American Invasion*, 1902; Jean-Jacques Servan-Schreiber, *Le défi américain*, trans. Ronald Steel, 1979.

23 Furness, *Industrial Peace and Industrial Efficiency*, 1908, p. 12.

24 Charles Wilson, *The History of Unilever: A Study in Economic Growth and Social Change*, 1954.

25 Deborah Cadbury, *Chocolate Wars: From Cadbury to Kraft, 200 Years of Sweet Success and Bitter Rivalry*, 2010.

26 Edward Cadbury, *Experiments in Industrial Organization*, 1912.

27 Cadbury, *Experiments in Industrial Organization*; see also his *Women's Work and Wages*, 1906.

28 Urwick and Brech, *The Making of Scientific Management*, vol. 2, pp. 183–4; Herbert N. Casson, *Creative Thinkers: The Efficient Few Who Cause Progress and Prosperity*, 1298, p. 165.

29 Edward Cadbury, 'Some Principles of Industrial Organisation; The Case for and against Scientific Management', *Sociological Review*, 1914.

30 J.A. Hobson, 'Scientific Management', *Sociological Review*, 1913.

31 Michael Rowlinson, 'The Early Application of Scientific Management by Cadbury', *Business History*, 1988.

32 Quoted in Basil H. Tripp, *Renold Chains: A History of the Company and the Rise of the Precision Chain Industry 1879–1955*, 1956.

33 Kevin Whitson, 'The Reception of Scientific Management by British Engineers 1890–1914', *Business History Review*, 1997.

34 'It is not recorded that Elbourne ever met Taylor, nor does his thought show any trace of having been influenced by Taylor doctrines', Urwick and Brech, *The Making of Modern Management*, vol. 1, pp. 148–9. I am not sure I would go quite that far, but certainly my reading of Elbourne, in both this and later works, is that he is trying to create a system of management that will be acceptable to his audience rather than pushing a particular dogma.

35 Sidney Webb and Beatrice Webb, *Problems of Modern Industry*, 1898.

36 Sidney Webb, *The Works Manager To-Day*, 1917, pp. 3–4.

37 Lawrence Appley, *Formula for Success: A Core Concept of Management*, 1974.

38 Webb, *The Works Manager To-Day*, p. 131.

39 Nelson, 'Scientific Management in Retrospect', p. 19. Webb himself, like most British contemporaries, was rather more critical of the state of British industry.

40 Webb, *The Works Manager To-Day*, p. 133.

41 Webb, *The Works Manager To-Day*, pp. 136–7.

42 Webb, *The Works Manager To-Day*, pp. 139–40.

43 Urwick and Brech, *The Making of Scientific Management*, vol. 2, pp. 187–8.

44 Lawrence R. Dicksee, *The True Basis of Efficiency*, 1922.

45 Edward T. Elbourne, *The Marketing Problem: How It Is Being Tackled in the USA*, 1926; *Fundamentals of Industrial Administration: An Introduction to Industrial Organization, Management and Economics*, 1934.

46 Elbourne, *Fundamentals of Industrial Administration*, p. 525.

47 Philip Sargant Florence, *The Logic of Industrial Organization*, 1933.

48 Alfred Marshall, *Industry and Trade*, 1919, p. 355.

49 Marshall, *Industry and Trade*, p. 364.

50 Oliver Sheldon, *The Philosophy of Management*, 1923, p. 27.

51 Sheldon, *The Philosophy of Management*, p. 33.

52 Sheldon, *The Philosophy of Management*, p. 33.

53 Sheldon, *The Philosophy of Management*, p. 259.

54 John Lee (ed.), *Pitman's Dictionary of Industrial Administration*, 1928; *Harmsworth's Business Encyclopedia*, 1925.
55 Child, *British Management Thought*, p. 87.
56 John Lee, *Management: A Study of Industrial Organisation*, 1921; Lee, *Industrial Organisation: Developments and Prospects*, 1923.
57 John Lee, 'The Pros and Cons of Functionalization', in Luther H. Gulick and Lyndall Urwick (eds), *Papers on the Science of Administration*, 1937.
58 John Spedan Lewis, *Partnership for All*, 1948.
59 John Spedan Lewis, *Fairer Shares*, 1954.
60 H. Gordon Selfridge, *The Romance of Commerce*, 1918.
61 Herbert N. Casson, *How to Get Things Done*, 1935, p. 13.
62 Herbert N. Casson, *Lectures on Efficiency*, 1917, p. 3; see also Casson, *Creative Thinkers*, 1928.
63 Benjamin Seebohm Rowntree, *The Human Factor in Business: Experiments in Industrial Democracy*, 1921, p. 156.
64 Schedule of papers from the Oxford Management Conferences, Borthwick Institute, University of York.
65 Edward Brech, Andrew Thomson and John F. Wilson, *Lyndall Urwick, Management Pioneer: A Biography*, 2010.
66 Brech *et al.*, *Lyndall Urwick*, p. 18.
67 A point made by Brech *et al.*, *Lyndall Urwick*, p. 75.
68 Lyndall Urwick, *Management of Tomorrow*, 1933. The quote is from Brech *et al.*, *Lyndall Urwick*, p. 86.
69 Urwick, *Management of Tomorrow*, p.21.
70 Urwick, *Management of Tomorrow*, p. 201.
71 Urwick, *Management of Tomorrow*, p. 80.
72 Robert Fitzgerald, *Rowntree and the Marketing Revolution 1862–1969*, 1995.
73 Urwick, *Management of Tomorrow*, p. xv.
74 Urwick, *Management of Tomorrow*, p. 201.
75 Luther H. Gulick and Lyndall Urwick (eds), *Papers on the Science of Administration*, 1937.
76 Henri Fayol, *Administration industrielle et générale*, 1916, trans. J.A. Coubrough, 1930.
77 Brech *et al.*, *Lyndall Urwick*, p. 81.
78 John C. Wood and Michael C. Wood (eds), *Henri Fayol*, 2002; see also Jean-Louis Peaucelle and Cameron Guthrie's forthcoming account of Fayol in Morgen Witzel and Malcolm Warner (eds), *Oxford Handbook of Management Thinkers*, 2012.
79 Peaucelle and Guthrie, 'Henri Fayol'.
80 Henry Mintzberg, *Mintzberg on Management*, 1989, p. 9; for a commentary, see David Lamond, 'A Matter of Style: Reconciling Henri and Henry', *Management Decision*, 2004.
81 Henri de Saint-Simon, *Selected Writings on Science, Industry and Social Organisation*, trans. Keith Taylor, 1975; Frank Manuel, *The New World of Henri de Saint-Simon*, 1956.
82 Auguste Comte, *The Positive Philosophy of Auguste Comte*, trans. Harriet Martineau, 1853.
83 Émile Durkheim, *De la division du travail social*, trans. George Simpson, *The Division of Labor in Society*, 1933; Frank Parkin, *Émile Durkheim*, 1992.
84 Peaucelle and Guthrie, 'Henri Fayol'.
85 Kennedy, 'Fayol' s Principles and the Rule of St Benedict'.
86 Mildred Golden Pryor and Sonia Taneja, 'Henri Fayol, Practitioner and Theoretician – Revered and Reviled', *Journal of Management History*, 2010.
87 Urwick, *Golden Book of Management*, pp. 209–12.
88 Sasaki Tsuneo, 'Campion, Gabriel', in Morgen Witzel (ed.), *Biographical Dictionary of Management*, 2001, p. 128.
89 Gabriel Campion, *Economie privée: organisation, financement et exploitation des entreprises* (Private Economy: Organization, Finance and Administration of Enterprises), 1941.
90 See Erik Grimmer-Solem, *The Rise of Historical Economics and Social Reform in Germany*, 2003; Yuichi Shinoya (ed.), *The German Historical School: The Historical and Ethical Approach to Economics*, 2001. A useful perspective too can be found in Geoffrey M. Hodgson, *How Economics Forgot History: The Problem of Historical Specificity in Social Science*, 2001.
91 F.G. Burton, *The Commercial Management of Engineering Works*, 2nd edn, 1905.
92 Moritz Weyermann and Hans Schönitz, *Grundlegung und Systematik einer wissenschaftlichen Privatwirtschaftslehre und ihre pflege an Universitaten und Hochschulen* (Theoretical Foundation

and System of Private Economics and Their Establishment in Universities and High Schools), 1912.

93 Heinrich Nicklisch, *Der Weg aufwarts! Organisation* (The Way Forward! Organization), 1920; Nicklisch, *Wirtschaftliche Betriebslehre* (Economic Theory of Business Administration), 1922. See also Udo Neugebauer, 'Business Ethics in Older German Administration: Heinrich Nicklisch, Wihelm Kalveram, August Marx', in Peter Koslowski (ed.), *Methodology of the Social Sciences, Ethics and Economics in the Newer Historical School*, 1997, and Sasaki Tsuneo, 'Nicklisch, Heinrich', in Witzel (ed.), *Biographical Dictionary of Management*, 2001.

94 Fritz Schonpflug, *Das Methodenproblem in der Einzelwirtschaftslehre* (Methodological Problems of Individual Economics), 1933. See also Sasaki Tsuneo, 'Schonpflug, Fritz', in Witzel (ed.), *Biographical Dictionary of Management*, 2001.

95 Bøje Larsen, 'German Organization and Leadership Theory: Stable Trends and Flexible Adaptation', *Scandinavian Journal of Management*, 2003.

96 Eugen Schmalenbach, *Über die Dienstellengliederung in Grossbetrieb* (On the Division of Departments in Big Business), 1941.

97 Weber, *The Protestant Ethic and the Spirit of Capitalism*; see also Weber, *Economy and Society*.

98 Weber, *The Religion of China*.

99 George Ritzer, *The McDonaldization of Society*, 1996; Jeffery D. Houghton, 'Does Max Weber's Notion of Authority Still Hold in the Twenty-First Century?', *Journal of Management History*, 2010.

100 Michel Foucault, *Discipline and Punish: Birth of the Prison*, 1977; George Orwell, *Nineteen Eighty-Four*, 1949.

101 Robert Michels, *Zur Soziologie des Parteiwesens in der modernen Demokratie*, 1911.

102 See in particular Joseph Schumpeter, *Business Cycles*, 1939.

103 Guido Buenstorf and Johann Peter Murmann, 'Ernst Abbé's Scientific Management: Theoretical Insights from a Nineteenth-Century Dynamic Capabilities Approach', 2005.

104 Nelson, 'Scientific Management in Retrospect'.

105 Walther Rathenau, *Von Kommenden Dingen*, 1917, trans. *In Days to Come*, 1921; Rathenau, *Die Neue Wirtschaft*, 1918; Rathenau, *Der Neue Staat*, 1919, trans. *The New Society*, 1921.

106 Rathenau, *In Days to Come*, p. 63.

107 Krupp was referred to in Chapter 4. On Bosch's methods of management, see Theodor Heuss, *Robert Bosch*, 1987.

108 Edmund Heinen, *Betriebswirtschaftliche Kostenlehre* (Cost Theory of Business Administration), 1959; Erich Gutenberg, *Einführung in die Betriebswirtschaftslehre* (Introduction to the Science of Business Administration), 1958; Erich Kosiol, *Anlagenrechnung: Theorie und Praxis der Abschreibungen* (Capital Accounting: Theory and Practice of Depreciation), 1955; Kosiol, *Organisation der Unternehmung* (Organization of the Enterprise), 1962.

109 Campion, *Economie privée*; Campion, *Traité des entreprises privées* (Introduction to Private Enterprises), 1945–8; Michel Crozier, *The Bureaucratic Phenomenon*, 1963; Crozier, *The World of the Office Worker*, 1965; Foucault, *Discipline and Punish*.

110 Hugh Clegg, *A New Approach to Industrial Democracy*, 1960; Allan Flanders, *Trade Unions*, 1952; Joan Woodward, *Industrial Organization: Theory and Practice*, 1965; Patrick Blackett, *Studies of War*, 1962; Peter Checkland, *Systems Thinking, Systems Practice*, 1981; Geoffrey Vickers, *The Art of Judgment*, 1965; Ronald Coase, 'The Nature of the Firm', *Economica*, 1937.

111 Phil Hodgson, 'In Search of European Leadership', *European Business Forum*, 2007.

112 See for example Kai-Alexander Schlevogt, *The Art of Chinese Management: Theory, Evidence and Applications*, 2002.

7 Management thought and human relations

1 Tripp, *Renold Chains*; Thomas J. Watson, 'To Make a Business Grow: Begin Growing Men!', *System*, 1926, p. 152.

2 Quoted in Lala, *For the Love of India*, p. 37.

3 Sawai, 'Araki Toichiro', p. 21.

4 Webb, *The Works Manager To-Day*; Siegfried, *Les Etats-Unis d'aujourd'hui*.

5 James B. Clark, 'More about Organization', *Industrial Management*, 1921, p. 229.

6 John H. Patterson, 'Altruism and Sympathy as Factors in Works Administration', *Engineering Magazine*, 1902.

7 Wren, *The Evolution of Management Thought*, pp. 225–8.

8 Sophonisba Preston Breckinridge and Edith Abbott, *The Delinquent Child and the Home,* 1912; Edith Abbott, *Women in Industry: A Study in American Economic History*, 1910; Abbott and Breckinridge, 'Employment of Women in Industries: Twelfth Census Statistics', *Journal of Political Economy*, 1906.

9 George, *The History of Management Thought*, p. 122.

10 Ernest Fox Nichols, 'The Employment Manager', *Annals of the American Academy of Political and Social Science*, 1916.

11 William C. Redfield, 'The Employment Problem in Industry', *Annals of the American Academy of Political and Social Science*, 1916, p. 11.

12 Meyer Bloomfield, 'The Aim and Work of Employment Managers' Associations', *Annals of the American Academy of Political and Social Science*, 1916, p. 76; see also Edmund C. Lynch, *Meyer Bloomfield and Employment Management*, 1970.

13 Meyer Bloomfield, *Management and Men: A Record of New Steps in Industrial Relations*, 1919.

14 Ordway Tead, *Instincts in Industry: A Study of Working-Class Psychology*, 1918.

15 James Sully, *Outlines of Psychology*, 1894; William James, *The Principles of Psychology*, 1890.

16 James, *The Principles of Psychology*; see also Ralph B. Perry, *In the Spirit of William James*, 1938.

17 Ordway Tead and Henry C. Metcalf, *Personnel Administration: Its Principles and Practice*, 1920, p. 2.

18 Tead and Metcalf, *Personnel Administration*, p. 1.

19 Tead and Metcalf, *Personnel Administration*, p. 19.

20 Ordway Tead, *The Art of Leadership*, 1935.

21 Charles A. Ellwood, 'The Instincts in Social Psychology', *Psychological Bulletin*, 1919.

22 Edward L. Bernays, *Propaganda*, 1928, p. 9.

23 Urwick, *The Golden Book of Management*, p. 132; Pauline Graham, *Mary Parker Follett: Prophet of Management*, 1995; Joan C. Tonn, *Mary P. Follett: Creating Democracy, Transforming Management*, 2003; John Child, 'Mary Parker Follett', in Morgen Witzel and Malcolm Warner (eds), *Oxford Handbook of Management Thinkers*, 2012.

24 Mary Parker Follett, *The New State: Group Organization, the Solution of Popular Government*, 1918.

25 The two most important collections are Henry C. Metcalf and Lyndall Urwick (eds), *Dynamic Administration: The Collected Papers of Mary Parker Follett*, 1941, and Lyndall Urwick (ed.), *Freedom and Co-ordination: Lectures in Business Organization by Mary Parker Follett*, 1949.

26 Mary Parker Follett, *Creative Experience*, 1924, pp. 167–8.

27 Follett, *Creative Experience*, p. 5.

28 Follett, *Creative Experience*, p. 3.

29 Follett, *Creative Experience*, p. 168.

30 Follett, *Creative Experience*, p. 67.

31 Mary Parker Follett, 'The Process of Control', in Luther H. Gulick and Lyndall Urwick (eds), *Papers on the Science of Administration*, 1937, p. 164.

32 Follett, 'The Process of Control', p. 161.

33 Follett, 'The Process of Control', p. 169.

34 Elton Mayo, *Democracy and Freedom: Essays in Social Logic*, 1919.

35 Fritz Roethlisberger and William J. Dickson, *Management and the Worker*, 1939.

36 Elton Mayo, 'The Human Effect of Mechanization', *American Economic Review*, 1933, p. 171. More detail on the experiments can be found in Mayo, *The Human Problems of an Industrial Civilization*, 1933, and Roethlisberger and Dickson, *Management and the Worker*.

37 Roethlisberger and Dickson, *Management and the Worker*, p. 138.

38 There have since been some doubts as to the validity of the conclusions of the study; for example, Ronald G. Greenwood, Alfred A. Bolton and Regina A. Greenwood discovered that some participants in experiments may have been paid extra to participate, which would almost certainly have skewed some findings. The question of whether this had a decisive result on the outcome is, in my view, debatable. See their 'Hawthorne: A Half Century Later', *Journal of Management History*, 1983.

39 Mayo, 'The Human Effect of Mechanization', p. 175.

40 Thomas North Whitehead, *Leadership in a Free Society: A Study in Human Relations Based on an Analysis of Present-Day Industrial Civilization*, 1936, p. 3.

41 Whitehead, *Leadership in a Free Society*, p. 21.

42 Whitehead, *Leadership in a Free Society*, p. 30.

43 Paul S. Adler, 'Toward Collaborative Interdependence: A Century of Change in the Organization of Work', in Kaufman *et al.*, *Industrial Relations to Human Resources and Beyond*, 2003.

44 Frank B. Gilbreth and Lillian Gilbreth, 'The Three Position Plan of Promotion', *Annals of the American Academy of Political and Social Science*, 1916.

45 Dexter S. Kimball, *Principles of Industrial Organization*, 1913.

46 Richard A. Feiss, 'Personal Relationship as a Basis of Scientific Management', *Annals of the American Academy of Political and Social Science*, 1916; Mary B. Gilson, 'The Relation of Home Conditions to Industrial Efficiency', *Annals of the American Academy of Political and Social Science*, 1916; Mary B. Gilson, *What's Past is Prologue*, 1940; see also Charles D. Wrege and Ronald D. Greenwood, 'Mary B. Gilson: A Historical Study of the Neglected Accomplishments of a Woman Who Pioneered in Personnel Management', *Business and Economic History* 1982; Phipps, 'Mary, Mary, Quite Contrary'.

47 Phipps, 'Mary, Mary, Quite Contrary', p. 14.

48 Gilson, book review of *Management and the Worker*, quoted in Wrege and Greenwood, 'Mary B. Gilson', p. 40.

49 Henry Post Dutton, *Principles of Organization*, 1931.

50 John Kenneth Galbraith, *A Life in Our Times: Memoirs*, 1981, p. 61.

51 Henry S. Dennison, 'Production and Profits', *Annals of the American Academy of Political and Social Science*, 1920; Dennison, *Organization Engineering*, 1931; Dennison and John Kenneth Galbraith, *Modern Competition and Business Policy*, 1938; Kyle Bruce, 'Henry S. Dennison, Elton Mayo and Human Relations Historiography', *Management and Organizational History*, 2006.

52 See for example his *More Profits from Merchandizing*, 1925.

53 Edward Filene, *Successful Living in This Machine Age*, 1932, p. 11.

54 Lee K. Frankel and Alexander Fleischer, *The Human Factor in Industry*, 1920, pp. 5–6. 'Employé' was a common alternative to 'employee', including amongst American writers.

55 Cornelia Stratton Parker, *Working With the Working Woman*, 1922, p. vii.

56 Quoted in Edwin P. Hoyt, *The Guggenheims and the American Dream*, 1967, p. 236.

57 Daniel Guggenheim, 'Some Thoughts on Industrial Unrest', *Annals of the American Academy of Political and Social Science*, 1915, p. 209.

58 Daphne Taras, 'The North American Workplace: From Employee Representation to Employee Involvement', in Bruce E. Kaufman *et al.* (eds), *Industrial Relations to Human Resources and Beyond: The Evolving Process of Employee Relations Management*, 2003, p. 303.

59 William Lyon Mackenzie King, *Industry and Humanity*, 1918; see also Taras, 'The North American Workplace'.

60 Esther Lowenthal, 'The Labour Policy of the Oneida Community Ltd', *Journal of Political Economy*, 1927.

61 Anna Kuokkanen, Aino Laakso and Hannele Seeck, 'Management Paradigms in Personnel Magazines of the Finnish Metal and Forest Industries', *Journal of Management History*, 2010.

62 Sasaki Jun, 'Ohara Magosaburo', in Morgen Witzel (ed.), *Biographical Dictionary of Management*, 2001.

63 Muhammad 'Abduh, *Risalat al-Tawhid*, trans. Ishaq Musa'ad and Kenneth Cragg, *The Theology of Unity*, 1966.

64 R.N. Bose, *Gandhian Technique and Tradition in Industrial Relations*, 1956.

65 Quoted in Shriman Narayan (ed.), *The Selected Works of Mahatma Gandhi*, vol. 6, p. 141.

66 Tim Wright, 'A Method of Evading Management: Contract Labor in Chinese Coal Mines Before 1937', *Comparative Studies in Society and History*, 1981.

67 Gail Hershatter, 'Flying Hammers, Walking Chisels: The Workers of Santiaoshi', *Modern China*, 1983.

68 Min Ch'ien Tuk Zung Tyau, *China Awakened*, 1922, p. 234.

69 Tyau, *China Awakened*, pp. 234–5

70 Wren, *The Evolution of Management Thought*, p. 298.

71 James D. Mooney and Alan C. Reiley, *Onward Industry! The Principles of Organization and Their Significance to Modern Industry*, 1931, p. 10.

72 Mooney and Reiley, *Onward Industry!*, p. 494.

73 Mooney and Reiley, *Onward Industry!*, pp. 14–15.

74 Mooney and Reiley, *Onward Industry!*, p. 526.

75 James D. Mooney, 'The Principles of Organization', in Luther H. Gulick and Lyndall Urwick (eds) *Papers on the Science of Administration*, 1937, p. 97.

76 It should be added that upon America's joining the war, Mooney served as a staff officer in the US Navy for the duration, thus fulfilling his social responsibilities in another sense.

77 Octavia Hill, *Colour, Space and Music for the People*, 1884; Howard, *Garden Cities of To-morrow*.

78 George B. Hopkins, 'The New York Bureau of Municipal Research', *Annals of the American Academy of Political and Social Science*, 1912.

79 Luther H. Gulick, 'Notes on the Theory of Organization', in Luther H. Gulick and Lyndall Urwick (eds) *Papers on the Science of Administration*, 1937.

80 Alfred D. Chandler, *Strategy and Structure: Chapters in the History of American Industrial Enterprise*, 1962.

81 Gulick, 'Notes on the Theory of Organization', p. 37.

82 Luther H. Gulick, *Administrative Reflections from World War II*, 1948.

83 Gulick, 'Notes on the Theory of Organization', p. 40.

84 Barnard's work has often been studied and there is a considerable literature on him. Good starting points are William B. Wolfe, *The Basic Barnard: An Introduction to Chester I. Barnard and His Theories of Organization and Management*, 1974, and Andrea Gabor and Joseph T. Mahoney, 'Chester Barnard', in Morgen Witzel and Malcolm Warner (eds), *Oxford Handbook of Management Thinkers*, 2012. William G. Scott's *Chester I. Barnard and the Guardians of the Managerial State*, 1992, is an in-depth account at times critical of his subject.

85 Chester I. Barnard, *The Functions of the Executive*, 1938, p. 5.

86 Gabor and Mahoney, 'Chester Barnard'.

87 Warren G. Bennis, *On Becoming a Leader*, 1989; Henry Mintzberg, *The Nature of Managerial Work*, 1973.

88 Chester I. Barnard, *The Functions of the Executive*, 1938, p. 282.

8 The growth of management disciplines

1 Elliott Jaques, *The Changing Culture of a Factory*, 1951.

2 Keith Davis, *Human Relations in Business*, 1957.

3 Crozier, *The Bureaucratic Phenomenon*, 1963.

4 Abraham Maslow, *Motivation and Personality*, 1954.

5 See especially Frederick Herzberg, *Work and the Nature of Man*, 1966.

6 Douglas McGregor, *The Human Side of Enterprise*, 1960.

7 Chris Argyris, *Personality and Organization*, 1957.

8 Rensis Likert, *Human Organization: Its Management and Value*, 1967.

9 David C. McClelland, *Power: The Inner Experience*, 1975; Amitai Etzioni, *The Active Society: A Theory of Social and Political Processes*, 1968.

10 See for example Philip Kotler, *Marketing Management*, 1997; Michael Baker, *Marketing: An Introductory Text*, 1992.

11 David D. van Fleet, 'Doing Management History: One Editor's Views', *Journal of Management History*, 2008.

12 Witzel, *Builders and Dreamers*; Witzel, *Management History*.

13 Gary G. Hamilton and Lai Chi-kong, 'Consumption and Brand Names in Late Imperial China', in Henry J. Rutz and Benjamin S. Orlove (eds), *The Social Economy of Consumption*, 1989.

14 Witzel, *Management History*, pp. 220–2.

15 Paul T. Cherington, *The Elements of Marketing*, 1920, pp. 13–14.

16 United States Census statistics.

17 Cherington, *The Elements of Marketing*, p. 6.

18 Cherington, *The Elements of Marketing*, p. 9.

19 Paul T. Cherington, *The Consumer Looks at Advertising*, 1928; Cherington, *People's Wants and How to Satisfy Them*, 1935.

20 Melvin T. Copeland, *Business Statistics*, 1917; Copeland, *Principles of Merchandising*, 1924.

21 Walter Dill Scott, *The Psychology of Advertising*, 1913, p. 2.

22 Elias St Elmo Lewis, *Financial Advertising*, 1908.

23 Fred E. Clark, 'Criteria of Marketing Efficiency', *American Economic Review*, 1921; Clark, *Principles of Marketing*, 1924.

24 Herbert N. Casson, *Advertisements and Sales: A Study of Advertising and Selling from the Standpoint of the New Principles of Scientific Management*, 1913, p. 145.

25 C. Bertrand Thompson, 'Scientific Management in Retailing', repr. in C. Bertrand Thompson (ed.), *Scientific Management*, 1914, p. 545.

26 Charles W. Hoyt, *Scientific Sales Management Today*, 1913.

27 Selden O. Martin, 'The Scientific Study of Marketing', *Annals of the American Academy of Political and Social Science*, 1915; John E.G. Bateson, *Managing Services Marketing*, 1999; Christopher Lovelock and Jochen Wirtz, *Essentials of Services Marketing*, 2009.

28 Arnold Brown, 'The Manufacturer as Advertiser', in T. Russell (ed.), *Harmsworth Business Library*, vol. 5, 1911.

29 George W. Orange and J. McBain, 'Mail Order Advertising', in T. Russell (ed.), *Harmsworth Business Library*, vol. 5, 1911.

30 Harry Tipper (ed.), *Advertising: Its Principles and Practice*, 1921.

31 Wesley Clair Mitchell, *Business Cycles*, 1913, pp. 27–32.

32 Arch W. Shaw, *Some Problems in Market Distribution*, 1912. This work is sometimes called the first American textbook on marketing, but in fact it discusses little more than distribution issues.

33 L.D.H. Weld, 'Marketing Functions and Mercantile Organization', *American Economic Review*, 1917.

34 W.D. Moriarty, *The Economics of Marketing and Advertising*, 1923.

35 See for example John Kenneth Galbraith and John Black. ' The Quantitative Position of Marketing in the United States', *Quarterly Journal of Economics,* 1935; E. Jerome McCarthy, *Basic Marketing: A Managerial Approach*, 1960.

36 Homer Vanderblue, 'The Functional Approach to the Study of Marketing', *Journal of Political Economy*, 1921.

37 Bernays, *Propaganda*, 1928.

38 Aldous Huxley, *Brave New World*, 1932; Frederick Pohl and C.M. Kornbluth, *The Space Merchants*, 1953.

39 Naomi Klein, *No Logo*, 2000.

40 Marshall McLuhan, *The Mechanical Bride: Folklore of Industrial Man*, 1951, p. v.

41 McLuhan, *Understanding Media: The Extensions of Man*, 1964; McLuhan, *Culture Is Our Business*, 1970.

42 Tim Ambler, *Marketing and the Bottom Line: The New Metrics of Corporate Wealth*, 2000, p. 1.

43 This is not the place for a detailed discussion of pre-modern strategy. For more on this subject, see Witzel, *Builders and Dreamers*; Witzel, *Management History*. See also the discussion on business policy in J.G.B. Hutchins, 'Business History, Entrepreneurial History and Business Administration' *Journal of Economic History*, 1958.

44 A point also made by Wren, *The Evolution of Management Thought*, p. 421. See James Brian Quinn, *Strategies for Change: Logical Incrementalism*, 1980

45 Peter F. Drucker, *The Practice of Management*, 1954, p. 352; Wren, *The Evolution of Management Thought*, p. 421.

46 Theodore Levitt, 'Marketing Myopia', *Harvard Business Review*, 1960, p. 4.

47 Levitt, 'Marketing Myopia', p. 10.

48 Peter Drucker, *Managing for Results: Economic Tasks and Risk-Taking Decisions*, 1964.

49 Chandler, *Strategy and Structure*, p. 314.

50 Geoffrey Jones and Alexis Lefort, 'McKinsey and the Globalization of Consultancy', 2005.

51 George Steiner, *Managerial Long-Range Planning*, 1963; H. Igor Ansoff, *Corporate Strategy*, 1965.

52 Bruce Smith, *The RAND Corporation: Case Study of a Nonprofit Advisory Corporation*, 1966.

53 Jonathan Barron Baskin and Paul J. Miranti, *A History of Corporate Finance*, 1997.

54 Gabriel Hawawini and Ashok Vora, 'A Brief History of Yield Approximations', in Geoffrey Poitras (ed.), *Pioneers of Financial Economics*, vol. 2, 2007.

55 Robert E. Wright (ed.), *The History of Corporate Finance: Developments of Anglo-American Securities Markets, Financial Practices, Theories and Laws*, 2003.

56 Richard L. Norgaard, 'The Evolution of Business Finance Textbooks', *Financial Management*, 1981.

57 Lloyd, *Wealth Against Commonwealth*.

58 Thomas L. Greene, *Corporation Finance*, 1897.

59 Meade, *Corporation Finance*, p. 366.

60 Edmund E. Lincoln, *Problems in Business Finance*, 1921.

61 W. J. Jackman, *Corporations: Organizing, Finance and Management*, 1910; Thomas Conway, *Investment and Speculation*, 1914; William H. Walker, *Corporation Finance*, 1917; Charles

260 *Notes*

Gerstenberg, *Financial Organization and the Management of Business*, 1924; Arthur S. Dewing, *Corporation Finance*, 1923.

62 Brian R. Cheffins, *Corporate Ownership and Control: British Business Transformed*, 2008.

63 Mark J. Roe, *Strong Managers, Weak Owners: The Political Roots of American Corporate Finance*, 1994, p. 22. A similar point is made by Richard Sylla and George David Smith, 'The Transformation of Financial Capitalism: An Essay on the History of American Capital Markets', *Financial Markets, Institutions and Instruments*, 1993.

64 William Z. Ripley, *From Main Street to Wall Street*, 1926, p. 85.

65 Adolph A. Berle and Gardiner C. Means, *The Modern Corporation and Private Property*, 1932, p. 312.

66 James Burnham, *The Managerial Revolution: Or, What is Happening in the World Now*, 1941, p.48.

67 Burnham, *The Managerial Revolution*, pp. 87–8, 90.

68 Caroline Fohlin, *The History of Corporate Ownership and Control in Germany*, 2005; see also Baskin and Miranti, *A History of Corporate Finance*.

69 Yumiko Morii, 'A Comparative Analysis of Corporate Finance in the United States and Japan from 1880 to 1930', 2008. See also Takeo Hoshi and Anil Kashyap, *Corporate Financing and Governance in Japan: The Road to the Future*, 2001; Juno Teranishi, 'Were Banks Really at the Center of the Prewar Japanese Financial System?', *Monetary and Economics Studies*, 2007; Tetsuji Okazaki, 'The Evolution of Corporate Finance and Corporate Governance in Prewar Japan: Comments on "Were Banks Really at the Center of the Prewar Japanese Financial System?"', *Monetary and Economic Studies*, 2007.

70 Andrea L. McElderry, *Shanghai Old-Style Banks (Ch'ien-chuang) 1800–1935*, 1976.

71 Yeh, *Shanghai Splendor*, p. 6.

72 Yeh, *Shanghai Splendor*, p. 31.

73 Yeh, *Shanghai Splendor*, p. 34.

74 Richard P. Mitchell, *The Society of the Muslim Brothers*, 1993.

75 Quoted in Jan Slomp, 'The "Political Equation" in *Al-jihad fi al-Islam* of Abul A'la Mawdudi (1903–79)', in David Thomas and Clare Amos (eds), *A Faithful Presence: Essays for Kenneth Cragg*, 2003. This passage is also quoted in Hans Visser, *Islamic Finance: Principles and Practice*, 2009, p. 2. Al-Mawdudi's own ideas are spelled out in detail in his *Economic System of Islam*, 1999, and 'Economic and Political Teachings of the Qur'an', 1963.

76 See his *Islam and the Theory of Interest*, 1991.

77 Visser, *Islamic Finance*.

78 Mark Casson and Howard Cox, 'International Business Networks: Theory and History', *Business and Economic History*, 1993; Geoffrey Jones and Tarun Khanna, 'Bringing History Into International Business', 2004. For an overview see Jones, *The Evolution of International Business*, 1996.

79 Barnard Ellinger, *Credit and International Trade: How They Work in Practice*, 1934.

80 Cleona Lewis and Karl T. Schlotterbeck, *America's Stake in International Investments*, 1938.

81 H.B. Morse, *The Guilds of China*, 1932.

82 Chong-Su See, *The Foreign Trade of China*, 1919; En-Sai Tai, *Central and Local Finance in China*, 1922; Chin Chu, *The Tariff Problem in China*, 1916; Tyau, *China Awakened*; Sun Yat-Sen, *The International Development of China*, 1922.

83 Chin-Ning Chu, *Thick Face, Black Heart: The Asian Path to Thriving, Winning and Succeeding*, 1995. There is also an rather erratic English translation of the original text by Zhao An Xin, 2009.

84 John Dunning, *American Investment in British Manufacturing Industry*, 1957; John Fayerweather, *Management of International Operations*, 1960; Richard D. Robinson, *International Business Policy*, 1966.

85 Peter Buckley's introduction to *International Business*, 2003, is an excellent survey of the development of this field.

86 E.J. Kahn, *The Problem Solvers: A History of Arthur D. Little, Inc.*, 1986.

87 Joel Dean, *The Management Counsel Profession*, 1940.

88 See Matthias Kipping and Lars Engwall (eds), *Management Consulting: Emergence and Dynamics of a Knowledge Industry*, 2001; Christopher McKenna, *The World's Newest Profession: Management Consulting in the Twentieth Century*, 2006; Patricia Tisdall, *Agents of Change: The Development and Practice of Management Consultancy*, 1982; Michael Ferguson, *The Rise of Management Consulting in Britain*, 2002.

89 Michael W. Sedlak and Harold F. Williamson, *The Evolution of Management Education: A History of the Northwestern University J.L. Kellogg Graduate School of Management 1908–1983*, 1983, p. 2.

90 Melvin T. Copeland, *And Mark the Era: The Story of Harvard Business School*, 1958; Sedlak and Williamson, *The Evolution of Management Education*.

91 Yeh, *Shanghai Splendor*, p. 36.

92 Quoted in Anthony J. Mayo, Nitin Nohria and Laura G. Singleton, *Paths to Power: How Insiders and Outsiders Shaped American Business Leadership*, 2006, p. 132.

93 Copeland, *And Mark the Era*; Sedlak and Williamson, *The Evolution of Management Education*.

94 Jeremy Holt, *Reinventing the CFO*, 1996.

95 Yoram (Jerry) Wind, 'The Integrative Thinking Challenge for Management Education and Research', *Rotman's Magazine*, 2002.

9 From scientific management to management science

1 Ludwig von Mises, *Human Action: A Treatise on Economics*, 1949.

2 Ayn Rand, *Atlas Shrugged*, 1957. See also Douglas Den Uyl and Douglas B. Rasmussen, *The Philosophic Thought of Ayn Rand*, 1984.

3 Ralph C. Davis, 'A Philosophy of Management', *Journal of the Academy of Management*, 1958, p. 37.

4 Gulick, *Administrative Reflections from World War II*, 1948, p. 32.

5 Harold B. Maynard, G.J. Stegemerten and John L. Schwab, *Methods–Time Measurement*, 1948, p. v.

6 For more on this export of ideas to Europe, see Matthias Kipping and Ove Bjarnar (eds), *The Americanisation of European Business: The Marshall Plan and the Transfer of US Management Models*, 1998.

7 S.M. Amadae, *Rationalizing Capitalist Democracy: The Cold War Origins of Rational Choice Liberalism*, 2003.

8 Mie Augier and James G. March, *The Roots, Rituals and Rhetorics of Change: North American Business Schools after the Second World War*, 2011, p. 97.

9 Robert Gordon and James Howell, *Higher Education for Business*, 1959. See also Rakesh Khurana, Kenneth Kimura and Marion Fourcade, 'How Foundations Think: The Ford Foundation as a Dominating Institution in the Field of American Business Schools', 2011; and for a broader overview, Rakesh Khurana, *From Higher Aims to Hired Hands: The Social Transformation of American Business Schools and the Unfulfilled Promise of Management as a Profession*, 2007.

10 Augier and March, *The Roots, Rituals and Rhetorics of Change*, p. 12.

11 Augier and March, *The Roots, Rituals and Rhetorics of Change*, p. 307.

12 Adler, 'Towards Collaborative Interdependence', 2003.

13 Patricia Genoe McLaren and Albert J. Mills, 'A Product of "His" Time? Exploring the Construct of the Ideal Manager in the Cold War Era', *Journal of Management History*, 2008, p. 396.

14 George T. Trundle (ed.), *Managerial Control of Business*, 1948; Marshall E. Dimock, *The Executive in Action*, 1945.

15 Quoted by Samuel Eilon, 'Management Science', in Malcolm Warner (ed.), *International Encyclopedia of Business and Management*, 1996, vol. 3, p. 3032.

16 See Blackett, *Studies of War*; see also Mary Jo Nye, *Blackett: Physics, War and Politics in the Twentieth Century*, 2004. For an overview of the entire subject of operational research, see Agatha C. Hughes and Thomas P. Hughes (eds), *Systems, Experts, and Computers: The Systems Approach in Management and Engineering, World War II and After*, 2000.

17 Norbert Wiener, *The Human Use of Human Beings: Cybernetics and Society*, 1950.

18 Claude Shannon and Warren Weaver, *The Mathematical Theory of Communication*, 1949.

19 See in particular Walter Shewhart, *Economic Control of Quality of Manufactured Product*, 1931.

20 Stafford Beer, *Cybernetics and Management*, 1959; Beer, *Decision and Control: The Managing of Operational Research and Management Cybernetics*, 1966; Beer, *Brain of the Firm*, 1972.

21 C. West Churchman, Russell L. Ackoff and Leonard Arnoff, *Introduction to Operations Research*, 1957.

22 C. West Churchman, *The Design of Inquiring Systems: Basic Concepts of Systems and Organizations*, 1971.

23 Russell L. Ackoff, *Creating the Corporate Future*, 1981; Russell L. Ackoff and Frederick E. Emery, *On Purposeful Systems*, 1972.
24 Jay Wright Forrester, *Industrial Dynamics*, 1961.
25 Manuel Laguna and Johan Marklund, *Business Process Modelling, Simulation and Design*, 2004; Michael Hammer and James Champy, *Reengineering the Corporation: A Manifesto for Business Revolution*, 1993; Thomas Davenport and James Short, 'The New Industrial Engineering: Information Technology and Business Process Redesign', *Sloan Management Review*, 1990.
26 Eilon, 'Management Science', p. 3033. See also Samuel Eilon, *Aspects of Management*, 1979.
27 Mol and Birkinshaw, *Giant Steps in Management*, p. 37.
28 See especially Alfred Marshall, *Principles of Economics: An Introductory Volume*, 1890; and Marshall, *Industry and Trade*.
29 Robert W. Dimand, 'Irving Fisher and His Students as Financial Economists', in Geoffrey Poitras (ed.), *Pioneers of Financial Economics*, vol. 2, 2007.
30 Harry Markowitz, *Portfolio Selection: Efficient Diversification of Investments*, 1959.
31 See for example Paul A. Samuelson, 'Proof that Properly Anticipated Prices Fluctuate Randomly', *Industrial Management Review*, 1965.
32 I have not attempted to define these concepts in any more detail here because it is in fact very difficult even to summarize them without getting into the mathematical concepts behind them. For an overview of how this field developed, see Geoffrey Poitras, 'Introduction' in *Pioneers of Financial Economics*, vol. 2, 2007, and Edwin J. Elton and Martin J. Gruber, 'Modern Portfolio Theory, 1950 to Date', 1997.
33 Poitras, 'Introduction', p. 4.
34 Poitras, 'Introduction', p. 7.
35 Pablo Triana, *Lecturing Birds on Flying: Can Mathematical Theories Destroy the Financial Markets?* 2009.
36 Triana, *Lecturing Birds on Flying*, pp. 267–8.
37 George, *The History of Management Thought*, p. 178.
38 Isaac Asimov, *Foundation*, 1951.
39 Peters, *Thriving on Chaos: Handbook for a Management Revolution*.
40 Lawrence LeShan and Henry Margenau, *Einstein's Space and Van Gogh's Sky: Physical Reality and Beyond*, 1982, p. xiii.
41 Philip Sargant Florence, *Labour*, 1949.
42 Ronald H. Coase, 'The Nature of the Firm', *Economica*, 1937.
43 Erich Kosiol, *Organisation das Unternehmung* (Organization of the Enterprise), 1962.
44 Philip Sargant Florence, *Investment, Location and Size of Plant*, 1948.
45 Kenneth Arrow, *Social Choice and Individual Values*, 1951.
46 Kenneth Boulding, *The Image*, 1956.
47 Hunter Crowther-Heyck, *Herbert A. Simon: The Bounds of Reason in America*, 2005; J.C. Spender, 'Herbert Simon', in Morgen Witzel and Malcolm Warner (eds), *Oxford Handbook of Management Thinkers*, 2012.
48 Hunter Crowther-Heyck, 'Herbert Simon and the GSIA: Building an Interdisciplinary Community', *Journal of the History of the Behavioral Sciences*, 2006, p. 330.
49 Herbert A. Simon, *Administrative Behavior: A Study of the Decision-Making Processes in Administrative Organization*, 1947
50 Spender, 'Herbert Simon'.
51 James G. March and Herbert A. Simon, *Organizations*, 1958, p. 28.
52 Richard M. Cyert and James G. March, *A Behavioral Theory of the Firm*, 1963; James G. March, 'The Technology of Foolishness', in March (ed.), *Decisions and Organizations*, 1971.
53 Ludwig von Bertalanffy, *General System Theory*, 1968.
54 LeShan and Margenau, *Einstein's Space and Van Gogh's Sky: Physical Reality and Beyond*, 1982.
55 Geoffrey Vickers, *Towards a Sociology of Management*, 1967.
56 Checkland, *Systems Thinking, Systems Practice*.
57 Chris Argyris and Donald Schön *Organizational Learning*, 1978.
58 Chris Argyris, *Management and Organizational Development*, 1971.
59 Woodward, *Industrial Organization: Theory and Practice*.
60 Joan Woodward, *Industrial Organization: Behaviour and Control*, 1970.
61 Tom Burns and George M. Stalker, *The Management of Innovation*, 1961

62 Tom Burns, 'Industry in a New Age', *New Society*, 1963, p. 103.
63 Thomas J. Peters and Robert H. Waterman, *In Search of Excellence: Lessons from America's Best-Run Companies*, 1982; Kanter, *When Giants Learn to Dance*.
64 Paul R. Lawrence and Jay W. Lorsch, *Organization and Environment: Managing Differentiation and Organization*, 1967.
65 Eric L. Trist and Frederick E. Emery, *Towards a Social Ecology: Contextual Appreciations of the Future and the Present*, 1973.
66 Elliott Jaques, *A General Theory of Bureaucracy*, 1976.
67 Elliott Jaques, *The Form of Time*, 1982, p. 215.
68 Elliott Jaques, *Requisite Organization*, 1988, p. 156.
69 Derek S. Pugh, 'The Measurement of Organization Structures: Does Context Determine Form?' *Organizational Dynamics*, 1973, pp. 27–8. See also Derek S. Pugh and David J. Hickson, *Organization Structure in its Context*, 1976.
70 Edgar H. Schein, *Organizational Psychology*, 1985.
71 Edgar H. Schein, 'From Brainwashing to Organisational Therapy', *European Business Forum*, 2007, p. 9.
72 James David Thompson, *Organizations in Action*, 1967, p. 159.
73 Michael T. Hannan and John Freeman, *Organizational Ecology*, 1989.
74 Jay R. Galbraith and Daniel A. Nathanson, *Strategy Implementation: The Role of Structure and Process*, 1978; Miles and Snow, *Organizational Strategy, Structure and Process*.
75 Miles and Snow, *Organizational Strategy, Structure and Process*, p. 18.
76 Harold R. Koontz and Cyril O'Donnell, *Principles of Management*, 1955.
77 W. Graham Astley, 'Administrative Science as Socially Constructed Truth', *Administrative Science Quarterly*, 1985, p. 508.
78 Marta B. Calás and Linda Smircich, 'Voicing Seduction to Silence Leadership', *Organization Studies*, 1991.
79 Charles E. Lindblom, 'The Science of Muddling Through', *Public Administration Review*, 1959.
80 Mintzberg, *The Nature of Managerial Work*.
81 Harold Geneen, *The Synergy Myth, and Other Ailments of Business Today*, 1997.
82 Andrew Grove, *High Output Management*, 1983, p. 3.
83 Matsushita Konosuke, *Quest for Prosperity: The Life of a Japanese Industrialist*, 1988; Rowland Gould, *The Matsushita Phenomenon*, 1970.
84 Paul M. Dauten, Homer L. Gammill and Stanley C. Robinson, 'Our Concepts of Controlling Need Re-thinking', *Journal of the Academy of Management*, 1958, p. 41.
85 Peter F. Drucker, *The New Realities*, 1989.
86 Peter Starbuck, 'Peter Drucker', in Morgen Witzel and Malcolm Warner (eds), *Oxford Handbook of Management Thinkers*, 2012; for views on Drucker see also Jack Beatty, *The World According to Drucker*, 1998; John J. Tarrant, *Drucker: The Man Who Invented Corporate Society*, 1976; Tony H. Bonaparte and John E. Flaherty (eds), *Peter Drucker: Contributions to Business Enterprise*, 1970. For Drucker's earlier ideas, see *The Future of Industrial Man*, 1942, and *Concept of the Corporation*, 1946.
87 Drucker, *The Practice of Management*, 1954; Drucker, *The Effective Executive*, 1967; Drucker, *Management: Tasks, Responsibilities, Practices*, 1974.
88 Drucker, *Management: Tasks, Responsibilities, Practices*, p. 88.
89 Drucker, *Management: Tasks, Responsibilities, Practices*, p. 89.

10 The age of the management gurus

1 Robert R. Locke, *The Collapse of the American Management Mystique*, 1996.
2 See Michael J. Hogan, *The Marshall Plan: America, Britain and the Reconstruction of Western Europe, 1947–1952*, 1989; Kipping and Bjarnar, *The Americanisation of European Business*; Marie-Laure Djelic, *Exporting the American Model: The Postwar Transformation of European Business*, 1998,
3 Alfred D. Chandler, *Scale and Scope: The Dynamics of Industrial Capitalism*, 1990. For descriptions of German management culture, see Charles Hampden-Turner and Fons Trompenaars, *The Seven Cultures of Capitalism*, 1993; Ronnie Lessem and Fred Neubauer,

European Management Systems: Towards Unity out of Cultural Diversity, 1994; Roland Calori and Philippe De Woot, *A European Management Model: Beyond Diversity*, 1994; Christel Lane, *Industry and Society in Europe: Stability and Change in Britain, Germany and France*, 1998.

4 Wilhelm Rieger, *Einführung in de Privatwirtschaftslehre* (Introduction to the Private Sector), 1984; see also David A.R. Forrester, 'Wilhelm Rieger and Cash Accounting: An Essay in Controversial Ideas', *Abacus*, 2000.

5 Gutenberg, *Einführung in die Betriebswirtschaftslehre*.

6 Rainer Marr, 'Management in Germany', in Malcolm Warner (ed.), *Management in Europe*, 2000.

7 See Edmund Heinen, *Einführung in die Betriebswirtschaftslehre* (Introduction to Business Administration), 1968.

8 Michael Crichton, *Rising Sun*, 1992.

9 Naoto Sasaki, *Management and Industrial Structure in Japan*, 1990. For more on Japanese industrial development, see Etsuo Abe and Robert Fitzgerald (eds), *The Origins of Japanese Industrial Power*, 1995; W. Mark Fruin, *The Japanese Enterprise System*, 1992; Yoshitaka Suzuki, *Japanese Management Structures*, 1991.

10 Shoji Kimoto, *Quest for the Dawn*, 1991.

11 See Kimoto, *Quest for the Dawn*; Toyoda Eiji, *Toyota: Fifty Years in Motion, an Autobiography by the Chairman*, 1987; James P. Womack, Daniel T. Jones and Daniel Roos, *The Machine that Changed the World: The Story of Lean Production*, 1990; Ohno Taiichi, *Toyota Production System: Beyond Large-Scale Production*, 1988; Shigeo Shingo, *A Study of the Toyota Production System from an Industrial Engineering Viewpoint*, 1989; Richard J. Shonberger, *Japanese Manufacturing Techniques: Nine Hidden Lessons in Simplicity*, 1982.

12 Ohno, *Toyota Production System*, p. 126.

13 Ronald Fisher, *Statistical Methods for Research Workers*, 1925. For Fisher's impact, see David Salsburg, *The Lady Tasting Tea: How Statistics Revolutionized Science in the Twentieth Century*, 2002.

14 Armand V. Feigenbaum, *Quality Control: Principles, Practices and Administration*, 1945; Feigenbaum, *Total Quality Control*, 1961.

15 Levitt, 'Marketing Myopia'.

16 P.C. Malahanobis, 'Walter A. Shewhart and Statistical Control in India', *Sankhya: The Indian Journal of Statistics*, 1948.

17 For more on the statistical movement in India see J.K. Ghosh, 'Malahanobis and the Art and Science of Statistics: The Early Days', *Indian Journal of the History of Science*, 1994; Ashok Rudra, *Prasanta Chandra Malahanobis: A Biography*, 1998.

18 Joseph M. Juran, *Quality Control Handbook*, 4th edn, 1988. See also Juran, *Juran on Leadership for Quality: An Executive Handbook*, 1989.

19 Peter B. Petersen, 'The Contribution of W. Edwards Deming to Japanese Management Theory and Practice', *Academy of Management Best Paper Proceedings 1987*, 1987.

20 Ishikawa Kaoru, *What Is Total Quality Control? The Japanese Way*, 1985.

21 See for example Robert L. Flood, *Beyond TQM*, 1993.

22 John Butman, *Juran: A Lifetime of Influence*, 1997.

23 Juran, *Juran on Leadership for Quality*, 1989.

24 W. Edwards Deming, *Out of the Crisis*, 1986; see also Andrea Gabor, *The Man Who Discovered Quality*, 1990; Cecilia S. Kilian, *The World of W. Edwards Deming*, 1992.

25 Deming, *Out of the Crisis*.

26 W. Edwards Deming, *The New Economics for Industry, Government, Education*, 1993.

27 Geert Hofstede, *Culture's Consequences: International Differences in Work-Related Values*, 1980.

28 Geert Hofstede and Michael Harris Bond, 'The Confucius Connection: From Cultural Roots to Economic Growth', *Organizational Dynamics*, 1988; Hofstede, *Culture and Organizations*.

29 Robert J. House *et al.* (eds), *Culture, Leadership, and Organizations: the GLOBE Study of 62 Societies*, 2004.

30 Nancy J. Adler, *International Dimensions of Organizational Behavior*, 1997.

31 To take two examples from many, see Taylor H. Cox and Stacy Blake, 'Managing Cultural Diversity: Implications for Organizational Effectiveness', *The Executive*, 1991; Ellen Ernst Kossek and Sharon A. Lobel (eds), *Managing Diversity: Human Resource Strategies for Transforming the Workplace*, 1997.

32 Zhang Deyi, *Diary of a Chinese Diplomat*, trans. Simon Johnstone, 1989.

33 Kenichi Ohmae, *The Next Global Stage: Challenges and Opportunities in Our Borderless World*, 2005.

34 Philip Kotler and Sidney J. Levy, 'Broadening the Concept of Marketing', *Journal of Marketing* 1969, p. 10.

35 Kotler and Levy, 'Broadening the Concept of Marketing', p. 10.

36 Kotler and Levy, 'Broadening the Concept of Marketing', p. 11.

37 David J. Luck, 'Broadening the Concept of Marketing – Too Far', *Journal of Marketing*, 1969, p. 53.

38 Philip Kotler and Gerald Zaltman, 'Social Marketing: An Approach to Planned Social Change', *Journal of Marketing* 1971; Philip Kotler and Alan Andreasen, *Strategic Marketing for Nonprofit Organizations*, 1996.

39 Kotler, *Marketing Management*, p. 29.

40 Kotler, *Marketing Management*, p. 4.

41 Levitt, 'Marketing Myopia'.

42 See for example A. Parasuraman, Valerie A. Zeithaml and Leonard L. Berry, 'A Conceptual Model of Service Quality and Its Implications for Future Research', *Journal of Marketing*, 1985; Parasuraman, Zeithaml and Berry, 'SERVQUAL: A Multiple-Item Scale for Measuring Customer Perceptions of Service Quality'. *Journal of Retailing*, 1988.

43 David A. Aaker, *Managing Brand Equity: Capitalizing on the Power of a Brand Name*, 1992; Aaker, *Building Strong Brands*, 1995.

44 Patrick Barwise. 'Brand Equity: Snark or Boojum?', *International Journal of Research in Marketing*, 1993; Mary Jo Hatch and Majken Schultz, *Taking Brand Initiative: How Companies Can Align Strategy, Culture and Identity Through Corporate Branding*, 2008.

45 See for example Jonathan Schroeder, 'The Cultural Codes of Branding', *Marketing Theory*, 2009.

46 Peter McKiernan (ed.), *Historical Evolution of Strategic Management*, 1996, p. xix.

47 Kenneth R. Andrews, *The Concept of Corporate Strategy*, 1971, p. 18.

48 Aaron Wildavsky, 'If Planning is Everything, Maybe It's Nothing', *Policy Sciences*, 1983, p. 127.

49 Wildavsky, 'If Planning is Everything, Maybe It's Nothing', p. 129.

50 Mintzberg, *Mintzberg on Management*, p. 189.

51 Omar Khayyam, *Rubaiyat*, trans. Edward Fitzgerald, 2009.

52 Ohmae, *The Mind of the Strategist*, p. 4

53 Ohmae, *The Mind of the Strategist*, p. 78.

54 Ansoff, *The New Corporate Strategy*.

55 De Geus, 'Planning as Learning'.

56 Pierre Wack, 'Scenarios: Shooting the Rapids', *Harvard Business Review*, 1985.

57 Lindblom, 'The Science of Muddling Through'; Lindblom, 'Still Muddling, Not Yet Through', 1979; Lindblom, *The Intelligence of Democracy*, 1965.

58 Quinn, *Strategies for Change*.

59 For example, Birger Wernerfeldt, 'A Resource-Based View of the Firm', *Strategic Management Journal*, 1984; David J. Teece, Gary Pisano and Amy Shuen, 'Dynamic Capabilities and Strategic Management', *Strategic Management Journal*, 1997; see also Robert M. Grant, 'The Resource-Based Theory of Competitive Advantage: Implications for Strategy Formulation', *California Management Review*, 1991.

60 Gary Hamel and C.K. Prahalad, *Competing for the Future*, 1994.

61 Joe S. Bain, *Industrial Organization*, 1968.

62 Bruce D. Henderson, *Henderson on Corporate Strategy*, 1979.

63 Michael E. Porter, *Competitive Strategy: Techniques for Analyzing Industries and Competitors*, 1980; see also Porter, *Competitive Advantage: Creating and Sustaining Superior Performance*, 1985.

64 See for example Henry Mintzberg, Bruce Ahlstrand and Joseph Lampel, *Strategy Safari: A Guided Tour Through the Wilds of Strategic Management*, 2002 which explores a dozen different schools.

65 See for example Nonaka and Takeuchi, *The Knowledge-Creating Company*.

66 Peters, *Thriving on Chaos*; Peters, *Liberation Management: Necessary Disorganization for the Nanosecond Nineties*, 1992.

67 Rosabeth Moss Kanter, *The Change Masters: Innovation for Productivity in the American Corporation*, 1983.

68 Kanter, *When Giants Learn to Dance*, p. 31.
69 Kanter, *When Giants Learn to Dance*, p. 354.
70 Charles Handy, *Understanding Organisations*, 1976.
71 Charles Handy, *The Age of Unreason*, 1989.
72 Charles Handy, *The Empty Raincoat*, 1994.
73 Morgan, *Images of Organization*.
74 Fred E. Fiedler, *A Theory of Leadership Effectiveness*, 1967.
75 For example, see Richard L. Hughes, Robert C. Ginnett and Gordon J. Curphy, *Leadership: Enhancing the Lessons of Experience*, 1996.
76 James MacGregor Burns, *Leadership*, 1978; Robert K. Greenleaf, *Servant Leadership*, 1977.
77 His major works on this subject are Warren G. Bennis and Burt Nanus, *Leaders: Five Strategies for Taking Charge*, 1985 and Bennis, *On Becoming a Leader*, 1989.
78 Bennis, *On Becoming A Leader*.
79 John P. Kotter, *A Force for Change: How Leadership Differs from Management*, 1990.
80 Stephen R. Covey, *The Seven Habits of Highly Effective People*, 1989.
81 Joseph C. Rost, *Leadership for the Twenty-First Century*, 1991; Max DePree, *Leadership Is An Art*, 1987.
82 See John Adair, *Action-Centred Leadership*, 1973; Adair, *Not Bosses But Leaders*, 1989; Jonathan Gosling, Peter Case and Morgen Witzel (eds), *John Adair: Fundamentals of Leadership*, 2007.
83 Laurence J. Peter, *The Peter Principle*, 1969.
84 Norman Dixon, *On the Psychology of Military Incompetence*, 1976.
85 Grint, Foreword to Gosling *et al.*, *John Adair*.

11 Management thought in the internet age

1 John Naisbitt, *Megatrends*, 1982.
2 Alvin Toffler, *The Third Wave*, 1981.
3 Kanter, *When Giants Learn to Dance*.
4 Bennis and Nanus, *Leaders*.
5 Tom Standage, *The Victorian Internet*, 1998.
6 Donald Read, *The Power of News: The History of Reuters, 1849–1989*, 1992.
7 Marshall McLuhan and Quentin Fiore, *War and Peace in the Global Village*, 1968.
8 Tim Berners-Lee and Mark Fischetti, *Weaving the Web*, 1999.
9 On a related subject but reflecting very much the prevailing uncertainties about the internet, see Steve Jones (ed.), *Doing Internet Research: Critical Issues and Methods for Examining the Net*, 1999.
10 Examples of books on e-commerce from the late 1990s include Ravi Kalakota and Andrew Whinston, *Electronic Commerce: A Manager's Guide*, 1997; Michael De Kare-Silver, *E-shock 2000*, 2000; James Slevin, *The Internet and Society*, 2000.
11 See for example Dave Chaffey, *E-Business and E-Commerce Management*, 2nd edn, 2003.
12 Neil Harvey, *The Chiapas Rebellion: The Struggle for Land and Democracy*, 1998.
13 Follett, *The New State*.
14 See for example Brendan Tutt, 'When Social Networking Meets Knowledge Management', 2007. My view of current research on social networks is conditioned by my experience as editor in chief of *Corporate Finance Review*, where I have read a number of manuscripts on this subject. Most describe the world as the authors would like it to be, rather than as it is.
15 Roger Parkinson, *The Late Victorian Navy: The Pre-Dreadnought Era and the Origins of the First World War*, 2008.
16 Victor K. McElheny, *Insisting on the Impossible: The Life of Edwin Land*, 1998; Glenn Rifkin and George Harrar, *The Ultimate Entrepreneur: The Story of Ken Olsen and Digital Equipment Corporation*, 1988.
17 Jay R. Galbraith, *Designing Matrix Organizations that Actually Work: How IBM, Procter & Gamble and Others Design for Success*, 2008.
18 Malcolm Warner and Morgen Witzel, *Managing in Virtual Organisations*, 2004.
19 Samuel E. Bleecker, 'The Virtual Organization', repr. in Gill Robinson Hickman (ed.), *Leading Organizations: Perspectives for a New Era*, 1998.

20 W. Chan Kim and Renée Mauborgne, *Blue Ocean Strategy: How to Create Uncontested Market Space and Make the Competition Irrelevant*, 2005.

21 Barwise and Meehan, *Beyond the Familiar*; Clayton Christensen, *The Innovator's Dilemma: When New Technologies Cause Great Firms to Fail*, 1997.

22 Michael Polanyi, *The Tacit Dimension*, 1966, p. 4. See also Polanyi, *Personal Knowledge: Towards a Post-Critical Philosophy*, 1958.

23 Max Boisot, *Information and Organizations: The Manager as Anthropologist*, 1987; Boisot, *Information Space: A Framework for Learning in Organizations, Institutions and Culture*, 1995; Nonaka and Takeuchi, *The Knowledge-Creating Company*.

24 Senge, *The Fifth Discipline*, p. 3.

25 Peter J. Buckley and Mark Casson, 'The Future of the Multinational Enterprise in Retrospect and in Prospect', *Journal of International Business Studies*, 2003; also Buckley and Casson, *The Future of the Multinational Enterprise*, 1976.

26 See for example Immanuel Wallerstein, *The Capitalist World Economy*, 1979.

27 John Dunning, 'Toward an Eclectic Theory of International Production: Some Empirical Tests', *Journal of International Business*, 1980; see also Dunning, 'The Eclectic Paradigm of International Production: A Restatement and Some Possible Extensions', *Journal of International Business*, 1988.

28 For more detail see Asif H. Qureshi, *The World Trade Organization; Implementing International Trade Norms*, 1996; Jeffrey J. Schott, *WTO 2000: Setting the Course for World Trade*, 1996; Bernard M. Hoekman and Petros C. Mavroidis, *The World Trade Organization: Law, Economics, and Politics*, 2007.

29 Kenichi Ohmae, *Triad Power: The Coming Shape of Global Competition*, 1985; Ohmae, *The Borderless World*, 1990. Ohmae continued this theme in *The Next Global Stage*, 2005.

30 Francis Fukuyama, *The End of History and the Last Man*, 1992; Samuel P. Huntington, *The Clash of Civilizations and the Remaking of the World Order*, 1996.

31 Huntington, *The Clash of Civilizations*, p. 51.

32 Christopher A. Bartlett and Sumantra Ghoshal, *Managing Across Borders: The Transnational Solution*, 2002.

33 Patrick Geddes, *Cities in Evolution: An Introduction to the Town Planning Movement and to the Study of Civics*, 1915.

34 Claudio Vignali, 'McDonald's: "Think Global, Act Local" – The Marketing Mix', *British Food Journal*, 2007.

35 Nassim Nicholas Taleb, *The Black Swan: The Impact of the Highly Improbable*, 2007.

36 Walter Lord, *Incredible Victory: The Battle of Midway*, 1998; Fuchida Mitsuo and Okumiya Masatake, *Midway: The Battle That Doomed Japan*, 1955.

37 Laudicina, *World Out of Balance*.

38 Ohmae, *The Mind of the Strategist*; Andrew Grove, *Only the Paranoid Survive: How to Exploit the Crisis Points that Challenge Every Company and Career*, 1996.

39 John Child, *Management in China in the Age of Reform*, 1994; S. Gordon Redding, *The Spirit of Chinese Capitalism*, 1993.

40 Elizabeth Croll, *China's New Consumers: Social Development and Domestic Demand*, 2006.

41 Rama Bijapurkar, *We Are Like That Only*, 2007.

42 C.K. Prahalad, *The Fortune at the Bottom of the Pyramid*, 2004. It should be pointed out that Prahalad was a professor at the University of Michigan at the time he wrote this work, but like many Indian expatriate academics he retained very strong ties with India; this can with some justification be claimed as an Indian idea.

43 Sangeeta Talwar of Tata Tea, pers. comm. 2009.

44 See for example David Bornstein, *The Price of a Dream: The Story of the Grameen Bank*, 2005.

45 Stuart L. Hart, *Capitalism at the Crossroads*, 2005; Ted London and Stuart L. Hart, 'Reinventing Strategies for Emerging Markets: Beyond the Transnational Model', *Journal of International Business Studies*, 2004.

46 James E. Austin, *Managing in Developing Countries: Strategic Analysis and Operating Techniques*, 1990; Moses N. Kiggundu, *Managing Organizations in Developing Countries: An Operational and Strategic Approach*, 1989; Monir Tayeb, *The Global Business Environment*, 1995; see also Alfred M. Jaeger and Rabindra N. Kanungo (eds), *Management in Developing Countries*, 1990.

47 Peter Blunt and Merrick Jones, *Managing Organizations in Africa*, 1992; Tayo Fashoyin (ed.), *Industrial Relations and African Development*, 1992.

48 P. Kassey Odubogun, *Management Theory: Relevance for Management Practice in Nigeria*, 1992; Mamadou Dia, *Africa's Management in the 1990s and Beyond: Reconciling Indigenous and Transplanted Institutions*, 1996; see also International Bank for Reconstruction and Development, *Indigenous Management Practices: Lessons for Africa's Management from the '90s*, 1993.

49 Piet Human and Frank M. Horwitz, *On the Edge: How South African Companies Cope with Change*, Kenwyn: Juta, 1992; Iyabo Olojde, *Women in Top Management in Nigeria*, 1995.

50 Vijay Mahajan, *Africa Rising: How 900 Million African Consumers Offer More than You Think*, 2008.

51 Farid A. Muna, *The Arab Executive*, 1980.

52 Abbas 'Ali, 'Decision Making Style and Work Satisfaction of Arab Gulf Executives', *International Studies of Management and Organization*, 1993; Monir Tayeb, 'Islamic Revival in Asia and Human Resource Management', *Employee Relations*, 1997; Muhammad Abdulrahman al-Tawail, *Public Administration in the Kingdom of Saudi Arabia*, 1995; M. Sami Kassem and Ghazi M. Habib (eds), *Strategic Management of Services in the Arab Gulf States*, 1989.

53 Thomas C. Cochran and Reuben E. Reina, *Entrepreneurship in Argentine Culture: Torcuato di Tella and SIAM*, 1962; Robert J. Shafer, *Mexican Business Organizations: History and Analysis*, 1973.

54 D. R. Shea, F. W. Swacker, R. J. Radway and S. T. Stairs (eds), *Reference Manual on Doing Business in Latin America*, 1979; Ernest Bartell and Leigh Payne (eds) *Business and Democracy in Latin America*, 1995; Eva Kras, *Management in Two Cultures: Bridging the Gap between US and Mexican Managers*, 1995.

55 João Carlos Ferraz, Howard Rush and Ian Miles, *Development, Technology and Flexibility: Brazil Faces the Industrial Divide*, 1992.

56 Rodolfo H. Terragno, *The Challenge of Real Development in Argentina in the Twenty-First Century*, 1998, p. 102.

57 Terragno, *The Challenge of Real Development in Argentina in the Twenty-First Century*, p. 101.

58 Thomas Robert Malthus, *An Essay on the Principles of Population*, 1798.

59 Donella H. Meadows *et al.*, *The Limits to Growth*, 1972.

60 Rachel Carson, *Silent Spring*, 1962.

61 For a summary of views, see Vaclav Smil, *Energy at the Crossroads: Global Perspectives and Uncertainties*, 2003.

62 James Lovelock, *Gaia: A New Look at Life on Earth*, 1979.

63 Kenneth E. Boulding, Elise Boulding and Guy M. Burgess, *The Social System of the Planet Earth*, 1977.

64 World Commission on Environment and Development, *Our Common Future*, 1987.

65 John Elkington, *Cannibals with Forks: The Triple Bottom Line of 21st Century Business*, 1997.

66 Nicholas Stern, *The Economics of Climate Change: The Stern Review*, 2007.

67 Herman Daly and John Cobb, *For the Common Good: Redirecting the Economy Toward Community, the Environment and a Sustainable Future*, 1989.

68 Hart, *Capitalism at the Crossroads*, 2005 and see also Stuart L. Hart and Mark B. Milstein, 'Creating Sustainable Value', *Academy of Management Executive*, 2003; Peter M. Senge *et al.*, *The Necessary Revolution: How Individuals and Organizations Are Working Together to Create a Sustainable World*, 2008.

69 Paul Hawken, *The Ecology of Commerce: A Declaration of Sustainability*, 1994; Paul Hawken, Amory Lovins and E. Hunter Lovins, *Natural Capitalism*, 1999.

70 'Saudi Dove in the Oil Slick', *Observer*, 14 January 2001; Amory B. Lovins, E. Kyle Datta, Odd-Even Bustnes and Jonathan G. Koomey, *Winning the Oil Endgame*, 2004.

71 See for example Michael Braungart and William McDonough, *Cradle to Cradle: Remaking the Way We Make Things*, 2009; Christian Seelos and Johanna Mair, 'Profitable Business Models and Market Creation in the Context of Deep Poverty: A Strategic View', *Academy of Management Perspectives*, 2007.

12 Conclusion

1 Lewis Mumford, *The Myth of the Machine*, 1967.
2 Alvin Toffler, *Future Shock*, 1970.
3 Polanyi, *The Tacit Dimension*, pp. 3–4.
4 Taylor, *The Principles of Scientific Management*, p. 4.
5 Ovid, *Metamorphoses*, trans. Denis Feeney and David Raeburn, 2004.

Bibliography

Note: This is by no means an exhaustive bibliography of the subject, and contains only those works which are directly referenced in the text of this book. The preparation of a full and complete international bibliography of the history of management is a task that awaits a scholar far more dedicated and persevering than myself.

Aaker, David A. (1992) *Managing Brand Equity: Capitalizing on the Power of a Brand Name*, New York: The Free Press.
—— (1995) *Building Strong Brands*, New York: The Free Press.
Abbott, Edith (1910) *Women in Industry: A Study in American Economic History*, New York: D. Appleton & Co.
Abbott, Edith and Breckinridge, Sophonisba Preston (1906) 'Employment of Women in Industries: Twelfth Census Statistics', *Journal of Political Economy* 14: 14–40.
'Abduh, Muhammad (1966) *Risalat al-Tawhid*, trans. Ishaq Musa'ad and Kenneth Cragg, *The Theology of Unity*, London: George Allen & Unwin.
Abdullah, Thabit A.J. (2000) *Merchants, Mamluks and Murder: The Political Economy of Trade in Eighteenth-Century Basra*, Albany, NY: SUNY Press.
Abe Etsuo and Fitzgerald, Robert (eds) (1995) *The Origins of Japanese Industrial Power*, London: Frank Cass.
Abu Ubayd (2005) *Kitab al-amwal* (Book of Revenue), trans. Imran Ahsan Khyan Nyazee, Reading: Garnet Publishing.
Ackoff, Russell L. (1981) *Creating the Corporate Future*, New York: John Wiley.
Ackoff, Russell L. and Emery, Fred E. (1972) *On Purposeful Systems*, London: Tavistock.
Ackoff, Russell and Rovin, Sheldon (2005) *Beating the System: Using Creativity to Outsmart Bureaucracies*, San Francisco: Berrett-Koehler.
Adair, John (1973) *Action-Centred Leadership*, London: McGraw Hill.
—— (1989) *Not Bosses But Leaders*, Guildford: Talbot Adair Press.
Adler, Nancy J. (1997) *International Dimensions of Organizational Behavior*, Cincinnati: South-Western Publishing, 3rd edn.
Adler, Paul S. (2003) 'Toward Collaborative Interdependence: A Century of Change in the Organization of Work', in Bruce E. Kaufman, Richard A. Beaumont and Roy B. Helfgott (eds), *Industrial Relations to Human Resources and Beyond: The Evolving Process of Employee Relations Management*, Armonk, NY: M.E. Sharpe.
'Ali ibn Abi Talib (1978) *Nahjul Balagha* (Peak of Eloquence), trans. S.A. Reza, Elmhurst, NY: Tahrike Tarsile Qu'ran.
'Ali, Abbas (1993) 'Decision Making Style and Work Satisfaction of Arab Gulf Executives', *International Studies of Management and Organization* 23 (3): 53–73.
Amadae, S.M. (2003) *Rationalizing Capitalist Democracy: The Cold War Origins of Rational Choice Liberalism*, Chicago: University of Chicago Press.
Ambler, Tim (2000) *Marketing and the Bottom Line: The New Metrics of Corporate Wealth*, London: FT-Prentice Hall.

Ambler, Tim, Witzel, Morgen and Xi, Chao (2009) *Doing Business in China*, London: Routledge, 3rd edn.

Ambrose, Stephen A. (1975) *Crazy Horse and Custer: The Parallel Lives of Two American Warriors*, New York: New American Library.

Andrews, Kenneth R. (1971) *The Concept of Corporate Strategy*, Homewood, IL: Irwin.

Ansoff, H. Igor (1965) *Corporate Strategy*, New York: McGraw-Hill.

—— (1988) *The New Corporate Strategy*, New York: John Wiley.

Appley, Lawrence (1974) *Formula for Success: A Core Concept of Management*, New York: Amacom.

Argyris, Chris (1957) *Personality and Organization*, New York: Harper & Row.

—— (1971) *Management and Organizational Development*, New York: McGraw-Hill.

Argyris, Chris and Schön, Donald (1978) *Organizational Learning*, Reading, MA: Addison-Wesley.

Arrian (1948) *The Campaigns of Alexander*, trans. Aubrey de Sélincourt, Harmondsworth: Penguin.

Arrow, Kenneth (1951) *Social Choice and Individual Values*, New York: John Wiley.

Arundhati, P. (1994) *Royal Life in Manasollasa*, New Delhi: Sundeep Publications.

Asimov, Isaac (1951) *Foundation*, New York: Doubleday.

Astley, W. Graham (1985) 'Administrative Science as Socially Constructed Truth', *Administrative Science Quarterly* 30: 497–513.

Atiya, Aziz S. (1962) *Crusade, Commerce and Culture*, Bloomington: Indiana University Press.

Aubet, Maria Eugenia (2001) *The Phoenicians and the West: Politics, Colonies and Trade*, trans. Mary Turton, Cambridge: Cambridge University Press, 2nd edn.

Augier, Mie and March, James G. (2011) *The Roots, Rituals and Rhetorics of Change: North American Business Schools after the Second World War*, Stanford: Stanford University Press.

Austin, James E. (1990) *Managing in Developing Countries: Strategic Analysis and Operating Techniques*, New York: The Free Press.

Babbage, Charles (1835) *The Economy of Machinery and Manufactures*, London: Charles Knight.

—— (1851) *The Exposition of 1851*, London: John Murray.

Bain, Joe S. (1968) *Industrial Organization*, New York: Wiley.

Baker, Michael (1992) *Marketing: An Introductory Text*, Basingstoke: Macmillan, 5th edn.

Barnard, Chester I. (1938) *The Functions of the Executive*, Cambridge, MA: Harvard University Press.

Bartell, Ernest and Payne, Leigh (eds) (1995) *Business and Democracy in Latin America*, Pittsburgh: University of Pittsburgh Press.

Barth, Carl (1926) 'The Barth Standard Wage Scale', *Manufacturing Industries*, 11 (5).

Bartlett, Christopher A. and Ghoshal, Sumantra (2002) *Managing Across Borders: The Transnational Solution*, Boston: Harvard Business School Press.

Barwise, Patrick (1993) 'Brand Equity: Snark or Boojum?', *International Journal of Research in Marketing* 10 (1): 93–104.

Barwise, Patrick and Meehan, Seán (2011) *Beyond the Familiar: Long-Term Growth Through Customer Focus and Innovation*, San Francisco: Jossey-Bass.

Baskin, Jonathan Barron and Miranti, Paul J. (1997) *A History of Corporate Finance*, Cambridge: Cambridge University Press.

Bat'a, Tomás (1992) *Knowledge in Action: The Bata System of Management*, Amsterdam: IOS Press.

Bateson, John E.G. (1999) *Managing Services Marketing*, New York: Thomson Learning.

Beasley, W.G. (1972) *The Meiji Restoration*, Stanford, CA: Stanford University Press.

—— (1995) *The Rise of Modern Japan: Political, Economic and Social Change Since 1850*, New York: St Martin's Press.

Beatty, Jack (1998) *The World According to Drucker*, London: Orion.

Becker, Tracy (1997) *Traditional American Indian Leadership: A Comparison with US Governance*, St Paul, MN: American Research and Policy Institute.

Bedaux, Charles (1918) *The Bedaux Efficiency Course for Industrial Application*, Cleveland, OH: Bedaux Industrial Institute.

Bedeian, Arthur G. and Philips, Carl R. (1990) 'Scientific Management and Stakhanovism in the Soviet Union: A Historical Perspective', *International Journal of Social Economics* 17 (10): 28–35.

Beer, Stafford (1959) *Cybernetics and Management*, Chichester: John Wiley.

—— (1966) *Decision and Control: The Managing of Operational Research and Management Cybernetics*, Chichester: John Wiley.

—— (1972) *Brain of the Firm*, London: Allen Lane

Beha ed-Din (1978) *What Befell Sultan Yusuf*, New York: AMS Press.

Benioff, Marc and Southwick, Karen (2004) *Compassionate Capitalism: How Corporations Can Make Doing Good an Integral Part of Doing Well*, Pompton Plains, NJ: Career Press.

Bennis, Warren G. (1989) *On Becoming a Leader*, Reading, MA: Addison-Wesley.

Bennis, Warren G. and Nanus, Bert (1985) *Leaders: Five Strategies for Taking Charge*, New York: Harper & Row.

Berdan, Frances F. and Anwalt, Patricia R. (1997) *The Essential Codex Mendoza*, Berkeley, CA: University of California Press.

Berle, Adolph A. and Means, Gardiner C. (1932) *The Modern Corporation and Private Property*, New York: Macmillan.

Berlin, Isaiah (1953) *The Fox and the Hedgehog: An Essay on Tolstoy's View of History*, London: Weidenfeld and Nicolson.

Bernays, Edward L. (1928) *Propaganda*, Port Washington, NY: Kennikat Press.

Berners-Lee, Tim and Fischetti, Mark (1999) *Weaving the Web*, New York: HarperCollins.

Bijapurkar, Rama (2007) *We Are Like that Only*, New Delhi: Penguin India.

Binfield, Kevin (2004) *Writings of the Luddites*, Baltimore: Johns Hopkins University Press.

Black Elk and Neihardt, John G. (1979) *Black Elk Speaks*, Lincoln: University of Nebraska Press.

Blackett, Patrick (1962) *Studies of War*, Edinburgh: Oliver & Boyd.

Bleecker, Samuel E. (1998) 'The Virtual Organization', repr. in Gill Robinson Hickman (ed.), *Leading Organizations: Perspectives for a New Era*, Newbury Park, CA: Sage.

Bliss, William D.P. (ed.) (1908) *The New Encyclopedia of Social Reform*, New York: Funk & Wagnalls; repr. Bristol: Thoemmes Press, 2002.

Bloomfield, Meyer (1916) 'The Aim and Work of Employment Managers' Associations', *Annals of the American Academy of Political and Social Science* 65: 76–87.

—— (1919) *Management and Men: A Record of New Steps in Industrial Relations*, New York: Century.

Blunt, Peter and Jones, Merrick (1992) *Managing Organizations in Africa*, Berlin: Walter de Gruyter.

Boisot, Max (1987) *Information and Organizations: The Manager as Anthropologist*, London: Fontana.

—— (1995) *Information Space: A Framework for Learning in Organizations, Institutions and Culture*, London: Routledge.

Bonaparte, Tony H. and Flaherty, John E. (eds) (1970) *Peter Drucker: Contributions to Business Enterprise*, New York: New York University Press.

Book of Dede Korkut (1964) trans. Geoffrey Lewis, London: Penguin.

Boris, Eileen (1986) *Art and Labor*, Philadelphia: Temple University Press.

Bornstein, David (2005) *The Price of a Dream: The Story of the Grameen Bank*, Oxford: Oxford University Press.

Bose, R.N. (1956) *Gandhian Technique and Tradition in Industrial Relations*, Calcutta: All-India Institute of Social Welfare and Business Management.

Bosworth, C.E. (1963) 'A Pioneer Arabic Encyclopedia of the Sciences: al-Khwarazmi's "Keys of the Sciences"', *Isis* 54: 97–111.

—— (1969) 'Abu 'Abdallah al-Khwarazmi on the Technical Terms of the Secretary's Art', *Journal of the Economic and Social History of the Orient* 12: 113–64.

—— (1982) *Medieval Arabic Culture and Administration*, London: Variorum.

Boulding, Kenneth (1956) *The Image*, Ann Arbor: University of Michigan Press.

Boulding, Kenneth, Boulding, Elise and Burgess, Guy M. (1977) *The Social System of the Planet Earth*, Reading, MA: Addison-Wesley.

Brandeis, Louis D. (1914) *Other People's Money and How the Bankers Use It*, New York: Stokes.

—— (1934) *The Curse of Bigness*, New York: Viking.

Braungart, Michael and McDonough, William (2009) *Cradle to Cradle: Remaking the Way We Make Things*, New York: Vintage.

Brech, E.F.L. (2002) *The Evolution of Modern Management*, Bristol: Thoemmes Press, 5 vols.

Brech, Edward, Thomson, Andrew and Wilson, John F. (2010) *Lyndall Urwick, Management Pioneer: A Biography*, Oxford: Oxford University Press.

Breckinridge, Sophonisba Preston and Abbott, Edith (1912) *The Delinquent Child and the Home*, New York: Charities Publication Committee.

Brewer, Anthony (1992) *Richard Cantillon: Pioneer of Economic Theory*, London: Routledge.

Brown, Arnold (1911) 'The Manufacturer as Advertiser', in T. Russell (ed.) *Harmsworth Business Library*, London: Educational Books Co., vol. 5.

Brown, Dee (1970) *Bury My Heart at Wounded Knee*, New York: Holt, Rinehart & Winston.

Bruce, Kyle (2006) 'Henry S. Dennison, Elton Mayo and Human Relations Historiography', *Management and Organizational History* 1 (2): 177–99.

Bryant, Miles T. (1996) 'Contrasting American and Native American View of Leadership', paper presented at the annual meeting of the University Council for Educational Administration, available as download from http://www.eric.ed.gov.

Buckley, Peter J. (ed.) (2003) *International Business*, Aldershot: Ashgate.

Buckley, Peter J. and Casson, Mark (1976) *The Future of the Multinational Enterprise,* London: Macmillan.

—— (2003) 'The Future of the Multinational Enterprise in Retrospect and in Prospect', *Journal of International Business Studies* 34: 219–22.

Buenstorf, Guido and Murmann, Johann Peter (2005) 'Ernst Abbé's Scientific Management: Theoretical Insights from a Nineteenth-Century Dynamic Capabilities Approach', *Industrial and Corporate Change* 14 (4): 543–78.

Burnham, James (1941) *The Managerial Revolution: Or, What Is Happening in the World Now*, London: Putnam

—— (1943) *The Machiavellians: Defenders of Freedom*, London: Putnam.

Burns, James MacGregor (1978) *Leadership*, New York: Harper & Row.

Burns, Tom (1963) 'Industry in a New Age', *New Society*, 31 January, 17–20; repr. in Derek S. Pugh (ed.), *Organization Theory: Selected Readings*, London: Penguin, 1997.

Burns, Tom and Stalker, George M. (1961) *The Management of Innovation*, London: Tavistock.

Burton, F.G. (1896) *The Naval Engineer and Command of the Sea: A Story of Naval Administration*, Manchester: The Technical Publishing Co. Ltd.

—— (1899) *The Commercial Management of Engineering Works*, Manchester: The Scientific Publishing Company; 2nd edn, 1905.

Butman, John (1997) *Juran: A Lifetime of Influence*, New York: John Wiley.

Cadbury, Deborah (2010) *Chocolate Wars: From Cadbury to Kraft, 200 Years of Sweet Success and Bitter Rivalry*, London: HarperPress.

Cadbury, Edward (1908) *Sweating*, London: Headley Brothers.

—— (1912) *Experiments in Industrial Organization*, London: Longmans, Green & Co.

—— (1914) 'Some Principles of Industrial Organisation; The Case For and Against Scientific Management', *Sociological Review* 7: 99–120.

Cadbury, Edward and Shann, George (1906) *Women's Work and Wages*, London: Headley Brothers.

Calás, Marta B. and Smircich, Linda (1991) 'Voicing Seduction to Silence Leadership', *Organization Studies* 12: 567–602; repr. in Calás and Smircich (eds), *Postmodern Management Theory*, Aldershot: Dartmouth, 1997.

Calhoun, Charles W. (ed.) (2006) *The Gilded Age: Perspectives on the Origins of Modern America*, Lanham, MD: Rowman & Littlefield.

Calori, Roland and De Woot, Philippe (1994) *A European Management Model: Beyond Diversity*, Hemel Hempstead: Prentice Hall.

Campbell, Bruce M.S. (2000) *English Seigniorial Agriculture 1250–1400*, Cambridge: Cambridge University Press.

Campbell, R.H. and Skinner, Andrew S. (1986) *Adam Smith*, London: Routledge.

Campion, Gabriel (1941) *Economie privée: organisation, financement et exploitation des entreprises* (Private Economy: Organization, Finance and Administration of Enterprises), Paris: Centre d'Information Interprofessionnel.

—— (1945–8) *Traité des entreprises privées* (Introduction to Private Enterprises), Paris: Press Universitaires de France, 2 vols.

Cannons, H.G.T. (1920) *Bibliography of Industrial Efficiency and Factory Management*, London: Routledge.

Cao Xueqin (n.d.) *A Dream of Red Mansions*, Beijing: Foreign Languages Press.

Carey, Henry C. (1853) *The Slave Trade, Domestic and Foreign: Why It Exists and How It May Be Distinguished*, repr. in David M. Levy and Sandra Peart (eds), *The Political Economy of Slavery*, Bristol: Thoemmes Press, 2004.

Carlyle, Thomas (1838) *Sartor Resartus*, repr. Oxford: Oxford University Press, 2000.

Carson, Rachel (1962) *Silent Spring*, Boston: Houghton-Mifflin.

Carus-Wilson, E.M. (1967) *Medieval Merchant Venturers*, London: Methuen.

Cary-Elwes, Charles (1988) *St Benedict and His Rule*, London: Catholic Truth Society.

Casson, Herbert N. (1907) *The Romance of Steel: The Story of a Thousand Millionaires*, New York: A.S. Barnes.

—— (1913) *Advertisements and Sales: A Study of Advertising and Selling from the Standpoint of the New Principles of Scientific Management*, London: Pitman.

—— (1917) *Lectures on Efficiency*, Manchester: Mather & Platt.

—— (1928) *Creative Thinkers: The Efficient Few Who Cause Progress and Prosperity*, London: Efficiency Magazine.

—— (1931) *The Story of My Life*, London: Efficiency Magazine.

—— (1935) *How to Get Things Done*, London: Efficiency Magazine.

Casson, Mark and Cox, Howard (1993) 'International Business Networks: Theory and History', *Business and Economic History* 22 (1): 42–53.

Castiglione, Baldesar (1959) *The Book of the Courtier*, trans. Charles S. Singleton, New York: Anchor.

Chaffey, Dave (2003) *E-Business and E-Commerce Management*, London: FT-Prentice Hall, 2nd edn.

Chan, Wing-tsit (1963) *A Source Book in Chinese Philosophy*, Princeton, NJ: Princeton University Press.

—— (1987) *Chu Hsi: Life and Thought*, Hong Kong: Hong Kong University Press.

Chandler, Alfred D. (1962) *Strategy and Structure: Chapters in the History of American Industrial Enterprise*, Cambridge, MA: MIT Press.

—— (1977) *The Visible Hand: The Managerial Revolution in American Business*, Cambridge, MA: Belknap Press.

—— (1990) *Scale and Scope: The Dynamics of Industrial Capitalism*, Cambridge, MA: Harvard University Press.

Chatfield, Michael (1977) *A History of Accounting Thought*, New York: Robert E. Krieger.

Chaudhuri, K.N. (1985) *Trade and Civilisation in the Indian Ocean: An Economic History from the Rise of Islam to 1750*, Cambridge: Cambridge University Press.

Checkland, Peter (1981) *Systems Thinking, Systems Practice*, Chichester: John Wiley.

Cheffins, Brian R. (2008) *Corporate Ownership and Control: British Business Transformed*, Oxford: Oxford University Press.

Chen Huan-Chang (1911) *The Economic Principles of Confucius and His School*, New York: Longmans, Green; repr. Bristol: Thoemmes Press, 2002, with an introduction by Morgen Witzel.

Chen, Min (1995) *Asian Management Systems*, London: Routledge.

Cheney, C.R. (1967) *Hubert Walter*, London: Thomas Nelson & Sons.

Cherington, Paul T. (1920) *The Elements of Marketing*, New York: Macmillan.

—— (1928) *The Consumer Looks at Advertising*, New York: Harper & Bros.

—— (1935) *People's Wants and How to Satisfy Them*, New York: Harper & Bros.

Child, John (1969) *British Management Thought*, London: George Allen & Unwin.

—— (1994) *Management in China in the Age of Reform*, Cambridge: Cambridge University Press.

—— (2005) *Cooperative Strategy: Managing Alliances, Networks and Joint Ventures*, Oxford: Oxford University Press.

—— (2012) 'Mary Parker Follett', in Morgen Witzel and Malcolm Warner (eds), *Oxford Handbook of Management Thinkers*, Oxford: Oxford University Press.

Child, Josiah (1694) *A Discourse of the Nature, Use and Advantages of Trade*.

Childers, Erskine (1903) *The Riddle of the Sands*, London: Smith, Elder.

Christensen, Clayton (1997)*The Innovator's Dilemma: When New Technologies Cause Great Firms to Fail*, Boston: Harvard Business School Press.

Chu, Chin (1916) *The Tariff Problem in China*, New York: Columbia University Press.

Chu, Chin-Ning (1995) *Thick Face, Black Heart: The Asian Path to Thriving, Winning and Succeeding*, London: Nicholas Brealey.

Church, Alexander Hamilton (1914) *The Science and Practice of Management*, New York: Engineering Magazine Co.

Churchman, C. West (1971) *The Design of Inquiring Systems: Basic Concepts of Systems and Organizations*, New York: Basic Books.

Churchman, C. West, Ackoff, Russell L. and Arnoff, Leonard (1957) *Introduction to Operations Research*, New York: John Wiley.

Çizakça, Murat (1996) *A Comparative Evolution of Business Partnerships: The Islamic World and Europe, with Specific Reference to the Ottoman Archives*, Leiden: Brill.

Clanchy, M.T. (1993) *From Memory to Written Record: England 1066–1307*, Oxford: Blackwell.

Clark, Fred E. (1921) 'Criteria of Marketing Efficiency', *American Economic Review* 11: 214–20.

—— (1924) *Principles of Marketing*, New York: Macmillan.

Clark, James B. (1921) 'More About Organization', *Industrial Management* 62: 228–31.

Clausewitz, Karl von (1819) *Vom Kriege*, ed. and trans. Michael Howard and Peter Paret, *On War*, Princeton: Princeton University Press, 1984.

Cleary, Thomas (trans.) (1992) *I Ching: The Book of Change*, Boston: Shambhala.

Clegg, Hugh (1960) *A New Approach to Industrial Democracy*, Oxford: Blackwell.

Coase, Ronald H. (1937) 'The Nature of the Firm', *Economica* 4: 386–405.

Cochran, Thomas C. and Reina, Reuben E. (1962) *Entrepreneurship in Argentine Culture: Torcuato di Tella and SIAM*, Philadelphia: University of Pennsylvania Press.

Coleridge, Samuel Taylor (1817) *A Lay Sermon*, London; repr. in John Morrow (ed.), *Coleridge's Writings*, vol. 1, *On Politics and Society*, Basingstoke, 1990, pp. 97–151.

Collins, John (1653) *An Introduction to Merchants Accounts, Containing Five Distinct Questions of Accounts*, London.

Comte, Auguste (1853) *The Positive Philosophy of Auguste Comte*, trans. Harriet Martineau, Cambridge: Cambridge University Press; repr. Cambridge: Cambridge University Press, 2009.

Conti, Robert (2012) 'Frederick Winslow Taylor', in Morgen Witzel and Malcolm Warner (eds), *Oxford Handbook of Management Thinkers*, Oxford: Oxford University Press.

Conway, Thomas (1914) *Investment and Speculation*, New York: Alexander Hamilton Institute.

Cooke, Morris L. (1918) *Our Cities Awake: Notes on Municipal Activities and Administration*, New York: Doubleday.

Copeland, Melvin T. (1917) *Business Statistics*, Cambridge, MA: Harvard University Press.

—— (1924) *Principles of Merchandising*, Chicago: A.W. Shaw.

—— (1958) *And Mark the Era: The Story of Harvard Business School*, Boston: Little, Brown.

Cottingham, John (1986) *Descartes*, Oxford: Blackwell.

Covey, Stephen R. (1989) *The Seven Habits of Highly Effective People*, New York: Simon & Schuster.

Cox, Taylor H. and Blake, Stacy (1991) 'Managing Cultural Diversity: Implications for Organizational Effectiveness', *The Executive* 5 (3): 45–56.

Crichton, Michael (1992) *Rising Sun*, New York: Knopf.

Croll, Elizabeth (2006) *China's New Consumers: Social Development and Domestic Demand*, London: Routledge.

Crowley, George R. and Sobel, Russell S. (2010) 'Adam Smith: Managerial Insights from the Father of Economics', *Journal of Management History* 16 (4): 504–8.

Crowther-Heyck, Hunter (2005) *Herbert A. Simon: The Bounds of Reason in America*, Baltimore: Johns Hopkins University Press.

—— (2006) 'Herbert Simon and the GSIA: Building an Interdisciplinary Community', *Journal of the History of the Behavioral Sciences*, 42 (4): 311–34.

Crozier, Michel (1963) *The Bureaucratic Phenomenon*, Chicago: University of Chicago Press.
—— (1965) *The World of the Office Worker*, Chicago: University of Chicago Press.
Cyert, Richard M. and March, James G. (1963) *A Behavioral Theory of the Firm*, New York: Prentice-Hall.
Dafforne, Richard (1636) *The Merchants Mirror, or Directions for the Perfect Ordering and Keeping of His Accounts*, London; repr. London: Scholar Press, 1978.
Daly, Herman and Cobb, John (1989) *For the Common Good: Redirecting the Economy Toward Community, the Environment and a Sustainable Future*, Boston: Beacon Press.
Danzin, André (2002) *Charles de Fréminville 1856–1936: pionnier de l'organisation scientifique du travail*, Paris: Aubin.
Dauten, Paul M., Gammill, Homer L. and Robinson, Stanley C. (1958) 'Our Concepts of Controlling Need Re-thinking', *Journal of the Academy of Management* 1 (3): 41–55.
Davenport, Thomas and Short, James (1990) 'The New Industrial Engineering: Information Technology and Business Process Redesign', *Sloan Management Review* Summer: 11–27.
Davis, John P. (1894) *The Union Pacific Railway: A Study of Political and Economic History*, Chicago: S. Griggs & Co.
—— (1905) *Corporations* (2 vols), New York: G.P. Putnam's Sons.
Davis, Keith (1957) *Human Relations in Business*, New York: McGraw-Hill.
Davis, Ralph C. (1958) 'A Philosophy of Management', *Journal of the Academy of Management* 1 (3): 37–40.
de Bary, William Theodore, Keene, Donald and Ryusaku Tsunoda (1958) *Sources of Japanese Tradition*, New York: Columbia University Press.
de Geus, Arie (1988) 'Planning as Learning', *Harvard Business Review* March–April: 70–4.
—— (1997) *The Living Company: Habits for Survival in a Turbulent Environment*, London: Nicholas Brealey.
De Kare-Silver, Michael (2000) *E-shock 2000*, London: Macmillan.
de Roover, Raymond (1955) 'Scholastic Economics: Survival and Lasting Influence from the Sixteenth Century to Adam Smith', *Quarterly Journal of Economics* 69 (2): 161–90; repr. in Mark Blaug (ed.), *St Thomas Aquinas*, Aldershot: Edward Elgar, 1991, 67–96.
—— (1958) 'The Concept of Just Price Theory and Economic Policy', *Journal of Economic History* 18: 418–34; repr. in Mark Blaug (ed.), *St Thomas Aquinas*, Aldershot: Edward Elgar, 1991, 97–113.
—— (1962) *The Rise and Decline of the Medici Bank*, Cambridge, MA: Harvard University Press.
—— (1967) *San Bernardino of Siena and Sant'Antonio of Florence: The Two Great Economic Thinkers of the Middle Ages*, Boston: Baker Library, Harvard Graduate School of Business Administration.
Dean, Joel (1940) *The Management Counsel Profession*, Bloomington: Indiana University.
Deming, W. Edwards (1986) *Out of the Crisis*, Cambridge, MA: MIT Center for Advanced Engineering Study.
—— (1993) *The New Economics for Industry, Government, Education*, Cambridge, MA: MIT Center for Advanced Engineering Study.
Dempsey, B.W. (1935) 'Just Price in a Functional Economy', *American Economic Review* 25: 471–86; repr. in Mark Blaug (ed.), *St Thomas Aquinas*, Aldershot: Edward Elgar, 1991, 1–16.
Den Uyl, Douglas and Rasmussen, Douglas B. (1984) *The Philosophic Thought of Ayn Rand*, Chicago: University of Chicago Press.
Dennison, Henry S. (1920) 'Production and Profits', *Annals of the American Academy of Political and Social Science* 66: 159–61.
—— (1931) *Organization Engineering*, New York: McGraw-Hill.
Dennison, Henry S. and Galbraith, John Kenneth (1938) *Modern Competition and Business Policy*, New York: Oxford University Press.
DePree, Max (1987) *Leadership Is An Art*, New York: Doubleday.
Devinat, Paul (1927) *Scientific Management in Europe*, Geneva: International Labour Office.
Dewing, Arthur S. (1923) *Corporation Finance*, New York: The Ronald Press.
Dia, Mamadou (1996) *Africa's Management in the 1990s and Beyond: Reconciling Indigenous and Transplanted Institutions*, Washington DC: The World Bank.

Dicksee, Lawrence R. (1910) *Business Organisation*, London: Longmans, Green & Co.

—— (1922) *The True Basis of Efficiency*, London: Gee & Co.

Diemer, Hugo (1914) *Factory Organization and Administration*, New York: McGraw-Hill.

Dimand, Robert W. (2007) 'Irving Fisher and His Students as Financial Economists', in Geoffrey Poitras (ed.), *Pioneers of Financial Economics*, vol. 2, Cheltenham: Edward Elgar.

al-Dimashqi, Abu al-Fadl (1995) *Al-ishara ila mahasin al-tijjarah* (Reference to the Virtues of Commerce), trans. Youssef Seddik, *Eloge du Commerce*, Tunis: MC Editions.

Dimock, Marshall E. (1945) *The Executive in Action*, New York: Harper & Bros.

Dixon, Norman (1976) *On the Psychology of Military Incompetence*, London: Pimlico.

Djelic, Marie-Laure (1998) *Exporting the American Model: The Postwar Transformation of European Business*, Oxford: Oxford University Press.

Donnachie, Ian (2000) *Robert Owen*, East Linton: Tuckwell Press.

Doz, Yves L. and Hamel, Gary (1998) *Alliance Advantage: The Art of Creating Value Through Partnering*, Boston: Harvard Business School Press.

Drucker, Peter F. (1942) *The Future of Industrial Man*, New York: John Day.

—— (1946) *The Concept of the Corporation*, New York: John Day.

—— (1954) *The Practice of Management*, New York: Harper & Row.

—— (1964) *Managing for Results: Economic Tasks and Risk-Taking Decisions*, New York: Harper & Row.

—— (1967) *The Effective Executive*, New York: Harper & Row.

—— (1974) *Management: Tasks, Responsibilities, Practices*, New York: Harper & Row.

—— (1989) *The New Realities*, New York: Harper & Row.

Drury, Horace B. (1915) *Scientific Management: A History and Criticism*, New York: Columbia University Press.

Dubs, Homer H. (1927) *Hsüntze: The Moulder of Ancient Confucianism*, London: Arthur Probsthain.

Duhamel, Georges (1930) *Scènes de la vie future* (Pictures of Life in the Future), Paris: Éditions Mercure.

Dunning, John (1957) *American Investment in British Manufacturing Industry*, London: George Allen & Unwin.

—— (1980) 'Toward an Eclectic Theory of International Production: Some Empirical Tests', *Journal of International Business*, 11 (1): 9–31.

—— (1988) 'The Eclectic Paradigm of International Production: A Restatement and Some Possible Extensions', *Journal of International Business* 19 (1): 1–31.

Durkheim, Émile (1933) *De la division du travail social*, trans. George Simpson, *The Division of Labor in Society*, New York: Macmillan.

Dutton, Henry Post (1931) *Principle of Organization*, New York: McGraw-Hill.

Edmunds, Russell D. (1984) *Tecumseh and the Quest for Indian Leadership*, Boston: Little, Brown.

Eilon, Samuel (1979) *Aspects of Management*, Oxford: Pergamon.

—— (1996) 'Management Science', in Malcolm Warner (ed.), *International Encyclopedia of Business and Management*, vol. 3, London: Routledge.

Elkington, John (1997) *Cannibals With Forks: The Triple Bottom Line of 21st Century Business*, Oxford: Capstone.

Ellinger, Barnard (1934) *Credit and International Trade: How They Work in Practice*, London: Macmillan.

Ellwood, Charles A. (1919) 'The Instincts in Social Psychology', *Psychological Bulletin* 16 (3): 71–5.

Elton, Edwin J. and Gruber, Martin J. (1997) 'Modern Portfolio Theory, 1950 to Date', New York University Stern School of Business Department of Finance working paper.

Ely, Richard T. (1900) *Monopolies and Trusts*, New York: Macmillan.

Emerson, Harrington (1909) *Efficiency as a Basis for Operations and Wages*, New York: John R. Dunlap.

—— (1913) *The Twelve Principles of Efficiency*, New York: The Engineering Magazine Co.

Epic of Gilgamesh, trans. N.K. Sandars (1960), Harmondsworth: Penguin.

Epstein, S.R. (2008) 'Craft Guilds in the Pre-Modern Economy: A Discussion', *Economic History Review* 61 (1): 155–74.

Epstein, S.R. and Prak, Maarten (eds) (2008) *Guilds, Innovation and the European Economy, 1400–1800*, Cambridge: Cambridge University Press.

Erdman, David V. (1991) *Blake, Prophet Against Empire: A Poet's Interpretation of His Own Times*, Princeton: Princeton University Press.

Etzioni, Amitai (1968) *The Active Society: A Theory of Moral and Political Processes*, New York: The Free Press.

Evans, G.R. (2000) *Bernard of Clairvaux*, Oxford: Oxford University Press.

Farber, Liana (2006) *An Anatomy of Trade in Medieval Writing: Value, Consent and Community*, Ithaca, NY: Cornell University Press.

Fashoyin, Tayo (ed.) (1992) *Industrial Relations and African Development*, New Delhi: Asia Publishers.

Fayerweather, John (1960) *Management of International Operations*, New York: McGraw-Hill.

Fayol, Henri (1916) *Administration industrielle et générale*, trans. Irwin Gray, New York: David S. Lake, 1984.

Feigenbaum, Armand V. (1945) *Quality Control: Principles, Practices and Administration*, New York: McGraw-Hill.

—— (1961) *Total Quality Control*, New York: McGraw-Hill.

Feiss, Richard A. (1916) 'Personal Relationship as a Basis of Scientific Management', *Annals of the American Academy of Political and Social Science* 65: 27–56.

Ferguson, Michael (2002) *The Rise of Management Consulting in Britain*, Aldershot: Ashgate.

Ferraz, João Carlos, Rush, Howard and Miles, Ian (1992) *Development, Technology and Flexibility: Brazil Faces the Industrial Divide*, London: Routledge.

Fiedler, Fred E. (1967) *A Theory of Leadership Effectiveness*, New York: McGraw-Hill.

Filene, Edward (1925) *More Profits from Merchandizing*, Chicago: A.W. Shaw.

—— (1932) *Successful Living in This Machine Age*, London: Jonathan Cape.

Fisher, Ronald (1925) *Statistical Methods for Research Workers*, Edinburgh: Oliver & Boyd.

Fitton, Richard S. (1989) *The Arkwrights: Spinners of Fortune*, Manchester: Manchester University Press.

Fitz Neal, Richard (1950) *Dialogus de Scaccario*, trans. Charles Johnson, Oxford: Blackwell; a translation can also be found in Ernest Henderson, *Select Historical Documents from the Middle Ages*, London: George Bell & Sons, 1896, or online at http://avalon.law.yale.edu/medieval/excheq.asp.

Fitzgerald, Robert (1995) *Rowntree and the Marketing Revolution 1862–1969*, Cambridge: Cambridge University Press.

Flanders, Allan (1952) *Trade Unions*, London: Hutchinson.

Fletcher, Richard (1997) *The Conversion of Europe: From Paganism to Christianity, 371–1386 AD*, London: HarperCollins.

Flint, Charles R., Hill, James J., Bridge, James H., Dodd, Samuel C.T. and Thurber, Francis B. (1902) *The Trust: Its Book*, New York: Doubleday, Page & Co.

Flood, Robert L. (1993) *Beyond TQM*, New York: John Wiley.

Florence, Philip Sargant (1933) *The Logic of Industrial Organization*, London: Kegan, Paul, Trench, Trubner.

—— (1948) *Investment, Location and Size of Plant*, Cambridge: Cambridge University Press.

—— (1949) *Labour*, London: Hutchinson.

Fohlin, Caroline (2005) *The History of Corporate Ownership and Control in Germany*, Cambridge, MA: National Bureau of Economic Research.

Follett, Mary Parker (1918) *The New State: Group Organization, the Solution of Popular Government*, New York: Longmans, Green.

—— (1924) *Creative Experience*, New York: Longmans, Green.

—— (1937) 'The Process of Control', in Luther H. Gulick and Lyndall Urwick (eds), *Papers on the Science of Administration*, New York: Institute for Public Administration.

Forrester, David A.R. (2000) 'Wilhelm Rieger and Cash Accounting: An Essay in Controversial Ideas', *Abacus* 36 (1): 108–21.

Forrester, Jay Wright (1961) *Industrial Dynamics*, Portland, OR: Productivity Press.

Foucault, Michel (1977) *Discipline and Punish: Birth of the Prison*, trans. Alan Sheridan, London: Allen Lane.

Fowler, W.W. (1880) *Twenty Years of Inside Life in Wall Street, or Revelations of the Personal Experience of a Speculator*, New York: Orange Judd; repr. Bristol: Thoemmes Press, 2001, with an introduction by Morgen Witzel.

Fréminville, Charles de la Poix de (1918) *Quelques aperçus sur le système Taylor* (Fundamental Principles of the Taylor Method), Paris: A. Maréchal.

Frontinus, Sextus Julius (1925) *Stratagemata*, trans Charles E. Bennett, New York: Loeb.

Fruin, W. Mark (1992) *The Japanese Enterprise System*, Oxford: Clarendon.

Fuchida Mitsuo and Okumiya Masatake (1955) *Midway: The Battle that Doomed Japan*, Washington DC: Naval Institute Press.

The Fugger News-Letters (1924), ed. Victor von Klarwill, trans. Pauline de Chary, with a foreword by H. Gordon Selfridge, London: John Lane.

Fukuyama, Francis (1992) *The End of History and the Last Man*, New York: The Free Press.

Fukuzawa, Yukichi (1876) *The Encouragement of Learning*, trans. David A. Dilworth and Umeyo Hirano, Tokyo: Sophia University, 1969.

Furness, Christopher (1902) *The American Invasion*, London: Simpkin, Marshall, Hamilton, Kent & Co.

—— (1908) *Industrial Peace and Industrial Efficiency*, West Hartlepool: Alexander Salton.

Furnham, Adrian (2004) *Management and Myths: Challenging Business Fads, Fallacies and Fashions*, Basingstoke: Palgrave Macmillan.

Gabor, Andrea (1990) *The Man Who Discovered Quality*, New York: Times Books.

Gabor, Andrea and Mahoney, Joseph T. (2012) 'Chester Barnard', in Morgen Witzel and Malcolm Warner (eds), *Oxford Handbook of Management Thinkers*, Oxford: Oxford University Press.

Galbraith, Jay R. (2008) *Designing Matrix Organizations that Actually Work: How IBM, Procter & Gamble and Others Design for Success*, San Francisco: Jossey Bass.

Galbraith, Jay R. and Nathanson, Daniel A. (1978) *Strategy Implementation: The Role of Structure and Process*, St Paul, MN: West Publishing.

Galbraith, John Kenneth and Black, John (1935) 'The Quantitative Position of Marketing in the United States', *Quarterly Journal of Economics* 49: 394–413.

Galbraith, John Kenneth (1981) *A Life in Our Time: Memoirs*, Boston: Houghton-Mifflin.

Galston, Michael (1990) *Politics and Excellence: The Political Philosophy of Alfarabi*, Princeton: Princeton University Press.

Gantt, Henry L. (1913) *Work, Wages and Profits*, New York: The Engineering Magazine, 2nd edn.

Geddes, Patrick (1915) *Cities in Evolution: An Introduction to the Town Planning Movement and to the Study of Civics*, London: Williams.

Geneen, Harold (1997) *The Synergy Myth, and Other Ailments of Business Today*, New York: St Martin's Press.

George, Claude S. (1972) *The History of Management Thought*, Englewood Cliffs, NJ: Prentice-Hall, 2nd edn.

Gerstenberg, Charles (1924) *Financial Organization and the Management of Business*, New York: Prentice-Hall.

Ghosh, J.K. (1994) 'Malahanobis and the Art and Science of Statistics: The Early Days', *Indian Journal of the History of Science* 29 (1): 89–98.

Gibbs, Richard and Humphries, Andrew (2009) *Strategic Alliances and Marketing Partnerships*, London: Kogan Page.

Gilbreth, Frank B. (1911) *Motion Study: A Method for Increasing the Efficiency of the Workman*, New York: Van Nostrand.

—— (1912) *Primer of Scientific Management*, New York: Van Nostrand.

Gilbreth, Frank B. and Gilbreth, Lillian E. (1916) *Fatigue Study*, New York: Sturgis & Walton.

—— (1916) 'The Three Position Plan of Promotion', *Annals of the American Academy of Political and Social Science* 65; repr. in *Applied Motion Study*, London: George Routledge & Sons, 1918.

Gilbreth, Lillian E. (1914) *The Psychology of Management*, London: Sir Isaac Pitman.

—— (1924) *The Quest of the One Best Way: A Sketch of the Life of Frank Bunker Gilbreth*, Chicago: Society of Industrial Engineers.

Gilson, Mary B. (1916) 'The Relation of Home Conditions to Industrial Efficiency', *Annals of the American Academy of Political and Social Science* 65: 277–89.

——*What's Past Is Prologue*, New York: Harper & Bros.

Gimpel, Jean (1976) *The Medieval Machine: The Industrial Revolution in the Middle Ages*, London: Penguin.

Gioia, Melchiorre (2010) *Nuovo Prospetto delle scienze economiche*, Charleston, SC: Nabu Press.

Goffee, Rob and Jones, Gareth (2006) *Why Should Anyone Be Led by You?* Boston: HBS Press.

Goleman, Daniel (2006) *Social Intelligence*, New York: Bantam.

Gordon, Andrew (1989) 'Araki Toichiro and the Shaping of Labour Management', in Tsunehiko Yui and Keiichiro Nakagawa, *Japanese Management in Historical Perspective*, Tokyo: University of Tokyo Press.

Gordon, Robert and Howell, James (1959) *Higher Education for Business*, New York: Columbia University Press.

Gosling, Jonathan, Case, Peter and Witzel, Morgen (eds) (2007) *John Adair: Fundamentals of Leadership*, Basingstoke: Palgrave Macmillan.

Gould, Rowland (1970) *The Matsushita Phenomenon*, Tokyo: Diamond Sha.

Graham, Pauline (1995) *Mary Parker Follett: Prophet of Management*, Boston: Harvard Business School Press.

Grant, Robert M. (1991) 'The Resource-Based Theory of Competitive Advantage: Implications for Strategy Formulation', *California Management Review* 33 (3): 114–35.

Gratton, Lynda (2009) *Glow: How You Can Radiate Energy, Innovation and Success*, London: Financial Times-Prentice Hall.

Graunt, John (1939) *Natural and Political Observations made upon the Bills of Mortality*, ed. W.F. Wilcox, Baltimore: Johns Hopkins University Press.

Great Plan, Chinese text and English translation, http://ctext.org/shang-shu/great-plan.

Greene, Thomas L. (1897) *Corporation Finance*, New York: G.P. Putnam's Sons.

Greenleaf, Robert K. (1977) *Servant Leadership*, Mahwah, NJ: Paulist Press.

Greenwood, Ronald G. and Ross, Robert H. (1982) 'Early American Influence on Japanese Management Philosophy: The Scientific Management Movement in Japan', in Sang M. Lee and Gary Schwendiman, *Management by Japanese Systems*, New York: Praeger.

Greenwood, Ronald G., Bolton, Alfred A. and Greenwood, Regina A. (1983) 'Hawthorne: A Half Century Later', *Journal of Management History* 9 (2): 217–31.

Grimmer-Solem, Erik (2003) *The Rise of Historical Economics and Social Reform in Germany*, Oxford: Oxford University Press.

Grove, Andrew (1983) *High Output Management*, New York: Random House.

—— (1996) *Only the Paranoid Survive: How to Exploit the Crisis Points that Challenge Every Company and Career*, New York: HarperCollins.

Grube, G.M.A. (1980) *Plato's Thought*, London: Athlone.

Grunebaum, Gustave E. von (1953) *Medieval Islam: A Study in Cultural Orientation*, Chicago: University of Chicago Press.

Guggenheim, Daniel (1915) 'Some Thoughts on Industrial Unrest', *Annals of the American Academy of Political and Social Science* 59: 209–11.

Guicciardini, Francesco (1969) *The History of Italy*, trans. Sidney Alexander, London: Collier Macmillan.

Guillén, Mauro (2006) *The Taylorized Beauty of the Mechanical: Scientific Management and the Rise of Modern Architecture*, Princeton: Princeton University Press.

Guilmartin, John (1976) *Gunpowder and Galleys*, Cambridge: Cambridge University Press.

Gulick, Luther H. (1937) 'Notes on the Theory of Organization', in Luther H. Gulick and Lyndall Urwick (eds), *Papers on the Science of Administration*, New York: Institute for Public Administration.

—— (1948) *Administrative Reflections from World War II*, University, AL: University of Alabama Press.

Gulick, Luther H. and Urwick, Lyndall (1937) *Papers on the Science of Administration*, New York: Institute for Public Administration.

Gurkan, Leyla (2007) 'Bostanzade, Yahya Efendi', in Oliver Leaman (ed.), *Biographical Dictionary of Islamic Philosophers*, London: Continuum.

Gutenberg, Erich (1958) *Einführung in die Betriebswirtschaftslehre* (Introduction to the Science of Business Administration), Wiesbaden: Gabler.

Guthrie, W.K.C. (1962–78) *A History of Greek Philosophy*, Cambridge: Cambridge University Press, 6 vols.

Habib, Irfan (1969) 'Potentialities of Capitalistic Development in the Economy of Mughal India', *Journal of Economic History* 29 (1): 32–78.

Hakeda Yoshito (1967), *The Awakening of Faith*, New York: Columbia University Press (translation of the *Dasheng qixunlun* [Awakening of Faith in Mahayana]).

Hall, David L. and Ames, Roger T. (1987) *Thinking Through Confucius*, Albany, NY: State University of New York Press.

Halsey, Frederick A. (1905) 'The Premium Plan of Paying for Labour', in John R. Commons (ed.), *Trade Unionism and Labour Problems*, Boston: Ginn & Co.

—— (1914) *Methods of Machine Shop Work*, New York: McGraw-Hill.

Hamel, Gary and Prahalad, C.K. (1994) *Competing For the Future*, Boston: Harvard Business School Press.

Hamilton, Gary G. and Lai Chi-kong (1989), 'Consumption and Brand Names in Late Imperial China', in Henry J. Rutz and Benjamin S. Orlove (eds), *The Social Economy of Consumption*, Lanham, MD: University Press of America, pp. 253–79; repr. in R. Ampalavanar Brown, *Chinese Business Enterprise*, London: Routledge, 1996, vol. 3.

Hammer, Michael and Champy, James (1993) *Reengineering the Corporation: A Manifesto for Business Revolution*, London: Nicholas Brealey.

Hammond, Bray (1957) *Banks and Politics in America from the Revolution to the Civil War*, Princeton: Princeton University Press.

Hampden-Turner, Charles and Trompenaars, Fons (1993) *The Seven Cultures of Capitalism*, London: Piatkus.

Hampson, Norman (1968) *Enlightenment*, London: Penguin.

Handel, Michael (2000) *Masters of War: Sun Tzu, Clausewitz and Jomini*, London: Routledge.

Handy, Charles (1976) *Understanding Organisations*, London: Penguin.

—— (1989) *The Age of Unreason*, London: Business Books.

—— (1994) *The Empty Raincoat*, London: Hutchinson.

Hannan, Michael T. and Freeman, John (1989) *Organizational Ecology*, Cambridge, MA: Harvard University Press.

Harmsworth's Business Encyclopedia (1925), London, 5 vols.

Harris, Frank R. (1925) *J.N. Tata: A Chronicle of His Life*, repr. New Delhi: Oxford University Press, 1958.

Hart, Stuart L. (2005) *Capitalism at the Crossroads*, Englewood Cliffs, NJ: Wharton School Publishing.

Hart, Stuart L. and Milstein, Mark B. (2003) 'Creating Sustainable Value', *Academy of Management Executive* 17 (2) 56–69.

Harvard Business Review on Strategic Alliances (2003), Boston: Harvard Business School Press.

Harvey, Charles and Press, Jon (1991) *William Morris: Design and Enterprise in Victorian Britain*, Manchester: Manchester University Press.

Harvey, Paul (1998) *The Chiapas Rebellion: The Struggle for Land and Democracy*, Durham, NC: Duke University Press.

Haskins, Charles Homer (1927), *The Renaissance of the Twelfth Century*, repr. Cambridge, MA: Harvard University Press, 1971.

Hatch, Mary Jo and Schultz, Majken (2008) *Taking Brand Initiative: How Companies Can Align Strategy, Culture and Identity Through Corporate Branding*, Chichester: John Wiley.

Hathaway, Horace K. (1911), 'Prerequisites to the Introduction of Scientific Management', *Engineering Magazine* 41; repr. in C. Bertrand Thompson (ed.), *Scientific Management*, Cambridge, MA: Harvard University Press.

Hawawini, Gabriel and Vora, Ashok (2007) 'A Brief History of Yield Approximations', in Geoffrey Poitras (ed.) *Pioneers of Financial Economics*, vol. 2, Cheltenham: Edward Elgar.

Hawken, Paul (1994) *The Ecology of Commerce: A Declaration of Sustainability*, New York: Harper Business.

Hawken, Paul, Lovins, Amory and Lovins, E. Hunter (1999) *Natural Capitalism*, Boston: Little, Brown.

Heck, Gene W. (2004) *Islam Inc.: An Early Business History*, Riyadh: King Faisal Center for Research and Islamic Studies.

Hee, Charles Chow Hoi and Gurd, Bruce (2010) 'Leadership Essentials from Sun Zi's Art of War and the Bhagavad Gita', *Journal of Management History* 16 (3): 396–414.

Heinen, Edmund (1959) *Betriebswirtschaftliche Kostenlehre* (Cost Theory of Business Administration), Wiesbaden: Gabler.

—— (1968) *Einführung in die Betriebswirtschaftslehre* (Introduction to Business Administration), Wiesbaden: Gabler.

Hemmings, John (1983) *The Conquest of the Incas*, London: Penguin.

Henderson, Bruce D. (1979) *Henderson on Corporate Strategy*, New York: HarperCollins.

Hershatter, Gail (1983) 'Flying Hammers, Walking Chisels: The Workers of Santiaoshi', *Modern China* 9 (4): 387–419; repr. in R. Ampalavanar Brown (ed.) *Chinese Business Enterprise: Critical Perspectives on Business and Management*, vol. 3, London: Routledge, 1996.

Herzberg, Frederick (1966) *Work and the Nature of Man*, Cleveland: World Publishing Company.

Heuss, Theodor (1987) *Robert Bosch*, Stuttgart: Deutsche Verlanganstalt.

Hill, Octavia (1884) *Colour, Space and Music for the People*, London: Kegan Paul, Trench, Trubner.

Hobson, J.A. (1913) 'Scientific Management', *Sociological Review* 13: 99.

Hodgett, Gerald A.J. (1972) *A Social and Economic History of Medieval Europe*, London: Methuen.

Hodgson, Geoffrey M. (2001) *How Economics Forgot History: The Problem of Historical Specificity in Social Science*, London: Routledge.

Hodgson, Geoffrey M. and Knudsen, Thorbjørn (2010) *Darwin's Conjecture: The Search for General Principles of Social and Scientific Evolution*, Chicago: University of Chicago Press.

Hodgson, Marshall G.S. (1977) *The Ventures of Islam*, 3 vols, Chicago: University of Chicago Press.

Hodgson, Phil (2007) 'In Search of European Leadership', *European Business Forum* 30.

Hoekman, Bernard M. and Mavroidis, Petros C. (2007) *The World Trade Organization: Law, Economics, and Politics*, London: Routledge.

Hofstede, Geert (1980) *Culture's Consequences: International Differences in Work-Related Values*, Beverly Hills, CA: Sage.

—— (1991) *Cultures and Organizations: Software of the Mind*, London: McGraw-Hill.

Hofstede, Geert and Bond, Michael Harris (1988) 'The Confucius Connection: From Cultural Roots to Economic Growth', *Organizational Dynamics* 16 (4): 4–21.

Hogan, Michael J. (1989)*The Marshall Plan: America, Britain and the Reconstruction of Western Europe, 1947–1952*, Cambridge: Cambridge University Press.

Holt, Jeremy (1996) *Reinventing the CFO*, Boston: Harvard Business School Press.

Homer, *The Iliad*, trans. Herbert Jordan (2008), Norman, OK: University of Oklahoma Press.

——*The Odyssey*, trans. Robert Fitzgerald (1998), New York: Farrar, Strauss and Giroux.

Hopkins, George B. (1912) 'The New York Bureau of Municipal Research', *Annals of the American Academy of Political and Social Science* 41: 235–9.

Hoshi, Takeo and Kashyap, Anil (2001) *Corporate Financing and Governance in Japan: The Road to the Future*, Cambridge, MA: MIT Press.

Houghton, Jeffery D. (2010) 'Does Max Weber's Notion of Authority Still Hold in the Twenty-First Century?' *Journal of Management History* 16 (4): 449–53.

Hourani, Albert (1970) *Arabic Thought in the Liberal Age*, Oxford: Oxford University Press.

—— (1991) *A History of the Arab Peoples*, London: Faber & Faber.

House, Robert J., Hanges, Paul J., Javidan, Mansour, Dorfman, Peter W. and Gupta, Vipin (eds) (2004), *Culture, Leadership and Organizations: the GLOBE Study of 62 Societies*, Newbury Park, CA: Sage.

Houtsma, M.T. *et al.* (eds) (1913) *Encyclopedia of Islam*, Leiden: Brill.

Howard, Sir Ebenezer (1902) *Garden Cities of To-morrow*, London: Swan Sonnenschein.

Hoxie, Robert F. (1915) *Scientific Management and Labor*, New York: D. Appleton & Co.

Hoyt, Charles W. (1913) *Scientific Sales Management Today*; repr. New York: The Ronald Press, 1929.

Hoyt, Edwin P. (1967) *The Guggenheims and the American Dream*, New York: Funk & Wagnalls.

Hsu, Mu-Lan and Chiu, Kwan-Yao (2008) 'A Comparison between I-Ching's Early Management Decision Making Model and Western Management Decision Making Models', *Chinese Management Studies* 2 (1): 52–75.

Hucker, Charles O. (1978) *China to 1850*, Stanford, CA: Stanford University Press.

Hudson, G.F. (1931) *Europe and China*, London: Edward Arnold.

Hughes, Agatha C. and Hughes, Thomas P. (eds) (2000) *Systems, Experts, and Computers: The Systems Approach in Management and Engineering, World War II and After*, Cambridge, MA: MIT Press.

Hughes, Richard (1972) *Foreign Devil*, London: Century.

Hughes, Richard L., Ginnett, Robert C. and Curphy, Gordon J. (1996) *Leadership: Enhancing the Lessons of Experience*, Homewood, IL: Irwin.

Human, Piet and Horwitz, Frank M. (1992) *On the Edge: How South African Companies Cope with Change*, Kenwyn: Juta.

Hume, David (1978) *Enquiry Concerning Human Understanding*, L.A. Selby-Bigge and P.H. Nidditch (eds) in *Enquiries Concerning Human Understanding and Concerning the Principles of Morals*, Oxford: Clarendon.

Humphreys, George G. (1986) *Taylorism in France 1904–1920: The Impact of Scientific Management on Factory Relations and Society*, New York: Garland.

Huntington, Samuel P. (1996) *The Clash of Civilizations and the Remaking of the World Order*, New York: Simon & Schuster.

Hutchins, J.G.B. (1958) 'Business History, Entrepreneurial History and Business Administration' *Journal of Economic History* 18 (4): 453–71.

Huxley, Aldous (1932) *Brave New World*, repr. London: HarperCollins, 1999.

Huxley, Julian (1944) *On Living in a Revolution*, London: Chatto & Windus.

Hwa, Lily (2008) 'State Building in the Government of Tang Taizhong', *Forum on Public Policy*.

Hyman, Anthony (1985) *Charles Babbage: Pioneer of the Computer*, Oxford: Oxford University Press.

Ibn Khaldun (1986) *The Muqaddimah*, trans. Franz Rosenthal, London: Routledge, 3 vols.

Imber, Colin (2002) *The Ottoman Empire 1300–1650: The Structure of Power*, Basingstoke: Palgrave Macmillan.

Inalcik, Halil (1994) *An Economic and Social History of the Ottoman Empire*, vol. 1, *1300–1600*, Cambridge: Cambridge University Press.

International Bank for Reconstruction and Development (1993) *Indigenous Management Practices: Lessons for Africa's Management from the '90s*, Washington, DC: IBRD.

Ishikawa Kaoru (1985) *What Is Total Quality Control? The Japanese Way*, Englewood Cliffs, NJ: Prentice Hall.

Iyer, Raghavan N. (1973) *The Political and Moral Thought of Mahatma Gandhi*, Oxford: Oxford University Press.

Jaeger, Alfred M. and Kanungo, Rabindra N. (eds) (1990) *Management in Developing Countries*, London: Routledge.

Jabotinsky, Vladimir (1945) *Prelude to Delilah*, New York: Bernard Ackerman.

Jackman, W. J. (1910) *Corporations: Organizing, Finance and Management*, Minneapolis: International Law and Business Institute.

James William (1890) *The Principles of Psychology*, Cambridge, MA: Harvard University Press.

Jaques, Elliott (1951) *The Changing Culture of a Factory*, London: Tavistock Publications.

—— (1976) *A General Theory of Bureaucracy*, London: Heinemann.

—— (1982) *The Form of Time*, London: Heinemann.

—— (1988) *Requisite Organization*; repr. London: Gower, 1997

Jay, Anthony (1967) *Management and Machiavelli*, London: Hodder & Stoughton.

Jefferson, Thomas (1984) *Writings*, ed. Merrill D. Peterson, New York: Library of America.

Jenks, Jeremiah W. (1900) *The Trust Problem*, New York: McClure, Philips & Co.

John of Salisbury (1927) *Policraticus*, trans. J. Dickinson as *Policraticus: The Statesman's Book*, New York: Knopf.

Johnson, E.A.J. (1939) *Predecessors of Adam Smith*, repr. New York: Augustus M. Kelley, 1980.

Jomini, Antoine-Henri (1805) *Traité des grandes opérations militaires, contenant l'histoire des campagnes de Frédéric II*, 5 vols, Paris; trans. S.B. Holabird, *Treatise on Grand Military Operations*, New York: Van Nostrand, 1865.

Jones, Edward D. (1912) 'Military History and the Science of Business Administration', *Engineering Magazine* 44: 1–6, 185–90, 321–6.

Jones, Geoffrey (1996) *The Evolution of International Business*, London: Routledge.

Jones, Geoffrey and Khanna, Tarun (2004) 'Bringing History Into International Business', Harvard Business School working paper.

Jones, Geoffrey and Lefort, Alexis (2005) 'McKinsey and the Globalization of Consultancy', Harvard Business School case study.

Jones, Steve (ed.) (1999) *Doing Internet Research: Critical Issues and Methods for Examining the Net*, Thousand Oaks, CA: Sage.

Juran, Joseph M. (1988) *Quality Control Handbook*, 4th edn, New York: McGraw-Hill.

—— (1989) *Juran on Leadership for Quality: An Executive Handbook*, New York: The Free Press.

Kahn, Charles H. (1979) *The Art and Thought of Heraclitus*, Cambridge: Cambridge University Press.

Kahn, E.J. (1986) *The Problem Solvers: A History of Arthur D. Little*, Boston: Little, Brown.

Kai Kaus ibn Iskandar (1951) *A Mirror for Princes*, trans. Reuben Levy, London: The Cresset Press.

Kalakota, Ravi and Whinston, Andrew (1997) *Electronic Commerce: A Manager's Guide*, Reading, MA: Addison-Wesley.

Kamandakiya Nitisara; or, The Elements of Polity, in English (1896), Calcutta: M.N. Dutt.

Kanigel, Robert (1997) *The One Best Way: Frederick Taylor and the Enigma of Efficiency*, New York: Viking Penguin.

Kant, Immanuel (1933) *Critique of Pure Reason*, trans. Norman Kemp Smith, 2nd edn, London: Macmillan.

Kanter, Rosabeth Moss (1983) *The Change Masters: Innovation for Productivity in the American Corporation*, New York: Simon & Schuster.

—— (1989) *When Giants Learn to Dance: Mastering the Challenge of Strategy, Management and Careers in the 1990s*, New York: Simon & Schuster.

Kassem, M. Sami and Habib, Ghazi M. (eds) (1989) *Strategic Management of Services in the Arab Gulf States*, Berlin: Walter de Gruyter.

Kay, John (2010) *Obliquity: Why Our Goals Are Best Achieved Indirectly*, London: Profile Books.

Kemp, Barry J. (1992) *Ancient Egypt: Anatomy of a Civilization*, London: Routledge.

Kennedy, Hugh (2007). *The Great Arab Conquests: How the Spread of Islam Changed the World We Live In*, Philadelphia: Da Capo Press.

Kennedy, Michael H. (1999) 'Fayol's Principles and the Rule of St Benedict: Is There Anything New Under the Sun?', *Journal of Management History* 5 (5): 269–76.

Kennedy, Paul (1980) *The Rise of Anglo-German Antagonism 1860–1914*, London: George Allen & Unwin.

Kessler, Ian (1998) 'Bedaux, Charles', in Malcolm Warner (ed.) *Handbook of Management Thinking*, London: International Thomson Business Press.

Khayyam, Omar (2009) *Rubaiyat*, trans. Edward Fitzgerald, Oxford: Oxford University Press.

Khurana, Rakesh (2007) *From Higher Aims to Hired Hands: The Social Transformation of American Business Schools and the Unfulfilled Promise of Management as a Profession*, Princeton: Princeton University Press.

Khurana, Rakesh, Kimura, Kenneth and Fourcade, Marion (2011) 'How Foundations Think: The Ford Foundation as a Dominating Institution in the Field of American Business Schools', Harvard Business School working paper.

Kiggundu, Moses N. (1989) *Managing Organizations in Developing Countries: An Operational and Strategic Approach*, West Hartford, CT: Kumarian Press.

Kilian, Cecilia S. (1992) *The World of W. Edwards Deming*, Knoxville, TN: SPC Press.

Kim, W. Chan and Mauborgne, Renée (2005) *Blue Ocean Strategy: How to Create Uncontested Market Space and Make the Competition Irrelevant*, Boston: Harvard Business School Press.

Kimball, Dexter S. (1913) *Principles of Industrial Organization*, New York: McGraw-Hill.

Kimoto, Shoji (1991) *Quest of the Dawn*, Milwaukee: Dougherty.

Kipping, Matthias and Bjarnar, Ove (eds) (1998) *The Americanisation of European Business: The Marshall Plan and the Transfer of US Management Models*, London: Routledge.

Kipping, Matthias and Engwall, Lars (eds) (2001) *Management Consulting: Emergence and Dynamics of a Knowledge Industry*, Oxford: Oxford University Press.

Klass, Gert von (1954), *Krupps: The Story of an Industrial Empire*, trans. James Cleugh, London: Sidgwick and Jackson.

Klein, Naomi (2000) *No Logo*, Toronto: Knopf.

Knoeppel, Charles E. (1918) *Organization and Administration*, New York: McGraw-Hill.

Kojiki, trans. Basil H. Chamberlain (1932), *Translation of the Ko-ji-ki, or Records of Ancient Matters*, 2nd edn, Kobe: J.L. Thompson & Co, 1932.

Koontz, Harold R. and O'Donnell, Cyril (1955) *Principles of Management*, New York: McGraw-Hill.

Kosiol, Erich (1955) *Anlagenrechnung: Theorie und Praxis der Abschreibungen* (Capital Accounting: Theory and Practice of Depreciation), Wiesbaden: Gabler.

—— (1962) *Organisation der Unternehmung* (Organization of the Enterprise), Wiesbaden: Gabler.

Kossek, Ellen Ernst and Lobel, Sharon A. (eds) (1997) *Managing Diversity: Human Resource Strategies for Transforming the Workplace*, New York: Wiley.

Kotler, Philip (1997) *Marketing Management*, Engelwood Cliffs, NJ: Prentice-Hall, 9th edn.

Kotler, Philip and Andreasen, Alan (1996) *Strategic Marketing for Nonprofit Organizations*, Engelwood Cliffs, NJ: Prentice Hall.

Kotler, Philip and Levy, Sidney J. (1969) 'Broadening the Concept of Marketing', *Journal of Marketing* 33 (January): 10–15.

Kotler, Philip and Zaltman, Gerald (1971) 'Social Marketing: An Approach to Planned Social Change', *Journal of Marketing* 35 (January): 3–12.

Kotter, John P. (1990) *A Force for Change: How Leadership Differs from Management*, New York: The Free Press.

Kras, Eva (1995) *Management in Two Cultures: Bridging the Gap between US and Mexican Managers*, Yarmouth, ME: Intercultural Press.

Kraut, Richard (1992) *Cambridge Companion to Plato*, Cambridge: Cambridge University Press.

Kreis, Steven (1995) 'The Diffusion of Scientific Management: The Bedaux Company in America and Britain', in Daniel Nelson (ed.) *A Mental Revolution: Scientific Management Since Taylor*, Columbus, OH: Ohio State University Press.

Kumar, Umesh (1990) *Kautilya's Thought on Public Administration*, New Delhi: National Book Organization.

Kuokkanen, Anna, Laakso, Aino and Seeck, Hannele (2010) 'Management Paradigms in Personnel Magazines of the Finnish Metal and Forest Industries', *Journal of Management History* 16 (2): 195–215.

Kuşpinar, Bilal (2007) 'Raghib Pasha, Mehmed', in Oliver Leaman (ed.), *Biographical Dictionary of Islamic Philosophers*, London: Continuum.

Laguna, Manuel and Marklund, Johan (2004) *Business Process Modelling, Simulation and Design*, Engelwood Cliffs, NJ: Prentice Hall.

Lai, Chi-kong (1992) 'The Qing State and Merchant Enterprise', in Jane Kate Leonard and John R. Watt (eds), *To Achieve Security and Wealth: The Qing Imperial State and the Economy 1644–1911*, Ithaca, NY: Cornell University Press.

Lal, Krishna (2005) *The Sukraniti*, Sanskrit and English edition, Calcutta: J.P. Publications.

Lala, R.M. (2004) *For the Love of India: The Life and Times of Jamsetji Tata*, New Delhi: Penguin.

Lamond, David (2004) 'A Matter of Style: Reconciling Henri and Henry', *Management Decision* 42 (2): 330–56.

Lane, Christel (1998) *Industry and Society in Europe: Stability and Change in Britain, Germany and France*, Aldershot: Edward Elgar.

Lane, Frederic C. (1934) *Venetian Ships and Shipbuilders of the Renaissance*, Baltimore: Johns Hopkins University Press.

Langlois, Richard N. (1999) 'The Coevolution of Technology and Organisation in the Transition to the Factory System', in P.L. Robertson (ed.), *Authority and Control in Modern Industry*, London: Routledge.

Larsen, Bøje (2003) 'German Organization and Leadership Theory: Stable Trends and Flexible Adaptation', *Scandinavian Journal of Management* 19 (1): 103–33.

Lau, D.C. (1970) *Mencius*, Harmondsworth: Penguin.

—— (1979) *Confucius: The Analects*, Harmondsworth: Penguin.

Lau, D.C. and Ames, Roger T. (1998) 'Confucius', in Edward Craig (ed.), *Routledge Encyclopedia of Philosophy*, London: Routledge, vol. 2, 565–70.

Laudicina, Paul A. (2005) *World Out of Balance: Navigating Global Risks to Seize Competitive Advantage*, New York: McGraw-Hill.

Lawrence (or Laurence), Edward (1731) *The Duty and Office of a Land-Steward*, 3rd edn, Dublin.

Lawrence, Paul R. and Lorsch, Jay W. (1967) *Organization and Environment: Managing Differentiation and Organization*, Boston: Harvard University Press.

Le Châtelier, Henri (1928) *Le Taylorisme*, Paris: Dunod.

Lee, John (1921) *Management: A Study of Industrial Organisation*, London: Pitman.

—— (1923) *Industrial Organisation: Developments and Prospects*, London: Pitman.

—— (ed.) (1928) *Pitman's Dictionary of Industrial Administration*, London: Pitman & Sons.

—— (1937) 'The Pros and Cons of Functionalization', in Luther H. Gulick and Lyndal Urwick (eds), *Papers on the Science of Administration*, New York: Institute of Public Administration, 171–9.

Lee, Pui Tak (1996) 'Understanding and Practice of "New Business" in Nineteenth-Century China', in R. Ampalavanar Brown (ed.), *Chinese Business Enterprise: Critical Perspectives on Business and Management*, London: Routledge.

Le Goff, Jacques (1980) *Time, Work and Culture in the Middle Ages*, trans.

Legge, James (1861–72) *The Chinese Classics*, repr. New York: Simon Publications, 2001.

LeShan, Lawrence and Margenau, Henry (1982) *Einstein's Space and Van Gogh's Sky: Physical Reality and Beyond*, New York: Macmillan.

Lessem, Ronnie and Neubauer, Fred (1994) *European Management Systems: Towards Unity out of Cultural Diversity*, Maidenhead: McGraw Hill.

Levitt, Theodore (1960) 'Marketing Myopia', *Harvard Business Review*; reprinted with a retrospective commentary, *Harvard Business Review* September-October, 1975, 1–14.

Lewis, Cleona and Schlotterbeck, Karl T. (1938) *America's Stake in International Investments*, New York: Ayer.

Lewis, Elias St Elmo (1908) *Financial Advertising*, Indianapolis: Levy Bros.

Lewis, John Spedan (1948) *Partnership for All*, London: Kerr-Cross Publishing.

—— (1954) *Fairer Shares*, London: Staples Press.

Lewis, Joseph Slater (1896) *The Commercial Organization of Factories*, London: Spon.

—— (1900) 'Works Management for Maximum Production', *Engineering Magazine* 19: 211–20.

Lichtheim, Miriam (1975) *Ancient Egyptian Literature: The Old and Middle Kingdoms*, vol. 1, *A Book of Readings*, Berkeley, CA: University of California Press.

Likert, Rensis (1967) *Human Organization: Its Management and Value*, New York: McGraw-Hill.

Lincoln, Edmund E. (1921) *Problems in Business Finance*, Chicago: A.W. Shaw.

Lindblom, Charles E. (1959) 'The Science of Muddling Through', *Public Administration Review* 19: 79–88.

—— (1965) *The Intelligence of Democracy*, New York: The Free Press.

—— (1979) 'Still Muddling, Not Yet Through', *Public Administration Review* 39: 517–26.

Littleton, A.C. (1981) *Accounting Evolution to 1900*, University, AL: University of Alabama Press.

Liversedge, Alfred J. (1912) *Commercial Engineering*, Manchester: Emmott & Co.

Livingstone, Marilyn (2001) 'Fitz Neal, Richard', in Morgen Witzel (ed.) *Biographical Dictionary of Management*, Bristol: Thoemmes Press.

—— (2001) 'Walter of Henley', in Morgen Witzel (ed.) *Biographical Dictionary of Management*, Bristol: Thoemmes Press.

Lloyd, Henry Demarest (1894) *Wealth Against Commonwealth*, New York: Harper & Bros.

Locke, Robert R. (1996) *The Collapse of the American Management Mystique*, Oxford: Oxford University Press.

London, Ted and Hart, Stuart L. (2004) 'Reinventing Strategies for Emerging Markets: Beyond the Transnational Model', *Journal of International Business Studies* 35: 350–70.

Longo, Bernadette (2000) *Spurious Coin: A History of Science, Management and Technical Writing*, Albany, NY: State University of New York Press.

Lopez, Roberto S. (1933) *Benedetto Zaccaria: Genova Marinara del Duecenta*, Milan: Messina.

—— (1971) *The Commercial Revolution of the Middle Ages, 950–1340*, London: Prentice Hall.

Lopez, Roberto S. and Raymond, Irving W. (eds) (1955) *Medieval Trade in the Mediterranean World*, repr. New York: Columbia University Press, 2001.

Lord, Walter (1998) *Incredible Victory: The Battle of Midway*, Ithaca, NY: Burford Books.

Lough, William H. (1909) *Corporation Finance*, New York: Alexander Hamilton Institute.

Lovelock, Christopher and Wirtz, Jochen (2009) *Essentials of Services Marketing*, Englewood Cliffs, NJ: Prentice-Hall.

Lovelock, James (1979) *Gaia: A New Look at Life on Earth*, Oxford: Oxford University Press.

Lovins, Amory B., Datta, E. Kyle, Bustnes, Odd-Even and Koomey, Jonathan G. (2004) *Winning the Oil Endgame*, Boulder, CO: Rocky Mountain Institute.

Lowenthal, Esther (1927) 'The Labour Policy of the Oneida Community Ltd.', *Journal of Political Economy* 35 (February): 114–26.

Luck, David J. (1969) 'Broadening the Concept of Marketing – Too Far', *Journal of Marketing* 33 (July): 53–65.

Luckenbill, Daniel D. (trans.) (1931) *The Code of Hammurabi*, ed. Edward Chiera, in J.M.Powis Smith (ed.) *The Origin and History of Hebrew Law*, Chicago: University of Chicago Press.

Luo Guanzhong (1991) *The Three Kingdoms*, trans. Moss Roberts, Beijing: Foreign Languages Press.

Lynch, Edmund C. (1970) *Meyer Bloomfield and Employment Management*, Austin: Bureau of Business Research, University of Texas.

Machiavelli, Niccolò (1961) *Il principe* (The Prince), trans. G. Bull, Harmondsworth: Penguin.

—— (1970) *Discorsi sopra la prima deca di Tito Livio* (Discourses on the First Decade of Livy), ed. B. Crick, trans. L.J. Walker as *The Discourses*, Harmondsworth: Penguin.

—— (2001) *The Art of War*, trans. Ellis Farneworth, Cambridge, MA: Da Capo Press.

Mackenzie King, William Lyon (1918) *Industry and Humanity*, Toronto: University of Toronto Press.

Maddison, Angus (2006) *The World Economy*, 2 vols, Paris: OECD.

Magnusson, Lars (1994) *Mercantilism: The Shaping of Economic Language*, London: Routledge.

Mahajan, Vijay (2008) *Africa Rising: How 900 Million African Consumers Offer More Than You Think*, Engelwood Cliffs, NJ: Wharton School Publishing.

Malahanobis, P.C. (1948) 'Walter A. Shewhart and Statistical Control in India', *Sankhya: The Indian Journal of Statistics* 9 (1): 51–75.

Malthus, Thomas Robert (1798) *An Essay on the Principles of Population*, repr. London: Everyman, 1972.

—— (1820) *Principles of Political Economy*, repr. Cambridge: Cambridge University Press, 1989, 2 vols.

Manning, Florence M. (1989) 'Carl G. Barth, 1860–1939: A Sketch', *Norwegian-American Studies* 13 (4), www.naha.stolaf.edu/pubs/nas/volume13/vol13_7.htm.

Manuel, Frank (1956) *The New World of Henri de Saint-Simon*, Cambridge, MA: Harvard University Press.

March, James G. (1971) 'The Technology of Foolishness', in James G. March (ed.), *Decisions and Organizations*, New York: Basil Blackwell.

March, James G. and Simon, Herbert A. (1958) *Organizations*, New York: John Wiley.

Marcinkowski, Muhammad Ismail (ed. and trans.) (2002) *Mirza Rafi'a's Dastur al-Muluk: A Manual of Later Safavid Administration*, Kuala Lumpur: International Institute of Islamic Thought and Civilization.

Markowitz, Harry (1959) *Portfolio Selection: Efficient Diversification of Investments*, New York: John Wiley.

Marmura, Michael E. (1997) *The Incoherence of the Philosophers: Tahafut al-Falasifah*, Provo, UT: Brigham Young University Press.

Marr, Rainer (2000) 'Management in Germany', in Malcolm Warner (ed.), *Management in Europe*, London: Thomson Learning.

Marshall, Alfred (1890) *Principles of Economics: An Introductory Volume*, London: Macmillan.

—— (1919) *Industry and Trade: A Study of Industrial Technique and Business Organization*, London: Macmillan.

Martin, Selden O. (1915) 'The Scientific Study of Marketing', *Annals of the American Academy of Political and Social Science* 59: 77–85.

Martin-Pardey, Eva (1999) 'Administrative Bureaucracy', in Kathryn A. Bard (ed.), *Encyclopedia of the Archaeology of Ancient Egypt*, London: Routledge, 115–18.

Marx, Karl (1933) *Das Kapital*, London: J.M. Dent.

Marx, Karl and Engels, Friedrich (1998) *The Communist Manifesto*, London: Penguin.

Maslow, Abraham (1954) *Motivation and Personality*, New York: Harper & Bros.

Mason, Paul (2008) *Live Working or Die Fighting: How the Working Class Went Global*, London: Vintage.

Masschaele, James (1997) *Peasants, Merchants and Markets: Inland Trade in Medieval England, 1150–1350*, New York: St Martin's Press.

Matsushita Konosuke (1988) *Quest for Prosperity: The Life of a Japanese Industrialist*, Tokyo: PHP Institute

Mauro, Francesco (1930) *Esperienze di Organizzazione Giapponese* (The Experience of Japanese Management), Rome: ENIOS.

al-Mawardi, Abdul Hasan (2005) *Al-akham al-sultaniyya* (The Ordinances of Government), trans. Walaa H. Wahaba, Reading: Garnet Publishing.

al-Mawdudi, Sayyid Abu'l A'la (1963) 'Economic and Political Teachings of the Qur'an', in M.M. Sharf (ed.) *A History of Muslim Philosophy*, Wiesbaden: Otto Harrassowitz.

—— (1999) *Economic System of Islam*, trans. Riaz Husain, Lahore: Islamic Publications, 4th edn.

Maynard, Harold B., Stegemerten, G.J. and Schwab, John L. (1948) *Methods–Time Measurement*, New York: McGraw-Hill.

Mayo, Anthony J., Nohria, Nitin and Singleton, Laura G. (2006) *Paths to Power: How Insiders and Outsiders Shaped American Business Leadership*, Boston: Harvard Business School Press.

Mayo, Elton (1919) *Democracy and Freedom: Essays in Social Logic*, Melbourne: Macmillan.

—— (1933) 'The Human Effect of Mechanization', *American Economic Review* 20: 156–76.

—— (1933) *The Human Problems of an Industrial Civilization*, New York: Macmillan.

McCann, J. (1937) *Saint Benedict*, London: Sheed & Ward.

McCarthy, E. Jerome (1960) *Basic Marketing: A Managerial Approach*, Homewood, IL: Irwin.

McClelland, David C. (1975) *Power: The Inner Experience*, New York: Irvington.

McCraw, Thomas (1984) *Prophets of Regulation: Charles Francis Adams, Louis D. Brandeis, James M. Landis, Alfred E. Kahn*, Cambridge, MA: Harvard University Press.

McDonald, Donald (1908) *Agricultural Writers from Sir Walter of Henley to Arthur Young, 1200–1800*, London: Horace Cox.

McElderry, Andrea L. (1976) *Shanghai Old-Style Banks (Ch'ien-chuang) 1800–1935*, Ann Arbor, MI: Centre for Chinese Studies, University of Michigan.

McElheny, Victor K. (1998) *Insisting on the Impossible: The Life of Edwin Land*, New York: Perseus.

McGregor, Douglas (1960) *The Human Side of Enterprise*, New York: McGraw-Hill.

McKenna, Christopher (2006) *The World's Newest Profession: Management Consulting in the Twentieth Century*, Cambridge: Cambridge University Press.

McKiernan, Peter (ed.) (1996) *Historical Evolution of Strategic Management*, Aldershot: Dartmouth, 2 vols.

McKillop, Margaret and McKillop, Alan D. (1920) *Efficiency Methods: An Introduction to Scientific Management*, London: George Routledge & Sons.

McKinsey, James O. (1922) *Budgetary Control*, New York: The Ronald Press.

McLaren, Patricia Genoe and Mills, Albert J. (2008) 'A Product of "His" Time? Exploring the Construct of the Ideal Manager in the Cold War Era', *Journal of Management History* 14 (4): 386–403.

McLaughlin, Raoul (2009) *Rome and the Distant East: Trade Routes to the Ancient Lands of Arabia, India and China*, London: Hambledon Continuum.

McLuhan, Marshall (1951) *The Mechanical Bride: The Folklore of Industrial Man*, New York: Vanguard.

—— (1964) *Understanding Media: The Extensions of Man*, London: Routledge & Kegan Paul.

—— (1970) *Culture Is Our Business*, New York: McGraw-Hill.

McLuhan, Marshall and Fiore, Quentin (1968) *War and Peace in the Global Village*, New York: McGraw-Hill.

Meade, Edward S. (1910) *Corporation Finance*, New York: D. Appleton.

Meadows, Donella H., Meadows, Dennis L., Randers, Jørgen and Behrens, William W. (1972) *The Limits to Growth*, New York: Universe Books.

Merkle, Judith (1980) *Management and Ideology: The Legacy of the International Scientific Management Movement*, Berkeley: University of California Press.

Metcalf, Henry C. and Urwick, Lyndall (eds) (1941) *Dynamic Administration: The Collected Papers of Mary Parker Follett*, London: Pitman.

Metcalfe, Henry (1885) *The Cost of Manufactures and the Administration of Workshops*, New York: John Wiley & Sons.

Meyenberg, Friedrich-Ludwig (1951) *Industrial Administration and Management*, London: Pitman.

Meyer, Stephen (1981) *The Five-Dollar Day: Labor Management and Social Control in the Ford Motor Company, 1908–1921*, New York: Charles Scribner.

Michels, Robert (1911) *Zur Soziologie des Parteiwesens in der modernen Demokratie*, trans. Eden and Cedar Paul, *Political Parties: A Sociological Study of the Oligarchical Tendencies of Modern Democracy*, New York, 1915: repr. New York: Dover, 1949.

Miles, Raymond E. and Snow, Charles C. (1978) *Organizational Strategy, Structure and Process*, New York: McGraw-Hill.

Mill, John Stuart (2008) *Principles of Political Economy*, ed. Jonathan Riley, Oxford: Oxford University Press.

Mintzberg, Henry (1973) *The Nature of Managerial Work*, New York: Harper & Row.

—— (1989) *Mintzberg on Management*, New York: The Free Press.

—— (1994) *The Rise and Fall of Strategic Planning*, New York: The Free Press.

Mintzberg, Henry, Ahlstrand, Bruce and Lampel, Joseph (2002) *Strategy Safari: A Guided Tour Through the Wilds of Strategic Management*, Engelwood Cliffs, NJ: Prentice Hall.

Mises, Ludwig von (1949) *Human Action: A Treatise on Economics*, Chicago: Henry Regnery.

Mitchell, Lynette (2008) 'The Education of Cyrus and the Obedience of the Willing', University of Exeter, Centre for Leadership Studies, Extended Essay Series.

Mitchell, Richard P. (1993) *The Society of the Muslim Brothers*, Oxford: Oxford University Press.

Mitchell, Wesley Clair (1913) *Business Cycles*, Berkeley: University of California Press.

Miyamoto Musashi (2005) *The Book of Five Rings: A Classic Text on the Japanese Way of the Sword*, trans. Thomas Cleary, Boston: Shambhala.

Mol, Michael J. and Birkinshaw, Julian (2008) *Giant Steps in Management: Creating Innovations that Change the Way We Work*, London: FT-Prentice Hall.

Montesquieu, Baron de (Charles-Louis de Secondat) (1973) *The Persian Letters*, trans. C.J. Betts, London: Penguin.

Mooney, James D. (1937) 'The Principles of Organization', in Luther H. Gulick and Lyndall Urwick (eds) *Papers on the Science of Administration*, New York: Institute of Public Administration.

Mooney, James D. and Reiley, Alan C. (1931) *Onward Industry! The Principles of Organization and Their Significance to Modern Industry*, New York: Harper & Bros.

Moore, Karl and Lewis, David (2000) *Foundations of Corporate Empire: Is History Repeating Itself?* London: Financial Times-Prentice Hall.

Moore, Karl and Lewis, David (2009) *The Origins of Globalization*, London: Routledge.

Morgan, Gareth (1986) *Images of Organization*, Newbury Park, CA: Sage.

Morgan, Stephen L. (2006) 'Transfer of Taylorist Ideas to China, 1910–30', *Journal of Management History* 12 (4): 408–24.

Moriarty, W.D. (1923) *The Economics of Marketing and Advertising*, New York: Harper & Bros.

Morii, Yumiko (2008) 'A Comparative Analysis of Corporate Finance in the United States and Japan from 1880 to 1930', PhD dissertation, Florida International University.

Morley, Neville (2007) *Trade in Classical Antiquity*, Cambridge: Cambridge University Press.

Morse, H.B. (1932) *The Guilds of China*, London: Longmans, Green.

Morse, Philip M. and Kimball, George E. (1951) *Methods of Operations Research*, Cambridge, MA: MIT Press.

Morson, Gary Saul (1998) 'Tolstoi, Count Lev Nikolaevich', in Edward Craig (ed.) *Routledge Encyclopedia of Philosophy*, London: Routledge, vol. 9, pp. 435–40.

Mortimer, Thomas (1761) *Every Man His Own Broker*, London.

—— (1772) *The Elements of Commerce, Politics and Finances*, London.

—— (1810) *A General Dictionary of Commerce, Trade and Manufactures*, London.

Mukhopadhyay, Sri Nabaniharan (2008) 'Swami Vivekananda's Thoughts on Industrialization', *Vivek-Javan*, July.

Mumford, Lewis (1934) *Technics and Civilization*, London: George Routledge & Sons.

—— (1967) *The Myth of the Machine*, London: Secker & Warburg, 2 vols.

Muna, Farid A. (1980) *The Arab Executive*, New York: Macmillan.

Münsterberg, Hugo (1913) *Psychology and Industrial Efficiency*, Boston: Houghton Mifflin.

Naisbitt, John (1982) *Megatrends*, New York: Warner Books.

Narayan, Shriman (ed.) (1968) *The Selected Works of Mahatma Gandhi*, Ahmedabad: Navajivan Publishing House.

Nath Dutt, Manmatha (2005) *Yajnavalkyasmrti: Sanskrit Text, English Translation*, New Delhi: Parimal Publications.

Nelson, Daniel (1995) 'Scientific Management in Retrospect', in Daniel Nelson (ed.) *A Mental Revolution: Scientific Management Since Taylor*, Columbus, OH: Ohio State University Press.

Neugebauer, Udo (1997) 'Business Ethics in Older German Administration: Heinrich Nicklisch, Wihelm Kalveram, August Marx', in Peter Koslowski (ed.), *Methodology of the Social Sciences, Ethics and Economics in the Newer Historical School*, Berlin: Springer.

Nevins, Allan N. and Hill, Frank E. (1954) *Ford: the Times, the Man, the Company*, New York: Charles Scribner's Sons.

—— *Ford: Expansion and Challenge, 1915–1933*, New York: Charles Scribner's Sons.

Nichols, Ernest Fox (1916) 'The Employment Manager', *Annals of the American Academy of Political and Social Science* 65: 1–8.

Nicklisch, Heinrich (1920) *Der Weg aufwarts! Organisation* (The Way Forward! Organisation), Stuttgart.

—— (1922) *Wirtschaftliche Betriebslehre* (Economic Theory of Business Administration), Stuttgart.

Nishikawa, Shunsaku (1998) 'Fukuzawa, Yukichi', in Malcolm Warner (ed.) *The IEBM Handbook of Management Thinking*, London: International Thomson Business Press, pp. 233–7.

Nizam al-Mulk (Abu 'Ali al-Hasan al-Tusi) (1960) *The Book of Government or Rules for Kings*, trans. Hubert Darke, London: Routledge and Kegan Paul.

Nonaka, Ikujiro and Takeuchi, Hirotaka (1995) *The Knowledge-Creating Company: How Japanese Companies Create the Dynamics of Innovation*, Oxford: Oxford University Press.

Norgaard, Richard L. (1981) 'The Evolution of Business Finance Textbooks', *Financial Management* 10 (2): 34–46.

Nye, Mary Jo (2004) *Blackett: Physics, War and Politics in the Twentieth Century*, Cambridge, MA: Harvard University Press.

Odubogun, P. Kassey (1992) *Management Theory: Relevance for Management Practice in Nigeria*, The Hague: Netherlands International Institute for Management, 1992.

Ohmae, Kenichi (1982) *The Mind of the Strategist*, New York: McGraw-Hill.

—— (1985) *Triad Power: The Coming Shape of Global Competition*, New York: The Free Press.

—— (1990) *The Borderless World: Power and Strategy in the Interlinked Economy*, New York: Harper Business.

—— (2005) *The Next Global Stage: Challenges and Opportunities in Our Borderless World*, Engelwood Cliffs, NJ: Wharton School Publishing.

Ohno Taiichi (1988) *Toyota Production System: Beyond Large-Scale Production*, Cambridge, MA: Productivity Press.

Okazaki, Tetsuji (2007) 'The Evolution of Corporate Finance and Corporate Governance in Prewar Japan: Comments on "Were Banks Really at the Center of the Prewar Japanese Financial System?"', *Monetary and Economic Studies* 25 (1): 89–94.

Olojde, Iyabo (1995) *Women in Top Management in Nigeria*, Nairobi: African Association of Public Administration and Management.

Orange, George W. and McBain, J. (1911) 'Mail Order Advertising', in T. Russell (ed.) *Harmsworth Business Library*, London: Educational Book Co., vol. 5.

Origo, Iris (1957) *The Merchant of Prato*, London: Jonathan Cape.

—— (1962) *The World of San Bernardino*, London: Jonathan Cape.

Orwell, George (1949) *Nineteen Eighty-Four*, repr. London: Penguin, 2008.

Oschinsky, Dorothea (1971) *Walter of Henley and Other Treatises on Estate Management and Accounting*, Oxford: Clarendon.

Ovid (2004) *Metamorphoses*, trans. Denis Feeney and David Raeburn, London: Penguin.

Owen, Robert (1812) *A Statement Regarding the New Lanark Establishment*, Edinburgh.

—— (1815) *Some Observations on the Effect of the Manufacturing System*, London.

Page, T.E. (1967) *Cato and Varro De Re Rustica "On Agriculture"*, trans. William Davis Hooper, London: William Heinemann.

Palmer, R.R. (1986) 'Frederick the Great, Guibert, Bülow: From Dynastic to National War', in Peter Paret (ed.), *Makers of Modern Strategy*, Princeton, NJ: Princeton University Press, pp. 91–119.

Pappas, Nickolas (1995) *Plato and the Republic*, London: Routledge.

Parasuraman, A., Zeithaml, Valarie A. and Berry, Leonard L. (1985) 'A Conceptual Model of Service Quality and Its Implications for Future Research', *Journal of Marketing* 49: 41–55.

—— (1988) 'SERVQUAL: A Multiple-Item Scale for Measuring Customer Perceptions of Service Quality'. *Journal of Retailing* 64: 12–40.

Paret, Peter, Craig, Gordon A. and Gilbert, Felix (eds) (1986) *Makers of Modern Strategy*, Princeton: Princeton University Press.

Parker, Cornelia Stratton (1922) *Working With the Working Woman*, New York: Harper & Bros.

Parkin, Frank (1992) *Durkheim*, Oxford: Oxford University Press.

Parkinson, C. Northcote (1958) *Parkinson's Law*, London: John Murray.

Parkinson, R.B. (2002) *Poetry and Culture in Middle Kingdom Egypt: A Dark Side to Perfection*, London: Continuum.

Parkinson, Roger (2008) *The Late Victorian Navy: The Pre-Dreadnought Era and the Origins of the First World War*, Woodbridge: Boydell.

Parry, J.H. (1964) *The Age of Reconnaissance: Discovery, Exploration and Settlement*, New York: Mentor.

Patterson, John H. (1902) 'Altruism and Sympathy as Factors in Works Administration', *Engineering Magazine* 20; repr. in Daniel A. Wren (ed.) *Early Management Thought*, Aldershot: Ashgate.

Payne, Stephanie C., Youngcourt, Satoris S. and Watrous, Kristen M. (2006) 'Portrayals of F.W. Taylor Across Textbooks', *Journal of Management History* 12(4): 385–407.

Peaucelle, Jean-Louis and Guthrie, Cameron (2012) 'Henri Fayol', in Morgen Witzel and Malcolm Warner (eds), *Oxford Handbook of Management Thinkers*, Oxford: Oxford University Press.

Pegolotti, Francesco di Balduccio (1936) *La pratica della mercatura*, ed. A. Evans, Cambridge, MA: Medieval Academy of America.

Perry, Ralph B. (1938) *In the Spirit of William James*, New Haven: Yale University Press.

Peter, Laurence J. (1969) *The Peter Principle*, London: Pan.

Peters, Thomas J. (1987) *Thriving on Chaos: Handbook for a Management Revolution*, New York: Knopf.

—— (1992) *Liberation Management: Necessary Disorganization for the Nanosecond Nineties*, New York: Knopf.

Peters, Thomas J. and Waterman, Robert H. (1982) *In Search of Excellence: Lessons from America's Best-Run Companies*, New York: Harper & Row.

Petersen, Peter B. (1987) 'The Contribution of W. Edwards Deming to Japanese Management Theory and Practice', *Academy of Management Best Paper Proceedings 1987*, 133–7.

Petty, William (1899) *The Economic Writings of Sir William Petty*, ed. Charles Henry Hull, Cambridge: Cambridge University Press.

Phipps, Simone T.A. (2011) 'Mary, Mary, Quite Contrary: In a Male-Dominated Field, Women Contributed by Bringing a Touch of Spirituality to Early Management Practice', *Journal of Management History* 17 (3).

Podmore, Frank (1924) *Robert Owen*, New York: Appleton Century Crofts.

Pohl, Frederick and Kornbluth, C.M. (1953), *The Space Merchants*, repr. London: Victor Gollancz, 2003.

Poitras, Geoffrey (2007) 'Introduction', in Geoffrey Poitras (ed.) *Pioneers of Financial Economics*, vol. 2, Cheltenham: Edward Elgar.

Polanyi, Michael (1958) *Personal Knowledge: Towards a Post-Critical Philosophy*, London: Routledge.

—— (1966) *The Tacit Dimension*, New York: Doubleday.

—— (1965) *The Genesis of Modern Management*, London: Penguin.

Pollard, Sidney and Robertson, Paul (1979) *The British Shipbuilding Industry 1870–1914*, Cambridge, MA: Harvard University Press.

Porter, Michael E. (1980) *Competitive Strategy: Techniques for Analyzing Industries and Competitors*, New York: The Free Press.

—— (1985) *Competitive Advantage: Creating and Sustaining Superior Performance*, New York: The Free Press.

Porter, Roy (2001) *Enlightenment: Britain and the Creation of the Modern World*, London: Penguin.

Postlethwayt, Malachy (1750) *The Merchant's Public Counting House, or New Mercantile Institution*, London.

—— (1751) *The Universal Dictionary of Trade and Commerce*, London.

Prabhupada, A.C. Bhaktivedante Swami (ed. and trans.) (1972) *Bhagavad-Gita As It Is*, New York: Collier.

Prahalad, C.K. (2004) *The Fortune at the Bottom of the Pyramid*, Engelwood Cliffs, NJ: Wharton School Publishing.

Prahalad, C.K. and Hamel, Gary (1990) 'The Core Competence of the Corporation', *Harvard Business Review*, May-June.

Prescott, William H. (1909) *The Conquest of Mexico*, London: Everyman's.

Pryor, Mildred Golden and Taneja, Sonia (2010) 'Henri Fayol, Practitioner and Theoretician – Revered and Reviled', *Journal of Management History*, 16 (4): 489–503.

Pugh, Derek S. (1973) 'The Measurement of Organization Structures: Does Context Determine Form?' *Organizational Dynamics*; repr. in Pugh (ed.), *Organization Theory: Selected Readings*, London: Penguin, 1997.

Pugh, Derek S. and Hickson, David J. (1976) *Organization Structure in its Context*, Farnborough: Aston House.

Quinn, James Brian (1980) *Strategies for Change: Logical Incrementalism*, Homewood, IL: Irwin.

Quirke, Stephen (1990) *The Administration of Egypt in the Late Middle Kingdom*, New Malden: SIA Publishing.

Qureshi, Anwar Iqbal (1993) *Islam and the Theory of Interest*, Lahore: Muhammad Ashraf.

Qureshi, Asif H. (1996) *The World Trade Organization; Implementing International Trade Norms*, Manchester: Manchester University Press.

Radhakrishnan, S. (1993) *The Bhagavad-Gita*, London: HarperCollins.

Rae, Ian and Witzel, Morgen (2008) *The Overseas Chinese of Southeast Asia: History, Business, Culture*, Basingstoke: Palgrave Macmillan.

Rand, Ayn (1957) *Atlas Shrugged*, New York: New American Library.

Rao, C.V. Ramachandra (1976) *Administration and Society in Medieval Andhra (AD 1038–1538)*, Nellore: Manasa Publications.

Rao, M.V.K. (1979) *Studies in Kautilya*, New Delhi: Munshiram Manoharlal.

Rathe, Alex W. (1961) *Gantt on Management*, New York: American Management Association.

Rathenau, Walther (1917) *Von Kommenden Dingen* (In Days to Come) trans. Eden and Cedar Paul, London: Allen & Unwin.

—— (1918) *Die Neue Wirtschaft* (The New Economy), Berlin: G. Fischer

—— (1919) *Der Neue Staat* (The New Society), trans. anon, London: Williams & Norgate.

Rawski, Thomas G. (1989) *Economic Growth in Prewar China*, Berkeley: University of California Press.

Read, Donald (1992) *The Power of News: The History of Reuters, 1849–1989*, Oxford: Oxford University Press.

Redding, S. Gordon (1993) *The Spirit of Chinese Capitalism*, New York: de Gruyter.

Redfield, William C. (1916) 'The Employment Problem in Industry', *Annals of the American Academy of Political and Social Science* 65: 9–14.

Refuge, Eustache de (2008) *Treatise on the Court*, trans. J. Chris Cooper, Boca Raton, FL: Orgpax Publications.

Reid, Anthony (1988–95) *Southeast Asia in the Age of Commerce, 1450–1680*, London: Yale University Press.

Richards, D.S. (2011) *Mamluk Administrative Documents from St Catherine's Monastery*, Leuven: Peeters.

Rieger, Wilhelm (1984) *Einführung in de Privatwirtschaftslehre* (Introduction to the Private Sector), Stuttgart: Palm & Enke.

Rifkin, Glenn and Harrar, George (1988) *The Ultimate Entrepreneur: The Story of Ken Olsen and Digital Equipment Corporation*, Chicago: Contemporary Books.

Rig Veda, in R.C. Zaehner (ed. and trans.) (1966) *From the Rig Veda; From the Atharva Veda*, London: Everyman.

Rindova, Violina P. and Starbuck, William H. (1997) 'Ancient Chinese Theories of Control', *Journal of Management Inquiry* 6: 144–59.

Ripley, William Z. (ed.) (1905) *Trusts, Pools and Corporations*, Boston: Ginn & Company.

—— (1926) *From Main Street to Wall Street*, New York: Harper & Bros.

Ritzer, George (1996) *The McDonaldization of Society*, Thousand Oaks, CA: Pine Forge Press.

Robinson, Richard D. (1966) *International Business Policy*, New York: Holt, Rinehart & Winston.

Rochefoucauld, François de la (1959) *Maxims*, trans. Louis Kronenberger, New York: Random House.

Roe, Mark J. (1994) *Strong Managers, Weak Owners: The Political Roots of American Corporate Finance*, Princeton: Princeton University Press.

Roethlisberger, Fritz and Dickson, William J. (1939) *Management and the Worker*, Cambridge, MA: Harvard University Press.

Roll, Erich (1930) *Early Experiments in Industrial Organization*, London: Longmans Green.

Roncaglia, Alessandro (1985) *Petty: Origins of Political Economy*, Armonk, NY: M.E. Sharpe.

Rost, Joseph C. (1991) *Leadership for the Twenty-First Century*, New York: Praeger.

Rost, Katja *et al.* (2010) 'The Corporate Governance of Benedictine Abbeys: What Can Stock Corporations Learn From Monasteries?', *Journal of Management History* 16 (1): 90–115.

Rouse, W.H.D. (trans.) (1956) *Great Dialogues of Plato*, New York: Mentor.

Rowlinson, Michael (1988) 'The Early Application of Scientific Management by Cadbury', *Business History* 30: 377–95.

Rowntree, Benjamin Seebohm (1921) *The Human Factor in Business: Experiments in Industrial Democracy*, London: Longmans, Green.

Rudra, Ashok (1998) *Prasanta Chandra Malahanobis: A Biography*, New Delhi: Oxford University Press.

Saint-Simon, Henri de (1975) *Selected Writings on Science, Industry and Social Organisation*, London: Croom Helm.

Salsburg, David (2002) *The Lady Tasting Tea: How Statistics Revolutionized Science in the Twentieth Century*, New York: W.H. Freeman.

Sampson, Henry (1874) *A History of Advertising from the Earliest Times*, London: Chatton & Windus; repr. Bristol: Thoemmes Press, 2002.

Samuelson, Paul A. (1965) 'Proof that Properly Anticipated Prices Fluctuate Randomly', *Industrial Management* 6 (1): 41–9.

Sasaki Jun (2001) 'Ohara Magosaburo', in Morgen Witzel (ed.), *Biographical Dictionary of Management*, Bristol: Thoemmes Press.

Sasaki Naoto (1990) *Management and Industrial Structure in Japan*, Oxford: Pergamon.

Sasaki Tsuneo (2001), 'Nicklisch, Heinrich', in Morgen Witzel (ed.), *Biographical Dictionary of Management*, Bristol: Thoemmes Press.

—— (2001) 'Campion, Gabriel', in Morgen Witzel (ed.), *Biographical Dictionary of Management*, Bristol: Thoemmes Press.

—— (2001), 'Schonpflug, Fritz', in Morgen Witzel (ed.), *Biographical Dictionary of Management*, Bristol: Thoemmes Press.

Savary, Jacques (1675) *Le parfait négociant, ou instruction générale pour ce qui regarde le commerce de toute sorte de marchandises de France et des pays étrangers* (The Perfect Merchant, or General Instruction regarding the Mercantile Trade of France and Foreign Countries), Paris.

Savino, David (2009) 'Louis D. Brandeis and His Role Promoting Scientific Management as a Progressive Movement', *Journal of Management History* 15 (1): 38–49.

Sawai Minoru (2001) 'Araki Toichiro', in Morgen Witzel (ed.), *Biographical Dictionary of Management*, Bristol: Thoemmes Press.

Schein, Edgar H. (1985) *Organizational Psychology*, New York: Prentice Hall.

—— (1997) 'From Brainwashing to Organisational Therapy', *European Business Forum* 31: 6–9.

Schlevogt, Kai-Alexander (2002) *The Art of Chinese Management: Theory, Evidence and Applications*, Oxford: Oxford University Press.

Schmalenbach, Eugen (1941) *Über die Dienstellengliederung in Grossbetrieb* (On the Division of Departments in Big Business), Leipzig: Opladen.

Schneirov, Richard, Stromquist, Shelton and Salvatore, Nick (eds) (1999) *The Pullman Strike and the Crisis of the 1890s: Essays on Labour and Politics*, Urbana, IL: University of Illinois Press.

Schonpflug, Fritz (1933) *Das Methodenproblem in der Einzelwirtschaftslehre* (Methodological Problems of Individual Economics), Stuttgart.

Schopen, Gregory (2004) *Buddhist Monks and Business Matters*, Honolulu: University of Hawaii Press.

Schott, Jeffrey J. (1996) *WTO 2000:Setting the Course for World Trade*, Washington DC: Institute for International Economics.

Schroeder, Jonathan (2009) 'The Cultural Codes of Branding', *Marketing Theory* 9 (1): 123–6.

Schumpeter, Joseph (1939) *Business Cycles*, New York: McGraw-Hill.

Schuyler, Robert L. (1931) *Josiah Tucker: A Selection from His Economic and Political Writings*, New York: Columbia University Press.

Scott, Walter Dill (1913) *The Psychology of Advertising*, Chicago: Dodd, Mead & Co.

Scott, William G. (1992) *Chester I. Barnard and the Guardians of the Managerial State*, Lawrence, KS: University Press of Kansas.

Sedlak, Michael W. and Williamson, Harold F. (1983) *The Evolution of Management Education: A History of the Northwestern University J.L. Kellogg Graduate School of Management 1908–1983*, Chicago: University of Illinois Press.

See, Chong-Su (1919) *The Foreign Trade of China*, New York: Columbia University Press.

Seelos, Christian and Mair, Johanna (2007) 'Profitable Business Models and Market Creation in the Context of Deep Poverty: A Strategic View', *Academy of Management Perspectives* 21: 49–63.

Selfridge, H. Gordon (1918) *The Romance of Commerce*, London: John Lane.

Senge, Peter M. (1990) *The Fifth Discipline: The Art and Practice of the Learning Organization*, New York: Doubleday.

Senge, Peter M., Smith, Bryan, Kruschwitz, Nina, Laur, Joe and Schley, Sara (2008) *The Necessary Revolution: How Individuals and Organizations Are Working Together to Create a Sustainable World*, London: Nicholas Brealey.

Senior, Nassau (1830) *An Outline of the Science of Political Economy*, London.

Servan-Schreiber, Jean-Jacques (1979) *Le défi américain*, trans. Ronald Steel, *The American Challenge*, New York: Holiday House.

Shafer, Robert J. (1973) *Mexican Business Organizations: History and Analysis*, Syracuse: Syracuse University Press.

Shannon, Claude and Weaver, Warren (1949) *The Mathematical Theory of Communication*, Urbana: University of Illinois Press.

Shaw, Arch W. (1912) *Some Problems in Market Distribution*, Cambridge, MA: Harvard University Press.

Shea, D.R., Swacker, F.W., Radway, R.J. and Stairs, S.T. (eds) (1979) *Reference Manual on Doing Business in Latin America*, Milwaukee: University of Wisconsin Press.

Sheldon, Oliver (1923) *The Philosophy of Management*, London: Pitman.

Shewhart, Walter (1931) *Economic Control of Quality of Manufactured Product*, New York: Van Nostrand.

Shibusawa Eiichi (1994) *The Autobiography of Shibusawa Eiichi: From Peasant to Entrepreneur*, trans. Teruko Craig, Tokyo: University of Tokyo Press.

Shigeo Shingo (1989) *A Study of the Toyota Production System from an Industrial Engineering Viewpoint*, Cambridge, MA: Productivity Press.

Shinoya, Yuichi (ed.) (2001) *The German Historical School: The Historical and Ethical Approach to Economics*, London: Routledge.

Shonberger, Richard J. (1982) *Japanese Manufacturing Techniques: Nine Hidden Lessons in Simplicity*, New York: The Free Press.

Sidani, Yusuf M. (2008) 'Ibn Khaldun of North Africa: An AD 1377 Theory of Leadership', *Journal of Management History* 14 (1): 73–86.

Siegfried, André (1927) *Les Etats-Unis d'aujourd'hui*, Paris: Armand Colin.

Sigler, Laurence E. (trans.) (2002) *Fibonacci's Liber Abaci*, Berlin: Springer-Verlag.

Simha, Aditya and Lemak, David J. (2010) 'The Value of Original Source Readings in Management Education: the Case of Frederick Winslow Taylor', *Journal of Management History* 16 (2): 233–53.

Simon, Herbert A. (1947) *Administrative Behavior: A Study of Decision-Making Processes in Administrative Organization*, New York: Macmillan.

Sinclair, Upton (1906) *The Jungle*, repr. London: Penguin, 2006.

Silver, Morris (1995) *Economic Structures of Antiquity*, Westport, CT: Greenwood Press.

Sircar, D.C. (1967) *Studies in the Society and Administration of Ancient and Medieval India*, Calcutta: Firma K.L. Mukhopadhyay.

Slevin, James (2000) *The Internet and Society*, Cambridge: Polity Press.

Slomp, Jan (2003) 'The "Political Equation" in *Al-jihad fi al-Islam* of Abul A'la Mawdudi (1903–79)', in David Thomas and Clare Amos (eds), *A Faithful Presence: Essays for Kenneth Cragg*, London: Melisende.

Smil, Vaclav (2003) *Energy at the Crossroads: Global Perspectives and Uncertainties*, Cambridge, MA: MIT Press.

Smiles, Samuel (1889) *Self-Help: With Illustrations of Character and Conduct*, London: John Murray; repr. Oxford: Oxford University Press, 2002.

Smith, Adam (1776) *Inquiry into the Nature and Causes of the Wealth of Nations*, repr. London: Penguin, 2004.

Smith, Bruce (1966) *The RAND Corporation: Case Study of a Nonprofit Advisory Corporation*, Cambridge, MA: Harvard University Press.

Solvay, Ernest (1900) *Etudes sociales: notes sur le productivisme et le compatibilisme*, Brussels: Lamertin.

Somadeva (1924) *The Katha Sarit Sagara*, trans. C.H. Tawney in N.M. Penzer, *The Ocean of Story*, London: Chas J. Sawyer, 10 vols.

Southey, Robert (1811) *On the Economical Reformers*, London; repr. in *Essays Moral and Political*, 1832, vol. 1, pp. 51–74.

—— (1812) *On the State of the Poor, the Principle of Mr Malthus's Essay on Population, and the Manufacturing System*, London; repr. in *Essays Moral and Political*, 1832, vol. 1, pp. 75–158.

Spender, J.C. (2012) 'Herbert Simon', in Morgen Witzel and Malcolm Warner (eds), *Oxford Handbook of Management Thinkers*, Oxford: Oxford University Press.

Spooner, Henry J. (1918) *Wealth from Waste: Elimination of Waste, A World Problem*, London: Routledge.

Standage, Tom (1998) *The Victorian Internet*, Gaithersburg, MD: Phoenix.

Stannard, J.W. (1911) *Factory Organisation and Management*, London: Harmsworth.

Starbuck, Peter (2012) 'Peter Drucker', in Morgen Witzel and Malcolm Warner (eds), *Oxford Handbook of Management Thinkers*, Oxford: Oxford University Press.

Starbuck, William H. (2005) 'The Origins of Organization Theory', in Haridimos Tsoukas and Christian Knudsen (eds), *The Oxford Handbook of Organization Theory*, Oxford: Oxford University Press, 143–82.

Steele, Darrell C. (2006) 'Leadership Lessons of Great American Indians: An Untapped Legacy for Today's Airmen', thesis submitted to the Air Command and Staff College, Air University, US Air Force.

Steiner, George (1963) *Managerial Long-Range Planning*, New York: McGraw-Hill.

Stern, Nicholas (2007) *The Economics of Climate Change: The Stern Review*, Cambridge: Cambridge University Press.

Stevenson, David (2005) *The First World War and International Politics*, Oxford: Oxford University Press.

Stone, David (2001) 'Medieval Farm Management and Technological Mentalities: Hinderclay Before the Black Death', *Economic History Review* 54 (4): 612–38.

Strouse, Jean (1999) *Morgan: American Financier*, New York: Random House.

Strudwick, Nigel (1985) *The Administration of Egypt in the Old Kingdom*, London: KPI.

Sugawara Makoto (1985) *Lives of Master Swordsmen*, ed. Burritt Sabin, Tokyo: The East Publications.

Sully, James (1884) *Outlines of Psychology*, London: Longmans, Green.

Sumner, William Graham (1885) *Collected Essays in Political and Social Science*, New York: Henry Holt & Co.

Sun Yat-Sen (1922) *The International Development of China*, New York: G.P. Putnams.

Sunzi (1963) *The Art of War*, trans. L. Giles, ed. Samuel B. Griffiths, Oxford: Oxford University Press.

Suzuki Yoshitaka (1991) *Japanese Management Structures*, London: Macmillan.

Swetz, F.J. (1987) *Capitalism and Arithmetic: The New Math of the 15th Century*, La Salle, IL: Open Court.

Sylla, Richard and Smith, George David (1993) 'The Transformation of Financial Capitalism: An Essay on the History of American Capital Markets', *Financial Markets, Institutions and Instruments* 2 (2).

Taber, John (1998) 'Duty and Virtue, Indian Conceptions of', in Edward Craig (ed.), *Routledge Encyclopedia of Philosophy*, London: Routledge, vo. 3, 183–7.

Tacitus (1948) *The Agricola and the Germania*, trans. H. Mattingly, Harmondsworth: Penguin.

Tadhkirat al-muluk (Memorial of the Kings) (1980) trans. Vladimir Minorsky, Cambridge: Gibb Memorial Trust, 2nd edn, 1980.

Tai, En-Sai (1922) *Central and Local Finance in China*, New York: Columbia University Press.

Takemura Eiji (1997) *The Perception of Work in Tokugawa Japan: A Study of Ishida Baigan and Ninomiya Sontoku*, Lanham, MD: University Press of America.

Taleb, Nassim Nicholas (2007) *The Black Swan: The Impact of the Highly Improbable*, London: Penguin.

Tanner, Marcus (2008) *The Raven King: Matthias Corvinus and the Fate of His Lost Library*, New Haven: Yale University Press.

Taras, Daphne (2003) 'The North American Workplace: From Employee Representation to Employee Involvement', in Bruce E. Kaufman, Richard A. Beaumont and Roy B. Hilfgott (eds), *Industrial Relations to Human Resources and Beyond: The Evolving Process of Employee Relations Management*, Armonk, NY: M.E. Sharpe.

Tarbell, Ida Minerva (1904) *The History of the Standard Oil Company*, New York: McClure's, 2 vols.

—— (1906) 'Commercial Machiavellianism', *McClure's* 23: 453–64.

—— (1916) *New Ideals in Business: An Account of Their Practice and Their Effect on Men and Profits*, New York: Macmillan.

—— (1921) 'The New Place of Women in Industry', six-part series published in *Industrial Management* 62.

—— (1932) *Owen D. Young: A New Type of Industrial Leader*, New York: Macmillan.

Tarrant, John J. (1976) *Drucker: The Man Who Invented Corporate Society*, London: Barrie & Jenkins.

al-Tawail, Muhammad Abdulrahman (1995) *Public Administration in the Kingdom of Saudi Arabia*, Riyadh: Institute of Public Administration.

Tayeb, Monir (1995) *The Global Business Environment*, London: Sage.

—— (1997) 'Islamic Revival in Asia and Human Resource Management', *Employee Relations* 19(4): 352–4.

Taylor, Frederick Winslow (1895) *A Piece-Rate System*, New York: American Society of Mechanical Engineers; repr. Bristol: Thoemmes Press, 2000.

—— (1903) *Shop Management*, New York: Harper & Bros.

—— (1911) *The Principles of Scientific Management*, New York: Harper & Bros; repr. Stilwell, KS: Digireads.com.

Tead, Ordway (1918) *Instincts in Industry: A Study of Working-Class Psychology*, Boston: Houghton Mifflin.

—— (1935) *The Art of Leadership*, New York: McGraw-Hill.

Tead, Ordway and Metcalf, Henry C. (1920) *Personnel Administration: Its Principles and Practice*, New York: McGraw-Hill.

Teece, David J., Pisano, Gary and Shuen, Amy (1997) 'Dynamic Capabilities and Strategic Management', *Strategic Management Journal* 18 (7): 509–33.

Teranishi, Juno (2007) 'Were Banks Really at the Center of the Prewar Japanese Financial System?', *Monetary and Economics Studies* 25 (1): 49–76.

Terragno, Rodolfo H. (1988) *The Challenge of Real Development in Argentina in the Twenty-First Century*, Boulder, CO: Lynne Rienner.

Théodoridès, Aristide (1999) 'Law', in Kathryn A. Bard (ed.), *Encyclopedia of the Archaeology of Ancient Egypt*, London: Routledge, 438–41.

Thompson, C. Bertrand (1914) *Scientific Management*, Cambridge, MA: Harvard University Press.

—— (1914) 'Scientific Management in Retailing', repr. in C. Bertrand Thompson (ed.), *Scientific Management*, Cambridge, MA: Harvard University Press.

Thompson, E.P. (1963) *The Making of the English Working Class*, London: Victor Gollancz.

Thompson, James David (1967) *Organizations in Action*, New York: McGraw-Hill.

Thompson, Paul (1967) *The Work of William Morris*, London: Heinemann.

Thompson, Stephen E. (1999) 'Textual Sources, Old Kingdom', in Kathryn A. Bard (ed.), *Encyclopedia of the Archaeology of Ancient Egypt*, London: Routledge, 801–2.

Tipper, Harry (ed.) (1921) *Advertising: Its Principles and Practice*, New York: The Ronald Press.

Tisdall, Patricia (1982) *Agents of Change: The Development and Practice of Management Consultancy*, New York and London: Heinemann.

Toffler, Alvin (1970) *Future Shock*, London: Bodley Head.

—— (1981) *The Third Wave*, London: William Collins.

Tolstoy, Leo (Lev Nikolaevich Tolstoi) (1957), *War and Peace*, trans. Rosemary Edmonds, London: Penguin, 1957.

Tonn, Joan C. (2003) *Mary P. Follett: Creating Democracy, Transforming Management*, New Haven: Yale University Press.

Towne, Henry Robinson (1886) 'The Engineer as an Economist', *Transactions of the American Society of Mechanical Engineers* 7: 428–32.

Toyoda Eiji (1987) *Toyota: Fifty Years in Motion, an Autobiography by the Chairman*, Tokyo: Kodansha International.

Trachtenberg, Alan (2007) *The Incorporation of America: Culture and Society in the Gilded Age*, New York: Hill & Wang.

Triana, Pablo (2009) *Lecturing Birds on Flying: Can Mathematical Theories Destroy the Financial Markets?* Chichester: John Wiley.

Tripp, Basil H. (1955) *Renold Chains: A History of the Company and the Rise of the Precision Chain Industry 1879–1955*, London: George Allen & Unwin.

Trist, Eric L. and Emery, Frederick E. (1973) *Towards a Social Ecology: Contextual Appreciations of the Future and the Present*, New York: Plenum.

Trundle, George T. (1948) *Managerial Control of Business*, Chichester: John Wiley.

Tsutsui, William M. (1998) *Manufacturing Ideology: Scientific Management in Twentieth-Century Japan*, Princeton: Princeton University Press.

—— (2001) 'The Way of Efficiency: Ueno Yoichi and Scientific Management in Twentieth-Century Japan', *Modern Asian Studies* 35: 441–67.

Tuchman, Barbara W. (1980) *The Proud Tower: A Portrait of the World Before the War 1880–1914*, London: Macmillan.

Tucker, Josiah (1755) *The Elements of Commerce, and Theory of Taxes*, London.

Tutt, Brendan (2007) 'When Social Networking Meets Knowledge Management', ZDNet.co.uk.

Tyau, Min Ch'ien Tuk Zung (1922) *China Awakened*, London: Macmillan.

Udgaonkar, Padma B. (1969) *The Political Institutions and Administration of Northern India During Medieval Times*, Delhi: Motilal Banarsidass.

Uglow, Jenny (2002) *The Lunar Men: The Friends Who Made the Future*, London: Faber & Faber.

Ure, Andrew (1835) *The Philosophy of Manufactures: or an Exposition of the Scientific, Moral and Commercial Economy of the Factory System of Great Britain*, London, 2nd edn, London: H.G. Bohn.

—— (1836) *The Cotton Manufactures of Great Britain*, London.

—— (1839) *Dictionary of Arts, Manufactures and Mines*, London.

Urwick, Lyndall (1933) *Management of Tomorrow*, London: Nisbet.

—— (ed.) (1949) *Freedom and Co-ordination: Lectures in Business Organization by Mary Parker Follett*, London: Management Publications Trust.

—— (1956) *The Golden Book of Management*, London: Newman Neame.

Urwick, Lyndall F. and Brech, E.F.L. (1947) *The Making of Scientific Management*, 3 vols, London: Management Publications Trust; repr. Bristol: Thoemmes Press, 1994.

Vaidya, R.V. (1967) *A Study of the Mahabharata*, Pune: A.V.G. Prakashan.

Van De Water, Thomas J. (1987) 'Psychology's Entrepreneurs and the Marketing of Industrial Psychology', *Journal of Applied Psychology* 82 (4): 486–99.

van den Boorn, G.P.F. (1988) *The Duties of the Vizier*, London: Kegan Paul International.

Vanderblue, Homer (1921) 'A Functional Approach to the Study of Marketing', *Journal of Political Economy* 29: 676–83.

van Fleet, David D. (2008) 'Doing Management History: One Editor's Views', *Journal of Management History* 14 (3): 237–47.

Varley, H. Paul (trans.) (1980) *A Chronicle of Gods and Sovereigns: The Jinno Shotoki of Kitabatake Chikafusa*, New York: Columbia University Press.

Vegetius (1993) *Epitoma Rei Militaris*, ed. and trans. N.P. Milner, Liverpool: Liverpool University Press.

Veith, Ilza (1972) *The Yellow Emperor's Classic of Internal Medicine*, Berkeley: University of California Press.

Verma, B.R. and Baskshi, S.R. (eds) (2005) *Administration and Society in Medieval India*, New Delhi: Commonwealth Publishers.

Vickers, Geoffrey (1965) *The Art of Judgment*, London: Chapman & Hall.

—— (1967) *Towards a Sociology of Management*, New York: Basic Books.

Vignali, Claudio (2007) 'McDonald's: "Think Global, Act Local" – The Marketing Mix', *British Food Journal* 103 (2): 97–111.

Visser, Hans (2009) *Islamic Finance: Principles and Practice*, Cheltenham: Edward Elgar.

von Bertalanffy, Ludwig (1968) *General System Theory*, New York: Braziller.

Wack, Pierre (1985) 'Scenarios: Shooting the Rapids', *Harvard Business Review*, November-December: 139–50.

Wade, Geoff (2009) 'An Early Age of Commerce in Southeast Asia, 900–1300 CE', *Journal of Southeast Asian Studies* 40 (2).

Wagner-Tsukamoto, Sigmund (2008) 'Scientific Management Revisited: Did Taylorism Fail Because of a Too Positive Image of Human Nature?', *Journal of Management History* 14 (4): 348–72.

Walker, Francis Amasa (1887) *Political Economy*, New York: Henry Holt & Co.

Walker, William H. (1917) *Corporation Finance*, New York: Alexander Hamilton Institute.

Wallace-Hadrill, J.M. (1952) *The Barbarian West, 400–1000*, London: Hutchinson.

Wallerstein, Immanuel (1979) *The Capitalist World Economy*, New York: Cambridge University Press.

Walter-Busch, Emil (2006) 'Albert Thomas and Scientific Management in War and Peace, 1914–32', *Journal of Management History* 12 (2): 212–31.

Walzer, Richard (1985) *Al-Farabi on the Perfect State: Abu Nasr al-Farabi's Mabadi' Ara Ahl al-Madina al-Fadila*, Oxford: Clarendon.

Warner, Malcolm (1994) 'Japanese Culture, Western Management: Taylorism and Human Resources in Japan', *Organization Studies*, 15 (4): 509–35.

—— (2010) 'In Search of Confucian HRM: Theory and Practice in Greater China and Beyond', *International Journal of Human Resource Management* 21 (12): 2053–78.

Warner, Malcolm and Witzel, Morgen (2004) *Managing in Virtual Organisations*, London: International Thomson Business Press.

Watson, Burton (2003) *Han Fei Tzu: Basic Writings*, New York: Columbia University Press.

Watson, Thomas J. (1926) 'To Make a Business Grow: Begin Growing Men!', *System* 50: 151–4.

—— (1931) 'Scientific Management and Industrial Psychology', *English Review* 52: 444–55.

Watts, Steven (2005) *The People's Tycoon: Henry Ford and the American Century*, New York: Alfred A. Knopf.

Webb, Sidney (1917) *The Works Manager To-Day*, London: Longmans, Green & Co.

Webb, Sidney and Webb, Beatrice (1898) *Problems of Modern Industry*, London: Longmans, Green & Co.

Weber, Max (1964) *The Religion of China: Confucianism and Taoism*, trans. Hans H. Gerth, London: Collier Macmillan.

—— (2002) *The Protestant Ethic and The Spirit of Capitalism*, trans. Peter Baehr and Gordon C. Wells, London: Penguin.

—— (2003) *The History of Commercial Partnerships in the Middle Ages*, trans. Lutz Kaelber, Lanham, MD: Rowman & Littlefield.

—— (2008) *Economy and Society*, trans. Keith Tribe, ed. Sam Whimster, London: Routledge.

Wee, Chow Hu, Lee, Kai Sheang and Hidajat, Bambang Walujo (1991) *Sun Tzu: War and Management*, Singapore: Addison-Wesley.

Weld, L.D.H. (1917) 'Marketing Functions and Mercantile Organization', *American Economic Review* 7: 306–18.

Wernerfeldt, Birger (1984) 'A Resource-Based View of the Firm', *Strategic Management Journal* 5 (2): 171–80.

West, Martin L. (ed. and trans.) (1978) *Hesiod: Works and Days*, Oxford: Oxford University Press.

Weyermann, Moritz and Schönitz, Hans (1912) *Grundlegung und Systematik einer wissenschaftlichen Privatwirtschaftslehre und ihre pflege an Universitaten und Hochschulen* (Theoretical Foundation and System of Private Economics and Their Establishment in Universities and High Schools), Karlsruhe.

Whitehead, Alfred North (1929) *Process and Reality*, repr. New York: The Free Press, 1979.

Whitehead, Thomas North (1936) *Leadership in a Free Society: A Study in Human Relations Based on an Analysis of Present-Day Industrial Civilization*, Oxford: Oxford University Press.

Whitson, Kevin (1997) 'The Reception of Scientific Management by British Engineers 1890–1914', *British History Review* 71 (2): 207–29.

Wiener, Norbert (1950) *The Human Use of Human Beings: Cybernetics and Society*, London: Eyre & Spottiswood.

Wildavsky, Aaron (1983) 'If Planning Is Everything, Maybe It's Nothing', *Policy Sciences* 4: 127–53.

Wilson, Charles (1954) *The History of Unilever: A Study in Economic Growth and Social Change*, London: Cassell.

Wilson, John F. (1995) *British Business History 1720–1994*, Manchester: University of Manchester Press.

Wilson, John F. and Thomson, Andrew (2006) *The Making of Modern Management: British Management in a Historical Perspective*, Oxford: Oxford University Press.

Wind, Yoram (Jerry) (2002) 'The Integrative Thinking Challenge for Management Education and Research', *Rotman's Magazine* Fall: 18–20.

Witzel, Morgen (ed.) (2001) *Biographical Dictionary of Management*, Bristol: Thoemmes Press.

—— (2002) *Builders and Dreamers: The Making and Meaning of Management*, London: FT-Prentice Hall.

—— (2004) 'Collins, John', in Donald Rutherford (ed.), *Biographical Dictionary of British Economists*, Bristol: Thoemmes Press.

—— (2005) 'Where Scientific Management Went Awry', *European Business Forum* 21: 89–92.

—— (2006) 'The Unsung Master of Management', *European Business Forum* 25: 62–3.

—— (2007) 'Early Contributors to Financial Management: Jeremiah Jenks, Edward Meade and William Ripley', in Geoffrey Poitras (ed.), *Pioneers of Financial Economics*, Cheltenham: Edward Elgar, vol. 2, 31–44.

—— (2009) *Management History: Text and Cases*, London: Routledge.

—— (2009) 'Why Management History Matters', *EFMD Global Focus*, 3 (3): 20–23.

—— (2010) *Tata: Evolution of a Corporate Brand*, New Delhi: Penguin Portfolio.

Wolfe, William B. (1974) *The Basic Barnard: An Introduction to Chester I. Barnard and His Theories of Organization and Management*, Ithaca, NY: Cornell University Press.

Womack, James P., Jones, Daniel T. and Roos, Daniel (1990) *The Machine that Changed the World: The Story of Lean Production*, New York: Macmillan.

Wong, Siu-lun (1985) 'The Chinese Family Firm: A Model', *British Journal of Sociology* 36 (1), 58–72.

Wood, John C. and Wood, Michael C. (eds) (2002) *Henri Fayol*, London: Routledge.

Woodward, Joan (1965) *Industrial Organization: Theory and Practice*, Oxford: Oxford University Press.

—— (1970) *Industrial Organization: Behaviour and Control*, Oxford: Oxford University Press.

World Commission on Environment and Development (1987) *Our Common Future*, Oxford: Oxford University Press.

Wrege, Charles D. and Greenwood, Ronald D. (1982) 'Mary B. Gilson: A Historical Study of the Neglected Accomplishments of a Woman Who Pioneered in Personnel Management', *Business and Economic History* : 35–42.

Wrege, Charles D. and Greenwood, Ronald G. (1991) *Frederick W. Taylor, the Father of Scientific Management: Myth and Reality*, Homewood, Il: Business One Irwin.

Wren, Daniel A. (1980) 'Scientific Management in the USSR, With Particular Reference to the Contributions of Walter N. Polakov', *Academy of Management Review* 5 (1): 1–11.

—— (1994) *The Evolution of Management Thought*, New York: John Wiley, 4th edn.

Wright, M.R. (1981) *Empedocles: The Extant Fragments,* New Haven: Yale University Press.

Wright, Patricia (1972) *Conflict on the Nile: The Fashoda Incident of 1898*, London: Heinemann.

Wright, Robert E. (ed.) (2003) *The History of Corporate Finance: Developments of Anglo-American Securities Markets, Financial Practices, Theories and Laws*, London: Pickering & Chatto, 6 vols.

—— (2005) *The First Wall Street: Chestnut Street, Philadelphia, and the Birth of American Finance*, Chicago: University of Chicago Press.

Wright, Robert E. and Cowen, David J. (2006) *Financial Founding Fathers: The Men Who Made America Rich*, Chicago: University of Chicago Press.

Wright, Tim (1981) 'A Method of Evading Management: Contract Labor in Chinese Coal Mines Before 1937', *Comparative Studies in Society and History* 23 (4): 656–78; repr. in R. Ampalavanar Brown (ed.), *Chinese Business Enterprise: Critical Perspectives on Business and Management*, vol. 3, London: Routledge.

Wu, John C.H. (trans.) (1990) *Tao Teh Ching (Daodejing)*, Boston and London: Shambhala.

Xenophon (2004) *The Persian Expedition*, trans. Rex Warner, Harmondsworth: Penguin.

Yamamoto Tsunetomo (1979) *Hagakure: The Book of the Samurai*, trans. William Scott Wilson, Tokyo: Kodansha International.

Yamey, Basil S. (1977) *Essays on the History of Accounting*, New York: Arno.

—— (ed.) (1994) *Luca Pacioli: Exposition of Double-Entry Bookkeeping Venice 1494*, Venice: Albrizzi Editorie.

Yarranton, Andrew (1678) *England's Improvement by Land and Sea*, London.

Yeh, Wen-hsin (2008) *Shanghai Splendor: Economic Sentiments and the Making of Modern China 1843–1949*, Berkeley: University of California Press.

Zaehner, R.C. (trans.) (1966) *Hindu Scriptures*, London: Dent.

Zhang Deyi (1989) *Diary of a Chinese Diplomat*, trans. Simon Johstone, Beijing: Panda Books.

Zhao An Xin (trans.) (2009) *Thick Black Theory*, privately published.

Zola, Émile (1885) *Germinal*, trans. Peter Collier, Oxford: Oxford University Press, 2008.

—— (1883) *Au bonheur des dames*, trans. Brian Nelson, Princeton: Princeton University Press.

Index